Market, Socialist, and Mixed Economies

CARMELO MESA-LAGO

Market, Socialist, and Mixed Economies

Comparative Policy and Performance

Chile, Cuba, and Costa Rica

with Alberto Arenas de Mesa, Ivan Brenes,
Verónica Montecinos, and Mark Samara

The Johns Hopkins University Press
Baltimore and London

© 2000 The Johns Hopkins University Press
All rights reserved. Published 2000
Printed in the United States of America on acid-free paper
9 8 7 6 5 4 3 2 1

The Johns Hopkins University Press
2715 North Charles Street
Baltimore, Maryland 21218-4363
www.press.jhu.edu

Library of Congress Cataloging-in-Publication Data will be found at the end
of this book.
A catalog record for this book is available from the British Library.

ISBN 0-8018-6172-1

This book is dedicated to several distinguished scholars who significantly influenced my own work:

Peter Thullen, who first taught me, with his social security studies and actions, to tell the truth despite the consequences

Carlos Díaz-Alejandro, Leví Marrero, and **Manuel Moreno Fraginals,** compatriots, colleagues, and friends, who aroused my interest in the economic history of Latin America and Cuba

Albert O. Hirschman, whose innovative books and articles I eagerly read as a student of economics and later as a teacher have assigned to my own students

Amartya Sen, for his preoccupation with and seminal works on ethics, poverty, and development, which have been illuminating and appealing

John M. Montias and **Frederic Pryor,** whose methodological works on comparative economic systems induced my concern for that field and tools

Contents

Tables

CUBA

COSTA RICA

COMPARISONS

Acknowledgments

There are many people who have collaborated in and institutions that have supported this long and complex project. I designed the entire study, wrote parts 1, 3, and 5, coauthored the other two parts, and undertook the final revision and reduction in the size of the entire book.

I am especially indebted to my former research assistant at the University of Pittsburgh in 1993–95 (now Director of the Office of Research of Budget at the Ministry of Finance in Chile), Dr. Alberto Arenas de Mesa; he is the principal author of part 2 on Chile and helped with many other tasks. Collection of the initial information and first set of data to 1988 and the updating of policies in 1994–96 (with the support of Arenas de Mesa) was done by Professor Verónica Montecinos, Department of Sociology, Penn State University. I designed the part, supervised the work of Arenas and Montecinos, added statistical information, reviewed three drafts of that part, and wrote its final version. Thus, authorship of that part is by Arenas de Mesa, Mesa-Lago, and Montecinos. Dr. Joseph Ramos read a preliminary version of this part and made many valuable comments, most of which were incorporated.

Ivan Brenes, my research assistant at Pitt in 1989–90 (now working in Kobe, Japan), did all the research and wrote two drafts of the part on Costa Rica up to 1990. A first draft of the section on the administration between 1990 and 1994 was prepared by Mark Samara, my research assistant at Florida International University in 1995. I designed the part, guided and supervised Brenes's and Samara's work, merged the latter's section into the part, standardized the analysis of performance to match the structure of the other two country parts, and wrote the final version. Thus, authorship of that part is by Brenes, Mesa-Lago, and Samara. Professor Jorge Rovira Mas read a preliminary version and provided many detailed, solid comments; other suggestions were made by Professor Manuel de Jesús Baldares and Dr. Herman Hess.

Fabio Bertranou, my research assistant in 1996–97 and Ph.D. candidate in Economics at Pitt, provided valuable help on the methodology for ranking performance in the concluding part and worked on the indices of performance. My last research assistant at Pitt, Matthew P. Ligozio, gathered last-minute bibliography information and statistics. Professor Thomas Rawski helped with the review of the literature on comparative economic systems in the introduction. An anonymous reader for the Johns Hopkins University Press read the entire manuscript and made many suggestions that improved it and helped in the process of cutting its size. Last but not least, my secretaries Jacqueline Janos, Eric Kiefer, and, particularly, Lauree Graham had the burdensome task of typing several versions of the manuscript, correcting numerous errors, and dealing with the complex tables and formatting.

I am grateful for the financial support given by the following institutions to complete various stages of this project: the Howard Heinz Endowment Research Program on Current Latin American Issues for a seed grant (1990); the University of Pittsburgh, which granted a sabbatical (1990–91) and a research leave (1994–95); the Instituto Universitario Ortega y Gasset for a Visiting Professorship (winter 1991); the Alexander von Humboldt Stiftung Senior Research Prize and the Max-Planck-Institut for ausländisches und internationales Sozialrecht in Munich, which provided financial and institutional support respectively (summers of 1991 and 1992); the Emilio Bacardi Moreau Cuban Chair at the University of Miami (fall 1994) and a Mellon Visiting Professorship at Florida International University (winter 1995); and the Alexander von Humboldt Stiftung Grant and the Lateinamerika Institut at the Freie Universität Berlin for financial and institutional support respectively (summer 1997). The research also benefited from field trips to the three countries, although not directly linked with this project: one visit to Cuba, in the summer of 1990, supported by a grant from the Andrew Mellon Foundation; visits to Costa Rica in 1988 and 1997 funded by the World Bank and the Friedrich Ebert Stiftung respectively; and four visits to Chile, in 1988 and 1989 as part of World Bank missions, and in 1992 and 1994 to participate in conferences sponsored by CIEDESS.

I take full responsibility for all that is said herein. My wife Elena is greatly relieved that this project, the longest in my forty-year career, is over, and she has my gratitude for her patience and cheerfulness throughout it. Now I am ready to retire and start the new millennium as a free man.

Abbreviations

AEC	(Anuario Estadístico de Cuba) Cuban Statistical Yearbook
AFP	(Administradora de Fondos de Pensiones) Administrator of Pension Funds
ANAP	(Asociación Nacional de Agricultores Pequeños) National Association of Small Farmers
BANHVI	(Banco Hipotecario de Vivienda) Home Mortgage Bank
BCCh	(Banco Central de Chile) Central Bank of Chile
BCCR	(Banco Central de Costa Rica) Costa Rican Central Bank
BE	(Boletín Estadístico) Statistical Bulletin
BEC	(Boletín Estadístico de Cuba) Cuban Statistical Bulletin
BNC	(Banco Nacional de Cuba) Cuban National (Central) Bank
CACM	Central American Common Market
CCSS	(Caja Costarricense de Seguro Social) Costa Rican Social Security Fund
CDR	(Comités de Defensa de la Revolución) Committees for the Defense of the Revolution
CeC	(Cuba en Cifras) Cuba in Figures
CEE	(Comité Estatal de Estadística) State Committee on Statistics
CELADE	(Centro Latinoamericano de Demografía) Latin American Center of Demography
CEV	(Comisión Especial para la Vivienda) Special Housing Commission
CIA	Central Intelligence Agency
CIEDESS	(Corporación de Investigación, Estudio y Desarrollo de la Seguridad Social) Corporation of Research, Study and Development of Social Security

CMEA	Council for Mutual Economic Assistance
CNI	(Consejo Nacional de Inversiones) National Investment Council
CNP	(Consejo Nacional de Producción) National Production Council
CODELCO	(Corporación Nacional del Cobre de Chile) National Corporation of Chilean Copper
CODESA	(Corporación Costarricense de Desarrollo) Costa Rica Development Corporation
COREC	(Comisión para la Reforma del Estado) Commission for State Reform
CORFO	(Corporación de Fomento de la Producción) Corporation for National Development
CPA	(Cooperativas de Producción Agropecuaria) Agricultural Production Cooperatives
CPT	(Centros de Perfeccionamiento Técnico) Technical Training Centers
CQER	Cuba Quarterly Economic Report
CTC	(Central de Trabajadores de Cuba) Confederation of Cuban Workers
CU	(Coalición Unidad) United Coalition
CUT	(Central Unitaria de Trabajadores) United Workers Federation
ECLAC	(Comisión Económica para América Latina y el Caribe) Economic Commission for Latin America and the Caribbean
ENAP	(Empresa Nacional de Petróleo) National Oil Corporation
FAO	United Nations Food and Agricultural Organization
FEC	(Fondo de Estabilización del Cobre) Copper Stabilization Fund
FONASA	(Fondo Nacional de Salud) National Health Fund
FONAVI	(Fondo Nacional de Vivienda) National Housing Fund
FONDEF	(Fondo de Fomento a la Investigación Científica y Tecnológica) Fund for Scientific and Technical Promotion
FONSUVI	(Fondo de Subsidios para la Vivienda) Housing Subsidy Fund

FONTEC	(Fondo de Desarrollo Tecnológico y Productivo) Fund for Technological and Production Development
FOSIS	(Fondo de Solidaridad e Inversión Social) Social Investment and Solidarity Fund
FP	(Programa Alimentario) Food Program
GATT	General Agreement on Tariffs and Trade
GDP	Gross Domestic Product
GSP	Global Social Product
HMO	Health Maintenance Organization
ICE	(Instituto Costarricense de Electricidad) Costa Rican Electricity Institute
IDA	(Instituto de Desarrollo Agrario) Institute of Agrarian Development
IDB	(Banco Inter-Americano de Desarrollo) Inter-American Development Bank
IE	(Informe Económico) Economic Report
ILO	(Oficina Internacional del Trabajo) International Labour Office
IMAS	(Instituto Mixto de Asistencia Social) Institute of Social Assistance
IMF	(Fondo Monetario Internacional) International Monetary Fund
INA	(Instituto Nacional de Aprendizaje) National Institute for Training
INE	(Instituto Nacional de Estadísticas) National Bureau of Statistics
INP	(Instituto de Normalización Previsional) Institute of Social Insurance Standardization
INRA	(Instituto Nacional de Reforma Agraria) National Institute of Agrarian Reform
INS	(Instituto Nacional de Seguros) National Insurance Institute
INVU	(Instituto Nacional de Vivienda y Urbanismo) National Institute of Housing and Urban Affairs
IP	(Institutos Profesionales) Vocational-Technical Institutes
ISAPRES	(Instituciones de Salud Previsional) Insurance Health Institutions

ISI	Import Substitution Industrialization
ITCO	(Instituto de Tierras y Colonización) Land and Colonization Institute
JAPDEVA	(Junta Administrativa Portuaria de la Vertiente Atlántica) Board of Port Administration and Economic Development of the Atlantic Region
JUCEPLAN	(Junta Central de Planificación) Central Planning Board
JUNJI	(Junta Nacional de Jardines Infantiles) National Board of Kindergartens
KTP-1, KTP-2	Sugar Cane Harvesters
LAICA	(Liga Agrícola e Industrial de la Caña de Azúcar) Agro-industrial Sugar Cane League
MECE	(Mejoramiento de la Calidad y Equidad de la Educación) Improvement of Equity and Quality of Education
MERCOSUR	(Mercado Común del Sur) South American Common Market
MIDEPLAN	(Ministerio de Planificación Nacional y Política Económica) Ministry of National Planning and Economic Policy
MINFAR	(Ministerio de Fuerzas Armadas Revolucionarias) Ministry of Revolutionary Armed Forces
MINSA	(Ministerio de Salud) Ministry of Health
MINSAP	(Ministerio de Salud Pública) Ministry of Public Health
MPS	Material Product System
NAFTA	North American Free Trade Agreement
NGO	Nongovernmental Organizations
OAS	Organization of American States
ODEPLAN	(Oficina de Planificación Nacional) National Planning Office
OFIPLAN	(Oficina de Planificación Nacional) National Planning Office
ONE	(Oficina Nacional de Estadísticas) National Statistical Office
PAHO	Pan American Health Organization
PCC	(Partido Comunista de Cuba) Cuban Communist Party
PEM	(Plan de Empleo Mínimo) Minimum Employment Plan

PLN	(Partido de Liberación Nacional) National Liberation Party
POJH	(Programa de Empleo para Jefes de Hogar) Employment Program for Heads of Households
PRC	(Partido Republicano Calderonista) Republican Calderonist Party
PRN	(Partido Republicano Nacional) National Republican Party
PROCHILE	(Promoción de Exportaciones de Chile) Chilean Exports Promotion
PSD	(Partido Social Demócrata) Social Democrat Party
PUfN	(Partido Unificación Nacional) National Unification Party
PUN	(Partido Unión Nacional) National Union Party
PUSC	(Partido Unidad Social Cristiana) Social Christian Unity Party
RECOPE	(Refinería Costarricense de Petróleo) Costa Rican Petroleum Refinery
RP	(Proceso de Rectificación) Rectification Process
SAFP	(Superintendencia de AFP) Superintendency of AFP
SDE	(Sistema de Dirección Económica) System of Economic Direction
SDPE	(Sistema de Dirección y Planificación de la Economía) System of Economic Direction and Planning
SERMENA	(Servicio Médico Nacional de Empleados) National Health Service for White-Collar Employees
SICA	(Sistema de Integración Centroamericana) Central American Integration System
SNA	(part II) (Sociedad Nacional de Agricultura) National Agricultural Association
SNA	(parts III, V) System of National Accounts
SNAA	(Servicio Nacional de Acueductos y Alcantarillados) National Service of Aqueducts and Sewers
SNS	(Servicio Nacional de Salud) National Health Service
SNSS	(Sistema Nacional de Servicios de Salud) National System of Health Services

SUSESO	(Superintendencia de Seguridad Social) Superintendency of Social Security
UBPC	(Unidades Básicas de Producción Cooperativa) Basic Units of Cooperative Production
ꓶ UF	(Unidad de Fomento) Monetary Unit Adjustable to Inflation
UN	United Nations
UNDP	United Nations Development Program
UNESCO	United Nations Education, Scientific and Cultural Organization
UNRISD	United Nations Research Institute for Social Development
VAT	Value-Added Tax
WB	World Bank

Part I

INTRODUCTION

1. A Brief Review of the State of the Fields of Latin American Development and Comparative Economic Systems

In spite of significant advances in the last three decades, the field of Latin American development still suffers from the lack of a systematic, sophisticated methodology to compare specific economic models (their policies and performance) among the various countries in the region or a selected group of them. The field of Comparative Economic Systems, despite its title's apparent comprehensiveness, initially centered on socialist economies and, after these disappeared, turned to transitional economies but basically maintained its original geographic focus. This field has certainly advanced much more than Latin American development in the systemic comparison, but its weakest feature continues to be the comparative measurement of performance. A quick look at the main literature in the two fields shows significant differences.

A. Comparative Latin American Development

A renowned Latin Americanist recently stated that "comparative analysis of Latin America is most conspicuous by its scarcity. Scholars have tended to focus their investigative energies on the region itself, or selected subregions, or, most commonly, on one country at a time. . . . Regional specialists, on the whole, have displayed substantial aversion to the comparative enterprise" (Smith 1995, p. 14). Textbooks on Latin American economies and development are incredibly few, cover the entire region, and usually deal with general topics, lacking a comparative approach. Between 1977 and 1997, the most important scholarly journal in this area *(Latin American Research Review)* published seven articles involving some type of economic comparison

1

but focusing on specific topics (e.g., the crisis of the 1980s, foreign invest-ment, multinational corporations, tax reform, income distribution, rural poverty); none of them compared socioeconomic models or global policies and outcomes.

In the last decade, several important books have significantly advanced this field: Hartlyn and Morley (1986), Ramos (1986), Sheahan (1987), Bul-mer-Thomas (1996), and Randall (1997). (In addition, the World Bank has a series comparing economies of pair countries, three on Latin America: Mad-dison et al. 1992; Rottenberg et al. 1993; Urdinola et al. forthcoming). All these books study economic policies and performance in a group of coun-tries (from six to eight, except three by Ramos and two by the World Bank), some identify political or economic models, and all use abundant statistics. But virtually all of them lack a common framework of analysis and do not utilize well-defined economic models or apply them systematically to all cases; the statistical data used vary greatly among countries, performance is not consistently evaluated in each case and compared with the same set of indicators among all cases, and there is not a clear linkage shown between policies and outcomes. Outstanding exceptions are Ramos, who compared variations of the neoconservative model (called neo*liberal* in Latin Amer-ica) in the Southern Cone, and Randall's team, who studied the implemen-tation of divergent models in three countries (but not in the other four cases).

These books have been elaborated by teams of experts, except two writ-ten by one author (Ramos and Sheahan). An advantage enjoyed by a single author is the potential control over the consistent treatment of cases with a common frame of analysis, while a disadvantage is the lack of enough time and knowledge to study in depth a relatively large number of countries. The opposite is true in the work done by a group of experts under the guidance of one or more editors.

All these books have advanced the field of comparative Latin American development and have substantially contributed to my own research, but I feel that there is still considerable space for improving the methodology of comparison in both policy and performance among representative (and, par-ticularly, diverse) economic models in the region.

B. Comparative Economic Systems

In contrast with Latin America, the field of comparative economic systems has abundant textbooks: at least a dozen published in the last decade, prob-ably the most successful—at least in the number of printed editions—being Gregory and Stuart (1995). The approach in virtually all of them is similar: they start with a general introduction on the theoretical models (neoclassic,

Marxist, market-socialist), then select a number of countries as "cases" or "prototypes" (the United States and the Soviet Union–Russia always, a couple from Eastern Europe, China and/or Japan, Germany or Sweden, rarely one from Latin America), and end with some general conclusions or future challenges but without a comparative evaluation of country performance (barring Gregory and Stuart). Few experts in the field have devoted themselves to the overall methodology of comparison; significant exceptions, among others, are Eckstein (1971), Montias (1975, 1994), Neuberger and Duffy (1976), and Pryor (1985). In spite of the wide title of the field, a small minority of articles published in its two major journals (*Journal of Comparative Economics* and *Comparative Economic Studies*) actually involved country comparisons. For instance, of 363 articles published in the 1980s, only 7% compared country economies or systems while the remaining 93% dealt with one single country or analyzed overall issues. Between 1990 and 1996, 360 articles were published in both journals, and the proportion comparing countries' systems increased to 19%, still a small minority.

The World Bank series cited above includes six global comparative economic studies of pairs of countries (outside of Latin America), virtually all market and mixed economies. This is an important effort, but most of these books do not undertake a systematic comparison (an exception is Pryor 1991). Recent analyses of economic policies and performance of China and India have been sponsored by the Asia Society and the International Center for Economic Growth respectively (Dernberger and Eckhaus 1988; Srinivasan 1993). The *World Development Report 1996* is devoted to a profound comparative analysis of transition in former socialist economies in Central and Eastern Europe, as well as the current socialist market economies of China and Vietnam. The *Report* deals with the key issues in transition and contains bounteous statistics, many of them standardized, but there is no global comparative study of the economies involved (a task obviously impeded by the large number of both countries and issues), albeit a couple of extremely brief comparisons, such as Russia and China. More surprising is the fact that in the 530 items included in the bibliography of the *Report* there is not a single one comparing global policies and performance among two or three countries; the works cited are either one-country studies or wide cross-country analysis on specific topics or comparison of one topic among a few countries (World Bank 1996).

With the collapse of socialism, the field of comparative economic systems faces the serious challenge of transformation or extinction (the professional association of the field—ACES—devoted part of its business national meeting in 1997 to discussing this problem). In spite of the pioneering role played by some Latin American countries in the transition to the market (particularly Chile), virtually none are included in this field's textbooks, monographs, and academic articles.

C. World Cross-Country Comparisons Based on Internationally Compiled Data

In Latin America, the Economic Commission for Latin America and the Caribbean (ECLAC) has been the longest and most important source of information. In the last fifteen years, nevertheless, there has been a remarkable explosion of all type of statistics, on most countries in the world, published as yearbooks by international organizations (World Bank, IMF, UNDP, IDB, etc.), conveniently presented in a comparative manner for easy use by scholars and policy makers, and in one case aggregated into a composite index. This is a most welcome and significant improvement in the availability of data (some of which have been productively used in this book), but I am skeptical about comparative studies (and their conclusions), largely based on those type of data and sophisticated economic modeling, without knowledge of the countries and their crucial institutional features (recent examples are Barro and Sala-i-Martin 1995; Sala-i-Martin 1997).

Furthermore, contrasting statistics from those yearbooks with data I have collected and refined after years of field research in many of the same countries, I have noted the following flaws: factual errors, figures that appear completely out of line with the country's level of development, equal treatment of data from countries with a solid statistical base and from others with primitive information, frustratingly wide variation among series produced by various organizations on the same indicator, and vagueness about the date for which the data are provided (and comparisons made among countries, sometimes with a significant time gap). In summary, there is no facile substitute for doing research in the traditional, hard way: international series should be carefully checked with information from the field as well as institutional knowledge.

2. Conceptual and Methodological Conundrums

There are important debates in the fields of comparative economics and development on both the concepts and the most appropriate methods of comparison and measurement. Three key issues are briefly discussed in this section: (1) the selection of one among various existing comparative research methods, (2) the choosing between the "most similar" and "most different" cases/countries, and (3) the concept of development and the selection of indicators to measure it.

A. Selection of the Most Appropriate Method

Four methods can be used in comparative studies in the social sciences: case study, experimental, statistical, and comparative (these first two sections are largely based on Collier 1991 and Smith 1995). The case-study approach is usually based on one or two observations or countries, which enhances depth but is quite limited to testing hypotheses and generalizing the findings (an example of this approach is the cited World Bank series comparing pairs of countries). The experimental method is normally not applicable to most topics in comparative social sciences because the appropriate experimental data are very difficult or impossible to generate. The statistical method relies on a very large number of cases and countries, which permits a wide spectrum in the comparison and heightens generalization of results, but it faces two major disadvantages: the difficulty in both gathering reliable and comparable data and having adequate institutional knowledge for all cases (resulting from limited time and resources) and, hence, reaching valid conclusions (problems already discussed in the previous section); and the problem of "conceptual stretching," that is, the desire to include as many cases as possible—with considerable differences—which usually leads to excessively broad, abstract, or second-rate findings.

The comparative method roughly involves from 3 to 10 cases; therefore, it is an intermediate approach between the case-study and statistical methods and avoids some of the predicaments of those two, but it faces its own quandaries: the relatively small number of cases/countries (more than in the case study but less than in the statistical method) and having more variables than cases/countries to observe. Innovations introduced in the last three decades, nevertheless, have improved this method and reduced its difficulties, thus making it more fruitful: (1) the rise of the "school of comparative historical analysis" that evaluates each case/country over a long period of time with an emphasis on "interpretative understanding" (also the challenge by economic historians who stress the role of institutions); (2) the careful selection (matching) of cases/countries, which acts as a partial substitute for experimental or statistical control; (3) the application of carefully thought-out, systematic comparative qualitative and quantitative techniques, within an adequate framework; and (4) the combination of variables focusing on a smaller number of explanatory factors.

B. Most Similar Versus Most Different Cases/Countries

In the selection of countries for comparison there are two conflicting approaches and an eclectic one. In order to have a relatively "controlled comparison" (reduce the impact of a substantial number of independent variables), one stand supports the careful selection of a few "matched" (very close) countries that share similar values or features in a preselected set of variables. Conversely it is argued that even a careful matching of most similar cases would fail to eliminate many rival explanations, hence it is preferable to select a set of countries as diverse as possible in which the scholar traces similar processes of change. The eclectic approach argues that "similar" and "different" concepts are relative and that the two previous methods can be combined: selecting a reasonable number of countries roughly matched on a number of variables (ensuring at least partial similarity and some controlled comparison) and analyzing groups, within the selected set, that are as different as possible (allowing for different processes of change).

Another debate is between choosing countries within a given geographic area (intraregional comparison) such as Latin America (which share some similarities in language, culture, and history), versus selecting countries from diverse geographical locations (cross-regional comparison) based on issues or analytical requirements (but the problem of controlled comparison is worse in the latter).

C. The Concept and Measurement of Development

Development is an elusive term whose definition has roused long and heated controversies (main sources of this section are Little 1982; Dréze and Sen 1989; Betancourt 1996). In the 1950s and the 1960s development was tantamount to economic growth or Gross Domestic Product (GDP) per capita, but at the end of the 1960s that conventionally accepted equivalence became the target of criticism for the following reasons: (1) economic growth does not necessarily bring improvement in the welfare of society (countries with a high GDP per capita may suffer from high unemployment and poverty); (2) the average GDP per capita may be meaningless if it conceals substantial inequalities in income distribution; and (3) the welfare of society is not exclusively measured by income but also by access to key social services such as sanitation, education, and health care.

The pendulum then oscillated to the social side, focusing on issues such as inequality, poverty, and unemployment, and yet alleviation of these social problems cannot be sustained in the long run without savings and investment needed to promote growth, and these resources may be depleted by excessive social expenditures. The size of investment, however, does not guarantee growth unless it is efficiently allocated and used; furthermore, investment in education and health contributes to a healthier labor force with better skills, thus improving productivity and promoting growth. In addition, it is argued that growth is not the exclusive result of efficient investment and application of science and technology to the production process but is also influenced by the role of institutions and economic policy.

The search for a more embracing concept of development and a better balance in the indicators to measure it led to new foci: satisfaction of "basic needs" (Organization for Economic Cooperation and Development) and the achievement of full employment (International Labor Office), which culminated in 1976 with the World Employment Conference "basic needs strategy." At the turn of the 1970s, the Overseas Development Council and some scholars construed a "quality of life index" comprising multiple indicators. The application of structural adjustment policies in many countries in the world (combined with the severe economic crisis of the 1980s) provoked an increase in poverty and an universal preoccupation to reduce it.

Basic needs

In the above debates, little attention has been given to incorporating external economic indicators in the measurement of development, such as the balance of payments, the burden of the foreign debt, export and trade partner concentration, terms of trade, and so forth. Interestingly, in the 1960s and 1970s the now discredited dependency theory explained underdevelopment in the "periphery" (developing countries) based on their dependency on the "center" (developed countries that extracted a "surplus" from the periphery) within the world capitalist system but failed to generate cross-country indicators to measure such external economic "dependency."

dependency theory

Currently two major international organizations rank most countries in the world based on distinct indicators. The World Bank in its annual *World Development Report* (first published in 1978) ranked 133 countries in its 1996 edition into three major groups based on real GNP per capita in U.S. dollars: low-income, middle-income (subdivided into lower and upper), and high-income, hence, still based on the conventional concept of development. The bank acknowledges that GNP per capita does not, by itself, measure welfare or success in development and in 1988 began to publish a yearbook companion on *Social Indicators of Development;* but, so far, it has not integrated them with its major indicator. On the other hand, the United Nations Development Program (UNDP) in 1990 began to publish the *Human Development Report,* which in 1996 ranked 136 countries based on a "human development index" (HDI) that integrates three indices: two social (life expectancy and education—adult literacy, educational enrollment) and one economic (real GDP per capita at purchasing power parity rates in U.S. dollars). The ranking of the countries differs significantly between the World Bank and the UNDP, as there are countries classified as middle-income by the former that are ordered at the top of the HDI, above some high-income countries.

World Bank

yearbook

UN report

The various concepts and indicators of development discussed above are related to diverse goals and approaches chosen to pursue it, as well as to divergent roles of the state, the market, and other institutions. The traditional goal/approach dichotomy was growth versus equity. The first approach allocates resources to promote economic expansion (usually with a predominant role of the market) with the assumption that there will be a "trickledown" effect that eventually will improve living conditions of all the population including the poor. The second approach assigns priority to public social services, employment promotion, reduction of poverty, and income inequality (normally with a crucial role of the state) with the presumption that there will be a "perk-up" effect on growth. More recent work has tried to combine both goals arguing that such a mix is both convenient and feasible (e.g, "growth with equity," "growth with a human face"), while the UNDP (1996, p. 6) argues that there is a "reinforcing relationship between equity and growth," but the controversy on whether the two are truly compatible or there is a trade-off between them lingers.

Drèze and Sen (1989) have modified the labels of these two approaches as "growth-mediated security" and "support-led security," but they went beyond a simple rechristening to show how simplistic and false the traditional *total* dichotomy was. The authors do not dismiss growth, as increasing private income may facilitate access to food, other essential commodities, and services; furthermore, more available resources generate the potential for public action to provide social services. This approach, however, faces two problems: if high growth is accompanied by increasing inequality (which thwarts access to food and services by the poor), and if the government does not seize the opportunity of greater available resources to improve the quality of life. The alternative approach involves important direct "public action" to fight deprivation and improve social welfare, but such action is not limited to the state, as it involves multiple and heterogeneous mechanisms including other social institutions, pressure groups, the private sector, and so forth. A potential problem with this approach arises if too many resources are allocated to social services, hence depleting them from growth.

The traditional *total* dichotomy on goals/approaches is false or Manichean, argue Drèze and Sen, for three reasons: (1) it is not absolutely state activism versus disengagement, because in the first approach the government may take public action to improve the quality of life; (2) it is not simply state versus market provision of social services, as both can occur in either approach although with different degrees; (3) it is not exclusively a goal of growth versus equity or satisfaction of basis needs, because in the first approach there are potential resources for social services, while in the second approach the goal of growth is not surrendered, as it is essential for sustainability. The authors conclude that there are major complementaries between the two goals/approaches, and it is important to strive for a balance and avoid extremes: the dilemma in the use of available resources is not between all or nothing but to give *preference* to one goal *complemented* by the other.

3. A New Approach to the Comparative Study of Latin American Economies

Building upon the existing scholarly work, herein I attempt to move forward the field of comparative Latin American development. The book was designed and mainly written by me, with the valuable collaboration of several research assistants who strictly followed my directions, hence securing a consistent application of a common framework. The book utilizes the comparative method (improving it with some of the innovations introduced in recent years), selects three countries from the same geographical area (Chile, Costa Rica, and Cuba, all in Latin America), and applies one version of the eclectic approach (these three countries share a set of similar features but have followed divergent economic models).

Virtually all the books on Latin American development briefly discussed above include in their comparisons either all three countries (Sheahan 1987), Chile and Cuba (Hartlyn and Morley 1986; Randall 1997), or Chile or Costa Rica (Ramos 1986; Rottenberg 1993; Bulmer-Thomas 1996). In addition, in the last decade, four other works have undertaken a brief, partial comparison among the three countries or at least two of them. Mesa-Lago and Díaz-Briquets (1988) compared Costa Rica and Cuba between 1960 and 1980, identifying their two models (but without any description less analysis of their policies) and briefly measuring their performance relying on ten socioeconomic indicators. Drèze and Sen (1989) studied Chile and Costa Rica (and very briefly touched on Cuba), comparing their strategies for improving living conditions between 1960 and 1985, and measuring their results with a few indicators mostly health-related. Following the same approach, Betancourt (1996) shortly contrasted the three countries, extended the period of analysis to 1960–90, and concentrated on three social indicators on health and education. González (1995) compared Costa Rica and Cuba between 1960 and 1990, constructing a socioeconomic development index based on multiple indicators, and ranking these countries with twenty-six others in the region (including Chile) but without any policy analysis. These were pioneer, useful works, but none accomplished the task of comprehensive analysis of models and policies of the three selected countries, combined with a thorough evaluation of their overall performance.

This book's approach is different from the existing literature in five ways:

(1) it carefully selects a manageable number of countries, three, that do not have wide differences in natural endowment, level of development, and other nonsystemic factors that could affect their performance; (2) it is circumscribed to a single economic model in each of the three countries, although showing its evolution and change through time; (3) it embraces a relatively long period of observation: about thirty-six years for Costa Rica and Cuba, and twenty-one years for Chile; (4) it compares socioeconomic policies (based on an ample rather than narrow concept of development), consistently applying a common and integrated framework of analysis to the three countries, through several policy stages in each; and (5) it constructs standardized statistical series for the three countries during the period of observation and uses these series to develop multiple indicators (going further than those currently used) and a combined index for the measurement of performance in the three countries. The first feature addresses the issue of minimum similarity and, hence, helps to achieve a relative controlled comparison, while the other four features improve the comparative method.

Following the "most different" country approach (but compensated by minimum similarity), the three economic models selected are completely diverse and represent two extremes and an intermediate position within a world continuum of economic systems between two abstract poles or theoretical models: the market and the plan. On one extreme is the neoclassic or neo-conservative (*neoliberal* in Latin America) or monetarist or "social market" model of Chile between 1974 and 1994; on the other extreme is the centrally planned, command, or socialist economy of Cuba between 1959 and 1995; and somewhere in the middle of the two extremes is the mixed economy of Costa Rica between 1958 and 1994. The political systems of the three countries are also quite distinct (the following characterizations are based on the situation in mid-1998 when this book was finished): an authoritarian military regime in Chile (1973–90), followed by a pluralistic democracy; an authoritarian socialist regime in Cuba for the entire period of observation; and a pluralistic democracy in Costa Rica during the entire period of observation. In spite of these significant regime differences, the three countries have been politically stable.

The book is divided into three major parts: (1) this introduction (part 1), which summarizes the theoretical foundations of the three models and their empirical application in each country, explains the methodology to be used, and identifies some of the problems confronted; (2) the three case studies (parts 2–4), where the socioeconomic policies and performance of Chile, Cuba, and Costa Rica are described and analyzed in an intertwined fashion; and (3) a comparative analysis of the system policies and evaluation of their outcomes in the three countries (part 5), using a standardized set of socioeconomic indicators and three types of rankings, and including a look at the future of those systems and policies.

Eight crucial issues or questions are analyzed in the book:

1. What is the relationship between political continuity and economic policy continuity;
2. Which of the three systems has performed better in economic and social areas and why;
3. Whether it is possible to achieve simultaneous success in both areas, or whether there are trade-offs between them;
4. Whether the performance of the three countries can be exclusively explained by the system and its policies or whether there are other nonsystemic explicatory factors;
5. How the regional crisis in the 1980s affected the three countries in different ways and with divergent social costs;
6. Why, after such a crisis, one country has experienced sustained high growth and recovery in some social indicators, while another is confronting sluggish growth but so far is preserving its social accomplishments, and the third is suffering a severe economic crisis that threatens its social accomplishments;
7. Whether it would have been possible to avoid or reduce economic-social costs during the transition by changing some of the policies or whether those results were inherent to the model; and
8. What is the feasibility of and prospects for the three models in the short and medium term.

4. The Selection of the Three Countries and Their Models

Most books written on Latin America are on the largest countries, such as Argentina, Brazil, and Mexico, which is logical in terms of the size of their territories, economies, populations, trade, and overall influence. Research findings from these countries were often generalized for the whole region with erroneous conclusions, but more recently there has been increasing recognition of the heterogeneity within the continent (Smith 1995). Furthermore, the overwhelming majority of the twenty Latin American countries (not to mention the fourteen Caribbean countries) are either small or middle-sized as are the three selected for this study. They were not mainly chosen for their size, of course, but for the uniqueness of the two extreme models (Chile and Cuba) and their disproportionate influence in view of their size, both in the region and in the world. Think, for instance, of the influence of Chile's neoconservative model and structural adjustment program not only in Latin America but also in shaping World Bank policies, and the Chilean pension-reform model being eagerly sold today by some international financial organizations and business conglomerates in Western and Eastern Europe, Asia, and even the United States. On the other hand, in the 1960s, 1970s, and part of the 1980s, Cuba's economic system was highly influential in Chile (under Allende's administration in 1971–73) and Nicaragua (under the Sandinistas in the 1980s) and inspired guerrilla movements in several countries of Central and South America that had Cuba as the model to follow. In the second half of the 1960s Cuba contested the Soviet Union, claiming to be more advanced in the construction of the ultimate communist system than its patron, and became one of the most egalitarian societies in the world. Cuba also played a key role in the wars in Africa (and provided economic and technical assistance to several countries in that continent and elsewhere), in the Nonaligned Movement, and among Marxist and leftist parties all over the world. Costa Rica ppears to be insignificant beside those two ideological giants and yet was able to achieve in the same period one of the highest social standards in the world without sacrificing its pluralistic democracy and civic freedoms.

Although it is impossible to find identical countries for a comparison in terms of equal size, natural endowment, level of development, and so forth, the three countries selected share many similarities, and their differences are not significant barriers for a comparison. Spanish is basically the only language spoken in the three countries (although an indigenous dialect is also spoken in the south of Chile), and they share a similar colonial, cultural, and religious heritage. Ethnically Costa Rica and Chile have a relatively homogenous population of European origin (the latter has indigenous pockets in the South), while in Cuba there is a substantial population of African origin.

Table I.1 selects thirteen key indicators to assess the comparability issue. In four of them the three countries are very similar: (1) GDP per capita (although there are comparability problems in Cuba); (2) foreign trade dependency (Cuba's is smaller than that of the other two, a mirage created by an inflated national product that results from accounting distortions to be explained later); (3) production of electricity (the proportions of hydroelectric versus thermal in the three countries, however, are quite different: Costa Rica 94.2% and 5.8%, Chile 51.3% and 48.7%, and Cuba 0.5% and 99.5%; ECLAC *Yearbook* 1993); and (4) public expenditures in social services (Cuba's percentage is lower than the other two, because the size of its budget in relation to the national economy is considerably higher).

In three other indicators (dependency on imported fuel, export concentration, and external debt per capita), Costa Rica and Chile are similar, but

Cuba's are higher. The latter benefited, however, from substantial Soviet price subsidies on oil imports as well as on sugar and nickel exports, and the island's bulk of its foreign debt was with the Soviet Union, which supplied it abundantly, under extremely generous conditions, and with virtually no payment demanded.

In terms of population size, Cuba and Chile are similar, but Costa Rica has a considerably lower population; more important is that the last's population growth rate is considerably higher than that of the other two (more than twice the Cuban rate), which imposes a heavy socioeconomic burden. Furthermore, Costa Rica's territorial area and agricultural land per capita are significantly lower than the corresponding indicators of the other two countries. Costa Rica has 40% agricultural land per capita (agricultural labor force) of Chile and 54% of Cuba's. Chile has the highest urban population, followed by Cuba (both ranking among the most urbanized in the region); Costa Rica's urban population is considerably lower than the other two, but there is significant equality in both income per capita and access to social services in the urban and rural sectors (something rare in the region). Finally, in trade partner concentration, the three countries have divergent indicators: Cuba the highest (at least until the beginning of the 1990s) and Chile the lowest.

A comparative study conducted among ninety-one developing countries to measure human development found that all the highly successful cases shared the following four among six common features: they began circa 1965 with a relatively high-quality human resource base, had a strong leadership committed to social policy and allocated substantial resources to education and health, were politically stable, and had linguistic homogeneity (Lindenberg 1993). The three selected countries in this book also share virtually all those features. A research project by UNRISD selected Chile, Costa Rica, and Cuba among seven case studies in the world to find out how they were able to achieve high social standards in spite of having a lower income per capita than many other countries with a poorer social record. Some common factors found to explain such exceptional social performance ratified most of the conclusions of the previous worldwide comparative study: (1) relatively high standards in health and education achieved in the past (1940s and 1950s); (2) early reformist movements that generated important positive changes in social policy; (3) leadership's commitment to expansion in social services, which led to virtual universal coverage in health, education, and social security in the 1960s or 1970s; (4) significant allocation of resources to social services at least until the crisis; (5) emphasis on primary social services first, as well as on vulnerable groups of the population, such as pregnant women and infants; and (6) a relatively homogenous population in Chile and Costa Rica, mainly of European origin, who placed high priority in education and health—in the case of Cuba, a mixed population but relatively integrated combined with early influence of the United States in improving health and education on the island (Ghai 1999).

In summary, I will be comparing three economies of fairly similar levels of development, which are quite dependent on foreign trade, with significant export concentration and dependency on fuel imports, and with traditional emphasis on expansion of social services and social standards above the average in the region. Chile's major advantages are the highest agricultural land per capita (close to Cuba's) and the most diversified trade partners, while Cuba has the lowest population growth rate and Costa Rica the smallest export concentration. Cuba's major disadvantages are the highest export and trade partner concentrations, and Costa Rica's is the highest population growth rate and the lowest agricultural land per capita, while Chile does not have any major disadvantage in terms of Table I.1 indicators. These advantages and disadvantages will be taken into account in the comparison of performance.

In terms of the state's power to implement fast and drastic economic change and policies, the Cuban government is undoubtedly the strongest, followed by Chile (under the authoritarian regime, which was a contradiction with its market ideology), while Costa Rica has the weakest state and had to implement change through democratic means. But overly strong state power might have adverse economic effects, such as committing large-scale errors in policy with disastrous results and excluding the majority of the population from the decision-making process needed to build a consensus.

5. Theoretical Foundations and Actual Application of the Three Economic Models

The main economic features of the three models are summarized and systematically compared in Table I.2: overall ideology, ownership of the means of production, roles of the market versus the state (planning, decision making, decentralization), finance (taxes, interest rate, credit, investment, state-budget balancing), prices (of goods and wages, fiscal subsidies, stabilization), distribution (social services, equity), incentives (material vs. nonmaterial stimuli, unions, collective bargaining, strikes), development strategy (inward versus outward), and economic freedoms (consumer sovereignty, consumer choice, equilibrium). The last row of Table I.2 describes the political system in each country.

There are two broad subperiods in each of the three countries: in Chile the authoritarian regime (1973–90) and the democratic one (since 1990), although the model has continued but with minor adjustments implemented to improve equity. In Costa Rica we see the establishment, consolidation, expansion, and crisis of the model (1958–82) and the following subperiod in which a gradual change toward the market is taking place, particularly in the 1990s. In Cuba there is the long subperiod of application of centralized planning, although with variations (1959–90) and the subperiod of the 1990s crisis, which brought timid, piecemeal, selective market measures, at least until mid-1995, when that movement appeared to be halted. A comparison of the countries at the end of the 1980s would have shown basically one model and unilinear trend, but the 1990s changed the picture with a slight or minor reversal in Chile against the market (in the social arena), an acceleration of the gradual move to the market in Costa Rica, and a timid (but still dramatic) trend toward the market in Cuba. In each of the country parts there will be a more detailed periodization in terms of policy changes.

Table I.2 makes clear that there is no "pure" model even in the two extremes: Chile obviously does not have a perfect competitive market (a theoretical abstraction) but imperfect competition, while Cuba never had a perfect centralized plan (another theoretical, although less elaborated abstraction) but an imperfect plan and only in certain stages. There is not a theoretical paradigm for Costa Rica, but basically the original model was that of a planned market (with indicative planning) going well beyond imperfect competition because of the growing role of the state in the provision of services and production of goods.

Important departures from a conventional neoclassic, monetarist model took place in Chile even during the military regime. For instance, the government decided, for strategic and economic reasons, not to privatize the copper industry (the most important in the country); wage fixing was not left to market forces in the 1970s but largely controlled by the government in an effort to reduce cost-push inflation (which, combined with banning of unions and strikes placed the burden of adjustment on labor); the exchange rate was not allowed to float in that stage either (which led to an overvalued currency and the first crisis); when open unemployment got out of hand (between 1975 and 1979 and even worse between 1982 and 1985) the government did not sit and wait for an automatic market correction but introduced Keynesian massive emergency employment programs; when the crisis of the early 1980s threatened to unravel the system, a new economic team was temporarily put in charge, and the state intervened in many enterprises and banks until the recovery began.

Exceptions to a conventional Soviet model of economic planning took place in Cuba also. Between 1966 and 1970 the central plan was replaced by sectorial and microplans (which led to a lack of central coordination and paralysis of investment); wide experimentation with nonmaterial ("moral") incentives and even an attempt to create a "New Man" occurred between 1966 and 1970 and again between 1986 and 1990 (although with less intensity), in both cases resulting in failure and contributing to the ensuing crisis; and, in general, until the crisis of the 1990s Cuba placed considerably more emphasis on egalitarianism than was done in the Soviet Union and was closer in some stages to the Chinese model of the Great Leap Forward.

The Costa Rican case is representative of the import-substitution-industrialization (ISI) model widely tried in the region (with ECLAC support) from the late 1950s until the crisis of the 1980s. But it was combined with social welfare policies typical of the more advanced countries of the region (Argentina, Chile, and Uruguay) in spite of the fact that Costa Rica's economy was fundamentally agricultural and trade unions were quite weak at the time. The result was one of the most advanced and unique welfare states in the region, without the adverse economic effects suffered by their counterparts: Costa Rica enjoyed moderate economic growth rates until the crisis of the early 1980s. The structural adjustment program did not copy the Chilean model either, as it has been a model of gradualist-slow change (at least until the mid-1990s) with social compensatory programs installed in the 1970s before they became fashionable in the region in the second half of the 1980s.

6. Methodology for Comparative Analysis of Policies and Evaluation of Performance

Although each of the three countries has a basic model during the period of observation, policies have changed in all of them with divergent degrees of importance: the Chilean model is the one that has least changes, followed by Costa Rica and, finally, Cuba (although the policies of the 1990s are dramatic, the Cuban model retains its fundamental features). These policy changes are clustered into stages (in each country), and in each stage there is a description of the corresponding socioeconomic policies as well as an evaluation of their outcomes.

The description of the model in the entire period, as well as policy changes in each stage, are summarized in the first table of each country part. Policies are systematically compared in eight major sectors: ownership, planning and market, financing, stability and prices, development strategy, external sector, labor and employment, and distribution and social services. Several topics are discussed in each of these sectors; for instance, in ownership I look at either the process of reprivatization of public enterprises, land, and services in Chile or the collectivization of virtually all means of production in Cuba; in this sector I also review state regulatory policies, government intervention of enterprises, and so forth.

A general distinction is made between economic organization and development strategy; the former refers to the way the system is structured (ownership, planning, financing, incentives, etc.), while the latter refers to the government's role in promoting development (the greatest role in Cuba and the least in Chile, with Costa Rica in between), with an "outward" or "inward" strategy, and assigning priorities to specific areas of the economy (agriculture, industry, tourism, financial services). The eight sectors combine economic and social policies in a balanced manner.

The framework described above facilitates the comparison of policy changes not only within one country (done in parts 2, 3, and 4 respectively for Chile, Cuba, and Costa Rica) but also among the three countries (an analysis done in the concluding part).

The description of policy and evaluation of performance in each part is based on twenty-six statistical tables for Chile and Costa Rica, but thirty-five for Cuba (because of the absence of internationally standardized data in this country for many macroeconomic indicators, peculiar features, and more frequent changes in policy). These tables combine economic and social data in series that cover the entire period of observation whenever feasible. Table I.3 lists twenty-six main topics covered in such statistical series and identifies the table number for each topic in the three countries, thus facilitating its location by the reader.

The final part of the book first summarizes and compares socioeconomic policies among the three countries and their outcomes. Second, it addresses most of the crucial issues listed in section 3. Third, it evaluates the performance of the three countries based on a set of twenty-three indicators (derived from the country statistical tables), grouped in four categories: (1) *domestic macroeconomic:* GDP growth and per capita, gross domestic investment, inflation, fiscal balance, composition of GDP; (2) *external economic:* export concentration/diversification, import composition, trade partner concentration, cumulative trade volume and balance per capita, foreign debt per capita; (3) *distribution and employment:* income distribution, real wages, poverty incidence, composition of and women's participation in the labor force, open unemployment; and (4) *social standards:* literacy, school enrollment, infant mortality, life expectancy, rate of contagious diseases, access to potable water and sewerage, social security coverage, and housing. A final selection of twenty indications (based on their reliability and comparability) is used to rank the performance of the three models. Three types of rankings among the countries are done with those indicators: absolute (e.g, degree of export concentration in the three countries in 1993), relative improvement (e.g., change in export concentration between the first and last year of the comparison), and indices that combine the twenty indicators. Finally, this part discusses the viability of the three models in the short and medium terms.

The comparison and evaluation of performance have faced three major problems that will be discussed in more detail in the final part: (1) different periods of operation for the model in Costa Rica and Cuba (about thirty-six years) and Chile (about twenty-one years), which creates a problem in the comparison of *relative* performance, because in the first two countries the model started around 1960, while in Chile it began in 1973–74; (2) lack of comparable data for some key variables in Cuba, due to its divergent methodology for calculating the national product vis-à-vis the other two countries; and (3) impossibility of quantifying and isolating nonsystemic factors in the evaluation of performance, which forces the use of qualitative analysis.

A final note on the period of observation. This book took ten years for completion and, to halt the time-consuming process of constant updating, I set the final year for the systematic comparison as 1994 for Chile and Costa Rica (the year of the conclusion of presidential terms) and 1995 for Cuba (particularly in terms of policy), because it was then that the process of reform appeared to be halted (a point that still held in July 1998 when the manuscript was finished). Even with that cut, the book covers about thirty-six years of economic history in these three Latin American countries, and it is quite long. Still the reader is entitled to know what happened in the 1994–98 presidential terms in Chile and Costa Rica, as well as developments in Cuba during the same period, but the systematic incorporation of those extra years would have postponed the book further. In order to satisfy the reader's curiosity, brief information on major changes in policy and performance in 1995–97 was incorporated in part 5, in the analysis of the future of the models.

Tables to Part I

Table I.1

Basic Indicators for the Three Countries, (Percentage) 1986–1990

	Chile	Costa Rica	Cuba
Population (millions, 1990)	13.2	3.0	10.7
Population growth rate[a]	1.8	2.9	1.4
Urban population (percent of total 1990)	85.6	53.6	74.9
Area (thousands, km²)	757	51	115
Agricultural land per capita (in ha. per one in agricultural labor force[b] 1990)	4.58	1.86	3.45
Foreign-trade dependency (transactions as percent of GDP in current prices 1989)	72.1	73.8	50.7[c]
Export concentration[d] (Percent over total exports 1988)	48.4	42.8	74.6
Oil dependence (Percent over total imports 1988)	12	12	34[e]
Production of electricity (kw/h per capita 1990)	1,400	1,249	1,505
Debt per capita (U.S.$ 1990)	1,443	1,163	3,546
Trade-partner concentration[f] (Percent over total trade 1988)	20.5	40.5	69.1
GDP per capita (U.S.$ 1990)	1,940	1,900	1,777[c,g]
Public expenditures in social services[h] (Percent of total public budget 1986)	61.1	62.2	44.0

Sources: Data for Cuba, unless specified, come from CCE, *AEC 1988* and *1989;* public expenditures from *Granma Weekly Review,* 1–12, 1986, p. 3; debt per capita (including Soviet Union, Eastern Europe, and hard currency) from Mesa-Lago 1993a; GDP per capita from BNC 1995 and population projection from author. Data sources for Chile and Costa Rica are: population from CELADE 1991; area, oil dependency, GDP per capita, and public expenditures from World Bank, *WDR* 1986b, 1992b; foreign-trade dependency, export, and trade-partner concentration from IMF, *IFSY 1989* and *1990* and *DTSY 1989;* debt per capita from IDB 1991. All figures on electricity output are from ECLAC, *Yearbook* 1993, and on urban population from UNDP 1996. Agricultural land per capita in the agricultural labor force are author's estimates: other indicators came from FAO 1987 and UNDP *HDR* 1994.

[a]Annual average for periods of study (1960–93). [b]Other indicator is arable land (ha) per one person in agricultural labor force: Chile 4.1, Costa Rica 1.0, and Cuba 4.7. The indicator agricultural land (ha) per inhabitant (total population) is the least meaningful: Chile 0.34, Costa Rica 0.18, and Cuba 0.31. I appreciate Prof. Mitchell Seligson's help in estimating these indicators. [c]Global Social Product instead of GDP. [d]Chile, copper; Costa Rica, coffee and bananas; Cuba, sugar. [e]Fuel and minerals. [f]U.S. for Chile and Costa Rica, Soviet Union, for Cuba. [g]In pesos. [h]Social services include education, health, housing, amenities, social security, and welfare; for Cuba, it also includes cultural and scientific activities.

Table I.2
Economic Models of the Three Countries

Country	Chile	Costa Rica	Cuba
Overall ideology	Neoclassic, neoliberal (neoconservative), monetarist, imperfect competition model in 1974–90. Some Neo-Keynesian influence in tax and social policies in 1990s.	Keynesian, Social-Democrat, ECLAC structuralist until early 1980s. Gradual change to Neoclassical, neoconservative, since mid-1980s and particularly in 1990s.	Marxist-Leninist, with alternative Stalinist, Mao-Guevarist and mild Soviet-type reforms until 1990. Very small neoclassical and monetarist influence in 1990–95.
Ownership of means of production	Basically private except mainly in copper. Privatization of public enterprises and most social services until 1990. No advance of state ownership in the 1990s.	Predominantly private but with increasing state ownership in social services and production until 1980s. Gradual process of privatization of state enterprises, banking, etc. in late 1980s and 1990s.	Basically public (state) except small agriculture sector until 1990. Agricultural crops, self-employment, expansion of informal sector and joint enterprises with foreign companies in 1990s.
Market vs. state: planning, decision making, decentralization	Market is dominant, subsidiary state role; very weak indicative long-term plan; decentralization of decision making; focus on micro-efficiency. Small increase in state role in social services and distribution in 1990s.	Market is predominant but growing state role, centralization and indicative plan (focus on macro-economic issues) until the early 1980s. Decreasing (some decentralization) in the 1990s.	Overwhelming state role with tiny illegal market pockets (black market), and centralized imperative plan until end of 1980s. Some decentralization, and growing legal and informal markets in 1990s.
Finance: Taxes, banking, interest rate, credit, investment, state	Basically free financial system with some controls by central banks and other state agencies;	Increasing state control of financial system; banks nationalized; crucial and growing role of central bank	All economy financed by state budget (budgetary vs. self-financing schools), state banking monopoly,

(continued)

21

Table I.2
(Continued)

Country	Chile	Costa Rica	Cuba
budget balance	banking is private; interest rate fundamentally set by market; consumption taxes predominate; state incentives for saving/ investment and promotion of financial markets.	and other state agencies; public credit for priority sectors; state-fixed interest rate. Gradual and partial reversal of these policies in 1990s.	few taxes, state provides investment (small role of credit) and fixes interest rate. Increasing taxes and concern with budget deficit in 1990s.
Prices: Goods, wages, fiscal subsidies, stabilization	Prices basically set by market with some exceptions, but wages partly fixed by the state to control inflation (in 1970s and part of 1980s); structural adjustment, elimination of subsidies to consumer goods and services.	Predominantly market-set but considerable role of the state in price fixing (goods, wages) and subsidies to public enterprises and essential consumer goods and services. Gradualist structural adjustment in 1980s and 1990s, much milder than in Chile.	Basically prices of all goods and wages fixed by the state; subsidies to public enterprises and essential consumer goods and services. Increasing market role in price (and to less extend wage) setting, and adjustment program in 1990s.
External Sector: Foreign trade, exchange rate, tariffs, investment	Liberalization of and opening to world trade and capital, unification and drastic reduction of import tariffs, elimination of protectionism to increase competition and efficiency; exchange rate temporarily controlled but since 1982 set by market; no regulation of foreign investment to freely compete with domestic.	Mainly market but state control through quotas/tariffs; exchange rate fixed by the state until 1981 (thereafter it largely floats); protection of domestic producers; regulation of foreign investment. Gradual liberalization in late 1980s and 1990s but not to the Chilean extent.	State monopoly of foreign trade, protection of domestic industry, exchange rate arbitrarily fixed by state; foreign investment banned until 1982 and liberalized in 1990s (in this period also some decentralization of trade in key state or pseudo-private enterprises).

22

Distribution	Virtually set by market with reduced ex-post state role to correct some major problems (through transfers and limited social policy). More emphasis on equity (tax reform) and poverty reduction in 1990s.	Mainly by market but with increasing state intervention through taxation, social services and welfare policies to reduce major inequalities.	By state through total control of wages and ownership; egalitarianism pursued in some stages. Increasing inequalities in the 1990s through money remittances, dollar circulation, state dollar shops.
Incentives: labor conditions	Utility maximization, material-individual incentives. Control of unions and collective bargaining and prohibition of strikes until 1980s. Labor freedoms fully restored in 1990s.	Predominant material-individual but moderated by state role to provide solidarity and equity. Full labor freedoms although with some limits in 1990s.	Alternative emphasis in moral-collective stimulation (1966–70, 1986–89) and moderate individual-material (significant increase in the 1990s). State-controlled unions and collective bargaining, strikes banned.
Development strategy	State provides legal framework and infrastructure for market to flourish; nontraditional export promotion based on comparative advantages (outward development).	State-guided plans for industrial expansion (ISI) and agricultural diversification supporting private sector and later with state as producer (inward development). Export promotion and external opening in the late 1980s and 1990s (outward development).	Initially state-directed industrialization and agricultural diversification program (inward development); later return to sugar with large crops, followed by a more balanced strategy (all three strategies with substantial Soviet support); development of hard-currency exports and tourism with foreign investment in the 1990s (outward development).

(continued)

Table I.2
(Continued)

Country	Chile	Costa Rica	Cuba
Economic freedoms: consumer sovereignty, freedom of choice, equilibrium	Consumer sovereignty (but with minor limitations); freedom of choice; equilibrium set by market with least feasible state participation.	Consumer sovereignty (but considerably more restricted than in Chile; less limited in 1990s); freedom of choice; equilibrium by market but with key state role (less in 1990s).	Planner's preferences and considerably limited freedom of choice (although increasing in 1990s); equilibrium set by plan (less so in 1990s).
Political system	Authoritarian military regime took enormous powers to implement change and severely restricted civic freedoms until 1990. Pluralistic democracy (with a few minor limitations) and full civic freedoms in the 1990s.	Pluralistic democracy and full civic freedoms, with a predominant political party (but frequent changes of party in power); reforms introduced in a democratic way.	"Dictatorship of the Proletariat," authoritarian socialist regime with single party, absolute powers and virtually no civic freedoms. No substantial change in 1990s.

Table I.3

Topics in Statistical Series in the Three Countries (Table Numbers)

Topics	Chile	Costa Rica	Cuba
Socioeconomic policies by stages	II.1	IV.1–IV.2	III.1
Collectivization and privatization	II.2		III.2
Basic macroeconomic data	II.3	IV.3	III.3–III.7
Composition of GDP/GSP	II.4	IV.4	III.8–III.9
Physical output	II.5–II.6	IV.5–IV.6	III.10–III.15
Trade balance and dependency	II.7	IV.7	III.16
Composition of exports	II.8	IV.7	III.17
Composition of imports	II.9	IV.9	III.18
World prices exports/imports	II.10	IV.10	III.19
Trade-partner concentration	II.11	IV.11	III.20
Dependency on fuel imports	II.12	IV.12	III.21
Foreign debt	II.13	IV.13	III.22–III.23
Labor force by economic sector	II.14	IV.14	III.24
Women in labor force	II.15	IV.15	III.25
Open unemployment	II.16	IV.16	III.26
Public social expenditures	II.17	IV.17	III.6
Income distribution	II.18	IV.18	III.27
Poverty incidence	II.18	IV.19	
Real wages	II.19	IV.20	III.28
Consumption	II.20		III.29
Demography and health	II.21	IV.21	III.30
Contagious diseases	II.22	IV.22	III.31
Potable water and sewerage	II.23	IV.23	III.32
Literacy and school enrollment	II.24	IV.24	III.33
Social security	II.25	IV.25	III.34
Housing	II.26	IV.26	III.35

Part II

CHILE
The Market Model

1

Introduction

1. Summary of Socioeconomic Conditions and Policies on the Eve of the Military Coup

Since the late 1950s, Chilean governments of different ideological persuasions attempted to make reforms in economic management in order to improve effectiveness and competitiveness, introduce changes in state institutions and in the public administration, and, more generally, modernize economic policy making. Between 1958 and 1973 Chile experienced the most diverse economic policies in its history, as three administrations with markedly different ideologies (but an increasing state role) came to power: Jorge Alessandri (conservative, 1958–64), Eduardo Frei (Christian Democrat, 1964–70) and Salvador Allende (socialist, 1970–73).

The Alessandri administration has been characterized as a frustrated attempt to implement a free-market economy. His administration tried to expand the participation of the private sector in the economy and to reduce the state planning and entrepreneurial roles developed since 1939, when the Corporation for National Development (CORFO) was created (Arellano 1985; Ffrench-Davis and Muñoz 1990).

The Frei and, especially, the Allende governments, however, strengthened the economic role of the state. Both administrations gave priority to income distribution policies, through the expansion of social services, which placed Chile in a high rank regionally concerning social indicators (Arellano 1985). Allende has been the only case in the Americas in which a socialist candidate was democratically elected as president. His administration was characterized by deep structural reforms and serious internal conflicts between labor and capital, as well as among political groups. (Data for 1970, at the beginning of the Allende administration, are scarce, making it difficult to analyze economic performance in 1970–73. When data for 1970 are not available, comparisons will be made between 1965, Frei's first year, and 1973, Allende's last year in power, or with the average of the 1960s.)

In 1970–73 the state became the main actor in the Chilean economy, as it played a predominant role in economic regulation, production, resource allocation, and conflict resolution. About 461 firms were seized or intervened by the government, which, at the end of 1973, controlled approximately 39% of GNP, compared with 14% in 1965, in both cases excluding the agricultural sector. Between 1965 and 1973 the state firms by economic sector increased as follows: from 25% to 100% in services, from 13% to 85% in mining, from an unknown proportion to 85% in finances, from 11% to 70% in communications, and from 3% to 40% in industry (Table II.2). The nationalization of the copper industry, the acceleration of the agrarian reform, and the intervention of banks increased to 70% the state's control of total investment. In addition, the state set prices and granted subsidies for basic products, regulated and oversaw foreign trade, controlled the labor market, and expanded the provision of free social services (Hachette and Luders 1987; Muñoz 1992).

As part of Allende's expansive fiscal policy, social expenditures rose by 30% in 1970–72. Tax collection, however, decreased annually by 6% in 1971–73 because of managerial flaws and the hyperinflation of 1972–73. As a result, the fiscal deficit reached 13% of GDP in 1972 and 24.7% in 1973 (Arellano 1985; Edwards and Edwards 1987; Larraín and Meller 1990; Table II.3).

Because of the expansionist policies, GDP grew by 9% in 1971, twice the 4.4% average rate of 1960–70, but this initial success was followed by declines of 1.2% in 1972 and 5.6% in 1973. Annual average GDP growth per capita in 1971–73 was −1% contrasted with 2.2% between 1960 and 1970. Gross investment, as a percentage of GDP, dramatically fell in 1970–73 from 16.4.% to 7.9%, the lowest since at least 1960; the annual average under Allende was 11.5%, compared with 15.1% between 1960 and 1970 (Table II.3).

Because of very low domestic savings and the small capital market at the time, the main source for financing government current expenditures was credit provided by the Central Bank. As a result, the total amount of money in circulation increased 30 times in 1970–73, creating acute macroeconomic disequilibria. There was a severe scarcity of essential consumer goods in the domestic market because of the high demand caused by the expansion in the money supply and the price controls imposed by the government on such goods, which created a parallel or illegal (black) market. Growing inflation rates were another adverse effect: between 1960 and 1970 the average annual inflation rate was 23%, in 1972 it reached 163%, and in 1973 it soared to 508% (Table II.3).

The composition of GDP by economic activity exhibited minor changes between 1960 and 1973: the primary sector declined from 10.6% to 6.8%; the secondary sector (including construction) rose little, from 39.1% to 39.8%; and the tertiary sector (transport, communication, commerce, and others) was the most dynamic, as it increased from 50.3% to 53.4% (Table II.4).

Allende's trade policy was characterized by too many import restrictions and excessive protectionism. For instance, 5,125 new custom tariffs were established, of which 63% were direct prohibitions; the 1973 nominal tariff averaged 94%, and the maximum was 600% (Edwards 1985). Copper production increased by an average of 3% between 1960 and 1970, but, under state management, the average dropped to 2% in 1971–73 (Table II.5). Dependency on copper exports (as a percentage of total exports) declined from 70.5% to 67.3% between 1960 and 1970 but jumped to 83.3% in 1973 (Table II.8). Dependency on oil imports (as a percentage of total oil supply) increased from 34% to 68% between 1960 and 1973 (there are no data for 1970). The last two indicators obviously made Chile more vulnerable to price fluctuations in the world market. On the other hand, there was an acceleration in the trend toward diversification of trade partners: between 1960 and 1970 trade with the United States declined from 42.6% to 24.1% of Chile's total trade; that percentage steadily declined to 12.3% in 1973—its lowest historical level—but this was largely a result of U.S. actions (Hachette and Luders 1987; Larraín and Meller 1990; Muñoz 1992; Fontaine 1993; Moguillansky and Titelman 1993; Tables II.11–12).

The decline in the world price of copper by 24% in 1970–72 (the price jumped 66% in 1973 but was partly offset by an oil price increase that year), the continuous and dramatic currency devaluations (the rate of devaluation averaged 31.2% between 1962 and 1970 but was 468% in 1973), the soaring inflation, and the increase in the value of imports by 53% in 1970–73 provoked a deficit in the merchandise trade balance of U.S.$174 million in 1972–73 and reduced international reserves by more than 50% in 1970–73 (BCCh *Indicadores* 1989; Larraín and Meller 1990; Tables II.7, II.10).

The national unemployment rate averaged 6.5% between 1960 and 1970; the latter was based on ODEPLAN, but this series ended in 1970, and there is not a continuous series for 1960–73; ILO and Balassa data, however, indicate that the 1970 rate was lower (3.4–3.5%), and, after a decline in 1972, it increased to 4.8% in 1973. All series on the unemployment rate in Santiago show a decline in 1971 and an increase in 1973 (Table II.16). The Allende government promoted unionization, regulated the labor market, and protected workers against arbitrary layoffs (which largely explains the decline of unemployment in 1971–72). Between 1965 and 1970, 17.7% of those employed were unionized, but the percentage increased to 29% in 1971–73 and 33.7% in 1973. Close to a half million workers, or 16.3% of the labor force, went on strike in 1971–73 (ILO *Yearbook* 1977).

Real wages increased by 21.5 points in 1971 because of government control and a 12.8% drop in inflation, but in 1972 they declined by 12.4 points and by 41.1 points more in 1973 (based on ECLAC; Table II.19). The government's policy of increasing nominal wages (aimed at raising the purchasing power of the population) was more than offset by inflation; hence real wages decreased by 53% in 1970–73 (Table II.19; Campero and Cortázar 1989; Larraín and Meller 1990; Meller 1992a, 1992b).

Allende tried to improve income redistribution with the following measures: agrarian reform and distribution of land to peasants, wage controls (which were defeated by inflation), and increases in social expenditures of 25.2% of GDP in 1971 and 25.8% in 1972, higher than the average of 18.6% between 1960 and 1970, but resulting in an expanded fiscal deficit (Arellano 1985). Consumption per capita increased in 1971–72 but dramatically fell in 1973, below the 1970 level (Table II.20).

Social security coverage increased from 73.8% of the labor force in 1965 to 75.6% in 1970 and 75.9% in 1973, but costs rose from 12.3% to 17.5% of GDP between 1965 and 1971 (the latter a historical record) and declined to 10.4% in 1973. Real pensions increased 38 percentage points in 1971 but declined 32 points in 1972 and 46 points in 1973 (Table II.25; Mesa-Lago 1985). Infant mortality dropped from 120 to 82 per thousand between 1960 and 1970 (at an annual rate of 3.8) to 66 in 1973 (at a faster rate of 5.3%). Life expectancy increased from 58.1 to 63.6 years between 1960 and 1970 and to 65.7 in 1973 (at similar annual rates; Table II.21). Enrollment in elementary school increased from 87% to 100% between 1960 and 1970 and continued to be universal in 1973; enrollment in secondary school rose from 23% to 38% between 1960 and 1970 and to 51% in 1973; and enrollment in higher education increased from 4% to 10% between 1960 and 1970 and to 17% in 1973 (in the last two indicators, the rate of annual expansion in 1971–73 was considerably higher than between 1960 and 1970; see Table II.24; Arellano 1985; Marcel and Arenas 1992).

In summary, after a brief positive economic start for the Allende administration and a good record on social services throughout it, Chile ended up at the end of 1973 with a state economic control equal to 39% of GDP, a hyperinflation rate of 508%, a fiscal deficit of 25% of GDP, a deficit in the trade balance of U.S.$174 million in 1972–73, international reserves reduced by 50% below the 1970 level, an average tariff of 94% with a maximum of 600%, a monetary supply increased 30 times in 1970–73, an increase in unemployment although still minor (less than 5%), and real wages reduced more than 28% under the 1970 level. Such a difficult situation, combined with strong internal social turmoil and external pressures, created an explosive economic and political environment that facilitated the breakdown of

Chile's long-standing democracy through a military coup on September 11, 1973 (Larraín and Meller 1990).

2. Periodization of Neoconservative Policies

The rest of this part will analyze the radical structural economic reforms implemented in Chile from September 1973 onwards, which transformed the country's mixed economy into the one most market-oriented and open to foreign trade in Latin America. This part will cover the 1973–94 period, divided into five stages: (1), Monetarism, Adjustment, and First Crisis (1973–76): initial steps of the neoconservative strategy and first economic crisis caused by growing inflation and decline in GDP. (2) Monetarism, Open Economy, Growth, and Indebtedness (1976–81): acceleration of the opening to foreign trade, declining inflation, increase in internal and external debt, and economic recovery. (3) Second Crisis and State Intervention (1981–83): state intervention in the economy, prompted by a severe economic crisis, characterized by a decline in GDP and a very high unemployment rate. (4) Corrections, Recovery, and Economic Boom (1984–90): inflation and the debt crisis are controlled, and sustained growth leads to a boom and a new inflationary spurt. (5) Democracy, Continuation of Economic Model, and Growth with Equity (1990–94): adjustments to reduce inflation and face the 1990 oil crisis, stabilization and sustained growth, and more equitable labor and social policies (for a summary of policies in each stage see Table II.1).

2

Monetarism, Adjustment, and the First Crisis

1973–1976

The Chilean economic reform was implemented by an authoritarian military regime that was in power for sixteen and a half years (from September 1973 to March 1990). This part will not analyze the politics of that regime but will refer briefly to its characteristics that facilitated the application of the drastic economic changes.

The military closed and dissolved the National Congress, whose powers were transferred to the military junta, made up by the four commanders of the armed forces, and all political parties and opposition activities were prohibited. Trade union headquarters were closed down and labor federations at the national level banned. The new government intervened in the universities, and professional associations were closed or debarred. General civil liberties were restricted (curfew, special controls on cars and homes), and the mass media was placed under government control. The economic reforms were thus implemented under strict governmental control and without any civic or political debate.

At the end of 1973, an ideologically coherent team of economic experts, the majority of them graduates of the University of Chicago, was incorporated into the government bureaucracy. The team pushed for numerous economic liberalization measures that had to overcome the military's mistrust of neoconservative policies and free markets, which were contrary to their strong sense of nationalism and the traditional protection granted to industry and domestic production. The team of economists explained the economic stagnation, hyperinflation, and crisis of the early 1970s as a result of the increase in state control and intervention in the economy, the erosion of the market, and the weakness of the private sector. To overcome these problems, the neoconservatives elaborated a well-structured, comprehensive, coherent package of reforms, whose central goal was the total transformation of Chile's mixed, regulated, and protectionist economy into an open and free-market system.

Under the influence of the neoconservative team, the military attempted to confront the acute economic crisis and macroeconomic disequilibrium inherited from the Allende government through the following measures: price liberalization; deregulation of custom duties, tariffs, and foreign trade; privatization of public enterprises; restrictive fiscal and monetary policies; and several monetary devaluations. These reforms laid the foundations of the most radical neoconservative model to be applied in Latin America in the last quarter of the twentieth century, much more orthodox than the models of Argentina, Brazil, and Uruguay. According to Ramos (1986), the Chilean process was the "most pure model" of the experiences of the Southern Cone. Sheahan (1987) asserts that in Chile "the economic policies introduced by the military regime from 1973 constituted a new extreme, the most all-out application of conservative free-market principles seen in Latin America since the 1920s." For Ffrench-Davis (1988), the Chilean case was the "most extreme model" implemented in the region. Authoritarianism was officially justified as due to the radical reform needed to overcome existing economic problems.

1. Policies

A. Ownership

"Reducing the state is to make the nation grow" was a common expression used in this stage. The neoconservative strategy was to gradually transfer the state's productive and some service activities to the private sector, which should control investment and lead economic growth. Such a goal was to be accomplished through privatization, not only of the firms intervened in by Allende but also of public enterprises created before 1970. Three reasons were given for privatization: to solve the financial problems of the public sector, improve the efficiency of state enterprises, and distribute ownership to the people through the sale of stocks (Marcel 1989).

The privatization process went through three stages. In the first (1973–81), it was massive and scarcely regulated, without adequate financial guarantees, and there were unlimited sales to a single buyer. All this led to concentration of ownership in a few economic conglomerates that had a high rate of indebtedness, hence contributing to the 1981–82 debt crisis. In the second stage (1983–85), enterprises intervened in by the state during the debt crisis, to avoid their bankruptcy, were reprivatized. In the third stage (1985–89), privatization of the remaining state enterprises was done gradually, through the sale of stocks in the capital market, more regulation of these transactions, and efforts to promote wider ownership (Marcel 1989; Hachette and Luders 1993).

In 1974, out of a total of 259 enterprises intervened in by the state in 1973, 202 were returned to the private sector, and in 1976 the number rose to 251. Some of the privatized enterprises received compensation, especially those that had not received any indemnification when they were expropriated (e.g., U.S.-owned mining corporations). In 1973–76, 100 manufacturing firms and 13 banks were sold to the private sector, at very low prices, because of the urgency of selling at a time of deep recession. The state lost around 30% of the book value of the sold assets; those who acquired public assets received a subsidy, and there was a transfer of resources from the state to the private sector. One of the first government actions at the end of 1973 was the return of agricultural lands previously expropriated to private owners (under the process of land distribution initiated by Frei in 1964 and continued under Allende until 1973): from 30% to 40% of the expropriated land, including peasants' parcels and cooperatives, was returned to its former owners (Ortega 1987; Sanfuentes 1987; Foxley 1988; Table II.2).

The above analysis and comparative studies indicate that the Chilean privatization process was one of the most radical, in both scope and speed, implemented in developing countries. The economic conglomerates, organized as an outcome of the privatization process, controlled the Chilean economy until 1982, when the financial collapse provoked by the debt crisis forced the government to intervene (Marcel 1989; Muñoz 1992). The government, nevertheless, retained ownership of a significant sector of the economy, including the copper industry (hence controlling 60% of Chilean exports), as well as 12 out of 15 large nonfinancial enterprises, such as steel, coal, telecommunications, computers, water, gas, electricity, railroads, and aerial transportation (Ramos 1986).

B. Planning

Three government economic agencies were the target of the deregulation and marketization processes: the National Planning Office (ODEPLAN), the Ministry of the Economy, and the Corporation for National Development (CORFO). The last, founded in 1939, was the first planning agency in Chile and had a key role in the promotion and development of productive and technological activities, functions that were dramatically reduced by the regime. The Ministry of the Economy's productive and regulatory roles were also diminished, and it became a secondary player in the design of economic policies.

Opinions within the government were divided regarding the fate of ODE-PLAN. Initially, some government officials favored the abolition or reduction of that agency, to eliminate the main instrument of centralization and state planning under Allende, and because they rejected planning as a managerial tool in a market economy. The neoconservative team who took over the control of ODEPLAN, however, wanted not only to keep that agency but also to increase its power in order to control public-sector operations and modify economic policy making. ODEPLAN had offices established throughout the country, which were used by the neoconservatives to participate in all the technical committees that the military government had established to restructure the public sector, design and evaluate projects, and elaborate new policies. Through the control of that fortress, neoconservative economists expanded their participation in the state bureaucracy and their influence in the government as a whole. They designed and managed cost-benefit norms that were applied to all evaluations of social projects, programmed the drastic reduction in public expenditures, and introduced measures of fiscal discipline that have been followed until the present (Montecinos 1988).

ODEPLAN economists, nevertheless, encountered resistance from military officers in charge of regional programs who resented their considerable power and control; the officers requested an expansion of their share of decision making within the government. In 1973–76 the struggle was resolved in favor of the economists, whose power in ODEPLAN and other government agencies was strengthened, and with it their control over the economy. The absence of democracy and public debate, among other factors, made this control possible without the checks typical of a democratic society (Montecinos 1988; Ffrench-Davis and Muñoz 1990; Fontaine 1993).

C. Financing

To increase public revenues and reduce the fiscal deficit, the first tax reform was implemented in 1974, with the following features: (1) introduction of the Value-Added Tax (VAT), which eliminated the multiple previous sales taxes; (2) elimination of taxes over property and capital gains; (3) reduction of taxes on profits of enterprises; (4) increased control on tax evasion; (5) improvement of the monetary adjustment system; (6) elimination of fiscal exemptions; and (7) merging of taxes imposed on individuals and firms (Ramos 1986; Yáñez 1992).

The progressive liberalization of both the domestic financial market and control on capital movement facilitated the inflow of foreign capital; thus, the reduction in domestic savings was offset by external savings. The development of capital markets made the operation of foreign financial institutions possible, which, together with the privatized national institutions, functioned with the sole restriction that they had to pay a maximum nominal interest rate of 25% per month. This rate was substantially higher than the one offered by the banks under government control (9.6% monthly nominal rate), hence stimulating the transfer of resources from the state to the private sector (Foxley 1988).

D. Stability and Prices

Stabilization policies in this stage were characterized by the use of the market as the main mechanism in economic decision making. At the end of 1973, the government's main target was to control macroeconomic disequilibria, especially inflation and the fiscal deficit, which neoconservative economists interpreted as being mainly "monetary" phenomena. Several measures were taken to control the inflationary process. Prices were no longer controlled (including the interest rate), thus ending shortages and the black market for domestic goods. The Central Bank implemented various unannounced devaluations with the purpose of stopping inflationary expectations and alleviating the deficit in the balance of payments. The dismantling of labor organizations helped to control wages, deemed necessary to avoid cost-led inflation (Ramos 1986; Foxley 1988; Fontaine 1993).

The huge fiscal deficit (30% of GDP at the end of 1973) was tackled with a restrictive monetary policy. The Central Bank made a serious effort to control the rate of growth of domestic credit. About 50,000 public jobs were cut in 1974, and salaries of public employees were controlled. Subsidies to public enterprises that the government had intervened in were eliminated, as they were considered the main cause of the fiscal deficit and escalation of inflation. Public expenditures were cut from 43.6% to 20.1% of GDP in 1973–76. Social expenditures were the most affected, as they were reduced by 9 points of GDP, reversing the growing trend in the allocation of resources for social services in the previous two decades. Conversely, defense expenditures increased (Ffrench-Davis 1983; Arellano 1985; Edwards and Edwards 1987; Foxley 1988; Larraín and Meller 1990; Meller 1992a, 1992b).

E. Development Strategy

Because of the high priority given to control inflation, there was no specific strategy of economic development in this stage. General policies, however, eliminated some of the bases for the previous strategy (centered on import substitution industrialization [ISI]), such as reduction in the size and role of the state, the greater participation of the private sector in all areas of the economy, and the liberalization of financial markets and foreign trade. In addition, some of the policies in the agrarian-forestry sector laid the basis for a future strategy, focusing on the expansion of nontraditional exports (see next section).

Neoconservative economists criticized the subordinate position given to agriculture in the previous ISI strategy. Agriculture and forestry, therefore, were given priority as keys to export development. The modernization of the agricultural sector was based on two basic principles: the market should determine the price of products, and there should be an opening to foreign trade. The new agricultural policies removed some of the old obstacles and created new incentives: the liberalization of prices in the agrarian market (with the exception of some essential grains like wheat, corn, and rice, whose prices remained temporarily fixed by the state); the reduction of protectionism (import tariffs were lowered and uniformed); and the elimination of labor pressures. The development of agriculture was led by the private sector, which took over the old state-owned agricultural enterprises, among them vegetable oil producers, fisheries, fruit processors, grain storage facilities (silos), refrigeration equipment, agribusiness conglomerates, and vineyards. The private sector also led the development of forestry, promoted by the government through three measures: the transfer from the National Forestry Corporation (CONAF) to the private sector of 60,000 sectors of forests, nurseries, and sawmills; a subsidy to the private sector equivalent to 75% of the cost of forestation; and some tax exemptions (Sanfuentes 1987; Silva 1987).

F. External Sector

The government liberalized foreign trade through the opening of the economy to external markets and capital, as well as through the creation of incentives for the participation of the domestic private sector in the international financial market. In order to maintain a neutral, nondiscriminatory policy between national and foreign investment, the government reduced the existing limits to foreign investment and credit. Furthermore, trade barriers were eliminated and customs regulations simplified to remove obstacles to foreign trade. A process of reduction and unification of tariffs was initiated in 1974: the average tariff decreased from 94% to 35.6% in 1973–76, while the maximum tariff shrank from 600% to 65% (Edwards 1985; Foxley 1988).

At the end of 1973, a single exchange rate replaced the existing 15 multiple exchange rates, and the peso sharply devalued. The latter was followed, from the start of 1974 to the beginning of 1975, by a series of unannounced mini-devaluations to control inflation. From early 1975 to mid-1976, devaluations had the purpose of solving the crisis in the balance of payments, as they were linked to fluctuations in the world price of copper. Thus, when the price of copper fell, a devaluation immediately followed in order to maintain the equilibrium in the trade balance and in the internal hard-currency market (Ramos 1986; Foxley 1988).

Two key objectives of the new economic policy were the development of exports and the increase of their competitiveness in the world market. These were stimulated by the new exchange policy and tariff reductions, as well as other measures taken at the end of 1974: modernization of the ports infrastructure, changes in the regulation of the merchant marine and air transportation (debureaucratization of the administrative system and greater participation of the private sector), and the creation of PROCHILE, a state agency for the promotion of exports with the following functions: (1) financing of special nontraditional exports programs, (2) establishment of an information network with 26 commercial offices in the most important world markets, (3) coordination of exports through an internal administrative structure of 51 sectoral committees, (4) defense against protectionist policies of other countries, and (5) support in the commercialization of export products (Moguillansky and Titelman 1993).

G. Labor and Employment

Adjustment policies and the opening of the economy to imports led to increased unemployment. Furthermore, in order to reduce inflation, the government decided to cut labor costs through the following measures: it banned or controlled unions, prohibited strikes and collective bargaining, fixed wages below inflation, made cuts in the minimum wage and unemployment compensation, and facilitated layoffs. Notice that there is a significant contradiction in the Chilean model: the state deregulated many economic activities and liberalized prices but tightly controlled labor and fixed wages, thus placing the burden of adjustment on the workers.

In 1975 the notable increase in unemployment forced the government to create the Minimum Employment Plan (PEM): work was concentrated in beautification activities, parks, and roads (all of them nonproductive, temporary, and requiring little skills), and salaries were 25% of the legal minimum wage. In addition, a special subsidy was granted to enterprises that hired new workers.

Changes in labor legislation to reduce labor costs and make the labor market more flexible included the unification of the minimum wage paid to blue- and white-collar workers (based on the minimum wage of blue-collars and paid only to workers who had three or more months in the job); the freedom to fire workers, without the need to justify the cause of dismissal; and reductions in unemployment compensation. Unions and other labor organizations were eliminated or restricted: the United Workers Federation (Central Unica de Trabajadores [CUT]), the most important trade union organization at the time, was dissolved in the first week after the coup. In addition, strikes and direct collective bargaining between employers and workers were prohibited. The government began to fix wages under the level of inflation; hence a decline in real wages occurred in this stage (Cortázar 1985; Meller 1992a, 1992b).

H. Distribution and Social Services

The government redefined social policy and the role of the state in it and reduced public social expenditures. The state's function in the social sector (as well as in the economy) would be a subsidiary one, restricted to correcting the negative effects of the operation of the free market. The government, therefore, would no longer intervene in income redistribution (e.g., through social expenditures), but the market would solely determine the price of production factors, and the state's role would be limited to providing a minimum base for the neediest and/or those affected by the economic reform. Because of this last role for the state, the Chilean model was officially labeled "social market." These measures prepared the conditions for the transfer of social services to the private sector (Arellano 1985; Ffrench-Davis and Raczynski 1987).

New social security policies included (1) the creation of a United Fund of Family Allowances, which unified the administration of several funds and equalized their benefits (based on the lowest amount, paid to blue-collar workers); (2) the introduction of a uniform and universal unemployment benefit; (3) the extension of welfare pensions to low-income individuals lacking social insurance coverage and aged 65 and older or disabled aged 18 and older; (4) the establishment of the National Fund of Welfare Pensions, which centralized the administration and accounting of all contributions from pension funds as well as state subsidies; (5) the increase in contributions to improve the financing of the social security system; (6) the implementation of more controls on evasion and payment delay of contributions; and (7) the augmenting of state contributions for the pension system (Arellano 1985; Mesa-Lago 1985).

State expenditures on health care were reduced more than in any other social service, but the diminished resources available were strictly targeted to primary care for children and pregnant women in order to improve the main health indicators, such as infant mortality and malnutrition. This targeting policy was in keeping with sound public health principles, and the government alleged that it was also more equitable: public funds had previously subsidized the middle class to the detriment of the poor. But the drastic cuts in current expenditures and investment eventually harmed some public health areas (e.g., contagious disease control), as well as secondary and tertiary care for the population as a whole. Last, a strong emphasis was given to the development of private health care, preparing the conditions for a broader reform to be implemented at the beginning of the 1980s (Arellano 1985; Vergara 1990).

In education, the government's priority was the depoliticization of the system. Arguing economic and political reasons, the government restructured the main institutions of higher education, dismissing many faculty and staff members for ideological reasons. University presidents ceased to be directly elected by the academic community (who did not always select the best) but were appointed by the government (the majority of the appointees were military officers), hence ensuring state control over universities. There were changes in priorities assigned to academic disciplines as well: technical fields, experimental sciences, biology, engineering, and business administration took the lead, at the expense of sharp cuts in the social sciences (sociology, anthropology, economics; Marxist economics were abolished) and the elimination of all political science programs. After health, education was the sector most affected by cuts in public expenditures, and the reduced resources were concentrated in preschool education, through food distribution programs for school children and the National Board of Kindergartens (JUNJI) (Arellano 1985; Cox 1985; Vergara 1990).

The Ministry of Housing and Urban Planning was reformed and decentralized, with massive employment cuts. There were changes in the regulation of urban land, allowing the private sector to invest with fewer state controls, while the design, construction, financing, and commercialization of housing were transferred to the private sector. The role of the public sector was limited to the establishment and supervision of new norms for the financing of housing, and the selection of the beneficiaries of state subsidies to buy houses (such subsidies existed since 1953). Other measures to liberalize the housing and real estate market were the reintroduction of indexation of mortgages to inflation, the authorization of private mortgage contracts, the liberalization of interest rates, and the elimination of lease controls, leaving the market to set them. Changes in housing mortgages and subsidies led to the increased participation of private firms in the construction and financing of state-subsidized and nonsubsidized housing, thus balancing the state's withdrawal in the housing market. In 1974–76 an average of 66% of the new homes were built by the private sector (Table II.26; Arellano 1985; Castañeda 1989).

2. Performance

A. Growth

In 1974 GDP grew by 1% (-0.7% per capita), and the drastic stabilization policies worsened the recession, provoking a 12.9% decline in GDP in 1975 (-14.4% per capita), the worst at least since 1960. Industrial production decreased by 25.6% in 1975, the most dramatic drop in 50 years. GDP increased in 1976 by 3.5% (1.8% per capita) as a result of a 63% expansion in exports, and a 6% growth in industry. Annual average GDP declined by 2.8% or 4.4% per capita in 1974–76 (Tables II.3, II.6).

Gross national investment as a percentage of GDP increased from 7.9% in 1973 to 21.2% in 1974; a good part of it was to replenish inventories that had been depleted in the last year of Allende's administration. Contrary to government expectations, however, the rate dropped to 13.1% in 1975 and 12.8% in 1976, the fourth lowest since 1960; still the 1974–76 annual average of 15.7% was higher than the 14.5% average of 1960–70 (Table II.3).

B. Inflation

The liberalization of most prices in the domestic market ended both the shortages in basic needs goods and the black market and promoted the replacement of industrial inventories. But price liberalization aggravated inflation to 700% in the last trimester of 1973; however, it declined to 376% in 1974, 341% in 1975, and 174% in 1976. The increase in taxation, cut in public expenditures, and rigid fiscal discipline imposed by ODEPLAN over most government projects reduced the fiscal deficit from 24.7% to 2.3% of GDP in 1973–76 (Table II.3).

The liberalization of the financial market and the creation of a dynamic capital market changed interest rates from negative to positive and increased the number of transactions in the capital market and financial institutions. But financial liberalization also created problems; for instance, high interest rates charged by banks generated heavy indebtedness in the industrial sector (oriented to import substitution) and in the traditional agricultural sector. In addition, the rapid growth in the financial market was not supervised by monetary authorities, and this would become a main cause of the later debt crisis (Edwards and Edwards 1987; Sanfuentes 1987).

C. Diversification

The opening to international trade and Chile's comparative advantages (various climates and location in the Southern Hemisphere) stimulated the production of fruits of excellent quality that were in high demand during the winter in the Northern Hemisphere. Devaluations and tariff reductions improved the competitiveness of the export fruit sector (63% of total agricultural exports in 1975) and provided incentives for private investment (fruit exports increased 330% between 1965 and 1975). The agrarian-forestry sector's share in GDP rose from 6.8% to 10.3% in 1973–75, although it declined to 9.8% in 1976. The traditional agricultural sector (oriented to the internal market), nevertheless, suffered huge losses because of cuts of subsidies, high interest rates, and low investment. But total agricultural exports increased by almost 300% between 1965 and 1975 (Ceron 1987; Sanfuentes 1987; Silva 1987; Cruz 1988).

The impact of tariff reductions, nevertheless, was negative for industry, especially manufacturing, which suffered simultaneously a reduction in internal demand, caused by the 1975 recession, and lowered external protection. In 1975 manufacturing production shrank by 25.6%, the worst decline since at least 1960. However, mining expanded in this stage; for example, copper output increased 36.7%, thus partly offsetting manufacturing decline. The industrial share of GDP (including manufacturing, mining, and public utilities) decreased only from 34.5% to 33.2% in 1973–76. Stabilization policies also affected the construction sector, which slightly decreased its share of GDP from 5.3% to 4.5% in this stage (Tables II.4–6; Muñoz 1988a, 1988b).

The financial and service sectors increased their share from 30.2% to 33.7%, as a result of the internal market deregulation and the liberalization of the capital market, which promoted the participation of new investors. Transportation and communication also increased, from 4.9% to 5.3% (Table II.4; Edwards and Edwards 1987).

D. Trade Balance and External Dependency

In the external sector, the increase in the world price of copper from 59 cents per pound in 1971–73 to 71 cents in 1974–76, combined with an average annual rate of devaluation of 435% in this stage, generated a substantial improvement in the trade balance (from a deficit of U.S.$13 million in 1973 to a surplus of U.S.$643 million in 1976) and a recovery of international reserves, which had been seriously reduced in 1972–73 (Tables II.3, II.7, II.10; Ramos 1986; Vial and Valdés 1991). The opening to world trade and jump of

35% in trade transactions in 1973–76 led to an increase of trade dependency: from 30% to 46% of GDP (in current prices); however, the increase in 1977 prices was only from 35% to 38.4% (Table II.7; BCCh *Indicadores* 1989).

The value of exports increased by 61% in 1973–76, stimulated by government incentives, the opening to world trade, low cost of labor, tax exemptions, and tariff reductions, which prompted increases in profits in this sector. The expansion in exports facilitated their diversification; thus in spite of rising output and world prices of copper, the share of copper in total exports declined from 83.3% to 60%. The combined shares of iron, meat, fish meal, grapes, and "other" nontraditional exports jumped from 16.7% to 40% of total exports in 1973–76 (Table II.8; Moguillansky and Titelman 1993).

The 1974 cut in the average tariff from 94% to 75.6% (the maximum tariff dropped from 600% to 150%) did result in a 43% increase of imports in that year. However, further cuts in tariffs (in 1976 the average was 35.6% and the maximum was 60%) did not stimulate more imports but a decline of 22% in 1974–76 (Table II.7; Edwards 1985). The composition of imports did not change significantly in this stage: shares of food and beverages, raw materials, and machinery/transportation were stagnant or increased very little; however, the oil shock of 1973 led to an increase in the oil import share from 7% to 12%, and the share of manufactured imports declined from 30% to 24% (Table II.9).

Chile's notable diversification of trade partners was basically maintained in this stage. The U.S. share increased from 12% to 16%, and it was Chile's largest trade partner; Germany's share declined from 12% to 11%, and Japan's was basically unchanged (Table II.11).

We lack data on Chile's foreign debt prior to 1975. In 1975–76 the real debt declined by 8%; the debt burden fell in relation to both GDP (from 56% to 48%) and exports (from 272% to 197%), and the debt per capita also decreased. The public share of the debt declined from 84% to 80%, while the private share increased from 16% to 20% (Table II.13).

E. Unemployment

The unemployment rate rose to the highest level ever registered. Between 1960 and 1973, the national rate fluctuated between 3% and 8% of the labor force; it increased from 4.8% in 1973 to 9.2% in 1974, 14.7% to 14.9% in 1975, and 12.7% to 14% in 1976. The rate in Santiago increased steadily from 4.8% in 1973 to 16.3% to 17.1% in 1976; if the emergency employment programs are included, the unemployment rate reached 22% in 1976 (Table II.16). The high rate of unemployment was the result of neither demographic factors nor probably the high cost of labor. Instead, it was provoked by the drastic reduction in employment caused by the structural adjustment.

The composition of the labor force by economic activity is difficult to estimate because we lack data for 1973 and 1976 (the following figures are for 1970 and 1975; Table II.14). The share of agriculture continued its decline (−4.3 points), the share of industry reversed its increasing trend (−1.7 points), and the share of services accelerated its increase (+3.5 points); other activities experienced very minor changes. The percentage of the labor force made up of women probably continued to increase, but we do not have data between 1970 and 1980 (Table II.15). The expansion of the urban informal sector was an important change in the labor market (Cortázar 1988). Finally, the activities of unions were reduced to a minimum, so their impact was none or very minor in the determination of wages and other working conditions (but there are no data on these issues, as well as strikes, for 1974–79).

F. Equality

There are no data on income distribution for 1973, but available indicators show a deterioration in both distribution and the living standards of the population in this stage. The Gini coefficient (personal income of the working population) worsened from 0.468 to 0.543 in 1974–76, while the Gini coefficient of the labor force deteriorated from 0.518 to 0.618; family income, however, improved. Per capita consumption diminished 26.8% in 1973–76, while the share of labor in the gross national income declined 13 points (Tables II.18, II.20).

According to ECLAC, real wages fell 7.4 percentage points in 1974, plus an additional 3 points in 1975, and recovered 1 point in 1976. But there are diverse estimates of the variation of real wages between 1973 and 1976: ECLAC estimates a decline of 9.4 points, while Meller calculates a 1.2 decrease, but INE a 6.6 point increase and Castañeda a 25.9 point jump. All sources (except INE) show a dramatic decline between 1971 and 1976, ranging from 41 to 63 points (Table II.19).

The social cost of the adjustment was concentrated in the lower income sectors. Unfortunately, we lack data for the 1971–75 period; however, the incidence of poverty among households jumped from 17% to 56.9% between 1970 and 1976, and the incidence of indigency increased from 6% to 28% (Table II.18).

G. Social Indicators

Social policies in this stage were characterized by a decline in public social expenditures (a reversal of an increasing trend since the 1920s) and targeting (both on programs and population) of the scarce resources available.

In 1972–75 social public expenditures declined by 7.5 points of GDP. The level reached by social expenditures in 1972 (25.8% of the GDP) was difficult to sustain with the growing fiscal deficit (13% of the GDP in that year). There are no data for 1973 and 1976, but expenditures in 1975 were 32% below the 1972 level and 31% below the 1970 level (Arellano 1985). Social services in general worsened, although there were some positive effects.

Social security benefited from a process of unification, standardization, and extension of some benefits (facilitated by the concentration of power in the hands of the reformers), but coverage of the labor force decreased from 76% to 73% in 1973–76 because of increased unemployment and informalization of the labor market (Table II.25). The extension of welfare pensions benefited approximately 300,000 older people in 1975–76, who were previously excluded, but the average real pension fell by 42% in 1973–76, equivalent to losing 5.3 months of pension payments. Family allowances, unemployment compensation, and minimum pensions were made uniform, thus eliminating the previous differences among public employees and private white- and blue-collar workers. But family allowances were made equal to the lowest amount paid to blue-collar workers and were not adjusted to inflation in 1973–76, despite a 505% inflation rate in 1974. Furthermore, differences in benefits between civilians and the military expanded in this stage, because the standardization of benefits excluded the armed forces (Arellano 1985).

Real public expenditures on health care were reduced by 28% in 1972–75 (from 4.3% to 2.8% of GDP in 1972–75; there are no data for 1973), which led to a decline in current and investment expenditures. Hospital beds per 1,000 inhabitants decreased slightly from 3.7 to 3.6 in 1973–76. But access of the urban population to potable water and sewerage expanded 20 and 15 points, respectively. Scarce resources targeted to primary health care, pregnant women and infants, and malnutrition (combined with better education of mothers and a decline in the number of births) resulted in improvement of some health indicators; for instance, infant mortality shrank from 65.8 to 56.6 per 1,000 in 1973–76. This helped cut the crude mortality rate from 8.1 to 7.7 per 1,000 and increase life expectancy at birth from 65.7 to 68 years (Table II.21 and 2.23; Raczynski and Oyaro 1981; Arellano 1985; Vergara 1990).

Public expenditures on education declined from 5.9% to 4.5% of GDP in 1972–75. Because of targeting, the preschool program tripled its national enrollment in 1973–76, and elementary education maintained a 100% coverage. Conversely, enrollment in secondary education decreased from 51% to 49%, and in higher education from 17% to 14%. The latter was caused by the reassignment of resources and cuts in some disciplines, as well as by the recession, which forced low-income students to enter the labor force largely in the informal sector (Table II.24; Arellano 1985; Vergara 1990).

Public housing was harmed by a significant reduction in fiscal expenditures (a decline from 4.1% to 2.9% of GDP in 1972–75), investment, and urban development. Conversely private housing increased because of the liberalization of the market and government incentives. We lack data for 1973, but new housing units decreased by 21% in 1975 but rose 116% in 1976, surpassing the 1965 level. However, the housing deficit increased 18% in 1973–76 (Table II.26; Arellano 1985; Castañeda 1989).

3

Monetarism, Open Economy, Growth, and Indebtedness

1976–1981

Because of the inherited economic crisis and the 1975 recession, the previous stage was characterized by strict controls and adjustment policies. After 1976, once the crisis was under control and a better coordination achieved between neoconservative economists and the military, new policies were implemented to accelerate the opening to foreign trade and free flow of capital, further reduce inflation, continue financial liberalization and the privatization of public enterprises, and promote a greater private role in the provision of social services. The ultimate goal was to have steady and stable growth.

1. Policies

A. Ownership

The privatization policy maintained the guidelines of the previous stage; hence by 1977 only 19 state enterprises, out of the 529 administered by CORFO in 1973, remained in the public sector: copper, steel, oil, electricity, transport, and communications (Table II.2). In 1979, 65% of the land expropriated during the agrarian reform of 1965–73 had been returned to its previous owners, divided into lots or sold at low prices to the private sector (Sanfuentes 1987; Foxley 1988). Furthermore, state enterprises began to reduce their deficits, and in 1977 12 of them started to pay dividends. The causes of such a positive outcome, explained the government, were higher productivity and administrative efficiency, as well as price increases in the goods and services provided by those firms (Cortázar 1985; Ramos 1986).

Between 1973 and 1983 (there are no data available for 1976 and 1981)

49

the state's participation in the economy declined from 39% to 24% of GDP (Table II.2). The state's participation by sector was reduced from 85% to 28% in financing, from 70% to 21% in transport, from 100% to 75% in services, from 40% to 12% in industry, and from 85% to 83% in mining. The only exception was communications, where the state increased its participation from 70% to 96%, which the government explained was due to the peculiar monopolistic nature of this sector. In addition, the market began to be introduced as a mechanism to rationalize and administer social services such as pensions, health care, education, and housing (Chile was a pioneer in Latin America in the privatization of social services).

A main cause of the very high concentration of financial assets in a few hands was the ideological conviction among the neoconservative technocrats of the need to minimize the state's economic intervention (even in antitrust regulation) and let the market alone. The private economic conglomerates, organized after the privatization process, established mutual linkages through the purchase of large enterprises in the domestic market (e.g., 10 of the most important banks), led the expansion of exports in agriculture and forestry, and controlled the new private pension and health-care systems. The high level of indebtedness of such conglomerates became one of the crucial causes of the debt crisis (Edwards and Edwards 1987; Muñoz 1992).

B. Planning

Planning changed its orientation: from conjunctural and short-term in the previous stage, to broader, longer-term, and pursuing the structural transformation of the economy in this stage. The reform of the Ministry of Economy was completed through a reduction of its direct production function and a shift to regulation and supervision of industrial activities as well as foreign investment and trade. The privatization of CORFO's enterprises weakened this agency, which previously was an important branch of the ministry. Within ODEPLAN, neoconservative economists consolidated their power, and from there they expanded their influence to all spheres of government. The successful halt of the 1975 crisis and reduction of inflation contributed to increasing the influence of this group both in policy making and with the military, who became more open to liberalization, deregulation, and lowering protectionism.

C. Financing

The tax reform of 1974 increased fiscal revenue to an annual average of 20% of GDP between 1976 and 1981, which, combined with the cut of public expenditures, allowed a reduction of the public deficit and eventually generated a surplus, thus making a new tax reform unnecessary. The state also received close to U.S.$700 million in revenue from the privatization of public enterprises in this stage (Table II.2; Marcel 1989; Hachette and Luders 1993).

The service of the debt, suspended and renegotiated in 1973–75, began to be paid regularly in 1976, thus increasing the capital outflow. The latter, however, was offset by an expansion of external credit in 1977, and to a surplus in 1978–81, 50% of which was used to accumulate international reserves (Ceron and Staplefield 1988; Foxley 1988).

The capital market continued its expansion, increasing its role in the economic opening. Contributing to such expansion was the opening of the capital account and the final liberalization of interest rates, which provoked a strong increase in the domestic rate, accentuated by the lack of state intervention in the financial market. Neoconservative economists argued that the financial market would quickly adjust itself and that state intervention would create unnecessary distortions and impede the operation of free-market mechanisms. Those expectations did not materialize, and the difference between international and domestic interest rates rapidly expanded. Such a gap benefited the conglomerates that had access to the external financial market and acted as intermediaries between foreign and domestic credit. The opening of the capital market, the gap in interest rates, and a nominal exchange rate fixed in 1979 created a false impression that external credits in dollars were cheap. All this promoted the inflow of foreign capital and the indebtedness in dollars, particularly in the private sector. The external debt, therefore, became the main source of financing, mostly of conspicuous consumption of imported luxury goods, rather than productive or investment activities. The government did not pay much attention to the increase in the external debt, because it was mainly contracted by the private sector (Arellano 1983; Cortázar 1985; Edwards and Edwards 1987; Ffrench-Davis 1988; Vial 1992).

D. Stability and Prices

The focus of the stabilization policies changed in this stage from the increase of fiscal revenue and reduction of aggregate demand, to the monetary policy and management of inflationary expectations through exchange rates, a key to controling inflation (Corbo 1985; Ramos 1986; Foxley 1988; for exchange policy see section F below).

According to monetarist principles endorsed by the neoconservatives, domestic inflation should rapidly converge with international inflation. Thus, a fixed exchange rate was established in 1979 in order to reduce domestic inflation to the level of international inflation. The monetarist approach to the balance of payments (popular in the United States at the beginning of the 1970s) ensured that the reduction would be automatic, but the theory was not corroborated by the Chilean experience. Cost pressures continued to be controlled by the state: general fiscal expenditures (excluding the public debt) were maintained on average at 20.7% of the GDP in 1976–81 (but social expenditures dropped an additional 3.1% of GDP), and employment in the public sector was reduced by more than 30,000 employees in 1975–79, but wage restrictions were relaxed somewhat after 1979 (Arellano 1985; Ramos 1986; Edwards and Edwards 1987; Foxley 1988).

E. Development Strategy

Unlike the previous stage (when the development strategy was not clearly defined), the strategy became more concrete and explicit in this stage: an aggressive external opening of the economy, through the liberalization of the capital account and economic policies that clearly favored the export sector (to lead development), and promotion of the domestic capital market to attract foreign investment. The previous strategy of protectionism and ISI was totally abandoned, and the role of the state in agriculture changed significantly. The government maintained a few regulations and price fixing in agriculture (in grains such as wheat, corn, and rice), but the trend was toward deregulation and price liberalization to allow market mechanisms to orient the allocation of resources. Financial services (credit) and technical assistance, which were traditionally provided by the state, were privatized, and the reduced state participation was focused on the export sector. For example, in 1978 a policy of technological transfer was exclusively directed to medium-sized fruit exporters, excluding the traditional agrarian sector (Sanfuentes 1987).

Agriculture and forestry, led by the private sector, became the cornerstone in the promotion of nontraditional exports in order to reduce both dependency on copper exports and the negative impact of its price fluctuations in the world market. To attract private investors to this sector, the government offered incentives such as tax exemptions and subsidies to production. In 1976–79 state forests were privatized, their planted area expanded, and new private mills established to raise the output of cellulose for export markets. In addition, the number of hectares sowed for fruit production increased by 5% annually between 1975 and 1980. Conversely, the traditional agricultural sector reduced its activity because of its high level of indebtedness and the decline in profits caused by the reduction in import tariffs and a 54%

cut of state expenditures between 1969 and 1979 (Silva 1987; Cruz 1988; Gómez and Echeñique 1988).

F. External Sector

In this stage there was a continuation of policies of trade liberalization, such as elimination of import barriers and quotas, reduction and standardization of import tariffs, and openness toward foreign investment, but a new exchange policy, influenced by the monetarist approach to the balance of payments, was introduced.

The average and maximum import tariffs were further and gradually reduced from 35.6% and 65% respectively to a 10% across-the-board tariff in June 1979, which continued through 1981 (Edwards 1985; Ffrench-Davis 1989). This policy brought an indiscriminate increase in imports, especially luxury goods such as cars, appliances, clothes, perfumes, and liquor (Ffrench-Davis 1980; Foxley 1988; Yáñez 1992).

The exchange policy was altered several times during this stage. In the first semester of 1976, the peso appreciated, ending three consecutive years of significant devaluations. From late 1976 until 1978, a system of minidevaluations based on a preannounced schedule was introduced attempting to address inflationary expectations. As the process of tariff reductions progressed, the mini-devaluations were intensified. In June 1979, once a uniform tariff of 10% was set, the exchange rate was fixed at 39 pesos; the dollar was unchanged for three years until June 1982. This policy was used as a stabilization mechanism, since a fixed exchange rate sought to transfer the lower international inflation to the domestic economy, a process that should be automatic according to the neoconservative predictions. The exchange policy created a growing antagonism between the export sector (opposed to the fixed exchange rate) and economic groups that were heavily indebted in dollars and, hence, wanted to maintain that policy (Corbo 1985; Ramos 1986; Edwards and Edwards 1987; Foxley 1988).

G. Labor and Employment

The restrictive wage policies, applied in the previous stage to minimize cost-induced inflation, were maintained in this stage, but the degree of state intervention in this process was gradually reduced. With the implementation of the Labor Plan in 1979 (which replaced the 1931 Labor Code), the state's role focused more on the regulation than on the fixing of wages.

For neoconservative economists, a free-market system required a totally free labor market, based on a series of principles that were incorporated in the Labor Plan of 1979. The plan brought a relative improvement in union organization, strikes, and collective bargaining over the existing de facto situation since the 1973 coup, because those rights were restored, although submitted to very strong restrictions rarely found in Latin America (wage adjustment became more beneficial as well); conversely there was a deterioration in terms of job security. In general the government abandoned the traditional role it had played between 1924 and 1973 of protecting the rights of workers and clearly tilted the balance in favor of employers (Arellano 1985; Cortázar 1985; Meller 1992a, 1992b).

The Labor Plan introduced several new policies: (1) voluntary union membership, which ended the obligatory affiliation typical of trade unionism before 1973 (various unions could be organized within one firm with the same type of work); (2) restoration of collective bargaining but with restrictions (authorized in a single enterprise but not by economic activity or group of enterprises within the same productive branch); (3) autonomy of trade union federations and confederations from political parties (to avoid political influence in collective bargaining); (4) reduction of legal protection of union leaders; (5) financing of unions exclusively from the quotas paid by the affiliated workers, excluding contributions from other unions; (6) reintroduction of the right to strike but with strong restrictions (after a 60-day period, workers on strike could be laid off without indemnization, employers could hire supplementary personnel during the strike, and workers had the possibility of individually disassociating themselves from the strike); (7) indexation of wages equal to 100% of the inflation rate in the year previous to the collective bargaining (that ceiling could be exceeded according to collective agreements signed in each enterprise); and (8) employers' freedom to lay off workers, paying compensation equivalent to one month's salary for each year worked for the same employer (a maximum indemnification of five months' salary was imposed in 1981), which liberated employers from the need to justify dismissals.

Although there are no data for 1974–79, the number of unionized workers declined 56% between 1971–73 and 1980–85 (from 29% to 12% of total employment), while the number of workers participating in collective bargaining dropped by 71% in the same periods (from 11% to 3% of total employment). The number of strikes and workers involved decreased by 96% between 1973 and 1980, and the number of workdays lost declined by 83% (ILO 1977–83).

Despite the economic growth in this stage, the emergency employment programs, created in 1975 to reduce high unemployment, were expanded. On average, the two programs covered 4.5% of the labor force between 1976 and 1981 but peaked in 1976 and declined until 1981 (Table II.16).

H. Distribution and Social Services

This stage was characterized by continued cuts in social-service expenditures, the privatization and decentralization of public social programs, and income distribution set through market mechanisms instead of by the government. Comparisons of social expenditures will be made between 1977 and 1981 because there are no available figures for 1976.

Public expenditures on social security dropped from 7.5% to 6.4% of GDP between 1977 and 1981 (Table II.17). In 1979 the first legal modifications of the pension system were introduced (the armed forces and the police were excluded from these regulations and maintained all their privileges): (1) the abolition of seniority retirement (based on years of work regardless of age); (2) the standardization of the retirement age at 60 years for women and 65 for men; (3) the authorization of early retirement according to number of years of work (for workers close to retirement); and (4) the elimination of the pension indexation privilege enjoyed by public employees (*perseguidora:* a pension adjusted to inflation based on the salary adjustment of the job that the pensioner had at the time of retirement).

These measures were followed by a comprehensive, radical pension reform law, enacted in May 1981, which closed the old social security system and replaced it by a new system; those already insured were given a five-year period to stay in the old system or move to the new one, and those entering the labor force for the first time are obliged to enter the new system. The new system is obligatory for all salaried workers and voluntary for self-employed workers; it excludes the armed forces and the police. It is based on capitalization (fully funded individual) instead of pay-as-you-go financing and is administered by private, for-profit associations called Administradoras de Fondos de Pensiones (AFPs), instead of the old social insurance funds. Wage contributions are paid by workers alone (employers are responsible only for occupational hazards), divided in two parts: 10% for the old-age pension, and a variable contribution for the administration of such pensions by the AFPs and for disability and death insurance by private insurance companies (initially from 3% to 3.7%). The total contribution to the new pension system was set 8 percentage points lower than to the old one, which enticed workers who were not yet close to retirement to move to the AFPs. The funds accumulated in the insured's individual account are administered and invested by the AFPs in the capital market and must pay a minimum capital return (investment yield) equivalent to the average yield in the whole system. The new system does not provide a "defined benefit" (the law does not establish a formula to calculate the pension as in the old system); thus the future pension is uncertain (it is based on the fund accumulated in the individual account), as it depends on variables such as the worker's income, the investment yield, the commissions paid to the AFPs, and the overall performance of the economy. To facilitate the transfer to the AFPs of those affiliated with the old system, a "recognition bond" was created to take into account the contributions they had made to the old system. The bond is adjusted to inflation, yields a 4% real interest annually, and must be paid by the state (deposited in the individual account) at the time the worker retires. The new pension system has several state guarantees, among them a minimum pension to all affiliates who have a minimum of contributions but do not qualify for a minimum pension, and government responsibility in case of the bankruptcy of an AFP (Mesa-Lago 1985, 1994; Bustamante 1988; Marcel and Arenas 1992).

State allocations to public health care slightly declined from 3% to 2.9% of GDP between 1977 and 1981. Until 1979 the public health-care system had two main branches: one took care of insured blue-collar workers and "indigents" and their dependents—free of charge for the poor (Servicio Nacional de Salud [SNS])—and the other covered public employees and private white-collar workers and their dependents (Servicio Médico Nacional de Empleados [SERMENA]). In 1979 these two institutions were merged into a new National System of Health Services (Sistema Nacional de Servicios de Salud [SNSS]), which has 27 regional agencies that provide public health care. The SNSS is financed with a wage contribution initially set at 4% and paid exclusively by workers (employers contributed until 1981), state subsidies, and fees for services by the high-income noninsured, administered by the National Health Fund (Fondo Nacional de Salud [FONASA]). Additionally, in 1979, primary health care was transferred to the municipalities.

In 1981 the government took a second step and created the Insurance Health Institutions (Instituciones de Salud Previsional [ISAPREs]), private, for-profit corporations (HMOs) that cover those insureds who freely decide to move from the public to the private sector, administer their wage contributions, and provide—for an additional payment—higher-quality health services (ISAPREs may own health installations but usually work as intermediaries between insured and clinics and health personnel). The public health-care system suffered a significant loss in revenue as the higher-income insureds (and their contributions) moved to ISAPREs (Arellano 1985; Vergara 1990; Mesa-Lago 1994).

The standardized family allowance, created in 1981, is paid by the state to low-income children younger than six years of age, previously excluded from the system because their parents had no social security coverage. The state also took full responsibility for and standardized unemployment compensation (Arellano 1985; Vergara 1990).

Education was the second most affected social service as state expenditures declined from 4.5% of GDP in 1977 to 3.6% in 1981 (Table II.17). State financing to the public educational system was cut from 80% of total revenue between 1965 and 1974 to 68% between 1977 and 1978. The government reallocated the diminished fiscal resources among the various educational levels. Between 1974 and 1979, the percentage going to higher education was reduced by 1% of GDP and transferred to the preschool, primary, and secondary levels. Priority was given to the preschool level, whose state support increased by 150% between 1976 and 1981 (Vergara 1990). Educational policies changed their orientation in this stage, from depoliticization (a priority in the previous stage) to administrative reform, decentralization, and greater private participation.

In 1978 neoconservative economists took over the administration of the Ministry of Education and began to implement the new policies. In 1980, 80% of primary and secondary education was provided by public schools, 14% by private schools receiving state subsidies, and 6% by private schools without subsidy. The new decentralization policy promoted the transfer of public schools (infrastructure, teachers, administration, students) to the municipalities. Educational personnel transferred to municipalities became subject to contracts regulated by the Labor Plan of 1979 (hence losing their benefits as public employees). The municipalization process was implemented with an improvised administrative system, scarce technico-managerial capacity, and insufficient state and municipal funds (linked to the average school attendance of students). The financial problems worsened, and, at the end of 1981, the state was forced to supplement the meager municipal budgets. The decentralization of the system was supervised by the Ministry of the Interior, which exercised strict political control over the municipalities (Cox 1985).

In 1981 a new higher education law restructured its administrative and financial systems. The law promoted decentralization, dividing the two state universities (the most important in the nation) into 12 regional autonomous university centers. Financing of university students was also modified, eliminating the centralized state credit and creating autonomous credit funds administered by each university (Sanfuentes 1986).

The housing sector was the most affected by the reduction in state expenditures: from 2.3% to 1.3% of GDP between 1977 and 1981. Housing subsidies were maintained in an indirect manner (via lower interest rates) rather than a reduction in the price of homes provided. In 1978 a new system of subsidies for nonowners with some savings facilitated access to commercial credit, thus supplementing state subsidies. In 1980 it was discovered that state subsidies were benefiting middle-income groups rather than the needy;

hence a new program of Social Housing (Vivienda Social) was geared to lower-income groups and the elimination of shanty towns. Under this program, the state provided a basic housing unit of 26 square meters in a 130 square meter lot, financed with a state subsidy equivalent to 75% of the value of the unit, while the remaining 25% was financed with a state credit to be paid in 12 years with no interest (Arellano 1985; Castañeda 1988).

2. Performance

A. Growth

Once the 1975 crisis was over, this stage was characterized by steady economic growth (the so-called Chilean economic miracle) due to a declining fiscal deficit that became a surplus, a sharp cut in inflation, decrease in unemployment, rising real wages, rapid growth of exports (particularly nontraditional ones, helped by high world prices), and expansion of the capital market and external credit. GDP grew 3.5% in 1976 (1.8% per capita) and boomed between 1977 and 1981 with an average annual rate of 8% (6% per capita). Industrial growth averaged 7% in this stage (8% in 1977–80), and agricultural exports increased fourfold. But the growth rate steadily declined from almost 10% in 1977 to 5.5% in 1981 (8% and 3.8% per capita, respectively) (Tables II.3, II.6; Cruz 1988).

Total gross investment increased from 12.8% to 22.7% of GDP between 1976 and 1981 because of the strong increase in the flow of external capital motivated by the capital market liberalization and the facilities given to foreign investors. While the external component of gross investment grew from −1.7% to 14.5% of GDP, domestic investment shrank from 14.5% to 8.2% in this stage; the latter was only slightly above the 1975 level and lower than that of 1972 (Table II.3).

In addition to the slowdown in GDP growth toward the end of this stage, there were other signs of the end of the boom and external trouble. Between 1977 and 1981, the average growth of the industrial sector was 7%, but in the last year it was only 2.6%, and in the last trimester of that year, there was an 8% drop in production (due to the high level of indebtedness with high interest rates; Table II.6). Furthermore the peso was overvalued, domestic investment declined, the terms of trade deteriorated, the trade surplus turned into a growing deficit, and the external debt more than doubled. These ominous signs did not alarm policy makers, who predicted an automatic adjustment in the balance of payments, but those problems eventually led to the severe 1982 crisis.

B. Inflation

The stabilization policies applied in this stage (continuation of cuts in public expenditures, huge state revenue from privatization, increase in tax revenue from 16% to 21% of GDP, and a nonexpansionist monetary policy) dramatically reduced the inflation rate from 174% to 9.5% between 1976 and 1981; the latter was the lowest inflation rate in Chile since 1961. The fiscal deficit was slashed from 2.3% to 0.8% of GDP in 1976–78 and turned into an average surplus of 2.2% in 1979–81 (Table II.3).

The liberalization and deregulation of the financial market allowed a free flow of capital and a significant increase in the participation of foreign banks in the domestic market: from only 1 in 1976 to 20 in 1981. Three-quarters of these banks initiated their operations in 1979 (Goñi 1988). In addition, the propitious conditions for external borrowing (low external interest rates, high internal interest rates, and a fixed exchange rate after 1979) motivated the inflow of foreign capital and an increase in international reserves. External borrowing grew dramatically (see section D below), and the domestic saving/investment rate declined sharply.

The liberalization of domestic markets and the heavy foreign borrowing benefited the largest economic conglomerates with access to external credit, which, in turn, facilitated the concentration of the operations in the domestic capital market. Despite high real internal interest rates (from 13% to 28% in 1981; BCCh *Indicadores* 1989), the financial market maintained high growth rates. The total volume of credit awarded between 1976 and 1981 increased 360%, from 10.4% to 50.4% of GDP. The first disequilibria in the financial markets occurred in 1977: three financial institutions went bankrupt, and the government was forced to intervene in one of the largest private banks. The weak state regulations on private borrowing, plus the high level of indebtedness, provoked in 1981 the bankruptcy of and intervention in four more banks and four financial institutions that represented 10% of the capital and reserves of the financial system. Finally, the unpaid loans (bad debts) increased from 10% to 23% of the capital and reserves of the system in 1980–81 (Arellano 1983; Ramos 1986; Edwards and Edwards 1987; Foxley 1988; Held 1990; Vial 1992; Yáñez 1992).

C. Diversification

Stimulated by government incentives, the nontraditional agricultural sector enjoyed an average annual growth of 32.6% in this stage. The growth of fruit exports was most notable, as it averaged 35%, increasing its share in agricultural exports from 63% to 70%, and its share in total exports from 2.5%

to 5%. Forestry continued the expansive trend of the previous stage: in 1976–81 cellulose and paper exports grew at an average annual rate of 16%. However, the traditional agricultural sector, oriented to the internal market, suffered the adverse consequences brought about by the reduction in import tariffs and the fixed exchange rate, which led to a strong increase in cheaper agricultural imports. The decline in traditional agriculture exceeded the increase in production for nontraditional exports. For example, in 1979, wheat imports alone accounted for as much as total resources generated by fruit exports, which represented 65% of the agricultural exports in that year. The participation of the agro-forestry sector in GDP, therefore, declined from 9.8% to 8.1% between 1976 and 1981 (Table II.4; Silva 1987; Cruz 1988; Moguillansky and Titelman 1993).

The industrial sector was affected by the external opening, and, although its average growth was strong (6.9% between 1977 and 1981), it was lower than GDP (8%), which led to a reduction in the industrial share in GDP from 33% to 30.3%, the lowest share since 1960. Conversely, commerce, construction, and financial sectors grew vigorously between 1976 and 1981: commerce by an average of 14.4% (increasing its share in GDP from 13.7% to 18.3%), and construction expanding its share from 4.5% to 6.1%. The financial sector also grew significantly, but social services declined sharply, and their combined share in GDP decreased from 33.7% to 31.8%. The strong growth in these sectors was not accompanied by adequate capital accumulation, but it was based on the expansion of consumption (Table II.4; Edwards and Edwards 1987; Foxley 1988).

D. Trade Balance and External Dependency

In this stage the economic opening to external trade led to a phenomenal increase of 188% in trade transactions. Dependency on trade, measured in total transactions at current prices, increased from 45.9% to 48% between 1976 and 1980 but decreased in 1981 because of stagnation in trade transactions (Table II.7); measured in constant prices (1977) there was a jump in the entire stage from 38.4% to 53.7% (BCCh *Indicadores* 1989).

Exports increased 122% between 1971 and 1980 but decreased in 1981; hence the export expansion in the entire stage was 81%. The share of exports in GDP (constant prices) increased from 20.2% to 22.3% between 1976 and 1980 but in 1981 declined to the 1986 level; in current prices the share decreased from 25% to 16.4%. Export diversification continued its expansion: copper exports declined from 60% to 44%, in spite of a significant increase in world prices, while nontraditional exports increased from 40% to 56% of total exports (mainly forest products, fruits, paper, cellulose, fish and seafood, and fish meal; Tables II.7, II.8, II.10; Moguillansky and Titelman 1993).

The fixed exchange rate and the progressive reduction in tariffs were an incentive for the massive 342% increase in imports between 1976 and 1981; the share of imports in GDP rose from 20.8% to 26.8%. The composition of imports changed as follows: (1) manufacturing imports jumped from 24% to 38% of total imports, as Chileans went crazy importing all kinds of manufactured products, such as cars and domestic appliances; (2) food and beverages declined from 24.6% to 10%; and (3) oil imports rose from 12% to 14% (actually there was a peak of 21% in 1979, a historical record, due to that year's jump in oil prices). Despite this increase in oil imports, the share of imported oil in domestic consumption dropped from 75% to 56.7% because of the 14% annual average increase in the domestic production of oil in this stage (Tables II.7–9, II.12).

The increase in imports (342%) exceeded the increase in exports (81%); hence, after a declining merchandise trade surplus in 1976–77, there was a deficit in 1978–81, which increased 528% and took an average of 2.2% GDP (Table II.7; Edwards and Edwards 1987; Ffrench-Davis and Raczynski 1987; Foxley 1988).

The external debt in real terms rose 120% between 1976 and 1981, from 47.9% to 52.5% of GDP and from 197% to 310% of the value of exports; in per capita terms the debt doubled from U.S.$801 to U.S.$1,621. The share of the private debt in the total debt catapulted from 20.3% to 64.8%. The abundance of external capital inflows, however, was partly used for the accumulation of international reserves, which increased 400% between 1976 and 1981 and averaged U.S.$1.1 billion annually in 1978–80 (Table II.13; Ramos 1986; Edwards and Edwards 1987; Foxley 1988; Hachette and Luders 1993).

The external commerce liberalization led to an expansion of trade with the United States, whose share increased from 16.4% to 21.6% of all external transactions (exports expanded much faster than imports). Trade with Japan, the second most important commercial partner, was stagnant at 11% of all transactions, while trade with Germany decreased from 11% to 8% during this stage. The remaining 59% of external transaction was very diversified (Table II.11).

E. Unemployment

Despite high and sustained growth, the employment growth rate (2%) was lower than the labor force growth rate (2.8%). According to the ILO, the rate of national open unemployment declined from 14% to 10.4% between 1976 and 1980 but increased to 11.3% in 1981; the latter was still double the average rate of the second half of the 1960s. Open unemployment in Santiago, based on ECLAC series, declined from 16.3% to 9%. When the underemployment in emergency programs is considered, the combined rate declined from 22% to 15% in this stage; the latter is almost triple the rates of the 1960s (Table II.16).

The diversification associated with the developmental strategy changed the percentage distribution by economic activity of the labor force between 1975 and 1980: increases in services from 27.7% to 30.5%, in commerce from 14.1% to 17.4%, and in finances from 2.6% to 3%; and reductions in agriculture from 17.5% to 15.3%, industry from 17.5% to 16.3%, construction from 5.4% to 5.1%, and nonspecified or unemployed from 5.8% to 3.1%. In 1980, 60% of the labor force was concentrated in the tertiary sector: services, commerce, transportation, and finances (Table II.14; Cortázar 1985; Ffrench-Davis and Raczynski 1987).

The participation rate of women in the labor market increased from 18.1% to 21.3% between 1970 and 1980, while the proportion of the EAP made up of women rose from 23% to 29.3% (data are not available for 1976 and 1981). The agrarian export sector massively hired rural women for manual jobs in seasonal activities, mostly in fruit production. In addition, women increased their participation in the informal labor market and in the activities of local, nongovernmental organizations (Table II.15; Raczynski and Serrano 1985; Serrano 1986; Montecinos 1993).

F. Equality

Between 1976 and 1981, the participation of labor in national income increased by 21.5 percentage points, but it was still 7 points below the 1970 level. Wage restrictions were maintained in this stage, but the strong decline in inflation, combined with the adjustment clause in the 1979 labor law, promoted the recovery of wages between 1976 and 1981. Virtually all estimates show that, in 1981, mean average wages were from 28 to 38 percentage points above the 1976 level, but still below the 1972 peak. Urban minimum wages jumped 48 points in this stage. Poverty declined from 57% to 44% of the population between 1976 and 1980, while indigence decreased from 27.9% to 14.4% in the same period. The Gini coefficient of family income worsened from 0.438 to 0.521 between 1976 and 1981, but the Gini coefficient for personal income improved from 0.618 to 0.579 (labor force) and from 0.543 to 0.531 (working population). Consumption per capita increased 20 percentage points between 1976 and 1981, recovering the 1973 level but still below the 1972 peak. Between 1969 and 1978, the poorest 20% of the households reduced their participation in consumption from 7.7% to 5.2%, while the richest 20% increased their participation from 44.5% to 51%; unfortunately we lack data for 1976 and 1979–81. Social expenditures per capita declined by 10% in this stage (Tables II.18–20; Foxley 1988; Meller 1992a, 1992b).

G. Social Indicators

The reduction of the state's role in social services and the corresponding increase in the private sector's role was characteristic of this stage. Social expenditures declined from 17.4% to 14.3% of GDP between 1977 and 1981 (Table II.17).

In the area of social security, the state transferred the majority of the administration of pension funds to the private sector: by the end of 1981, 58% of the contributors insured in the old public system had moved to the new system. But virtually all pensions remained in the old system, which saw an increase of 264,000 pensioners between 1976 and 1981, and the loss of more than half of its contributors expanded its deficit from 4.6% to 6.2% of GDP in 1980–81. Furthermore, because of high unemployment and expansion of the informal sector, social security coverage declined from 73% to 65.4% between 1976 and 1981, and yet costs increased from 10.7% to 12.3% of GDP (Table II.25). Some social security benefits increased in this stage, but, because of high inflation in 1973–76, the 1981 real level was still below that of 1970; for example, minimum pensions rose 30% between 1976 and 1981 but still remained 17.5% below the 1970 level, while real average pensions increased 28.8%, still 27% below 1970. The distribution of benefits within the old system worsened also: blue-collar workers (55% of the pensioners in the old system) received a pension equal to 54% of the average pension in that system in 1976 but 46% in 1981. Conversely pensioners from the armed forces and the police (5% of the pensioners in the old system) in 1981 received a pension 350% above the average pension paid in that system (Arellano 1985; Mesa-Lago 1985; Marcel and Arenas 1992).

By the end of 1981, the system of family allowances had expanded its coverage to 100,000 children and made the payment uniform; the real value of this benefit, however, declined by 13% between 1976 and 1981 (Arellano 1985; Vergara 1990).

The previous health-care policies of reduction in state expenditures and targeting of certain diseases as well as mothers and infants were maintained in this stage, with similar positive results. Between 1976 and 1981, infant mortality declined from 56.6 to 27 per 1,000, the general mortality rate decreased from 7.7 to 6.2 per 1,000, and life expectancy rose from 68 to 71 years. The percentage of the urban population with access to potable water expanded from 78% to 91.5% and access to sewerage from 52% to 68%; rural access to water grew from 34.5% to 47.5%. Indicators of public health facilities, however, either declined or stagnated: hospital beds per 1,000 inhabitants decreased from 3.6 to 3.3, matching 1975 as the lowest figure registered for this index since 1960, and the ratio of doctors per 10,000 inhabitants increased slightly, from 6.1 to 6.2 in 1977–79 (Tables II.21, II.23).

In this stage there were no reported cases of malaria and polio, while cases of tetanus remained almost nonexistent, and tuberculosis declined; diphtheria and hepatitis first increased and then decreased. But there were two epidemic outbursts. The first was typhoid, which increased from 59 cases per 100,000 in 1976 to 122 cases in 1978 and declined to 98 cases in 1979–80 (there are no data for 1981). The second epidemic was measles, which jumped from 10 cases per 100,000 inhabitants in 1977 to 315 cases in 1979, forcing the implementation of a national vaccination program that lowered the cases to 34 in 1980. The epidemic outbursts may have been caused by the cut in public resources and the neglect of preventive medicine and some vaccination programs directed to segments of the population other than children and mothers (Table II.22; Vergara 1990).

Public expenditures on education were cut from 4.5% to 3.6% of GDP between 1977 and 1981, the decentralization of education encountered financial difficulties, and public employees in the sector suffered a cut in their salaries and fringes. And yet most indicators improved. The national illiteracy rate decreased from 10.7% to 8.3% between 1970 and 1982: from 6.8 to 5.8 in urban areas and from 24% to 20% in rural areas (there are data for neither 1976 nor 1981). Changes in school enrollment at the various educational levels were as follows: preschool education increased from 9.1% to 15.7% (maintaining the 1973–76 trend); elementary education continued to be universal; secondary education increased from 49% to 63% (a reversal of the 1973–76 trend); and higher education declined from 14% to 11% (continuing the trend initiated in 1973). The latter was largely due to a 35% increase in real terms of tuition in this stage (Table II.24; Arellano 1985; Sanfuentes 1986; Vergara 1990).

In the housing sector, the supply of mortgage loans dropped and public alternatives for housing credits declined because of the sharp cut of state expenditures (from 2.3% to 1.3% of GDP between 1977 and 1981) as well as a reduced supply of private financial resources, the latter partly explained by high interest rates in this stage. Furthermore, the system of savings for housing that had been initiated in 1976 was reduced, which led to a suspension of new mortgage credits from 1981 onwards. All this led to a 40% decline in the number of houses approved for construction in 1976–78; those permits rose by 48% in 1979–81, because the economic growth was an incentive for housing construction, and yet many of those houses were never built as the economic crisis virtually paralyzed all construction at the end of 1981. In spite of the goal for the new system of housing subsidies to allocate them to the neediest, 93% of its beneficiaries were in the highest 40% income bracket in 1980, compared with 68.5% in 1969; conversely, the program of social housing was more progressive: in 1981, 88% of their beneficiaries were in the poorest 60% of the population. The housing deficit increased from 665,000 to 888,000 houses between 1976 and 1981, although units built per 1,000 inhabitants increased somewhat. Contributing to the deficit was the heavy increase in the number of homeless indigents who joined shanty towns (Table II.26; Arellano 1985).

4

Second Crisis and
State Intervention

1981–1983

In 1981–83 Chile confronted the most acute economic recession since the 1930s. This domestic crisis forced the government to take drastic measures and to intervene in the internal markets, contradicting the neoconservative principles of nonintervention and a subsidiary role for the state. The situation was aggravated by the international recession of the early 1980s, a decline in the world price of copper, and the Latin American debt crisis, which provoked a suspension of international loans and an increase in external interest rates.

1. Policies

A. Ownership

In the two previous stages, privatization and deregulation led to a reduction in the state's economic participation. In this stage the government had to intervene in areas of the economy that had been transferred to the private sector before the crisis, to avoid the collapse of both the financial system and enterprises dependent on commercial banks and other financial institutions. Between November 1981 and December 1983, the state intervened in 14 banks and 4 financial institutions, including two of the largest private banks in the nation. As part of a program of regulation and financial stabilization initiated in early 1982, five of these banks were subjected to a provisional administrative regime and later liquidated. The state was left in control of more than 60% of all the deposits in the financial market and 69% of the deposits in the just established private funds. While intervening in the financial system, the state found firms without sufficient backup capital ("paper firms") that were related to the banks and financial institutions that belonged to the large economic conglomerates. The short-term goal of state intervention was to prevent the collapse of the financial system, while the medium-term goal was to reprivatize the system. The state, therefore, absorbed the losses of the private banking system, plus the expenditures of making the intervened firms attractive to new private investors (Arellano 1983, 1984; Foxley 1988; Valenzuela 1989; Meller 1990; Muñoz 1992; Vial 1992).

B. Planning

During this stage there were two changes in the economic team in power. The initial neoconservative team continued until June 1982, when it was briefly replaced by a more moderate team. Opposed by the more radical, original neoconservatives, as well as by powerful groups of businessmen and economic conglomerates, the second team was dismissed at the beginning of 1983. The radical neoconservatives (with different leaders) integrated a third team that lasted until the end of this stage.

The original neoconservative economic team claimed that the market was capable of handling the crisis and that state intervention was unnecessary. Consequently, despite the negative economic indicators, this team did not modify its policies, which contributed to the worsening of the crisis in 1982–83. But the crisis weakened the power and image of the government and provoked street demonstrations; hence a change in strategy was finally accepted after considerable "internal" debate. The government and part of the opposition (Christian Democrat, Radical, and Social Democrat parties) initiated a dialogue. The original team of neoconservative economists was removed from the Ministries of the Economy (including ODEPLAN) and Finance. The new (second) team that took control of these institutions believed in free-market principles but also in the need for state interventionism such as protection of productive sectors, particularly industry and traditional agriculture, in recessive periods. The new team was viewed with suspicion by the other ministries and by those who advocated more "pure" free-market policies: exporters opposed protectionist measures, some entrepreneurs mistrusted state intervention, and conservative parties feared a retreat to the interventionist policies of the past. In 1983 a third economic team was appointed that resumed neoconservative policies: tariffs were lowered, special credits for industries were eliminated, and the stabilization program applied basically followed neoconservative policies. The state intervention of the financial system was an exception, considered necessary to avoid its bankruptcy and that of its related enterprises, among them, the large firms connected to the troubled banks, AFPs, ISAPREs, and so forth (Montecinos 1988; Muñoz 1988a, 1988b; Meller 1990; Fontaine 1993).

C. Financing

In the two previous stages, the government benefited from the revenue generated by the privatization of public enterprises, the tax reform of 1974, and the enormous flow of external capital that went to the private sector and prevented the state from higher levels of indebtedness. In 1981–83, however, the state did not have access to those sources of funds: the recession reduced tax revenues by an annual average of 1.5% of GDP in 1981–83, and the flow of external credits to the private sector decreased dramatically because of the international recession and the insolvency of the domestic financial sector. The state budget was another source, but it was insufficient and could create serious disequilibria. The government, therefore, resorted to three revenue sources: international reserves, external loans (the public debt increased from 19% to 50% of GDP in 1981–83), and internal debt.

The internal debt became the most serious fiscal problem in 1982. The Central Bank played a key role as moneylender, providing a continuous flow of credit to avoid the collapse of the financial system and the related enterprises. The private sector, burdened with external and internal debts in dollars, benefited with the Central Bank's introduction of a preferential exchange rate lower than the market rate. Private debtors used the preferential rate to pay their debts, thus saving the costs created by exchange devaluations in this stage, but this procedure led to a fiscal subsidy that averaged U.S.$772 million annually in 1982–83. Despite those subsidies, the private financial system was technically bankrupt in 1983. The nonrecoverable debt was equal to 3.5 times the total capital and reserves of the national banks, and the Central Bank, pressured by foreign banks, had to guarantee that debt. The "nationalization" of the private debt, initiated in 1983, was financed through the central government budget, at a cost of 11% of GDP. To make this financial operation possible, the Public Treasury had to transfer funds to recapitalize the Central Bank, which, even after that capital injection, was left with a high level of indebtedness. The International Monetary Fund (IMF), the World Bank, and the Inter-American Development Bank (IDB) came to the rescue, granting U.S.$1 billion in loans to support a stabilization program initiated in 1983 (Arellano 1983, 1984, 1988; Edwards and Edwards 1987; Ffrench-Davis 1989; Larrañaga 1989; Meller 1990; Muñoz 1992; Vial 1992).

D. Stability and Prices

The first neoconservative team argued that the structural changes in the economy had already been made in the previous stage. The monetarist approach to the balance of payments predicted an automatic adjustment, which, in the case of Chile, was the interest rate. After a year (June 1981 to June 1982) of inaction, despite the economic decline unchecked by the automatic adjustment, the change in economic team took place in 1982, and a new approach was embraced to confront the recession. The main stabilization measures implemented by the more moderate economic team (which was in charge less than one year) were: (1) a tariff increase (to protect domestic industries), (2) expansion of state transfers to the Central Bank to properly cover the debt of the commercial banks, (3) regulation of some prices in the domestic market (especially in traditional agriculture), and (4) public loans to support some economic activities (mainly in the industrial sector).

In 1983, with the return of the radical neoconservative team, a five-year stabilization program proposed by the IMF was accepted. According to this program, the main problem of the Chilean economy was its enormous external debt, which had to be rapidly reduced through four principal measures: (1) a cut in fiscal expenditures to eliminate the private-sector deficit, (2) control of the money supply, (3) elimination of wage indexation (more liberalization of the labor market), and (4) rapid payment of the foreign debt (Arellano 1983, 1988; Corbo 1985; Edwards and Edwards 1987; Ffrench-Davis 1989; Meller 1990; Muñoz 1992).

E. Development Strategy

The essence of the development strategy was not altered in this stage (an open economy and aggressive promotion of exports, particularly nontraditional), but the crisis forced state intervention, hence contesting the theory of automatic adjustment of the economy (Ramos 1986; Edwards and Edwards 1987; Muñoz 1988a, 1988b; Meller 1990). The industrial and construction sectors were the most seriously affected by the crisis; hence state intervention and subsidies were necessary to bail them out. Despite these measures, however, industrial bankruptcies increased from an annual average of 252 cases between 1976 and 1980 to 621 in 1981–82 (Table II.6; Foxley 1988; Meller 1993).

Most of the traditional agricultural sector, already in decline in the previous stage, entered a deep recession in this stage because of high interest rates, heavy debts incurred by producers, and reduction of loans from commercial banks. The situation prompted the government to adopt a number of emergency policies: (1) loans from the Central Bank, at rates lower than those of the market; (2) payment of debts in dollars with a preferential exchange rate; (3) extension of government price regulation to cooking oil, beets, milk, and other dairy products (wheat, corn, and rice were already regulated); and (4) opening regional state purchasing centers for traditional products (Ortega 1987; Gómez and Echeñique 1988). Concerning promotion of nontraditional exports, the state subsidy to forestry was increased from 75% to 90% of the cost of production at the end of 1982, in order to maintain the incentives for the export of wood, cellulose, paper, and products derived from paper.

F. External Sector

In this stage the state sector suffered the impact of the national debt crisis and adverse international factors, such as the rise of domestic and international interest rates, reduction in the inflow of foreign capital, and decline in world prices of copper. As a result, financial resources of the external sector were reduced, which led to external disequilibria in the current and balance of payments accounts.

The fixed nominal exchange rate, which began in 1979 and continued until mid-1982, was one of the causes of the external financial disequilibrium, because it reduced the competitiveness of exports and decreased the cost of imports. Changes were made in the exchange policy from mid-1982 throughout 1983. First, the fixed exchange rate was abandoned and a 18% devaluation imposed in June 1982; an additional 40% devaluation took place in September, and successive devaluations that averaged 55% occurred in 1983. Second, a schedule of daily mini-devaluations (*tablita*) was introduced in July 1982 with the purpose of containing expectations regarding the exchange rate and speculations on the rise of the parallel market for dollars. Third, a free-floating exchange rate was established in August 1982 but lasted only three days and was replaced by a "dirty" flotation (free exchange rate but with state intervention in the dollar market). Finally, a preferential exchange rate (lower than the market rate) was initiated in 1982 to subsidize private debtors in dollars (Arellano 1983; Corbo 1985; Ramos 1986; Edwards and Edwards 1987; Ffrench-Davis 1989; Meller 1990, 1992a, 1992b).

Import tariffs had been reduced and standardized at 10% in 1981, a level maintained until March 1983, when they were raised to 20% (an average of 17.9% in 1983). This measure attempted to reduce the accelerated growth in imports and protect the national industry. It was taken by the second economic team that briefly replaced the neoconservative economists, but it was reversed when the latter returned to power. Finally, in 1983, the government adopted an IMF stabilization program, which imposed strict payments of the foreign debt, creating additional financial restrictions in the external sector (Yáñez 1992; Fontaine 1993).

G. Labor and Employment

As in previous stages, the new stabilization program placed the brunt of the adjustment on labor and lower-income groups. After an increase in the real urban minimum wage in 1982, it was cut by 23 percentage points in 1983. Wage indexation was abandoned in June 1982, and nominal wages were reduced by a decree that established a ceiling equal to the wage level of June 1979. The third neoconservative team argued that the reduction in real wages would lead to an increase in employment and a decline in the unemployment rate. Contrary to those expectations, the severe economic crisis provoked a notable increase in unemployment, which forced the state to create a second emergency employment program in 1982 (Programa de Empleo para los Jefes de Hogar [POJH]), which paid about 60% of the minimum salary to heads of households. In 1982–83 the two emergency employment programs (PEM and POJH) covered 500,000 unemployed at an average annual cost of 1% of GDP (Cortázar 1985, 1988; Ffrench-Davis and Raczynski 1987; Meller 1990, 1992a, 1992b).

H. Distribution and Social Services

This stage consolidated the neoconservative policies in distribution and social services. In 1981–83 public expenditures on social services remained constant in real terms, but, because of the decline of GDP, their percentage increased from 14.3% to 17.1% of GDP (Table II.17).

In the area of social security, the state increased the subsidy to the old pension system from 6% to 8.2% of the GDP because of the huge deficit generated by the massive transfer of contributing insureds from the old system to the new private pension system (AFPs). In 1981–83 the minimum pension (fixed by the state) was adjusted below inflation and was paid to 60% of total pensioners in the old system. Family allowances were also adjusted below inflation in 1982 and not adjusted at all in 1983. In the new pension system, the real average fixed commission charged by AFPs was raised by 8.5%, while the variable one for old-age, disability, and survival insurance was increased from 2.4% to 3.6%. Such increases elevated the average monthly cost of the new pension program from 13.4% to 14.8%. Finally, AFPs had to increase their investment in the public sector (to bail out the state) from 28% to 45% of their total portfolio; for example, investment in Public Treasury bonds jumped from zero to 30% of total investment (Table II.25; Arellano 1985; Marcel and Arenas 1992; Mesa-Lago 1994).

The public health-care system began to suffer a deficit, because its revenues from wage contributions diminished because of the transfer of higher-income groups to the private system (ISAPREs). The state increased its public health-care budget by 0.7% of GDP in 1981–82, but lowered it to 0.7% in 1982–83, thus aggravating the deficit. Investment and current expenditures in this area continued to decline: in 1983 they were 11% and 90% of the 1970 levels, respectively. To cope with the deficit, the obligatory wage contribution to health insurance was raised from 4% in 1981 to 6% in 1983, increasing the burden on the workers in the midst of the crisis. Fiscal resources allocated to health care continued to be targeted to programs for mothers and infants (Oyarzo 1981; Marcel 1984; Arellano 1985; Mesa-Lago 1988, 1989; Vergara 1990; Arenas de Mesa 1991).

Real public expenditures in education decreased by 4% annually in 1981–83, but, because of the economic decline, the percentage of such expenditures in GDP increased from 3.6% to 3.9%. In 1982, 87% of all public schools had been transferred to the municipalities, 33% of public industrial schools were handled through the industrialist association (SOFOFA), and all agricultural schools went to the agricultural association (SNA). The transfer of elementary and secondary education to the municipalities was temporarily paralyzed at the end of 1982 because of the recession and the technico-administrative problems that decentralization brought, especially in small and medium-sized municipalities (Castañeda 1989).

An evaluation of the higher education system carried out by the Ministry of Education concluded that: (1) universities covered only 7.4% of the 18 to 24-year-old population, (2) high-school graduates had no alternatives other than university education, (3) public universities neglected the development of their regional centers, and (4) public subsidies to higher education were not adequately targeted. In order to correct these problems, the higher education system was restructured in 1981 through the following measures: (1) decentralization to reduce the politization of universities and create regional universities and autonomous vocational-technical institutes (the number of all higher education institutions rose from 8 to 23 in 1981); (2) introduction of a new higher education system with three main pillars: conventional universities, technical training centers (CPTs, which offer nonuniversity occupations for low-qualified students), and vocational-technical institutes (IPs); (3) maintenance of 12 disciplines within the universities and transfer of the rest to the IPs; (4) creation of private universities by easing state approval; (5) introduction of competition for the allocation of public funds among universities (a new transitional system was created for that purpose, which received 5% of total state resources to higher education); and (6) establishment of a new financing system, which tried to make the university system independent from the state. Starting in 1981, the universities were financed through four sources: tuition paid by students, fiscal credits granted to students, direct allocations (reduced by 0.3% of the GDP in 1981–83), and indirect fiscal contributions based on competition. The restructuring of the higher education system, however, was slowed down because of the economic crisis, the reduction in public expenditures, and the resistance from traditional universities and the majority of the academic community. These factors led to the gradual abandonment of the competitive approach among universities from 1983 onwards (Cox 1985; Sanfuentes 1986, 1988, 1990; Castañeda 1989).

Previous housing policies continued in this stage. Real public expenditures on housing were reduced by 21% annually in 1981–83, from 1.3% to 0.9% of the GDP. Incentives for the participation of the private sector were maintained, and 98% of the total number of houses built in this stage were by private constructors (Table II.26). Subsidies to housing and the program of basic housing were maintained, but the government transferred resources from public housing to financing of mortgages in the private sector. In 1982 a new program to eradicate slums in Santiago was launched, moving the inhabitants to the city outskirts (Arellano 1985; Ffrench-Davis and Raczynski 1987).

2. Performance

A. Growth

The severe 1982–83 recession (worse than the one in 1974–75) was partly provoked by the inertia of the neoconservative economists in the face of slowdown in growth, rising private indebtedness, and expanding external financial disequilibrium. Nonintervention by the state was an outcome of the monetarist belief in an automatic adjustment of the balance of payments. The Chilean recession was aggravated by the world recession, declining world prices of copper, and the Latin American debt crisis, which virtually halted all external loans and credits (Ramos 1986; Edwards and Edwards 1987; Foxley 1988; Meller 1990).

GDP declined by 14% (−15.5% per capita) in 1982, and an additional 0.7% drop (−2.4% per capita) occurred in 1983; the average annual decrease in this stage was 7.4% or −9% per capita. After the second half of 1983, however, the economy began to recover; thus after suffering a 21% decline in

1982, the industrial sector grew 3.1% in that year. The gross investment rate abated from 22.7% to 9.8% of GDP in 1981–83, mainly explained by the reduction in the foreign component (from 14.5% to 5.4%); the domestic component declined from 8.2% to 2.1% in 1981–82 but grew to 4.4% in 1983. The declines of GDP in 1982, the gross investment in 1983, and the domestic investment rate in 1982 were the lowest since the 1930s (Tables II.3, II.6; Ffrench-Davis 1989).

B. Inflation

The rate of inflation jumped from 9.2% in 1981 to 20.7% in 1982, while the fiscal surplus of 1.7% of GDP turned into a deficit of 2.3%. Initially the automatic adjustment was expected to solve the crisis, but one of its consequences was the sharp increase in the internal real interest rate, which reached 28.7% in 1981 and 22.4% in 1982, compared with a 4.9% average between 1979 and 1980. Eventually the state's intervention in the financial system prevented its collapse and that of the related productive sectors, but the government had to take over the debt of the national private banks and transfer funds to them: in 1982 the fiscal transfer was tantamount to 15% of GDP in 1982 and 11% in 1983. The five-year stabilization plan of the IMF began in 1983 and gave high priority to control inflation and the fiscal deficit, but it had no positive results in the first year, since inflation grew to 23.1% and the deficit increased to 3.8% of GDP (Table II.3; Arellano 1983; BCCh *Indicadores* 1989; Corbo 1985; Ramos 1986; Edwards and Edwards 1987; Foxley 1988; Ffrench-Davis 1989; Meller 1990, 1992a, 1992b).

C. Diversification

The crisis negatively affected all productive sectors, although with divergent intensity. Changes in the composition of GDP were not significant. The construction, commercial, industrial, and financial sectors were the most affected by the crisis. In 1981–83 construction activity decreased by 27%, and its share in GDP contracted from 6.1% to 5.2%. Commerce declined 20%, and its share in GDP went from 18.3% to 17.1%. Industry diminished its production by 21% in 1982 but grew by 3.1% in 1983 (industry recovered before all other sectors), and its share of GDP increased from 30.3% to 31.4%. Traditional agricultural production shrank by 4%, whereas the nontraditional sector maintained its level of activity, and some products increased their output, for example, grapes by 61%, apples by 22%, and fish and seafood by 19%. As a whole, agricultural output dropped by 2.8%, but this was the smallest decrease in all sectors; hence agriculture increased its share of GDP from 8.1% to 9.2% (Tables II.4–6).

D. Trade Balance and External Dependency

The trade deficit reached 13% of GDP in 1981, the highest ever; such a severe disequilibrium discredited the theory of automatic adjustment and led to the restrictive trade policies of 1982–83. Despite the economic crisis, the total value of exports remained constant in 1981–83, mainly because of the peso devaluations from June 1982 onward (which made exports more competitive). Conversely, imports declined in real terms by 56% in 1981–83, caused by the devaluations (over 54% in 1982–83) and the rise in tariffs from 10% to 20% in 1983, which made imports more expensive. The outcome was a trade surplus in 1983 close to U.S.$1 billion (the highest ever), equal to 4% of GDP. In spite of the huge trade surplus, however, the decline in external capital inflow led to a drop of international reserves by U.S.$1.2 billion in 1982 and U.S.$541 million in 1983 (Table II.7; Ramos 1986; BCCh *Indicadores* 1989; Hachette and Luders 1993).

Export diversification reversed slightly in this stage. Copper output increased 16% (one of the few activities that grew), and although world prices declined in 1982, they recovered somewhat in 1983. The share of copper exports in total exports, therefore, increased from 44% to 48% in 1981–83. Nontraditional exports were successful, despite the crisis, and grew by 15%. Fresh fruit exports expanded their share in total exports from 4.9% to 6%, and the fish and fish-meal export share also grew from 5.4% to 8%. But the share of "other" exports (including manufacturing) declined from 44.7% to 38.2% (Table II.8; Moguillansky and Titelman 1993).

The composition of imports varied according to the goods that were most affected by the devaluation process and the increase in tariffs. Machinery and transportation were the most afflicted and declined by 73% in real terms; hence their share in total imports dropped from 34% to 23% in 1981–83. The second most affected imports were manufactures, whose share declined from 38% to 35%. Domestic production of oil rose, thus expanding its supply for internal consumption and reducing dependency on imported oil; but the overall decrease in total imports resulted in an increase in the share of oil imports from 14% to 21%. Finally, the share of food and beverage imports that had declined to an all-time low of 10% in 1981 increased to 17% in 1983, also an outcome of the overall decline in imports (Tables II.9, II.12).

In this stage the share of Chilean trade with the United States continued to expand: from 21.6% to 27.1% of all transactions, mainly because of a favorable increase from 15% to 28% in Chilean exports to the United States, which led to a healthy surplus (total trade with Germany rose from 7.9% to 10.2%, but with Japan declined from 10.7 to 7.7%). It should be noted, nevertheless, that the share of trade with U.S. in 1983 equaled the share in 1969, and that 55% of all trade transactions in 1983 were conducted with other countries other than the three major trade partners (Table II.11).

Chile's total external debt in constant prices was virtually stagnant in 1981–83 because of the halt in foreign loans and credits. Because the economy declined sharply in this stage, however, the debt burden increased from 52.5% to 88.2% of GDP. The state absorption of Chilean private debt led to an increase in the public-held debt from 35% to 56% (Table II.13).

E. Unemployment

The national unemployment rate, according to the ILO, rose from 11.3% in 1981 to 19.6% in 1982 but declined to 14.6% in 1983. In Santiago the unemployment rate increased from 11% to 22% in 1981–83. If underemployed workers enrolled in the emergency employment programs (PEM and POJH) are added, open unemployment increased from 15% in 1981 to 31% in 1983. Half of the unemployed belonged to the lowest income quintile; 33% of the unemployed workers were in the emergency programs, and another 15% received unemployment compensation, but the remaining 52% lacked any protection. Industry was one of the sectors most affected by the crisis: employment in this sector declined by 23% in 1981–83, which affected 25% of industrial workers (Tables II.6, II.16; Cortázar 1988; Muñoz 1988a, 1988b; Meller 1990, 1992a, 1992b).

Available data on the composition of the labor force by economic activity in 1980 and 1985 show a continuous decline in the agriculture share by 2 percentage points, a combined decline of 1.2 points in the secondary sector, and stagnation in the tertiary sector—actually minor declines in commerce and transportation offset by minor increases in services (Table II.14). In the same period, the percentage of the labor force made up by women increased from 29.3% to 30.7%, about one-half the annual pace of expansion between 1970 and 1980 (Table II.15).

F. Equality

State intervention in the 1982–83 crisis had regressive effects on income distribution. The cost of emergency employment programs was 1% of GDP, benefiting 500,000 workers, whereas the 10,000 debtors of the private sector received a state subsidy equivalent to 3.5% of the GDP, through the preferential exchange rate. Thus, in the midst of the economic crisis, the capital sector received considerably more state funds than did the unemployed (Ffrench-Davis and Raczynski 1987; Meller 1990, 1992a, 1992b; Ffrench-Davis 1991). The suspension of wage indexation and the ceiling imposed on wages in 1982 (back to the wage level of 1979) brought about, according to ECLAC, a 12 percentage point reduction in real wages in 1981–83 and a 22 point cut in the urban minimum wage (Table II.19).

Government surveys indicated that, between 1980 and 1982, poverty incidence among families declined from 44.3% to 30.8%, while indigence incidence went down from 14.4% to 10.8%; these figures are questionable in view of the high rates of unemployment and reduction in real wages during those years. But data for 1984 show increases of poverty incidence to 48.2% and indigence to 23%. The Gini coefficient based on family income (calculated by nongovernmental experts) worsened, from 0.521 to 0.542 in 1981–83 (the Gini for personal income for the labor force worsened from 0.579 to 0.639, but that for the working population was stagnant). Per capita consumption declined by almost 17 percentage points in this stage (Tables II.18, II.20).

G. Social Indicators

Despite the serious economic crisis, social expenditures did not increase. The old social security pension system was closed to new entrants to the labor force after May 1981, but the system was kept in operation for those who decided to remain affiliated, as well as pensioners. More than 1.2 million contributors to the old system moved to the AFPs in 1981–83, but the number of pensioners in the old system continued to increase and reached 1.2 million in 1983. The two opposite trends led to a growing deficit in the old system: 4.1% or 7.5% GDP in 1981–83 according to different analysts (Arellano 1985; Marcel and Arenas 1992; Mesa-Lago 1994).

A comparison of key assumptions of the new pension system with its real outcomes in 1981–83 gives the following results (for more details see chapters 5 and 6 in this part). The first assumption was that the AFPs would foster competition, thus reducing both administrative costs and the commissions charged to the insureds. In 1983 the administrative cost per beneficiary (combining actives and passives) was 40% lower in the old pension system than in the new. Insureds' contributions to AFPs rose from 13.4% to 14.8% in 1981–83 (mainly because of increasing commissions), but they were lower than the contributions charged by the old system, which ranged from 19% to 21% in 1983. The lower contributions to the AFPs, however, were not based on their higher competition and efficiency in cost reduction but resulted from legislation, which mandated a reduction of those rates in the new system but not in the old. The number of AFPs was stagnant at 12 in 1981–83, and there was a high concentration in the system: 59.4% of total insureds were affiliated in three AFPs.

A second assumption of the new system was that a strict relationship between contributions and benefits would reduce evasion and increase population coverage. The percentage of affiliates actively contributing in the old system averaged 70% in 1980–81, but two years after the APFs began to operate the percentage in the new system declined to 68%. Because of high unemployment, coverage of the labor force decreased from 65% to 59% in 1981–83, while coverage of the employed also dropped from 74% to 69%.

A third assumption was that the new system would attract most insureds from the old system because the AFPs would be financially solid and pay higher pensions through better efficiency and higher investment yields. Indeed, 1.8 million insureds moved, but it appears that they did so mainly motivated by higher net wages (as the contribution in the new system was 6 percentage points lower), as well as by the massive public campaign, which "sold" the new system.

A fourth assumption was that the creation of the AFPs would vigorously increase domestic savings and develop the capital market. The annual real investment yield of the AFPs averaged 20.6% in 1981–83 (3 points above the real interest rates of banks), and the accumulated pension fund grew, reaching 6% of GDP in 1983. And yet there is no evidence that the global social security pension system (combining the old and the new) generated a net increase in domestic savings; actually the domestic investment rate sharply declined in 1981–83. Social security benefits were not adjusted to inflation in this stage and suffered a decline in real terms: minimum pension and average pensions in the old system lost 5 percentage points, while family allowances declined by 22 percentage points (Tables II.3, II.23; Arellano 1985, 1989; BCCh *Indicadores* 1989; Mesa-Lago 1985, 1988, 1991, 1994; Guillion and Bonilla 1992; Marcel and Arenas 1992).

Real public health expenditures per capita shrank by 14.5 percentage points in 1981–83, but targeting mothers and infants continued. Hence there were improvements and deterioration in health indicators: the infant mortality rate further declined from 27 to 22 per 1,000; the general mortality rate was virtually stagnant (6.2 and 6.3 per 1,000 inhabitants); life expectancy at birth remained stable at 71 years; the ratio of doctors per 10,000 inhabitants increased from 6.2 to 8.8 between 1979 and 1983 (no data are available for 1981); the ratio of hospital beds per 1,000 inhabitants was stagnant at 3.3; and access of the urban and rural population to potable water continued its expansion (the latter from 47.5% to 54.7% and the former from 91.5% to 92.7%), and access to sewerage increased (Tables II.21, II.23; Arenas de Mesa 1991).

Rates of contagious diseases per 100,000 inhabitants in 1981–83 show no cases reported of malaria and polio, tetanus almost nonexistent, declines in diphtheria and tuberculosis, and a rise in cases of measles in 1982 but a decline in 1983. Two epidemic outbursts occurred in this stage. Typhoid increased from 97.9 cases per 100,000 in 1980 to 111.0 cases in 1982. This forced the implementation of a national vaccination program, which in 1983 did not have the expected results, since the cases increased to 119.8 per 100,000 (the reduction of this indicator did not begin until 1984). Hepatitis increased from 38.8 per 100,000 to 69.7 in 1982 and to 90.9 in 1983 (Table II.22). These two outbursts, according to health authorities, were caused by the use of contaminated water in agriculture and a decline in sanitary inspections and pediatric control (PAHO 1986).

Enrollment at the various educational levels in 1981–83 was as follows: (1) preschool education increased slightly from 15.7% to 15.9%, (2) elementary education continued its universal coverage, (3) secondary education remained stagnant at 63% coverage, and (4) higher education increased from 11% to 15%. These levels of coverage were consistent with the resources allocated to each level and policies implemented in this stage. The allocation to preschool education increased 15%, while the budget of elementary and secondary education were not changed, and the transfer to municipalities did not expand coverage of secondary education. The expansion in coverage of higher education was the result of changes in incentives and budgetary structure; for instance, the new emphasis in student tuition led universities to increase their enrollments in order to improve their revenues (Sanfuentes 1986, 1988, 1990).

There were four policy outcomes in housing in 1981–83: (1) the government reduced public expenditures for social housing programs (from 1.3% to 0.9% of GDP) to finance mortgages in the private sector with regressive effects, (2) the housing deficit increased 8.6%, (3) the number of houses approved for construction dropped by 31%, and (4) state targeting of subsidies for basic housing helped low-income groups, as 60% of the beneficiaries of this program belonged to the poorest 40% of the population, a measure that had progressive effects (Table II.26; Arellano 1985).

5

Corrections, Recovery, and Economic Boom

1984–1990

The next stage in Chile's economic history may be divided into two sub-stages: recovery in 1984–85, and sustained economic growth between 1985 and 1990. After the end of the crisis of 1981–83, a fourth team of economists took over from April 1984 to February 1985, but they did not make any significant policy changes. In February 1985 Hernán Buchi was appointed finance minister, and a fifth team, also integrated by neoconservative economists, took over and corrected some of the mistakes that had caused and deepened the crisis. The new team consolidated the free-market model and went further in pushing economic opening, privatization, promotion of foreign investment, export-based development, and expansion of the financial market. But the hard lessons learned from the 1975 and 1982–83 crises moved them in this stage, unlike the previous three ones, to assign a more important role to the state in the regulation and supervision of the economy. The political opening was another divergent variable in this stage. In 1988 a national plebiscite asked the population to approve or reject the continuation of General Pinochet's rule: the answer was negative, which meant that Pinochet could not be a candidate in the 1989 presidential elections. The candidates then were Hernán Buchi for a coalition of right-wing parties that supported the continuation of the status quo, and Patricio Aylwin for a coalition of center-left parties that wanted some change; the latter won the presidency. Legislative elections were held on December 1989 to reopen the National Congress in March 1990. Although the opposition's triumph in both elections opened a new democratic stage, the implementation of neoconservative policies continued until March 11, 1990, the last day of Pinochet's administration.

1. Policies

A. Ownership

In the 1984–85 substage, enterprises intervened in by the state during the debt crisis of 1981–83 were reprivatized, and in the 1985–1990 substage there was a massive privatization of public enterprises that the government had previously kept in the public sector because of their strategic importance for the national economy.

At the beginning of 1985, two laws were enacted that initiated the so-called popular capitalism, with two objectives: the rapid privatization of intervened financial institutions and enterprises, and the disaggregation or dissemination of conglomerates property to various sectors of the population. Neoconservatives claimed that the second objective would be in line with modern capitalism and give an opportunity to the people to own part of the enterprises. Critics of the privatization process noted that the ultimate goal of the dispersion of ownership was to avoid or make more difficult any future reversal, such as the one that briefly took place in 1982–83. If future governments wanted to intervene in or nationalize those enterprises, they would have to face a large number of stockholders (Marcel 1988, 1989; Valenzuela 1989; Muñoz 1992).

In the second substage, Buchi implemented an even more ambitious privatization program. State ownership was reduced from 24.1% of GDP in 1983 to 15.9% in 1988 (there are no available data for 1984–85; Table II.2). The initial goal, set in 1985, was to sell between 30% and 49% of 22 public enterprises that still belonged to CORFO. The privatization program included large enterprises that had traditionally been state owned and suffered neither serious financial disequilibria nor operational inefficiencies: steel, sugar, pharmaceuticals, and electricity. In addition, enterprises that were not in the initial privatization plan were later included: insurance, coal, energy, and sanitation. There were two significant exceptions to the state-enterprise privatization goal: copper (CODELCO) and oil (ENAP); the privatization of the former confronted the stern opposition of the military, and not necessarily for nationalistic reasons: the annual budget of the armed forces was tied to cooper exports. The initial goals of privatization in 1985 had been amply surpassed in 1989, because the process was accelerated after the government's electoral defeat in the 1988 plebiscite. For instance, in 1985, 11 enterprises were to be excluded from privatization, but only 6 remained in state hands by 1989; and no enterprises were supposed to be privatized from 71% to 100% in 1985, but 22 were eventually in that category by 1989 (Table II.2).

Some specialists argue that, unlike the privatization program of 1976–81, between 1985 and 1990 there was more state regulation and control of selling prices (to avoid losses) and over the concentration of property. And yet estimates show that actual selling prices were low, leading to state capital losses equivalent to 37% to 56% of the real, potential value of the assets sold (Marcel 1989). The privatization methods seemed to ensure that sold property would be well distributed, as the following percentage distribution suggested: 50% by transactions in the stock exchange, 23% by stock sales to workers in public enterprises, 18% by stock sales to AFPs, and 9% by auctions. Several studies demonstrate, however, that such a variety of selling methods did not impede the concentration of property of the large public enterprises that were privatized. The total revenue from sales of state enterprises was close to U.S.$1.2 billion. Half of it was allocated to investments in the public sector; the other half was used to finance fiscal current expenditures and the macroeconomic program at the time, which included tax cuts and an increase in public expenditures, both prompted by the electoral process preceding the 1988 plebiscite (Marcel 1988, 1989; Vial et al. 1990; Muñoz 1992; Bitrán and Sáez 1994).

Several studies claim that there was a denationalization process, as the majority of privatized assets became owned or controlled by foreign firms or multinational corporations; for instance, seven banks and two financial institutions (plus participation in the board of two of the largest banks through the popular capitalism scheme), the largest insurance corporations, the three largest AFPs (whose capital in 1989 was equal to 11.6% of GDP), and three of the six largest exporting firms of fruits and forestry products. Toward the end of the military government, the privatization of public enterprises became a target of criticism of opposition groups, based on the following arguments: (1) the rapidity of the privatization process (Chile sold in 4 years what England did in 8 years, measured as a percentage of the GDP in each country); (2) the secrecy of the process (the government released very little information and refused to discuss the issue publicly); and (3) the selling of enterprises that were in good financial shape, that did not confront serious inefficiency problems, and, rather than being a burden for the state, that actually contributed to the surplus CORFO generated in the second half of the 1980s (Muñoz 1988a; Délano and Traslaviña 1989; Marcel 1989).

In sum, the 1985–90 wave of privatization of public enterprises differed from the previous waves in three ways. First, in the target: between 1985 and 1990 the goal was to privatize enterprises that had historically belonged to the state as well as public social services; the 1973–76 wave reversed statization; the 1976–81 wave centered on financial institutions and public enterprises that had been recently placed under state control; and the 1984–85 wave was geared toward enterprises intervened in by the state during the 1981–83 crisis. Second, in the amount of revenue resulting from the privatization: between 1985 and 1990 it amply surpassed the revenue of previous privatization waves. Third, in the state's regulation of the privatization process (to preclude potential abuses and adverse effects on the economy): the 1985–90 rules were considerably greater and stricter than in previous waves (Marcel 1988, 1989; Muñoz 1988a, 1992, 1993; Hachette and Luders 1993; Bitrán and Sáez 1994).

B. Planning

As has been said, during this stage there were two changes in the economic team. The third neoconservative team continued in power until April 1984, when it was replaced by a fourth team. Unlike the previous three teams, the fourth was not made up by graduates from the Chicago School, and some observers have said the team members were "anti-neoconservatives." The main reason for this apparent dramatic change was political: the government and the oppositions began to talk, but, when such discussions failed, the economic team was removed (in February 1985) without being able to introduce any significant changes. A fifth economic team, led by Minister Buchi, maintained the principles of the neoconservative model. However, after 1986, adjustments were made in macroeconomic policy in a pragmatist move on the eve of the 1988 plebiscite. Exporters, especially nontraditional ones, continued to receive technical assistance and financial aid from the state (special lines of credit were made available both at the State Bank and from commercial banks). Favorable arrangements were offered to debtors in the rescheduling and renegotiation of their debts: lengthening the terms, modifying interest rates, and changing the currency from pesos to an adjustable monetary unit (Unidades de Fomento [UF], adjusted daily for inflation over the previous 60 days) (Montecinos 1988; Muñoz 1988a; Solimano 1990b).

Despite the previous rigorous policies for containment of public expenditures and fiscal austerity, the following measures were taken, before the 1988 plebiscite and the 1989 elections, to accelerate growth and show stability and economic strength: increases in public expenditures, cuts in taxes (on income, profits, and consumption—VAT), and reductions in import tariffs. These measures were facilitated by the high world price of copper (which in 1988–89 generated 48% of export value), which made possible economic growth and financial equilibrium (Meller 1990; Vial et al. 1990).

After the government's defeat in the 1988 plebiscite and on the eve of the December 1989 elections (when all public opinion polls were favorable to the opposition), there was a 180 degree turn in policy. The government rushed to implement several measures in order to guarantee that the neoconservative model would remain in place after it left power. In October 1989 the Central Bank was transformed into a permanent autonomous agency in charge of monetary policy, independent from the Executive, with a technical staff and its own patrimony and resources. The goal of such a transformation was the preservation of macroeconomic stability and the avoidance of inflationary mandatory increases in the money supply to finance fiscal deficits. In March 1990 a law guaranteed the job stability of top public officials occupying key decision-making posts, hence forcing the incoming administration to govern with appointees of the previous regime (Larrañaga 1991; Muñoz and Celedón 1993).

C. Financing

A major source of domestic financing in this stage was the privatization of state enterprises, which generated approximately U.S.$1.2 billion, 30% more than between 1976 and 1981; half of this revenue was used to finance the macroeconomic program, which expanded public expenditures (and economic growth) with stability. Another source of domestic financing was the funds accumulated in the private pension system (AFPs), which grew fast, but their investment in state instruments proportionally declined, after a 1985 reform to diversify and privatize AFPs' portfolio (see section H below). Three tax changes took place, but, unlike the tax reforms of previous stages, they brought a net reduction in tax revenue. The first reform, implemented in 1984, changed the income tax (reduced the tax rates and increased the income tax brackets) and introduced a tax on the distribution of business profits; it resulted in a regressive reduction of direct taxes from 5.2% to 3.7% of GDP in 1984–87. The second reform, made in 1988, cut the VAT rate from 20% to 16%, with a reduction in fiscal revenue but progressive on distribution. Third, in 1989, incentives were provided for the reinvestment of business profits, exempting them from the corresponding tax, with a decline in revenue and regressive effects (Yáñez 1992; Carciofi et al. 1993).

Foreign sources of financing played divergent roles. Foreign bank loans shrank from U.S.$1.3 billion in 1983 to U.S.$370 million in 1986, and new loans were not granted in 1987–88; the banks only lengthened the terms previously agreed for interest payments. External financing came from multinational agencies with whom Chile maintained excellent relations in this stage and that strongly supported Chilean neoconservative policies, for example, the IMF's five-year program and the World Bank's three-year program. In addition, the IDB gave U.S.$300 million annually in 1985–87, the single largest IDB disbursement to Latin America in that period (Ffrench-Davis 1987, 1988; Meller 1990; Solimano 1990a).

A potential external source of revenue was the increase in the world price of copper from 62.5 to 129 cents per pound between 1984 and 1989. According to restrictions imposed by the World Bank, revenues from copper exports had to be deposited in the Copper Stabilization Fund (FEC) and used in servicing the foreign debt, but, at the end of 1989, funds accumulated in the FEC were only U.S.$20 million, while they should have been U.S.$1.7 billion; the difference was used for internal financing (Arellano 1988; Vial et al. 1990). Debt-equity swaps became an important mechanism to both reduce the external debt and attract foreign investment (see section F below).

D. Stability and Prices

The IMF five-year stabilization program (1983–87), supported by the new economic team headed by Minister Buchi, recommended the following measures: (1) renegotiation with foreign banks of the terms for the payment of the debt, (2) flexibility in important tariffs, (3) partial control of exchange rates ("dirty" floatation), (4) restrictive monetary policy, (5) preferential dollars for debtors, (6) reprivatization of banks and large enterprises, (7) financial support and technical assistance for the main domestic banks, (8) maintenance of low real wages, (9) cuts in public expenditures, and (10) a further reduction in the size of the state. The World Bank program (1985–87) reaffirmed almost all the IMF measures, but it added an exchange-rate policy: the maintenance of a low value of the peso vis-à-vis the U.S. dollar to give incentives for the increase in exports in order to generate a surplus in the trade balance and reduce the foreign debt; this recommendation was also followed by the new economic team (Arellano 1988; Ffrench-Davis 1989; Meller 1990, 1992a. 1992b, 1993; Solimano 1990a; Dornbusch and Edwards 1994).

From 1985 onwards, Buchi's team implemented the structural adjustment based on the recommendations from the IMF and the World Bank. Unlike the 1976–81 stabilization program, the new one attempted to reduce the need for external financing with the following policies: (1) a reduction in the fiscal deficit to control inflation and the deficit in the balance of payments, (2) a further cut in the size of the state through a new and broader wave of privatization of public enterprises, (3) export promotion, especially nontraditional exports, through improvements in competitiveness via real devaluations of the exchange rate, and (4) encouragement of domestic and foreign investments (Ffrench-Davis and Muñoz 1990; Cariofi et al. 1993; Corbo and Fischer 1994).

To stimulate domestic and foreign investment, and reduce dependency on external indebtedness, Buchi implemented the following policies starting in 1985: (1) an increase in public investment; (2) a rise in real interest rates from 2.3% to 5.1% between 1984 and 1989; (3) an active monetary policy coherent with maintaining an interest rate in equilibrium that would promote investment and would not jeopardize growth; and (4) a reduction in taxes on enterprise profits from 46% to 10%, plus exemptions over profits reinvested in the firms (BCCh *Indicadores* 1989; Meller 1990; Solimano 1990b; Vial 1990). A new aspect of Buchi's economic program was the creation of a system of regulation, control, and supervision of transactions in the financial and banking systems, to avoid a repetition of the 1981–83 crisis, caused in part by the lack of regulation in financial activities. The state, therefore, increased its role in this area. For example, new powers were given to the AFP Superintendency, and a commission to classify risks was created to regulate capital markets and diversify AFP portfolios (see section H below). Although price liberalization continued in this stage, the government fixed prices of traditional agricultural products, not only basic grains but also others such as sugar and vegetable oils, in an effort to stimulate output (see next section).

Finally, the reduction of inflation was no longer the main macroeconomic target in this stage (as it had been in the stabilization process of 1976–81). Between 1984 and 1988 inflation was kept under control through fiscal austerity and the new monetary policy. But fiscal expansion and a 50% increase in the money supply led to a new inflationary burst in 1989–90. The economic authorities tried to control inflationary pressures through a reduction in the amount of money and a slowdown in the devaluation of the exchange rate in the second semester of 1989 (Table II.3; BCCh *Boletín Mensual,* March 1994).

E. Development Strategy

The previous development strategy was strengthened in this stage, but Buchi's team was more flexible and pragmatic in order to encourage traditional agricultural production. Another feature of this stage was the increasing foreign ownership of Chilean businesses, through the mechanisms of conversion of the foreign debt. The government also nationalized the remaining foreign debt of the private sector and supported the domestic banking system.

As in previous stages, however, the development strategy between 1984 and 1990 continued to lack a long-term industrial policy. Government critics noted that such a vacuum could affect future economic growth, because the experiences of successfully industrialized countries was against the concentration of efforts in the export of raw materials. In the Chilean case, 80% of exports were concentrated in mining, agriculture, forestry, and fishing in 1989 (Muñoz 1986, 1988a, 1988b, 1992; Cruz 1988; Ffrench-Davis and Muñoz 1990).

An important change in this stage was state protection of traditional agriculture, to increase its output and reduce imports, through the following policies: (1) price fixing of traditional agricultural products in 1984–85 (e.g., wheat, sugar, corn and vegetable oils), due to higher costs of domestic production over imports; (2) an increase in import tariffs of those products and periodic devaluations of the exchange rate, which made imports even more expensive, thus increasing the competitiveness of domestic agricultural products and the profits of exporters; and (3) opening preferential credit lines by the State Bank for traditional agricultural producers.

The nontraditional agricultural sector (fruit and forestry) continued to receive government support for their exports, through specialized technical assistance, credit from both the State Bank and commercial banks, and subsidies to reforestation and forest products. The policy of continuous periodic devaluations made nontraditional exports more competitive. Starting in 1985, taxes paid by nontraditional exporters were annually returned to them; accumulated returns between 1985 and 1989 were U.S.$181 million; in 1986 the payment of tariffs and the VAT for imported inputs used in the production of goods for export was suspended. The agro-forestry sector became an area of external investment through the mechanisms of debt conversion explained earlier. Thus, in 1986 transnational corporations controlled three of the six largest export firms, which generated more than 30% of fruit and forestry exports and brought new technology that was incorporated in the sector (Gómez and Echeñique 1988; Meller 1992b, Moguillansky and Titelman 1993).

F. External Sector

The recovery and economic boom of this stage were partly the result of the continuation of previous external policies (open foreign trade, incentives to foreign investment, and export promotion), combined with the flexible tariff and exchange-rate policies.

The tariff policy responded actively to the needs of the economic program of 1984–90. When it was necessary to reduce imports (September 1984) and protect industries during the recovery phase, import tariffs were increased from 20% to 35% (averaging 24.4% in the year). With Buchi's economic team in place and the recovery under way, import tariffs returned to a low level for all products (except for automobiles, alcohol, traditional agricultural products, etc.). Tariffs were reduced from 35% to 30% in March 1985 and to 20% in June of the same year (averaging 25.8% in the year), maintained at 20% from June 1985 to December 1987, lowered to 15% in January 1988, and kept at that level for the rest of the stage (Meller 1990, 1992b; Muñoz and Celedón 1993; Yáñez 1992).

Periodic devaluations of the peso continued, leading to an average real increase in the exchange rate of 23.8% between 1984 and 1989. The objectives of these policies were to strengthen the competitiveness of the external sector and promote exports (particularly nontraditional ones), make traditional agricultural products cheaper than imports, restore the equilibrium in the trade balance, and generate resources for the servicing of the foreign debt. The liberalization of external trade was consolidated during the economic boom of 1985–90, and the economy became more open. A new policy to reduce the external debt and attract foreign investment was the debt-equity swaps, and from 1985 onwards multinational corporations entered the market for export agricultural products (Arellano 1988; Cruz 1988; Gómez and Echeñique 1988; Muñoz 1988a, 1992; Muñoz and Celedón 1993; Dornbusch and Edwards 1994; Yañez 1992).

The total external debt increased from 88% to 127% of GDP in 1983–85 but was reduced after 1986 because of strong economic growth, high prices of copper in the international market, aid from international financial organizations, reconversion of part of the foreign debt, and full payment of principal and interest of such debt. Unlike some Latin American countries that, at the time, rejected or resisted the tough schedule of payments established by the IMF because of the high social costs that the adjustment imposed on low- and middle-income groups, the Chilean government faithfully fulfilled its obligations with the IMF (which, in turn, prompted aid from the IMF, World Bank, and IDB). The authoritarian regime facilitated the heavy social costs, which were not as feasible in democratic countries (Ffrench-Davis 1987, 1989; Vial et al. 1990; Ministerio de Hacienda 1992; Carciofi et al. 1993; Muñoz and Celedón 1993).

One of the innovative mechanisms used to reduce the external debt in this stage was the conversion of foreign debt into investment. Designed by the Central Bank in 1985, debt-equity swaps had two mechanisms: foreign-debt promissory notes were sold by the creditor to Chile's Central Bank, which in turn sold them in the international secondary market at a discount rate (which averaged 40% between 1985 and 1989); and foreign-debt paper was used to buy Chilean domestic enterprises, and interest payments on the debt were replaced by future profits from the acquired enterprises, payable in four years. About 19% of the external debt was converted through these two mechanisms concentrated on the most dynamic economic sectors: mining, fisheries, forestry, and financial services. Debt-equity swaps, however, were controversial in Chile. Supporters claimed they had two advantages: increases in foreign investment and incentives for economic growth through expanded financial resources. Critics pinpointed disadvantages: (1) the conversion of foreign debt was used for the selling of state enterprises at low prices; (2) the conversion did not attract new capital but "paper" investment that was not necessarily transformed into new productive capacity (this point is supported by the low and declining rate of foreign gross investment in this stage); and (3) initially the Chilean government accepted excessively high valuations of the IOUs (prices close to 88% of their face value), which, added to the 40% average discount rate of the IOUs in the secondary market, led to net losses for the state and subsidies for the investors. In 1984 the government offered the possibility of converting the debt of the private sector from dollars to Chilean pesos, at a cost of U.S.$230 million according to the Central Bank's estimates (Fontaine 1986; Shinke 1987; Ffrench-Davis 1989; ECLAC 1993b).

G. Labor and Employment

The 1979 labor law was not modified in this stage, and the adjustment programs harmed workers. At the end of 1983 and throughout 1984, massive popular protests against the military government were organized by university students and workers and spread to other segments of the population. As a result, in October 1984 the government declared a state of siege.

Average and minimum wages were kept under the level of inflation and further deteriorated in 1984–87 but began to recover in 1988–89 because of the economic boom and government's concessions prompted by public pressure and the elections. The emergency employment programs (PEM and POJH) continued during most of this stage but lost importance in 1988–89 and disappeared because of the significant decline in unemployment (Ffrench-Davis and Raczynski 1987; Jadresic 1990; Meller 1992a).

In 1988, the year of the plebiscite, various workers' organizations, in particular, the copper, coal, oil, and construction unions, created the United Confederation of Workers (Central Unitaria de Trabajadores [CUT]), which grouped together all unionized workers. The main opposition parties were represented in this umbrella labor organization, which had a broad and diverse political composition, unlike the previous federation, controlled by the communist and socialist parties and dissolved by the military in 1973. In spite of ideological differences, CUT had a common objective: the defense of workers' interests vis-à-vis the neoconservative adjustment policies. In addition, CUT played an important role in the triumph of the opposition in both electoral contests.

The number of workers unionized increased by 22% in 1986–89 over 1980–85, but in terms of the employed labor force the proportion declined from 12% to 10.6%, and the number of workers involved in strikes kept declining (ILO 1980–83, 1989–90). But period averages hide increases in the number of strikes (40%), workers involved (219%), and workdays lost (242%), all in 1989 (ILO 1989–90).

H. Distribution and Social Services

In this stage there was no change in previous policies: income distribution through market mechanisms with the state playing a subsidiary role in social policy, and the private sector increasing its role in social security (majority of pensions), health, education (excluding preschool education), and housing. Social spending was reduced from 17.1% to 14% of GDP between 1983 and 1989 (Table II.17).

The fiscal subsidy to the social security system as a whole declined from 9.4% to 7.6% of GDP to cover two expenses: the deficit in the old system generated by the transfer of the majority of their active contributors to the private pension system, and the full cost of programs previously financed by employers (unemployment compensation and family allowances). The cost of social security decreased from 14.7% to 11.4% of GDP because of erosion in the real value of benefits in the old system (Table II.25; Dirección de Presupuestos 1993; SUSESO 1993). The minimum and welfare pensions in the old system were adjusted below inflation between 1984 and 1989; hence in real terms they declined by 11% and 21%, respectively, while family allowances suffered a 92% drop in real value. In 1988–89, 19 pension funds in the old system were merged into the new Institute of Social Insurance Standardization (Instituto de Normalización Previsional [INP]), which began to standardize their entitlement conditions and benefits. The pension systems of the armed forces and the police continued to be excluded from unification and standardization. Measures were taken in the new private pension system regarding the composition and diversification of the AFP portfolio because it was dangerously concentrated in state and debt instruments. In 1985 a law authorized investments in bonds and stocks of firms that met certain minimum requirements. These transactions were regulated and controlled by the SAFP, through rules enforced by its Commission for Ranking Risks (Comisión Clasificadora de Riesgos). The commission classified and ranked private stocks and bonds by degree of risk (specifying which was the lowest allowed for investment) and supervised the investment of AFPs. In 1986–88, 95% of the total AFP investment was concentrated in public enterprises in the process of being privatized; thus, in 1989, restrictions to investments in bonds and stocks were made more flexible. The purpose of these measures was to diversify the investment portfolio, prevent a repetition of the 1981–83 danger of AFP bankruptcy, and generate more, varied investment opportunities for the growing amount of pension funds. The AFP commissions exhibited a declining trend between 1983 and 1989: the average fixed commission went from 784 to 245 pesos (in constant pesos of 1990), the average commission for old-age, disability, and survival insurance from 3.6% to 3.3%, and the average monthly cost for the insureds from 14.8% to 13.5%. Finally, in 1988, responding to the high yields of the private pension system, new system voluntary savings accounts were created and administered by the AFPs (Mesa-Lago 1985, 1993, 1994; Ffrench-Davis 1991; Iglesias, Acuña, and Chamorro 1991; Marcel and Arenas 1992; Meller, Lehmann, and Cifuentes 1993; SAFP 1993).

The state budget for public health care was cut from 2.9% to 2.4% between 1983 and 1989, a deterioration made worse by the continuous transfer of contributors from the public to the private system (ISAPREs). As in previous stages, the reduced resources of the public sector were targeted to mother-infant care. In 1989 ISAPREs' population coverage was 13.5%, but their revenues exceeded 50% of the public-system revenues (because those who moved were the higher-income contributors). In 1985 these financial problems forced an increase in the mandatory health contribution from 6% to 7%, a measure that improved the finances of the public system but increased the burden on the insureds, most of whom were low and middle income. The contribution increase was less of a burden to the high-income insureds in the ISAPREs. In 1985 a reform was implemented to partly privatize the public health-care system, allowing those covered by it to choose care at the public institutions or at private clinics and ambulatories registered with FONASA ("free-choice"). Before 1985 all those covered by the public system facilities (SNSS) received free care, but in that year a reform created four groups (identified by the letters A–D) according to the insureds' taxable income: A (indigents and those without taxable income), does not pay for services; B (income lower than U.S.$100 per month), also receives free attention; C (between U.S.$100 and U.S.$160 dollars per month), pays 25% of the service cost; and D (more than U.S.$160 dollars per month), pays 50% of the service cost. In the free-choice modality, the insured must buy from FONASA a voucher for medical care, whose value depends on the level or quality of attention demanded by the insured; the voucher is used to pay in the private clinics, which are later reimbursed by FONASA (Arellano 1987; Oyarzo 1989; Vergara 1990; Arenas de Mesa 1991; Covarrubias 1991).

Public expenditures on education declined from 3.9% to 2.9% of GDP between 1983 and 1989. After the 1981–83 crisis was over and the recovery ensued, the government resumed the transfer of elementary and secondary education to the municipalities, a process completed in 1986. The private sector responded rapidly to the granting of fiscal subsidies in exchange for the delivery of educational services: the number of private educational institutions increased by 50% in this stage (Table II.17; Castañeda 1989). Several changes occurred in the higher-education sector. Enrollment increased because of the creation of new private universities and professional institutes; total tuition in the latter more than doubled that of the former. The structure of university financing was unchanged: state contributions were divided into direct subsidies, indirect subsidies, and student credits. Direct subsidies reached 70% of total state resources allocated to higher education in 1989, but, according to the 1981 budgetary plan, they should have been only 30%. Indirect subsidies (fiscal credit) to universities were targeted to finance low-income students, and a new system of student credit was created in 1988. The administration of fiscal credit was transferred to the universities, which also received the power to allocate the student credits under a new revolving credit fund (Arriagada 1989; Sanfuentes 1990; Brunner et al. 1991).

Housing was an exception in social policy, as its public-expenditure allocation increased from 0.9% to 1.1% of GDP between 1983 and 1989, but the real funds allocated in 1989 were 11% lower than those of 1981 and 63% lower than those of 1970 (Table II.17). In 1984 a new program of state subsidy for "marginality housing" consolidated all existing public subsidies geared toward low-income groups (social housing and basic housing in previous stages). The new program targeted groups in extreme poverty, providing houses at a maximum cost of U.S.$6,000, financed with state nonrepayable subsidies that covered up to 75% of the house's value, and the remaining 25% with state credits and bank savings accumulated by the beneficiaries. All government housing programs delivered an annual average of 35,000 houses between 1984 and 1989, built by the private sector through public bidding. The share of houses built by the private sector reached more than 98% of total houses (public and private) constructed in this stage. In Santiago the program to eradicate indigent neighborhoods (initiated in 1981) continued, and 87,000 families in conditions of extreme poverty were relocated outside the capital. Mortgage debts affecting more than 100,000 families became a priority after the 1981–83 crisis; the government created a program to reschedule those loans in 1983–84 (especially for middle-income families), based on two features: the debtor had to reschedule the mortgage but with a real debt higher than the initial value of the mortgage; and the debt currency was changed from pesos to UF, the daily adjusted currency

(Table II.26; Castañeda 1989; Délano and Traslaviña 1989; Vergara 1990; Ffrench-Davis 1991).

2. Performance

A. Growth

This stage encompassed a rapid economic recovery in 1984–85 and sustained growth in 1986–89, as a result of the following policies and factors: control of the fiscal deficit, coherence between restrictive monetary and fiscal policies (until 1987), continuous devaluation of the exchange rate, the high world price of copper, which facilitated the equilibrium in the external accounts and balance of payments, continuous growth in the nontraditional export sector, development of domestic investment and the capital market (the latter crucial to opening new investment opportunities for the growing pension funds), and the strong support received from international financial agencies. (When not specified, the date in this section covers the period from December 1983 to December 1989; when the data presented are not comparable it will be noted.)

GDP grew by 6.3% in 1984 (4.6% per capita) but declined to 2.4% in 1985 (0.8% per capita); thereafter GDP steadily increased to a peak of 9.9% in 1989 (8.1% per capita). The latter was largely the result of the expansive fiscal policy of 1988–89, a futile political move taken to influence the electoral processes. The average annual growth rate of GDP in this stage was 6.4% (4.6% per capita); the latter was much higher than the rates of the 1960s (2.5%) and the first half of the 1970s (−3%), but lower than the rate of the earlier boom between 1977 and 1981 (6%) (Table II.3). There were important differences between the two stages of economic growth under Pinochet, 1977–81 and 1984–89. In the first, there was rapidly increasing consumption and indebtedness, while in the second domestic investment was promoted and rose, with the aims of reducing both dependency on external financing and the heavy external indebtedness that provoked the crisis in 1981–83. In the first stage, the average annual consumption was 6.6% and the real external debt increased 121%, while in the second stage the respective figures were 2.4% and −23% (Tables II.13, II.20; Solimano 1990a; Meller, Lehmann, and Cifuentes 1993).

The gross investment rate increased from 13.6% to 19.1% of GDP. The most important component was the domestic one, which increased from 2.9% to 17.2% of GDP; with the exception of 1974, the latter was the highest in the 1974–89 neoconservative period. Conversely, the external component of gross investment declined from 10.7% to 1.9% in the stage, one of the three lowest in the period (Table II.3).

B. Inflation

The IMF five-year structural adjustment program accepted by the government succeeded in stabilizing the economy, opened the door to World Bank and IDB credits, reduced external disequilibrium, and facilitated the servicing of the external debt. Real interest rates rose from 2.3% to 5.1%, an incentive that contributed to increased savings and investment (Marcel 1989; Dirección de Presupuestos 1993).

The fiscal deficit rose from 3.8% to 6.3% of GDP in 1983–85, but, because of the restrictive monetary and fiscal policy, it was almost wiped out (−0.1%) in 1987. On the eve of the elections, however, the government applied an expansive economic policy, and public indebtedness reached 52% of GDP in 1989, despite the abundant fiscal revenue coming from the privatization of state enterprises and the doubling of world copper prices. The fiscal deficit, therefore, rose to 1.7% in 1988 and 3% in 1989. The annual average of the deficit for the entire stage was −3%, equal to that during the crisis, but contrasted with a surplus of 0.8% during the 1977–81 boom (Table II.3).

Inflation rose from 23% in 1984 to 26.4% in 1985 and kept declining (except for 1987) to 12.7% in 1988 because of the restrictive fiscal and monetary policies. Inflation rose to 21.4% in 1989 because of the growth in fiscal expenditures before the presidential elections, and a 50% increase in the amount of money in circulation (Table II.3). The inflationary spiral of 1989, combined with the significant public indebtedness and the substantial payments of foreign debt that the government was to face in 1990, would create important domestic and external restrictions for the incoming democratic administration and contributed to the 1990 economic decline (Marcel 1989, 1991; Ffrench-Davis 1989, 1991; Vial, Butelmann, and Celedón 1990; Muñoz and Celedón 1993).

C. Diversification

All economic activities grew in this stage, although the structural adjustment program impacted them in divergent ways; differences among activities resulted from their rate of growth vis-à-vis that of GDP, which rose at an annual average of 6.4%. The agricultural-forestry-fishing sector increased 5.9% annually, less than GDP, and hence its share of GDP declined from 9.3% to 9%; but there were significant differences among agricultural subsectors and specific activities. Traditional agriculture decreased annually by 1% (despite government support), while nontraditional agriculture swelled 18% per year (three times the GDP growth rate): grapes rose by 30%, while fishing rose by 29%. Between 1985 and 1989 agricultural exports jumped 80%; fruits (mainly grapes and apples) contributed 69% to all agricultural exports in 1989, despite growing protectionist barriers in the United States and in Europe (Cruz 1988; Gómez and Echeñique 1988).

The industrial sector (including mining, electricity, gas, water) grew annually at 6.2% (slightly below GDP growth), and its share of GDP slightly decreased from 31.4% to 31.1% between 1983 and 1989; but because of the redirection of domestic output to export markets, industrial exports doubled in this stage and reached U.S.$2.5 billion in 1989 or 9.5% of GDP. The construction sector expanded annually by 8.2% (more than GDP), the second highest rate of all sectors, and its share of GDP increased from 5.2% to 5.8%. Transportation and communications grew 9.2% per year (the highest rate of all sectors) and increased their share of GDP from 5.4% to 6.4%. Commerce expanded at an annual rate of 7.3% (also higher than GDP), and its share of GDP rose from 17.1% to 18%. Services, which include banking and financial services, grew 5.1% annually (less than GDP), reducing their share of GDP from 31.7% to 29.7%; such a decrease is explained by the cut in the volume of credits that followed the heavy expansion in the 1981–82 crisis (Tables II.–6; Cruz 1988; Ffrench-Davis and Muñoz 1990).

D. Trade Balance and External Dependency

The continuation in the free-trade model led to a trade surplus, as in the previous stage, but with an important difference: after an initial decline, both exports and imports grew at very high rates (the external debt crisis forced the government to generate a trade surplus to service the debt). After a decline of 20% of exports in 1983–85, successive devaluations promoted an annual increase of exports (mainly nontraditional) by 27.6% in 1986–89, and their share in GDP expansion (current prices) from 24% to 37.7% between 1983 and 1989. Imports stagnated in 1983–85, responding to peso devaluations and increases in tariffs, but, once the process was reversed and tariffs lowered, imports grew continuously at a 20.2% annually in 1986–89 (in the latter year recovering the 1981 peak) and expanded their share in GDP in current prices from 21.3% to 34.4% between 1983 and 1989. The increase in exports amply surpassed that of imports, so that the trade surplus jumped 125% between 1983 and 1988 (a record of U.S.$2 billion in 1988, which declined to U.S.$1.6 billion in 1989 vis-à-vis less than U.S.$1 billion in 1981). As trade transactions grew by 118% in the stage, external dependency of the economy increased from 45% to 72% of GDP in current prices, and from 46% to 57% in constant prices (Table II.7; BCCh *Indicadores* 1989).

The IMF program demanded the timely payment of the external debt, and Chile complied. The debt service averaged U.S.$1.9 billion annually between 1984 and 1989, or 36% of export value. The real total external debt, therefore, was reduced by 26% in the stage, from 115% to 69% of GDP and from 420% to 201% of export value. The public component increased from 56% to 74% of the total debt, while the private component declined from 44% to 26% as a result of the state's absorption of part of the private debt. International reserves increased annually by U.S.$400 million, mainly because of the very high world prices of copper and the inflow of foreign capital (Table II.8; Ffrench-Davis 1989; Meller 1990, 1992b; ECLAC 1993b; Hachette and Luders 1993; Meller et al. 1993).

Export diversification resumed between 1983 and 1987, as world copper prices declined. Therefore, copper reduced its share of total exports from 48% to 41% between 1983 and 1987, while the share of other exports increased from 52% to 59%. In 1987–89, however, world copper prices increased 60%, establishing a historical record in 1989 (production also increased and set a record that year), leading for the first time in 15 years to a reversion in export diversification. The share of copper exports increased from 41% to 50% in 1987–89, while the share of other exports decreased from 59% to 50% (Tables II.7–8; Ffrench-Davis and Muñoz 1990; Moguillansky and Titelman 1993).

The development of the nontraditional export sector established Chile as the most important exporter of grapes, apples, and fish meal in the Southern Hemisphere. Chile became the main supplier of fruit to the North American and European markets, serving these markets for six months uninterruptedly. Nontraditional exports grew annually by 22% and increased their share in total exports from 15.6% to 30% between 1983 and 1989. The growth in the export market promoted an increase of 50%, in 1986–88, of new export firms in agriculture, forestry, fishing, and industry (Arellano 1988; Ffrench-Davis and Muñoz 1990; Meller 1992b).

The composition of imports changed because of the peso devaluation and variations in import tariffs, as follows: (1) food and beverages decreased from 17% to 3% (an indication of the policy's success in increasing output of traditional agriculture); (2) oil decreased from 21% to 12% (mainly because of a decline in oil world prices, but also because of a decline in domestic production; oil imports increased annually at 11%, hence raising the dependency on imported oil from 49% to 64% between 1983 and 1987); (3) imports of machinery and transportation dramatically jumped from 23% to 44% (going back to the 1968 level in the midst of ISI; this was largely because of the importing of new technology and equipment for agriculture, and to a lesser extent industry); and (4) manufactures increased from 35% to 37%, as tariffs were reduced (Tables II.9, II.12; Lavín 1987; Muñoz 1988a). The search for new markets led to a resumption of trade-partner diversification. The U.S. share decreased from 27% to 19% between 1983 and 1989, and Germany's declined from 10% to 9%; conversely Japan's trade share rose from 7.7% to 12.6% (Table II.11).

E. Unemployment

Economic growth between 1984 and 1989 led to a sustained decline in open unemployment. According to the ILO, the national unemployment rate shrank from 14.6% to 5.3% between 1983 and 1989; ECLAC estimated a decrease of unemployment in Santiago from 19% to 7.2%. These rates began to approximate the average of the 1960s but were still higher than those in the early 1970s. Estimates for 1988–89 indicate that 33% of urban workers were in the informal sector, compared to 20% in 1980. Emergency employment programs (PEM and POJH) reduced enrollment from 336,000 to 124,100 workers, and, beginning in 1988, these programs were gradually eliminated (Table II.16; Ffrench-Davis and Raczynski 1987; Meller 1990; Mesa-Lago 1990; Ffrench-Davis 1991; ECLAC 1993b).

The distribution of the labor force was influenced by incentives given to the development of labor-intensive export activities (agriculture-forestry and industry). Shares of these sectors increased as follows between 1985 and 1990 (data are not available for 1983–84 and 1989): agriculture from 18.6% to 19.4%, industry from 13.2% to 15.6%, transportation from 5.7% to 6.4%, construction from 4.6% to 6.9%, and financial services from 4% to 4.3%. Leading job expansion was the industrial sector, which, after suffering the impact of the 1981–83 crisis and a 25% reduction in employment, increased jobs by 88% between 1983 and 1989. The share of other activities declined: mining from 2.2% to 2% and services (personal, social) from 31.6% to 26.6% (Tables II.6, II.14).

The proportion of the labor force made up of women remained stable: 30.7% in 1985 and 30.8% in 1989. Their participation rate increased from 21.3% to 24.2% between 1980 and 1985 and 27% in 1990. In the agricultural sector there was a strong increase in female employment, especially in export activities that hired rural women temporarily at low wages (Table II.15; Muñoz 1988a; Montecinos 1994).

F. Equality

Economic growth in this stage led to a 14 percentage point increase in household consumption; actually it was stagnant between 1983 and 1987 and then increased in 1988–89. Still, consumption in 1989 remained 2.7 points below the 1981 level and 8.5 points below the 1972 level. Between 1978 and 1988 (there are no data for 1979–83 and 1989), the poorest 20% of the population in the capital reduced their share in total consumption from 5.2% to 4.4%, whereas the wealthiest 20% increased their share from 51% to 54.6%. Poverty incidence increased from 30.8% to 50.9% of the population between 1982 and 1986 but improved slightly to 48.6% in 1987. The incidence of indigency increased from 10.8% to 24.7% and declined to 22.6% in the same period (Tables II.18, II.20).

According to ECLAC, real mean wages declined by 2.3 percentage points between 1983 and 1987 (continuing the downward trend since 1982) but increased by 8.2 percentage points in 1987–89, although still remaining 6 points lower than the 1981 level and 30 points lower than the 1971 level. The construction sector suffered the worse decline in real wages (23 points between 1983 and 1989) followed by agriculture and industry (a decline of 14.4 points). The real urban minimum wage declined by 10 points between 1983 and 1989, 32 points below the 1981 level. Sectoral indexes indicate that the real minimum wage in the manufactured sector decreased by 16% in 1983–84 and 8% in 1985–88; it increased in 1988–89 but remained 14.5% below the 1983 level and 25% lower than the 1980 level. In the construction sector, the real minimum wage dropped by 23% in 1988–89. Sustained growth in this stage therefore led to only a small recovery of real wages during the election period of 1988–89 (Table II.19; Jadresic 1990; Meller 1990, 1992a; Ffrench-Davis 1991; ECLAC 1993b; Meller, Lehmann, and Cifuentes 1993; SAFP 1993).

Unfortunately there are no data on either the Gini coefficient or the labor share in gross national income after 1983–84. But the economic policies of 1974–89 appear to have a regressive impact on income distribution. A study based on nonpublished data estimates that the poorest 40% of the population had an average share of 10.5% total income between 1959 and 1973 (14 years under the Alessandri, Frei, and Allende administrations), but this share declined to an average of 9.1% between 1974 and 1989 (15 years under Pinochet). Conversely, the wealthiest 20% of the population increased its income share from an average of 57.3% to 62% in similar periods (Marcel and Solimano 1994).

G. Social Indicators

Previous social policies continued in this stage, and the adjustment program had some adverse effects. Despite economic growth, social expenditures decreased from 17.1% to 14% of GDP between 1983 and 1989; in per capita terms, they declined by 4% annually, further deteriorating the living standards of the lower-income groups, although the improvement in some social indicators continued (Table II.17; Ffrench-Davis and Raczynski 1987; Marcel and Solimano 1994).

As in the previous stage, here assumptions versus actual performance of pensions are contrasted concerning the role of competition in cost reduction; incentives to cut evasion, payment delays, and underreporting of income; real level of benefits; portfolio diversification; and impact on the capital market and domestic savings (the following discussion is based on Cheyre 1988; Arellano 1989; Vergara 1990; Arrau 1991; Ffrench-Davis 1991; Iglesias, Acuña, and Chamorro 1991; Piñera 1991; Guillion and Bonilla 1992; Marcel and Arenas 1992; CIEDESS 1992; Dirección de Presupuestos 1993; Meller, Lehmann, and Cifuentes 1993; Mesa-Lago 1993, 1994; SAFP 1983–89).

The first question is whether competition really worked, as assumed, and reduced the costs of administration, insureds' wage contributions, and commissions charged by AFPs. The number of AFPs increased from 12 to 13 between 1983 and 1989, but the concentration of insureds affiliated with the three largest AFPs rose from 59.4% to 65.2%. The two largest AFPs controlled 53% of the market in 1983 and 52% in 1989, despite long periods in which they charged the highest commissions and paid the lowest investment yields in the system. Annually, between 17% and 22% of all affiliates changed AFPs, and approximately 90% of the transfers were made by salespersons hired by the AFPs, who received a commission for each transfer. It appears that the insureds did not choose the AFPs on the basis of low commissions and high investment yields (the two main indicators for judging competition and efficiency in the system) but because of publicity or direct marketing (the interest of AFP personnel is not necessarily the same as that of the insureds). Contributions to the new system dropped from 14.8% to 13.5% between 1983 and 1989, almost returning to the 13.4% level of 1981, but contributions to the old system were maintained between 19% and 21%. Administrative costs of the AFPs were cut from 20% to 16% of all contributions, compared to 8% in the old system before the reform in 1981. Such a difference was largely due to the high costs of publicity in the new system (marketing personnel in AFPs made up 35% of their total employment in 1989), but advertising was not needed in the old system. Finally, managing two pension systems (public and private) increased administrative costs, a situation that will remain until the disappearance of the public system (it will start losing its importance in 2020 and will disappear between 2035 and 2040).

The second question is whether, as alleged, the strict relationship between contributions and benefits reduced evasion and payment delays, thus increasing population coverage. Coverage indeed increased from 59% to 79% between 1983 and 1989, reversing the 1981–83 decline, facilitated by employment growth and reduction in unemployment. The percentage of active contributors in relation to the total number of those affiliated to the system, however, further declined from 68.2% to 65.3% (or 53%, depending on the estimate). In the public system, this percentage increased from 68% to 86% between 1980 and 1987, because insureds in the old system are closer to retirement age than those in the new system. In 1989, 51% of the labor force was affiliated and made contributions, 28% was affiliated and did not contribute, and close to 21% was not covered; 47% of the affiliated had a record of a year without contributions to their individual accounts. Another problem that persisted in the private system was the very low coverage (voluntary) of self-employed workers: only 5% of total self-employed in 1989. Furthermore, declared wages that year averaged 20% less than real wages in the economy (a significant underreporting), and 26% of the insured paid contributions equal to or lower than the legal minimum, which will increase the number of people receiving a minimum pension guaranteed by the state (Table II.25).

Third, did the social security reform result in higher real benefits? Average pensions in the new system indeed were higher than average pensions in the old system, but the same was not true of other social security benefits between 1983 and 1989: family allowance beneficiaries declined by 180,000, and the real value of the allowance dropped 34% because of the lack of indexation. The number of welfare pensioners decreased 10%, and their real value shrank 23%; also, the real minimum pension declined by 12%, and the average real pension of the public system was cut by 5%.

The fourth issue is whether the investment portfolio of the private pension system became truly diversified. The composition of the pension funds portfolio changed as follows between 1983 and 1989. The overall share of state instruments declined from 44.5% to 41.6% of total investment, but, if investment in stocks of state enterprises being privatized (still with a state ownership above 50%) had been included, the share in public instruments would have climbed to 51.1% in 1989. The public portfolio changed in this stage, reducing investment in Treasury paper from 30.4% to 3.5%, but increasing Central Bank debt paper from 14.1% to 38.1%; hence the net reduction was about only 3 percentage points. Finally, investment in private instruments increased from 55.5% to 58.4% of the total: the share of mortgage promissory notes declined from 50.6% to 17.7%; the share in bonds and bank deposits rose from 4.9% to 30.6%; and investment in stocks increased from zero to 10.1% (95% of which was in state enterprises being privatized).

In summary, there was some diversification, particularly following the 1985 law, but about half of the investment was still in public instruments (including public enterprises with less than 50% private ownership); most instruments were debt, and only 10% was in stocks of private enterprises.

Fifth, did the private pension system significantly contribute to develop the capital market and increase domestic savings? The initial high real yield of AFP investment (20% annual average in 1981–83) declined to 7.7% between 1984 and 1989; this yield, however, was 1.5 percentage points higher than Chile's average banking interest rate in this stage and the highest yield in Latin America. Thus, the real value of the pension funds increased from 5.8% to 17.8% of GDP between 1983 and 1989. The latter could be interpreted as supporting the claim by the founders of the system (see, e.g., Piñera 1991) that the transformation of the pay-as-you-go system into a fully funded system would increase capital accumulation. This point was contested by scholars (e.g., Arellano 1989; Mesa-Lago 1994), who argued that to have a net positive effect, capital accumulation in the AFPs would have to be higher than the fiscal deficit originated by the social security reform. For instance, the number of active contributors to the old public pension system declined from 478,000 to 348,000 between 1983 and 1989, but the number of pensioners was 1,200,000 in 1989, thus creating a fiscal deficit that averaged 8% of GDP. Several studies concluded that, in the 1980s, there was no evidence that the new private system helped to increase the national savings rate, as it was rather the product of external savings and the restrictive fiscal policy in this stage.

In the area of health care, between 1983 and 1989 ISAPREs increased their population coverage from 2% to 13.5%, but the latter contributed to the private system 53% of the total contribution revenue of the entire (public and private) healthcare system. Between 1983 and 1989 the state's share of the total revenue of the public health sector declined from 46% to 35% (public expenditures decreased by 0.5% of GDP annually in this stage), while the insureds' share increased from 35% to 45% (as contributions rose from 6% to 7%); the remaining 20% came from revenue generated by the system itself and the external debt, both being stagnant during this period. As a result, the financial burden on the lower-income insureds increased, and the regressiveness in health-care financing was reinforced (Oyarzo 1989; Arenas de Mesa 1991).

The quantity and quality of public health-care services generally declined in the stage because of the growing financial deficit, the obsolescence of equipment and technology (especially in some regions and rural areas), the shortage of material inputs and basic drugs, and the wearing out of hospital infrastructure. (The deficit in public health-care investment in this st?

would demand a high amount of resources between 1990 and 1994.) Administrative procedures for surgery and access to public hospital beds increased; thus the waiting list for public hospital beds ranged from one to two years, which, in turn, provoked an annual increase of 10% in emergency consultations between 1983 and 1987. The ratio of hospital beds per 1,000 inhabitants decreased from 3.3 to 2.8 between 1983 and 1989; the annual number of consultations for children between 1 and 15 years of age dropped from 1.78 to 1.48 between 1985 and 1989; and the medical ambulatory consultations of adults per inhabitants 15 and older were reduced from 1 to 0.83. Conversely, the ratio of physicians per 10,000 covered in the public sector increased from 3.7 to 5.1 between 1982 and 1989 because of the shift of insureds from the public to the private sector—without a reduction in the number of physicians working in the former. A significant improvement was the increase in access of the population to potable water and sewerage services: from 92.7% to 96.2% (water) and from 70.6% to 81.5% (sewerage) in the urban sector, and from 54.7% to 78.5% (water) in the rural sector (Table II.21 and 2.23; Arellano 1987; Oyarzo 1989; Vergara 1990; Ministerio de Salud 1991; Arenas de Mesa 1991; Raczynski and Romaguera 1993).

The continuous targeting of public health expenditures on primary care (especially infants and pregnant women) sustained improvements in this area: pre- and postnatal consultations increased by 26% in 1984–87; and the supplementary nutrition program (focused on poor children) expanded its share in total public-health expenditures from 6.7% to 9.2% between 1983 and 1989. But, as in previous stages, there was an erosion in the secondary and tertiary levels. According to PAHO the main causes of mortality were circulatory diseases, tumors, cancer, accidents, and poisoning. There were no preventative or curative programs for those diseases, since all the state's efforts were focused on infant mortality, which was further reduced from 21.9 to 17.1 per 1,000 between 1983 and 1989. But the national average concealed significant inequalities: in 1987, out of the 12 regions, the 7 that concentrated 35% of the population had infant mortality rates from 21.9 to 32.5 while the national rate was 18.5. Other health indicators improved between 1983 and 1989: general mortality declined from 6.3 to 5.8 per 1,000, and life expectancy at birth increased slightly from 71.3 to 71.9 years. Data on morbidity for 1983–89 is incomplete for several diseases, which impedes a comprehensive evaluation. Available figures, however, suggest that most rates remained stable with the following exceptions: hepatitis and tuberculosis rates decreased, while the measles rate rose from 57.8 to 336.7. According to PAHO, the latter was because of the epidemiological cycle that takes place every four years and that had not occurred since 1979 (Tables II.21–22; PAHO 1986, 1990).

The decentralization process and the transfer of elementary and secondary education to the municipalities was completed in this stage, and the private sector responded promptly to the law covering school subsidies by increasing its population coverage from 14% to 29% between 1980 and 1986. State allocation to education further decreased from 3.9% to 2.9% of GDP between 1983 and 1989, while educational expenditures per capita declined by 11%. The latter was partly compensated for by the increase in private educational expenditures and the targeting of public resources except in higher education (Arellano 1985; Castañeda 1989; Ffrench-Davis 1991; Dirección de Presupuestos 1993; Meller et al. 1993).

Illiteracy was reduced, between 1982 and 1990, from 8.9% to 6.6% of the population 15 and older (data are not available for either 1983 or 1989). Population coverage in all educational levels increased between 1983 and 1989. Preschool coverage rose from 15.9% to 20.2%, maintaining the trend in previous stages, but the JUNJI and the Ministry of Education estimated that 60–86% of lower-income children at this level were not enrolled. Coverage of elementary education continued to be universal. In secondary education, coverage was increased from 63% to 75% because of the participation of subsidized private schools. Higher education expanded its coverage from 15% to 19% because of the increase in enrollment in private universities (1,800%) and professional institutes (106%) between 1982 and 1987; but enrollment in public universities declined by 11% (Table II.24; Arriagada 1989; Castañeda 1989; Sanfuentes 1990; Vergara 1990; ECLAC 1993b).

Public expenditures in higher education decreased by 46.4% between 1983 and 1989, maintaining the previous trend and the transferring to and targeting of public resources on preschool education. Research was especially harmed, as its public financing decreased by 0.13% of GDP. The change from fiscal credits to university credits, financed autonomously by each university after 1988, did not solve the financial problems of university students. Payment delays and default remained at 40%, very high compared with similar systems in South America. Credit administered by the universities decreased by 40.3% between 1984 and 1988, and in 1989 it accounted for only 25% of the amount mandated by the 1981 law. Furthermore, more than 50% of the credit was allocated to students in the two highest income quintiles. In order to have access to subsidized transportation and free health care in the universities, students had to receive credit, thus encouraging excessive demand for credit and its inadequate allocation, which led to student protests (Sanfuentes 1986, 1990; Arriagada 1989; Castañeda 1989; Hachette 1990).

Public funds allocated to housing rose from 0.9% to 1.1% of GDP in this stage or from 2.7% to 5.6% of total government expenditures. In addition, units built by the state increased from 2.9 per 1,000 to 6.5, and housing subsidies provided incentives to the private sector to increase housing construction (more than 98% of the total between 1983 and 1989). According to some specialists such increases helped to reduce the housing deficit, especially in lower income sectors. Conversely, the Association of Architects estimated that 500,000 new families were added to the housing deficit between 1974 and 1989. In 1983 the estimated housing deficit was 964,000 homes; to solve this problem 80,000 homes had to be built annually, but only 49,000 actually were (combining the state and private sectors). The housing deficit, therefore, rose to 1,031,000 in 1988; the count would have been larger if families housed in the homes of relatives and the destruction caused by the 1985 earthquake were taken into account. About one-third of the new families established between 1985 and 1989 did not have a home (Table II.26; MacDonald 1983, 1994; Castañeda 1989; Délano and Traslaviña 1989; Vergara 1990; Raczynski and Romaguera 1993).

6

Democracy, Continuation of the Economic Model, and Growth with Equity

1990–1994

After more than 16 years of military government, on March 11, 1990, Patricio Aylwin became president for a four-year term, supported by a center-left coalition (*Concertación*) made up mostly of Christian Democrats and Socialists. With the return to democracy, the people had high expectations for a rapid response to unsatisfied social demands that had accumulated in the Pinochet years. But in 1990 there were serious economic problems due to the sharp increase in expenditures in 1989. The first economic team under the restored democracy, therefore, was forced to implement a severe adjustment program, which restricted social benefits in the first year of the administration.

Aylwin's program was also limited by the institutional framework (legal, political, economic) set by the military and their allied political forces, which retained an important share of power in this stage. The president's strategy was to partly reform the legal framework, develop political pacts, establish stable institutions for the development of economic activity, and introduce gradual small changes in the neoconservative economic model. Aylwin signed an agreement with a conservative party (Unión Demócrata Independiente), which won him a majority in the National Congress to gain the presidencies of the Senate and the Chamber of Deputies, hence facilitating the enactment of crucial legislation. A tax reform was negotiated and approved in 1990 with the principal party of the conservative opposition (Renovación Nacional), representative of businessmen who accepted higher taxes, including those on business profits. Labor reforms were possible due to agreements reached, through government mediation, between the main organiza-

105

tions representing business and workers; the latter accepted postponing many of their demands (Vial, Butelmann, and Celedón 1990; Foxley 1993; Ministerio de Hacienda 1993; Muñoz and Celedón 1993).

According to Minister of Finance Alejandro Foxley (1993), the new economic program introduced a truly "social market economy": it maintained the economic policies of the 1984–89 neoconservative stage (capital markets, open economy, active participation of the private sector) but introduced a tax reform and increased state action in social and labor areas, as well as in the regulation of private businesses, in order to reduce excessive inequalities generated by the previous free-market model. Revenue from the tax reform was largely used to incorporate marginalized groups into the benefits of economic development, as well as to augment social expenditures. Labor legislation was modified to restore workers' rights suppressed or reduced by the military government. The privatization process was halted, and the state took new supervisory and regulatory roles over some private economic activities.

There are four different viewpoints concerning the impact of Aylwin's socioeconomic policies on the neoconservative model: such policies (1) deepened the model (Fontaine 1990), (2) were essential and modified the model significantly (Muñoz and Celedón 1993; Bosworth et al. 1994), (3) created a new model (Cortázar 1993; ECLAC 1993b; Foxley, 1993), or (4) were not essential and failed fundamentally to alter the model (Petras et al. 1994). The following analysis indicates that the second viewpoint is the proper one.

1. Policies

A. Ownership

The privatization process was halted by Alywin, but he respected privatizations carried out until March 1990, when he took power. Legislation was enacted, nevertheless, to regulate certain private economic activities, but it was neither a return to the "state entrepreneur" of the 1960s and early 1970s nor a continuation of the policies of privatization and deregulation of 1974–89. The new state regulatory and supervisory functions were applied by the Ministry of Economics and a new National Anti-trust Agency to (1) large public enterprises (conglomerates) privatized between 1984 and 1989; (2) natural monopolies and activities that provoked negative externalities (e.g., damage to the environment); (3) exploitation of forests, protection of national parks, and intensive reforestation; (4) bans or restrictions on fishing species in danger of extinction; and (5) tariffs for public utilities such as electricity, fuel, and telecommunications (Ministerio de Hacienda 1992, 1993; CORFO 1993).

B. Planning

In 1990 the National Planning Office (ODEPLAN) was restructured and became the Ministry of Planning (MIDEPLAN), a change that enhanced social-policy planning. The government pursued modernization of the public sector, by increasing the efficiency and productivity of some public services. In 1993 a pilot project of five state services began with the aid of the Ministry of Finance, which established an evaluation program to assess the performance of the agencies and their employees; in 1994 this program was extended to five other services. The National Development Corporation (CORFO) continued operating during this stage, and its director was also granted ministerial rank. After seven years of losses, the 41 enterprises affiliated with CORFO generated a profit of U.S.$11.5 million in 1992, an improvement attributed by the government to better planning and management of those enterprises (CORFO 1993; Ministerio de Hacienda 1993, 1994).

The functions of the Central Bank (autonomous from the Ministry of Finance since 1989), in charge of monetary policy, and the Ministry of Finance, in charge of fiscal policy, were coordinated. The composition of the board of directors of the Central Bank was decided, prior to Aylwin's becoming president, by an agreement between the outgoing and incoming administrations, achieving a balance between the two parties, which facilitated communication of the Central Bank with the Ministry of Finance controlled by Alywin's coalition. The Ministry of Finance transferred U.S.$700 million to the Central Bank in this stage to finance the debt that commercial banks had with the Central Bank since they were bailed out following the economic crisis of 1981–83 (Larrañaga 1991; Ministerio de Hacienda 1993).

A central issue in this administration was the increasing role of the state and planning to alleviate poverty and improve social equity, because economic growth was considered necessary but not sufficient to achieve those social goals. The government therefore designed, implemented, and expanded social policies, reversing the trend of the state's withdrawal from this area that occurred during the military government. Finally, I have already discussed the state regulation of certain private economic activities, including enterprises privatized between 1984 and 1989 (Marcel and Solimano 1994).

C. Financing

The return to democracy, combined with strong economic growth and stability in this stage, became a powerful incentive for keeping foreign investment and aid. Incentives to domestic investors were also maintained to expand their share in total investment. The Aylwin administration's aim was to increase independence from foreign financing and make the economy less vulnerable to external shocks, such as international recessions, increases in oil prices, reductions in world market prices of copper, and so forth. As a result of these policies there was a significant increase in both fiscal revenue and foreign capital in this stage that generated more than U.S.$9 billion: (1) U.S.$3.5 billion engendered by the tax reform, (2) U.S.$753 million in Chilean government bonds, (3) U.S.$4 billion in foreign investment, and (4) more than U.S.$1 billion in soft loans from the World Bank and IDB.

The tax reform of 1990 generated additional fiscal revenue from U.S.$750 to U.S.$950 million annually or 2% of GDP, through the following measures: (1) an increase in taxes on enterprises' capital gains from 10% to 15%, (2) an increase in the value-added tax (VAT) from 16% to 18%, (3) the introduction of a top 50% tax bracket for the highest-income taxpayers, and (4) the incorporation into the system of accounting-assessed income of some productive sectors that previously had no or poor accounting and paid taxes based on a grossly estimated income. In negotiations with the opposition, in 1990, the government pledged to end the tax increases in 1994, when the tax burden would return to the 1989 level. In 1993, however, there was a second round of negotiations with the opposition, which brought the following results: the 18% VAT was maintained, but the government promised to reduce it to 17% in 1996; the capital gains tax was kept at 15%, and from 1995 onwards income taxes would gradually return to the 1989 level (Ministerio de Hacienda 1991, 1992, 1993, 1994).

Foreign investment averaged near U.S.$1 billion per year, attracted by lucrative opportunities, political stability, and high rates of economic growth, as well as by the signing of investment treaties with 12 countries. Multilateral financial organizations, mainly the World Bank and the IDB, provided substantial resources to finance the following social programs: employment and training for young workers; improvement of educational equity and quality in preschool, elementary, and secondary educational levels (MECE); and modernization of productive capacity through an improvement of the infrastructure. With the restoration of democracy, financial and technical aid (donations, soft loans) from many foreign governments (which had been suspended for political reasons during the military government) were reestablished by, among others, Belgium, France, Germany, Italy, Japan, Malaysia, Spain, Sweden, and Switzerland. Japan alone contributed U.S.$180 million for irrigation and sewerage projects (Ministerio de Hacienda 1992, 1993, 1994; Ministerio de Educación 1993; Ministerio de Salud 1994).

D. Stability and Prices

The sharp increase in fiscal expenditures in 1989 led to a projected annual inflation rate of 31% (based on September 1989 to January 1990), as well as an increase of the state deficit from 1.7% to 3% of GDP, and a rise in the real interest rate from 2% to 5% (Table II.3; BCCh *Boletín Mensual,* March 1994).

The military government started stabilization measures in December 1989, but it was not until March 1990, when Aylwin's stabilization program was implemented, that domestic spending and aggregate demand growth began to be reduced. Fiscal and monetary policies were coordinated by the Ministry of Finance and the Central Bank. The stabilization program looked for macroeconomic equilibria, and its main goal was to limit spending (growth in aggregate demand) in accordance with economic growth. The new economic team used the interest rate as an adjustment variable: in 1989–90 the real interest rate increased from 5.1% to 9.7% (BCCh *Boletín Mensual,* March 1994; the rate averaged 16.4% in March-June 1990). The following exogenous or "inherited" factors deepened the 1990 crisis, aggravated inflation, and made the new adjustment program more difficult: (1) the high level of indexation of the economy (in 1990, 80% of labor contracts had indexation clauses equivalent to 100% of the consumer price index), (2) the abrupt increase in oil world market prices provoked by the Persian Gulf War, and (3) a severe drought in 1990, which reduced agricultural supply.

Factors that helped to promote the recovery were the relatively high world price of copper in 1990 (although lower than in 1989 it was still the second highest in recent history); the successful renegotiation of the foreign debt (and inflow of external capital) and the reduction in domestic spending; the government's agreement in October 1990 with public employees to a 25% wage increase in 1991 (which was lower than the projected inflation rate for the year 1990); the end of the Persian Gulf War (with the consequent decline in international oil prices); and the confidence created by a peaceful transition to democracy with political and economic stability. The real interest rate dropped from 9.7% to 3.0% in 1990–91. The stabilization program ended in December 1990, paving the way for a new stage in which economic policies were aimed at sustained growth and a gradual reduction of inflation (Foxley 1993; Muñoz and Celedón 1993; BCCh *Boletín Mensual,* March 1994).

E. Development Strategy

As its strategy for economic development, the Aylwin administration adopted the formula of "economic growth with equity" in distinction to the

1984–89 stage of growth without equity. The essence of the development strategy of 1984–89 was maintained but halting the process of reduction in the state's size and functions, increasing some state functions and modifying others. Three components of the previous development strategy (which had proven to be effective in promoting vigorous and stable growth) were left virtually untouched in this stage: an open economy, with continuous emphasis on export promotion, especially nontraditional exports, the predominant participation of the private sector in economic activity and as the main generator of domestic savings, and preservation of macroeconomic equilibria. But there were three new elements added to the previous strategy that involved changes in the role of the state to become the economic regulator of major private economic activity, play a more dynamic role in the development of the infrastructure to increase export competitiveness and support productive modernization, and improve distribution. This was a strategy similar to that implemented in Japan, Germany, France, and Scandinavian countries. Finally, economic growth was considered a necessary but not sufficient condition by itself to improve equity; therefore, state intervention in the social area increased in this stage (Ffrench-Davis 1991; Meller 1992b, 1993; Vial 1992).

I have already discussed the maintenance of the mechanisms to increase domestic savings. The increase in public spending (especially in the social sector) was not financed with monetary expansion, which in the long run would have provoked adverse consequences such as inflation, especially for the lower-income groups. All government economic policies required, therefore, adequate financing (domestic and/or external) to preserve macroeconomic equilibria and avoid inflationary pressures. Once macroeconomic stability was achieved, sustained economic growth would be possible, with higher flows of foreign investment and increased employment, and control of inflation (Ministerio de Hacienda 1992, 1993; Marfán and Bosworth 1994).

The expansion of external trade was based on government support for further development of the export sector infrastructure and capacity in order to maintain and increase international competitiveness and exports. For that purpose a national program of public investment in infrastructure was funded with U.S.$1,660 million in this stage, averaging U.S.$553 million annually, almost twice the average at the end of the 1980s.

The agricultural sector, especially fruits and wine, forestry, and fishing, received a boost from the development of transportation, ports, and other infrastructure facilities in this stage. The reconstruction and remodeling of the main two ports (Valparaíso and San Antonio), which had been damaged by the 1985 earthquake and not repaired, were finished in 1991. In the same year a five-year program began to increase the area of irrigated agricultural land by 200,000 ha; 100,000 ha more were added to the program in 1993 supported with a U.S.$80 million credit from the World Bank. The forestry sector, especially in the South, benefited from repairs of existing ports and the building of new ones near the forestry areas; the new facilities led to a U.S.$6 million annual reduction in the cost of delays in shipments. A railroad network was also developed by the government to support private investment in forestry, which amounted to U.S.$3 billion. The fishing sector was a direct beneficiary of the port repairs, as coastal trade costs were reduced, which, in turn, facilitated and promoted exports. In addition, the government increased by U.S.$10 million the allocation to help small and medium-sized fishing enterprises. Public funds for road and railroad infrastructure were increased by U.S.$150 million, and a new international airport for Santiago was finished in 1994 (Ministerio de Hacienda 1992, 1993, 1994).

The policy of modernization of production was also supported with the creation of two public funds: one for technological and production development (FONTEC) and another for scientific and technical promotion (FONDEF). Contributions from the state, universities, and private sector, plus an IDB credit, financed technological research applied to productive sectors for a total of U.S.$153 million in 1992–93.

F. External Sector

Policies in the external sector maintained the following previous principles: open economy, free trade, low import tariffs, export increases and diversification (incentives for nontraditional exports and imports related to productive/technological improvements), and openness to foreign investment. But there were new policies as well: tighter controls of the exchange rate and foreign capital inflow, reduction in the vulnerability to external shocks and price fluctuations, new incentives for nontraditional exports, trade agreements with many countries and entrance into regional trade groups, authorization for enterprises to invest abroad, and successful renegotiation of the external debt with foreign banks and continuation of debt-equity swaps.

Tariffs were maintained at low levels for the majority of products; free trade was promoted with the reduction of import tariffs from 15% to 11% in 1991, a level maintained for the rest of the stage. The exchange rate played a growing role in economic policy mainly because external financing was no longer a constraining factor, as it was before. The increase in the flow of external capital (largely stimulated by the interest-rate differential between LIBOR and the domestic rate) was such that, in 1991, the Central Bank established a tax on external credit, as well as a reserve of 20% in 1991 and 30%

in 1992, and restricted the flow of short-term foreign capital. Such controls were imposed because the dramatic increase in the amount of dollars in circulation had begun to appreciate the real exchange rate (overvaluing the peso), which could have negatively affected exports. The Central Bank also intervened in the foreign exchange market by buying foreign currency and increasing international reserves. This generated a monetary expansion, and, to avoid inflationary pressures, the Central Bank issued debt bonds, thus contracting the amount of money in circulation. Finally, the Ministry of Finance made prepayments to the Central Bank on the bad debts that the latter held since the nationalization of the private banking system (Ministerio de Hacienda 1993, 1994; Bianchi 1994).

The growing transnationalization of the economy and the efforts to open and consolidate new markets were part of a global strategy in external trade. Several trade agreements were reached within the pursuit of expanding foreign markets: (1) the free-trade agreement with Mexico (1991), the first of its kind in Latin America, which included a gradual elimination of tariffs (in 10 years), investment protection, and elimination of all barriers to free trade between the two countries; (2) the trade agreement with Venezuela (1993), which reduced tariffs and facilitated commercial exchanges; (3) the economic cooperation treaties with Argentina (1991) and Bolivia (1993), which included trade agreements, investment protection, development of communications and air/land transportation, and integration in energy production; (4) negotiations with Colombia, Brazil, and Uruguay (in 1993), which expanded trade relations with these countries; (5) the negotiation of a free-trade agreement (initiated in 1992) with the United States that would follow NAFTA negotiations and be carried out in the context of the fast-track authority (Chile was admitted to NAFTA during the Summit Meeting of the Americas in Miami in December 1994, but its entrance has not been approved yet by the three member countries); and (6) the negotiations for Chile's incorporation into MERCOSUR, which began in 1994. The successful foreign economic policy gave new impetus to economic development with the expansion of business abroad by domestic enterprises; investment of domestic capital abroad was therefore authorized in 1990 and amounted to U.S.$400 million that year (Ministerio de Hacienda 1992, 1993, 1994; CORFO 1994).

Policies aimed at promoting export diversification to reduce vulnerability to fluctuations in the world market, especially the price of copper exports, added new incentives for nontraditional exports: (1) strict control of inflation and intervention in the foreign exchange market, which kept the dollar at a high level (thus making exports more competitive); (2) tax returns on nontraditional exports; (3) opening of special lines of credit (at CORFO) for small and medium-sized enterprises, to stimulate the adoption of new technologies in the production of nontraditional exports; (4) expansion of technical and financial assistance programs (through CORFO) to small and medium-sized entrepreneurs; and (5) tariff reductions in imported technology to be applied in the production of exports (Foxley 1993; Ministerio de Hacienda 1993).

The 1990 external-debt negotiation with foreign banks resulted in the following agreements: (1) 1991–94 payments of commercial bank debt were rescheduled, postponing debt service until 1995; (2) interest payments were fixed annually instead of biannually; (3) debt contracts with international agencies and foreign commercial banks were made more flexible; (4) Chile was reintegrated into voluntary credit markets; and (5) Chilean government bonds were issued (in agreement with international financial institutions) in 1991 and 1993 for a total of U.S.$753 million (Muñoz and Celedón 1993; ECLAC 1994b).

G. Labor and Employment

One of the main changes in the previous economic model was the increasing role of the state in the regulation of the labor market through a series of legal reforms whose overall objectives were to increase workers' participation in the benefits of growth and to revoke restrictions on unions and workers' rights imposed under the military government. The reforms involved social pacts among workers and employers, modifications to the 1979 Labor Plan, and additional labor legislation and programs. The reforms were implemented gradually to avoid negative effects on the international competitiveness of exports. Petras, Leiva, and Veltmeyer (1994) argue, however, that the government actually disarticulated popular mobilization (in search of wage increases) in order to achieve better export competitiveness.

The reforms dealt with seven main areas: (1) the concentration of national agreements between the main organizations of workers and employers, which led to a stable labor market, promotion of economic growth, and consolidation of democracy; (2) the new labor legislation, which avoided a return to confrontations between workers and entrepreneurs, typical of 1970–73, corrected the restrictions against and lack of protection of unions and workers existing between 1974 and 1989, improved the balance in bargaining power between workers and employers, and provided regulations for the negotiation of labor contracts and for hiring and firing practices; (3) the improvement of workers' protection concerning dismissals; (4) the regulation of individual labor contracts and minimum labor conditions; (5) incentives for women's incorporation into the labor force and reduction of discrimination against women in labor conditions; (6) the occupational training of young workers, one of the groups most affected by unemployment; and (7) improvements in the social security system (discussed below)(Ministerio de Hacienda 1992, 1993; Cortázar 1993).

Two months after Aylwin took office, the first national agreement between the Central Unitaria de Trabajadores (the major workers' federation), the Confederación de la Producción y el Comercio (the main business organization), and the government was signed. Other national agreements were signed, in 1991, 1992, and 1993. Those agreements brought the following results: (1) an increase in the real minimum wage by 28%; (2) a rise in real family allowances by 85%; (3) increments in minimum pensions, welfare pensions, and family subsidies (see next section); (4) expansion of state housing subsidies for workers; and (5) creation of tripartite commissions (businesses, workers, and government) to discuss and elaborate proposals for educational, health, and labor market reforms.

There were four modifications to the 1979 Labor Plan. The first, enacted in 1990, changed the norms regulating the firing of workers: it (1) required a justified cause for dismissals (previously workers could be fired without just cause); (2) granted workers dismissed without cause the right of appeal to labor courts and imposed on employers found guilty a compensation equal to 125% of indemnization of dismissal; (3) increased the maximum of indemnization for dismissal from 5 to 11 months' wages; (4) created an indemnization for dismissal or resignation of workers with a minimum of seven years of service (workers are paid one month for each year of service in indemnizations for dismissal but only a half month for dismissal or resignation; the worker must select beforehand between the two alternatives); and (5) granted protection to union leaders, prohibiting their dismissal without approval by a labor court.

In 1991 two new laws modified the Labor Plan, dealing with labor unions and the right to strike. They (1) reestablished the right to organize union federations, thus eliminating the previous prohibition, (2) required approval by 5% of the total union membership for the formation of such federations, (3) allowed unions to organize AFPs and ISAPREs, (4) reduced the minimum number of workers required to organize a union in small and medium-sized enterprises, (5) allowed the organizations of unions in the agricultural sector, a revocation of the existing restriction, (6) established new rules for union financing (if the benefits gained in a contract by the union are extended by the employer to nonunion members in the enterprise, they must pay 75% of the union contribution through the duration of the contract), (7) revoked the maximum of 60 days for strikes and set no time limit for their duration, and (8) restricted the replacement of striking workers (such replacement was previously permitted, thus reducing the workers' bargaining power).

The third modification to the Labor Plan introduced in 1993 dealt with individual labor contracts and workers' protection: it (1) established maximum working hours and minimum rest periods for commerce, transportation, and fishing workers (groups that never had been entitled to these benefits); (2) introduced a national minimum wage for workers 65 years old or older; (3) universalized the right to paid vacations for all workers (previously several groups were excluded); (4) created paid leaves for birth or death of a worker's child and death of a spouse; and (5) established new rules and increased sanctions for employers' labor violations and facilitated workers' access to labor courts (Vial 1990; Vial, Butelmann, and Celedón 1990; Meller 1990, 1992a, 1992b; Cortázar 1993; Muñoz and Celedón 1993).

Labor conditions for working women were also improved. Regulations (1) abolished their exclusion from certain occupations; (2) granted to female domestic servants (more than 20% of all working women) a minimum monthly wage equal to 65% of the minimum wage, an obligatory indemnization for dismissal or resignation (though 4.1% of wages paid by the employer to individual accounts at the AFPs), increased the hours of rest for working women residing in the employer's household from 10 to 12 and established a maximum 12-hour working day, with at least one hour of rest, for those not living in the employer's household; (3) imposed on the employers of women in seasonal agricultural jobs (especially those in the export sector) the obligation of signing labor contracts during their first month of work; and (4) established that employers must provide workers with food, transportation, lodging (in some cases), and hygienic working conditions (Meller 1992a; Cortázar 1993; Foxley 1993).

A training program for workers between the ages of 15 and 24 was created in 1991–94, in order to reduce unemployment and improve labor skills. The goal was to train 100,000 youths; financing of U.S.$80 million came half from the IDB and half from the government (Cortázar 1993).

Finally, the following measures benefited public employees: an overall increase in real salaries, salary increases above the sector average for the 25 agencies with the lowest salaries, and authorization and regulation of associations of public employees (which were previously forbidden) (Ministerio de Hacienda 1992, 1993, 1994).

H. Distribution and Social Services

In this stage the state, with both external financing and domestic resources, resumed a leading role in income distribution and social policies. Real cumulative social spending rose more than U.S.$1.4 billion or by 32% (24% per capita; equivalent to an increase from 6% to 12% of total public spending in the stage) (Ministerio de Hacienda 1993, 1994).

Social security real cumulative spending increased by 23% or from 7.6% to 7.9% of GDP (Table II.17). Benefits in the public system were improved as follows: (1) public pensions were increased in real terms by 10.6% (minimum and welfare pensions in 1990—above the inflation level—and the rest of pensioners in 1991–92); (2) minimum pensions were standardized in 1990 and welfare pensions in 1993, ending unjustified differences (the number of welfare pensioners rose by 5%); (3) beneficiaries of family allowances were expanded by 100,000 in 1991–92, targeting lower-income workers (eliminating the subsidy for higher-income workers), and the allowance real value was increased by 85%; (4) the formula for calculating pensions of public employees was changed, and the total salary became the basis for the contribution, thus ending unjustified differences; and (5) punctualality of payments to 1.3 million pensioners in the public system was improved by doubling the number of payment offices through subcontracts with private banks and sending checks by mail or making direct deposits into bank accounts (Cortázar 1993; Ministerio de Hacienda 1993, 1994).

The private pension system (AFP), established in 1981, was maintained but improved with the following measures: (1) AFPs must start paying a preliminary pension within 15 days from the time of application (the previous average time was six months); (2) the information provided by AFPs to their affiliates became more accessible, complete, and clear (e.g., investment yields and commissions were standardized, and the quarterly AFP report was simplified); (3) to reduce evasion and payment delays, fines and interest were increased, and judicial procedures for collection of due contributions were expedited; (4) a new computer system reduced the time in the state's payment of recognition bonds from 9 to 3 months (the average cost of those bonds was U.S.$340 million or 0.8% of GDP between 1990 and 1994, and it will increase rapidly in the next 20 years as the system matures); and (5) the operation of capital markets was improved through a 1994 law (discussed below) (Arenas de Mesa and Marcel 1993; Cortázar 1993; Foxley 1993; Ministerio de Hacienda 1993, 1994).

A 1994 law added financial instruments for AFP investment: stocks in public corporations approved by the Commission for Ranking Risks, debt instruments and bonds convertible into stocks for the financing of investment projects, recognition bonds, and new public debt securities certificates authorized by the Central Bank. Ceilings for investment in various instruments were either introduced or modified to improve flexibility and security. Finally, the following changes were implemented in the administration of

AFPs: members of the board of directors of corporations bought with pension funds must be elected, and they cannot have an interest in investments made by the pension fund that they operate; and trade unions were authorized to have AFPs, and their membership were granted participation in their administration (Bitrán and Saavedra 1993; Cortázar 1993; SAFP 1993, 1994; CORFO 1994).

There was an increase in state action in terms of development, regulation, financing, and expansion of public health, as well as in the supervision of private-sector activities. Real cumulative public spending in health care increased by 50% or from 2.4% to 2.9% of GDP in this stage. New policies were aimed at extending emergency programs, primary care, and immunizations, reducing the waiting time for service, protecting the environment, solving the crisis in the hospital infrastructure, and improving labor conditions of health personnel (Ministerio de Hacienda 1993, 1994; Ministerio de Salud 1994).

Measures on health prevention included: (1) 45 new emergency primary care units, which offered 1.2 million additional ambulatory consultations; (2) maintenance of the previous priority of infants and mothers, but increasing resources for nutrition and preventing neglect of other health programs as happened in the past; (3) expansion in coverage of immunization programs (especially among those under 15 years of age); (4) a new national emergency program to combat the cholera epidemics; and (5) new teams of psychosocial counselors for young and female workers, especially in rural areas and among low-income groups (Ministerio de Salud 1994).

The prolonged waiting time for the delivery of health services at the secondary and tertiary levels (e.g., one or two years for surgery) contributed to a deterioration of the population's health status and increased the complexity of the cases that were cared for in the public health system (e.g., repetition of exams and patients hospitalizations). Several steps were taken to improve the situation: (1) granting priority to the services that had deteriorated the most and the poorest sectors, (2) increasing health personnel by 5,300 or an increase of 9.2% in the stage, (3) expanding on-duty hours for doctors in emergency centers and rural clinics, (4) increasing real salaries of personnel by 43% in 1991–93, and (5) creationing the opportunity for international financing to coordinate projects supported with domestic and external resources. Programs to reduce contamination included controls of air pollution in Santiago and of using contaminated water for agricultural irrigation, as well as of waste treatment in the mining and industrial sector (Arenas de Mesa 1991; Ministerio de Salud 1994).

Several investment programs to improve the hospital infrastructure were funded for a total of U.S.$530 million (between 1991 and 1997), about one-half from external sources (World Bank, IDB, the German government) and the other half from domestic funds. The objective was to build, expand, rehabilitate, and equip hospitals in the three regions with the worst deficits in the infrastructure (including the capital), largely geared to the lowest income sector (Ministerio de Hacienda 1993; Ministerio de Salud 1994).

The transfer of affiliates from the public to the private health-care system continued during this stage. The number of those affiliated with the ISAPREs (which rose from 31 to 36) increased from 705,638 to 1,460,000; thus population coverage expanded from 13.5% to 28.1%. A Superintendency of ISAPREs was created in 1990 as a technical state agency that supervises, regulates, and promotes improvements in the private health-care system and operates as an arbiter between the beneficiaries and the ISAPREs (in 1991–92 questions and complaints increased by 66%). In 1991 the Superintendency of ISAPREs submitted a legal draft to the National Congress regulating their operation and increasing equity and transparency in the system, but the opposition blocked its approval until 1995 (Ministerio de Salud 1994; Sapag 1994; Cartin 1995).

In education, the government undertook new planning and supervisory functions, expanded access through more equitable opportunities, improved the quality of some levels, and increased funds. Public spending to education rose by 10% annually, from 2.9% to 3.1% of GDP in this stage. The World Bank provided U.S.$245 million, between 1992 and 1996, for a new program on Improvement of Equity and Quality of Education (Mejoramiento de la Calidad y Equidad de la Educacion [MECE]). The program's aims are to increase coverage and quality at the preschool level, improve the quality of primary education, and modernize the techno-vocational secondary level. Program funds were distributed as follows: 16% to preschool education, 70% to elementary education, and 14% to secondary education (Ministerio de Educación 1993; Ministerio de Hacienda 1994).

The JUNJI implemented several programs to further expand preschool coverage in this stage. There was a 52% increase in funds for conventional child-care centers (located in urban areas and geared to children 4 and 5 years of age), which targeted malnourished children or those in conditions of extreme poverty. Coverage of nonconventional child-care centers (located in rural or semirural areas and geared to children under age 4) was extended through the following measures: (1) the number of these centers increased from 200 to 641, and expenditures per child rose from U.S.$340 to U.S.$1,400 annually in this stage; (2) a new program provided child-care and educational services at home, especially for families living in conditions of extreme poverty or in geographical isolation and for children up to age 2; (3) special programs were established to incorporate indigenous communities previously excluded; (4) day-care centers were also created to service mothers working in seasonal agricultural activities (3 or 4 months of the year); and (5) a radio program for children in day-care centers was organized to cover the most isolated areas in three regions. To improve the quality of services, the personnel at JUNJI was augmented by 13% in this stage, expenditures in maintenance of child-care centers jumped by 300% (200 centers were remodeled and teaching materials modernized), and real expenditures in food for preschoolers increased by 63%, and its nutritional level was improved (Ministerio de Educacion 1993; JUNJI 1994).

MECE's goal in elementary education was to maintain the high population coverage achieved in the 1980s and improve the quality of teaching in the low-income areas (investing U.S.$30 million annually between 1992 and 1996) through the following policies: an emergency program gave support to 969 schools with significant deficiencies, 3,500 new libraries were created, delivery of free textbooks increased from 1.9 to 6.1 million, free school meals rose by 39%, 1,000 elementary schools were repaired, and computers were given to elementary schools, targeting those areas in conditions of extreme poverty. In secondary education, priority was given to the modernization of techno-vocational training. In 1992, for the first time, 100,000 free meals began to be distributed in techno-vocational schools located in areas of extreme poverty. Labor conditions of teachers were improved through new statutes agreed on between the government and the teachers association, which, among other things, introduced a minimum salary.

University authorities were democratically elected (thus ending the system of appointments by the government), and they recognized the associations of professors, administrative employees, and students. The government regulated private universities to correct flaws in the existing legislation and because 18 new private universities were created in the last three years of the military regime. The 1981 law continued to be applied in financing higher education, but with the following changes: public funds devoted to student credits and the development of scientific research were increased, 15,000 new scholarships for students in extreme poverty or in the low-income bracket were created, and students had their debts rescheduled by a law approved in 1991 (another law enacted in 1994 expanded financing to university students).

The state took on again the role of regulator of urban development and provider of housing, functions that had been transferred to the market. Real cumulative public expenditures allocated to housing increased by 43% or from 1.1% to 1.4% of GDP in this stage; international organizations (e.g., IDB and World Bank) contributed 25% of total public housing expenditures in 1990–92 and 6% in 1993; and foreign governments donated U.S.$27.3

million. The number of homes constructed by the public and private sectors increased from 83,891 in 1989 to 105,000 in 1993, thus reducing the housing deficit. Housing subsidies to low- and middle-income groups averaged 47,000 per year in this stage, compared with 37,000 in the 1980s. Changes in credit regulations by the Ministry of Housing reduced the mortgages of 227,588 debtors to the public sector, and public loans alleviated the burden of 10,000 mortgage debtors to private banks and the vanished savings and loans associations. Finally, public housing programs improved the level of service and information to the public through increased personnel and information offices established all over the country (Ministerio de Hacienda 1994; Ministerio de Vivienda 1994).

The Social Investment and Solidarity Fund (Fondo de Solidaridad e Inversión Social [FOSIS]) was created in 1990 as a decentralized public agency to finance projects on behalf of low-income groups and microenterprises, in order to reduce structural poverty, indigence, and unemployment. FOSIS must coordinate its projects with other central and local government programs and NGOs (FOSIS 1992a, 1992b).

2. Performance

This stage, when the date is not specified, covers from January 1990 to December 1993 (although the new administration took over in March 1990, it is impossible to exclude the first two months of that year); comparisons between the previous stage and this one are based on the years 1989 and 1993 (unless specified). Cases in which the information presented is not comparable will be noted.

A. Growth

In its first year the democratic government had to impose a severe adjustment program to control the inflationary spiral and overheated economy created, at the end of 1989, by the previous government in a failed attempt to win that year's elections. As a result, there was an economic decline in the second and third quarters of 1990, and GDP decreased from 9.9% in 1989 to 3.3% in 1990. Aylwin's domestic and external policies, nevertheless, successfully stabilized the economy, and GDP increased 7.3% in 1991, 11% in 1992, and 6.3% in 1993. The average rate of growth in 1990–93 was 7% compared with 6.4% between 1984 and 1989. Per capita GDP averaged 5.3% in this stage, above the rates for 1974–77 (−4.4), 1982–83 (−9%), and 1984–89 (4.6%), but lower than the rate for 1977–81 (6%) (Table II.3).

The rate of total gross investment rose from 19.1% of GDP in 1989 to 26.2 in 1993. The successful policies to promote domestic savings led to an increase from 17.2% to 21.3% of GDP, while foreign investment increased from 1.9% to 4.9% of GDP because of the massive inflow of external capital. The annual average rate of total gross investment in this stage was 21.6%% of GDP, compared with 15.8% in the previous stage and 16% between 1974 and 1989 (Table II.3).

The high and sustained economic growth in this stage was due to several factors: (1) the coordination between fiscal and monetary control policies, which resulted in a reduction of inflation after 1991 and a fiscal surplus after 1990; (2) the jump in total gross investment, which averaged 21.6% of GDP; (3) an annual average increase in exports of 9.3% (especially nontraditional), resulting from a rise in export value, opening of new external markets, and export diversification; (4) the successful foreign debt negotiation, which postponed the debt service until 1995 and generated additional external financing; and (5) the IDB's and World Bank's financial support to the growth with equity program. As between 1984 and 1989, economic growth between 1990 and 1994 was more an outcome of expanding investment and exports rather than increasing consumption, as had happened between 1976 and 1981.

B. Inflation

The adjustment policies implemented at the start of the Aylwin administration attempted to control the inflationary spurt of late 1989 (an annual average of 21.4%), but in the last quarter of 1990 inflation soared, and the annual rate was 27.3%. A tight fiscal policy kept inflation under control, and the rate declined gradually to 12.2% in 1993; the annual average in the stage was 17.7%, compared with 20.4% between 1984 and 1989. The new policy turned the fiscal deficit of 3% of GDP in 1989 into a surplus between 1990 and 1994, which averaged 1.4% of GDP. Furthermore, the public debt, which had reached 52% of GDP in 1989 was lowered to 33% in 1993 (Table II.3; Ministerio de Hacienda 1993, 1994).

C. Diversification

Policies to promote exports led to continuous growth of that sector, which, on average, generated 31.6% of GDP, higher than the 28.1% of 1982–89 (Ffrench-Davis and Muñoz 1990). All economic activities expanded in this stage, but their rate of growth varied compared with the 7% average increase of GDP. The agricultural sector (including forestry and fishing) grew annually by 4.8% in this stage; hence its participation in GDP declined from 9% to 8.5% in 1990–93. However, the various activities within agriculture had a different performance. Policies to expand production of nontraditional agriculture were successful with a 49% cumulative growth in this stage. Specific products for exports increased as follows: table grapes 61%, forestry 42%, fishing 14%, and apples 32%. The amount of land planted to produce fruit expanded by 7.7% in the stage. Conversely traditional agriculture (oriented to the domestic market) reduced planted land, and its production declined annually by 6% in this stage (Tables II.3–5; BCCh *Boletín Mensual,* March 1994; ECLAC 1991b, 1994b; CORFO 1993, 1994).

The industrial sector (which includes manufactures, mining, electricity, gas, and water) grew annually by 5.2%, and its share of GDP declined from 31.1% to 30.1% between 1989 and 1993. Although output of copper jumped 30% in this stage, the dramatic fall in the world price of copper resulted in a lower export value, and that impeded a higher growth rate in industry. Conversely the construction sector's annual growth was 8.1%, and its share in GDP rose from 5.8% to 6.2%. Domestic and foreign investment in communications and infrastructure pushed growth in the transportation and communications sector by 13.4% annually (the highest rate of all sectors), and its share in GDP expanded from 6.4% to 8.3%. Commerce grew at an annual rate of 5.1% and reduced its share in GDP from 18% to 17.2%, mostly because of the impact of the economic adjustment of 1990. The service sector was also affected, but its recovery was more accentuated, fueled by the growth of financial services; hence this sector grew at an annual rate of 7%, maintaining its share of GDP (Tables II.4–5; BCCh *Boletín Mensual,* March 1994; Frei 1994).

D. Trade Balance and External Dependency

The government continued and expanded the previous model of an economy open to external markets, with a leading role for the private sector in exports, especially nontraditional ones. The policy of low tariffs across the board, combined with a high and competitive exchange rate, was effective and increased participation of exports in GDP from 29.5% to 36.4% between 1989 and 1993 (in constant prices). Imports increased even more than exports, and their participation in GDP expanded from 27.5% to 40.3%, responding positively to a rising GDP and the reduction of import tariffs in 1991. Trade transactions increased at an annual rate of 7.4% (a record U.S. $10 billion in 1993), and their share of GDP expanded at the fastest rate ever, from 57% to a peak of 76.6% in constant prices, hence increasing external dependency (Table II.7; BCCh *Indicadores* 1989; BCCh *Boletín Mensual,* March 1994; Muñoz and Celedón 1993).

In 1990–92 the value of exports surpassed that of imports, generating a surplus in the balance of trade, which averaged more than U.S.$1 billion annually (similar to that of 1984–89) or 3.6% of GDP. But in 1993 the price of copper fell by 16%; furthermore, the domestic currency appreciated (a fall in the exchange rate or the value of the U.S. dollar) because of an excess of hard currency in the domestic market. Exports declined by 0.8%, while imports increased by 10.2%, hence beginning a deficit in the trade balance close to U.S.$1 billion or 2.2% of GDP that year. Reversing the 1985–88 trend of improvement in the terms of trade (largely resulting from increasing world prices of copper and declining world prices of oil), a deterioration began in 1989 and continued through 1993 (because of the decrease in copper prices, and the increase in oil prices in 1990–91) (Tables II.7, II.10).

The policies to promote nontraditional exports were successful, leading to an annual average increase of 26% per year, and the number of export firms grew by 35% in this stage. These changes, combined with the decline in the world price of copper, resulted in a greater export diversification: the share of copper declined from 49.8% to 35.3% (the lowest on record), while the share of nontraditional exports expanded from 48.3% to 57.4% in 1989–92. (Table II.8; BCCh *Boletín Mensual,* March 1994; Ministerio de Hacienda 1993, 1994; CORFO 1994).

The composition of imports was influenced by the decrease in tariffs, the growth of production, and the need to incorporate new technologies. Manufactures decreased from 37% to 33% in 1989–90 as a result of the economic adjustment in 1990, but they increased to 38% in 1993 as tariffs were reduced. Machinery and transportation declined from 44% to 38% in 1989–91, but they rose to 44% in 1993 as production and the economy grew. The most important decline was in the share of oil imports from 12% to 9%, due to the drop in the price of crude oil in the world market after the Persian Gulf War. The share of food and beverage imports increased from 3% to 5% as output of traditional agriculture declined in this stage (Table II.9).

As an outcome of success in searching for new external markets, the concentration of foreign trade partners (combining the main partners: the United States, Japan, and Germany) decreased from 41.2% to 31.5%. The Japanese and German shares of total transactions declined sharply, while the U.S. share increased slightly. Conversely the Latin American share rose from 39.2% to 43.1%, as a result of free trade and economic cooperation agreements signed with the major countries in the region. There was also an increase from 18.9% to 24.6% in exports to Southeast Asia (Table II.11; BCCh *Boletín Mensual* 1989–94; Ministerio de Hacienda 1993, 1994).

The external debt declined from 69% to 43.8% of GDP because of a strict control of external borrowing, the growth of GDP, and the punctual servicing of the debt. The last reached 19% of the average value of exports in this stage (a significant reduction compared with the 36% registered between 1984 and 1989), but the debt as a percentage of exports was basically stagnant in this stage. The public external debt declined from 50% to 28% of GDP, reducing its share in the total external debt from 74% to 47%, while the private share increased from 26% to 53%. Despite the payment of the external debt, the decline in the value of exports in 1993, and the deficit in the trade balance in that year, foreign reserves increased from U.S.$2.95 billion to U.S.$9.75 billion in the stage because of the massive inflow of external capital. The foreign reserves accumulated in 1993 were equivalent to 12 months of imports (Table II.13; Ministerio de Hacienda 1994).

E. Unemployment

Changes introduced in the labor market alleviated the adverse effects of the structural adjustment policies of the 1980s. The model of growth with equity focused on labor, employment, and vulnerable groups such as women, young workers, and pensioners.

The generation of 600,000 new jobs (a 3.1% annual rate of employment creation in the stage, twice the rate of population growth) further pushed down the open unemployment rate, which, according to ECLAC, declined in Santiago from 7.2% to 4%, the lowest since the early 1970s; national rates also decreased (based on ILO) from 5.3% to 4.5%. The emergency employment programs were terminated, but FOSIS began a new program emphasizing skills and productivity. The training program for young workers incorporated 72,000 individuals in 1991–93; approximately 75% of them finished the program and found jobs at an average salary 50% above the minimum wage or enrolled in more advanced studies (Table II.16; Cortázar 1993).

The distribution of the labor force changed because of the stability of the labor market and the increase in real wages. There was a decline in labor supply in rural areas and in personal services, and an increase in the labor supply in urban sectors, characterized by more stable occupations. The following sectors increased their share in the labor force in 1990–93: commerce from 17% to 18.6%, financial services from 4.3% to 5.8%, industry from 15.6% to 16.8%, construction from 6.9% to 8.1%, and transportation/communication from 6.4% to 7.1%. Shares declined in agriculture from 19.4% to 16.6%, personal services from 26.6% to 24.7%, and mining and public utilities only slightly (Table II.14).

The percentage of women in the labor force increased from 30.8% to 32.5% between 1989 and 1993; and the participation rate rose from 24.2%

to 28.1% between 1985 and 1992 (no data are available for 1989 and 1993). About 211,000 women found employment in this stage, at an annual average rate of growth of 4%, doubling the male rate (Table II.15; Ministerio de Hacienda 1993, 1994).

F. Equality

Income distribution improved somewhat in this stage but remained extremely unequal. Between 1973 and 1989, the income of the wealthiest quintile was 23.3 times higher than that of the poorest quintile, but in 1990–93 that ratio declined to 18 times, closer to the ratio of the 1970s. The share of the poorest quintile in total income averaged 3.4% in 1990–92 and showed only a minimal increase over the shares of 1959–64 (3.2%), 1965–70 (3.2%), and 1971–73 (3.1%), but it was better than that of 1974–89 (2.7%). The richest quintile still had a very high share of total income in 1990–92 (61.5%), slightly lower than between 1974 and 1989 (62%), but higher than between 1959 and 1964 (57.9%), 1965 and 1970 (58.6%), and 1971–73 (55.4%) (Marcel and Solimano 1994).

According to ECLAC, real mean wages increased 21.5 percentage points between 1989 and 1994, thus surpassing the 1972 level but still 8.9 percentage points below the 1971 level. In the public sector mean real wages increased even more (by 25 percentage points), reversing the previous decreasing trend. Minimum urban wages increased by 21.8 percentage points between 1989 and 1993 but remained 11.4 points below the 1982 level (Table II.19; Ministerio de Hacienda 1994).

These statistics, however, do not provide a full picture of the situation. The active participation of the state in social policy improved equity as the following indicators show: (1) poverty incidence of households declined from 48.6% to 24% between 1987 and 1994 (no data are available for 1988–89), and indigent incidence from 22.6% to 7%, the lowest since 1970 (comparisons for 1990–94 show declines from 35% to 24%, and from 12% to 7%, respectively); (2) family income in the poorest quintile increased by 26%, and the real wage rose by 17 percentage points, while the real minimum wage in urban areas increased 20 points; (3) the unemployment rate of lower income sectors decreased from 23% to 14%; (4) real public social spending increased 32% or 26% per capita and was targeted on vulnerable groups such as children, unemployed youth, female heads of household, and microentrepreneurs and rose 160% within these groups; and (5) monetary subsidies for extreme poverty groups grew by 25% and was somewhat targeted (the 40% of the population with higher incomes decreased their share in those subsidies from 27% to 22% between 1987 and 1992 but still was being considerably subsidized) (Tables II.18–20; Foxley 1993; Ministerio de Hacienda 1993, 1994; ECLAC 1994b).

Furthermore, the policy section suggested that most of the social service policies of the Aylwin administration had a progressive effect on distribution: (1) increases in welfare and minimum pensions, as well as in family allowances (these were restricted to low-income groups); (2) new primary health-care programs (nutrition, immunization) targeted at low-income strata and improvement of hospital infrastructure in the three regions with the worst deficit; and (3) expansion of preschool coverage among the poor, isolated regions, indigenous populations, and female seasonal agricultural workers, as well as improved quality of elementary education in low-income areas (free meals and textbooks, etc.) and scholarships for higher-education students with low-incomes or in extreme poverty. However, other social policies might have had a regressive effect: (1) transfer of affiliates from the public health system to ISAPREs and fiscal resources to improve benefits in the latter, (2) payment of recognition bonds to pensioners of AFPs, and (3) credits for and rescheduled debts of low- and middle-income university students as well as mortgage reduction of housing loans not targeted toward low-income groups.

G. Social Indicators

The expansion and targeting of social expenditures on the lower-income and poverty groups improved social indicators in this stage, in some cases recovering the 1970 level.

In social security, the old pension system continued to endure a decline in the number of active contributors (from 390,061 to 336,000 in this stage), while pensioners began to decline (from 1,293,000 to 1,282,000). The annual yearly average deficit of the old system decreased from 8% of GDP between 1984 and 1989 to 7% in 1990–93. Real public expenditures allocated to social security rose by 23% or 24% per pensioner. In 1993, after 23 years, per capita expenditures in social security surpassed by 6% the 1970 level. Real social security benefits increased in this stage as follows: 5.7% in family allowances for indigents and 52% in family allowances for low-income groups, 21.5% in welfare pensions, 21.3% in minimum pensions, and 10% in average pensions in the old system (Table II.25; Cortázar 1993; Ministerio de Hacienda 1993, 1994; SUSESO 1994).

The private pension system was not modified. As in previous stages I contrast assumptions versus performance of that system between 1990 and 1994, concerning cost reduction through competition, increases in coverage by controlling evasion, portfolio diversification and yields, and expansion of the capital market and domestic savings (I add an analysis on gender discrimination, not touched on before).

The average percentage commission charged by AFPs decreased from 3.5% to 3% and the real fixed commission by 64%. Legal changes allowed workers to own and participate in the administration of AFPs, which provided an incentive for the creation of 10 new AFPs in 1992–93 (some by unions), increasing their number from 13 to 22 (two merged into one) in this stage. But real administrative costs per insured increased by 38% because of a 55% jump in marketing expenditures, to avoid a decline in affiliates in this more competitive stage. The larger number of AFPs did not reduce the concentration of affiliates in the system either; on the contrary, the three biggest AFPs increased their combined share of the total from 65% to 68%, although they had lower investment yields than the system average. In 1993 the 10 new AFPs had only 1.9% of the affiliates and 5.1% of the pension funds. Affiliates who changed AFPs increased 29% annually, and there was an increasing trend in shifts; this high turnover was the result of the increased marketing effort, especially of the larger AFPs, and the work of salespersons who charge a commission and whose numbers rose fourfold, from 2,615 to 10,771 (SAFP 1989–94). The above analysis shows that competition did not function properly as a higher number of AFPs increased commissions, market share, and salesperson profits but did not benefit the affiliates.

Another presumed advantage of the private pension system is the increase in coverage and reduction in evasion and payment delays because of the alleged affiliates' incentive to augment their individual accounts. Affiliation in the system rose from 74.3% to 90.2% of the labor force, and from 78.4% to 94.9% of total employment, but part of that increase was because of double counting of one affiliate in two AFPs (because of frequent changes and slow updating of registration); other reasons were the creation of new jobs, reduction in unemployment, and expansion of labor contracts in agriculture. Active contributors in the system rose from 48.5% to 53.5% of the labor force. But the percentage of affiliates who did not contribute to the system increased from 35% to 41% (the increase in affiliates was higher than that of contributors, and these, in turn, were higher than the increase of the labor force). Coverage of the self-employed remained low, and only 5% of them made contributions (Table II.25; SAFP 1989–94).

The expansion of domestic savings and the capital market are other presumed effects of the private pension system. The percentage distribution of the portfolio by instrument became more diversified in this stage with a rising private share: (1) state instruments declined from 42% to 39.3%, (2) domestic private instruments increased from 58% to 60.1% (long-term deposits and mortgage debts decreased, but stocks and bonds jumped from 19.2% to

39.4%), and (3) foreign instruments were legally allowed in 1991 up to 12% but represented only 0.6% of total investment of the pension funds in 1993. AFPs are now able to invest in public bonds convertible in stocks for investment, for example, in infrastructural projects probably generating more portfolio diversification and investment in the capital market. The profitability of the system continued to be the highest in Latin America: its annual average real yield increased from 7.7% between 1984 and 1989 to 16.9% between 1990 and 1994 (SAFP 1989–94, 1994b; Ministerio de Hacienda 1992, 1994; Bitrán and Saavedra 1993; Marfán and Bosworth 1994).

The average growth of the private pension funds almost tripled GDP growth; hence the value of the funds jumped from 18.5% to 39.4% of GDP between 1989 and 1993. But the annual public deficit in social security created by the 1981 reform has been estimated at 5% of GDP, larger than the average 3% of GDP that the pension funds contributed annually to total domestic savings in this stage. Domestic savings were led by public and private savings outside of the AFP system, and there is no evidence that the pension system was the major force in domestic savings in this stage. The capital market also developed considerably, with stocks and bonds of private enterprises reaching 39.4% of the pension funds, but there is no solid evidence that such market expansion has been significantly influenced by the pension reform (SAFP 1989–94, 1994b; Mesa-Lago 1994).

Unlike the public pension system, which does not discriminate by gender, pensions in the private system are considerably lower for women than for men because of the lower salaries of women and their longer periods of absence from the labor market because of maternity and family care, which results in a smaller fund accumulated in their individual accounts; and a five-year lower legal retirement age for women (which reduces their contributions) as well as an average of seven more years in their life expectancy (both compared with men), which requires a larger fund to finance the longer life period of women's pensions. The public system also has different ages of retirement by sex but pays equal pensions regardless of gender (except for divergent remuneration only based on sex); this is feasible because the additional cost is financed by contributors and mainly by the state. The elimination of any solidarity and redistribution within the private system (based on individual capitalization) impedes the equalization of pensions by sex, particularly with a combined difference of about 12 years for women (five for legal retirement age plus seven for life expectancy). If women decide to postpone their retirement to age 65 in the private system (and it is assumed that other differences are eliminated, except for life expectancy), their pension would still average 90% of men's pension. If other differences persist (lower remuneration, less participation in the labor force), the average would be even lower (Arenas de Mesa 1995; Arenas de Mesa and Montecinos 1995).

In health care, the state reestablished its leading role in the development of policies and increased real expenditures by 11.6% per year, equal to a 30% increase in real spending per user in this stage (Ministerio de Hacienda 1993, 1994). The program for the rehabilitation of public hospitals and the construction of new health centers in this stage added 1.5 million people receiving health-care services in those establishments. The program to reduce waiting lists developed 284 units to make access more expeditious in the services with the highest deficits. The 45 new primary and emergency service facilities and the increase of new medical laboratories installed in them from 24 to 72 expanded the number of people served in those establishments from 196,185 to 1.2 million. Also, the ratio of hospital beds per 10,000 inhabitants grew from 2.8 to 3.2 in 1989–92, the number of physicians per 100,000 in the public sector increased from 5.1 to 5.8 in 1989–90, and personnel in public health was increased by 9.2% (Table II.21; Ministerio de Salud 1994).

Largely because of these policies, health indicators improved in this stage: (1) the infant mortality ratio declined from 17.1 to 13.9 in 1989–92; (2) malnourishment among children aged 5 and younger dropped from 8.3% to 6.3% in 1989–92; (3) the general mortality rate decreased from 5.8% to 5.6% in 1989–91 (there are no data for 1992–93); (4) the wide immunization program showed positive effects on morbidity indicators of contagious diseases: year after year no cases of polio and malaria, as well as almost zero rates for diphtheria and tetanus, and sharp declines in hepatitis, measles, tuberculosis, and typhoid (the cholera epidemic was an exception: rates increased in 1990–92 but declined in 1993, and there were no cases reported in the first quarter of 1994); (5) coverage of potable water and sewerage continued its improvement in this stage: in urban areas increasing from 96.2% to 96.7% (water) and from 81.5% to 85% (sewerage), while access to potable water in rural areas jumped from 78.5% to 90.7%; and (6) life expectancy at birth increased from 71.9 to 72.1 in 1989–91 (no data are available for 1992–93) (Tables II.21–23; Ministerio de Salud 1994).

Despite these results, the health sector was one of the most criticized in the stage, as it was affected by strikes and protests. Health-care workers halted their activities in demand for increases in their salaries, which provoked the resignation of the Minister of Health in 1992. Critics point out that the lack of reform in the health-care system had been responsible for confusion and almost no interaction between the public and private sectors. These problems caused paralysis in the projects for institutional development, a decline in the coverage of the public system, and an expansion of the private sector. The absence of agreement in the National Congress delayed the approval of the legal draft to reform the ISAPREs until 1994, allowing them to continue discriminatory policies against old age people, women (particularly during their fertility period), and those suffering from chronic and terminal diseases, forcing them to pay higher premiums or be excluded from coverage. Such discrimination was even more blatant, taking into account that in 1990 the state subsidy to ISAPREs was tantamount to 100% of their profits (Arenas de Mesa 1991; Oyarzo 1994; Cartin 1995).

The decentralization and municipalization of the educational system was consolidated. Real public expenditures on education increased by 10% annually, a 32% cumulative increase in real spending per student in this stage. The illiteracy rate declined from 6.6% to 5.4% in 1990–92 (no data are available for 1989 and 1993). Preschool education increased its coverage from 20% to 23%, thanks to the programs of the MECE and JUNJI. Conventional programs were strengthened, and new nonconventional programs were introduced targeting vulnerable groups such as indigenous and rural populations, those geographically isolated, and those in extreme poverty. Resources allocated to nutrition and improvement in the nutritional diet given to infants (since 1992) decreased undernourishment among preschoolers. Elementary education continued its universal coverage in 1989–92 (no data are available for 1993). Public resources were concentrated in elementary education (66% of MECE funds were spent at this level), targeting 969 schools located in areas of extreme poverty. In 1992 only 28% of those schools needed the special support of MECE, while students in the remaining 72% schools had grades above or equivalent to the national average. In secondary education, enrollment remained constant at 75%. The program for the modernization of 95 techno-vocational schools benefited 52,800 students in 1990–92 through labs and libraries. Higher education increased enrollment from 19% to 24%. The financing of universities was not modified, but real public spending allocated to them was increased by 43% in this stage. Credits and tuition scholarships for low-income university students benefited 70% of them, and the rescheduling of fiscal credits for low- and middle-income students helped 120,000 who rescheduled their debts through new 10-year loans with generous terms. Some 810 university students who had been expelled for political reasons during the military regime were readmitted, received credit for their previous courses, and were allowed to complete their educations (Table II.24; JUNJI 1993; Ministerio de Educación 1993; Ministerio de Hacienda 1993, 1994).

Real per capita spending in housing increased by 35% in this stage. The number of homes built grew from 6.5 to 8.6 per 1,000 inhabitants between 1989 and 1993, the housing deficit declined from 1,030,828 to 888,861 homes between 1988 and 1992, and the problem of the families housed in the homes of relatives was reduced from 25% to 16% of families in the nation between 1988 and 1992 (there are no data for 1989 and 1993 in most of these indicators). Savings for housing were promoted in this stage, and the number of banking savings accounts for that purpose grew from 450,000 to 870,000 (Table II.26; Mac Donald 1994; Ministerio de Hacienda 1994; Ministerio de Vivienda 1990–93).

FOSIS implemented 2,076 projects in 1990–92 but reached only 0.4% of the population. FOSIS has shown a great ability to mobilize external funds, and it has successful programs on nutrition and strengthening the community's abilities. Available data on the composition of the beneficiaries are not precise, but it seems that at least half of the projects go to the poorest population. Recent surveys show a strong support from the beneficiaries to this program and a recovery of their confidence in public action to alleviate poverty. However, some problems remain: (1) very small population coverage, (2) long and complex procedures in some projects, (3) lack of coordination with other public programs, (4) a need to improve targeting, and (5) absence of precise information for evaluating the program effects in general and on the poor (FOSIS 1992a, 1992b).

Several international and regional agencies, with different policy orientations (ECLAC, IDB, World Bank), have made positive evaluations of Chile's economic and social performance between 1990 and 1994, comparing it with that of other countries in Latin America and the developing world (ECLAC 1994b, 1995b; IDB 1994; World Bank 1995). But Aylwin's economic policies have been criticized from both the extreme right and left. Neoconservatives assert that the 1990–94 economic performance was fundamentally a result of the reforms introduced by the Pinochet government in the 1980s. Furthermore, they argue that the outcome would have been even better if the privatization of public enterprises had not been halted (the reduction of the state had continued), if taxes had not been raised, and if the labor reforms had not been enacted (Büchi 1992). The opposite extreme argues that the Alywin policy of growth with equity did not solve the problems inherent in the neoconservative model: "promoting the super-exploitation of labor" (real salaries have not recovered the early 1970s level), increasing external dependency and vulnerability to international economic shocks, growing foreign and multinational investment, and intensification of the careless use of natural resources and ecological depredation (Petras, Leiva, and Veltmeyer 1994).

The above analysis of socioeconomic indicators clearly shows that there was significant improvement in the large majority, and, hence, that the criticism from both extremes of the ideological spectrum is unfounded. In spite of the impressive progress made, however, in 1994 there were still some serious problems in the model of growth with social equity, among them a decline in traditional agriculture output, a slowdown in industrial growth, a trade deficit, about 4 million people living in poverty, significant income inequalities, insufficient infrastructure and personnel in the public health sector, persistent flaws in the private pension scheme (e.g., very low coverage among the self-employed, high noncompliance), and close to 900,000 families without a home. Some of these issues will be taken up again in the final part of this book.

Tables to Part II

Table II.1
Summary of Socioeconomic Policies by Stages in Chile, 1973–1994

Economic Policies	Monetarism, Adjustment, and First Crisis (1973–76)	Monetarism, Open Economy, Growth, and Indebtness (1976–81)	Second Crisis and State Intervention (1981–83)	Corrections, Recovery, and Economic Boom (1984–90)	Democracy; Continuation of the Economic Model and Growth, and Equity (1990–94)
Ownership	Privatization: Return of expropriated firms to owners, particularly those that were private before 1970; return to agricultural lands that had been expropriated to private-sector owners in 1970–73.	Directives of previous period are maintained; most enterprises under CORFO before 1970 are transferred to the private sector; key enterprises are maintained in public sector because of their strategic value (copper). State participation in the economy decreases sharply.	Temporary halting of privatization. State intervention to prevent the bankruptcy of the private sector (especially the financial one): control of financial institutions; government absorbs the losses of private banking. Long-term goal is to reprivatize.	In 1984–85, firms intervened by the state during the 1981–83 crisis are reprivatized. In 1985–89 occurs a massive privatization of public enterprises previously declared of national strategic value. "Popular capitalism" allows the people to own shares of privatized enterprises.	End of privatization process. The gov't begins regulation of privatized public enterprises of national strategic value, as well as natural economic monopolies and other activities.
Planning and market	The Ministry of Economy reduces its productive and regulatory roles and becomes a secondary player in economic policies. Neoconservative economists use ODEPLAN to modify economic policy-making and control public sector operations. CORFO role in the development of productive and	Ministry of Economy and CORFO further reduced. Neoconservatives' control of ODEPLAN is consolidated and their influence increased. Change from short-term, conjunctural stabilization policies to broader, structural-reform policies.	Neoconservatives oppose state intervention despite economic deterioration. But the crisis weakens the power of the gov't and a change in strategy is adopted. A new team of moderates replaces the neoconservatives and goes for state intervention but without changing the principles of the neocon-	Neoconservative model is maintained by a new team but with higher state regulatory and supervision powers. However, to win popular support for the gov't (facing elections in 1988–89), expenditures are increased, tax and tariffs reduced, and credit granted (high world	Continuation of market economy, but increasing state role in social and labor policies, as well as regulation of some private activities. ODEPLAN is transformed into a ministry (MIDEPLAN). CORFO also becomes a ministry and their enterprises' management is improved and generate a

134

technological activities is reduced. The administration is decentralized.	servative model. The moderate team is opposed by powerful groups and neoconservatives eventually return.	copper prices facilitate this move). When gov't realizes they will lose power, policies are reversed, and steps taken to assure continuation of the model.	profit. The Central Bank and the Ministry of Finance coordinate their functions.	
Financing Deregulation of the capital market, allowing international banks to participate in the domestic market. A tax reform is implemented in 1974 to increase public revenues and reduce fiscal deficit. Interest rate liberalized.	Privatization generates $1 billion in the period; further opening of the economy and liberalization of the capital market; interest rates are liberalized (but still higher than external); international credits to private and public sectors are expanded, offsetting resumed debt-service payments.	Halting of privatization, reduction of state's revenues due to the crisis, and lack of external credit generate a significant fiscal deficit; the gov't turns to domestic debt and foreign reserves. Interest rates are reduced, WB began to provide credits and loans.	Privatization is a major source of internal finance, as tax reforms have a net revenue loss. Private foreign banks gradually reduce and finally halt loans (1984–89). High world price of copper is a source of external finance. Debt-equity swaps do not bring new capital. IMF, WB, and IDB provide substantial loans.	Democracy, political stability, and continuous growth promotes national savings and attracts more foreign investment and international aid (WB, IDB, foreign governments). A tax reform (1990) raises tributes on capital gains, VAT, and highest income groups; revenue is used for social programs.
Stability and prices Orthodox short-term stabilization: cut in public expenditures and increase revenue in order to reduce fiscal deficit. Restrictive monetary policy. But price liberalization leads to booming prices. Shock treatment in 1975 further reduces inflation but still high in 1976.	Exchange rate becomes key anti-inflationary tool; control of the gov't budget leads to elimination of the fiscal deficit and sharp reduction of inflation. Gap between foreign and domestic interest rates expands but automatic market adjustment is expected. Macroeconomic policy dominated by	Neoconservatives believe in an automatic adjustment (the market, by itself, would solve the crisis), but the crisis worsens and forces the gov't to increase control of the economy through a moderate economic team. When this team is removed, the neoconservatives agreed a tough stabilization program	IMF, WB, and gov't adjustment programs: cuts in state size, public expenditures, public-employees wages; increase in interest rate since 1989; restrictive monetary policy. After peaking in 1985 budget deficit and inflation decline. Public investment is raised, and later taxes are cut and	A stabilization program is introduced in 1990 to control the increase in inflation largely provoked by the previous administration. Fiscal and monetary policies curb spending and aggregate demand and increase the interest rate. The state budget generates a surplus and inflation

(continued)

Table II.1
(Continued)

Economic Policies	Monetarism, Adjustment, and First Crisis (1973–76)	Monetarism, Open Economy, Growth, and External Indebtness (1976–81)	Second Crisis and State Intervention (1981–83)	Corrections, Recovery, and Economic Boom (1984–90)	Democracy, Continuation of the Economic Model and Growth, and Equity (1990–94)
		monetarist approach to balance of payments.	with the IMF, to reduce growing inflation.	tariffs reduced; price of agricultural products are state-fixed; in 1989 money supply increases renewing the inflationary process and budget deficit.	abates. The interest rate is reduced, and a new policy of sustained growth and gradual cut in inflation is applied in 1991–93.
Development strategy	Movement away from import-substitution industrialization (ISI), excessive state intervention, and protectionism. The new development strategy is not defined yet but relies on the market as the main instrument in economic decisions and the private sector as the main agent of development; domestic efficiency is encouraged through external competition; protectionism is reduced and exports grow in new sectors, but traditional agriculture is harmed.	Total abandonment of ISI and protectionism. A more defined development strategy is applied made up by progressive liberalization of the financial market, free flow of external capital, and export promotion of agricultural-forestry products (especially nontraditional) through gov't incentives.	The crisis, economic liberalization, and stabilization lead to industrial and traditional-agriculture deterioration. Many bankruptcies in industry result despite state subsidies (largely because of inability to pay loans with high interest rates). The gov't controls prices of some traditional agricultural products and provides incentives to this sector. The strategy based on nontraditional exports continues with further state incentives.	Export promotion continues (concentrated in natural resources) without an industrialization strategy. Nontraditional exporters are granted more incentives, and traditional agricultural producers and exporters began to receive state protection and incentives. There is increasing foreign ownership of national business, including nontraditional exports.	The "economic growth with equity" strategy keeps elements of the previous model: open market, promotion of nontraditional exports, private-sector generation of savings, and macroeconomic equilibrium. But new policies are added: state regulatory and distributive functions, more public financing of infrastructure (e.g., ports, highways, railroads for exports of fruits, forestry, fishing), and modernization of production (two new development funds were created for that purpose).

External sector	Liberalization of foreign trade, monetary devaluation, lower import tariffs, and promotion of exports lead to a reduction in trade deficit. In spite of liberalization of capital markets and authorization for operation of foreign banks, the external debt is stagnant and few external credits are granted.	Continuation of trade liberalization. Considerable opening to foreign investment; limitations to private external borrowing are reduced. After minidevaluations, the peso is pegged to the dollar at a fixed rate (1979–81). Tariffs are reduced and unified; the trade deficit increases. The exchange rate is used as a stabilization mechanism. The external debt grows.	External disequilibria is caused by debt crisis, cut in foreign loans and capital flight, rise in interest rates (until 1982), and fall in world-market price of copper. Automatic adjustment is abandoned. Increased devaluations are followed by a table of daily mini-devaluations; a free-floating rate is replaced by dirty flotation. Tariff increases are reversed. The IMF stabilization program is implemented.	Continuous application of IMF program and payments; agreement with WB and IDB. The exchange rate is gradually devalued and import tariffs decreased after a brief raise. Central Bank starts to promote debt-equity swaps. The external debt is decreased.	Elements of past policies continue, but new measures are added: continuous devaluations of the exchange rate, tight control of foreign capital inflow, intervention in foreign capital market, trade agreements with Latin America, and joining of regional trade groups; expanded incentives for nontraditional exports, and negotiation of the debt with foreign commercial banks.
Labor and employment	Gov't controls and reduces real wages. Open unemployment grows. Trade unions are suppressed and collective bargaining and strikes prohibited. In 1975, the sharp increase in unemployment forces the gov't to create an emergency employment program.	The labor plan of 1979 grants employers the right to dismiss workers without a cause, but with compensation; reintroduces right to organize unions, strikes, and collective bargaining but with strict restrictions; and wages adjust upward. High unemployment and emergency employment program continues but declining.	Wage indexation is abandoned in 1982. The crisis provokes higher unemployment and decline in real wages. In 1982 a new employment emergency program for heads of households is created.	Economic growth leads to declines in unemployment, and emergency employment programs end. Real wages decline until 1987 but increase in 1988–1989 (years of elections). The United Confederation of Workers (CUT) is created in 1988 with a broad political composition. The number of workers unionized and strikes rise, particularly in 1989.	State regulation of labor market increases significantly through social pacts, amendments to the 1979 labor plan, etc.: restoration of unions' and workers' rights, regulation and expansion of minimum labor conditions, protection on dismissals, improvement in woman working conditions, and training of young people. The open unemployment rate decreases further.
Distribution and social	The gov't decreases: expenditures on social policies, role	Further cuts in social expenditures. Income distribution is	Social expenditures are kept constant but state size role	Income distribution continues to be set by market, but	The state retakes its role of leader in social services

(*continued*)

Table II.1
(Continued)

Economic Policies	*Monetarism, Adjustment, and First Crisis (1973–76)*	*Monetarism, Open Economy, Growth, and External Indebtness (1976–81)*	*Second Crisis and State Intervention (1981–83)*	*Corrections, Recovery, and Economic Boom (1984–90)*	*Democracy, Continuation of the Economic Model and Growth, and Equity (1990–94)*
services	of the public sector, investment, and benefits. Social security contributions are increased, and the gov't creates unified, uniform funds for family allowances, unemployment compensation, and welfare pensions. Health resources are reduced but focused on maternity and child care. Depolitization of education. Liberalization of housing market, declining role of state and increased private sector functions.	determined by market, eliminating state role. The gov't fully privatizes the pension system (AFPs) and partly the health system (ISAPRES) and reforms and decentralizes all levels of education. The role of the private sector in housing increases, but state creates new subsidized house program for low-income groups.	continues to decline. The real value of minimum pensions and family allowances decrease. Because of rising deficit, contributions for health insurance are increased; targeting of resources on maternity and child care continues. New legislation for university systems; transfer of educational services to municipalities is halted. Private sector builds 98% of housing; new program for eradication of Santiago slums.	new state programs target poor. All social expenditures decline except housing; reduced resources target poor/low income, health, higher education, and housing; but real minimum and welfare pensions and family allowances decrease. New state agencies unify/uniform old pensions and regulate investment in private system; new public health system allows selection between public and private facilities (contribution is increased again); municipalization of elementary and secondary education is completed; new program unifies all housing subsidies.	and significantly increases public social expenditures. The WB, IDB, and foreign governments give support to new social policies. Increase in public-sector, minimum, and welfare pensions (the latter are standardized) and family allowances. New rules for AFP investment. Emphasis on primary care, emergency care, and improvement of public hospital infrastructure; regulation of ISAPRES. Coverage of preschool education, improvement of quality in elementary, regulation of private universities. Targeting of poor and low-income groups; creation of social investment fund (FOSIS).

138

Table II.2

The Processes of State Collectivization and Reprivatization in Chile, 1965–1990

A. The Process of Collectivization, 1965–73

Sectors	Number of Firms Totally or Partially State-Controlled[a]				Share of State Enterprises in Product	
	1970	Sept. 1973			1965	1973
		Added	Total	%		
Agriculture, forestry, fishing[b]	18	108	126	24.9		
Mining	3	24	27	5.3	13.0	85.0
Industry	24	259	283	55.8	3.0	40.0
Construction	1	24	25	4.9		
Banking	0	19	19	3.8	0	85.0
Other services	0	27	27	5.3		
Transport					24.0	
Communication					11.1	70.0
Other public					25.0	100.0
Total	46	461	507	100.0	14.2[c]	39.0[c]

B. The Process of Privatization, 1974–89

1.	1974–82	Number of "Intervened" Firms Returned to Owners	Number of Firms Sold	Sales of Bank Stock Packages	Total Sales (Million U.S.$)
	1974	202	49		15.7
	1975	39	28	9	224.1
	1976	10	22	4	106.8
	1977	6	7		124.2
	1978	2	8	6	114.8
	1979		8	1	164.6
	1980[c]		6	1	69.6
	1981		3		112.0
	1982		4		11.4
	Total	259	135	21	943.2

(continued)

2.	1985–89 (Percent of Privatization)[d]	Number of Enterprises	
		Goals 1985	Actual 1989
	0	11	6
	1–30	20	5
	31–49	2	0
	50–70	0	0
	71–100	0	22

C. Comparisons for 1970–1990

State Enterprises	1970	1973	1983	1989	1990
Number[e]	67	529	47	45	41
Percent GDP[f]	14.2[g]	39.0	24.1	15.9[h]	
Total investment	15.2	5.2	4.4	17.2	17.5
National employment	4.8	5.6	3.3		

Sources: Based on Wisecarver 1985; Edwards and Cox Edwards 1987; Marcel 1989; Larraín and Meller 1990; Hachette and Luders 1993; Bitrán and Sáez 1994.

[a]Includes enterprises with state partial or total control of stocks as well as enterprises requisitioned or placed under state management (*intervenidas*). [b]Firms such as agro-industrial enterprises. [c]According to one source, by 1980 all land expropriated by the state in 1971–73 had been returned to previous owners; another source reports that only 66% was returned. [d]Degree of privatization planned (goals) and actually accomplished among 33 enterprises; e.g., in 1985, 11 enterprises were not going to be privatized at all, but in 1989 the number was actually lower: 6. [e]Another source gives 90 in 1970, 529 and 620 in 1973, and 66 in 1981. [f]Excludes agriculture. [g]1965. [h]1988.

Table II.3
Basic Macroeconomic Indicators of Chile, 1960–1993

Year	GDP Rate[a] (Percentage)		Gross Investment (Percentage of GDP)[b]			Annual Inflation Rate (Percentage)[c]	State Budget Balance[d] (Percentage of GDP)	Official Exchange Rate[e] (Pesos per U.S. $)
	Absolute	Per Capita	Total	National	Foreign			
1960	6.5	4.1	13.9	10.1	3.8	5.5	-4.6	0.001
1961	6.1	3.7	15.3	9.8	5.5	9.6	-4.5	0.001
1962	4.5	2.0	12.4	9.4	3.0	27.7	-5.8	0.001
1963	4.9	2.5	14.8	10.5	4.3	45.3	-4.9	0.002
1964	4.7	2.3	14.2	11.5	2.7	38.5	-3.9	0.002
1965	5.0	2.8	15.0	13.7	8.4	25.8	-4.1	0.002
1966	6.9	4.8	16.3	14.9	1.4	17.0	-2.5	0.004
1967	2.5	0.5	16.1	14.5	1.6	21.9	-1.3	0.005
1968	2.9	0.9	16.3	14.3	2.0	27.9	-1.5	0.007
1969	3.3	1.4	15.1	14.5	0.6	29.3	-0.4	0.009
1970	1.4	-0.5	16.4	15.2	1.2	34.9	-2.7	0.012
1971	9.0	7.1	14.5	12.4	2.1	22.1	-10.7	0.012
1972	-1.2	-2.9	12.2	8.3	3.9	163.4	-13.0	0.019
1973	-5.6	-7.1	7.9	5.2	2.7	508.1	-24.7	0.111
1974	1.0	-0.7	21.2	20.7	0.4	375.9	-10.5	0.832
1975	-12.9	-14.4	13.1	7.9	5.2	340.7	-2.6	4.911
1976	3.5	1.8	12.8	14.5	-1.7	174.3	-2.3	13.054
1977	9.9	8.0	14.4	10.7	3.7	63.5	-1.8	21.536
1978	8.2	6.5	17.8	12.6	5.2	30.3	-0.8	31.656

(continued)

Table II.3
(Continued)

Year	GDP Rate[a] (Percentage)		Gross Investment (Percentage of GDP)[b]			Annual Inflation Rate (Percentage)[c]	State Budget Balance[d] (Percentage of GDP)	Official Exchange Rate[e] (Pesos per U.S. $)
	Absolute	Per Capita	Total	National	Foreign			
1979	8.3	6.7	17.8	12.4	5.4	38.9	1.7	37.246
1980	7.8	6.2	21.0	13.9	7.1	31.2	3.1	39.000
1981	5.5	3.8	22.7	8.2	14.5	9.5	1.7	39.000
1982	−14.1	−15.5	11.3	2.1	9.2	20.7	−2.3	50.909
1983	−0.7	−2.4	9.8	4.4	5.4	23.1	−3.8	78.788
1984	6.3	4.6	13.6	2.9	10.7	23.0	−4.0	98.478
1985	2.4	0.8	13.7	5.4	8.3	26.4	−6.3	160.860
1986	5.6	3.8	14.6	7.7	6.9	17.4	−2.8	192.930
1987	6.6	4.8	16.9	12.6	4.3	21.5	−0.1	219.470
1988	7.3	5.5	17.0	16.3	0.7	12.7	−1.7	245.012
1989	9.9	8.1	19.1	17.2	1.9	21.4	−3.0	266.954
1990	3.3	1.6	20.3	17.5	2.8	27.3	1.4	304.903
1991	7.3	5.6	18.8	19.0	−0.2	18.7	1.6	349.216
1992	11.0	9.3	21.3	19.6	1.7	12.7	2.7	362.576
1993	6.3	4.6	26.2	21.3	4.9	12.2	1.8	404.166

Sources: GDP and exchange rates from IMF, *IFSY* for 1960–89; BCCh, *Boletín Mensual*, March 1994; and Ministerio de Hacienda 1994. GDP per capita is author's estimates based on IMF population data and Ministerio de Hacienda 1994. Inflation, investment, and budget balance from BCCh, *Indicadores* 1989; *Boletín Mensual*, March 1994; and Ministerio de Hacienda 1993, 1994.

[a]1985 prices. [b]Current prices. [c]For 1970–78 there is a series for the annual inflation rate from Cortázar and Marshall 1980: 1970 = 36.1; 1971 = 28.2; 1972 = 260.5; 1973 = 605.1; 1974 = 369.2; 1975 = 343.3; 1976 = 179.9; 1977 = 84.2; 1978 = 37.2. This series gives an average annual inflation rate of 167.2% in 1970–78; the official series gives 145.5% for the same period. [d]1976 prices. There is a series in current prices derived from IDB, *Economic and Social* 1972–90. [e]Annual average.

Table II.4

Percentage Distribution of GDP by Economic Activity in Chile, 1960–1993

Year	Including Other Services						Excluding Other Services				
	Agriculture[a]	Industry[b]	Construction	Transport/ Communications	Commerce	Other Services[c]	Agriculture[a]	Industry[b]	Construction	Transport/ Communications	Commerce
1960	10.6	31.5	7.6	4.2	17.1	29.0	14.9	44.4	10.7	5.9	24.1
1961	9.9	32.4	6.7	4.3	18.0	28.7	13.9	45.4	9.4	6.0	25.3
1962	9.1	33.8	8.2	4.4	17.5	27.0	12.5	46.3	11.2	6.0	24.0
1963	9.1	32.9	9.6	4.5	16.9	27.0	12.5	45.1	13.2	6.2	23.2
1964	9.0	33.9	8.2	4.5	17.0	27.4	12.4	46.7	11.3	6.2	23.4
1965	9.0	34.0	7.8	4.7	15.9	28.6	12.6	47.6	10.9	6.6	22.3
1966	9.8	33.8	6.7	4.5	16.9	28.3	13.7	47.1	9.3	6.3	23.6
1967	9.7	33.7	6.6	4.5	17.0	28.5	13.6	47.1	9.2	6.3	23.8
1968	9.9	33.6	6.8	4.6	16.8	28.3	13.8	46.9	9.5	6.4	23.4
1969	8.4	33.3	7.2	4.7	17.1	29.3	11.9	47.1	10.2	6.6	24.2
1970	8.5	32.9	7.5	4.9	16.5	29.7	12.1	46.8	10.7	7.0	23.4
1971	7.7	33.9	6.9	4.7	17.6	29.2	10.9	47.9	9.8	6.6	24.8
1972	7.2	34.8	5.6	4.8	18.4	29.2	10.2	49.2	7.9	6.8	25.9
1973	6.8	34.5	5.3	4.9	18.3	30.2	9.7	49.4	7.6	7.0	26.3
1974	8.6	35.0	6.6	4.9	14.5	30.4	12.4	50.3	9.5	7.0	20.8
1975	10.3	31.7	5.6	5.2	13.9	33.3	15.4	47.5	8.4	7.8	20.9
1976	9.8	33.0	4.5	5.3	13.7	33.7	14.8	49.8	6.8	8.0	20.6
1977	9.8	32.0	4.1	5.3	15.6	33.1	14.7	47.8	6.1	7.9	23.5
1978	8.7	31.7	4.1	5.4	17.3	32.8	12.9	47.2	6.1	8.0	25.8
1979	8.6	31.4	4.7	5.4	17.7	32.2	12.7	46.3	6.9	8.0	26.1
1980	8.3	30.9	5.3	5.5	18.5	31.5	12.1	45.1	7.7	8.0	27.1
1981	8.1	30.3	6.1	5.4	18.3	31.8	11.9	44.4	8.9	7.9	26.9

(continued)

143

Table II.4
(Continued)

Year	Including Other Services						Excluding Other Services				
	Agriculture[a]	Industry[b]	Construction	Transport/ Communications	Commerce	Other Services[c]	Agriculture[a]	Industry[b]	Construction	Transport/ Communications	Commerce
1982	9.3	30.7	5.4	5.5	17.6	31.5	13.6	44.8	7.9	8.0	25.7
1983	9.2	31.4	5.2	5.4	17.1	31.7	13.5	46.0	7.6	7.9	25.0
1984	9.3	31.9	5.1	5.4	16.9	31.4	13.6	46.5	7.4	7.9	24.6
1985	9.6	31.7	5.8	5.6	16.7	30.6	13.8	45.7	8.4	8.1	24.0
1986	9.9	31.8	5.5	5.7	16.7	30.4	14.2	45.7	7.9	8.2	24.0
1987	9.6	31.2	5.8	6.0	17.0	30.4	14.0	44.8	8.3	8.6	24.0
1988	9.4	31.3	5.7	6.2	17.4	30.0	13.4	44.7	8.1	8.9	24.9
1989	9.0	31.1	5.8	6.4	18.0	29.7	12.8	44.2	8.3	9.1	25.6
1990	9.5	30.6	5.7	7.5	16.0	30.8	13.7	44.2	8.2	10.8	23.1
1991	9.2	30.9	5.6	7.7	16.0	30.6	13.3	44.5	8.1	11.1	23.0
1992	8.9	30.8	5.7	8.1	16.7	29.8	12.7	43.9	8.1	11.5	23.8
1993	8.5	30.1	6.2	8.3	17.2	29.7	12.1	42.8	8.8	11.8	24.5

Sources: BCCh, *Indicadores* 1989; *Boletín Mensual,* March 1994.

Note: GDP in 1977 pesos in 1960–89 and 1986 pesos in 1990–93. [a]Includes forestry and fishing. [b]Includes manufacturing, mining, electricity, gas, and water. [c]Includes financial sector, bank charges, import taxes, home ownership, and social services.

Table II.5
Physical Output of Principal Products in Chile, 1960–1993 (Thousand Tons)

Year	Copper	Iron	Nitrates	Fish[a]	Table Grapes	Apples	Wine (Million Liters)
1960	532	3,804	930	340			
1961	546	4,426	1,110	430			
1962	586	5,160	1,102	643			
1963	601	5,481	1,136	762			
1964	622	6,361	1,173	1,161			
1965	585	7,756	1,158	709		102	
1966	625	7,788	1,062	1,383			
1967	660	6,853	869	1,053			
1968	657	7,428	679	1,393			
1969	688	7,161	782	1,095			
1970	692	6,940	674	1,181		161	
1971	708	6,851	829	1,487			
1972	717	5,303	707	792			
1973	735	5,797	697	664	55	120	
1974	902	6,299	739	1,128	58	120	
1975	828	6,772	727	899	59	125	
1976	1,005	6,186	619	1,379	63	130	
1977	1,054	4,941	562	1,347	69	150	
1978	1,034	4,769	530	1,929	75	175	
1979	1,063	4,978	621	2,560	79	210	
1980	1,068	5,344	620	2,891	85	245	586
1981	1,081	5,190	624	3,503	122	298	594
1982	1,242	3,874	577	3,847	63	345	610
1983	1,258	3,602	622	4,162	196	365	520
1984	1,291	4,250	713	4,674	225	410	400
1985	1,356	3,945		4,987	276	425	450
1986	1,399	7,009		5,696	318	515	350
1987	1,413	6,690		4,932	397	580	400
1988	1,472	7,866		5,375	516	630	350
1989	1,628	8,761		6,633	547	660	335
1990	1,616	8,248		5,426	710	780	330
1991	1,855	8,414		6,166	800	830	328
1992	1,976	7,224		6,628	880	840	278
1993	2,116	7,409		6,191	880	870	320

Sources: BCCh, *Indicadores* 1989; *Boletín Mensual,* March 1994; *Síntesis Estadística* 1994.

[a]Includes all types of fish and seafood.

Table II.6

Statistics on Industrial Sector of Chile, 1960–1993

Year	Annual Growth Industrial Product (Percentage)	Annual Growth GDP (Percentage)	Employment Industry (Thousands)	Exports (U.S.$ Millions)
1960			370.1	39.0
1961	7.4	4.8	391.5	44.9
1962	9.4	4.7	399.3	36.9
1963	3.9	6.3	409.9	38.4
1964	5.1	2.2	419.6	83.2
1965	4.4	0.8	442.6	103.3
1966	12.6	11.2	458.7	116.4
1967	2.9	3.2	470.9	83.7
1968	3.2	3.6	477.8	91.2
1969	2.7	3.7	481.7	103.0
1970	2.0	2.1	492.2	128.5
1971	13.6	9.0	534.5	119.6
1972	2.2	−1.2	554.1	82.4
1973	−7.7	−5.6	545.0	89.4
1974	−2.6	1.0	515.3	241.7
1975	−25.6	−12.9	467.8	366.5
1976	6.0	3.5	446.4	471.4
1977	8.5	9.9	454.6	634.0
1978	9.3	8.2	462.4	723.5
1979	7.9	8.3	480.9	1,198.1
1980	6.2	7.8	503.5	1,490.3
1981	2.6	5.5	516.9	1,098.5
1982	−21.0	−14.1	409.4	1,023.4
1983	3.1	−0.7	396.1	971.3
1984	9.8	6.3	454.0	1,024.6
1985	1.2	2.4	493.0	956.5
1986	8.0	5.6	570.7	1,202.6
1987	5.3	6.6	606.9	1,824.1
1988	8.7	7.3	669.8	2,273.1
1989	10.9	9.9	745.5	2,475.3
1990	0.5	3.3	789.1	2,741.1
1991	5.7	7.3	826.4[a]	3,315.6
1992	11.0	11.0	813.2	4,032.9
1993	3.6	6.3	835.3	4,056.1

Sources: Hachette 1988; BCCh, *Boletín Mensual,* March 1994; ILO, *Yearbook* 1994.

Note: Includes manufacturing; excludes mining, electricity, gas, and water. [a]March 1991.

Table II.7

Trade Merchandise: Balance and Dependency in Chile, 1960–1993
(Millions U.S.$)

Year	Exports (f.o.b.)	Imports (c.i.f.)	Trade Transactions	Trade Balance Total	Per Capita U.S. $	Trade Dependency Percentage of GDP in Current Prices Exports	Imports	Transactions
1960	488	526	1,014	−38	−5.0	13.8	16.7	30.5
1961	506	598	1,104	−92	−11.9	12.1	16.3	28.4
1962	484	512	996	−28	−3.5	12.0	13.4	25.4
1963	493	490	983	3	0.4	12.9	15.4	28.3
1964	592	529	1,121	63	7.6	12.8	13.7	26.5
1965	692	530	1,222	162	19.0	13.9	13.1	27.0
1966	860	661	1,521	199	22.9	15.0	13.9	28.9
1967	883	651	1,534	232	26.2	14.7	13.4	28.1
1968	908	726	1,634	182	20.2	14.3	13.5	27.8
1969	1,172	786	1,958	386	42.0	16.9	14.5	31.4
1970	1,113	867	1,980	246	26.3	15.0	14.4	29.4
1971	1,000	927	1,927	73	7.8	11.3	12.4	23.7
1972	851	1,012	1,863	−161	−16.6	10.0	13.6	23.6
1973	1,316	1,329	2,645	−13	−1.3	13.9	15.9	29.8
1974	2,152	1,901	4,053	251	25.0	20.4	19.7	40.1
1975	1,590	1,520	3,110	70	6.9	25.5	27.4	52.9
1976	2,116	1,473	3,589	643	62.0	25.1	20.8	45.9
1977	2,186	2,151	4,337	35	3.3	20.6	22.4	43.0
1978	2,460	2,886	5,346	−426	−39.7	20.6	23.9	44.5
1979	3,835	4,190	8,025	−355	−32.5	23.3	26.1	49.4
1980	4,705	5,469	10,174	−764	−68.6	22.8	27.0	49.8
1981	3,836	6,513	10,349	−2,677	−236.5	16.4	26.8	43.2
1982	3,706	3,643	7,349	63	5.5	19.4	21.3	40.7
1983	3,831	2,845	6,676	986	84.2	24.0	21.3	45.3
1984	3,650	3,288	6,938	362	30.4	24.3	25.3	49.6
1985	3,084	2,920	6,004	164	13.5	29.1	26.3	55.4
1986	4,191	3,099	7,290	1,092	88.6	30.6	26.8	57.4
1987	5,224	3,994	9,218	1,230	98.2	33.5	29.4	62.9
1988	7,052	4,833	11,885	2,219	174.2	37.4	30.2	67.6
1989	8,080	6,502	14,582	1,578	121.8	37.7	34.4	72.1
1990	8,310	7,037	15,347	1,273	96.7	34.3	31.1	65.4
1991	8,929	7,353	16,282	1,576	117.7	33.3	28.7	62.0
1992	9,986	9,237	19,223	749	55.1	30.8	29.2	60.0
1993	9,202	10,181	19,383	−979	−70.9	27.8	30.1	57.9

Sources: IMF, *IFSY* 1992; BCCh, *Indicadores* 1989; *Boletín Mensual,* March 1994.

Table II.8

Percentage Distribution of Exports by Major Products in Chile, 1960–1993

Year	Copper	Iron Ore	Fish Meal	Grapes	Other
1960	70.5	7.2			22.3
1961	66.6	8.7			24.7
1962	69.2	10.6			20.2
1963	72.4	10.9			16.7
1964	74.3	11.8			13.9
1965	78.6	12.2			9.2
1966	84.3	9.5			6.2
1967	76.9	8.0			15.1
1968	79.7	8.4			11.9
1969	86.1	6.6			7.3
1970	67.3	5.7	1.3	0.3	25.4
1971	70.3	6.8	3.0	0.5	19.4
1972	73.8	5.3	2.1	0.5	18.3
1973	83.3	3.7	1.1	0.3	11.6
1974	66.7	2.9	1.4	0.2	28.8
1975	57.3	5.9	1.5	0.8	34.5
1976	59.9	4.1	2.9	0.7	32.4
1977	54.2	3.7	3.7	0.9	37.5
1978	51.3	3.2	4.3	1.2	40.0
1979	48.8	3.2	4.1	1.2	42.7
1980	46.1	3.4	4.9	1.1	44.5
1981	43.9	4.1	5.4	1.9	44.7
1982	46.7	4.3	7.1	2.7	39.2
1983	47.9	2.9	8.0	3.0	38.2
1984	43.4	3.0	7.6	3.6	42.4
1985	46.1	2.4	7.6	4.9	39.0
1986	41.9	2.1	8.0	4.4	43.6
1987	41.3	2.8	7.3	4.4	47.0
1988	48.4	2.4	6.6	4.0	40.1
1989	49.8	2.2	6.3	3.4	38.6
1990	45.7	4.4	4.5	4.6	40.8
1991	40.5	4.6	5.4	5.6	43.9
1992	38.9	3.7	5.5	4.3	47.6
1993	35.3				

Sources: Copper and iron ore from IMF, *IFSY* 1987, 1990; BCCh, *Boletín Mensual,* March 1994. For meat/fish meal and grapes: 1970–81 from UN, *ITSY* 1974–84; 1982–89 from ECLAC, *Yearbook* 1991; 1990–92 from BCCh, *Boletín Mensual,* March 1994.

Table II.9
Percentage Distribution of Imports by Major Products in Chile, 1962–1993

Year	Food and Beverages[a]	Non-Food Agricultural Products and Minerals	Fuels	Machinery and Transportation	Other Manufactures	Other
1962	18	8	7	40	27	0
1966	18	8	6	37	30	1
1967	16	8	8	41	26	0
1968	16	8	6	44	25	1
1969	16	7	7	41	28	1
1970	18	9	7	38	28	0
1971	16	6	9	39	31	0
1972	21	7	9	31	32	0
1973	24	5	7	34	30	0
1974	29	6	14	25	26	0
1975	16	4	20	34	26	0
1976	24	5	12	35	24	0
1977	11	4	20	35	30	0
1978	15	4	17	31	33	0
1979	11	3	21	29	36	0
1980	13	3	18	31	35	0
1981	10	3	14	34	38	1
1982	13	4	18	31	34	0
1983	17	4	21	23	35	0
1984	13	4	18	27	38	0
1985	8	3	19	32	38	0
1986	4	3	15	36	40	2
1987	4	3	12	40	41	0
1988	4	3	12	41	38	2
1989	3	2	12	44	37	2
1990	4	2	16	44	33	1
1991	5	3	15	38	37	2
1992	5	2	12	41	38	2
1993	5	2	9	44	38	2

Source: UN, *ITSY* 1964, 1969, 1972–73, 1976–88, 1991, 1992, and 1995.

Note: The World Bank also publishes this series, but figures are not always comparable to those of the U.N. For example, the *World Development Report* (1988) gives the respective percentages as 12, 3, 9, 40, 37 for 1986, and the 1989 edition gives 12, 4, 10, 39, 36 for 1987. [a]Data for 1962–70 include tobacco.

Table II.10
World Prices of Principal Export Products and Purchasing Power of Exports in Chile, 1970–1993

Year	Average Annual Prices (in U.S.$)			Purchasing Power of Exports (1980 = 100)	Terms of Trade[a]	
	Copper (London) (U.S. cents/ton)	Iron (U.S.$/ton)	Fish Meal (U.S.$/ton)		(1970 = 100)	(1980 = 100)
1970	64.0	15.2	196.8		100.0	
1971	49.0	13.5	168.1		78.2	
1972	48.6	12.8	238.7		72.0	
1973	80.6	17.1	542.0		83.3	
1974	93.2	19.0	372.0		88.1	
1975	56.1	22.8	245.3		53.2	
1976	63.6	22.2	376.2		57.1	
1977	59.4	21.6	453.9		51.3	
1978	61.9	19.4	409.9		49.8	
1979	89.5	23.4	394.9		53.4	
1980	98.6	28.1	504.4	100	49.0	100
1981	79.0	24.6	467.5	82	38.6	

Year					
1982	67.2	26.2	353.8	82	34.4
1983	72.2	24.0	452.5	94	
1984	62.5	23.1	373.2	88	
1985	64.3	26.6	280.1	97	
1986	62.1	21.9	320.6	109	
1987	80.8	22.2	383.4	126	
1988	117.9	23.1	544.4	160	
1989	129.1	26.4	409.1	172	
1990	120.9	30.8	412.2	165	
1991	106.1	33.3	478.0	179	
1992	103.6	35.4	481.5	198	
1993	86.7		364.7	186[b]	

Sources: Prices from IMF, *IFSY* 1990; ECLAC, *Survey* 1980, 1981, 1982, 1988, 1993; ECLAC, *Preliminary* 1983, 1986, 1990, 1992, and 1993; BCCh, *Síntesis Estadística* 1994.

[a]Relationship of prices of exchange of goods (imports/exports). [b]Preliminary figure.

Table II.11

Trade Concentration with Main Commercial Partner (U.S.) in Chile, 1960–1993 (Percentage of Trade)

	U.S.			West Germany			Japan		
Year	Total	Exports	Imports	Total	Exports	Imports	Total	Exports	Imports
1960	42.6	37.3	47.8	13.6	15.5	11.6	2.1	1.9	2.3
1961	38.4	36.7	39.7	13.1	12.4	13.8	4.2	5.2	3.5
1962	35.3	36.6	34.2	11.4	11.5	11.3	4.4	6.4	2.5
1963	37.2	34.3	40.1	12.6	11.3	13.9	4.7	7.3	2.2
1964	35.6	34.6	36.7	11.7	12.3	11.1	5.5	8.9	2.0
1965	34.9	31.1	39.2	12.0	13.2	10.5	6.5	10.8	1.5
1966	31.8	25.1	39.7	11.3	9.6	13.2	6.7	10.4	2.3
1967	26.1	18.5	35.7	10.0	7.8	12.7	7.2	11.9	1.2
1968	29.5	22.5	38.4	9.5	8.1	11.3	8.2	13.3	1.8
1969	27.0	17.3	38.5	9.8	9.5	10.3	8.3	13.6	2.0
1970	24.1	14.4	36.9	11.6	10.9	12.4	8.2	12.1	3.0
1971	17.4	7.7	27.3	11.4	12.3	10.5	11.5	18.4	4.5
1972	13.5	9.6	17.1	11.4	13.7	9.4	10.1	17.3	3.6
1973	12.3	8.6	16.4	12.2	14.0	10.3	10.8	17.7	3.2
1974	16.0	11.5	21.8	11.1	13.5	7.9	10.4	16.4	2.5
1975	18.6	8.8	29.1	11.5	14.4	8.3	8.3	11.2	5.1
1976	16.4	10.2	24.3	10.9	14.9	5.9	11.0	10.7	11.4
1977	16.5	12.3	20.5	10.8	13.6	8.1	11.5	12.0	11.0
1978	20.6	13.0	27.0	10.2	13.6	7.4	9.2	11.2	7.5
1979	16.9	10.7	22.6	10.7	15.4	6.4	9.1	10.7	7.6
1980	21.0	12.6	28.6	9.4	13.1	6.0	9.0	10.8	7.2
1981	21.6	15.2	25.6	7.9	11.6	5.6	10.7	10.9	10.6
1982	23.7	21.6	26.0	8.9	11.5	6.1	9.3	11.9	6.5
1983	27.1	28.2	25.5	10.2	12.6	6.7	7.7	9.1	5.9
1984	24.8	26.0	23.4	8.5	10.0	6.8	10.5	11.1	9.8
1985	23.3	22.9	23.9	8.8	9.7	7.6	8.7	10.1	6.9
1986	21.8	21.8	20.7	9.3	10.5	8.1	9.8	10.0	9.6
1987	21.4	21.8	19.3	8.8	9.3	8.4	10.2	10.7	9.7
1988	20.5	19.8	20.7	9.6	11.6	7.6	10.3	12.5	8.1
1989	19.3	18.0	20.7	9.3	11.3	7.4	12.6	13.9	11.3
1990	18.7	17.9	19.5	9.3	11.3	7.4	12.6	16.7	8.4
1991	19.0	17.6	20.6	7.2	7.8	6.5	13.7	18.2	8.4
1992	18.4	16.3	20.5	6.2	6.0	6.5	13.5	16.9	10.0
1993	18.4	17.6	19.4	2.5	5.2	0.1	7.5	16.0	0.2

Sources: IMF, *Direction of Trade* 1960–92; BCCh, *Boletín Mensual,* March 1994.

Table II.12

Dependency on Crude Oil Imports in Chile, 1960–1987 (Thousand Barrels)

Year	Imports[a]	Domestic Production	Total Supply	Dependency on Imports (Percentage)
1960	3,699	7,231	10,930	33.8
1972	26,728	12,506	39,234	68.1
1973	24,210	11,430	35,640	67.9
1974	29,937	10,040	39,977	74.9
1975	19,788	8,946	28,734	68.9
1976	25,260	8,371	33,631	75.1
1977	26,902	7,120	34,022	79.0
1978	27,117	6,291	33,408	81.1
1979	33,421	7,572	40,993	81.5
1980	23,867	12,140	36,007	66.3
1981	19,810	15,104	34,914	56.7
1982	8,950	14,965	23,915	37.4
1983	13,839	14,365	28,204	49.0
1984	14,479	14,069	28,548	50.7
1985	15,135	13,048	28,183	53.7
1986	19,093	12,205	31,298	61.0
1987	19,682	10,922	30,604	64.3

Source: IDB, 1975, 1978, 1980–81, 1985, 1989.

Note: IDB stopped the publication of statistics on oil dependency in 1989 with data until 1987.
[a]Chile also imports refined oil, but declined from 7.8 to 1.8 million bareels between 1982–87. If those imports are added, the degree of dependency increases to 52.8% and 66% in those two years. Chile refines almost all the crude oil it imports.

Table II.13
Total Disbursed External Debt of Chile, 1975–1993 (Million U.S. Current Dollars)

Year	Total External Debt		Percentage Distribution		Debt as Percentage of		Real Debt per Capita
	Current	Real (Prices 1985)	Public	Private	GDP	Exports Goods and Services	
1975	4,854	9,073	83.8	16.2	55.8	272.4	889.5
1976	4,720	8,310	79.7	20.3	47.9	197.4	801.4
1977	5,201	8,583	75.3	24.7	42.7	197.4	813.6
1978	6,664	10,237	70.7	29.3	43.6	224.6	954.1
1979	8,484	11,983	59.7	40.3	40.6	182.6	1,097.3
1980	11,084	14,339	45.7	54.3	43.1	185.7	1,287.2
1981	15,542	18,350	35.2	64.8	52.5	310.3	1,621.0
1982	17,153	19,038	38.8	61.2	70.5	369.5	1,654.0
1983	17,431	18,623	56.2	43.8	88.2	378.6	1,590.4
1984	18,877	19,400	65.4	34.6	115.0	420.0	1,628.9
1985	19,444	19,444	72.4	27.6	127.0	435.0	1,604.3
1986	19,501	18,988	80.8	19.2	110.1	387.7	1,541.2
1987	19,208	18,104	85.3	14.7	92.9	304.3	1,444.9
1988	17,638	16,137	83.3	16.7	73.0	213.4	1,266.6
1989	16,250	14,279	74.0	26.0	69.0	201.1	1,101.8
1990	17,425	14,401	67.7	32.3	62.7	209.7	1,093.5
1991	16,364	13,233	64.5	35.5	52.2	183.3	988.3
1992	18,242	14,219	52.8	47.2	44.2	182.7	1,046.2
1993	19,186	14,586	47.1	52.9	43.8	208.4	1,056.2

Sources: BCCh, *Indicadores* 1989; *Boletín Mensual,* March 1994; Ministerio de Hacienda 1994. Real external debt calculated with U.S. GNP deflator from IMF, *IFSY* 1992.

Table II.14

Percentage Distribution of the Labor Force by Economic Activity in Chile,
1960–1993

Economic Activities	1960	1965	1970	1975	1980	1985	1990	1992	1993
Agriculture	28.6	26.2	21.8	17.5	15.3	18.6	19.4	19.2	16.6
Mining	3.7	3.4	3.3	2.8	2.2	2.2	2.0	2.3	1.9
Industry	16.5	18.2	18.7	17.0	16.3	13.2	15.6	16.0	16.8
Electricity, gas, water	0.4	0.4	0.4	0.8	0.8	0.6	0.6	0.5	0.3
Construction	5.2	6.6	5.9	5.4	5.1	4.6	6.9	6.4	8.1
Commerce	10.4	10.9	13.8	14.1	17.4	16.7	17.0	17.7	18.6
Transportation and communication[a]	4.9	5.3	5.8	6.4	6.3	5.7	6.4	6.9	7.1
Financial services				2.6	3.0	4.0	4.3	4.5	5.8
Services	23.2	22.6	24.2	27.7	30.5	31.6	26.6	26.4	24.7
Nonspecified, unemployed, other[b]	7.1	6.4	6.1	5.8	3.1	2.8	1.2	0.1	0.1
Total	100.0	100.0	100.0	100.0	100.0	100.0	100.0	100.0	100.0

Sources: 1960–70 from ODEPLAN 1973; 1975–88 based on BCCh, *Indicadores* 1989; 1990–93 based on BCCh, *Boletín Mensual,* March 1994.

[a]For 1960–70 include transportation only. [b]For 1960–70 includes unemployment; for 1975–88 includes non-specified and those seeking jobs for the first time.

Table II.15

Percentage of Women in the Labor Force
and Women's Participation Rates in Chile, 1960–1993

Year	Percentage of Labor Force	Participation Rate[a]
1960		19.7
1965	22.0	
1970	23.0	18.1
1980	29.3	21.3
1985	30.7	24.2
1989	30.8	
1990		27.0
1991	30.7	
1992	32.0	28.1
1993	32.5	

Sources: Percent in 1965 from WB, *Social Indicators* 1987; percent in 1992 from UNDP, *Human Development Report* 1994; the rest from ILO, *Yearbook* 1976–94. Rates from ECLAC, *Yearbook* 1992, 1995.

[a]Economically active female population aged 10 years and over as a percentage of total female population in that age bracket.

Table II.16

Open Unemployment Rates in Chile, 1960–1993 (Percentage of the Labor Force)

| | Santiago | | | | | National | | |
| | University of Chile | ECLAC | ILO | Ffrench-Davis Open | Open with PEM and POJH | ODEPLAN | ILO | Balassa |
Year								
1960	7.4					7.1		
1961	6.6					8.0		
1962	5.2					7.9		
1963	5.0					7.5		
1964	5.3					7.0		
1965	5.4					6.4		
1966	5.3					6.1		
1967	6.1					4.7	4.7	
1968	6.0					4.9	4.8	
1969	6.2		4.6			6.0	4.7	
1970	7.1	4.1	4.1	5.9	5.9	6.1	3.4	3.5
1971	5.5	4.3	4.2	5.2	5.2		3.8	3.3
1972	3.8	3.2	3.3	4.1	4.1		3.1	3.3
1973	4.6	4.8	4.8	4.8	4.8			4.8
1974	9.7	8.3	8.3	9.1	9.1			9.2
1975	16.2	15.0	15.0	15.6	17.6[a]		14.7	14.9
1976	16.8	16.3	17.1	16.7	21.9		14.0	12.7
1977	13.2	13.9	13.9	13.3	18.9		11.6	11.8
1978	14.0	13.3	13.7	13.8	18.0		13.9	14.1
1979	13.6	13.4	13.4	13.5	17.3		13.6	13.6
1980	11.8	11.7		11.7	17.0		10.4	10.4
1981	11.1	9.0		10.4	15.1		11.3	11.3
1982	22.1	20.0		19.6	26.1[b]		19.6	19.4
1983	22.2	19.0		18.7	31.3		14.6	
1984	19.2	18.5		16.3	24.7		13.9	
1985	16.4	17.0		14.1	22.0		12.1	
1986	13.5	13.1		12.1	17.3		8.8	
1987	12.2	11.9		11.1	13.9		7.9	
1988	10.9	10.2					6.3	
1989	9.1	7.2					5.3	
1990	9.6	6.5					5.6	
1991	8.5	7.3					5.3	
1992	5.7	4.9					4.4	
1993	5.9	4.0					4.5	

Sources: University of Chile from Vial 1990; ECLAC, *Yearbook* 1995; ECLAC, *Survey* 1981, 1993; ECLAC, *Preliminary* 1983, 1984, 1989, 1990, 1992, 1994; ILO, *Yearbook* 1977, 1980, 1988, 1992, 1994; Ffrench Davis and Raczynski 1987; ODEPLAN 1973; Balassa 1985.

[a]PEM is created. [b]POJH is created.

Table II.17

Real Public Social Expenditures by Sectors in Chile, 1961–1993
(Percentage of GDP)

Year	Pension	Health	Education	Housing	Total
1961	8.7	3.2	3.1	2.0	17.0
1963	7.6	3.3	3.0	2.5	16.3
1965	9.1	3.6	3.7	3.6	20.0
1967	9.2	3.2	4.1	3.6	20.1
1969	8.2	3.0	4.2	3.3	18.7
1970	9.0	3.3	4.5	3.2	19.9
1971	11.6	4.0	5.8	4.1	25.2
1972	11.5	4.3	5.9	4.1	25.8
1974	6.4	2.9	3.8	4.5	17.6
1975	8.2	2.8	4.5	2.9	18.3
1977	7.5	3.0	4.5	2.3	17.4
1979	7.6	2.2	4.1	1.5	15.4
1981	6.4	2.9	3.6	1.3	14.3
1983	9.4	2.9	3.9	0.9	17.1
1987	9.3	2.6	3.7	1.2	16.7
1988	8.0	2.6	3.2	1.3	15.2
1989	7.6	2.4	2.9	1.1	14.0
1990	7.8	2.3	2.8	1.1	14.0
1991	7.6	2.6	3.0	1.3	14.5
1992	7.4	2.8	3.1	1.3	14.7
1993	7.9	2.9	3.1	1.4	15.3

Sources: 1961–74 from Arellano 1985; 1975–83 from Arellano 1985, Oyarzo 1989, and Arenas de Mesa 1991; 1987–88 from Ffrench-Davis 1991 and Raczynski and Romaguera 1993; 1989–93 from Dirección de Presupuestos 1994.

Note: The series 1961–74, 1975–83, 1987–88, and 1989–93 are not strictly comparable.

Table II.18

Income Distribution and Poverty Incidence in Chile, 1964–1994

| | Gini Coefficient (Greater Santiago) | | | Percentage of Poor Families[a] | | Labor Share in Gross National Income[b] (1970 = 100) |
| | Personal Income | | | | | |
Year	Working Population	Labor Force	Family Income	Poverty	Indigence	
1964	0.490	0.496	0.462			
1970	0.526	0.571	0.571	17.0	6.0	100.0
1973						84.1[c]
1974	0.468	0.518	0.450			64.9
1975	0.484	0.566	0.471			71.8
1976	0.543	0.618	0.438	56.9	27.9	71.1
1977	0.534	0.599	0.526			73.7
1978	0.524	0.588	0.520			77.5
1979	0.526	0.589	0.518			81.8
1980	0.522	0.578	0.526	44.3	14.4	86.1
1981	0.531	0.579	0.521			92.6
1982	0.534	0.624	0.539	30.8	10.8	99.1
1983	0.530	0.639	0.542			97.1
1984				48.2	23.0	
1986				50.9	24.7	
1987				48.6[d]	22.6[d]	
1990				35.0	12.0	
1992				28.0	7.0	
1994				24.0	7.0	

Sources: Gini coefficients from Edwards and Cox Edwards 1987; poverty from Tironi 1989 and ECLAC, *Yearbook* 1995, 1997; labor share from Ramos 1986.

[a]1970, 1990 and 1992 percentage of households; 1976, 1980, 1982, and 1986–87 percentage of total population. [b]Index reflects changes in the share with respect to base year. [c]First eight months of the year. [d]For 1987 ECLAC gives 37% of households on poverty and 14% on indigence.

Table II.19
Real Wage Indices in Chile, 1970–1994

| Year | ECLAC (1980 = 100) | | Meller (1970 = 100) | Castañeda (1980 = 100) | INE (1990 = 100) |
	Mean[a]	Urban Minimum			
1970	111.9		100.0	102.3	
1971	133.4		122.3	122.0	
1972	121.0		108.5	102.1	
1973	79.9		66.6	54.7	68.7
1974	72.5		65.1	66.6	61.4
1975	69.5	60.9	62.9	63.9	59.6
1976	70.5	67.5	64.8	80.6	75.3
1977	79.6	79.6	71.5	81.6	76.2
1978	84.7	100.7	76.0	86.8	81.1
1979	91.8	99.8	82.3	91.9	87.8
1980	100.0	100.0	89.4	100.0	95.4
1981	108.9	115.7	97.4	108.9	103.9
1982	108.6	117.2	97.7	108.7	103.7
1983	97.1	94.2	87.0	98.0	92.6
1984	97.2	80.7	87.1	98.1	92.7
1985	93.5	76.4	83.2	93.8	88.8
1986	95.1	72.9	84.9	95.7	90.6
1987	94.8	68.4	84.7	95.5	90.4
1988	101.1	73.2	90.3		96.4
1989	103.0	84.0	92.0		98.2
1990	104.8	86.8	93.7		100.0
1991	110.1	95.0			104.9
1992	115.1	99.5			109.6
1993	118.9	105.8			113.8
1994	124.5				

Sources: ECLAC, *Survey* 1970–93 and *Preliminary* 1994, 1996; Castañeda 1989; Meller 1992a; INE, *Indicadores* 1994.

[a]For 1970–74 I recalculated the series, shifting the base from 1970 to 1980 (1970–78 averages for January, April, July, and October; the rest averages for all 12 months).

Table II.20
Growth of Consumption per Capita and Distribution of Household Consumption in Chile, 1960–1993

	Consumption per Capita			Consumption per Capita			Consumption per Capita	
Year	Annual Percentage Variation	Index (1970 = 100)	Year	Annual Percentage Variation	Index (1970 = 100)	Year	Annual Percentage Variation	Index (1970 = 100)
1960	6.0	86.7	1972	5.6	117.2	1984	−0.4	93.5
1961	2.5	88.9	1973	−7.1	110.1	1985	−2.7	90.8
1962	1.7	90.4	1974	−15.7	94.5	1986	2.1	92.7
1963	1.2	91.5	1975	−12.6	81.9	1987	2.1	94.7
1964	−2.5	89.0	1976	−1.3	80.6	1988	7.2	101.5
1965	−1.2	87.8	1977	12.1	90.4	1989	6.4	108.0
1966	8.8	95.5	1978	5.9	95.7	1990	0.6	108.7
1967	1.0	96.5	1979	5.4	100.9	1991	5.4	114.6
1968	1.8	98.2	1980	2.7	103.6	1992	7.7	123.4
1969	3.4	101.6	1981	6.9	110.7	1993	3.4	127.6
1970	−1.6	100.0	1982	−12.2	98.5			
1971	11.0	111.0	1983	−4.6	93.9			

Percentage Distribution of Household Consumption
(Santiago)

Income Quintiles	1969	1978	1988
Lowest 20%	7.7	5.2	4.4
20%	11.7	9.3	8.2
20%	15.6	13.6	12.7
20%	20.6	21.0	20.1
Highest 20%	44.5	51.0	54.6
Total	100.1	100.1	100.0

Sources: Consumption per capita from ODEPLAN 1973; BCCh, *Indicadores* 1989, and *Boletín Mensual* 1989–90. Distribution of consumption from INE, *Encuestas* 1969–88, and Vial, Butelmann, and Celedón 1990.

Table II.21

Demographic and Health Indicators in Chile, 1960–1993

Year	Population (Millions)	Growth Rate (Percentage)	Doctors per 10,000 Inhabitants	Public Sector Doctors per 10,000 Public-Sector Inhabitants	Hospital Beds per 1,000 Inhabitants[a]	Mortality Rates (per 1,000) General	Mortality Rates (per 1,000) Infant[b]	Life Expectancy (Years at Birth)
1960	7.58	1.2	6.1		4.0	12.5	119.5	58.1
1961	7.76	2.4			3.7	11.7	106.4	58.6
1962	7.95	2.4			3.9	11.9	109.2	59.1
1963	8.14	2.4			3.7	12.0	100.3	59.6
1964	8.33	2.3	5.8		3.7	11.2	103.7	60.1
1965	8.51	2.2			4.2	10.7	97.3	60.6
1966	8.68	2.0			4.1	10.4	98.5	61.2
1967	8.85	2.0			4.1	9.7	94.7	61.8
1968	9.03	2.0	5.5		4.0	9.2	87.0	62.4
1969	9.20	1.9			3.7	9.0	83.1	63.0
1970	9.37	1.8	5.1	4.6	3.8	8.7	82.2	63.6
1971	9.53	1.7			3.8	8.6	73.9	64.3
1972	9.70	1.8			3.8	8.9	72.7	65.0
1973	9.86	1.6	5.4		3.7	8.1	65.8	65.7
1974	10.03	1.7			3.8	7.7	65.2	66.5
1975	10.20	1.7	4.3	4.3	3.3	7.2	57.6	67.2
1976	10.37	1.7			3.6	7.7	56.6	68.0
1977	10.55	1.7	6.1		3.5	6.9	50.1	68.7
1978	10.73	1.7			3.5	6.7	40.1	69.5

(continued)

Table II.21
(Continued)

Year	Population (Millions)	Growth Rate (Percentage)	Doctors per 10,000 Inhabitants	Public Sector Doctors per 10,000 Public-Sector Inhabitants	Hospital Beds per 1,000 Inhabitants[a]	Mortality Rates (per 1,000) General	Mortality Rates (per 1,000) Infant[b]	Life Expectancy (Years at Birth)
1979	10.92	1.8	6.2		3.5	6.8	37.9	70.2
1980	11.14	1.7			3.4	6.6	33.0	71.0
1981	11.32	1.7			3.3	6.2	27.0	71.1
1982	11.51	1.8		3.7	3.3	6.1	23.6	71.2
1983	11.71	1.7	8.8		3.3	6.3	21.6	71.3
1984	11.91	1.7	9.3		2.8	6.3	19.6	71.4
1985	12.12	1.6		5.0	2.8	6.1	19.5	71.5
1986	12.32	1.7		5.4	2.7	5.9	19.1	71.6
1987	12.53	1.6		5.3	2.6	5.6	18.5	71.7
1988	12.74	1.6		5.0	2.7	5.8	18.9	71.8
1989	12.96	1.5		5.1	2.8	5.8	17.1	71.9
1990	13.17	1.6		5.8	2.9	6.0	16.0	72.0
1991	13.39	1.7			3.1	5.6	14.6	72.1
1992	13.59	1.5			3.2		13.9	
1993	13.81	1.6						

Sources: Population 1960–85 from UCLA 1989; 1986–90 from BCCh, *Boletín Mensual*, March 1990 and Sept. 1991. Hospital beds, mortality rates, and life expectancy from BCCh, *Indicadores* 1989, and *Boletín Mensual* 1989–93. Doctors from WHO, *WHSA* 1964, 1968, 1973–76, 1980, 1984, PAHO 1981–84, and Ministerio de Salud 1994.

[a]Bed availability of the National Health Service is given for 1960–64, 1969, and 1987–88. [b]Infant deaths under age 1 per 1,000 born alive.

Table II.22

Rates of Contagious Diseases in Chile, 1961–1992 (Reported Cases per 100,000 Inhabitants)

Year	Diphtheria	Hepatitis	Malaria	Measles	Polio	Syphilis	Tetanus	Tuberculosis	Typhoid
1961	34.4	1.1	—[a]	489.6	8.2	—		—	58.8[b]
1962	25.2	3.1	—	468.9	5.5	—		—	45.9
1963	18.5	3.0	—	347.4	1.4	—		—	50.9[b]
1964	14.3	7.4	—	428.3	4.3	—		—	54.8
1965	12.7	14.6	—	151.7	2.4	51.8	0.7	—	64.8
1966	11.5	12.8	—	265.7	1.6	40.6	0.5	—	51.5
1967	7.2	19.8	—	172.5	0.9	43.8	0.4	—	49.8
1968	5.4	16.1	—	76.4	0.7	46.0	0.4	—	75.8
1969	3.8	37.2	—	99.7	0.7	34.3	0.5	—	56.0
1970	3.4	13.9	—	227.5	2.1	15.1	0.3	86.0	54.9
1971	4.7	29.0	—	178.1	0.6	32.4	0.4	88.5	48.2
1972	6.5	24.3	—	62.2	0.1	29.5	0.3	86.5	44.7
1973	5.5	44.4	—	39.1	—	27.2	0.3	82.4	37.3[b]
1974	4.1	27.1	—	166.8	—	38.9	0.3	79.9	46.2[b]
1975	4.2	44.0	—	82.1	—	51.2	0.4	90.7	59.6[b]
1976	4.7	46.2	—	24.3	—	54.7	0.3	7.4	59.1[b]
1977	5.3	85.6	—	10.1	—	65.0	0.2	76.9	109.3[b]
1978	5.0	56.0	—	143.3	—	95.5	0.3	74.2	122.2[b]
1979	3.2	56.6	—	315.0	—	76.9	0.2	74.2	98.6[b]
1980	2.3	38.8	—	34.6	—	73.8	0.3	76.8	97.9[b]

(continued)

Table II.22
(Continued)

Year	Diphtheria	Hepatitis	Malaria	Measles	Polio	Syphilis	Tetanus	Tuberculosis	Typhoid
1981	1.7		—	54.6	—	c	0.2	65.0	
1982	1.1	69.7	—	82.9	—		0.3	60.4	111.0
1983	0.7	90.9	—	57.8	—		0.3	59.8	119.8
1984	1.3	107.6	—	40.3	—		0.2	55.2	c
1985	1.8	c	—	141.1	—		0.2	55.0	
1986	2.2		—	102.0	—		0.2	56.5	
1987	1.3		—	21.2	—		0.2	50.0	44.4
1988	1.0		—	336.7	—	30.4	0.2	49.6	40.4
1989	0.4	80.9	—	100.4	—		0.1	51.9	50.7
1990	0.3	66.5	—	14.1	—		0.2	46.7	39.3
1991	0.2	66.6	—	15.5	—		0.1	41.1	31.6
1992		38.8	—		—			39.0	13.8

Sources: PAHO, *Health Conditions* 1961–64, 1965–68, 1969–72, 1973–76, 1977–80, 1981–84, 1990, and 1994; *Health Statistics* 1992, 1997.

[a]—No cases reported or negligible rates. [b]Includes paratyphoid fever. [c]PAHO, ceased or interrupted publication of this series on rates of contagious diseases.

Table II.23

*Access to Potable Water and Sewerage Service
in Chile, 1960–1993*

Year	Percentage of Urban Population		Percentage of Rural Population[a]
	Water[b]	Sewerage[c]	Water[d]
1960			9.5
1961			10.0
1962			10.4
1963	44.8	21.3	10.8
1964	49.2	23.4	11.3
1965	53.5	25.4	12.2
1966	56.3	26.0	17.1
1967	59.1	26.8	21.0
1968	61.7	27.8	25.8
1969	64.1	29.5	29.5
1970	66.5	31.1	34.2
1971	67.2	33.0	34.4
1972	67.9	34.8	34.6
1973	68.6	36.5	34.8
1974	69.2	38.2	35.0
1975	77.4	43.5	34.8
1976	78.2	51.5	34.5
1977	82.6	55.9	35.1
1978	86.0	56.3	37.6
1979	90.1	62.4	40.9
1980	91.4	67.4	44.2
1981	91.5	68.2	47.5
1982	92.1	70.0	51.5
1983	92.7	70.6	54.7
1984	94.3	72.9	60.3
1985	95.2	75.1	69.3
1986	97.0	77.2	70.2
1987	97.2	78.8	70.6
1988	97.7	80.1	76.0
1989	96.2	81.5	78.5
1990	96.1	80.6	81.1
1993	96.7	85.0	90.7

Sources: BCCh, *Indicadores* 1991; Ministerio de Salud 1994.

[a]Figures for coverage of sewerage service for rural populations are unavailable. [b]Piped water; ECLAC *Yearbooks* give higher percentages, probably including other sources of potable water. [c]Probably sewerage only. ECLAC *Yearbooks* give higher figures, possibly including other sources of excreta disposal. [d]Probably piped water and all other sources: ECLAC *Yearbooks* give much lower figures for piped water only.

Table II.24

Illiteracy Rates and Percentage of Age Group Enrolled by Educational Level in Chile, 1953–1992

Year	Illiteracy Rates (Percentage)			UNESCO National	Enrollment in Education[a] (Percentage)		
	National	Urban	Rural		Elementary	Secondary	Higher Education
1953	19.8						
1960	16.4	9.2	33.6		87	23	4
1965				16.4[b]	98	30	6
1970	10.7	6.8	24.0	11.0	105	38	10
1971					115	46	12
1972					118	49	15
1973					120	51	17
1974					121	50	16
1975					118	48	16
1976					116	49	14
1977					117	50	13
1978					118	52	13
1979					119	55	12
1980					113	61	11
1981					107	63	11
1982	8.3	5.8	20.0	8.9	106	63	10
1983					109	63	15
1984					108	66	15
1985				7.8	105	67	16
1986					105	68	17
1987					105	70	18
1988					102	75	19
1989					100	75	19
1990				6.6	99	74	
1992[c]	5.4	3.7	14.0	5.7	106	75	24

Sources: ECLAC, *Yearbook* 1980–93; a few figures from secondary and higher education have been taken from BCCh, *Indicadores* 1989; *Síntesis Estadística* 1994; INE 1992; UNDP, Human Development Report 1994; UNESCO 1994.

Note: Percentages for 1953, 1960, 1970, 1982, and 1992 are from population census; 1960 is based on people 15 years and older; and the rest are based on people 10 years and older. UNESCO is based on people 15 years and older with the following percentages by urban/rural areas: 1964: 9.2% and 33.6%; 1970: 6.6% and 25.6%; 1982: 6.2% and 20.9%. [a]Elementary is 6–13 years of age (rates go over 100% because of mismatch between population and education ages); secondary is 14–17; and higher is 20–24. [b]1964. [c]Enrollment in education estimated by the author.

Table II.25

Social Security Population Coverage and Costs in Chile, 1960–1993

	Percentage of Population Covered		Percentage Covered by		Cost of Social Security as Percentage of GDP	
Year	Labor Force[a]	Employed[a]	Old System	New System	Total Expenditures	State Subsidy
1960	70.8		100.0	0		
1965	73.8		100.0	0	12.3	4.4
1971	75.6[b]		100.0	0	17.5	6.9
1973	75.9		100.0	0	10.4	4.7
1976	73.0		100.0	0	10.7	3.9
1980	61.2	68.4	100.0	0	11.1	4.6
1981	65.4	73.8	42.0	58.0	12.3	6.2
1982	57.0	70.9	31.0	69.0	15.6	8.8
1983	59.0	69.1	27.1	72.9	14.3	8.2
1984	65.5	76.1	22.4	77.6	14.7	8.9
1985	70.0	79.6	18.9	81.1	13.5	8.6
1986	72.8	79.8	16.7	83.3	13.1	8.9
1987	71.3	76.8	14.9	85.1	12.2	8.0
1988	70.0	74.6	12.1	87.9	11.4	7.6
1989	74.3	78.4	10.1	89.9	11.4	6.9
1990	79.1	83.9	9.0	91.0	11.7	7.3
1991	85.7	90.5	7.9	92.1	12.2	7.3
1992	88.9	92.9	7.0	93.0	11.0	6.6
1993	90.2	94.9	6.2	93.8	11.4	6.6

Sources: Mesa-Lago 1978, 1988, 1989; SSS, *Estadísticas* 1990–93; *Costo* 1993, 1994.

[a]Based on INE. [b]1970.

Table II.26

Government Expenditures in Housing, Dwellings Built, and Housing Deficit in Chile, 1960–1993

Year	Government Expenditures in Housing		Housing Units Built			Units Built per 1,000 Inhabitants	Housing Deficit
	Percentage of Total Expenditures[a]	Index[b] (1973 = 100)	Total	Percentage Distribution			
				Public	Private		
1960	3.0						
1965	9.3		30,576[c]	52.4	47.6	3.5[c]	
1968	7.6						
1972	11.0						590,000[d]
1973	17.4	100.0					563,000
1974	17.0	91.6	20,034	14.7	85.3	2.0	571,000
1975	8.6	37.4	15,845	19.6	80.4	1.6	615,000
1976	7.5	32.9	34,220	66.3	33.7	3.3	665,000
1977	7.1	37.4	21,347	55.7	44.3	2.0	712,000
1978	5.3	27.8	20,423	14.9	85.1	1.9	766,000
1979	5.8	30.5	33,762	0.8	99.2	3.1	820,000
1980	5.5	34.1	43,310	3.7	96.3	3.9	857,000
1981	4.0	32.8	49,802	1.1	98.9	4.4	888,000
1982	1.3	11.7	24,139	1.3	98.7	2.1	912,000
1983	2.7	22.8	34,322	2.5	97.5	2.9	964,000
1984	3.9	35.3	41,675	0.5	99.5	3.5	1,009,000
1985	4.4	40.1	51,303	0.6	99.4	4.2	1,068,000
1986	4.4	40.7	52,082			4.2	1,095,000
1987	5.5	41.9	60,316			4.8	1,131,000
1988	7.7	55.8	77,501			5.9	1,031,000
1989	5.6	53.1	83,891	1.7	98.3	6.5	
1990	8.1	53.0	78,904	0.4	99.6	6.0	
1991	8.8	63.0	88,481	0.6	99.4	6.6	
1992	8.7	69.3	105,669	0.4	99.6	7.8	888,600
1993	8.7	75.9	117,392	0.3	99.7	8.6	

Sources: Percentage of expenditures 1960–68 from ODEPLAN 1973; 1972–93 from BCCh, *Boletín Mensual,* March 1994. Index based on Délano and Traslaviña 1989; Ministerio de Hacienda 1990–93. Units built from Ffrench-Davis and Raczynski 1988; Ministerio de Vivienda 1993. Housing deficit from Ffrench-Davis and Raczynski 1988; Raczynski Romaguera 1993; MacDonald 1994.

[a]Between 1960 and 1968 "housing and urbanism"; between 1972 and 1986 "housing and community amenities."
[b]Index based on expenditures in million U.S. dollars 1976. [c]1960–70 annual average. [d]1971.

Part III

CUBA
The Socialist Model

1

Introduction

1. Summary of Socioeconomic Conditions and Policies on the Eve of the Revolution

Several comparisons of Cuba with other Latin American countries in the 1950s ranked the island among the top two or three countries in socioeconomic development. But the Cuban economy suffered from serious problems that were not corrected by either the market or the government. (This chapter is mostly based on CERP 1965 and Mesa-Lago 1981.)

Compared with other Latin American countries at similar levels of development, in 1958 the Cuban state had a very low degree of ownership in production and services: none in industry and agriculture, and very small proportions in banking, construction, transportation, and trade. Public utilities such as electricity and telephones were owned by U.S. corporations that also controlled a significant share of banking. The only extensive state ownership was found in education and health facilities. Although overwhelmingly a market economy, after the Revolution of 1933 the Cuban state began to intervene in the regulation of labor conditions as well as in economic affairs. In the late 1940s and 1950s, several important institutions were established such as the National (Central) Bank of Cuba (BNC), the Agricultural and Development Bank, and the Economic and Social Development Bank. The last two banks provided credit for industrial promotion and agricultural diversification, while a Law of Industrial Stimulation introduced fiscal and tariff incentives for the creation of new industries. The state also expanded public construction and social services. In the 1950s the National Economic Council was created to program economic policies, but it lacked real power to become an effective planning agency.

Dependency on sugarcane was very high: in the 1950s the agricultural and industrial branches of sugar generated 28–29% of GNP, sugar exports accounted for 81% of total exports, and 20–25% of the labor force was employed in the sugarcane fields and mills (Pérez-López 1991). The price fluctuations of sugar in the world market, as well as the shifting sugar quota and prices fixed by the United States, were exogenous factors that Cuba could not control. Because of the dominant role of sugar, these fluctuations had a serious impact on GNP, provoking instability. The sugar sector was basically stagnant and could not provide the dynamism needed to make the economy grow vigorously. There were some signs, however, that sugar dependency was slowly declining; thus in 1957–58 that sector originated only 25% of GNP in spite of the high sugar output and exports during those years, and nonsugar industrial output grew 47% between 1947 and 1958.

GNP per capita in constant prices increased at a very low annual rate (1%) between 1950 and 1958, and inflation averaged 1% yearly. The investment ratio averaged 18% and showed an upward trend, eliciting hope that the rate of growth would rise in the future.

Cuban legislation on labor conditions and social security was among the most advanced in the region, and the trade union movement, as well as collective bargaining, were strong although usually controlled by the government. In 1956–57, nevertheless, 16% of the labor force was openly unemployed and approximately 14% underemployed. Furthermore, open unemployment increased more than twofold in the annual slack period of the sugar sector ("dead season") over the period of the harvest. The expansion of employment in construction, commerce, and industry was insufficient to absorb both the rapidly growing labor force and rural-to-urban migration. Scarce data from 1943–57 indicate that open unemployment was increasing (CERP 1963; Mesa-Lago 1972).

There are no data on income distribution, but between 1949 and 1958, the labor share of national income was 65%, the highest in the region: those employed enjoyed sufficient power to capture a significant share of national income, but their gains were largely obtained at the expense of the unemployed and the peasants. In 1957–58 Cuba's national averages in education, sanitation, health care, and social security were among the three highest in Latin America, but social service facilities were mainly concentrated in the capital and urban areas, whereas their availability and quality declined sharply in rural areas. For instance, in 1953 the illiteracy rate in rural areas was 3.6 times higher than in urban areas (41.7% and 11.6%, respectively) and similar disparities existed in income, infant mortality, access to potable water/sanitation, and housing. Most rural migrants to Havana lived in shanty towns, found low-paid work in the tertiary sector (domestic service, peddling), or became beggars. The high and growing percentage of the labor force engaged in tertiary activities was an indication of underemployment and a large informal sector.

Cuba's economy was remarkably open: in 1957–58 the trade turnover (exports plus imports) equaled more than half of GNP. Two-thirds of Cuban foreign trade was with the United States and invariably resulted in a deficit in merchandise trade (U.S. investment in Cuba was possibly the second highest in Latin America). The Cuban peso was exchanged par with the U.S. dollar, and it was freely convertible in the world market. According to one critical view, the Cuban economy was totally dependent on the United States (a situation that impeded a satisfactory degree of domestic integration on the island) and that perpetuated sugar dependency, obstructed industrialization, and induced significant inequalities (Boorstein 1968). An opposing view contends that Cuba's small size and proximity to the most powerful world economy made integration inevitable and that U.S. investment and transfer of technology were largely responsible for the relatively high development achieved on the island (CERP 1965).

In summary, during the decade prior to the Revolution, the Cuban economy had a small rate of growth that largely benefited capital and employed labor. The dominant sugar sector was basically stagnant while the nonsugar sector, although expanding, was not dynamic enough to generate vigorous economic growth and absorb the labor transfer from agriculture. Open unemployment and underemployment were high and apparently increasing. The island ranked among the top countries in the region in provision of social services, but national averages hid significant differences between urban and rural areas. Because of the openness of the Cuban economy as well as its heavy dependence on sugar exports and U.S. quotas and preferential prices, fluctuations in the sugar world price and shifts in U.S. policies had significant repercussions on the island's economy, creating considerable instability. The Cuban economy was fully integrated with the U.S. economy and had very little independence, but there is no consensus on whether that situation was avoidable as well as on its overall consequences. Although successive Cuban governments after 1933 gradually increased their intervention in the economy, particularly in the 1940s and 1950s, both state ownership and regulation were considerably low in comparison with Latin American countries at the same level of development.

2. Periodization of Revolutionary Socialist Policies: 1959–1995

There is a fair consensus among foreign experts on the economic periodization under the Revolution (one exception is Zimbalist and Eckstein 1987). Cuban economists generally follow the same periodization but stress the continuity of the process (Rodríguez 1989). Herein I identified seven stages in Cuban economic policy concerning the model of organization: (1) 1959–60, liquidation of capitalism and market erosion; (2) 1961–63, attempt to introduce an orthodox (Stalinist) central planning model; (3) 1964–66, debate over and test of alternative socialist models; (4) 1966–70, adoption and radicalization of the Guevarist model; (5) 1971–85, introduction of a moderate Soviet (pre-Gorbachev) model of economic reform; (6) 1986–90, the Rectification Process and movement away from the market; and (7) 1991 onward, collapse of the Soviet block, economic crisis, and slow move to the market. More than three decades of revolutionary policies are characterized by pendular shifts between the plan and the market but with an overwhelmingly predominance of the former. Intertwined with the policy stages on economic organization were shifting policies concerning the development strategy: (1) 1959–63, antisugar bias, industrialization, and agricultural diversification; (2) 1964–70, return to focus on the sugar sector with emphasis on huge crops; (3) 1971–90, a more balanced strategy with continuous predominance of sugar but with a better allocation of resources among various economic sectors; and (4) 1991 onward, the opening to foreign investment, technology, and capitalist markets, still with sugar dependency but increasing emphasis in tourism and other hard-currency earnings (Mesa-Lago 1971, 1978, 1981, 1988a, 1990a, 1994b, 1994c). A summary of the specific policies in each stage is given in Table III.1.

2

Liquidation of Capitalism and Market Erosion

1959–1960

1. Policies

At its inception the Revolution lacked an explicit ideology, although Fidel Castro referred to a vague doctrine of "humanism." Some scholars have noted that ECLAC's structuralism (which favored a mixed economy, decentralized-indicative planning, import substitution industrialization [ISI], agrarian and tax reforms, and progressive redistribution of income) exerted influence in this stage through well-known advisors to the Cuban government. Other scholars have attempted to prove that most revolutionaries were crypto-Marxists. Whether or not there was an underlying ideology, the new leaders soon showed nationalist, statist, antimarket, antibureaucratic, and distributional preferences. Fidel Castro and his close associates did not have any knowledge of economics (most of them were lawyers), and the few economists occupying government posts were soon dismissed and their jobs passed to enthusiastic but inexperienced revolutionaries. For example, Ernesto Guevara, a physician, first became the head of the Industrialization Department of the National Institute of Agrarian Reform (INRA), then president of the National Bank of Cuba, and finally the Minister of Industry. Bureaucrats and technicians were viewed as opportunists who deliberately complicated economic and administrative matters in hopes of making themselves indispensable. Partly because of their ignorance in economic matters and partly because they were captivated by the Revolution's almost magical success against the supposedly technical army of the overthrown dictatorship, the revolutionary leaders proposed the application of guerrilla techniques to the Cuban economy. It was widely believed that the nation's major socioeconomic problems

175

would be rapidly and simultaneously resolved by the power of the Revolution, the zeal and hard work of the leaders, the audacity of the improvisation, and the enthusiasm and support of the people. Willingness, consciousness, morale, austerity, and loyalty were emphasized over material and human resources, technology, and knowledge and expertise (Mesa-Lago 1981).

A. Ownership

Collectivization of the means of production slowly increased in 1959 and gained momentum in the second half of 1960. This occurred either because the leadership believed it was a necessary step toward achieving their developmental goals or because they were forced to do it by domestic and international events or by a combination of both. In 1959 several means were used in the collectivization process: confiscation of property and assets embezzled by officials of the overthrown dictatorship; expropriation of *latifundia* (farms exceeding a ceiling of 400 ha) through the first Agrarian Reform Law; expropriation of rental housing; state intervention in enterprises (factories, warehouses, transportation) abandoned by their owners or in which labor conflicts disrupted production; confiscation of assets of those who failed to pay taxes; and confiscation of all property belonging to those convicted of counterrevolutionary crimes or who had become political exiles. Expropriated farms under the Agrarian Reform of 1959 were to be divided and distributed to landless peasants. Although about 200,000 of them were indeed entitled to property, the bulk of the expropriated land (particularly sugarcane plantations and cattle ranches) was not divided but organized in state-controlled cooperatives with the argument that the partition of *latifundia* would provoke declines in productivity and output.

In successive waves between June and October 1960, the collectivization process was rapidly extended. All foreign-owned oil refineries, U.S.-owned sugar mills, banks, and telephone and electricity corporations were involved, as were all remaining U.S. properties as well as most domestically owned major industries, banks, and transportation businesses. By the end of 1960 all domestic wholesale and foreign trade and banking, and most transportation, industry, construction, and retail trade as well as more than one-third of agriculture was in state hands (Table III.2). This swift transfer of ownership liquidated the capitalist system and brought about the erosion of the automatic mechanisms of the market; as a result, production and distribution of goods and services partly ceased to be determined by the laws of supply and demand (CERP 1965; Mesa-Lago 1981).

B. Planning, Financing, Stability, and Prices

Several government agencies were created during this stage to regulate or dominate economic activities. The first was INRA, which gradually grew to become a bureaucratic giant controlling one-third of agriculture and a significant part of industry and which developed the first experiments with central planning. The Central Planning Board (JUCEPLAN) was initially established in March 1960 to coordinate government policies and to guide the private sector through indicative planning; however, these functions were never exercised, and, in the second stage, JUCEPLAN would become the agency for state central planning. Financing of the economy was increasingly done by the state, with private financing largely restricted to agriculture. The Ministry of Finance began to control financing through the state budget, while the National Bank expanded its command over credit and foreign exchange. The Ministry of Labor played an increasing role as labor arbiter and fixer of labor conditions, a step toward taming trade unions. During most of this stage, prices were mainly set in the market, but the government began to control prices, largely through collectivized public utilities (electricity, telephones, transportation). Increasing state expenditures were partly offset by augmented fiscal revenues, mostly through a more efficient tax system and profits of collectivized businesses; still there was a significant increase in the money supply, probably exceeding production. The collectivization process and the dissatisfaction of managers and technicians provoked the exodus of this vital group. Their jobs were promptly filled with loyal but inexperienced revolutionaries, the cadres that in the early 1960s would become responsible for the implementation of central planning as a substitute for the market forces (Boorstein 1968; Mesa-Lago and Zephirin 1971).

C. Development Strategy

Cuban leaders associated the island's economic problems with sugar dependency, hence their first development strategy (which began in 1960, gained momentum in 1961, and ended in 1963) had a distinct antisugar bias. The goal of diversification was to be achieved by two means: a rapid process of import substitution industrialization and agricultural diversification away from sugar and toward rice, tubers, fruits, and vegetables. State investment gave priority to these economic sectors, and agrarian reform plus nationalization of industry was to provide the necessary premises for the ambitious program of diversification (Mesa-Lago 1971; Ritter 1974).

D. External Sector

One of the Revolution's major targets was to reduce economic dependency on the United States. Early in 1960 a Soviet industrial fair was held in Havana, and a five-year (1960–64) trade agreement was signed with the Soviet Union that granted preferential status to the island, and committed the Soviets to buy one million tons of sugar annually and to supply oil, machinery, and chemicals. The Soviet Union also opened a credit line for U.S.$100 million to supply needed capital goods, construct factories, and undertake geological exploration. Other trade and economic agreements were signed with the German Democratic Republic (GDR) and Czechoslovakia. In mid-1960 U.S. refineries refused to process imports of Soviet oil crude; hence they were nationalized and began to refine Soviet oil. By the end of that year practically all Cuba's oil was imported from the Soviet Union. The United States reacted by suspending the sugar import quota from Cuba; the Soviet Union and China in turn made commitments to buy (at world market prices) most of that sugar. Soviet imports of Cuban sugar were actually higher than the island's loss of U.S. imports, and all socialist imports combined significantly surpassed U.S. imports in the early part of that year. The nationalization of all U.S. investment in October led to the imposition of an U.S. economic embargo on the island and the termination of trade between the two countries. By the end of 1960 the Cuban government tightly controlled foreign trade. In this stage the Cuban peso was still freely exchanged par with the U.S. dollar (Mesa-Lago 1971, 1978; Mesa-Lago and Gil 1989; Pérez-López 1991).

E. Labor and Employment

Unions held free elections in 1959, but government interference and pressure began at the end of that year, and open control measures were imposed in 1960. Collective bargaining was suspended at the end of 1959, and in 1960 the Ministry of Labor started to set wages and regulate labor conditions. Because of the collectivization process, employment in the state sector grew from 9% to about half of the labor force in 1959–60. With such control, an important target of public policy was to reduce unemployment. In agriculture, seasonal unemployment was cut by rural-to-urban migration partly encouraged by peasant mobilizations in the largest cities. Thus, the population of Havana increased in 1960 more than twice the average annual growth of the 1950s. Part of the migrants were hired by the armed forces, state security and police, unions and other mass organizations, public works and social services; others joined the ranks of urban unemployed and underemployed. Thousands of young peasants received scholarships that delayed their immediate entry into the labor force. Land ownership granted by the agrarian reform did not significantly increase rural employment because most of the new farm owners worked the same land before as sharecroppers, lessees, and so forth (Mesa-Lago and Hernández 1971; Mesa-Lago 1972).

F. Distribution and Social Services

Distributional policies included increases in overall wages, the minimum wage in agriculture, and minimum pensions. The disposable income of the poorest sector was augmented by reduction of electricity rates and urban housing rent by as much as 50%: the urban reform law of 1960 also entitled lessees to buy the house in which they were living by paying the rent to the state for a period ranging from 5 to 20 years. Disposable income also grew because of the expansion of free education and health care and subsidized public housing. The collectivization of land, real estate, banking, and most means of production virtually eliminated dividends, rent, and interest except in agriculture. The net result of these two sets of policies was a decrease in extreme income differentials. Furthermore, the expansion in social services was concentrated in rural areas, which helped to reduce the gap in living standards with urban areas. These policies ensured wide popular support for the Revolution but sharply reduced the investment share of GDP; furthermore, consumption increased faster than production and imports, rapidly depleting stocks (Mesa-Lago 1971, 1981).

2. Performance

A. Growth

Socioeconomic performance in the first two years of the Revolution is extremely difficult to assess because of lack of data. Statistical series usually begin in 1962 with the introduction of planning and usually omit data from 1959 to 1961. Apparently economic growth continued in the first two years of the Revolution, accomplished by fair sugar crops, full utilization of installed equipment, accumulated stocks and inventories, and foreign exchange reserves. Nonofficial estimates of the investment share indicate a significant decline in this stage. Sugar output increased 3% in 1959 (because of the end of the civil war) and slightly declined in 1960, but it was still above the 1958 level (Table III.11). Nickel output sharply declined in 1960 after the two U.S. nickel plants were nationalized; the largest, most modern plant in Moa was paralyzed for several years because managers and technicians had fled. With the exception of tobacco and cigars, output of most agricultural and industrial products increased in this stage (Table III.10). The FAO index of agricultural output per capita increased in 1959 and was stagnant in 1960, while two indices of industrial output suggest steady increases in both years (FAO 1970).

B. Inflation

Accurate figures on inflation are not available; it probably increased by the sharp expansion of disposable income and government expansionary policy, but it did not get out of hand because state revenue boomed from collecting delinquent taxes. A Cuban estimate released in 1989 sets the average annual inflation rate in 1959–61 at 2%.

C. Diversification, Trade Balance, and External Dependency

Since Cuba's macroeconomic series began in 1962 there are no data on diversification for this stage, but probably there was little or none. The new diversification strategy was launched in 1960 and did not have enough time to produce significant results. The value of exports declined in 1959–60, but so did the value of imports; hence the deficit in the trade balance in 1959 was similar to that of the previous year, and a tiny trade surplus was generated in 1960. Trade with the Soviet Union increased from 1% to 16% (17% including other Eastern European countries) in 1959–60 and generated healthy surpluses (Tables III.16, III.20). The Soviet Union and other socialist countries prevented the collapse of the Revolution under U.S. retaliatory trade policies.

D. Unemployment, Equality, and Social Indications

Open unemployment was either stagnant or reduced somewhat by growth of employment in rural areas, but it probably increased in urban areas. A 1960 labor census noted an increase in open unemployment, while annual surveys suggested some decline (Table III.26). Social expenditures gradually increased in this stage in social security, education, health care, and housing. Income distribution probably became more equal through reduction of non-wage income at the top of the income ladder and increase of disposable income at the bottom (but no data are available). The birth rate steadily rose while the crude mortality rate was almost stagnant; hence the population growth rate increased in 1959, but a first wave of emigration reduced the rate in 1960 (Tables III.27, III.30; Mesa-Lago 1994b).

3
Orthodox (Stalinist) Central Planning Model

1961–1963

The year 1961 brought the break of diplomatic relations with the United States, the defeat of the U.S.-sponsored Bay of Pigs invasion, which consolidated the Revolution, and the declaration that the Revolution was socialist and its maximum leader a Marxist. Facing the collapse of the market and having established a close politico-economic alliance with the Soviet Union (which secured the survival of the Revolution), the Cuban leaders decided to copy the extant Soviet model of planning. The Cuban strategy of industrialization, initiated in the first stage, fit the Soviet development model as well and hence remained in place. But multiple factors would soon render both approaches unfeasible.

1. Policies

A. Ownership

In spite of the warnings against too broad and rapid collectivization by some Western Marxist planners (e.g., Charles Bettelheim and René Dumont), that process continued unabated in the second stage (Table III.2): in 1961 all private educational institutions and large hospitals were nationalized; in 1962 rationing was introduced and most of the remaining private retail trade stores were collectivized into a state network of groceries and shops; and also in 1962 private agricultural cooperatives established after 1959 on nationalized latifundia were transformed into state farms. In 1963 the second Agrarian Reform Law expropriated land of farms having more than 67 ha, hence eliminating the midsized farmer; in the meantime, the state secured control of private agriculture through the INRA introducing procurement quotas (*acopio,* that is, compulsory sale of part of the crop to the state at prices set below the market price) and the incorporation of all private peasants into the state-controlled National Association of Small Farmers (ANAP). Finally, in 1963 the process of collectivization of private social insurance funds was completed, and all funds were integrated into a united state social security/health-care system.

By 1963 only 30% of agriculture and 25% of retail trade (mostly street vendors) were in private hands; the rest of the economy was virtually in state hands (Table III.2). The process of collectivization, therefore, was completed with extraordinary velocity (five years) and scope, avoiding bloody confrontations as in other socialist countries, although in 1963–65, small groups of peasants fought in the mountains and were crushed (Mesa-Lago 1971, 1981).

B. Planning

The shift from the market to the plan was influenced by Western Marxist scholars such as Leo Huberman, Paul Sweezy, Paul Baran, and Ernest Mandel, but most technical advice came from the Soviet Union and Czechoslovakia. The Cuban leadership rejected the alternative of market socialism (theoretically developed in the West in the late 1920s and 1930s, and first tried in Yugoslavia in the 1950s), which had a few domestic supporters as well as the backing of French economist René Dumont. Instead, Cuba copied the highly centralized physical planning model typical of command economies. Introduced by Stalin in the Soviet Union at the end of the 1920s, central planning was applied there until the mid-1960s, when a timid infusion of very limited market mechanisms took place; it was weakened by Gorbachev's *perestroika* and vanished in the 1990s. From the Soviet Union the Stalinist model spread throughout Eastern European and Asian communist countries until the market-oriented economic reforms, which began in the 1950s and gained momentum in those regions in the 1970s and 1980s.

The Stalinist model began to be introduced in Cuba early in 1961 with the creation of a new administrative structure. At its center was JUCEPLAN, now modified and in charge of the formulation and implementation of annual and medium-range economic plans. A network of central ministries and agencies was created to take over the recently collectivized economic sectors, mostly organized as state monopolies. In the industrial sector, a new ministry was created combining INRA's factories with new nationalized industries. Eventually, the Ministry of Industries would be subdivided into several smaller ministries: dealing with sugar, basic industry, light industry, mining and metallurgy, and food production. INRA remained in charge of agriculture, but later its sugar sector would be transferred to a new Ministry of Sugar, and INRA would become the Ministry of Agriculture. A Ministry of Construction was put in charge of all public building activity. The National Bank of Cuba (BNC) became the treasury, issuer, and controller of currency, depository bank, and manager of credit. In turn the Ministry of Finance was given responsibility for the state budget, which became the national financial plan for investment. The Ministry of Domestic Trade took over the national network of state stores and the administration of rationing as well as the distribution of nonrationed goods. The Ministry of Foreign Trade exercised direct control over virtually all imports and exports. The Ministry of Labor began to set wages and output standards nationally. Previously existing ministries in the social services became the sole administrators of such services as education and health care.

State enterprises producing the same type of goods (or providing similar services) were merged into trusts controlled by the corresponding central ministry. In 1958 there were about 38,300 industrial firms; by 1961, 18,500 industrial enterprises accounting for 80% of industrial output had been combined into several trusts. In agriculture, state farms (similar to the Soviet *sovkhoz*) became integrated with either INRA or the Ministry of Sugar. The average size of the state farm in 1961 was 8,870 ha, but it increased to about 10,000 ha within two years (Bernardo 1971). The ministries and central agencies were hastily organized and staffed with inadequate personnel, as most technicians and managers had fled the country after mid-1960 (after the big nationalization wave) and particularly after the defeat of the Bay of Pigs invasion in 1961.

Three medium-range plans, all following Soviet techniques, were rapidly drawn up: one at the end of 1960 by the Polish planner Michael Kalecki and two by mid-1961 by the Frenchman Bettelheim and the Russian A. Efinov. The last covered 1962–65 in order to adjust it to ongoing five-year plans in the Soviet Union and Eastern Europe. This plan became a theoretical study divorced from reality, which did not work in practice because of the planners' lack of real knowledge of the Cuban economy, the absence of sectorial studies as well as comprehensive and reliable statistics, and the fact that the leaders did not define economic directives well enough to allow the elaboration of concrete targets by the planners. Furthermore, the development strategy of diversification failed in 1963, making the 1962–65 plan unfeasible.

In March 1961 work began on the 1962 annual plan with the aid of Czech advisors. Their efforts were hindered though by the short time they had, the lack of both accurate statistics and trained cadres, and the fact that the Czech model was inappropriate. It was too centralized, shaped by a developed, industrialized economy, and was rigidly applied with no effort to adapt it to Cuba's insular, monoculture, developing economy. Figures were grossly estimated or invented, there was no real input and feedback from lower echelons, and hence production goals were too optimistic with no basis in reality. This problem was aggravated because planning targets were mostly measured by gross output and disregarded enterprise efficiency and profitability as well as quality of products. When the final version of the plan was ready (in May 1962), its gross miscalculations made it practically useless. Apparently, other plans were elaborated for 1963 and 1964, but we lack information on whether or not they were applied.

Cast in the old Soviet die, Cuban planning involved five steps: (1) basic economic directives consisting of highly aggregated guidelines (desirable growth rate, overall shares of consumption and investment) decided by the Executive and handed down to the planners; (2) a "global model" or aggregated projections and overall targets prepared by JUCEPLAN, which also ought to ensure their consistency (mainly through material and financial balances); (3) "control figures" or desegregated preliminary targets set by successive approximation in discussions of JUCEPLAN with the central ministries and between the latter and the corresponding enterprises; (4) "directive figures" or final desegregated targets determined on the way up as the control figures are revised and then discrepancies and inconsistencies are eliminated by JUCEPLAN; and (5) control of execution and revisions. This process suffered from the typical flaws experienced by central plans elsewhere; for instance, the needed interrelations among enterprises were not always developed, or consistency among targets not achieved, hence creating bottlenecks, surpluses, and shortages. Lack of fulfillment of a target by a crucial unit (whose output was input for other units) unleashed a chain reaction of nonfulfillment. Optimistic targets of domestic production combined with failure or delay in imports introduced additional problems. Last but not least, the information on evolving changes was not processed and transmitted rapidly enough to avoid some of the problems described above.

Other reasons peculiar to Cuba contributed to the failure of planning in this stage. The collectivization was too widespread and too rapid; hence millions of economic microrelations were destroyed at once, breaking the automatic mechanisms of the market when the state was not ready to take over these functions. The new central ministries and agencies lacked coordination among themselves, were hastily organized and staffed with inexperienced personnel, and operated in a freewheeling manner with no control procedures. Economic decisions were taken by the political leadership without consultation with JUCEPLAN, which resulted in serious inconsistencies. No investment plan existed, and investment decisions were not coordinated.

Land collectivization and the *acopio* system dislocated the flow of supplies from the countryside to the towns. Because of lack of information or managerial control, agricultural products badly needed in the cities were lost in the ground, forgotten, or, after being harvested, spoiled because of unavailable transportation (Boorstein 1968; Mesa-Lago and Zephirin 1971; Bernardo 1971).

C. Financing

Financing of the state economy was done through the national budget and central allocations from the Ministry of Finance to all public enterprises, farms, and agencies. This system, called budgetary finance (*sistema presupuestario*), began late in 1960 in INRA's Department of Industry, controlled by Guevara. Several laws enacted in 1961–63 organized all the new planning and central agencies around the budgetary finance system (this system is described further in chapter 4 below).

The government tried to reduce consumption (mostly through rationing) in order to augment capital formation. In addition, the investment share of the productive sector increased from 70.7% to 74.6% in 1962–63, while the corresponding share of the "nonproductive" sector (social services) declined from 29.3% to 25.4% (JUCEPLAN, *BEC* 1966). In the same vein, state budget allocations to finance production rose from 32.9% to 41.6% while the corresponding proportion of social services shrank from 35.7% to 33.7% (Table III.6). In the allocation of capital between alternative projects the Cubans used neither the Stalinist "coefficient of investment effectiveness" (based on the "payoff period") nor the interest rate; instead, investment decisions were made by the top leadership in an arbitrary manner. Lacking mechanisms to ensure efficiency, part of the increase in investment was wasted because of poor capital productivity (Bernardo 1971; Mesa-Lago 1971).

D. Stability and Prices

Beginning in 1962 annual state budgets with enormous scope (practically embracing all of the nation's economy) were prepared by the Ministry of Finance. But the necessary integration between the budget and the plan was not always accomplished, and budget accounting techniques were primitive. More than one-third of the budget was allocated to finance production, another third to social services, and most of the remaining third to defense and public administration (Table III.6). In the preliminary version of the budget, revenue and expenditures were in equilibrium, and no further information was published on the execution of the budget.

Most prices began to be centrally fixed by 1962, and physical allocation of consumer goods through rationing started that year (Table III.29). Rationed consumer goods were subsidized, and their prices remained basically frozen after 1961. According to the government's logic, if the market had been allowed to set the price of essential consumer goods, the substantial excess of demand over supply (due to expanding disposable income and stagnant or declining output) would have provoked skyrocketing inflation, thus hurting the lowest income groups, who were the strongest supporters of the regime. Rationing and subsidies, therefore, had both equalitarian and political purposes. Following the Soviet example, prices for *acopio* were set below the market as an indirect tax on private farmers to generate revenue for industrialization and to keep that group from getting excessive earnings (Mesa-Lago 1971, 1981).

E. Development Strategy

As part of the program of agrarian diversification and to decrease dependence on sugar, large estates producing sugarcane were cleared and replanted with rice, fruits, or vegetables; hence between 1958 and 1963, the total planted area of sugarcane was reduced by 25%. In 1961, 175,000 ha of cooperative sugar land were shifted to the cultivation of beans, peanuts, rice, cotton, tubers, and pasture, and in 1959–62, nine sugar mills, which amounted to almost 3% of grinding capacity, were dismantled. But two other reasons for this strategy could have been a decline in the world market price of sugar (due to Cuba's exceptionally high sugar crop of 1961 and high sugar production in Western Europe), and Cuba's poor sugar export opportunities in hard currency, after the loss of the U.S. market. A steady expansion of Cuba's fishing fleet took place in this stage: in 1962, 17 Soviet and East German long-range trawlers began to fish in more remote waters, while 100 wooden vessels built in 1963 fished closer to home.

In 1962–63 the investment share of industry was sharply increased from 23% to 31.6%, while the corresponding share of agriculture was cut from 29.4 to 24.3% (JUCEPLAN, *BEC* 1966). A substantial amount of domestic investment, together with foreign loans, was used to purchase manufacturing equipment from the Soviet Union, Czechoslovakia, and East Germany. In 1961 Minister of Economy Regino Boti forecast that by 1965 Cuba would lead Latin America in per capita output of electricity, steel, cement, tractors, and refined petroleum. In turn, Minister of Industries Guevara spoke of plans to produce trucks, internal combustion engines, and even automobiles (Mesa-Lago 1971; Ritter 1974; Pérez-López 1991). The ambitious industrialization plans did not materialize for various reasons. Some of the manufacturing equipment for the new factories imported from the socialist bloc was obsolete, which made competition by Cuban-manufactured products difficult in the international market. The lack of technicians hindered the Cubans in installing the new equipment as quickly as it was received; hence, machinery often piled up on the docks and rusted while waiting to be put into use. Some of the new factories required raw materials that were not produced domestically and had to be imported from socialist countries, reinforcing Cuba's external dependence. Petroleum exploration by Soviet geologists was unsuccessful; the island lacks coal, and its rivers do not have sufficient volume to generate enough hydroelectric energy; and the supply of oil from the Soviet Union (98% of Cuban needs) was very costly and required shipping it via tankers every 2 1/2 days. The island has a very small domestic market and almost no opportunity to export manufactured goods to the Western Hemisphere because of the U.S. economic embargo, which also made it difficult to obtain spare parts for U.S. equipment. The U.S. threat combined with Cuba's subversion in Latin America led Cuba to spend 13.3% of the 1962 budget in defense, which took resources away from development. Finally, the least industrialized countries of the socialist bloc also pursued the same industrialization strategy and, therefore, were not logical buyers of Cuba's manufactured goods.

F. External Sector

The shift of trade and aid away from the United States toward the Soviet Union was completed during this stage. Two events in 1962 accelerated this trend: the Missile Crisis, which led to the halt of all U.S. airline flights to the island, and the decision by the Organization of American States (OAS) to oust Cuba, thus beginning the nation's gradual isolation in the Western Hemisphere.

In 1961 the Soviet Union bought 51% of Cuban sugar exports, and all socialist countries combined bought 75%. And yet, when world sugar prices skyrocketed in 1963, these proportions declined to 28% and 59%, respectively, as Cuba took advantage of higher world market prices. In 1961–63 Soviet loans for U.S.$54 million plus technical assistance were awarded to Cuba for a fishing port and fleet, irrigation facilities, the nickel industry, and fertilizer factories; and more than 1,000 Soviet technicians started to work on the island (Mesa-Lago and Gil 1989). Additional trade and aid came from Eastern Europe and China. The Soviet agreement with the United States to withdraw the missiles in 1962 (without consulting Cuban leaders) provoked the first political skirmish between the two socialist partners.

G. Labor and Employment

The government completed its control of the labor movement by removing democratic leaders and installing old communists in the Confederation of Cuban Workers (CTC). A law on trade union organization, enacted in 1961, among various union objectives set out to help managers of state enterprises to fulfill production plans and promote efficiency. The new labor leaders argued that, under capitalism, the main function of the union movement was to fight for labor demands, but under socialism and the dictatorship of the proletariat, such a struggle lost its meaning (because the state administration and the workers were united); hence the shift in union objectives. In 1962 the Ministry of Labor, theoretically representing the workers, was empowered to fix all wages and labor conditions; therefore, collective bargaining also changed its goals from regulation of labor conditions to fulfillment of production plans and improvement of productivity. Government leaders also stated that strikes had become anachronistic, as it was unthinkable that the workers would strike against themselves. In 1961 a movement began, led by the controlled unions, to exhort the workers with high wages and fringe benefits to stop demands for wage increases and to renounce some of their "privileges" resulting from the strategic nature of their trades or enterprise profitability. In 1963 a pilot plan was begun to establish output or work quotas (*normas*) and wage scales. The former specify how many items of standard quality a worker must produce in a given time period. The scales fix national uniform wages for the performance of the same type of work regardless of enterprise profitability. Quotas and scales were set by the Ministry of Labor and gradually became interconnected: a worker must completely fulfill his or her corresponding quota in order to draw the corresponding wage rate from his or her wage scale. If the quota was overfulfilled, a bonus was paid (at a ratio of 0.5% for each 1% in excess); conversely, if the quota was underfulfilled, the wage would be cut proportionally. In 1962 workers began to be mobilized by the government and unions to perform voluntary (unpaid) labor after the work schedule and on weekends and vacations; the main target was to help with the sugar harvest and other crops that suffered a manpower deficit (Mesa-Lago and Hernández 1971).

State employment increased from half of the labor force in 1960 to two-thirds in 1963 because of the process of collectivization in agriculture and services. State farms provided stable employment throughout the year to many peasants previously affected by seasonal unemployment. Most of the unemployed found jobs in the state service sector, which increased twofold between 1958 and 1964, including social services, the armed forces (which reached 16% of the labor force in 1963), and the state bureaucracy. Apparently, there was also a growth of self-employment in personal services (such as repair work, tailoring, hairdressing) as well as in the booming black market. But employment shrank in commerce, tourism, insurance, real estate, and legal offices as a result of collectivization. The labor surplus accumulated in the cities could not be productively employed in the industrial sector, partly because of the contraction in the old U.S.-built industry. In addition, Guevara acknowledged that none of the basic industries acquired from the socialist camp would be in operation between 1961 and 1965 and hence could not reduce unemployment. Furthermore, the new factories were highly mechanized and required relatively little manpower. The policies of merging factories into trusts (which eliminated redundant jobs) and promoting mechanization (in cigar manufacturing, sugar packing, and bulk loading) also generated a labor surplus. However, these policies were not followed by massive layoffs as most redundant workers were kept on the payroll as surplus (*excedentes*) waiting for a transfer to productive jobs or to be retrained.

Subsidies paid to thousands of *excedentes* through the enterprises payroll must have led to a decline in productivity in industry. A similar effect occurred in agriculture, where state farmers reduced their labor effort, as they no longer feared unemployment, enjoyed a guaranteed wage, and lacked incentives and checks. The slackened labor effort created an artificial manpower deficit, particularly acute in the sugar harvest, which previously was handled by the seasonally unemployed. In a typical vicious circle, managers of state farms hired more employees, thus expanding overstaffing and reducing productivity further (Mesa-Lago and Hernández 1971; Mesa-Lago 1972, 1981).

H. Distribution and Social Services

Through the continued process of collectivization, income inequality was further reduced in this stage: private owners of educational and health services lost their high income, midsized farmers were wiped out, and the *acopio* limited the income of small farmers. Because most means of production became state owned (except 30% in agriculture and 25% in retail trade—mostly street vendors), practically all income earned in Cuba was paid and fixed by the government as wages and salaries (as well as *acopio* to peasants, and pensions). The freezing of wages and yielding of "privileges" enjoyed by the "labor aristocracy" and the introduction of wage scales helped to reduce wage differences (particularly reducing the income of those at the top). The continuous expansion of free social services (although at a slower pace in this stage) benefited the lowest income groups. Finally, rationing was an equalizer, as it assured a minimum supply of essential consumer goods to all the population regardless of income.

Two important social events occurred during this stage. In 1961 the government launched a national campaign to wipe out illiteracy, mobilizing thousands of students, particularly in the countryside. In 1963 a social security law completed the unification and standardization of the system (except for the armed forces), extended coverage of pensions to the entire salaried labor force, and created an universal and unified national health-care system for the entire population. The number of doctors per 10,000 inhabitants, which had declined from 9.2 to 5.4 between 1958 and 1962 because of the exodus of physicians, increased to 8.9 in 1963, but this might have been the result of incorporation of private physicians into the public sector (Mesa-Lago 1971, 1981, 1990b; Table III.30).

2. Performance

A. Growth

Although we lack statistics, it is clear that economic growth continued in 1961, fueled by the second largest sugar crop in history; the harvest took place during the first four months of the year, when the full impact of collectivization and administrative reform had not yet occurred. But during the next two years, the situation rapidly deteriorated, provoking the first recession under the Revolution. The 25% reduction of the cultivated area of sugarcane, the scarcity of professional cane cutters (who moved on to easier jobs), and the disorganization created in this sector by the new state farm structure had a heavy toll on sugar output: a decline of 28% in 1962 and another 21% in 1963 (the latter was the second lowest crop under the Revolution). In addition, several agricultural products (tobacco, coffee, beans, tubers) suffered output declines, and although the number of cattle and poultry reportedly increased, that of pigs declined. According to FAO (1970), agricultural output per capita in 1963 was 38 percentage points below that of 1961. (The devastating effects of hurricane Flora, which hit the eastern provinces of Cuba, also contributed to the negative outcome in 1963.) Conversely, fish output increased 13% in 1960–63. In mining, nickel output almost recovered the 1957 level, but, after an increase in 1962, production of crude oil sharply declined in 1963. The output of key industrial products such as electricity, cigars, textiles, and beer decreased or was stagnant, while cement increased and then declined. Contributing to this failure was the lack of spare parts—virtually all Cuban factories were still U.S. made—the exodus of foreign and domestic industrial managers and technicians, and the poor planning and delays in the installation of the newly purchased factories. Contrary to the leaders' forecasts, in 1963 Cuba was not producing tractors, trucks, or combustion engines, and the dream of leading Latin America in industrial output per capita was shattered. In services, the number of tourists was cut in half in 1959–60, and statistics were discontinued thereafter until 1970.

Hard data on macroeconomic indicators for this stage are very scarce. The only figure on economic growth in this period is available for 1963; it shows that the global social product (GSP)[1] per capita in constant prices declined 3.7% that year. Because of restrictions in consumption and social services, however, the share of gross domestic investment in GSP apparently increased from 11.1% to 12.4% in 1962–63 (Table III.3; data are not available for 1961), but investment productivity probably declined because of inefficiencies in the allocation and use of capital.

B. Inflation

In spite of rationing, inflation in 1963 reached 10.2%, possibly the second highest rate under the Revolution until the 1990s (Table III.3). In 1962 the cumulative monetary surplus in the population (or "monetary overhang": excess money in circulation and bank deposits with which practically nothing could be bought) was close to the total population income that year (Table III.5), a fact that adversely affected labor motivation and incentives. Black market prices were from five to ten times higher than official prices. Furthermore, the lack of a sufficient supply of goods to meet the established rationing quotas for the entire population led to long lines in front of state stores. Low *acopio* prices became a disincentive for private farmers, who tried to avoid selling their crops to the state and largely shifted their surpluses to the black market. Finally, price rigidity in state stores prevented the reduction of prices of perishable goods.

1. GSP is based on the Soviet-style "material product system" (MPS), which significantly differs from GNP, based on the "system of national accounts" (SNA), typical of market economies. GSP excludes the value of "nonmaterial services" (e.g., social services, defense, bureaucracy) and, in this sense, is smaller than GDP. Conversely GSP does not use the "value-added" method typical in the calculation of GDP; therefore, GSP is usually "inflated" by the double counting of the same item and, hence, is larger than GDP. It is debatable which is the net result of these two opposite distortions. The conversion of Cuban GSP into GDP (or GNP) is available only for 1974, although some data exist for other years in the 1970s and the 1990s but lacking information on the conversion (Mesa-Lago and Pérez-López 1985a). These authors maintained that GSP was smaller than GDP because double counting was larger than the exclusion of nonmaterial services, while other scholars argued the opposite view (Zimbalist 1988).

C. Diversification, Trade Balance, and External Dependency

Cuba was able to reduce its dependency on sugar in 1962–63 (because of a decline in sugar output) at least in terms of GSP but not in its export concentration, which actually increased (Tables III.11, III.17). Furthermore, decreasing sugar output and exports created a bottleneck in the industrialization program. The decline in output of the principal exports (sugar, tobacco) cut the value of total exports by 13% in 1961–63 while the value of imports increased 27%. Although there was a small trade surplus in 1960, in 1961 a small trade deficit appeared, and the cumulative deficit in 1962–63 surpassed a half billion pesos (the peso-dollar exchange continued to be par in this stage). The share of Cuba's turnover trade with the Council of Mutual Economic Assistance (CMEA: the Soviet Union/Eastern European common market) reached 67% in 1962 and almost 50% with the Soviet Union; 92% of Cuba's trade deficit in 1963 was with the Soviet Union (Tables III.16, III.20). (In 1963 world sugar prices boomed—largely because of Cuba's bad crop and lower exports—while Soviet prices remained unchanged, resulting in a 2.3 to 1 price ratio against Cuba.) The Soviets provided credits to back up Cuba's trade deficit, but this aid rapidly increased the island's foreign debt. Dependency on Soviet oil was unabated: there was a vigorous increase in domestic production in 1962 but it met only 0.8% of total supply, and domestic oil output declined in 1963 (Table III.21). These external constraints, combined with the domestic problems already discussed, made it clear that the development strategy of rapid industrialization was unfeasible. Cuba achieved full economic independence from the United States (and survived the U.S. economic embargo as well as increasing hemispheric isolation) only to become dependent on the Soviet Union. It is true that the latter did not have direct investment in Cuba and provided it with generous aid, but still the island was heavily dependent on the vital Soviet pipeline of oil, credit, weapons, and a myriad of other imports.

D. Unemployment

By 1963 open unemployment in Cuba had probably been cut to one-half the prerevolutionary rate, but this was achieved by transforming most of the open unemployment into underemployment. Such a shift meant solving in the short run the social problem but spreading the economic costs to the entire population and negatively affecting labor productivity and economic growth. State farmers enjoyed guaranteed jobs and wages year-round, but their productivity was one-half that of private farmers. In 1963 employees of state farms worked only an average of 4.5 to 5 hours per day but were paid for 8. Industrial mergers and shutdowns should have generated unemployment, but unneeded workers remained on the enterprise payroll. The tertiary sector became hypertrophied with the expansion of the bureaucracy, social services, the armed forces, and internal security. (The only available figure on labor productivity shows stagnation in 1963; see JUCEPLAN, *BEC* 1966.) An artificial manpower deficit appeared in 1962 in the main crops, particularly sugar; to cope with it, the government resorted to mobilization of voluntary labor trying to transfer the urban labor surplus to the countryside. In many cases, however, the cost of mobilizing the inexperienced volunteers was higher than the value of the product created by them. The initial hope of productively employing the urban sector in the new industries was gone in 1963.

E. Equality

There are no official data on income distribution prior to and under the Revolution but only gross speculative estimates elaborated by Western scholars (occasionally quoted in Cuban publications without adding any new data). Two of these estimates indicate a substantial redistribution of income in the first four years of the Revolution but with some important differences: one estimate, based on family income in 1958 and 1962, calculated that about 8% of income from the wealthiest quintile was mostly transferred, in similar proportions, to the poorest and next poorer quintiles, while the income of the middle quintile increased only slightly; the other estimate, based on personal income in 1953 and 1962, showed that 16.5% was transferred from the wealthiest quintile but with the smallest proportion (4.1%) going to the poorest quintile and higher proportions going to the second (6.6%) and third poorest quintiles (5.2%) (Table III.27). Whatever the flaws of these estimates, the analysis of the previous section leaves no doubt that there was a dramatic redistribution of income in the first four years of the Revolution and that such a process continued in the second stage although possibly at a slower pace than in the first stage. On the other hand, high prices in the black market (realistically reflecting supply and demand) discriminated against the lowest brackets who could not afford these goods. It has been impossible to measure real wages in this stage because of the lack of a comprehensive and consistent series on inflation.

F. Social Indicators

Social services continued their expansion in this stage but at a much lower pace (as showed by declining shares of that sector in the budget and invest-

ment) because of the economic recession and the effort to increase investment. In education, the government claimed that the illiteracy rate (23.6% in
1953) had been reduced to 3.9% in 1961 (Table III.33) as a result of the anti-
illiteracy campaign, but the 1970 census would prove that rate to be grossly
exaggerated. The enrollment in education continued to expand at the primary
level and, to a lesser extent, at the secondary level. The nationalization of private educational facilities in 1961 gave a statistical boost to public enrollment because former private enrollment (not previously reported) suddenly
began to be counted as public enrollment. More than half of the university
professors left, thus harming the quality of higher education. In spite of
improvements in health care, most indicators showed a deterioration in
1960–62: the general mortality rate increased from 6.1 to 7.1 per 1,000, and
the infant mortality from 35.9 to 41.5 per 1,000; the rates of most contagious
diseases also rose in this stage. The exodus of about one-half of the physicians, the huge mass mobilizations, and the scarcity of medicines were partly
responsible for those phenomena, but better reporting of deaths and diseases
might also have contributed. The birth rate steadily rose and peaked at 35.1
per 1,000 in 1963; however, the increase in infant mortality and the huge emigration in 1960–62 (close to 200,000) reduced the rate of population
growth. And yet, the halting of U.S. flights to Cuba after the 1962 Missile
Crisis sharply cut emigration in 1963 and led that year to the highest population growth rate under the Revolution (Table III.30).

4
Debate over and Test of Alternative Socialist Models

1964–1966

The double failure of the development strategy and economic organization in 1963 raised serious doubts about whether the Soviet model was appropriate for an insular plantation economy; it was therefore decided to postpone heavy industrialization and return to sugar as the engine for development. Accompanying this change in the development strategy, there was a lively ideologico-economic debate in this stage between two alternative models of economic organization: Guevarism and Libermanism.

Ernesto Che Guevara and a group of devoted followers, indirectly influenced by War Communism (tried in the Soviet Union in 1918–20) and by the Maoist Great Leap Forward (applied in China in 1958–60), endorsed an idealistic line of thought contrary to the conventional Soviet doctrine. Guevara believed that "subjective conditions" (ideas, consciousness, willingness; all belonging to the superstructure in Marxist terms) could decisively influence "objective conditions," that is, the material base, the forces of production, the structure, which, in the orthodox interpretation of Marxism, determines the superstructure. This group argued that a successful raising of consciousness ahead of the material-base development could enable a country to skip the transitional, socialist stage between capitalism and communism or to build socialism and communism simultaneously.

Two sets of actions were proposed to achieve the Guevarists' goal. In the material realm, the ultimate goal was the total elimination of the market or the law of supply and demand, through the following measures: full collectivization of all means of production, highly centralized planning with enterprises operating as government offices, budgetary financing, elimination of mercantile relations among enterprises, gradual eradication of money, downplaying of material incentives (which should be mostly collective), and physical allocation and central pricing of consumer goods to replace the law of supply and demand. In the ideal realm, to ensure productivity, quality, investment efficiency, and reduction in costs, economic incentives should be largely replaced by raising the consciousness of managers and workers. This would require the creation of a "New Man" who, contrary to the economic man, would be unselfish, frugal, egalitarian, and motivated by patriotism and solidarity instead of greed and who would give his maximum labor effort to the collectivity in exchange for the basic satisfaction of needs (distribution according to needs). This ideal human being would be the product of mass consciousness-raising through education, mobilization, unpaid voluntary labor, moral incentives, and the gradual expansion of state-provided free social services. If conducted simultaneously, the two sets of actions would be reinforcing rather than conflicting and result in both economic and consciousness development.

Confronting the Guevarists was a moderate, pragmatist group led by the economist Carlos Rafael Rodríguez (then director of INRA) and made up mostly of members of the prerevolutionary pro-Soviet Communist Party. This group believed in some principles of "market socialism"—the application of selected market mechanisms within the framework of a socialist economy—that had influenced economic reform, first in Eastern Europe and later the Russian economist E. G. Liberman's timid program that Khrushchev experimented with in the early 1960s and that was implemented to a moderate extent by Brezhnev-Kosygin in 1965 to unsuccessfully revive the sluggish Soviet economy. Rodríguez's group, sticking to the conventional interpretation of Marxism, argued that subjective conditions cannot ignore objective conditions, a socialist country cannot go farther than its structure allows it to go, the material base has to be developed first and will in turn raise consciousness, and the transitional-socialist stage between capitalism and full communism cannot be skipped.

In the necessary transitional stage, there will be traits of the capitalist past and some features of the communist future. It would not be possible in this stage to eliminate the law of supply and demand, and hence some market mechanisms should be used (for example, money, profit, interest, and differential rent). Rodríguez's group was not favorable to further collectivization, and while supporting central planning, it attempted to improve efficiency by using selective market tools. Local enterprises would have much more autonomy than in the Guevarist approach in hiring and dismissing labor, making investment decisions, and so forth, and they could buy and sell among themselves using money as a means of exchange. The pragmatist group was against budgetary financing and instead advocated "self-financing." To foster labor productivity, the group advocated material rather than moral incentives in the transitional stage. They believed that to ignore the law of supply and demand and cut down material incentives would have a negative effect on production and the development of the material base. They advocated distribution according to work and were willing to accept some degree of inequality (Mesa-Lago 1978).

1. Policies

A. Ownership

The Guevarists favored full collectivization of the means of production, while the pragmatists were reluctant to further expand the state sector particularly in small agriculture, retail trade, and personal services. Foreign supporters of the pragmatists, including Dumont and Bettelheim, were critical of Cuba's excessive collectivization and in favor of midsized industrial firms and private cooperatives (in agriculture and small industry) rather than gigantic state firms and huge industrial trusts. Bettelheim argued that the Cuban economy suffered from a fundamental disorder because productive relations were not as developed as the productive forces (including ownership of the means of production), and hence the state lacked real economic control; to correct this problem, Cuba should adopt those forms of ownership adequate to its level of development. Either because the pragmatists' arguments were convincing or simply because the government needed time to absorb all the means of production collectivized in the previous two stages, there were no new steps toward collectivization in this stage (Table III.2; Mesa-Lago 1971, 1981).

B. Planning

Both sides of the debate advocated central planning and the use of mathematics and cybernetics, but they had different conceptions. Guevara conceived the ideal plan as a perfect clock mechanism, highly centralized, with allocation done physically, all the enterprises and farms operating as branches of the central government, and directive indicators based on gross output. His opponents endorsed selective use of market tools to improve planning efficiency; they also advocated some decentralization of economic decision making through increased power of enterprise administrators, competition among enterprises, market price formation of nonstrategic goods, and use of profit and costs as the best indicators of managerial performance. Several of these policies were endorsed by Dumont, who also recommended the use of differential rent on state land as well as monetary and fiscal measures to promote domestic equilibrium.

The two models operated at the same time in different sectors of the Cuban economy, although the Libermanist one was adulterated with features of the Guevarist model. The former was tried in one-third of Cuban enterprises (mostly agriculture and domestic and foreign trade), while the latter operated in two-thirds of the state sector, primarily in industry. Guevara's centralistic model could work in the concentrated small industrial sector in which labor is skilled and its output relatively easy to check. But in agriculture, there are natural factors impossible to predict and control, and production is dispersed and in the hands of hundreds of thousands of unskilled workers and peasants whose output is difficult to monitor. The Cuban economy is essentially agrarian and depends heavily on foreign trade; hence market mechanisms seemed more appropriate; furthermore, in foreign commerce, Cuban officials faced the real outside world of internationally set market prices, tough competition based on costs, and the need for foreign exchange. Each of the two groups also controlled the key financing institution akin to its respective model: the Guevarists had the Ministry of Finance, which was in charge of the budget and capital grants, while Rodríguez's group had the National Bank, the traditional dispenser of loans to be repaid with interest.

In practice, annual plans were not apparently enforced in this stage; the 1962–65 plan was discontinued, and there was no discussion, much less elaboration, of a 1966–70 medium-range plan. Instead, sectorial plans began to proliferate in sugar, cattle raising, electricity, and so forth (for further details see the next stage). The official explanation was that, because of the lack of cadres and data, it was better to concentrate all resources and efforts on sectorial, practical plans instead of macroeconomic abstractions. Lacking an effective central planning apparatus, key economic decisions were made by the political leadership. In 1965 then President Dorticós took over JUCEPLAN and Prime Minister Castro assumed control of INRA; by the end of that year, practically all economic power was concentrated in Castro's office. The process of merging state enterprises continued in this stage; thus in 1966 about 86% of industrial output was generated by 26 enterprises and the remaining 14% by 30 other enterprises. These were various attempts at decentralization, in both industry and agriculture but with few practical consequences. The division of the economy into two sectors with divergent organizational models, the decline of central planning, and the continued enterprise concentration left the responsibility of decision making to a small group at the top of the leadership (Mesa-Lago and Zepherin 1971; Bernando 1971).

C. Financing, Stability, and Prices

Each of the two divergent systems of financing became the center of debate and the backbone of the opposing models. The Guevarists used budgetary financing in 69% of the nation's enterprises, mostly industries. Under this system, all economic activities of the nation are conceived as a huge single state enterprise of which factories, farms, and service agencies are mere branches. Transactions among enterprises cannot take the form of purchasing and selling (as all property belongs to the state) but are conducted as accounting transfers, and competition among enterprises is not allowed. Enterprises own neither property nor capital and receive all funds for their expenditures from the state budget (controlled by the Ministry of Finance) in the form of nonrepayable free-interest grants or "gifts." All enterprise surpluses (profits) go automatically to the state, and if there is a deficit, it is canceled and absorbed by the budget. There is no relationship between enterprise income and expenditures, the two being independent; expenditures may exceed the established limits, whereas revenue may fall below expectations. Planners decide how to invest the surpluses generated by the enterprise regardless of its profitability but taking into account national needs. Managers of enterprises have to follow strict specific orders from the center, and their performance (and that of workers) is evaluated by fulfillment of production targets and work quotas without taking enterprise profitability into account. Money is not used as a means for assessing profitability but only as a unit for accounting purposes: to reduce divergent elements (wages, inputs) into a common denominator. No market mechanism is used to achieve supply and demand equilibrium; hence this task must be fulfilled through physical measurement and control. There is no set of economic levers and incentives to increase production, improve quality, meet deliveries on schedule, reduce costs, use investment efficiently, or make innovations. The only internal motivation to achieve those objectives is the managers' or workers' degree of consciousness and response to moral (nonmaterial) stimuli. Guevara believed that such a centralized and idealistic system could work in Cuba because of the small size of the country and good communications system combined with mathematical and computer techniques as well as moral stimulation (Bernardo 1971).

The Libermanists used self-financing (*autofinanciamiento*, equivalent to the Soviet *khozraschet*) in about 31% of Cuban enterprises, mostly in agriculture and foreign and domestic trade. This system allows the development of as many enterprises as necessary and as autonomous as possible; transactions and competition among state enterprises are permitted. The system is controlled by the National Bank, and enterprises receive credit from the banking network in the form of repayable loans with interest. Enterprises must cover their costs with their own revenues and be profitable or face closure. Part of the enterprise's profit is kept for internal distribution (as an incentive), and part is devoted to decentralized investment proposed by the enterprise and approved by the central planning apparatus. Managers are empowered to determine the ultimate specifications of their orders from the center, and evaluation of managerial performance is largely done based on monetary-mercantile indices such as costs and profits. The partial use of money facilitates transmission of information at various levels. Material incentives are employed to motivate managers and workers, connecting their performance with enterprise profits through bonuses, premia, or deliverance of enterprise services (social clubs, libraries, day-care centers). According to some observers, Cuba lacked the needed conditions to develop self-financing; hence the system never had a chance to mature and became, in practice, disguised budgetary financing: there was a disconnection between revenues and expenditures, deficits were covered with budget grants or bank loans that were not repaid, investment funds were taken by the government, and the system of material incentives was not really developed (Bernardo 1971).

D. Development Strategy

The postponement of the heavy industrialization program forced a return to sugar as the most promising source of exports and foreign exchange. (There was practically no public discussion of this important shift, as the two sides of the debate concentrated on the model of economic organization.) In view of their previous critical stand against sugar dependency, the Cuban leaders justified the new strategy with the following rationale. The return to sugar was to be temporary, and sugar output would increase steadily in the second half of the 1960s, allowing Cuba to accomplish three crucial goals in the 1970s: (1) provide resources to resume the industrialization effort (hence diversifying production); (2) reduce the trade deficit and repay the external debt with socialist countries and obtain foreign exchange to import needed goods from the West (thus diversifying trade partners); and (3) significantly increase the population's standard of living. Because of the good quality of its soil and climate it would be much cheaper to produce sugarcane in Cuba than to cultivate sugar beets in the Soviet Union, East Germany, or Czechoslovakia. In these three countries, technological advances and skilled personnel made it more economical for them to produce machinery and equipment than it was in Cuba. Based on the theory of comparative advantages, both Cuba and its partners would mutually benefit through specialization and trade. Furthermore, international socialist solidarity would prevent the Soviet Union and other developed CMEA countries from taking advantage of their privileged position in their trade with Cuba, as the United States had done in the past: the socialist countries would pay fair prices for Cuban sugar in exchange for fuel, machinery, and manufactures of good quality at reasonable prices. The change in development strategy was publicly announced by Castro in mid-1963, after coming back from his first trip to Moscow, and defined more concretely in 1964 upon the return from his second trip.

The most important of the sectorial plans was the Prospective Sugar Plan (1965–70) developed for the sugar industry with a projected investment of more than one billion pesos. This plan included a 50% expansion of the sugarcane land to be planted with a higher-yield sugarcane variety and different maturity, the almost total mechanization of the sugar harvest to solve the shortage of manpower, the irrigation and fertilization of sugar fields in order to increase their yield, and the expansion of the grinding capacity through the modernization of existing sugar mills and the construction of three new sugar mills. The plan anticipated a gradual increase of sugar production from 6 million tons in 1965 to 10 million tons in 1970.

A second objective of the development program was the expansion of land under cultivation as well as irrigation, mechanization, and fertilization. A third target was the development of cattle raising through artificial insemination and of fishing through the expansion of the fishing fleet. A fourth goal was to increase the production of electricity, nickel, and cement (these plans are discussed in detail in the discussion of the next stage). The agricultural share of state investment increased from 24.3% to 40.5% in 1963–65, while the industrial share declined from 31.6% to 18.1% (JUCEPLAN, *BEC* 1966).

According to the new development strategy, the increase in sugar output and agricultural products in general would result in a sharp rise in exports with the consequent improvement of the balance of payments and the expansion of the country's capacity to import. This would make it possible to acquire fertilizer plants, irrigation equipment, and agricultural machinery (e.g., tractors, loaders), breeding bulls and artificial insemination equipment, fishing vessels (a new fishing fleet was launched in 1964), machinery for the extraction of minerals including petroleum, and electric-power and cement plants. In summary, Cuba was attempting to apply the unbalanced economic development theory, centering all the nation's effort around sugar production with the hope that the expansion of this sector would generate an overall development of agriculture and connected lines of industry (Mesa-Lago 1971, 1981; Ritter 1974; Brunner 1977).

Although the state budget allocation to defense and internal security declined from 13.3% to 8.4% in 1962–65 (Table III.6), still a disproportionally high share was devoted to military activities (partly a result of the U.S. threat and partly because of Cuba's subversive activities abroad), hence depleting these resources from use in development.

E. External Sector

The two sides in the debate took different positions concerning foreign trade. The Guevarists were strongly in favor of a monopoly exercised by the corresponding central ministry, while their opponents endorsed more freedom of enterprises to conduct direct commerce with partners abroad, although under central supervision.

In 1963–64 sugar prices in the world market increased largely because of the decline of Cuban sugarcane production and exports in those years. At that time Cuba had a valuable product (sugar) to trade with market economies, and, as a result, trade with socialist countries decreased. Such an important shift in commercial partners called into question the new development strategy assumption that trade with socialist countries was always more advantageous than with capitalist countries. Partly to correct that situation and to help Cuba with its new strategy, the Soviet Union signed a six-year trade and economic agreement (1965–70) in which the Soviets were committed to increase annual imports of Cuban sugar from 2 to 5 million tons in that period (hence buying most of the planned increase in Cuban production) for a total of 24 million tons at 6.11 cents per pound, an increase of almost 50% over the previous price. (China's buying of Cuban sugar also increased in this stage.) Furthermore, the Soviet Union granted Cuba technical aid for U.S.$138 million to expand and modernize the sugar industry and later an additional U.S.$46 million for the same purpose as well as geological prospecting. Finally, the Soviet Union and other CMEA countries promised to supply Cuba with most imports needed to implement the new policy.

In 1964 the OAS agreed to impose a collective embargo on Cuba, which was applied by all members except Mexico. Hence overall trade with market economies declined both for that reason and because of falling world sugar prices and rising Soviet subsidized prices. Cuban trade with market economies concentrated in Western Europe and to a lesser extent Canada and Japan (Mesa-Lago 1971, 1978, 1981; Mesa-Lago and Gil 1989).

F. Labor and Employment

A new law of labor justice, enforced since 1965, removed the right to strike, introduced sanctions for violation of labor discipline, and empowered enterprise managers to directly impose many of those sanctions. The system of work quotas and wage scales was completed at the end of 1965 or early 1966 for virtually all of the economy although its application in agriculture was weak.

Open unemployment continued to be tackled with similar policies in this stage, although there was a new concern with labor productivity. The postponement of the industrialization plan ended the expectation that the urban labor surplus would become productively employed in the industrial sector. On the other hand, the return to sugar and agriculture boosted the demand for manpower in the countryside. The Cuban leaders faced a manpower surplus in urban areas (made up by the remaining unemployed, subsidized laid-off workers in industry, and excessive bureaucrats in services), along with an artificial manpower deficit in agriculture. A vigorous effort began in 1964 to correct the labor imbalance by curtailing rural-to-urban migration, measuring the maximum labor force to be efficiently employed, dismissing redundant employees, and transferring the urban labor surplus to the countryside.

The state monopoly over employment was the key for migration control. Three measures were mainly used: (1) issuance of a compulsory identification labor card, indispensable for requesting employment, followed later by a labor booklet with a complete file of the workers' activities; (2) requirement of authorization from the Ministry of Labor for employment transfers; and (3) restriction of ration cards for one specific location, thus limiting labor mobility. Selective incentives were also given to countryside workers in the form of better housing, schools, and hospitals. These steps led to the slowdown of the population growth rate for the city of Havana: while in 1960–61 it grew by an average rate of 4.4%, the rate slowed to 2.1% in 1964, 1.5% in 1965, and 0.9% in 1966.

Real manpower needs were to be measured by work quotas expanded in 1964–65. It was then estimated that 2.4% of the labor force (some 60,000 workers) was redundant. Protests in some factories badly hit by layoffs prompted a reaction from the Minister of Labor, who said that it was necessary to dispose of the redundant manpower because, since the factories belonged to the workers, they had to be placed where they were most needed. The task of reducing the number of administrative jobs was entrusted to Commissions for the Struggle against Bureaucracy, established beginning in 1965 throughout the country, especially in Havana. Laid-off workers were sent to a "labor reserve" and paid their full salary until they could be retrained and transferred to other jobs (a policy similar to that with *excedentes* in 1961–63). Close to 1% of the labor force (22,000 workers) was determined to be redundant and laid off, half of them in Havana; however, only one-third were reemployed (mostly shifted from one bureaucratic job to another), and the rest kept waiting or studying while paid by the state.

The transfer of part of the urban surplus to the countryside was attempted through three measures: (1) introduction in 1964 of the Compulsory Military Service, which recruited an annual average of 100,000 youngsters (ages 16 to 20, delaying their entrance into the labor market), using most of them in agricultural work throughout the three-year draft; (2) organization of labor brigades integrated with some 50,000 young people recruited in nonproductive jobs who signed three-year contracts to work in agriculture; and (3) an increase in the mobilization of voluntary labor (mostly urbanites in nonproductive jobs) for the sugar and other harvests (Mesa-Lago and Hernández 1971; Mesa-Lago 1972).

G. Distribution and Social Services

The Guevarists supported a steady move toward distribution according to individual needs by gradually reducing the monetary wage and extreme wage differentials and expanding the "social wage," that is, social services freely provided by the state. There were strong egalitarian overtones in this approach and the belief that a change in human values would help achieve the rapid transformation of the old economic man into the New Man. Nonmaterial incentives were to be gradually replaced by moral incentives; the latter can be individual (e.g., a medal to a worker) and collective (a banner to workers in a factory), positive (the awarding of a medal to one worker or a banner to a factory, won in socialist emulation) and negative (publicly posting the name of the worst worker in an enterprise).

Conversely, Guevara's opponents believed that, in the transitional period, distribution must be done according to work, and hence they accepted some degree of inequality. They endorsed material incentives: individual (for instance, a bonus for overfulfilling work quotas) and collective (a share of the enterprise's profit), positive (as the two examples given) or negative (a cut in wage proportional to nonfulfillment of the work quota). Libermanists were cautious about the further expansion of free social services, and some in this group endorsed moderate user charges to cut down social-service waste and costs. We have noted, however, that a full system of material incentives (particularly profit sharing) was not implemented.

Both sides supported work quotas and wage scales (possibly the Guevarists less enthusiastically), and the implementation of this system contributed to a further reduction in inequality. In 1965 the extreme wage differential ratio between the highest and lowest paid worker in the wage scales—an unskilled agricultural peon earning 70 pesos monthly and a cabinet minister making 700 pesos—was 10 to 1, although another scholar reported 4.3 to 1 (Mesa-Lago 1981; Zimbalist and Brundenius 1989). However, when the old wage received by a worker was higher than the corresponding new wage, the old wage was not cut but officially maintained, the government calling it a "historical wage": in 1965, 70% of the nonagricultural labor force received this payment. In the competition for most skilled workers, enterprises disguised payments above the proper wage scale as historical wages. Those workers who performed well or gave an extra effort were rewarded with production bonuses and overtime payments. Private farmers increased their income as a result of better *acopio* prices in agriculture. Expansion in the number of rationed goods was an equalizer, but booming prices in the growing black market had the opposite effect. Finally, the budget share of social services was stagnant in this period, while the investment share of such services further declined from 25.4% to 21.3% in 1963–65 (Table III.6; JUCEPLAN, *BEC* 1966; Mesa-Lago 1971, 1981).

2. Performance

A. Growth

The 1962–63 recession ended as constant GSP per capita increased 4.7% in 1964, although it slowed to 1.5% in 1965 (Table III.3; as the year 1966 is split into this stage and the next, it was decided to analyze it in the following stage). Estimates of annual average economic growth between 1961 and 1965 are not consistent: they range from 2.7% to 7.1% based on different magnitudes and techniques (Table III.4). These data suggest, however, that the good performance of 1961, combined with the recovery of 1964–65, more than compensated for the decline of 1962–63 (but the level of output in 1965 might have been below that in 1961; see below).

The output target for the first year of the Prospective Sugar Plan (6 million tons in 1965) was surpassed by 2.6%, but it did not demand an increase in output above the 1959 and 1961 levels. Performance in nonsugar agriculture was mixed: there were slightly more products with declining or stagnant output than increasing output (however, the number of heads of cattle, pigs, and poultry as well as the number of fish caught rose). The impact of the second agrarian reform law (fully felt in 1964) plus the shift toward sugar production may explain the mixed agricultural performance in this stage. The FAO (1970) index of agricultural output per capita improved in this stage, but 1965 output was still 17 percentage points below the 1961 level. Output of nickel and petroleum as well as electricity, cigars, and fishing rose in this stage, while a smaller number of key industrial goods stagnated or declined. Various indices of nonsugar industrial output indicate steady growth in this stage. However, a combined agriculture and industry output index in constant prices suggests that, in spite of the recovery, the 1965 level was considerably below that of 1961. The share of investment in GSP declined in 1964 but recovered its 1963 level in 1965 (Tables III.3, III.10, III.12; Mesa-Lago 1971).

B. Inflation

Inflation continued to be very high in 1964 although lower than in 1963 (respectively 8.5% and 10.2%), but in 1965 a deflation of 1.7% was reported. The only available estimate of inflation in 1963–65 gives an annual rate of 5.7% (Tables III.3–4). The state budget was apparently in equilibrium. In 1965 the cumulative monetary surplus had been reduced to 73% of the population income (down from 91% in 1962), but it was still very high (Table III.5).

C. Diversification

The overall distribution of GSP by economic branch does not include data for this stage (only the year 1962 is available for the 1960s; Table III.8). As an outcome of the return to sugar (as well as better crops and prices), however, the share of sugar output in GSP increased from 9.8% to 13.8% in 1963–65, while the share of sugar exports/GSP increased from 8.4% to 8.8% (Table III.11).

D. Trade Balance and External Dependency

Mostly because of increasing sugar exports (both in quantity and higher prices in the Soviet and world markets), the value of Cuban exports rose by 31% in 1964; and although it declined in 1965, it still was 27% above the 1963 level. The value of imports increased by 17% in 1964 and in 1965 declined to the same level as in 1963. Hence, Cuba's trade deficit decreased slightly in 1964 and was cut sharply in the following year. Taking advantage of the high price of sugar in the world market, Cuba expanded its share of trade with market economies (from 17.5% to 35.7% in 1962–64), while the trade share with the Soviet Union declined from 49.4% to 39.5% (from 67% to 51.8% with CMEA). But in 1965 the increase in the Soviet price for Cuban sugar and the decline in the world price resulted in a price ratio of 2.9 to 1 in favor of Cuba. This price incentive, combined with associated credits provided by the Soviet Union, prompted an expansion in Cuban trade with that country in 1965 to 48.2% (61.5% with CMEA) but a precipitous decline in the share with market economies (down to 23.2%). Also, because of the increase in Soviet prices, Cuba's trade deficit with the Soviet Union was cut to one-third in 1963–65, and the Soviet share in Cuba's trade deficit declined from 92% to 60%. Export concentration remained unchanged in this stage: sugar exports accounted for 87% of the island's total exports. Dependency on Soviet oil imports continued unabated despite the increase in domestic production (in 1965 the Soviet Union provided 98.4% of Cuban supply); the Soviets basically charged the same oil price as the world market (Tables III.16, III.19, III.21; Pérez-López 1979; Mesa-Lago 1981).

E. Unemployment

In 1965 open unemployment had probably been reduced to 6.5%, about 40% of the prerevolutionary rate (Table III.26). The implementation of work quotas and wage scales might have helped in the reported increases in productivity in 1964–65 (JUCEPLAN, *BEC* 1966). And yet, disguised unemployment and underemployment continued in this stage: the total number of unnecessary workers, measured in 1965 by both work quotas and the Commissions against Bureaucracy, represented 3.4% of the labor force. If this figure is added to that of open unemployment, a combined rate close to 10% of the labor force is obtained.

F. Equality

Estimates of income distribution are not available for this stage, and it is impossible to assess the net result of the divergent policies applied. However, the extreme differential between the highest and lowest wage means by economic branches declined from 4.1:1 in 1962 to 3.6:1 in 1966. No data are available on real wages.

G. Social Indicators

Enrollment in secondary school in 1965 was 11 percentage points higher than in 1960. Most of this progress was due to real expansion of educational facilities, but the nationalization of private education in 1961 helped to boost public enrollment figures. Infant mortality peaked at 37.8 per 1,000 in 1965, while the overall rate of mortality increased slightly in this stage (the ratio of doctors per 10,000 inhabitants declined a little). Cuba did not publish any data on life expectancy at birth in this stage, but ECLAC reported an increase of 3.3 years over the previous quinquennium, debatable in view of the rise in infant mortality. The rate of five contagious diseases increased (hepatitis, chicken pox, measles, syphilis, and tetanus), while the rate of five diseases (diphtheria, malaria, polio, tuberculosis, and typhoid) decreased because of massive vaccination campaigns. The number of pensioners rose 40% in 1962–65 because of the expansion of social security coverage and retirement of many farmers expropriated under the second agrarian reform law (many *excedentes* decided to retire as well). Housing construction declined from an annual average of 17,000 units between 1959 and 1963 to 5,000 units in 1965. Emigration was more controlled and reduced, yet the birth rate was still high (it peaked in 1963 and thereafter slowly declined); hence the rate of population growth was quite high in this stage (2.5%), adding pressure to the demand for social services (Tables III.30–31, III.33, III.35).

5

Adoption and Radicalization of the Guevarist Model

1966–1970

For three years Castro abstained from open participation in the ideological controversy between the two competing organizational models, but by the end of 1965 Guevara had resigned as Minister of Industry and left Cuba (to lead the revolution in South America where he eventually met his death), and Rodríguez quit as director of INRA but cleverly stayed in Cuba as a minister without portfolio. In the summer of 1966 Castro announced the new directions in economic organization, basically following Guevara's model, but he implemented it in a more radicalized and idealistic fashion.

1. Policies

A. Ownership

The process of collectivization resumed with brio in this stage, concentrating on the two major pockets of private ownership left: agriculture and services. At the end of 1968 only one-fifth of agriculture and 2% of transportation remained in private hands (Table III.2). In 1967 four steps were taken to increase state control in agriculture: (1) workers on state farms were dispossessed of their tiny family plots on which they produced for their own consumption, barter, and sales to the black market; (2) private land tenure was limited to the lifetime of the farmer; hence he could not pass tenure to his heirs, and the state had priority to buy a private farm if the owner decided to sell it; (3) ANAP agreed not to sell agricultural surpluses from private farms on the market but to turn over all production to the government on the basis of the low *acopio* prices; and (4) private farmers were encouraged to join collective work brigades and mutual aid groups, thereby putting their manpower and equipment into common use.

The remaining 25% of retail trade left in private hands plus most of the 2%–5% in industry and transportation was collectivized in one single stroke in March 1968 under the "Revolutionary Offensive." More than 58,000 small businesses were confiscated including retail food outlets, consumer service shops, restaurants and bars, repair and handcraft shops, and even street vendor stands. In addition to expanding the state sector, the new collectivization wave officially aimed at eradicating the illicit purchases that the small businessmen made from private farmers, purchases that reduced *acopio* sales to the state and boosted the black market. Most of these businesses were turned over to inexperienced housewives who were members of the Committees for the Defense of the Revolution (CDR), or else the government tried to manage them directly. In 1970, however, Castro acknowledged that most of these businesses were managed with primitive accounting methods but with high efficiency because the owners knew all the details about supply, demand, and distribution; furthermore, the state was unable to gather, aggregate, and use all the needed information, and the newly appointed managers had neither enough skills nor knowledge of the local conditions; therefore, inefficiency spread rapidly. Later a Cuban scholar explained that an underlying reason for the 1968 collectivization of small businesses was that many of them successfully competed with the state because of their greater initiative and flexibility; hence their products were preferred even by the state sector. Following Bettelheim's previous argument but without citing him, the scholar criticized such "nationalization" for not being truly "socialization," as it was limited to a formal legal act, and businesses were not efficiently managed, so output and productivity declined (Mesa-Lago 1971, 1981; Ayala 1982; Castro 1982).

B. Planning

In this stage the macro-central plan virtually vanished, as the most important economic decisions were not grounded in a "scientific and objective" central planning apparatus but made by the political leadership. By the end of 1966, JUCEPLAN activities were reduced to research and two logistic functions: ensuring the inputs necessary to meet the output targets fixed by the political leaders and solving eventual inconsistencies. Medium-range and annual macroplans were replaced by sectorial or miniplans (in one sector such as sugar), and special or extra plans were also introduced in an ad hoc manner to tackle urgent economic problems. The administration of these plans was usually entrusted to loyal revolutionaries and the allocation of resources done by "superior order" (outside of JUCEPLAN); the latter led to a cut in resources allocated to central projects already in operation but ranked lower in priority than the special or extra plans; any resulting incompatibilities and conflicts were resolved in an arbitrary manner by the political leadership.

The absence of both a central plan and coordination among special plans provoked shortages in inputs, bottlenecks, shutdowns, and proliferation of incomplete projects. Advances in certain sectors were offset by declines in others. Imported equipment lay unutilized for years (often rusting on the docks) because the building to house it had not been finished. Nearly completed factories could not operate because of a missing component or part. The construction of small dams was not matched by the development of irrigation; hence most of the accumulated water could not be used. The lack of centralized information compounded with poor management had damaging effects: perishable goods spoiled on the docks or in warehouses; certain crops were lost because of excessively wet terrain while others dried up because of lack of water; still others were partly lost because of a lack of manpower; and valuable seedlings were stored and forgotten. Negligence of depreciation costs and maintenance resulted in the deterioration of physical plant and equipment, which led, in turn, to slowdowns or shutdowns; for example, electricity blackouts and water supply shortages (Mesa-Lago 1971).

C. Financing

In 1966 the Ministry of Finance was abolished and all its functions consolidated into the National Bank, but, instead of signaling the demise of the budgetary financing system, such action facilitated its expansion to all the economy because the National Bank was changed from a lender to an overseer of the financing of the economy. The number of state enterprises was reduced to 300, some of them embracing entire industrial branches—for example, the sugar industry was made up of well over 100 mills and related operations. The use of monetary calculation and market mechanisms in agriculture and trade was discontinued. But the state budget, which was supposed to play a key role in the Guevarist model, also lost importance (together with accounting techniques) and apparently disappeared for a decade (1967–77). In 1969 student enrollment in economics and management at universities and technical schools was one-twelfth that of 1965.

The emphasis on capital accumulation at the price of reducing consumption reached a climax in this stage. A sharp increase in national savings was to be generated by a cut in consumption through the expansion of rationing, the exporting of products previously assigned for internal consumption, and the reduction of imports considered unnecessary. In addition, material incentives sharply decreased, and the population was exhorted to work harder, save more, and accept deprivation with revolutionary spirit. Because the state budget was discontinued in this stage, it is impossible to know the share of the budget allocated to financing production; however, the investment share going to the productive sphere increased from 78.7% to 85.8% between 1965 and 1970, the latter being the highest proportion ever reached under the Revolution (JUCEPLAN, *BEC* 1966; CEE, *AEC* 1984a).

Foreign and Cuban economists noted a decline in efficiency in the allocation and use of the capital so draconicly saved, for several reasons: (1) arbitrary decisions made by political leaders that used neither central planning nor market tools to improve the efficiency in capital allocation; (2) generalization of budgetary financing, based on capital gifts and disconnected with profitability, which led to financial irresponsibility; (3) proliferation of sectorial and extra plans lacking an overall central investment plan to ensure minimum coordination; and (4) lack of skills and/or responsibility among workers who did not know how to operate costly and complex imported equipment, carelessly handled it, did not maintain it properly, or discarded it because of ignorance about how to repair it; for instance, half of the locomotives in existence were wrecked by careless workers, and the number of imported tractors was reduced to 14% in terms of years of service (Lataste 1968; Bernardo 1971; Mesa-Lago 1971).

D. Stability and Prices

Prices of expanding rationed goods continued frozen in this stage despite increasing costs of domestic production and imports after 1962; hence state subsidies to rationed goods rapidly grew, and a rising number of enterprises became more subsidized. All personal taxes were eliminated, more social services became virtually tax free or saw their rates reduced, and a considerable proportion of the population achieved ownership of their previously rented homes and stopped paying rent to the state. The money in circulation substantially grew, and with fewer consumer goods available, money began to lose value as both a means of exchange and incentive for labor effort. The reduction in black market operations after 1968 shut down another way to spend money. Prices became increasingly distorted, and lines in front of state stores grew longer (Mesa-Lago 1971).

E. Development Strategy

Concentration on sugar production peaked in this stage, as 70% of investment was targeted for the sugar industry (but there were other plans to expand heads of cattle, nonsugar agricultural production, the fishing catch, and the output of nickel, electricity, and cement). The Prospective Sugar Plan's (the most important sectorial plan) annual output targets steadily increased between 1966 and 1970 to 6.5, 7.5, 8, 9, and 10 million tons. Combined output of sugar and molasses was expected to surpass 25 million tons by the end of the 1970s. The initial target set for 1970 was 7.5 million tons, but Castro raised it to 10 million without a previous technical feasibility study; planning was hastily done ex post. Meeting the colossal target became a politico-economic battle, a crucial test of the Revolution, as Castro labeled any output level below that goal a moral defeat.

A series of factors conspired against the success of the plan. The length of the harvest was 334 days (50% more than in the previous record crop of 1952); it began in October when the cane was not ripe and ended in August in the midst of the rainy season, which begins in May. The planted area of cane did increase from 1 to 1.5 million ha, but this target was accomplished in the 18 months prior to the harvest, hastily done and causing considerable seed losses. The new sugarcane was of an improved variety with a higher yield, but it needed a minimum period of 18 months to mature, a condition not met in a high proportion of the planted seed. Irrigation facilities were planned to cover 385,000 ha, but only 40% or less were already installed in the spring of 1969, and nonfulfillment of the fertilization target was even worse. Out of 350,000 cane cutters needed, only one-fourth were professional cutters, and the rest were mobilized volunteers coming from the cities who lacked experience and had very low productivity (furthermore, old technicians in the sugar mills left the country in the early 1960s or were fired under the antibureaucracy campaign). Part of the harvest was to be mechanized, but the imported Soviet combines were too heavy and broke down easily (spare parts were very scarce), while very few Cuban-made combines were produced. Thus cane cutting was mechanized by only 1%; furthermore, plowing was mechanized by less than 40%. Because most combines did not clean the cane of leaves and trash, this process had to be done mechanically in new cane-conditioning centers, which were not built in sufficient numbers (only 25% of the cane was cleaned this way); hence the volume of cane transported increased significantly, adding pressure on the available equipment. The planned industrial yield (percentage of raw sugar produced in relation to the weight of the cane ground) was 12.3%, exactly the yield average of the 1960s; but conspiring against that target were excessive leaves and trash in the cane, low sugar content, problems with the milling equipment, and neglect of productivity indicators. The actual yield was only 10.7%, the lowest in three decades, and production costs were higher than the prevailing price of sugar in the world market. Only 40% of the required investment of one billion pesos had been accomplished at the beginning of the harvest, and none of the planned three new sugar mills was built; the resulting gap was to be filled with expanded grinding capacity of the existing mills, but only half of that target was actually reached. Imported equipment for the mills was delayed or received without enough time for installation and training of personnel; in addition, maintenance of the old equipment was neglected, and the considerable extra effort required led to frequent breakdowns. From 4,000 to 5,000 kilometers of railroads and highways had to be built, but only part of them were finished on time; and yet the transportation system had to handle the extra volume of uncleaned cane, plus the transfer of cane from problem-plagued mills to overburdened old mills (Mesa-Lago 1971; Roca 1976; Brunner 1977).

An important premise of the sugar plan was that it should not hurt production elsewhere, particularly in agriculture. Actually, the new development strategy contemplated an expansion of land, equipment, and other inputs in nonsugar agriculture, but most of the targets did not materialize. The area of cultivated land had to be increased by 900,000 ha, but only two-thirds was accomplished. Dam construction was expected to add one billion cubic meters of water between 1965 and 1970 alone, but only 86% of that volume was ultimately developed in the entire 1959–70 period. The planned annual number of imported tractors in this stage was 7,000, and it was probably reached, but careless utilization and lack of maintenance sharply reduced the actual number of tractors in operation. Fertilizer consumption was to be expanded significantly through domestic output and imports. Finally, the sugar sector depleted significant resources from the rest of agriculture.

The cattle plan set a target of 8 million heads for 1970, an increase of 18% over the 1965 number as well as a fourfold raise of milk output in 1968–70. This was to be achieved with (1) artificial insemination (two million cows had been inseminated by 1968); (2) breeding of Cuban native stock (Cebu, a poor milk producer) with imported bulls (Holstein, Brown Swiss) to develop a new resistant and higher-milk producer breed (the F-1); (3) the use of pasture and sugar molasses as cattle fodder, to cut imports of expensive corn; and (4) reduction of domestic beef consumption through smaller rationing quotas. According to Cuban data, the F-1 produced four times more milk than the Cebu, while a second generation of that hybrid (the F-2) showed a twofold milk increase over the F-1. But at a congress of animal science held in Havana in 1969, a team of British geneticists, advisors to the Cuban government, presented a report proving that the F-1 milk output was only 16% that of the Holstein and that the F-1 cows dried out after 100 days of nursing their calves. Another British report criticized the use of pastures and molasses as cattle feed, insisting that corn was the best fodder for cattle. Castro strongly criticized both reports, offering new data to show their inaccuracy and arguing that it was very cheap to produce grass and molasses in Cuba but very expensive to grow or import corn. And yet, in 1970 Castro acknowledged that the birth rate of cattle had not been high enough, pasture lands had not received proper attention in several years, and the rate of slaughtering had increased because of the low weight of cattle.

In early 1966 Cuba had a political confrontation with China, the main supplier of rice, a crucial staple in the Cuban diet. As a proportion of Cuba's total imports, Chinese imports (mainly rice) declined from 14.2% to 7.3% in 1965–67. This forced Cuba to rapidly prepare a rice plan to meet consumption demands; as a result, large mechanized rice plantations were developed in this stage.

Perhaps the most successful program in this stage was fishing. To the three fleets successively developed in 1962–64, a new fleet was added in 1968 made up of 90 Spanish vessels, 30 French freezing vessels, and 15 East German cutters for the manufacture of fish meal. The number of vessels in this new fleet surpassed the combined total number of the previous three fleets. In addition, Cuban shipyards built 500 small wooden vessels between 1959 and 1968. By 1968 there were more than 3,500 fishing vessels in operation: 93% of them were small, mostly made of wood, organized in cooperatives and producing 58% of total output (slightly above the 1961 level). The remaining 7% were imported vessels (rather advanced, with a small number of well-trained fishermen) that operated in the state fleet, which turned out 42% of the catch.

Cuba has the fourth largest reserves of nickel in the world and by 1958 had an extractive capacity of 40,000 metric tons of this mineral (in two U.S.-built plants). After the initial decline in output, Cuban technicians were able to recover the prerevolutionary output level in 1963–64 and set as a goal for 1970 to fully utilize the installed capacity. Electricity capacity was to expand by 570 million kwh through the addition of two new thermoelectric plants. Finally, output of cement was to increase also through expansion of installed capacity (Mesa-Lago 1978, 1981).

F. External Sector

In this stage the Soviet Union continued honoring the 1965–70 trade and economic agreement (except on oil in 1967) despite conflicts over Cuba's unorthodox economic model and foreign policy. The number of Soviet-Cuban agreements of all types signed in 1967–68, however, was the lowest since 1960. Furthermore, in 1967 the Soviet Union reduced by 3% the supply of oil to Cuba, instead of proceeding with a planned increase. Castro denounced this action at the beginning of 1968 and in retaliation put on trial several pro-

Soviet members of Cuba's prerevolutionary Communist Party (the "Micro-faction"), accusing them, among other things, of providing information to the Soviet Union on negative factors that made the 1970 sugar crop target unfeasible (in 1970 many of these factors proved to be correct and were publicly acknowledged by Castro). The Soviet invasion of Czechoslovakia in the summer of 1968 was a turning point in Soviet-Cuban relations. Castro supported the invasion (although with some reservations), and the island's foreign policy became closer to that of the Soviet Union (Che Guevara's death in Bolivia led to a halt in guerrilla warfare in Latin America and facilitated a more moderate Cuban foreign policy).

The price for Cuban sugar paid by the Soviet Union was maintained at U.S. 6.11 cents per pound during this stage. The world price of sugar, however, declined from U.S. 5.87 to U.S. 1.86 cents per pound in 1964–66 (the lowest since the Great Depression) because of Cuba's and other countries' increasing sugar production and exports. And yet, in 1969–70, the world price rose again, reaching U.S. 3.75 cents per pound in the last year (that increase was influenced by low Cuban crops in 1968–69); still, that price was much lower than the average price of U.S. 4.38 cents between 1957 and 1964 (Table III.19). Throughout this stage, the Soviet world market sugar price ratio stood at more than 2 to 1; hence Cuba continued exporting about 40% of its sugar to the Soviet Union (67% to socialist countries). More than half of Cuba's trade was with the Soviet Union and about two-thirds with CMEA. The political conflict with China significantly reduced trade with that country, mainly sugar exports and rice imports.

Cuba significantly expanded its merchant marine in this stage. The number of Cuban ships increased from 18 with a deadweight of 106,000 tons in 1965 to 37 ships with 282,000 tons in 1970, making Cuba's the fifth largest merchant marine in Latin America. But, because of the long distances that Cuban ships have to travel, in 1970 only 6% of foreign trade was carried by Cuban ships (Mesa-Lago 1971, 1978, 1981).

G. Labor and Employment

In this stage part of the urban labor surplus was transferred to agriculture (through the application and expansion of policies discussed in the previous stage), which was suffering from a manpower shortage, and open unemployment was virtually eliminated. And yet disguised unemployment was still present, and problems of labor productivity, misuse of voluntary work, and absenteeism became more acute. The government attempted to correct such problems with moral rather than material stimulation and, when it did not work, resorted to militarization of labor and control measures.

Castro announced the shift in Cuba's economic organization model at the CTC congress held in 1966, which quickly replaced its secretary general, an old communist and pro-Soviet leader, with a loyal *Fidelista*. In a rapid declaration of principles, the unions confirmed that their task was to increase output and productivity, improve quality, reduce costs, take proper care of socialist property, and organize voluntary labor and socialist emulation. According to an official statement, the unions became transmission belts of Cuba's Communist Party (PCC) directives. A Vanguard Workers movement composed of those who excelled in consciousness, militancy, and productivity gradually absorbed union functions, leaving the CTC with even more limited tasks, such as education of the labor force, promotion of discipline, and fighting selfishness. Cuban officials later acknowledged that by 1970 the trade union movement was withering away.

In 1970, 86.3% of the civilian labor force (excluding the military and security forces) was employed by the state. The 13.7% of nonstate employment was mostly private farmers (11%), and the rest were self-employed and private salaried workers (Table III.24).

Labor mobilization rapidly increased from 106,000 workers in 1966 to 302,000 in 1968 to 700,000 in 1970. Poor organization of voluntary labor and the volunteers' lack of skills resulted in considerable waste of time and resources. Voluntary labor was often used without real need for it, and in other cases the volunteers spent hours waiting to be transported to the fields, only to remain idle when arriving because of the lack of needed tools. The cost of mobilizing, feeding, and providing the volunteers with seeds and tools was often higher than the meager product created by that inefficient labor force. A CTC document, released in mid-1970 after the announcement that the sugar crop target would not be met, led to a revision of previous policies: it (1) criticized the general practice among union leaders of pressuring workers to increase production based on voluntary labor after the normal daily schedule and on weekends; (2) ensured that, after the extraneous effort of the harvest, the workers' vacations would be respected; and (3) exhorted managers and unions to raise production in the future by better labor organization, full utilization of the work schedule, and productivity increases instead of voluntary labor. A few months later, Castro acknowledged that poor organization of voluntary labor had resulted in a waste of time and effort.

Enforcement of work quotas was weakened in this stage, and by 1970 the levels achieved in 1965 had been lost. The connection between work quotas and wage scales was also gradually eroded. According to an official report, the wage policy during these years was not based at all on enterprise efficiency but just the opposite: industrial productivity generally had an inverse relationship with the wage share of the value added. In addition, the report said that production bonuses and other material incentives were suppressed or reduced and that there was a futile effort to replace them with moral incentives and political education. When this task failed, the leadership resorted to militarization of labor, particularly in agriculture: most state farms were headed by military officers, military discipline was enforced, and militarized labor brigades (also in construction) were presented as models.

At the end of 1966 Castro denounced the bureaucratization of the Commissions of Struggle against Bureaucracy and appointed an investigative committee that found that 43% of all dismissed employees since 1965 had been reemployed in enterprises that had just been cleansed of bureaucrats. A new wave of 31,500 layoffs followed, reaching 1.2% of the labor force in 1967. At the end of that year, one-third of those dismissed (who continued receiving their salaries) were still waiting to be transferred to other jobs or were studying, while two-thirds were reemployed, probably in agriculture, in construction, or back in the bureaucratic heaven.

According to a Party report released in 1969, labor absenteeism steadily increased because the socialist system had not developed tools of its own to replace the incentives and checks of the market system: wages had ceased to be an incentive, because there was more money in circulation than goods to spend it, and unemployment was no longer a fear. In September 1970 absenteeism reached 20% of the labor force because the workers were able to stay home and still be able to buy (with the money they earned) the scarce rationed goods available. The Minister of Labor acknowledged that the introduction of labor control measures in 1968–69 had not been effective in reducing absenteeism and that more stringent policies were necessary. A law against loafing enacted in 1971 established a work obligation for all able-bodied men from ages 17 through 60, severely sanctioned absenteeism, reduced the possibility of working outside of the state sector, and labeled as vagrants those wage earners temporarily employed in the private sector. A mass campaign to detect potential violators of the law got 100,000 men to join the labor force, half of them in agriculture (Mesa-Lago and Hernández 1971; Mesa-Lago 1971, 1981, 1982).

H. Distribution and Social Services

In this stage a big push was made toward further equalization in Cuba. Workers were asked to waive overtime pay, bonuses for the fulfillment of work quotas, and historical wages. The implementation of extra payment for work done under extremely arduous conditions was postponed. In-kind awards (trips, refrigerators, motorcycles) granted to sugar workers as incentives to increase production were stopped. Authors' royalties were abolished. Family plots enjoyed by state farmers were eliminated, and pressure was put on private farmers to sell all their crops to the state at low *acopio* prices. In 1970 state payments to private farmers were 60% below the 1965 level, which led the farmers to sell as much produce as possible on the black market; when the latter was suppressed in 1968, the farmers cut their output. Wage differentials were to be reduced in a gradual manner by raising the lowest wages and pensions and freezing the higher wages. Eventually every worker would earn the same wage, be he a cane cutter or engineer, and even food and clothing would be free, thus making wages and money virtually unnecessary. At the same time, free social services were expanded, including public phone calls, burials, day-care centers, and sports events, and it was promised that housing, recreation, transportation, and public utilities would soon be free. (Access of urban dwellings to potable water and sanitation increased little or was stagnant between 1953 and 1970—from 82% to 88%, and from 95% to 93%—but expanded considerably among rural dwellings—from 15% to 24% and from 46% to 61%; Table III.32.) Housing rent was set at 6% of family monthly income, but families with an income below 25 pesos monthly were exempted from paying rent. The percentage of investment going to social services, however, shrank from 21.3% to 14.2% between 1965 and 1970; and social expenditures per capita, which had risen 127% between 1960 and 1965, increased by only 35% between 1966 and 1970. Rationing was expanded, and subsidies to essential consumer goods rose; thus, the scarce goods available were equally distributed to the population (Table III.29; JUCEPLAN, *BEC* 1966; Mesa-Lago 1971, 1981, 1993d).

2. Performance

A. Growth

Macroeconomic indicators in this stage are scarce and unreliable. The Cuban government did not publish a single GSP series in constant prices for the entire 1966–70 period. Instead, there were three official series that cannot be connected: 1962–66 in constant prices, 1967–69 in current prices, and a third starting in 1970, also in current prices. According to these scattered data, constant GSP growth per capita in 1966 declined by 2%, while in current prices the decline was 0.1% in 1968 and 2.9% in 1969 (Table III.3). Cuban and foreign scholars elaborated rough estimates of average annual economic growth in constant prices for the entire 1966–70 period, but either they failed to show their calculations or their methodology was flawed. The wide divergence among such estimates increased doubt about their reliability: in absolute terms they ranged from 0.4% (GSP) to 7.1% (GDP) and, in per capita terms, from −1.3% to 5.4% (Table III.4). Although it is impossible to have a sound estimate for this stage, scattered production data to be discussed below indicate either stagnation or economic decline.

None of the annual output targets of the sugar plan for 1966–70 were met; total accumulated output during this period was 12 million tons less than (70% of) the planned target. The 1970 harvest set a historical record (8.5 million tons), but it was still 15% below target and was achieved by borrowing uncut sugarcane from the 1969 crop (4.5 million tons, half the target for that year). Furthermore, this was a Pyrrhic victory, as it was achieved by drawing on resources from other sectors of the economy, which in turn suffered output declines that partly or totally offset the increase in sugar output. Finally, the target of producing a sugar surplus of 1.5 million tons in 1970 did not materialize; this surplus was crucial to reducing the trade deficit and debt with the Soviet Union, resuming the industrialization program, and increasing living standards. Doubling the output of sugar and molasses at the end of the 1970s became an impossible dream. The fiasco of the sugar plan brought failure to both the development strategy and organizational model in the second half of the 1960s.

Production in nonsugar agriculture was even more disappointing. The cattle plan target of 8 million heads was not just unfulfilled, but the number of heads declined by 20% in 1967–70. The ratio of heads of cattle per inhabitant deteriorated from 0.87 in 1967 to 0.67 in 1970, and the weight of cattle also declined (Table III.12). Major causes of such negative performance were the failure of the cattle breeding, artificial insemination, and fodder programs that had been strongly criticized by British geneticists. Production of beef, milk, tobacco, pork, coffee, citrus, beans, tubers, and green vegetables declined, and the number of pigs decreased by 18% in 1967–70. The output of rice increased seven times, but the output level in 1970 was only slightly above that of 1959–60. Cuba let domestic rice output fall between 1961 and 1966, based on profitable barter of sugar for Chinese rice, but after the quarrel with China, it hurriedly pushed rice output again. The best steady performance in agriculture was in eggs, which showed an impressive increase of 64% in those five years. Even more remarkable was the 2.6 times jump of fish and seafood output supported by the rapid expansion and technological advances of the fishing fleet (Tables III.10, III.12). According to FAO, Cuba's index of agricultural output per capita declined 18 percentage points between 1965 and 1969; however, the index jumped 38 percentage points in 1970 (8 points above 1961) because of the record sugar harvest that year (FAO 1970–86).

Nickel output continued increasing steadily in this stage for a 32%

growth between 1965 and 1970; output in the last year was only 7.5% below total installed capacity, and hence the nickel plan was successful. Conversely, most of the manufacturing sector had a dismal performance: the output of cement, fertilizers, textiles, cigars, soap, beer, canned fruits, refrigerators, and radios in 1970 was considerably lower than in 1965 (in some products the decline ranged from 20% to 45%). However, steel output increased almost fourfold between 1965 and 1970 and electricity 44% (Table III.10).

There was a decline in the quality of goods, and in some cases a total loss due to serious deficiencies. These goods were stockpiled, but nobody wanted to buy them; therefore, material inputs, labor, and warehouse space were wasted. In other cases, the goods were sold, but their deficiencies shortened their life span. Finally, the number of tourists declined to less than 2,000 (from 272,000 in 1957), reaching a low point (Table III.15). The deterioration in other services cannot be measured, but it must have been significant.

The annual average share of investment in GSP was slightly higher between 1966 and 1970 than in 1962–65. However, that share declined from 14.3% in 1967 to 12.5% in 1968 and 9.6% in 1970; the last year had the lowest share since the series began in 1962 (Tables III.3, III.7). Furthermore a good part of investment was lost because of the decline in capital efficiency.

In summary, with the exception of sugar in 1970 and a few agricultural and industrial products, there was a generalized decline in output in the Cuban economy during this stage. In August 1970, in a somber assessment of the failure of the development strategy, Castro acknowledged that the enemy was right when it warned that the sugar crop of 10 million tons would cause the problems that arose. He blamed the leadership, including himself, for such a serious setback and offered to resign if the people so wanted. The only administrative official dismissed, however, was the minister of the sugar industry. Two months later Castro, forgetting his main responsibility in deciding the 10 million ton target and trying to achieve it at all costs, blamed the ministry's technicians for assuring him that they knew how to achieve the target and for shifting resources from the rest of the economy to the sugar sector, provoking an overall decline in nonsugar output (Mesa-Lago 1971).

B. Inflation

Estimated annual averages of inflation for this stage suggest a slowdown from 5.7% in 1963–65 to 1.3% between 1966 and 1970 (Table III.4). And yet Castro described this period as one of tremendous inflation, resulting from having more money in circulation than the value of goods and services available. Indeed, the cumulative monetary surplus peaked in 1970, reaching 83% of population income, almost twofold the value of the available supply of goods and services; the surplus per capita was 388 pesos, the highest during the Revolution until the 1990s (Table III.5). These figures highlight the shrinking value of money and explains why absenteeism boomed to 20% that year. The state budget either was nonexistent or was not published in this stage.

C. Diversification

A comparison of the overall distribution of GSP by economic sector in 1962 and 1970 (the only years available; Table III.8) shows the following declines (in percentage points) of the shares in: agriculture (3.1), industry (0.3), construction (2.0), and communication (0.1). The only sectors that increased were transportation (3.8) and trade (1.7). Part of these increases were attributed to foreign inflation (Zimbalist and Brundenius 1989). The share of sugar output in GSP increased from 10.1% to 15.1% in this stage, while the share of sugar exports/GSP rose from 7.4% to 9.7%, both clear indicators of the renewed dependency on sugar (Table III.11).

D. Trade Balance and External Dependency

One of the targets of the development strategy was to correct the imbalance of trade. But data show that the external disequilibrium further deteriorated in this stage except in 1970. The value of Cuban exports was basically stagnant between 1965 and 1969 but increased by 57% in 1970 because of the record sugar crop and higher world market prices that year. The value of Cuban imports steadily increased in this stage: in 1970 imports were 51% over the 1965 level. The trade deficit steadily grew in 1966–69 (a 69% increase in this stage), reaching more than a half billion dollars in 1969 (establishing another record), but the jump in exports in 1970 cut the trade deficit in half that year (Table III.16).

The inability to fulfill the sugar plan targets rather than generate a substantial surplus created a huge deficit in export commitments, particularly with the Soviet Union. Sugar export commitments to the Soviet Union between 1965 and 1970 totaled 24 million tons, but actual deliveries were 13 million (45% less than the target); hence a cumulative deficit of 11 million tons ensued, which was equivalent to two good sugar crops (Pérez-López 1991). Rationing of domestic sugar consumption (introduced in 1969 to save 200,000 tons for export) and buying sugar in the international market made only a dent in the deficit. The Soviet Union had to defer part of Cuba's export obligations so that the island could fulfill other commitments, particularly with the West (Mesa-Lago 1971).

Dependency on the Soviet Union increased, and so did Cuba's trade deficit. Stimulated by the beneficial Soviet preferential prices to sugar, the Soviet Union's share in Cuba's trade turnover averaged 52% in this stage, while the CMEA share was 66%. However, Soviet imports increased twice as fast as Cuban exports, and the cumulative trade deficit between 1966 and 1970 reached U.S.$1.4 billion, twice the size of the deficit between 1961 and 1965 (the official Cuban peso/U.S. dollar exchange was artificially maintained par in this stage). Almost 75% of Cuba's deficit during this period was with the Soviet Union (Table III.20). Soviet credits to cover the deficit increased twofold, hence dramatically augmenting Cuba's debt with the Soviet Union. Between 1960 and 1970 Cuba received the equivalent of U.S.$2.4 billion in Soviet loans to cover the trade deficit and for development, which constituted 68% of total Soviet aid (Table III.22).

An estimate of Soviet price subsidies to sugar (nonrepayable gifts) is more difficult because of different bases for the calculation. If the world market price is used, the cumulative Soviet subsidy between 1966 and 1970 was U.S.$778 million or 2.5 times the subsidy in the previous quinquennium. Based on the European Economic Community preferential import price, the subsidy was U.S.$162 million. If the preferential U.S. import price was used, the subsidy was −U.S.$339 million. If sugar would have been sold to the United States under the former quota and preferential prices, Cuba would have earned U.S.$339 million more than it did selling that sugar to the Soviet Union. Based on world market prices, Soviet price subsidies totaled U.S.$1.1 billion, accounting for 32% of total Soviet aid (Table III.22). Trade with market economies averaged 24% of Cuba's turnover (mostly with Japan and Western Europe), while trade with China declined from 14.3% to 6.6%.

Dependency on Soviet oil imports was slightly reduced from 97% to 92% of total supply in 1966–69 as Cuban domestic output tripled and Soviet imports increased only slightly (in 1967 the Soviet oil supply was cut). But the combination of a sharp decline in domestic output in 1970 and increased Soviet imports in 1969–70 led to a reversal in oil dependency to 94% in 1970 (Table III.21). Soviet oil prices remained basically the same as world prices (Table III.19). In spite of increasing dependency on the Soviet Union, Castro stated (at the time of the Soviet invasion of Czechoslovakia) that numerous socialist countries maintained trade practices with developing countries (including deliveries of deficient or technologically backward goods) similar to those used by capitalist countries (Mesa-Lago 1971, 1981; Pérez-López 1979; Mesa-Lago and Gil 1989).

Export concentration decreased during this stage in spite of the return to sugar: the share of sugar in total exports declined from 85% to 77% (Table III.17). The increase in nickel exports after 1968 and low world sugar prices determined that outcome. This indicator, however, is in conflict with the share of sugar exports in GSP, which, as we saw, increased in this period. Available data for only 1958 and 1970 on the composition of imports show positive changes: reductions in the shares of manufactured goods (down 6 percentage points) and fuels (2 points), and increases in the shares of machinery and transportation equipment (5 points) and chemicals (3 points). Conversely, imports of food and fats increased 1 percentage point, an indication of less self-sufficiency in domestic food production (Table III.18).

E. Unemployment

Full employment was practically achieved in 1970 when only 1.3% of the labor force was reported as openly unemployed (Table III.26). This feat was accomplished together with an increased participation by women in the labor force: from 12.6% in 1956–57 to 18.3% in 1970 (Table III.25). A comparison of the distribution of the labor force in 1956–57 and 1970 indicates that the share of the primary sector declined (8.8 percentage points); hence most employment was created in the tertiary sector (an increase of 5.3 points), particularly in services (3.6 points), as well as in the secondary sector (5.1 points). Therefore, the most dynamic sector was services instead of industry (Table III.24). Women found employment mostly in commerce, which experienced an increase of 15.8 percentage points between 1953 and 1970, but the largest majority still remained employed in the tertiary sector, which accounted for 67.5% of total female employment in 1970 (Table III.25). These figures hide the serious problem of underemployment and disguised unemployment, which must have risen in this stage. Thus, 1.2% of the labor force was found to be redundant in 1967, and in 1968–69 a survey in two-thirds of all state enterprises showed that from one-fourth to one-half of the workday was wasted, mostly because of flaws in labor organization and time lost in absenteeism, political activities, and malingering. Labor productivity declined by 2.1% in 1966 (JUCEPLAN, *BEC* 1966), and although statistics have not been published for 1967–70, abundant information indicates that productivity deteriorated further in that period because of weakening of work quotas, labor mobilizations, increasing absenteeism, and so forth. In 1970 Castro acknowledged that although open unemployment had been eradicated, there were still many people without jobs who received government subsidies (Mesa-Lago 1971, 1972, 1981).

F. Equality

Foreign estimates of income distribution are not available for 1970 but only for 1962 and 1973 (these estimates, presented in Table III.27, are not accurate because of both methodological flaws and the comparison of different groups). Such estimates indicate a further cut in the income share of the wealthiest quintile (-6.9), which went to the middle quintile (2.9) and the poorest two quintiles (about 1.5 each). No data on wage scales are available for this stage. The extreme differential between the highest and lowest wage among economic sectors further declined in this stage, from 3.6:1 in 1966 to 2.6:1 in 1971. Rationing expanded significantly between 1962 and 1969: out of 20 selected products, the rationing quotas of 12 declined (or they shifted from free distribution to rationed) while 5 were unchanged and only 3 increased (Table III.29).

G. Social Indicators

The illiteracy rate, reportedly reduced to 3.9% in 1961, was revealed to be 12.9% in the 1970 population census, still an important achievement but not as much as initially claimed. The gap between urban and rural illiteracy rates was cut in half from 12% and 42% in 1953 to 7% and 22% in 1970. Enrollment in secondary education was stagnant between 1965 and 1970, while enrollment in higher education increased from 4% to 5% (Table III.33). The general mortality rate was basically stagnant during this stage, while infant mortality rose from 37.2 to 46.7 per 1,000 between 1965 and 1969 and then declined to 38.7 in 1970. If the increase in infant mortality in the early period of the Revolution could be partly explained by better reporting of deaths, such an argument lost weight after 10 years. The rate of acute diarrhea significantly increased, as did four contagious diseases, while another six declined. Cuba did not publish data on life expectancy at birth in this stage, but ECLAC reported an increase in three years over the previous quinquennium, a figure contradicted by the significant increase in infant mortality (Tables III.30–31). Social security coverage of the population became universal in health care and reached almost 89% of the labor force on pensions (Table III.34). Beginning in the mid-1960s the government applied pressure on older workers to keep them in the labor force in order to save on pensions (the number of pensioners was stagnant in 1965–67), but the collectivization of small businesses in 1968 provoked an increase of 14% in the number of pensioners in two years (Mesa-Lago 1990b). Housing construction peaked at 10,257 units in 1967 (still below the 17,089 annual average between 1959 and 1963) but precipitously declined to 4,004 in 1970, the lowest on record. The housing deficit was estimated at 755,000 units (Table III.35). Rather than expanding social services (the share of investment in this sector was reduced from 21.3% to 14.2% between 1965 and 1970; JUCE-PLAN, *BEC* 1966; CEE, *AEC* 1984a), the government increased those that were free (burials, public phones, sports) or reduced their rates (public buses).

The population growth rate steadily declined from 2.5% to 1.5% between 1965 and 1970 as a result of a decrease in the birth rate from 34.3 to 27.7 per 1,000 combined with a higher net emigration—an annual average of about 50,000 (Table III.30). Contributing to the lower birth rate were factors such as the growing participation of women in the labor force, increasing education, and restrictions in consumption and housing.

6

Introduction of a Moderate Soviet (Pre-Gorbachev) Model of Economic Reform

1971–1985

In 1970 the Cuban leaders faced an economic debacle and had few alternatives with which to cope with it. A radical return to the market was blocked both by domestic ideological resistance and by the impossibility of reestablishing economic relations with the United States or receiving substantial aid from Western Europe or Japan. The option of further radicalizing the revolutionary economy along the line of 1966–70 was blocked by the chaos unleashed by the failure of the Guevarist-Castroite experiment. Finally, Cuba's ongoing quarrel with China and the devastating effect of the Great Proletarian Cultural Revolution in that country were impediments to Cuba's receiving aid. The Soviet Union was the only country economically capable and willing to help Cuba, but obviously on its own terms. It was only logical, therefore, that the Soviet model of timid economic reform (which had been endorsed in Cuba by the pragmatist group in the 1964–66 debate and introduced in the Soviet Union in 1965) was the one adopted by the Cuban leaders in the 1970s. The new stage, the longest under the Revolution (it lasted 15 years contrasted with an average of 3 years in the previous four stages), was characterized by economic pragmatism and politico-administrative institutionalization. But before introducing that change, it was necessary to discredit the previously exalted model.

In several speeches delivered in the 1970s, Castro criticized the preceding stage as utopian and explained the mistakes committed as follows. Cuba lacked good economists, scientists, and theoreticians to make a significant contribution to the construction of socialism, but its leaders tried to invent a new approach, showing contempt for positive experiences of other more ad-

vanced socialist countries. The Cuban approach in those years was highly
idealistic, minimized actual serious difficulties, and pretended that will-
power could overcome the absence of objective conditions. The leadership
was guilty of idealism in assuming that the attitude of a conscious vanguard
minority was typical of the overall society, and this misconception proved
detrimental to the economy. In the new pragmatist stage, it was realized that
it was easier to change the economic structure than man's consciousness, that
the latter had a long way to go, and that material-base development should
precede efforts to raise the consciousness of society. It was therefore accepted that the transitional stage between capitalism and communism could
not be skipped; it was folly to believe that the Cuban society could leave capitalism and enter, in one bound, into a society in which everyone would be-
have in an ethical and moral manner. When it might have seemed (at the Guevarist-Castroite stage) that Cuba was drawing nearer to communistic forms
of production and distribution, it was actually pulling away from the methods proper to the stage of development the island really was at. At the new
stage, it was acknowledged that Cuba was only building the foundations of
socialism while the Soviet Union had gone beyond full socialism and was
building the foundations of communism. Measures of a communist charac-
ter that were previously put into effect were eliminated or revised in the new
stage. In the future Cuba had to advance slowly, carefully, and realistically;
if it tried to go farther than possible, it would soon be forced to retreat (for
Castro sources see Mesa-Lago 1978, 1981).

1. Policies

A. Ownership

Despite a few trends to decentralize and timidly introduce some market
mechanisms, the process of land collectivization continued in this stage.
However, in the first half of the 1980s, some liberalization measures were introduced in agriculture, services, and housing. In any event, the 1975 program of the PCC stated that, in the long run, the construction of socialism
would require the government to take over the private property of all the
means of production.

In agriculture the state's goal was to gradually eliminate the private farms
by purchasing the land when the owners died or retired or through political
pressure so that the individual farms became integrated into state farms or
cooperatives. As a consequence of this policy, between 1967 and 1981 the
number of private farmers declined by 58%, from 233,679 to 98,113. The

Fourth Congress of the ANAP, held in 1971, agreed to encourage the progressive incorporation of the private farms into the state sector (in a voluntary manner but through political education), and this target was incorporated in the 1976 constitution. But in 1977 the Fifth Congress of ANAP acknowledged that the previous policy would take too long to achieve the goal and promoted the incorporation of the private farms into agriculture production cooperatives (CPAs) similar to the Soviet *kolhkoz*. Between 1977 and 1983 the number of cooperatives increased from 44 to 1,472, their total land area rose from 6,000 to 938,000 ha, and the number of cooperative farmers jumped from a few hundred to 82,611. The share of cooperative land as a percentage of total agricultural land increased from 0.4% to 10.2% between 1977 and 1986; 80.8% of the land was controlled by state farms in 1986 and only 6.5 % was left in the hands of private farmers and 2.5% in family plots on state farms. Contrary to the continuous collectivization trend, family plots on state farms, eliminated in 1967, were reinstated in the 1970s. And yet they were fused into collective plots in the early 1980s; these plots were not cultivated individually but by brigades, and their output was intended for self-consumption and state deliveries only. An increasing number of retired cooperative members in 1983–85 reduced the number of cooperatives to 1,378 and the number of cooperative members to 69,896. State prices for *acopio* were increased, and the government began to pay more punctually for its *acopio* purchases.

The most important liberalization measure in agriculture was the introduction of free peasant markets in 1980, in which small private farmers could sell their agricultural surpluses (after meeting state *acopio*) at prices freely set by supply and demand. These markets, the government argued, should encourage private farmers to increase their output with the resulting benefits of improving the supply of agricultural products (in quantity, assortment, and quality), and gradually eliminating the black market and rationing. Furthermore, the markets would provide incentives to the labor force to work harder in order to earn more money and buy more products in the free markets. In spite of these goals and a positive reaction by the farmers, the government prohibited them from selling their surpluses outside of the zone where they lived and banned middlemen ("intermediaries") who bought produce from the farmers and sold it in the markets. These rules obviously worked against the government's own goals of competitiveness and reduced prices. The acceptance of the middlemen would have allowed the farmers to concentrate on cultivating the land, instead of spending time transporting and selling their produce at the markets (especially when the surplus was small). Permitting farmers to sell outside their zones would have helped to correct market disequilibria. In 1982 a policy reversal occurred: Castro accused the farmers of charging very high prices and making juicy profits (thus expanding inequality); he threatened to increase their taxes and fix maximum prices to their produce and predicted the disappearance of private farms (and the free markets) in the long run. He also attacked middlemen who reportedly hired trucks to transport agricultural products and earned as much as 40,000 pesos a year selling at the peasant markets (the annual average wage at that time was 2,160 pesos). The police, alleging violations of the established rules, arrested numerous sellers at the free markets and confiscated their products. Two Cuban economists argued, however, that benefits accrued from the free markets compensated for their alleged flaws, some of which could be controlled by taxes. In addition, they reasoned that high prices of produce in such markets were partly caused by three factors: insufficient supply by the state and cooperative sectors, inflation in 1980–81, and extremely bureaucratic government rules to control the markets. The latter continued (until 1986), but severe damage was inflicted to the private farmers' incentives and their trust in the government.

In 1978–81 the government also legalized and encouraged self-employment in services, for example, hairdressers, tailors, gardeners, taxi drivers, photographers, electricians, carpenters, and mechanics, as well as professionals such as architects, engineers, physicians, and dentists. Under a new system of free labor hiring, state enterprises could contract with artisans and the self-employed, providing them with inputs in exchange for 30% of their profits. In large cities like Havana, small manufacturers began to sell their products in free markets. As in the case of the farmers markets, the government sent contradictory signals: it imposed a tax on self-employment income, recommended the creation of self-employment cooperatives to facilitate tax collection and other forms of control, and in 1982 launched a strong attack on those self-employed who were becoming "rich." The attack was led by Castro, who gave several examples of improper behavior: engineers and architects charged 800 to 1,000 pesos to draft a plan for home repairs, something he considered to be a "prostitution of the self-employment concept"; state managers hired teams of skilled workers to do private jobs in their free time, which he criticized as a "repulsive violation" of the rules and an "example of corruption"; artisans sold handmade manufactures for ten times the official price on the Havana free market (a pair of pants for 90 pesos, equal to half the average monthly wage), which had to be stopped, he said, to prevent the city from becoming crowded with selling stands. Some of these activities could be technically considered illegal, but others were not. In any event they showed the need for those goods and services and that the public was willing to pay a high price for them. But Castro accused the small businessmen of being robbers, becoming a "new bourgeoisie with capitalist attitudes," a "spoiled lumpen proletariat which was corrupting the masses." Thus, 250 of the self-employed were arrested, and Castro proposed doubling taxation on self-employment income. As in the case of farmers' free markets, the clampdown on self-employment and micro-entrepreneurs damaged incentives and contradicted the government's goal of improving the supply and quality of goods and services to the population.

Finally, in the first half of the 1980s, the state relaxed previous restrictions on private housing construction, and this policy, combined with expanding self-employment and easier access to construction materials, generated a robust housing market between 1980 and 1985 and the strongest dwelling construction boom in the history of the Revolution: two-thirds of the houses built in this period were private homes (Mesa-Lago 1981, 1982, 1988a, 1990a).

B. Planning

Central planning was reinstated in this stage as the principal economic tool, and mini-, sectorial, and special plans were subordinated to it. Annual macroplans were elaborated and implemented after 1973, as well as a global economic model (1973–75), the first and second five-year plans (1976–80 and 1981–85), and a 20-year development plan (1980–2000). Beginning in 1977 all statistical activity was centralized in the State Committee on Statistics (CEE), and the use of computer techniques was expanded with equipment imported from CMEA and Western Europe. There was a revival of economic, accounting, and managerial studies, all of which had suffered a serious setback between 1966 and 1970; enrollment in these fields increased sevenfold between 1970 and 1976, and a National School of Management and three provincial schools were established in 1976.

The new economic model, named the System of Economic Direction and Planning (SDPE), was gradually introduced beginning in 1976 and was scheduled to be fully in force nationally by the end of 1980. The SDPE was a moderate version of the timid economic reform introduced in the Soviet Union in 1965 with poor results, and many of its goals and features resembled those of the pragmatist model partly tested in 1964–66: (1) decentralization of state enterprises by breaking them down into smaller units (the number of enterprises expanded from 300 to 3,000 between 1968 and 1979); (2) transfer of many decisions from the central planners to enterprise managers; (3) a greater role of scarcity prices in allocations (a global price reform was planned); (4) complete replacement of self-financing for budgetary financing; (5) use of profit as a major indicator of managerial performance together with other indicators such as output, cost, quality, and productivity;

(6) reintroduction of interest and depreciation, as well as greater use of taxes and cuts in subsidies; and (7) reinforcement of work quotas and wage scales and restoration of material incentives as well as creation of an enterprise collective incentive fund based on enterprise profitability. But when 1980 arrived, the target year for national implementation of the SDPE, none of its elements were fully in operation: for instance, work quotas covered 59% of the labor force, and their full implementation was postponed to 1982; the collective incentive fund functioned in only 7% of enterprises and it was delayed until 1981–85; and the overall price reform had not been undertaken and was deferred until 1986–90.

Evaluations of the implementation of the SDPE were annually conducted, and information is available for those carried out in 1979, 1980, and 1985. These evaluations revealed serious flaws in the SDPE (some of them repeatedly reported without signs of improvement): *Overall:* poor discipline in enforcing the plan and applying its methodology; unreliable, inconsistent, and obsolete data; constant changes in the plan and lack of coordination between allocated inputs and goals; and overly aggregated targets that needed specific policies to be implemented. *Directive indicators:* their number was higher than 500, and they were not integrated into a unified system, thus resulting in lack of consistency both among them and between them and other indicators (such as the budget and the financial plan); indicators were centrally defined, hence, restricting the enterprise manager's autonomy; physical output indicators (such as material balances and gross output targets) received priority over financial indicators (profits, costs). *Decision making:* the noted flaws impeded decentralization and led to a disconnection between producers and consumers and a lack of producers' responsibility as suppliers; in turn, these flaws provoked a constant demand for resources (the more inputs a manager had, the easier it was to fulfill the targets) that led to idle resources in the enterprise and increased imports. *Inventories:* more than one-third of the enterprises did not report inventories, and one-half did not submit lists of unused inventories; as a result, some enterprises were shut down for lack of supplies that sat idle in other enterprises. *Contracts:* nonfulfillment of contracts among enterprises was widespread, largely because violators were not punished, thus creating delays and a chain reaction of bottlenecks. *Prices:* 500 violators of state-fixed prices were prosecuted in 1980; however, because of price rigidities, out-of-fashion or unattractive merchandise was stockpiled in inventories, and perishable goods were lost. *Quality:* almost one-third of enterprises lacked quality controls in 1980, and 90% of the products did not meet quality standards. *Paperwork:* regulations reached unprecedented levels; for instance, 102,047 regulations on material consumption, 334 volumes to partly cover wholesale prices, and three million work quotas. *Personnel:* between 1973 and 1984, administrative personnel increased almost threefold (from 90,000 to 250,000); about half of enterprise managers and central agency directors had not been trained in management schools; overstaffing and overspending increased production costs, and these led to price increases. *Participation:* feedback and participation of lower echelons in the elaboration and control of the plan were poor, too formal, and relegated to marginal issues. *Priorities:* the annual evaluations pinpointed hundreds of flaws but failed to elaborate a concrete plan of action and set priorities to tackle them.

The criticisms summarized above clearly show that the SDPE's failure was largely attributed to its own complexity and inefficiency. But an additional cause was the resistance of political leaders and directors of central agencies to relinquish part of their power and allow the needed decentralization to become a reality. Although in this stage there was much more progress in planning than in 1961–63 and in economic reform than in 1964–65, both approaches were still not fully implemented, and many of the old vices and defects persisted. Even if the combination of central plan and mild economic reform had been thoroughly applied in Cuba, it would probably have not been successful as its Soviet counterpart model (Mesa-Lago 1981, 1982, 1988a, 1990a).

C. Financing

Beginning in 1976 it was expected that self-financing would gradually replace budgetary financing in the Cuban economy, but the deadline to achieve such a goal was successively postponed from 1980 to 1985. Furthermore, the SDPE evaluations uncovered that self-financing—when applied—was formally superposed over budgetary financing and that the latter was still predominant in 1985. The fundamental source of financing was still the state budget instead of the enterprise's own resources and bank credit; the budget promoted spending rather than curtailing it, and enterprise deficits were often covered by state grants. The credit system was too complex and cumbersome, and repayment of bank loans was not properly done: in 1979, 20% of loans were 45 to 90 days behind payment deadlines, and in 1980 the proportion increased to 26% for a total of 1.4 billion pesos in unpaid loans. As in 1964–66 self-financing was corrupted by elements of budgetary financing.

At the beginning of this stage, emphasis was placed—at least rhetorically—on the efficiency of investment rather than on its size. Later it was asserted that both capital formation and its productivity had increased. But many of the previous investment flaws—which reduced capital efficiency—were still found in the 1980 SDPE evaluation, such as an excessive number of investment projects, absence of research, too much centralization of investment without adequate coordination, failure to ensure all required elements and imports, lack of a policy of depreciation and replacement, and absence of objective assessment of the efficiency of projects. For the 1981–85 plan there seemed to be a commitment to the following corrective measures: avoid spreading investment among too many projects (as many of them were previously left uncompleted because of insufficient funds), concentrate investment in a small number of important projects, complete those projects initiated between 1976 and 1980 before starting new ones, and reduce the period of maturation of investment. And yet the 1985 evaluation of the SDPE (as well as Castro's criticism in 1986) noted that such goals had not been realized; for instance, managers preferred to initiate new investment projects in order to fulfill plans in an easier way rather than complete existing projects; as a result, completion of such projects was delayed by as long as 22 years. Furthermore, the SDPE initially included a "development fund" (endorsed by the Second PCC Congress) fed by part of the enterprise profits and used for reinvestment in its expansion, but such a fund was discarded, and those resources were absorbed by the state budget. Therefore, investment was not made according to enterprise profitability but by central decision making according to national needs and priorities (Mesa-Lago 1981, 1982, 1988a, 1990a).

D. Stability and Prices

The state budget was reintroduced in 1978 after being discarded for almost a decade, and an attempt was made to promote fiscal equilibrium. In order to reduce excessive money in circulation, at the start of the 1970s the decision was made to decrease consumer demand and increase the supply of goods. To cut demand, several steps were taken: the previously scheduled abolition of house rents was canceled, the promised increase in minimum wages was halted, the granting of 100% salary to sick or retired vanguard workers was slashed, free social services such as public phone calls and day-care centers were charged a fee, and prices were raised for many goods and services, including cigarettes, beer, rum, electricity, water, worker-canteen meals, restaurants, and long-distance transportation. To increase the supply, the government expanded domestic output of some consumer durables (e.g., refrigerators, gas ranges, radios, pressure cookers) or imports (e.g., cars, TV sets, air conditioners, and fans) and raised their prices significantly. An official parallel market was introduced in 1973 in which surplus products were sold at a state-fixed price, reflecting supply and demand, from three to eight times the rationing price for the same item. Finally, in 1980 free peasant markets began to sell surplus produce at equilibrium prices, two to four times higher than the corresponding rationing price.

In 1972 it was claimed that there was a reduction in the cumulative monetary surplus and that money was starting to have some value. But world inflation, which accelerated after 1973 because of the oil shock, had an impact on Cuba, and it was officially acknowledged that after 1976 excess money in circulation began to expand again. This forced the halt of a series of measures that would have pushed inflationary pressures further, such as granting of bonuses for extremely dangerous work, payment of accumulated unused vacations, and so forth. The second oil shock in 1979, combined with expansionary domestic policies, further increased the surplus money in circulation in the 1980s.

As I have already noted, prices of most consumer goods were frozen in the early 1960s and remained largely unchanged for almost two decades; in addition, Cuba is heavily dependent on imports, and world inflation grew significantly during those years. By 1980 the gap between international and domestic prices had expanded dramatically, and the latter were so distorted that they became largely useless for planners and managers. For instance, evaluation of efficiency in investment allocation and in the appropriate choice of exports and imports became an almost impossible task. Furthermore, state subsidies to consumer goods (to protect low-income groups and avoid inequalities in distribution) were very large: 1,887 million pesos between 1976 and 1980 or 11% of the average GSP in those years.

In the 1970s and 1980s there was a move to close the price gap somewhat: the parallel and the free-peasant markets were tools to restore equilibrium prices and to provide incentives to medium and higher income groups. And yet low-income groups could hardly afford prices in these two markets and even less on the black market; good restaurants in Havana also were prohibitive for the average wage earner, and the cheapest refrigerator or television set cost the equivalent of five-months average wages. In 1981 there were partial reforms of wholesale and retail prices; the latter generated price increases—ranging from 7% to 525%—in 1,510 rationed consumer goods including most essential foodstuffs and manufactures, as well as many services (the average unweighted price increase was 65%, and the officially reported average increase was 10%). The price increase, however, did not completely eliminate state subsidies, which were estimated at 671 million pesos for 1982–85.

Available data on the distribution of retail trade of consumer goods by suppliers are contradictory. In 1970 about 90% of these goods were allocated through rationing; this share gradually declined as the share of the parallel market increased, and the farmers' free markets were introduced. Estimates for the parallel market share in the mid-1980s fluctuate from 14.4% to 58.7% (the latter including free sales in state stores), while figures for the share of rationing range from 20% to 40%; there was a consensus that the share of the free peasant markets was small, about 1.3%. I have grossly estimated the following shares in 1985: parallel market, 15%; peasant market, 1%; and rationing and others, 84% (probably disaggregated as 60% rationing and 24% free state) (Mesa-Lago 1981, 1982, 1988a).

E. Development Strategy

The economic strategy in this stage continued to be fundamentally based on sugar but with a more balanced approach: to produce as much sugar as possible with the resources allocated to that sector without depleting them from other economic sectors. In addition, sugar production would rely on technological advances—including mechanization of the harvest and expansion/modernization of milling capacity—rather than on labor mobilization. In the nonsugar sector, the emphasis was focused on fishing, citrus, nickel, a few industrial lines (electricity, cement, steel, textiles), and the revival of tourism.

In the sugar sector, three substages can be identified during this stage corresponding to the five-year sugar plans for 1971–75, 1976–80, and 1981–85. In the first, technicians were brought back with proper incentives, statistical gathering and data reliability improved, the use of computers was expanded, employment of voluntary cane cutters was reduced (in 1975 there were 174,400 fewer than in 1970), and both the length of the harvest and grinding were decreased significantly. To cope with less manpower and a shorter harvest, the Cubans resorted, in 1971, to the Australian system of burning and cutting the cane because burnt cane did not have to be cleaned of leaves, weighed less, and was cheaper to transport. But for the system to work effectively, the terrain had to be leveled off, a special variety of cane planted, the mechanical lifting modified, and the burnt cane rapidly ground to avoid sugar loss. Multiple difficulties led to a modified Australian system, which was thoroughly applied in the 1972 harvest with disastrous results; hence the Cubans turned to mechanization. After unsuccessfully trying several combines, in 1972 Soviet and Cuban engineers designed a new harvester (KTP-1), which was tested successfully in 1973, modified in 1974 to produce an improved version (KTP-2), and began to be produced in Cuba in 1977 with key components imported from the Soviet Union. Mechanical cutting increased from 1% to 26% between 1970 and 1975 (even before production of the KTPs began), plowing from 40% to 53%, cleaning from 25% to 34%, and lifting from 83% to 96%. These improvements led to some increases of sugar production and industrial yields in 1973–75.

The 1976–80 sugar plan set a target of 8.7 million tons in 1980 without the dislocation suffered in 1970. This task required an investment of 700 million pesos to build four new sugar mills, rebuild 21 existing mills, and modernize other mills in order to add a 1.5 million ton grinding capacity. Moreover, it was necessary to expand the cultivated and irrigated land area, replant all sugarcane with higher yielding seed, augment the use of fertilizers and pesticides, and mechanize cane cutting by 100%. Finally, the plan called for the repair of 9,500 kilometers of railway track, full mechanization of cart transport, building of 15 port terminals (to automate sugar bulk loading for exports), and construction of 16 sugar refineries. These ambitious targets did not materialize: only two out of the four new sugar mills were completed in 1980, but none of them in time for the harvest; modernization of the existing sugar mills fell behind schedule, and frequent breakdowns of old mills became a headache; there were delays in receiving imported equipment, and the production of the KTP-2 was about half of the planned target. Although all plowing and lifting of the cane was virtually mechanized by 1980, only 45% of cane cutting and 50% of cane cleaning was. To cope with some of these problems, both the harvest and grinding periods were expanded again, and industrial yields declined. The final blow to the plan was the rapid spread of a sugarcane blight (cane rust, a fungus that paralyzes the growth of the plant), which caused a loss of 1.5 million tons of sugar in the 1980 harvest. The pest apparently came from Angola and spread all over the Caribbean; in Cuba it hit one of the high-yield varieties of sugarcane planted on one-third of sugarcane land. Although sugar output slightly increased in this stage, delays in the plan combined with the epidemic blocked the fulfillment of the ambitious goals.

In the 1981–85 plan a target of 10 to 10.5 million tons of sugar was initially set for 1985 but then scaled down to 9.5 or 10 million tons. In order to reach such a target, several conditions had to be met: all the fungus-infected sugarcane seed had to be extracted, all fields disinfected, and pest-resistant new cane varieties planted; at least 7 new sugar mills were to be built, 23 expanded, and 18 modernized, for a combined new capacity of 2 to 2.5 million tons; and cane cutting and cleaning were to be fully mechanized. Most of these premises did not materialize: in addition to the four mills included in the 1976–80 plan and completed in the early 1980s, only three more new mills were built in 1985–86, and only 62% of cane cutting was mechanized by 1985 (no data were provided on cleaning). Furthermore, the new mills were quite large by Cuban standards and performed less satisfactorily (in capacity utilization and technical efficiency) than smaller mills, apparently because of more frequent breakdowns and hastily scheduled downtime. Although the 1985 output target was not met, the annual average output of sugar increased in this period, and yet the industrial yield continued to decline because of longer harvests and grinding periods (Mesa-Lago 1981, 1982, 1988a; Radell 1987; Pérez-López 1991).

In nonsugar agriculture, the main policies were to gradually expand the state sector and apply modern techniques, such as mechanization and fertilizers. Until the end of the 1970s, private farmers also had to cope with low *acopio* prices. Several epidemics badly affected tobacco and coffee crops, as well as pig raising. The results of collectivization were disastrous in crops difficult to mechanize, such as tobacco, coffee, and indigenous tubers. Private land on which tobacco was grown declined from 92% to 77% between 1963 and 1976, and so did production; in 1978 the government tried to reverse the damage, increasing prices of *acopio* and providing more credit to private farmers, and raising salaries to state farmers. But an epidemic of "blue mold" (a fungus endemic to Cuba) rapidly spread because of high temperatures and heavy rains, destroying as much as 27% of the 1978–79 harvest and 95% of the 1979–80 crop. As a result, in 1980 Cuba had to import tobacco, shut down all cigar factories, and tighten rationing of tobacco products. Economic incentives helped to restore output after the pest was controlled but did not increase production thereafter. Private land on which coffee was grown declined from 82% to 45% between 1967 and 1978, provoking a precipitous decline in output; economic incentives were not strong enough to promote significant increases in production. Two tubers important in the Cuban diet (*malanga* and yucca) followed the same pattern. Conversely, output of rice and potatoes, mostly produced in the state sector and largely mechanized, steadily increased. Significant investment in citrus led to an impressive expansion of production in the 1980s, but the selection and quality of this fruit was poor, and world competition was tough; hence practically all Cuba's citrus exports went to CMEA.

Three reports published in Cuba in the 1970s (authored by Cuban and foreign experts) identified the causes for the bad performance in cattle raising: fodder was not sufficiently nutritious, which resulted in underfeeding and loss of cattle weight, high production costs, and the nonprofitability of cattle raising; cattle illnesses spread rapidly (because of disorganization and lack of care), thus provoking an increase in mortality, and the artificial insemination program had serious flaws, which led to declining fertility rates. In addition, the number of cattle raised on private farms shrank together with the number of such farms. Finally, an outbreak of porcine cholera or African swine fever wiped out hogs in one province and infected pigs in two others. Success in poultry raising continued during this stage with the expansion of installations.

In the first half of the 1970s, the growth of Cuba's fishing fleet was sustained: by 1976, 262 modern deep-sea vessels had been imported, and Cuban shipyards built 6,000 small and medium-sized wood vessels, 400 steel reinforced medium vessels, and 90 large steel vessels. Cold storage, canning, freezing, and fish meal processing facilities were enlarged as well. Thus, Cuba's fishing fleet became the seventh largest in Latin America, and the fish catch steadily rose. But in the second half of the 1970s, there was a slowdown with erratic oscillations in output, mainly caused by the universalization of the 200-mile maritime zone, which restricted Cuba's fleet's access to traditional fishing waters and forced its transfer to areas farther out with higher costs and less predictable returns. Furthermore, in 1979 Peru canceled a profitable fishing agreement with Cuba, and the informal U.S.-Cuban fishing agreement of 1978 was halted.

The initial nickel plan involved quadrupling output at the start of the 1980s, thus making Cuba the fourth largest nickel producer and the second largest exporter in the world. The value of nickel production and hard-currency exports would amount to 30% and 50% of sugar production and exports, respectively. Plans for achieving these targets included modernization of the two existing U.S.-built plants (Nicaro and Moa), with Soviet aid, to increase their combined output to 47,000 tons in 1980; construction of a third plant (Che Guevara) in Punta Gorda, with CMEA aid, expected to produce 30,000 tons in 1980; and construction of a fourth plant in Camariocas, also with CMEA aid and a capacity of 30,000 tons. The combined planned output of the four plants at the beginning of the 1980s was to be 107,000 tons, almost three times the average output in the 1970s. But delays and technical problems in construction forced successive postponement of this target (Table III.13). Moreover, nickel production in Cuba was handicapped by the low quality of the ore and relative high cost of extraction: nickel is mixed with other elements, and its variety is the worst among 27 existing ores. In addition, the ore found on the island is laterites, which are processed by leaching, while in other exporting countries the ore is sulfites, which are processed by burning; not only does sulfur contribute to the combustion process, thus reducing costs, but the burning technology has also become increasingly more competitive. Cuba predominantly uses leaching with water and ammonium carbonate, a less efficient technique than others available in the West that had to be bought with hard currency that Cuba lacked and the Soviet Union was unwilling to spend. In 1979 Castro candidly acknowledged that Cuba's nickel industry was ruined because of its obsolete technology. Finally, international marketing of nickel is controlled by an oligopoly in which the United States plays a key role, making it extremely difficult for Cuba to enter (in addition, U.S. pressure on some buyers of Cuban nickel resulted in cancellation of imports). About ten new oil deposits were discovered in the 1970s, but none of them supported large-scale output (Mesa-Lago 1982, 1990a).

Plans for industry set equally ambitious output targets for 1985 based on promised Soviet and CMEA aid. Electricity output was to reach 15,000 million kwh (a 50% increase over 1980) with the addition of four new thermal plants. Moreover, with Soviet aid, Cuba would build a nuclear plant in Juraguá-Cienfuegos with four reactors so that output would increase 50%; but the discovery that the plant's location was in a seismic region, combined with technical difficulties, led to considerable delays. Planned cement output was approximately 5 million tons (a 76% increase over 1980) based on the construction of two new plants with East German aid. Steel output was expected to reach 1.6 million tons (more than a sixfold increase over 1980) with the expansion of the one existing mill and the construction of a new mill with Soviet aid in Holguín. Textile output would rise to 325 million square meters (more than a twofold increase over 1980) with the construction of two new plants, with Soviet aid, and the expansion of one existing plant.

In the 1970s Cuba began a serious effort to attract tourists to the island. It was helped by an inflow of Canadians and West Europeans, a brief lifting of U.S. barriers for American tourists (during the Carter administration), Cuban authorization for Cuban-Americans to visit the island (more than 100,000 did so in 1979–80), and a modest inflow of Latin American tourists as Cuba's diplomatic and trade relations were reestablished with countries in that region. The target for the early 1980s was to recover the prerevolutionary number of 300,000 tourists, who would generate revenues about twice the value of the fishing catch and three times that of nickel production. By 1978 Cuba had built 23 small hotels; 13 more were scheduled for inauguration in 1980 and 13 more for 1985. Domestic tourism was sacrificed to provide rooms for foreign tourists and hard-currency earnings. In 1982 a foreign investment law authorized joint ventures, giving special concessions in tourism. And yet two events in the 1980s slowed the tourist boom of 1979–80. The massive exodus of 125,000 Cubans from Mariel port in April 1980, partly attributed to the demonstration effect of the exiles' visits, led to a sharp decrease in their visits thereafter, and the Reagan administration issued an executive order prohibiting U.S. citizens from traveling to Cuba as tourists.

At the same time that Cuba was engaged in a new ambitious effort at development and diversification, it also became involved—beginning in 1975—in military activities in Africa and in other countries. This happened at a time during the Carter administration when the U.S. military threat had been significantly diminished, as diplomatic relations began to be reestablished and several agreements were signed. And yet the share of Cuba's state budget assigned to defense, which was 8.4% in 1965 (and probably lower in

1975), increased to 8.9% in 1979. The Reagan administration again raised the threat against Cuba, which reacted by doubling the size of its troops and increasing the military share of the budget to 11.6% in 1984 (expenses of the militia are not included in the budget). Therefore, resources that could have been devoted to development went to foreign wars and domestic defense (Table III.6; Mesa-Lago 1981, 1982, 1988a, 1990a).

F. External Sector

During this stage the Cuban leadership accepted a much higher degree of integration and dependency on the Soviet Union in order to obtain the desperately needed aid to save the island's economy from the 1970 debacle. The shift began when both countries established an Intergovernmental Commission for Economic and Scientific-Technical Cooperation, and the Soviet Union promised substantial aid. In 1972 Cuba became a full member of CMEA, receiving special member status as a developing country, which included preferential trade treatment by more developed members. In the same year four Soviet-Cuban agreements granted significant concessions and aid to the island: (1) payments on Cuban debt with the Soviet Union incurred between 1960 and 1972 were postponed until 1986 free of interest, with such debt to be paid in 25 years; (2) a credit was granted to cover Cuban trade deficits with the Soviet Union in 1973–75, whose payment was also postponed until 1986, interest free; (3) a development loan was awarded (U.S.$362 million to be paid over 25 years starting in 1976) for mechanization of the sugar harvest, expansion of nickel, textiles, and electricity, geological exploration, and so on; and (4) subsidized prices for Cuban sugar and nickel were set for 1973–75. In this period several bilateral agreements were signed, and a new Soviet loan was granted (U.S.$387 million) to develop the areas specified above plus the expansion and modernization of sugar mills, construction of the sugarcane-harvester factory, production of TV sets, and so forth.

In 1976 the first of a series of Soviet-Cuban five-year economic and trade agreements was signed. The 1976–80 agreement set a twofold increase of trade and subsidized prices for sugar, nickel, and oil. Other pacts signed that year committed additional Soviet aid to the construction of a steel mill and the nuclear power plant as well as other industrial and agricultural projects (for a total of U.S.$1.5 billion). Furthermore, they adjusted the value of Cuban imports from the Soviet Union to the value of Cuban major exports in order to reduce Cuba's trade deficit; after four years, that adjustment mechanism was abolished in 1979.

Between 1981 and 1985 Soviet-Cuban economic relations reached a zenith with the signing of numerous agreements: (1) a ten-year CMEA program (1981–90) for the economic and scientific-technological development of Cuba (extending low-interest loans), which focused on sugar, nickel (U.S.$870 million for this alone), citrus, nuclear and thermo-electric energy, and geological prospecting; (2) three agreements with CMEA for 1981–90, which included new credits totaling U.S.$1.8 billion (part in hard currency) to be repaid in 14 years, with low interest, to build the new sugar mills and modernize existing ones and expand nickel and citrus output (part of the expanded output was to be sent to the Soviet Union and other CMEA members as payment for their investments); (3) a second five-year economic and trade agreement (1981–85) with the Soviet Union, which increased the volume of trade, awarded new credits to cover trade deficits plus development loans, and fixed subsidized prices for that period; and (4) a Soviet-Cuban long-term cooperation agreement (1985–2000), which was aimed at strengthening Cuba's integration in CMEA and independence from market economies, creating Soviet-Cuban joint enterprises and joint exports to third countries, promoting Cuba's exports, increasing the efficiency of Cuba's utilization of socialist aid as well as savings in fuel and inputs, and achieving the island's self-sufficiency in foodstuffs. The 1985–2000 agreement was signed in 1984 when the Soviet Union was beginning to face severe economic constraints and Cuba's trade deficits reached historical records. Toward the end of that year, Castro declared that absolute priority would be given to investments that would increase Cuban exports to the Soviet Union and CMEA, and that the practice of diverting exports, earmarked for socialist countries to hard-currency countries, would be terminated (Mesa-Lago and Gil 1989).

As a result of all these agreements, Cuban trade with CMEA absorbed more than four-fifths of the island's total trade in the first half of the 1980s, but trade deficits and the debt kept expanding in spite of more generous Soviet price subsidies. Sugar prices in the world market escalated—from U.S. 3.8 to U.S. 29.7 cents per pound between 1970 and 1974—largely because of the sharp decline of Cuban production and exports in 1971–73. As the Soviet price paid for Cuban sugar remained unchanged at U.S. 6.1 cents per pound in 1971–72, in the latter year this price fell below the world market price. The Soviet Union steadily increased the price to U.S. 19.2 cents in 1974 but still did not match the world price, which reached a historical record that year. As had happened in 1963–64, Cuba took advantage of the high price of sugar to shift a considerable part of its trade away from the Soviet Union and CMEA toward developed market economies. But an increase in the Soviet price to U.S. 26.4 cents in 1975 (at a time that the world price began to fall because of Cuba's and other producers' increasing sugar exports) reestablished a favorable Soviet/world price ratio of 1.29 to 1.00 in favor of

Cuba. That ratio reached 3.79 to 1.00 in 1979, as Soviet prices climbed and world market prices declined; hence Cuba shifted its trade back to the Soviet Union and CMEA. In 1980, however, the world price boomed again because of the epidemic of sugar rust that affected Cuba and other sugar producers in the Caribbean, combined with a terrible sugar beet crop in the Soviet Union and a decline of Brazilian and Peruvian sugar exports. And yet, a new increase in the Soviet price maintained it above the world market level. Between 1981 and 1985 Soviet prices increased, and world prices declined (resulting from increasing world output and exports, combined with the development of a sugarcane substitute in the United States, and a slowdown in sugar consumption in developed countries), which generated a favorable ratio of 11.87 to 1.00 in Cuba's behalf and strengthened Cuba's trade integration with the Soviet bloc. Throughout this stage, Soviet sugar prices were considerably higher than world market prices except for a two-year period, and the same was true for nickel prices: by 1985 the Soviets were paying more than twice the world nickel price. Beginning in 1971 the Soviet Union sold crude oil to Cuba at prices considerably lower than the world price (in 1974 the Soviet price was 28% of the booming world market price). However, because of dwindling Soviet oil production, in 1983 the latter began to increase the price charged to Cuba, and this action, together with declining world prices, practically made the two prices alike in 1985 (Table III.19). The Soviet Union made another important concession: to pay Cuba in hard currency for the oil committed for delivery that the island was able to save; the Soviet Union exported that oil to other countries and passed the revenue on to Cuba, which, in turn, reported it as "oil reexports." The combination of all these subsidies resulted in a significant net gain for Cuba throughout this stage.

Cuba's strong economic recovery in the first half of the 1970s and the brief but significant shift of its trade toward developed market economies in 1974–75 allowed an access to credit from the West and Japan. Hence, the island's debt in hard currency (public and private) rapidly expanded. Most loans had a short maturity (one year), and interest rates escalated. These harsh conditions were compounded by the island's economic slowdown in the second half of the 1970s, and hard-currency loans began to decline during this period. Shrinking world sugar prices in the early 1980s and lack of sufficient fresh money forced Cuba to request a renegotiation of the terms of part of its hard-currency debt in 1982. Although an agreement to reschedule principal payments was reached with the creditors in 1983–84, giving the island a break, fresh loans became even rarer and practically stopped in 1986, thus increasing Cuban dependency on Soviet capital. In 1982 Cuba tried to overcome that dependency by enacting a foreign investment law that allowed investment from market economies in the form of joint ventures with domestic enterprises with special concessions in the case of tourism. But the law resulted in virtually no response in this stage because of foreign concerns about investment security, lack of access to the domestic market, unattractive fiscal and financial incentives, and U.S. prohibition of investment in Cuba (Mesa-Lago, 1981, 1982; Pérez-López 1985, 1986a; Mesa-Lago and Gil 1989).

G. Labor and Employment

During this stage, despite some early hope of improvement, there was no significant change in union objectives and degree of autonomy vis-à-vis the state. However, it was officially accepted that the previous policy of nonproductive employment creation, moral stimulation, and labor mobilization had resulted in low labor productivity and a burden to the economy. The SDPE labor policy emphasized productivity increases; hence it reintroduced work quotas and wage scales, revived old economic incentives and added new ones, facilitated a more flexible allocation of labor, practically eliminated voluntary labor, and created stimuli and mechanisms to release unneeded labor. At the beginning of the 1970s, several political leaders criticized the decline of trade unions in the 1960s, their lack of true democracy, and the illusion of identical interests between the unions and the administration of state enterprises. To change that situation, free elections and a return of the union's role as a defender of the workers' interests were promised. And yet the initial open discussion of these issues unleashed criticism that moved the government to reconsider these reforms and take steps to control the situation. In local elections held in 1971, only half of the expected voters participated; there were only 1.5 candidates for each post (instead of the promised 2 or 3 candidates); close to one-half of the incumbent leaders in Havana were reelected; and the government openly criticized those elected who did not fulfill the criteria of revolutionary loyalty and militancy. In a national congress of the CTC held in 1973 (after more than seven years without such an event), a series of conditions laid down by the government established limits for the discussion (ruling out criticism against the administration), and the voting on the congress's resolutions was done by public raising of hands. These resolutions and the newly enacted union statutes did not alter the role and objectives of the trade union movement, ratified the power of state administrators, and kept strikes virtually prohibited. In 1975 a survey conducted among union leaders and workers asked them what was the most important role of the unions: 60% answered production, 44% education, and only 4% defense of workers' interests.

The SDPE and the renewed emphasis on labor productivity led to the reenforcement and tightening of work quotas and their linkage to wage scales as well as a return to material incentives. Bonuses for exceeding work quotas were reinstated with a higher rate than in the 1960s: a 1% basic wage increase for each percent that the quota was exceeded. When reestablishing overtime payments, the previous policy of renouncing this benefit was criticized on the basis that unpaid overtime was more costly than regular paid hours because workers performed poorly while operating costs were fixed. Extra payments for work performed under dangerous or strenuous conditions as well as awards in kind and authors' royalties were restored. A new system of bonuses or *premios* rewarded groups of workers who surpassed quality standards, saved on raw materials and energy, developed new products, or increased production for export. To attract more manpower and increase productivity in the sugar sector, a new system of incentives for sugar workers included: a 15% wage increase, payment of 10% for exceeding work quotas, priority for buying scarce consumer goods (such as motorcycles, air conditioners), and better work clothing and housing. Other special wage systems were created to reward airplane pilots, ship captains, and qualified technicians. A new enterprise incentive fund (profit sharing) was established; the size of the fund was decided according to labor productivity, cost savings, size of the self-financed profit, and importance of production for exports. About two-thirds of the fund was paid in prizes (*premios* or cash payments to personnel at the end of the year), and one-third was for sociocultural activities (clubs, gymnasiums, vacations, entertainment, housing). Efforts to curb the old historical wage and prohibit the creation of a "new" historical wage (an increase not connected with productivity) were reportedly successful as such an increase was received by only 25% of the nonagricultural labor force in 1973 and by 11% in 1981. Incentives to private farmers (particularly those engaged in key crops) to increase output and sales to the state included higher prices for *acopio,* better credit facilities, authorization to hire salaried aid, and free markets to sell their produce. Self-employment was authorized to improve the quantity and quality of services.

The new system of incentives was a significant step forward over the previous "moral economy," but it was harmed by several factors: (1) managerial and technical personnel were not eligible for production bonuses and *premios;* (2) the linkage of work quotas to wages did not begin until 1974, and it proceeded very slowly, the revision of old quotas actually reducing the number of workers associated with them from 80% to 33% between 1973 and 1981; (3) most work quotas were so low that in 1979 almost 96% of those workers under the system either met or exceeded them; (4) the system of *premios* was very complex and overlapped with other incentives; (5) the enterprise incentive fund was conditioned by factors not related to the work effort, such as interruptions of supply and delays in the execution of investment, and as a result, only half of the enterprises under this program had a fund in operation; (6) although from one-fourth to one-third of the labor force received extra payments over the basic wage, all of them combined in 1985 accounted for only 10.6% of the basic wage, the lowest proportion within CMEA (Zimbalist and Brundenius 1989).

Fraud and corruption were also problems highlighted at the end of the 1970s by both Fidel and Raul Castro: foremen and workers made deals to exceed the work quota in half a day, there were slowdowns to avoid exceeding a very low quota too often (hence preempting its increase), and two quotas were met in one day in order to get an extra day free. The two leaders also complained that the spirit of austerity was flagging, a softening process was developing, work discipline had dropped, and signs of corruption appeared: high officials took advantage of their rank to get privileges, enterprise revenues were not deposited on time thus facilitating illegal appropriation, employees robbed their enterprises, and the masses adopted delinquent attitudes. In 1982 both free peasant markets and self-employment were also severely criticized. These "deviations" would eventually be given as reasons for the demise of the SDPE in the mid-1980s.

Unpaid voluntary labor was drastically curtailed in the 1970s, because it was contrary to enterprise efficiency. Those enterprises that provided volunteers had to keep paying their wages with a potential loss in production, cost increases, and fewer profits. Conversely, many enterprises that used volunteers did not reimburse the mobilizing agency, thereby increasing their output without a corresponding wage expenditure and thus boosting their profits. In the first half of the 1980s, these negative traits led to the practical elimination of voluntary labor.

In the 1970s the leadership officially acknowledged the existence of pockets of unemployment, and in 1980 it warned that such a problem would become worse in the 1980s, because of a decline in the demand for labor compounded by a sudden increase in labor supply. The latter was a result of the entrance into the labor market—beginning in 1977—of the baby boom of 1959–65 (birth rates climbed from 2.8% to 3.5% in that period), and labor supply was not expected to dwindle until the 1990s. There were several causes for the decline in labor demand. The SDPE emphasis on reducing labor costs (to increase productivity and profits), combined with the increased power and incentives of managers to fire redundant labor and the expansion and tightening of work quotas, led to the dismissal of thousands of workers (55,232 in 1980 alone) who were declared available or *disponibles,* similar to the *excedentes* of the 1960s. The slowdown in economic growth between

1976 and 1980 forced the postponement of investment projects (and the cancellation of some imports), creating a shortage of inputs and construction materials that led to the dismissal of thousands of construction workers and from 60,000 to 70,000 industrial workers in factories that had to be temporarily shut down. In addition, the tobacco blue mold pest caused the temporary unemployment of 26,000 workers. All these workers were declared temporarily jobless (*interruptos*). Finally, the size of the armed forces was cut by 15,000 men between 1970 and 1974 because of both a diminished threat of U.S. invasion and cuts in military activities abroad.

Several measures were taken to cope with the unemployment problem: (1) retirement laws were made more flexible in 1971, leading to a twofold increase in the number of those retiring in the 1970s compared with the 1960s, thus opening new jobs; (2) after 1973 service jobs that previously had been reserved for women were reopened for men, and in 1976 there was an expansion in the number of jobs from which women were barred because of health or safety reasons; (3) payment of 70% of salary was granted to both *disponibles* and *interruptos,* and the former were expected to be retrained and transferred to productive jobs (however, in 1976 a time limit was established for that compensation, and it was conditioned by the obligation to accept an adequate job offer); (4) the armed forces were significantly expanded after 1975 (at least by 50,000 men) as Cuba became involved in warfare in Africa; (5) professionals and skilled workers in abundant supply (e.g., physicians, construction workers) were exported to work abroad under government contracts paid in hard currency (in 1980 about 20,000 of them were performing services in Libya, Iraq, Algeria, and other countries); (6) low-skilled Cuban surplus manpower was hired under contracts by the Soviet Union, Czechoslovakia, East Germany, and Hungary to perform jobs needed in those countries (e.g., 10,000 Cubans went to cut timber in Siberia) in exchange for a share of the goods they produced or other goods needed by Cuba; (7) beginning in 1978 the private practice of personal services was allowed out of either state employment time or even full time in certain cases providing they registered and paid a modest tax, and to that effect the 1971 vagrancy law was made more flexible; (8) in the first half of the 1980s, private farmers were allowed to hire salaried workers, and self-employment in services and small manufactures was further expanded, with both farmers and urban handicraft markets providing extra jobs; and (9) the huge exodus from Mariel port in 1980 (more than 100,000 people) included an average of 6% of those unemployed (25% among the women), which significantly reduced the labor surplus. As has been explained already, some of these measures, particularly the expansion of private activities, received a severe blow in 1982 from the criticism and punitive measures taken by the government. In any event, the percentage of civilian employment continued its decline (from 13.7% to 4.7% between 1970 and 1985) in spite of the brief liberalization; however, a small increase was reported in self-employment and private salaried work in 1981 over 1979 (0.8 percentage points combined), to decline again in 1985. State civilian employment increased from 86.3% to 93.2% of the civilian labor force between 1970 and 1985 (Table III.24; Mesa-Lago 1978, 1981, 1982, 1988a).

H. Distribution and Social Services

Previous emphasis on egalitarianism came under criticism during this stage, paving the way for the expansion of wage differences, the reintroduction or strengthening of material incentives, the increasing use of markets and prices as a partial substitute for rationing, and the halt or curtailment of some free social services, all of which induced some stratification and inequality. The pursuit of wage equality and the communist principle of distribution according to need were criticized during this stage as idealistic errors (or petty bourgeois egalitarianism) that did not take into account the worker's productive effort; hence, wage differentials were defended as an incentive for those with labor skills, heavy responsibilities, and tough or dangerous jobs. In 1973 the CTC proclaimed the return to the socialist principle of distribution according to work. The old wage scale was considered too egalitarian; hence a wage reform in 1981 increased relative wages of highly skilled labor. The additional payments to the basic wage (even if they accounted for only 10.6% of the basic wage) must have enlarged income differences. Other sources of inequality during this stage were the growing incomes of small private farmers, self-employed workers, small manufacturers, and middlemen.

There was steady improvement in the supply of consumer goods during this stage (except for the stagnation during the recession of 1979–80), which was reflected by an increase in the rationing quotas of many products. In addition, the farmers, handicraft workers, and parallel markets increased the supply of goods, although at considerably higher prices than the rationing price, and hence could not be afforded by the lowest income brackets. The new markets had several objectives: to siphon out excess money in circulation, provide incentives for the labor force to work harder (to earn more and hence be able to buy more and better goods), reduce or compensate government subsidies to consumer goods, gradually eliminate rationing, and combat the black market. Beginning in 1973 some manufactured goods such as cameras and cosmetics were freed from rationing while others were put in limited distribution. Other consumer durables (refrigerators, television sets, sewing machines, bicycles) were withdrawn from stores but allocated to state enterprises, farms, and agencies. The agencies advertised the available goods to their workers, and those who were interested filled out forms to buy them; applications were then ranked by a committee of workers, mainly taking productivity into account. Most of these goods were out of reach of the lowest income strata; for instance, a TV set or refrigerator cost from four to five months average wages.

According to the Institute of Domestic Demand, created in 1971 to survey consumers' tastes and preferences, less than one-third of all goods (measured in value) were rationed by 1979, and the rest were distributed free or by the parallel market, the other two markets, and the system of allocation to enterprises. (Without disregarding the advance in the use of rational prices during this stage, it should be noted that the one-third of the goods still rationed in 1979 included the most important foodstuffs, beverages, and tobacco, all of which had a low price, while most nonrationed goods were very high-priced and hence accounted for the remaining two-thirds.) The significant price increases of consumer goods and services in 1981 was another attempt to adjust them somewhat to real market prices and to cut state subsidies. To somewhat protect low-income groups, nevertheless, the government increased the prices of the top-quality and out-of-season goods more than the prices of low-quality and seasonally abundant goods. Finally, several gratuities were eliminated, like free meals in workers' cafeterias, school uniforms, free public telephone calls, and free admittance to museums, zoos, botanical gardens, and some sporting events. The government then raised the lowest wages but not enough to compensate for the loss in purchasing power of the lowest income group caused by price increases and suppression of gratuities. Although the lowest income strata were still protected by a minimum of goods rationed and the dual tier of price increases, it was obvious that the wealthier became able to buy many goods and services not affordable by the poor as well as to choose from a wider assortment and better quality of products.

Expansion of social services became vigorous again during this stage after the slowdown suffered in the previous period. The share of the budget for social services was stagnant at 33% in 1965, 1978, and 1981 (no data are available for 1970) but increased to 42% in 1984–85. Investment in social services climbed from 14% in 1970 to 23% in 1975 but gradually slowed to 18% in 1985 (Table III.6; CEE *AEC* 1984a, 1985a). Social expenditures per capita (not adjusted for inflation), which had increased by 35% in the previous stage, jumped by 60% between 1971 and 1975, but the rate slowed to 42% between 1976 and 1980 and 32% between 1981 and 1985. The fastest-growing service expenditures were social security and welfare, followed by education and health care, with housing lagging behind (Rodríguez 1990a; O. Castro 1992; Mesa-Lago 1993d).

In 1979 the entire social security system exclusive of health care was integrated under the State Committee on Labor and Social Security. Coverage of pensions were extended to agricultural cooperatives, and there was a twofold increase in the number of pensioners in the 1970s due to more flexible retirement to open jobs for the unemployed, aging of the population, and maturation of the pension program. By 1985 social security costs (excluding health care) approximated one billion pesos, and the number of pensioners was close to 800,000 for a rough ratio of one pensioner per five active workers in the labor force (Table III.34; Rodríguez 1990a).

The number of physicians graduating from medical schools accelerated in the 1970s and by 1975 had recovered the prerevolutionary ratio; in 1985 there were 22.5 physicians per 10,000 inhabitants compared to 7.1 per 10,000 in 1970. The number of hospital beds per 10,000 inhabitants, which had declined from 5.3 to 4.1 between 1965 and 1977, increased to 4.8 by 1985 (Table III.30). The government made an enormous investment in health care to recover the prerevolutionary standards, and such efforts paid off in the 1970s and by the 1980s had achieved remarkable progress. Furthermore, the distribution of health resources was made more equal between urban and rural areas: in 1958 there was only one rural hospital, while in 1978 there were 57, and in 1968, 60% of physicians and 62% of hospital beds were in Havana, while in 1978 the proportions had declined to 36% and 29%, and the city had 21% of the population. Later, however, there was an increase in Havana's share again, and, in spite of the improvement, there were still significant differences among provinces.

In the 1960s most investment in education went to combat illiteracy and expand enrollment at the elementary level, in the 1970s the focus shifted to the secondary level, and in the 1980s it went to the higher level as well. However, the considerable physical plant and personnel already developed in the 1970s, together with the aging of the population, resulted in a significant slowdown in the rate of growth of educational facilities in the 1980s. A remarkable effort was done to also reduce inequalities between urban and rural areas in the 1960s but not as much in the 1970s, although a special program for peasants was created through scholarships, which cover costs of housing, food, clothing, and transportation.

In the first half of the 1980s, the relaxation in the previous restrictions on housing construction, combined with a higher proportion of the budget devoted to housing, easier access to construction materials, and authorization of self-employment, generated the biggest construction boom under the Revolution. A 1984 law established that tenants could convert their leases with the state into long-term purchase contracts with monthly installments equal to the rent they used to pay. By 1988 from 200,000 to 500,000 deeds had been turned in to comply with the law.

Until the mid-1970s the government argued that population was not a limiting factor in development and hence was critical of birth control and family planning. But the entrance of the baby boom in the labor market and the increasing burden of social services caused Castro in 1975 to acknowledge this problem and ask the Party to design a population policy. And yet Cuba's population growth in the mid-1970s became the lowest in Latin America without a specific government policy: growing urbanization, education, and women's incorporation into the labor force combined with a severe housing scarcity, rationing, and emigration were explanations for this phenomenon. Furthermore, the pill, the diaphragm, and other contraceptives began to be purchased and imported, and the number of abortions dramatically increased: in 1978 at the Havana Hospital 20 abortions were done daily versus 12 births (Mesa-Lago 1981, 1982, 1988a; Díaz-Briquets 1983).

2. Performance

A. Growth

For this stage there are two series on GSP growth at constant prices, but they cannot be connected because of divergent base years and methodologies. The first series (1971–75) gives an annual average GSP growth rate of 13.6% (11.9% per capita), but an alternative official figure is only half (7.5% or 5.8% per capita), and other estimates are even smaller. The second series starts in 1975, uses one single methodology and base year (1981), and provides abundant data on GSP and most of its components; hence it is significantly better than all previous series. However, there is no way to assess the reliability of the second series as details on its calculations, particularly on the deflators, have never been released. In addition, there is considerable debate on the selection of 1981 as the base year for the series because it was an abnormal year, as it registered some of the highest inflation rates under the Revolution (due to the jump in prices after 19 years of price freezing). Furthermore, the year 1981 was kept as a base for more than a decade, a practice that contradicted a methodological document of the United Nations (cited by Cuba as a reference) that recommends that a period base (rather than one year) be used and be changed every five years. The GSP rate in constant prices for 1981 was 16%, the highest ever reported under the Revolution, almost four times the average annual rate of growth between 1976 and 1989.

According to this series, annual GSP growth between 1976 and 1980 was 3.5% (2.7% per capita), while other growth estimates range from −0.3% to 4% (−1% to 3.3% per capita). For 1981–85 the same series gives a GSP growth rate of 7.3% (6.4% per capita), while alternative growth estimates fluctuate from 3.9% to 7.9% (3% to 7% per capita). The official rate for the entire 1976–85 stage is 5.4% (4.6% per capita), but, if the controversial 1981 rate is deleted, it declines to 4.2% (3.4% per capita); other estimates for the stage range from 1.2% to 2% (0.4% to 1.2% per capita) (Tables III.3–4; Mesa-Lago and Pérez-López 1992).

Although it is impossible to give a reliable GSP rate for 1971–85, the available data suggest that growth was higher than in any previous stages, but that there were significant fluctuations in the rate among the three quinquennia in this stage. Between 1971 and 1975 the rate was high because of the recovery after the 1966–70 debacle, booming world sugar prices, increase in Soviet aid and Western credit, and domestic economic rationalization measures. Between 1976 and 1980 there was a slowdown in the growth rate caused by declining sugar prices in the world market (although attenuated by Soviet subsidies), agricultural plagues, difficulties in the nickel and fishing industries, the heavier burden of servicing the hard-currency debt, and delays and complications in the implementation of the SDPE. Between 1981 and 1985 there was substantial growth, influenced again by the sharp increase in Soviet subsidies and loans, a brief boom in sugar world prices in 1981, and economic liberalization measures.

Average annual sugar output between 1971 and 1975 was 5,548 thousand tons, a 4% decline vis-à-vis the 1966–70 average, because of low sugar harvests in the first four years (with a low in 1972) caused by the failure of the Australian system and fewer resources allocated to the sugar sector. But by 1975 the sugar crop surpassed 6 million tons because of expanding mechanization and better organization and incentives. Sugar output steadily increased in the following two quinquennia to annual averages of 6,929 thousand tons between 1976 and 1980 and 7,777 thousand tons between 1981 and 1985 (the 8 million mark was surpassed in three years), largely as an outcome of successful mechanization of the harvest and some modernization of the mills. And yet actual production fell below the planned targets: in 1980 it was 8.7 million tons, but only 6.7 million tons were produced (because of the cane rust pest); and in 1985 the target was initially set at 10 to 10.5 million tons and then reduced to 9.5 to 10 million tons, but actual output was 8 million tons. The reason for the nonfulfillment was the failure to implement key premises of both five-year plans, compounded by the expanding length of the harvests from 99 to 126 days and declining industrial yields from 12.44% to 10.47%, both between 1975 and 1984 (Tables III.11, III.14).

Performance in nonsugar agriculture was mixed but much better than in the previous stage. There were remarkable increases in output of citrus (eightfold), milk (144%), and eggs (67%); but production of coffee, tobacco, and beans was stagnant or sluggish and by 1985 was below either the 1958 output level or the peak reached in the 1960s. The number of head of cattle was 12% lower in 1985 than in 1970, but the number of pigs (state sector) had risen almost four times and that of poultry almost twofold. The FAO index of agricultural output per capita showed an increase of 21% in 1985 over 1971, but, if the base year had been 1970 instead of 1971 (when sugar output declined sharply), such an increase would have been only 7% or 8%. The fish and seafood catch jumped twofold between 1970 and 1985, but it oscillated after 1974, and by 1985 it was only slightly higher than in 1978 (Tables III.10, III.12; FAO 1970–86).

In spite of the grandiose nickel plan, production was basically stagnant throughout this stage; the 1985 target of 69,500 metric tons was unfulfilled by one-half, and output that year was 8% below the 1970 level. Conversely, oil production steadily increased (particularly after 1982), and in 1985 it was 5.5 times higher than in 1970 (Tables III.13, III.21). Aided by equipment imported from the Soviet Union and CMEA, industrial output showed impressive growth between 1970 and 1985 in most lines: cement (329%), steel (186%), textiles (163%), electricity (150%), fertilizers (100%), and refrigerators, radios, and TV sets (almost tripled). But, with the exception of cement and electricity, that accomplishment was attenuated by two facts: production of durable consumer goods began in the 1960s, and hence their recorded growth between 1970 and 1985 was related to a very low base; and in other lines (textiles, fertilizers) output declined in the second half of the 1960s, and the 1970 base was actually a low; hence if 1960 or 1965 had been used as a base, the 1970–85 increase would have been much more modest. Furthermore, the production of several traditional manufactured goods for domestic consumption (shoes, soap, detergent) or for export (cigars) was either stagnant or declined in this stage. Western-estimated indices of overall industrial output give an increase of 2.4 to 3.7 times in this stage (Table III.10; Pérez-López 1987b; Zimbalist and Brundenius 1989).

The number of tourists grew from practically zero in 1971 to 34,000 in 1975 and then jumped to 83,000 in 1979 and 101,000 in 1980. Most of these tourists were Cuban-Americans but, after their visits were severely cut, the number fell in 1981. By 1985, however, 168,000 tourists were reported, who generated 100 million pesos in gross revenue, but still only 60 million pesos in net revenue or 0.22% of GSP (Table III.15).

Another way to evaluate economic performance in this stage is to contrast actual output with projected targets under the 1976–80 and 1981–85 plans; targets were not available for 1971–75 (Table III.14). Most macroeconomic targets were drastically underfulfilled in 1980 (for instance, −42% in GSP) and were subsequently set at a lower level for 1985 (e.g., the labor productivity goal was cut from 7% to 3%) and then overfulfilled by large margins (e.g., 46% in GSP). Even more revealing is to assess the fulfilment of physical output targets in key agricultural and industrial production lines, for both domestic consumption and exports. In 1980 the targets of only 2 products were overfulfilled (eggs and electricity), but those of 14 products were nonfulfilled, 8 of them by more than one-third (including nickel, cement, steel, textiles, fishing, and tobacco). For 1985 about half of the output targets were set below the level of the previous plan, but still most were not fulfilled and by larger margins: 2 targets were overfulfilled (eggs and pork), but 18 were underfulfilled, 8 of them by more than one-third (including nickel, cement, steel, textiles), and another 3 by one-fourth or more (fishing, citrus, and electricity). If most physical output targets in 1985 were underfulfilled by such a large margin, it is questionable that the GSP growth target was overfulfilled by 46% in that year.

The share of investment in GSP steadily increased from 9.6% in 1970 to 18.7% in 1977, declined to 13% in 1982, and grew to 15.9% in 1985. Throughout this stage the share averaged 14.7% annually, considerably higher than in any previous stage. Between 1971 and 1980 there are rare official estimates of the share of investment over GDP that exhibit an increasing trend until 1977 and a decline thereafter, averaging 20% for the entire period (Tables III.3, III.7). It is not possible to assess capital efficiency in this stage, but it was probably higher than between 1966 and 1970.

B. Inflation

Estimates of annual inflation give an average of 6.1% between 1971 and 1975. Since 1976 Cuba has published deflators that allow us to calculate annual inflation as 1.2% for 1976–80 and 1.6% for 1981–85. Inflation officially reached 8.5% in 1981 but reported deflation or almost no inflation in the following four years sharply reduced the 1981–85 average. If the two series could be combined (which is not technically feasible), the annual rate of inflation between 1970 and 1985 would be 3% (Tables III.3–4). Data on the cumulative monetary surplus do not match the inflation data trend. Between 1970 and 1975 the surplus per capita was cut from 388 to 215 pesos as excess money was siphoned out of circulation by price increases and elimination of gratuities, hence partly restoring the value of money. The surplus per capita was virtually stagnant between 1975 and 1980 but began to increase again and, by 1985, had reached 305 pesos (Table III.5). A significant proportion of that surplus was deposited in banks, which paid a 2% rate of interest. Still the sudden jump of the surplus in the first half of the 1980s was an indication of growing inflationary pressures.

Data on the budget balance, available since 1981, showed deficits in three years, which reached almost 1% of GSP in 1985 (Table III.3). Between 1976 and 1981 the state subsidized consumption for a total of 1,887 million pesos, but because of the 1981 price increases, the government estimated that such a subsidy would be cut between 1981 and 1985 to 671 million pesos. And yet the 1982 budget deficit was largely blamed on state subsidies to consumer goods and deficit-prone enterprises (Table III.6; Mesa-Lago 1982).

C. Diversification

An assessment of changes in diversification is obscured by three different series on the percentage distribution of GSP by economic sectors (Table III.8). The longest series (available since 1962) shows that the industrial share shrank from 47.9% (1970) to 37.6% (1975) and 36.1% (1985); the agricultural share first declined from 14.7% to 11.8% and then increased to 13.9%; the trade share steadily grew from 20.3% to 22% and 33.2%; and the remaining shares (construction, transportation, and communication) showed little change and were similar to those in the two new series (which began in 1980 and went back to 1975). The second series shifted about 10 percentage points (reportedly tax value) from the trade sector to the industrial sector (leaving the remained sectors virtually unchanged); that reshuffling resulted in an industrial share higher than in the first series but also declining from 47.8% (1975) to 45.8% (1985), a rising agricultural share (similar to those in the first and third series), and a lower and stagnant trade share (23.5% and 23.1%). The third series transferred an additional, gradually increasing proportion (from 1 to 10 percentage points) from the trade sector to the industrial sector (through another unclear redistribution of tax value), therefore conveying the exact opposite result from the first series: a growing industrial share, from 48.7% (1975) to 55.1% (1985), but a shrinking trade share from 22.5% to 14%. Although it is difficult to determine which of the three series is the most accurate, the first has been selected for five reasons: (1) the first series is the longest in existence (the other two lack data from 1962 to 1974), and, if inaccurate, it would have been dropped; (2) the third series does not explain what taxes were transferred that were not reshuffled already in the second series; (3) the reallocation of the tax value was virtually done only to industry with practically nothing going to the other four sectors; (4) the last two series might have been a fabrication to support the official claim of fast industrialization; and (5) data on employment trends (to be discussed later) confirm a declining share of industry.

Indicators on sugar dependency are not consistent either but, in general, suggest stagnation or increasing dependence. The share of sugar output in GSP declined from 15.1% to 8.2% between 1971 and 1980 but then increased again and by 1985 was 10.2%, the same proportion as in 1964. The share of sugar exports in GSP grew from 9.7% in 1970 to 15.8% in 1985, or almost twice the share of 1964 when the return to growing sugar began. Finally, we can compare sugar dependency prior to and under the Revolution based on the official GDP series available for 1971–80: the sugar export share in GDP was 22.2% in 1958 and 10.2% in 1971, but it increased to 23.3% in 1980, showing a higher degree of dependence than in 1958 (Table III.11).

D. Trade Balance and External Dependency

Historical comparisons of Cuba's foreign trade are complicated between 1971 and 1985 because the value of the peso ceased to be par with the U.S. dollar, as the Cuban government arbitrarily fixed the former above the latter, peaking at 0.71 pesos for U.S.$1 in 1980 (Table III.3). This exchange rate was artificial, and on the domestic black market several pesos were exchanged for U.S.$1 (e.g., 5 to 1 in 1979). We also lack a historical series on imports, exports, and trade balance in constant prices except for 1976–80 (Mesa-Lago and Pérez-López 1992).

The positive accomplishments in economic growth in this stage were offset by a significant worsening in the external disequilibria, aggravating the previous problem. Aided by growing sugar exports and booming world market prices in the first half of the 1970s, as well as rapidly increasing Soviet subsidies, the value of Cuban exports (except for 1971–72 when sugar output and exports sharply declined) jumped 470% in this stage. And yet the value of imports increased even more, 513%; actual imports between 1981 and 1985 surpassed the planned target by 80%. Except for a tiny trade surplus in 1974, there were trade deficits throughout this stage for an increase of 681%, or 752% if the official dollar conversion is used. A comparison among the three quinquennia within this stage shows that the cumulative deficit between 1971 and 1975 was reduced by 26% vis-à-vis that of 1966–70 but increased by 43% between 1976 and 1980 and by 196% between 1981 and 1985. The trade deficit amply surpassed U.S.$1 billion in 1981 and U.S.$2 billion in 1985, establishing historical records (Table III.16).

Dependency on the Soviet Union accelerated in this stage (based on Soviet price subsidies and trade credit); thus the Soviet share of Cuba's total transactions grew from 51.7% to 70.5% between 1970 and 1985 (from 64%

to 83% with CMEA), higher than the planned targets for 1985 of 65% with the Soviet Union and 69% with CMEA. One negative effect of this increasing trade dependency was that cargo vessels had to cover longer distances (than if trade was with the Americas or Western Europe); hence in spite of the impressive expansion of Cuba's merchant marine, it could handle only one-tenth of total trade, and the bulk of it had to be done with Soviet or CMEA ships (paid in soft currency or barter) as well as Western ships rented in hard currency. Cuba's trade deficit with the Soviet Union increased 767% (950% in U.S. dollars), and the Soviet share of Cuba's total trade deficit averaged 68% in this stage. In 1975–78, however, Cuba enjoyed a surplus due to the adjustment in the value of the island's exports with Soviet imports, but in 1979 the Soviets halted that arrangement, alleging that it was too costly, and thereafter the deficit grew steadily, surpassing U.S.$1 billion in 1985 (Table III.20; Mesa-Lago 1981).

Between 1971 and 1985 Cuba received U.S.$11.7 billion in Soviet loans: U.S.$6.8 billion to cover trade deficits and U.S.$4.9 billion in development aid (Table III.22, segment A). The debt accumulated up until 1972 was postponed to 1986, free of interest. Even more important were the price subsidies paid by the Soviet Union; it has been noted that, between 1966 and 1970, there was a significant difference in the estimation of the amount of such subsidies to the price of sugar, depending on the price used for the calculation. Although such a divergence continued between 1971 and 1975, it was dramatically reduced between 1976 and 1985 because of a closing of the gap between world prices and preferential prices. Based on the world market price, the Soviet subsidy between 1971 and 1985 was U.S.$22 billion (proportionally 9.5 times the subsidy paid between 1966 and 1970); based on the U.S. preferential price, the subsidy was U.S.$20 billion; and based on the U.S. preferential import price, the subsidy was U.S.$17 billion. The huge Soviet sugar subsidy (as well as smaller subsidies paid by other CMEA members) led Cuba to increase the percentage of its sugar exports to the Soviet Union from 40% between 1966 and 1970 to 52% between 1976 and 1985, and 73% to all socialist countries (however, between 1971 and 1975, because of the booming sugar prices in the world market, this percentage dropped to 36%). Cuba's share in the open sugar world market consequently declined from 15% to 9% in this stage (Pérez-López 1991).

In spite of a fivefold jump in oil domestic production in this stage, Cuba's growing fuel needs required a substantial increase in Soviet oil imports, which, by 1985, met 98.2% of the island's oil imports compared with 94.1% in 1970 (Table III.21). Triangular agreements with oil exporters such as Venezuela and Mexico had little impact and were charged to the Soviet Union anyway. Between 1971 and 1983 Soviet oil prices charged to Cuba were significantly lower than the world price; hence the island was protected from the devastating effects that escalating oil prices had on oil-importer developing countries; however, the price gap began to close in 1983 and disappeared by 1985 (Table III.19). Cuba's "reexports" of unused Soviet oil deliveries, nevertheless, accounted for the island's highest source of hard currency after sugar exports.

Total Soviet economic aid to Cuba, combining loans and price subsidies (to sugar, nickel, and oil, all based on world market prices) but excluding revenues from "reexports," amounted to U.S.$39.8 billion between 1971 and 1985. A comparison by quinquennia shows that Soviet aid increased 100% between 1971 and 1975, 300% between 1976 and 1980, and 55% between 1981 and 1985. Furthermore, while between 1971 and 1975 two-thirds of the aid was in repayable loans (debt) and one-third in nonrepayable subsidies, between 1981 and 1985 the proportions had reversed in Cuba's favor (Table III.22).

After a brief expansion of trade with market economies in 1974–75 (up to 41% of Cuba's total trade) stimulated by the booming sugar world prices, the market economies' trade share gradually declined to 13% in 1985 (trade with China also shrank from 6.6% to 2.7% during this stage). That reality contrasted with the 1981–85 plan, which forecast that the Cuban trade share with market economies would increase to 31%. Data on foreign exchange reserves are available since 1981; they show a decline from 403 to 350 million pesos between 1981 and 1985 and that dwindling reserves were increasingly made up of transferable rubles (ECLAC *Survey* 1989b). Cuba's debt in hard currency increased (in billion U.S. dollars) from U.S.$1.3 (1976) to U.S.$1.8 (1979) to U.S.$2.7 (1982) to U.S.$3.6 (1985). Beginning in the late 1970s and early 1980s, such increases were not as much an outcome of new loans as of rising interest rates and appreciation of the principal. About half of the debt was with governments and the rest with financial institutions and other creditors (the share of the latter—having the toughest terms—gradually increased). In 1984 Cuba's debt in hard currency was equal to 11.4% of its GSP, and the debt service represented almost 29% of the island's export value (Table III.23). Cuba's total external debt in 1985 was calculated as U.S.$16.7 billion, combining an estimate of the Soviet debt (U.S.$13.5 billion) and the debt in hard currency (U.S.$3.2 billion), but excluding the debt to other socialist countries. In that year Cuba's total debt was the fifth largest in Latin America; it was equal to 57% of GSP and 281% of total export value (Mesa-Lago and Gil 1989).

Export concentration on sugar increased from 77% to 90% between 1970 and 1975 (largely because of booming prices of sugar) and then declined to 74.5% in 1985. But part of that decline resulted from growing oil "reexports" from 0.1% to 9.5%—actually hard-currency transfers from the Soviet Union instead of real Cuban exports. When properly excluding oil "reexports," the share of sugar in total exports increased to 82%, similar to the percentage in 1962 and higher than that in 1959 (Table III.17). Cuba's ongoing sugar dependency was reinforced, as already discussed, by its increasing share of sugar exports in GSP (Table III.11). Sympathetic Western scholars argued, nevertheless, that both export and trade-partner concentration were outcomes of subsidized Soviet prices and meant neither continued dependency on sugar nor increased dependency on the Soviet Union (Zimbalist and Brundenius 1989). But if that argument were accepted, then one would have had to adjust downward both Cuban GSP and trade-transaction value (to eliminate the contribution of Soviet subsidies) and the value of Cuba's sugar exports to, and degree on dependency on, the United States prior to the Revolution (to eliminate the U.S. preferential prices paid to Cuba).

Most changes in the composition of Cuban imports in this stage appear to be positive, such as the decline in the shares of foodstuffs (from 22% to 12% between 1970 and 1985) and manufactures (from 25% to 16% between 1975 and 1985). These might suggest increasing self-sufficiency but could also be the result of consumption restrictions, particularly in manufactured goods. The equally sharp decline in the import share of machinery and transportation (from 42% to 30% between 1977 and 1985) could have been an indication of slowdown in the process of industrialization. The only increasing import share in this stage was that of fuels (from 9% to 33%), and this in spite of generous Soviet price subsidies; Cuba, therefore, had to proportionally reduce all other imports to raise oil imports and keep the economy functioning (Table III.18).

E. Unemployment

In spite of the policies to combat unemployment, official data on the open unemployment rate show that it increased from 1.3% in 1970 (population census) to 5.4% in 1979 (demographic survey) and to 5.5% in 1981 (population census) (Table III.26). According to official statistics, the rate of growth of state civilian employment slowed from 6.2% to 1.3% between 1977 and 1979 and declined by 1.2% in 1980; and yet the rate rose again (from 2% to 4%) in 1981–84. The expanding private sector must have played a role in this trend (Mesa-Lago 1988a). A comparison of the distribution of the labor force by economic sectors in 1970, 1979, and 1981 (no data are available for 1985) shows that the primary sector declined from 30% to 21.9% and then increased to 22.3%; the secondary sector increased from 26.3% to 27.8% and then stagnated (the industrial-mining share actually declined from 20.3% to 18.9%); and the tertiary sector steadily grew from 41.3% to 42.9% and 46.3% (Table III.24). These figures confirm that the service sector was the most dynamic in employment creation while the industrial sector either stagnated or declined. Female participation in the labor force rose from 18.3% to 31.4% between 1970 and 1981; women found employment mostly in the tertiary sector (although in a declining percentage, particularly in trade) and to a lesser extent in the secondary sector (also in a decreasing percentage, particularly in industry) and in the primary sector (although in a growing percentage). The highest degree of participation of women (exhibiting an increasing trend) was in administration and services; a very small degree of participation was found in executive and blue-collar jobs (Table III.25).

According to official figures, labor productivity in constant prices grew at an annual average rate of 4.2% between 1976 and 1980 (versus a planned target of 7% and probably at a lower rate that between 1971 and 1975), and at 5.1% between 1981 and 1985 (above the planned target of 3%). The latter average, however, included a great leap of 13.6% in 1981, unparalleled in Cuba's socialist history (compared with an average rate of 2% between 1976 and 1989, excluding 1981). No explanation was ever given for that feat, another indication of the inflated nature of the 1981 data. The productivity rate slowed to an average of 3% in 1982–85. If the suspicious 1981 rate is excluded, there was a declining average productivity rate in the three quinquennia in this stage. Between 1976 and 1980 the average annual net gain in productivity (contrasted with increases in real wages) was 3.7%, but it declined to 0.6% in 1982–85 (CEE, *AEC* 1977a–89a). Top Cuban leaders referred on multiple occasions to underutilization of labor in all sectors: agriculture (only four or five hours were worked daily in sugarcane fields and production cooperatives), construction (from 25% to 30% of the workday was wasted), industry (machinery was utilized by 50% to 60%, but a second labor shift was added), and services (offices were "full of people doing nothing"). The waves of *excedentes* released during this stage were another indication of underemployment (Mesa-Lago 1988a).

F. Equality

No Cuban data are available on income distribution, but it has been grossly calculated for the years 1973, 1978 (two variants with significantly different estimates), and 1986. Aside from serious methodological flaws, these distributions are not comparable (e.g., the private sector was included in some years and excluded in others), and the results were discrepant, which made them worthless (Table III.27). The distributions of 1973 and the first variant of 1978 were quite similar, except for a transfer of about 1 percentage point from the wealthier quintile to the two middle quintiles, while the two poorest quintiles remained unchanged. Conversely, the distributions of 1973 and the second variant of 1978 showed results opposite to the previous comparison: the two middle quintiles lost 6 percentage points, three-fourths of which went to the poorest two quintiles and one-fourth to the wealthiest. Finally, the 1986 distribution resembled the first variant of 1978 in the wealthiest quintile but was similar to the second variant of 1978 in the remaining four quintiles.

The scant and confusing data available on wage scales show that between 1979 and 1981, the ratio of the highest to the lowest wage rate rose from 4.9:1 to 5.5:1, as the lowest wage rate increased from 71 to 82 pesos, and the highest rate increased from 350 to 450 pesos (Brundenius 1984; Zimbalist and Brundenius 1989). And yet in 1979 the director of the Institute of Domestic Demand told me in Havana that the highest wage rate was 700 pesos, a salary often paid to cabinet ministers. In addition, there were special wage systems for sugar workers, pilots, and other groups (probably including the armed forces and internal security). Other differences were created by extra payments (bonuses, *premios,* prizes, overtime, strenuous working conditions) and the historical wage. Even before the 1981 reform, there were salaries in Cuba ranging from 500 to 750 pesos paid to top physicians, university professors, and highly skilled technicians. Last but not least was the increased income of the private sector; Castro reported incomes as high as 30,000 to 150,000 a year, although these were probably earned by few (Mesa-Lago 1981, 1990a). All this suggests that there was an increase in income inequality in this stage.

The real average wage increased about 8 percentage points between 1975 and 1980, and it gained 17 additional points by 1985 (Table III.28). Rationing improved between 1969 and 1971–72 as the quotas of nine products were increased or put in free distribution. However, the recession of 1979 led to a decrease in the quotas of four products, although two improved (Table III.29). The gradual replacement of rationing by the parallel and free markets (with much higher prices), as well as the significant price increases in 1981, must have contributed to inequality in this stage.

G. Social Indicators

The national illiteracy rate was reported as 4% by the demographic survey in 1979 (2.3% in urban areas and 7.1% in rural areas) and as 1.9% by the 1981 census. These were dramatic cuts from the 12.9% national rate (7.1% urban and 21.5% rural) given by the 1970 census. But these figures are not comparable because in 1970 they referred to the population 10 years and older, while in 1979 and 1981 the population 49 years and older were excluded (the segment in which the remnants of illiteracy were concentrated). UNESCO reported a rate of 7.6% in 1985 among those 15 years and older, the first figure comparable with the 1953 rate of 22%. Enrollment in secondary education rose from 25% to 85%, a remarkable feat in 15 years, while enrollment in higher education grew from 5% to 21%, also quite impressive (Table III.33). But the 1985 target was even more ambitious (39%) and was not met (Table III.14).

Infant mortality was cut from 38.7 to 16.5 per 1,000 in this stage, one of the most important improvements under the Revolution and a performance better than the planned target; for example, in 1980 the target was 24 and the actual rate was 19.6 (Table III.14). The overall mortality rate declined from 6.3 to 5.4 per 1,000 between 1970 and 1975 and then climbed to 6.4 in 1985, mostly because of the aging of the population. ECLAC estimated an increase in life expectancy from 71 years between 1971 and 1975 to 74.3 between 1981 and 1985. Cuba reported, for the first time, data on life expectancy: it increased from 73 years in 1977–78 to 74.3 in 1983–84 (both similar to ECLAC's average and compatible with improvements in infant mortality). Access of urban dwellers to potable water and sanitation increased slightly between 1970 and 1981 (from 88% to 90%, and from 93% to 96%, respectively); the expansion of rural access to water and sanitation was even more significant: from 24% to 33%, and from 61% to 80%, respectively. And yet advances in these indications vis-à-vis 1953 were relatively small compared with other progress in the area of health (Table III.32). The rates of six contagious diseases (preventable through vaccination) decreased or no cases were reported, but the rates of seven diseases increased, mostly those not preventable such as acute diarrhea and respiratory, hepatitis, syphilis, and gonorrhea, but also malaria (Table III.31). Social security coverage of the labor force on pensions was estimated to increase from 88.7% to 93% between 1970 and 1981 (Table III.34).

The average annual number of houses built by the state for the civilian population steadily rose during this stage: from 6,361 (1966–70) to 15,937 (1971–75), 16,485 (1976–80), and 22,114 (1981–85). In spite of this notable improvement, the planned targets for state housing construction in 1980 and 1985 were not met by about one-half (Table III.14). Between 1981 and 1985, an annual average of 41,445 houses were built by the population (one-fourth with certificate of habitability), and 4,858 more were constructed by the state for the military and by cooperatives. This housing boom must have reduced the deficit of 877,000 houses reported for 1981 (Table III.35). In 1972, 75% of all families owned their home, 10% were in the process of buying, 8% paid rent, and 6% were exempted from paying rent because of low income (Mesa-Lago 1981). Unfortunately, similar data are not available for the mid-1980s, but the proportion of ownership must have increased by then because of the large number of houses built by the population, the positive effects of the 1984 housing law, and the gradual process of converting leased houses into owned ones.

The population growth rate continued its declining trend: from 1.5% to 1.1% between 1970 and 1985, partly a result of a steady decrease in the birth rate from 27.7 to 18 per 1,000. Emigration fluctuated widely in this stage: it declined from 50,000 in 1971 (when a U.S.-Cuba airlift agreement for émigrés ended) to less than 1,000 in 1977. The Mariel exodus induced an increase to 141,742 emigrants in 1980 (the largest in Cuban history, 1.5% of the population, leading to a negative population growth rate of 0.6%), but in 1982–85 the annual average rate decreased to 8,700 (Table III.30).

7
Antimarket Rectification Process

1986–1990

In 1986 Castro launched the Rectification Process (RP), which, during the rest of the decade, set Cuba against the trend toward market-oriented reform within the socialist camp and elsewhere. Theoretically the RP was expected to find an optimal middle point between the "idealistic errors" of the Guevarist-Castroite model between 1966 and 1970 and the "economist mistakes" of the SDPE between 1976 and 1985. In practice, many of the RP policies resembled those applied in the 1966–70 stage: virtual elimination of the macro-central plan and recentralization of decision making under Castro; reduction of material incentives and expansion of moral stimulation; reintroduction of voluntary labor and military-style construction brigades, combined with massive use of labor mobilization in agriculture; excessively optimistic programs and targets basically set by Castro; and application of military managerial techniques in civilian production. The SDPE was the subject of strong criticism by Castro, who dismissed the head of JUCEPLAN and accused the moderate reformists of the sin of mechanically copying from socialist countries a model not suitable for Cuba.

The causes of the RP were the subject of debate. The Cubans mainly put the blame on domestic factors: widespread corruption, crime and waste under the SDPE, a declining revolutionary spirit, and expanding inequalities (Rodríguez 1990a). Some foreign scholars justified the RP and added external causes, among them the expanding deficit in the balance of trade and other external constraints, as well as domestic fiscal disequilibria and the state's need to assert its control to correct such problems (Zimbalist and Eckstein 1987; Zimbalist and Brundenius 1989; Eckstein 1990, 1991). Without discarding some of those causes, I identified ideological-political variables as well: the economic decentralization under the SDPE implied political del-

264

egation of power, something that Castro was unwilling to yield, and—according to his view—material incentives and corruption led to a weakening of the revolutionary defense against imperialism (Mesa-Lago 1990a, 1990d, 1991).

A major flaw of the RP was that it did not produce an integrated economic-organization model to substitute for the SDPE, something fundamental for a socialist command economy, especially one that eschewed markets. As a result, there was confusion and contradictions on the role of economic tools, for example, the nature of the central plan, the role of profit as an indicator of managerial performance, price reform, the ways to measure efficiency, and so forth. In spite of these problems, it is possible to summarize economic features and policies in this stage (Table III.1) as follows: (1) continued collectivization and virtual elimination of private-sector activities (except in a few foreign enclaves), the resulting vacuum to be filled by the state; (2) recentralization of decision making and emphasis on physical allocation but practical disappearance of the macroplan; (3) an unclear system of enterprise financing in spite of approval of self-financing; (4) an expanding budgetary deficit and price distortions; (5) promotion of nontraditional exports (such as biotechnology) and foreign tourism combined domestically with a food program to achieve self-sufficiency; (6) tighter control of the labor market, plus labor mobilization, and use of labor brigades and contingents; and (7) increasing egalitarianism through rationing, reduction of material incentives, and expansion of moral stimuli. (This chapter is based, unless otherwise specified, on Mesa-Lago 1988a, 1990a, 1990d, 1991, 1992, 1993a and 1994d.)

1. Policies

A. Ownership

The RP further restrained private property and the market, through the abolition of free peasant markets and acceleration of the process of integration of small private farms into state-controlled cooperatives; elimination of activities of small private manufacturers, truck owners, and street vendors, and reduction of self-employment; and restrictions on private construction, selling, rentals, and inheritance of housing.

In the spring of 1986 Castro launched a new, stronger attack against both free peasant markets and private farmers: (1) the farmers were allegedly making enormous profits by selling to the markets (he gave examples of incomes of 50,000 and 150,000 pesos per year); (2) the farmers resisted integration into cooperatives (CPAs) and tantalized the latter by making evident the farmers' better circumstances and income, hence becoming an obstacle to the success of the co-ops (the CPAs were pressured by the government to sell all their output surplus to the state instead of to the market where they could get a higher price); (3) "some" farmers delivered only 10% of their crops to the state or even nothing at all; and (4) only "12 or 13 farmers," out of a total of 98,000, paid taxes. In order to stop those "abuses," free peasant markets were abolished, and additional tough measures were announced against private farmers. Castro publicly opposed the reintroduction of the free markets until the end of 1993, adding that the private farmers (1) diverted state resources provided to them (fertilizers, seeds) to produce for the black market or gave away such resources to relatives and friends; hence the cost of state inputs was higher than the value of produce (*acopio*) delivered by the farmers to the state; (2) offered wages three times higher than those paid by the state (sometimes stealing manpower from state farms and cooperatives), which could not raise salaries because of other social costs; and (3) got very high prices on the black market because of the unsatisfied demand for agricultural products (Castro 1992b).

According to Castro, working with tens of thousands of private farmers was "terrible, virtually insolvable," because the government had to discuss and make agreements with them, while it was much easier to deal with one thousand cooperatives, and he forecast that soon all private farmers would be integrated in cooperatives. (Previously it had been theoretically argued that the state was already capable of truly socializing the private farms into "superior forms of agricultural production" such as the cooperative and the state farm.) Castro announced that some measures were under study against private farmers, including confiscation of the land of those who used it incorrectly or engaged in share cropping or leasing; elimination of all forms of absentee ownership in the countryside; creation of a tax of 5% on gross income (there was also talk about a progressive income tax with a top rate of 20%); increase in the prices of inputs and services supplied by the state; prohibition on buying cars and motorcycles and assignment of a lower priority to private farmers' access to restaurants (vis-à-vis state farm workers and co-op members); and adjustment of state deliveries to the private farmers according to the amount and quality of *acopio* and co-op yields. Some of these measures were implemented, and others were not but remained as ominous threats against private farmers. By 1989 the nonprivate agricultural sector had increased to 97% of all agricultural land (Table III.2), 78% were state farms, and 18.7% were cooperatives tightly controlled by the state (10.2% in CPAs and 8.5% in credit and service co-ops); only 3.3% remained in the hands of small farmers (CCE, *AEC* 1989a).

The described policies against the private farmers had deleterious effects on agricultural output, while the government was not capable of increasing production. It would have been more sensible to control the true legal violations by the farmers and enforce the law (on *acopio,* taxes) instead of eliminating the incentive of the free markets and pushing the integration of the farmers. It is true that these control measures would not have been easy to enforce, but the government ultimately threw out the baby with the bath water. A survey conducted among private farmers in Havana province revealed that many of them stopped cultivating some crops because they became unprofitable. In general, *acopio* did not increase, and the black market boomed. Even worse, integration into CPAs was hardly a solution as many of them became unprofitable for the following reasons: (1) 35,000 co-op members retired between 1983 and 1987, creating a deficit of 32 million pesos in the pension fund; (2) co-op members had no or poor managerial skills; (3) labor effort in the co-ops was low, as some reportedly worked half the normal time; (4) co-ops bought machinery and equipment on credit, but, lacking adequate personnel and proper maintenance, part of those resources were wasted, and the co-ops were unable to pay back the loans; and (5) there were excessive expenditures on housing and unjustified payments to members. In the late 1980s the government tried to correct some of these problems, but the number of co-op members kept declining: from 69,896 to 63,000 between 1985 and 1990 (Añé and Pérez 1989; Lugo 1989).

Small private manufacturers, transporters, street vendors, and other self-employed workers also came under attack. Castro reported that micro-entrepreneurs sold their output to state enterprises, and cooperatives became sales agents of those entrepreneurs, some of whom set up their own shops, began to use machinery, obtained raw materials (sometimes from state enterprises and cooperatives), and hired workers to expand production and distribution. Castro acknowledged that these activities flourished because the state did not produce those goods. About 10,000 private truck owners transported agricultural products from private farms, merchandise from the manufacturers, and people, earning 50,000 to 100,000 pesos annually. Teachers worked privately for money, and this allegedly enabled children of high-income families to be better prepared for entry exams, which led to privilege and inequality. Finally, painters and other visual artists were selling some of their works to state agencies and enterprises, which paid substantial sums for them. As in 1982, some of the denounced activities were illegal, but others were perfectly legal. Between 1985 and 1989 the proportion of self-employment in the labor force declined from 1.2% to 0.5% (Table III.24). The resulting gap in production and services was expected to be filled by the state agencies, which by 1988—according to Castro—would produce ten times more and sell about ten times more cheaply than the private sector, and on top of that contribute from 250 to 300 million pesos to the state treasury (JUCEPLAN, *BEC* 1966). Finally, Castro denounced the more flexible rules on housing construction introduced in 1980, claiming that they were ways to become rich: people purchased lots and construction materials (often illegally) to build houses and sell them for a healthy gain, or they simply bought and sold houses for a profit. He cited house prices as high as 80,000 pesos, a fortune by Cuban standards. A new law on housing prohibited those practices and increased the government's control on housing transactions.

The government promised that the vacuum left by the elimination and reduction of the private activities would be filled by the state through the expansion of procurement (*acopio*), marketing agencies, the parallel market, and production of state enterprises, as well as the resurrection of construction minibrigades and new construction contingents. However, those mechanisms were not successful: (1) the system of *acopio* continued to be inefficient, and state enterprises and farms, as well as cooperatives, were not able to increase production; (2) the parallel market virtually disappeared, and rationing expanded to all consumer goods; and (3) construction minibrigades and contingents were criticized as inefficient. These aspects will be analyzed later.

B. Planning

In the mid-1980s the SDPE was criticized by Castro as follows: it (1) was copied from other socialist countries without adapting it to Cuban conditions, (2) became a panacea to build socialism by itself, disregarding workers' participation, (3) encouraged managers of state enterprises to act as capitalists but without their efficiency, and (4) led to widespread corruption and waste. The chief of JUCEPLAN, Humberto Pérez, was dismissed from his job, expelled from the Party's Central Committee, and submitted to a criminal trial for his "deviations" in handling the economy.

As between 1966 and 1970, in this stage Castro took full control of the economy, but the process of recentralization of decision making was paralleled by a decline in central planning compounded by the absence of a clear model of economic organization. In 1986 a new System of Economic Direction (SDE, which dropped the word "planning" from the SDPE) was created, and its appointed president immediately declared that his work was guided by Castro's ideas. He warned that the RP should not be adjusted to the SDE, but just the opposite, and that the economic mechanisms could not replace the role of politics, ideology, and conscience. Castro asserted that central decision making would totally control key economic tools such as investment and hard currency, and the 4th Party Congress ratified that statement.

The RP pushed further vertical merging of state enterprises into trusts (*uniones lineales*). In the 1970s there was a move to disaggregate enterprises whose number increased from 700 to 3,000. In the 1980s the opposite occurred, first with the aggregation of agricultural enterprises and, since the mid-1980s, with the organization of bigger trusts and the intertwining of agricultural and construction brigades with factories and transportation facilities. In 1989 there were 61 *uniones,* which employed one-third of the labor force and generated 60% of output in agriculture, industry, construction, and transportation.

Parallel to centralization of decision making, central planning was partly dismantled, and there was no plan for 1986–90. Instead, an experiment of "continuous planning" began in 1988 to avoid "abstract" planning and entrust managers and workers with the initiative to elaborate the plan, without waiting for directions from above. The enterprise staff was encouraged to use past figures, work with projections (they lacked data on future supplies), maximize available resources, correct shortages and other problems that emerged during the plan implementation, and incorporate new solutions into the next plan. A top official of the SDE candidly acknowledged that continuous planning was "just a name, almost a pretext," and the 4th Party Congress failed even to mention "continuous planning," probably because it was not successful.

The new system of directive indicators, key in a central planning process, was not specified. In 1986 Castro said that instead of being the most important goal of an enterprise, profit should be subordinated to the "national interest," but he did not operationalize the latter into indicators. In 1989 the 500 indicators previously used had been reduced to 90, but the SDE president stated that a new integrated system of indicators was needed. The 4th Party Congress ratified that "private interest" would not replace the "national interest" but, again, failed to define the latter.

A new "integral system of enterprise improvement" began in the weapon factory of the armed forces (MINFAR) and from there extended to the rest of military and some civilian enterprises. Under this system the manager made all decisions, and workers had to stick to the duties stipulated in their labor contracts or otherwise faced severe sanctions (see below). All state enterprises were expected to implement the system in 1992 or 1993 but failed to do so because of difficulties in its application to civilian enterprises, concerns about unemployment, and delays in the revision of output quotas. The 4th Party Congress praised the MINFAR experiments but did not asses the results of the "integral" system.

One feature of the SDE appeared to be its lack of evaluation. Checks of the SDE were expected to be done monthly, but, to the best of my knowledge, not a single report was publicized. Early in 1990 the Party's Central Committee declared the need to correct mechanisms that had become bureaucratic. A declaration was followed by important changes in the leadership of the Party Political Bureau, the National Assembly, mass organizations, and, last but not least, in the removal of the president of the SDE. A restructuring of the latter followed, but the 4th Party Congress did not give any information on such changes and their outcomes.

Despite these policies, some Cuban economists and a few foreign experts claimed that the RP did not reverse the decentralization process initiated in the mid-1970s under the SDPE (Zimbalist and Brundenius 1989; Eckstein 1990; Rodríguez 1992). But a Cuban journalist asked how there could be decentralization in Cuba if even the most trivial issues could end up at the Executive Council of Ministers, for example, the approval of the creation of each construction contingency and discussion of petty robbery on buses (Mesa-Lago 1994d).

C. Financing

Under the former SDPE, financing of all enterprises was to shift completely from budgetary to self-financing, and yet we have seen that both methods were mixed and that, by 1985, budgetary financing was still predominant. After launching the RP, Castro claimed that he was not against self-financing provided it was understood that "political work is what makes efficiency possible." After two years of secret debate, the Party Political Bureau approved in 1988 the extension of self-financing, but the publication of that resolution was delayed one year, and the mandate apparently was not enforced. In 1990 I asked Cuban Vice President Carlos Rafael Rodríguez what proportion of enterprises were self-financed; he said it was impossible to determine, but that serious inefficiencies blocked progress, and that in most of the economy there was not budgetary financing but something between it and self-financing, which he failed to elaborate (Mesa-Lago 1993a).

Decisions on domestic investment were probably more centralized than ever. Early in the RP it was said that investment would not be spread among too many projects and that priority would be given to finish those under construction, before starting new ones (the same goal was set in the 1981–85 plan but did not materialize). In 1986 Castro launched numerous new projects, several of which had to be halted later because of the crisis and lack of resources. Investment efficiency probably was as bad or worse than between 1966 and 1970 because of the complete centralization of investment decisions, arbitrarily made by the political leadership without any objective mechanisms to select the most productive projects.

D. Stability and Prices

The budgetary deficit steadily increased in the second half of the 1980s, and in 1990 reached almost 2 billion pesos. On the income side, between 1986 and 1990 the circulation or turnover tax decreased from 45% to 37% of fiscal revenue because of the fall in domestic output and imports, while enterprise profits shrank from 13% to 8% because of increasing losses; data on other revenue were not published in 1990. On the expenditure side, state subsidies to enterprises and for rationed consumer goods (sold below cost) expanded almost twofold in 1987–88 and were the major culprits of the budget deficit in those years. In 1989 the total subsidy was 3.3 billion pesos (80% of which went to enterprises suffering losses and 20% to prices); this subsidy took 24% of state budget expenditures and was increasing. More than 44% of the budget went to social services, because the government was reluctant to cut those expenditures. Financing production absorbed close to 38% of the budget as the government wanted to increase output. Defense and security took more than 10% of the budget, and it was even more difficult to cut that line (Table III.6; BNC 1995).

In 1989 a Cuban economist explained that budgetary deficits in socialist countries could be financed with domestic resources (population savings in fixed-term deposits), external debt, or by printing currency. The Cuban government encouraged people to save by increasing the interest rate on bank deposits from 2% to as much as 5%; as there was little to spend money on, savings increased 28% in 1989–90, but the deficit grew by 40% (BNC 1995). Cuba did not receive hard-currency loans after 1986 when it suspended debt-service payments. The conclusion was that deficit financing in socialist countries was increasingly done through printing additional currency, which in Cuba was greater than both economic growth and saving accounts, thereby fueling inflation. In 1990 Castro asserted that there was an abundance of money in the hands of the population, which had many disadvantages because little could be done with it.

Some Cuban economists said that inflation is derived from insufficient consumer goods production (due mainly to managerial inefficiency) and the impossibility of covering that gap with imports. Price increases could be used to promote equilibrium only up to a point (because they would cut consumption among the lowest income stratum); hence it was necessary to increase supply. And yet both production and efficiency declined in Cuba in this stage.

The full price reform to be accomplished by the SDPE in 1986 never occurred. Castro's statements on price reforms during the RP were confusing and contradictory; he announced a wholesale price reform for 1990, which did not take place. Many Cuban economists believed that such reform was urgently needed, but there was virtually no public discussion on this important issue. The 4th Party Congress postponed price reform until the economic crisis was overcome; in the meantime, central physical allocation was generalized to virtually the entire economy.

E. Development Strategy

The development strategy continued to rely on sugar but in a more balanced way, as in the previous stage. Cuba's most important project under the RP was the Food Program (FP), which aimed at achieving self-sufficiency in the two largest provinces, but also at increasing production of sugar and citrus for export. In addition, there were new bio-technology and substitute fodder programs, continuation of the nickel plan, and expansion of tourism.

In the sugar sector, in spite of increasing production since the mid-1970s, output targets for 1985 had to be scaled down from 10.5 to 9.5 million tons and yet were not met. For 1990 the target was 9.5 million tons, and for 1995 the FP set a target of 11 million tons, which would have required an increase of 45% over the average output of 1986–90. There were, and still are, several chronic limitations to increasing sugar output well above 8 million tons: (1) little additional arable land is available without cutting into food and other export crops; (2) the rain pattern blocks the extension of the length of the sugar harvest, and irrigation covers only one-fifth of the total planted area of sugarcane; (3) sugarcane yields are below those of other competitors, and the increase of such yields demands new cane varieties and improvements in cultivation and fertilization; (4) about 70% of the crop is harvested by more than 4,000 combines, which leave considerable amounts of cane in the fields, and shortages of spare parts combined with poor maintenance reduce the efficiency of the combines and extend the harvest period; (5) cleaning centers process only half of the cane, do not function well, and still leave considerable trash, which increases fuel consumption in transportation and grinding; (6) two-thirds of the sugar mills are small, and over 85% were built prior to 1913; old equipment, poor maintenance, and lack of spare parts causes constant grinding stoppages; and (7) deficiencies in organization and transportation provoke delays and losses in recoverable sucrose. Because of the last three flaws, Cuban industrial yields are well below those of other producers.

The FP was probably the most ambitious agricultural program launched by the Revolution; its goals for 1995 were to (1) increase the output of export crops (sugar by 38% and citrus by 100%), (2) raise the domestic production of foodstuffs for domestic consumption (from 14% to 121% in rice, tubers, vegetables, plantains, bananas, beef, milk, pork, poultry, eggs, and fish), and (3) make the cities and provinces of Havana and Santiago self-sufficient in tubers and vegetables and, in addition, produce a surplus for other provinces. The requirements to make the FP successful were equally colossal, for instance, an expansion of irrigation to one million ha of cultivated land to be achieved in five years (1991–95), when it took 31 years (1959–89) for developing an irrigated area of about 900,000 ha. Other optimistic goals were new irrigation and drainage systems to be applied to close to one million ha of sugar and rice, 114 new cattle development centers (using embryo transplants, artificial insemination, and genetic techniques) plus 32 breeding centers and 325 dairies, 50 hog-breeding centers, 1,950 poultry sheds, and so forth.

Existing constraints to achieving the FP goals were enormous: insufficient land, the mobilization of hundreds of thousands of urban workers to the countryside (requiring housing, feeding, and transportation), the development of new, complex technology, the simultaneous construction of hundreds of projects, the limitations in the importation of the needed equipment, fertilizer, and other inputs, and the need to improve both *acopio* (to collect the increased output) and distribution (to deliver it to consumers). The chances of meeting the FP targets were therefore slim; for instance, planned increases in output from 14% to 121% between 1991 and 1995 contrasted with actual decreases in output of 1% to 15% between 1984 and 1989 in the same products.

It was not until 1992 that Castro acknowledged that fuel and cement limitations had forced a halting of several key elements of the FP: (1) the construction of new dams and embankments as well as irrigation systems; (2) the new irrigation and drainage system for sugar and rice (in the latter, 15 out of the projected 17 labor brigades were not operational because each required 1,000 tons of fuel annually); and (3) the construction of 44 permanent labor camps in Havana province, essential to solving the manpower shortage in agriculture. In spite of these problems Castro predicted that the output of tubers, fruits, and vegetables in Havana province would increase twofold in 1990–92 and double again by 1994; he concluded: "These are facts and realities that help us discuss with those who are confused, who do not understand, who oppose [us]" (Castro 1992a). But the economic crisis of the 1990s killed any remaining hope of success of the FP.

Because of insufficient imports of fodder, the FP sponsored the use of domestic substitutes for feeding livestock (e.g., molasses, saccharine) and a liquid fodder for pigs made up of sugar-cane by-products and food leftovers. Experts warned that it was vital to mix the new products properly with the traditional fodder to avoid weight loss and increased mortality of cattle and pigs. In 1991, because of the sharp decline in imports of fodder as well as domestic output lagging two-thirds behind target, a substitute cattle feeding was introduced: the Voisin rational pasture method. Invented by a French scientist who worked and died in Cuba, that method had been tried on the island in 1964 but abandoned because it required the installation of electric fences for land division, irrigation, and skilled personnel. The substitute cattle fodder combines pastures, saccharine, and leguminous plants, a formula similar to that unsuccessfully tried in the second half of the 1960s (which mixed pasture and molasses). All cattle ranches were ordered to implement the new method in ten months (March-December 1991); however, in April 1992 Castro said that the shift would not be completed until July 1993. There were no more references to the Voisin method after that, a clear indication of its failure.

Three other areas given priority between 1986 and 1990 were biotechnology, tourism, and nickel. An impressive Center of Genetic Engineering and Biotechnology was built in 1986 and reportedly produced 136 items including interferon, AIDS diagnostic kits, and meningitis and hepatitis B vaccines. In 1990 the Soviet Union bought more than U.S.$500 million in those products as well as high-tech medical items and rehabilitation services for victims of the Chernobyl accident; the value of those goods and services reportedly increased to U.S.$900 in 1991. Small amounts of biotechnological goods were sold to Brazil and a few other developing countries. Although these gains were remarkable, biotechnology exports were and are constrained by several problems: (1) doubts about the quality and efficacy of these drugs, resulting from improper testing, (2) the unknown profitability of such exports, (3) impediments to developing new technology, (4) the legal impossibility of selling those products to countries that honor patents because Cuba does not pay for foreign patents, and (5) difficulties in penetrating the international market, an oligopoly tightly controlled by a few industrialized countries.

The tourist industry received priority for both domestic and foreign investment in pursuit of badly needed hard currency. In 1988 a holding company, Cubanacán, was organized to operate as a vertically integrated unit controlling its own finances, and it was authorized to import supplies, keep foreign exchange, establish joint ventures, and hire foreign managers. The first joint venture with foreign capital was with Spain (Group Sol Meliá), which completed a hotel at Varadero Beach in 1990. Nickel production received a small boost in 1988 with the opening of the first unit of the Che Guevara plant; but technical difficulties and lack of fuel forced its shutdown in 1990. Oil production confronted technical difficulties as well because of poor technology for drilling deeper into the wells.

The share of defense and security expenditures, which peaked at 11.6% in 1984, declined to an average of 10.4% between 1985 and 1989 and fell to 9.6% in 1990 (Table III.6). Contributing to that decline was the deployment of Cuban troops from Africa and the beginning of the economic crisis at home.

F. External Sector

The value of Cuba's total trade transactions peaked in 1985 and steadily declined between 1986 and 1990; exports exhibited a decreasing trend, which was true of imports as well, except for the year 1989. Reasons for that trend were declining trade with CMEA (mainly due to economic difficulties in the Soviet Union, which cut price subsidies to Cuba) and a decrease in trade with market economies (due to a halting of fresh credit from the Club of Paris after 1986).

The last Soviet-Cuban five-year trade and economic cooperation agreement was the 1986–90 one, which was to increase credit to Cuba by 50% over the previous quinquennium. The shares of trade with the Soviet Union and CMEA peaked in 1987, and the trade deficit with the Soviet Union kept increasing and reached a zenith in 1989. Cuba reported delays and cuts in numerous Soviet imports in 1989–90. The Russian supply of oil and oil by-products peaked in 1987 and declined by 25% in the rest of this stage (Tables III.20–21). A deterioration in the terms of trade against Cuba took place in this stage concerning the three major products in the exchange with the Soviet Union: sugar, oil, and nickel. The world price of sugar increased from U.S. 4.1 to U.S. 12.8 cents per pound between 1985 and 1989 and slightly declined in 1990. The average Soviet price paid for Cuban sugar remained virtually stagnant between 1981 and 1985 and 1986 and 1990 (about U.S. 42 cents, but in pesos it increased from 36 to 40 centavos). The maximum Soviet/world sugar price ratio of 11.87 to 1:00, reached in 1985, declined gradually to 3.34 to 1:00 in 1990. Conversely, the price paid by Cuba for Soviet oil imports, which was below the world price between 1981 and 1985, surpassed the latter between 1986 and 1990. The Soviet/world oil price ratio in dollars increased from almost par in 1985 to 1.20 to 1:00 in 1990. There was also a deterioration in the Soviet/world nickel price ratio: from 2.41 to 1:00 in 1985 to 1.23 to 1:00 in 1990 (Table III.19). Although the combined net result of Soviet pricing for the three products was still quite favorable for Cuba (compared with world prices), the subsidy declined between 1986 and 1990.

In 1986 Cuba suspended payments on the service of its hard-currency debt, and the Club of Paris immediately suspended new credits. Cuba's position was (and still is, at least until mid-1998) that fresh credit is needed to restart paying the debt service, but debtors request that servicing of the debt precedes the granting of new credits; hence there was a stalemate. The halting of credit led to a reduction in trade with market economies. Beginning in the late 1980s Cuba began to apply, in a much more flexible manner, the 1982 foreign investment law in search of hard currency.

G. Labor and Employment

RP overall goals were to increase labor productivity, strengthen discipline at the workplace, and fight corruption. Specific policies were to cut down the labor surplus; tighten output quotas (normally increasing them); revise wages, production bonuses, *premios,* prize funds, and overtime payments (usually reducing them); revive unpaid voluntary work, labor mobilization, and construction brigades and create new construction contingents; increase the use of moral stimuli, although selectively use material incentives (e.g, in contingents, tourism); and impose tougher measures against corruption and crime.

In spite of rhetorical calls for increased workers' participation in economic functions (e.g., in "continuous planning"), there was a strengthening of managerial control over workers. The CTC Congress held in 1989 complained about the inadequacy of mechanisms set up for workers' participation in planning, and that managers did not give importance to that issue and consider production assemblies as mere formalities. Under the "integral system of enterprise improvement" (where the enterprise manager is a "production sergeant"), a worker who repeatedly fell below the output quota was demoted or dismissed. The colonel in charge of military enterprises was asked if they did not have an advantage over their civilian counterparts because the former could get around hundreds of labor regulations. He answered that labor legislation overprotects the bad worker and demoralizes the good one; hence the law must be changed because job security should be granted only to workers who fulfill their duties. A subsequent question was whether enterprise efficiency should be increased at the cost of firing unneeded workers. The colonel replied positively, saying that 258 workers had been dismissed in the Che Guevara military enterprise and assigned to other factories or labor brigades in agriculture to produce food for that enterprise's workers; hence everybody benefited.

Increasing militarized labor mobilization took place mostly in construction and agriculture. Construction brigades, eliminated under the SDPE because of their inefficiency, were reintroduced by Castro in 1987 as a keystone for solving the construction deficit (in housing, dams, roads, etc.). He argued that the previous inefficiency problem was solved in the new approach because (1) brigade members were surplus workers released from enterprises; (2) the remaining workers kept production up at the enterprise and fulfilled the output quotas without charging overtime; and (3) the state reimbursed the enterprise for wages paid to brigade members and provided them with proper supplies. In 1988 Castro praised the brigades for creating a new labor spirit and working miracles, but in 1989 he dramatically reversed that optimistic judgment: the brigades were disorganized, fell apart, were anarchic, mishandled the equipment, and lacked cost control (they spent 2.40 pesos for every peso produced, partly because most members were not professional construction workers).

Castro decided that construction contingents would be the solution to the above flaws. Instead of recruiting surplus workers from enterprises, contingent members were carefully selected and very well paid, fed, and housed; in return they had to work very hard and produce "labor miracles." Initially contingents were rapidly organized; then it became mandatory that they be authorized by the Council of Ministers. Later, new contingents were not established (because of lack of fuel and supplies and because of the re-creation of "old vices"), and finally, some members were sent home or elsewhere to work on other projects. Castro first claimed that the contingents were very productive (0.70 cost per peso produced), but problems soon appeared. Members were paid higher wages than most workers, and hence their production costs were higher; Castro argued that this was not a problem because costs were still below one peso. Special food, air-conditioned housing, and other perquisites, many of which were imported, added to salary costs. Shortages of construction materials caused bottlenecks, an obstacle initially pinpointed by Cuban technicians but disregarded by Castro. And the Cuban Institute of Economic Research found that producing one peso in the labor camps cost as much as 11 pesos in hidden costs. Castro discredited all criticism as being made by "worms" who look only "at the negative side" of things. When the new secretary general of the CTC complained in 1990 that contingent workers earned more than the Minister of Construction, Castro replied that "ministers do not have to break stones or drive bulldozers."

Echoing his speeches of the 1966–70 idealistic stage, Castro said in 1986 that it was a mistake to think that socialism could be built with material incentives because only capitalism could be developed that way: "Socialism must be built with awareness and moral incentives." He then criticized the following distortions in material incentives: (1) wages were paid disproportionately to the work done, payments were set according to six different work quotas instead of one, workers were paid two or three times the legal rate, and wage differentials were excessive (a 10 to 1 ratio); (2) only 25% of the work quotas were technically justified, and quotas were not adjusted for three years and became too easy to fulfill; (3) bonuses were very easy to get, often new technology was introduced, and since the work quota was not adjusted upward, everybody got bonuses; (4) enterprises used bonuses to steal workers from key state agencies such as the Council of State; (5) authors' royalties were paid by the page rather than by quality; and (6) managers did not control workers' absences, physicians illegally granted sick leaves, and labor absenteeism increased (25% in a textile plant in Santiago).

Several policies were implemented to correct some of these problems. Recentralization in fixing work quotas and wages was preferred because—according to Castro—these decisions "should not be left to thousands of people." There was a trend toward adjusting work quotas upward and reducing wages except those at the bottom. Prizes, *premios,* and production bonuses were reviewed to determine which ones were proper and which ones were not. In the second half of the 1980s, workers started to "spontaneously" reject bonuses, and, in national meetings, Castro and union leaders exalted these actions as exemplary. But, still in 1990, Castro complained that such "garbage" (bonuses) had not been legally changed yet. By 1987 *premios* had been cut by one-half, declining from 1.9% to 0.9% of the basic wage. But the process of reviewing national work quotas faced difficulties: in 1989 (three years after the RP began) 81% of the 2.5 or 3 million quotas had not been revised, without which it was impossible to establish cost systems programmed by the SDE for 1990. There was also a search for new incentives, but the payment formulas (used in the "integral system") were applied to only 1% of the labor force. The 4th Party Congress did not give specifics on any of these subjects, as the severe crisis probably halted all these experiments.

The government launched a fight against corruption and crime. New economic and administrative crimes were introduced in the penal code and sanctions made more severe, but Castro acknowledged that such measures had not been entirely successful. The "economic police" reported continued violations of the penal code, fraud, and robberies: in 1990, 25 million pesos were uncovered in 91 enterprise audits. According to Castro, scarcity of goods was not due only to cuts in imports but also to domestic lack of control and stealing: "There are some who would be willing to die in battle, and yet, when they are assigned to manage a store, they steal money from the till." He reported that financial troubles in transportation were caused by passengers who did not pay the fare. A public survey conducted in 1990 on People's Power revealed that its delegates used their posts to obtain crucial goods or services that the population lacked. In the same year, Cuba's State News

Agency asserted that crime and corruption were more dangerous than the CIA. Citizens were exhorted to help the government fight corruption through constant vigilance, even of leaders and members of the Ministry of Internal Security. Those people who had expenditures or a living standard above their means, particularly after being appointed to a job (e.g., buying a car or a motorcycle or expensive electric appliances), should be denounced, regardless of their rank.

The RP initially aspired to eliminate the labor surplus, but that target soon became politically unfeasible because of the reduction of private employment and the negative effects of the recession on state employment. Between 1985 and 1989 employment in the state civilian sector increased one percentage point (to 94%) while private employment declined proportionally; this happened before the crisis hit (Table III.24). In 1987–88 some 50,000 workers were estimated as surplus in factories alone and hundreds of thousands throughout the economy. The question was where to employ all these people. Castro first suggested that they could be shifted to new factories and other activities, an old trick used in the 1960s and 1970s. A Cuban scholar asserted that 600,000 new entrants in the labor force between 1986 and 1990 were absorbed in an inefficient manner to avoid an increase in open unemployment, which led to more underemployment and lower labor productivity (Carranza 1993).

H. Distribution and Social Services

Under the RP, Castro reluctantly accepted the need to continue with the socialist distribution formula (to each according to his or her work) but under strict control to prevent violations. The RP, however, had clear egalitarian elements such as the emphasis on moral incentives and reduction in material incentives, criticism of extreme wage differentials, denunciation of high earnings of private farmers and the self-employed, and elimination of the peasants' free markets. The crisis and ensuing severe scarcity forced an expansion of rationing, which operated as an egalitarian tool. The wage policy tried to decrease differences too: in 1987 the lowest rates on the wage scale were increased from 75/85 pesos monthly to 100, from 82/93 to 107, and from 95/107 to 118; all other rates remained frozen, and additional payments were reduced (Zimbalist and Brundenius 1989).

Initially the RP aimed at expanding social services, but the crisis tempered that policy. The share of social services in the state budget increased from 41.8% in 1985 to a record 45.5% in 1988 but decreased to 43.7% in 1990. Investment in social services rose from 17.7% of total investment in 1985 to 21.5% in 1988 but declined to 20% in 1989. Social expenditures per capita were planned to grow by 13% between 1986 and 1990, compared with 32% between 1981 and 1985 and 50% between 1976 and 1980 (Table III.6; CEE *AEC* 1985a–89a).

In this stage there was a relaxation of Cuba's entitlement conditions for pensions: retirement ages were reduced, and in 1987 the minimum monthly pension was increased, benefiting 690,000 pensioners (Mesa-Lago 1993c). This liberalization, together with the aging of the population, added a cumulative 1.3 billion pension costs between 1986 and 1990 (Masso 1992). Social security costs (including health care) surpassed 9% of GSP in 1990, the highest ever, and total social security expenditures exceeded the one billion peso mark in 1986 and kept growing. The number of pensioners surpassed the one million mark in 1990, 64% more than in 1979 (Table III.34). The number of physicians per 10,000 inhabitants increased from 22.5 to 36.4 between 1985 and 1990, mainly because of the rapidly growing number of physicians and the new family doctor program. The latter is based on 7,000 small offices, each staffed with a doctor and a nurse, who provide primary health care for 600 to 700 inhabitants; 25% of the population was covered in 1987, but the program was too costly (Mesa-Lago 1993c). The number of hospital beds per 1,000 inhabitants rose from 4.8 to 5.3 between 1985 and 1990 (Table III.30). Hospital inefficiency, however, was poor: bed occupancy was 76.9% in 1988 (low by international standards) and decreased to 73.9% in 1989; furthermore the average length of a hospital stay was 9.9 days, which was high by international norms (CEE, *BEC* 1990).

Emphasis on raising student enrollment in secondary and higher education continued at least until 1989. As discussed already, a new housing law imposed tougher regulations for private housing construction as well as dwelling transactions. The state, through construction brigades and contingents, was expected to fill the gap created by the decline in private construction. There was no change in the terms of population policy in this stage, and the huge exodus in 1980 was not been repeated in spite of the growing scarcity of consumer goods.

2. Performance

A. Growth

Measurement of the impact of the RP and other policies in this stage is obstructed by the lack of data. The latest Cuban statistical yearbook available at the time of finishing this book was the 1989 one (CEE, *AEC* 1989; also see chapter 8); until 1995 only occasional figures were available, most from Castro's speeches and scholars' estimates. In spite of the scarce statistics, there is no doubt that in this stage the Cuban economy began to enter the worst crisis under the Revolution. The negative economic performance started in 1986 when the RP was launched, long before the downfall of the socialist camp. There was a debate on whether the economic deterioration between 1986 and 1990 was caused by the RP, external factors, or a combination of both.

Cuban officials blamed exogenous, conjectural variables as exclusive causes of the 1986–90 recession, such as drought, decline in world prices of sugar, deterioration of the terms of trade with the Soviet Union, and lack of fresh hard-currency credit, while arguing that the RP had a positive, compensatory effect. Most U.S. scholars, without disregarding external variables, pinpointed harmful effects of the RP, such as the decline in private output and services, the state's inability to replace the eliminated market mechanisms, and the lack of a coherent economic model. Some Cuban economists eventually acknowledged that the crisis was not explainable by external factors alone; for instance, they admitted that the state—overburdened with too many functions—was unable to fill the vacuum left by the eradication of free peasant markets and reduced self-employment. Conversely, Carlos Aldana (the third most powerful political figure in Cuba until he was dismissed in the fall of 1992) declared that the crisis was "not a consequence of inefficiency or incompetence on our part but has been imposed on us by external factors beyond our control."

According to CCE, *AEC* (1989a), the GSP annual rate in 1986–89 was 0.2% or −0.8% per capita, but other Cuban estimates gave average declines of 0.5% and 0.6% absolute or −1.5% and −1.6% per capita. In 1995 the National Bank published a series on GDP, which showed worse annual averages for this stage than in GSP: −1.3% absolute and −2.3% per capita (Tables III.3–4). These figures clearly prove that the RP was a failure and that a serious recession began in this stage before the crisis hit in the 1990s.

Average annual sugar output between 1986 and 1990 was 7,582 thousand tons, 195,000 tons less than between 1981 and 1985. The output goal for 1990 was 9.5 million tons, but only 8 million tons were produced, 16% short of the target. The average sugar industrial yield between 1986 and 1990 continued the previous declining trend; it was 10.8 compared to 11.0 between 1981 and 1985 (Table III.11). Performance in nonsugar agriculture in 1986–89 was poor. In 1989 the output of tobacco, milk, and eggs was below the 1985 level, and the output of citrus fruits, beans, and coffee was either lower or similar to that of 1988. Output of rice in 1989 was below the 1984 level. Only pork production showed systematic gains in 1986–89. The number of heads of cattle diminished 4.4% between 1986 and 1990; heads per capita of population were 0.49 in 1985 and 0.45 in 1990. On the other hand, the number of pigs rose by 24% in 1986–89 and that of poultry by 8%. The FAO index of agricultural output per capita shows a decline of 6.8 percentage points between 1985 and 1990 (FAO 1995). The fish and seafood catch sank by 13% in 1986–89; the catch per 100 inhabitants fell from 2.16 tons in 1986 to 1.82 in 1989 (Tables III.10, III.12). These figures demonstrate that the food program was a fiasco.

Nickel output jumped 35% in 1986–89, mostly a result of the opening of the new Che Guevara plant in 1987, but it was shut down in 1990. The planned target output for 1990 was 106,500 tons, but only 41,000 tons were produced, 62% short of the target and 13% less than in 1989 (Table III.13). Oil production peaked at 938,000 metric tons in 1986 and steadily declined thereafter: output in 1990 was 671,000, 28% lower than in 1986 (Table III.21). Industrial output in 1989 was below the 1985 level in most lines: steel and fertilizers (−22%), cigars (−16%), refrigerators (−65%), radios (−27%), shoes (−19%), and soap (−5%). Conversely, electricity, cement, and textile output in 1989 were respectively 25%, 18%, and 7% higher than in 1985, but textile production fell 15% in 1989 (Table III.10).

In contrast to the dismal performance in industry and agriculture, the tourist sector experienced a boom. The number of tourists increased twofold (from 168,000 in 1985 to 327,000 in 1990) while the gross revenue grew 2.4 times (from 100 to 243 million pesos). But *net* tourist revenue was only 150 million in 1990 and represented 0.59% of GSP (0.98% if *gross* revenue is used) (Table III.15). Despite its positive performance, therefore, tourism was a small generator both of hard-currency revenue and national income.

The contrast of actual output with projected targets under the 1986–90 plan (Table III.14) clearly indicated a generalized failure, worse than in the two previous quinquennia. All output targets for which information is available (17 altogether) were unfulfilled, the majority by a large margin; for instance, from 20% to 64% in oil, nickel, steel, fertilizers, shoes, citrus, tobacco, textiles, milk, fish, and beer. The GSP growth target was missed by 96%. Such a terrible performance, combined with the crisis, partly explains why economic plans were dropped after 1990.

The share of investment in GSP averaged 15.9% in 1986–89, an important increment over the 14.7% average of the previous quinquennium (Table III.7). Still this was 27% lower than the plan target (Table III.14). Furthermore, efficiency in the allocation and use of capital declined in this stage (from 0.53 centavos of increment in production per peso invested, to 0.02 centavos) because of excessive centralization and absence of efficiency criteria (Carranza 1993).

B. Inflation

According to official figures, in 1986–88 the economy deflated at an annual average of 0.7%, probably the lowest quinquennium rate under the Revolution (Table III.3). The 1989 statistical yearbook did not publish inflation data for that year, and no information is available thereafter. In 1995 the National Bank published a series of GDP in constant prices for 1985–89 but did not give it in current prices (BNC 1995). I have estimated an average annual rate of deflation of 1.2% (GDP) in 1986–88, almost twice the official rate of GSP (Table III.4). Deflation figures do not match data on the monetary surplus, which continued its expansion in this stage: in 1990 it reached almost 5 billion pesos, a 60% increase over 1985 and almost twice the surplus of the crisis year of 1970 (Table III.5). The severe scarcity of consumer goods produced a phenomenal expansion of the black market with skyrocketing prices. The lowest-income groups could not supplement the meager rations by buying in the black market. After 1987 the value of the peso was set par with the U.S. dollar (Table III.3). In the domestic black market, however, 8 pesos were exchanged for U.S.$1 in 1990. The deficit in the state budget steadily worsened between 1986 and 1990, reaching almost 2 billion pesos in 1990 compared with a surplus of 16 million pesos in 1985 (Table III.6). As a percentage of GSP the deficit rose from 0.7% to 7.5% between 1986 and 1990.

C. Diversification

The three available series on the percentage distribution of GSP by economic sectors in 1986–89 show similar trends (declines in industry and trade, but an increase in agriculture and no changes in the rest) although with divergent magnitudes. The longest series indicate (for 1985–88, no data are available for 1989) a decline in the industrial share from 37.1% (1986) to 35.9%, an increase in the agricultural share from 13.9% to 15.7%, and a decrease in the trade share from 33.2% to 31.3%. The second series shows (for 1985–89) a diminishing industrial share from 47.2% (1986) to 46.6%, a rising agricultural share from 14.2% to 16.1%, and a declining trade share from 23.1% to 19.7%. Finally, the third series describes (1985–89) a declining industrial share from 56.3% (1986) to 55.3%, a growing agricultural share from 14.1% to 15.9%, and a shrinking trade share from 14% to 11.3% (Table III.8). Sugar dependency continued in this stage (Table III.11): the share of sugar output in GSP remained unchanged at 10.2% in 1986–89, while the share of sugar exports in GSP slightly declined from 15.5% to 14.9% (the 1989 share was still almost twice that of 1962).

D. Trade Balance and External Dependency

Overall trade dependency continued unabated: the value of total transactions as a proportion of GSP rose from 48.7% to 50.7% in 1986–89. External disequilibria worsened significantly: the value of exports declined 9.6% between 1986 and 1990 (mainly because of a decline in the size of the sugar crops and exports and no significant increase in Soviet subsidies), while the value of imports declined 7.7%. The trade deficit increased almost 34% in 1986–89 and reached U.S.$2.7 billion dollars, a new historical record, although it declined somewhat in 1990. The cumulative deficit between 1986 and 1990 was almost three times that in the previous quinquennium and equaled 52% of the total cumulative deficit since 1959 (Table III.16). Planned targets were unfulfilled by large margins: −148% in exports and −80% in imports (Table III.14).

Trade dependency on the Soviet Union and CMEA peaked in 1987 when Cuba's trade shares with them reached 72% and 86.6%, respectively (compared with 70.5% and 83% in 1985). But such shares declined to 64.7% and 78.9% in 1989 as trade with Eastern European countries and the Soviet Union diminished. Cuba's trade deficit with the Soviet Union expanded 144% between 1985 and 1989 (124% in U.S. dollars) and surpassed U.S.$2 billion in 1989, although it sharply declined in 1990. The Soviet share of Cuba's total trade deficit steadily rose from 45.9% to 83.6% between 1985 and 1989 (Table III.20). These data prove that the RP goals of reducing the external disequilibrium did not materialize, at least in the second half of the 1980s. Between 1986 and 1990 Cuba received U.S.$11.6 billion in Soviet loans (U.S.$8.2 billion to cover trade deficits and U.S.$3.4 billion in development aid), a sum similar to the total Cuba had received in the previous fifteen years. In addition, Cuba benefited from U.S.$10 billion in Soviet nonrepayable price subsidies, but this sum was about one-third the amount received between 1971 and 1985 (Table III.22). The reason was that the Soviet Union dramatically shifted the composition of aid—against Cuba—from nonrepayable subsidies to repayable loans: while between 1976 and 1980 the distribution was respectively 21% and 79%, between 1986 and 1990 it changed to 53.4% (loans) and 46.6% (subsidies). Although there was a rapid closing of the gap between Soviet and world sugar prices (a declining ratio of 11.8 to 3.3 between 1985 and 1990), Cuba still benefited from Soviet prices that were three times higher. The percentage of Cuban sugar exports going to the Soviet Union, therefore, kept growing and peaked at 76.7% in 1987, although it fell to 67% in 1989 (CCE, *AEC* 1989a). The terms of trade with the Soviet Union continued their deterioration against Cuba between 1986 and 1990, at least concerning the three major trade products: sugar, nickel, and oil. Despite this deterioration, Cuba still enjoyed an estimated net gain of U.S.$10 billion in that period, but it was 36% lower than between 1981 and 1985 (Table III.22).

Cuba's debt with the Soviet Union was disclosed for the first time by the Soviets at the end of 1989: 15.5 billion rubles or U.S.$24.5 billion dollars at the official exchange rate at that time. Cuba also owed at least U.S.$2.2 billion to four Eastern European countries. Official Soviet exchange rates were too high when compared with either commercial or tourist rates, but Cuba had to reach a reasonable agreement on both the exchange rate and form of repayment if trade was going to continue with those countries. My estimates of Cuba's debt with the Soviet Union and Eastern Europe in 1990 ranged from U.S.$10 to U.S.$30 billion, depending on the exchange rates used (Table III.23).

Cuba's domestic oil output peaked in 1986 and diminished throughout the rest of this stage; thus by 1990 production was 28% lower, and dependency on Soviet oil became higher, and in 1988 the Soviet Union was supplying 92% of Cuban oil imports. But the Soviet supply of oil and oil products steadily decreased from 13.5 to 10.2 million tons in 1987–90 (Table III.21). Subtracting the 1.5 to 2 million tons that Cuba "reexported" between 1984 and 1989, there was still a need for 5 to 8 million tons of fuel. There was no probability of meeting part of that gap, in the short and medium range, with domestic oil production or nuclear energy.

Cuba's trade share with market economies kept diminishing until it reached a low of 12.9% in 1988, but it increased to 16.8% in 1989 (CEE, *AEC* 1989a). Foreign exchange reserves declined by one-third in 1985–88, from 350 to 234 million pesos; furthermore, the reserves' share of hard-currency deposits in foreign banks sank from 61% to 33.5% while the share of transferable rubles rose from 35% to 58.4% (ECLAC, *Survey* 1989b). Cuba's debt in hard currency increased almost twofold between 1985 and 1989, from U.S.$3.6 to U.S.$6.4 billion, mainly as a result of the island's suspension of the debt service after 1986. The proportion of that debt owed to creditors with the toughest terms jumped from 12% to 22.8% between 1985 and 1989 (Table III.23). I have estimated Cuba's total external debt in 1990 (including both the hard-currency and nonconvertible parts) to be U.S.$37.6 billion, the highest per capita debt in Latin America and the Caribbean (Mesa-Lago 1993a).

Export concentration on sugar increased from 74.5% to 75.2% between 1985 and 1990. When adjusted to properly exclude the value of oil "reexports," the sugar share increased but exhibited a decreasing trend: from 82.3% to 75.9% in the same period. Three major reasons for that decline were the fall in sugar production and exports in 1986–88, the growth in world prices and exports of nickel in 1987–90 (which increased the nickel export share), and the rise in the share of nonoil exports other than sugar by almost 4 percentage points. In spite of some minor improvement, sugar export concentration in 1990—adjusted—was similar to that in 1959 (Table III.17). There were no major changes in the composition of Cuban imports at least between 1985 and 1989: the shares of fuel and manufactures decreased (respectively one and two percentage points), while the shares of food, chemicals, and machinery augmented one percentage point each (Table III.18).

E. Unemployment

No official statistics on open unemployment have been released since 1981, but a Cuban economist reported a rate of 6% in 1988, a slight increase over the 5.5% rate of 1981 and the highest since the mid-1960s. The reduction in private-sector activities by 1% between 1985 and 1989 probably contributed to that increase (Tables III.24–25). Female participation in the civilian labor force increased from 33.8% to 38.2% between 1981 and 1988, hence expanding the labor supply even more. Between 1985 and 1989 female participation in executive and administrative positions increased 8% and 6%, respectively, while it declined by 1% in technical positions and increased by 2% in traditional services (Table III.25).

According to official statistics, labor productivity declined at an annual average rate of 2.5% in 1986–89, contrasted with a planned increase of 3.5% in that period (CEE, *AEC* 1988a; *Economía y Desarrollo* various issues). The real average annual net gain in productivity (related to increases in real wages) dwindled at a rate of 3% in 1986–88 (author's calculations based on CEE, *AEC* 1986a–89a). The RP goals of improving labor productivity did not materialize.

F. Equality

There are no Western estimates on income distribution after 1986, but information analyzed above indicates that inequality was reduced. For instance, the ratio of the highest to the lowest wage rate fell from 5.5:1 to 4.5:1 between 1981 and 1987 as the bottom wages were increased and the rest remained frozen (based on Zimbalist and Brundenius 1989). The real average wage in 1989 was at the same level as in 1986 compared with a significant expansion in the previous quinquennium (Table III.28). Cuts in other payments (bonuses, *premios,* prizes, overtime), elimination of free peasant markets, and reduction in self-employment also must have contributed to shrink income differences.

The availability of consumer goods shrank between 1986 and 1990 because the state was not able to fill the gap created by declining private output and because of import cuts. In order to protect low-income groups, the government decided to expand rationing instead of allowing prices to increase. But as consumer goods become more scarce and the black market boomed, the poor were less protected, as they could not afford the high black-market prices. Conversely, the gap between the elite and the masses expanded as the former preserved its privileged access to goods and services through special stores, separate hospitals, recreational villas, and trips abroad (Mesa-Lago 1994d).

G. Social Indicators

UNESCO reported a 6% illiteracy rate in 1990 among those 15 years and older, a decline vis-à-vis the UNESCO 7.6% rate of 1985. Enrollment in secondary and higher education kept increasing in this stage, reaching 88% and 23% of the respective age groups in 1989 (Table III.33). But the 1990 target for enrollment in higher education was 35%, obviously not met, and there was a decline in enrollment to 21% in 1990 (Table III.14). Total student enrollment in education (all levels combined) peaked in 1977–78 at 3.6 million, but by 1989–90 it had declined by one million because of the halving of population growth rates and the parallel aging process. The number of teachers kept increasing and reached 241,923 in 1989–90, but the ratio of students per teacher, which was 16:1 in 1979–80, fell to 10:1 in 1989–90. Fellowships (including free tuition, food, clothing, and shelter) were awarded to 43% of all students enrolled in secondary school in 1989–90 and to 28% of all students enrolled in higher education—6,029 Cubans had fellowships for higher education abroad (CCE, *AEC* 1989a).

Infant mortality continued its impressive falling trend between 1985 and 1990: from 16.5 to 10.7 per 1,000. The 1990 planned target was a rate of 15; therefore, actual performance was 29% better, one of the rare cases in which a goal was surpassed in this stage. The overall mortality rate increased from 6.4% to 6.7% between 1985 and 1990, largely an outcome of an aging population. ECLAC reported an increase in life expectancy from 74.3 years between 1981 and 1985 to 75.2 in 1986–90, the latter higher than the Cuban average of 74.6 for 1986–89 (Tables III.14, III.30). Although statistics are not available, it seems that sanitation conditions did not advance, which may explain some morbidity problems (Mesa-Lago 1993c). The rates of seven contagious diseases decreased, or no cases were reported (mostly in diseases controllable through vaccination), but the rates of three diseases increased or were stagnant (mostly diseases uncontrollable through vaccination such as syphilis and gonorrhea). Finally, rates of acute diarrhea, hepatitis, and respiratory diseases peaked in 1986–88 and then declined. The population growth rate was stagnant at 1% in 1986–90: the birth rate diminished slightly while the mortality rate and emigration were basically unchanged (Tables III.30–31).

There are no data on social security coverage and number of pensioners for 1986–90, but pension expenditures increased 44% in this stage; hence the number of pensioners must have increased too. The latter, combined with the slowdown in population growth and employment, led to a decline in the ratio of active workers per pensioner from 5.2 to 4.2. Growing costs of social security raised the burden on GSP to 9.3%, and 63% of that cost had to financed by the state (Table III.34).

At the beginning of the RP, Castro incorrectly stated that the number of dwellings built between 1981 and 1985 was the lowest under the Revolution (when it was actually the highest: an annual average of 22,144) and asserted that construction brigades alone would build 100,000 houses annually. Subsequently, statistical series were changed, and no comparable total data are available after 1987. Scattered figures show, however, that total housing construction (including state and private) diminished from 74,437 to 69,107 in 1985–87: private housing construction from 45,119 to 40,535 in the same period, and state housing construction from 27,265 to 22,516 between 1985 and 1990 (Table III.35). The brigades built only 18,315 housing units in 1986–89, contrasted with Castro's annual goal of 100,000 units. In summary, all comparable statistics show a fall in housing construction after 1985, hence aggravating the housing deficit.

The RP intended to halt crime, which reportedly had risen under the SDPE, but scarce data indicate an increase of it in 1987–90. The growing scarcity of consumer goods became a fertile ground for robbery, black marketing, and exchange of pesos for foreign currency, even prostitution. Despite the introduction of harsh penal sanctions in the late 1980s, there were many reports of people stealing food from state farms and cooperatives, assaulting warehouses and cafeterias, attacking trucks, and even robbing a huge container on the docks (Mesa-Lago 1994d).

8

Market-Oriented Reform

1991 and Following

Cuba's seventh shift in economic organization and fourth in development strategy are taking place in the 1990s. In this stage the ideological pendulum has moved farther to the market than ever before under the Revolution, and the opening and concessions to foreign capitalist investment, trade, and technology are unparalleled. Furthermore, these policies combined with the worst economic crisis since 1959 have eroded the foundations of Cuban socialism: collectivization of virtually all means of production, absolute state control over the economy, equality, full employment, and universal free access to social services. Some eradicated evils of the past such as prostitution, mendacity, and corruption are back. Many foreign experts, and probably a good part of the Cuban people, question whether the Revolution and socialism are still alive or dead on the island. The leaders, nevertheless, insist that such dramatic changes do not constitute a transition to capitalism, but undesired albeit necessary tactical steps to save both socialism and crucial revolutionary gains.

The causes of the new stage are multiple and, as in previous dramatic shifts, have been both internal and external. First, the previous chapter showed that the Rectification Process (RP) was a fiasco: it provoked a severe economic recession and did not achieve any of its ambitious goals. Second, the Food Program (FP), the keystone of the RP development strategy, was equally unrealistic and based on continued aid from and trade with the Soviet camp. (It was not until April 1992 that Castro admitted that fuel and other limitations had forced a halting of some of the FP components, and it was not until December 1993 that he acknowledged that "all was lost.") Third, the collapse of socialism in the Soviet Union and Eastern Europe, the dissolution of the former, and the disappearance of CMEA led to termination of economic aid and price subsidies to Cuba and a drastic reduction of trade with the former allies and Soviet oil deliveries. Fourth, the end of the socialist pipeline generated severe scarcities in Cuba of foodstuffs, fuel, fertilizers, chemicals,

289

spare parts, and other inputs needed for agricultural and industrial production (some of these scarcities were aggravated by the ill-conceived RP and FP), which, in turn, provoked drastic cuts in mining, industry, transportation, and part of agricultural activities, as well as a significant expansion of the labor surplus and state subsidies to state enterprises. Fifth, the enactment of the Cuban Democracy Act (Torricelli Law) in 1992 and, particularly, the Helms-Burton Act (1996) tightened the U.S. embargo on Cuba, this time more effectively than before, because of the lack of aid and trade with the Soviet camp. As in 1963 and 1970, therefore, in 1991 the Cuban leaders faced a double failure: in economic organization and development strategy. But, unlike on those two previous occasions, the Soviet Union no longer existed to help Cuba, and the disappearance of CMEA left only the world capitalist market for trade, investment, and technology. China could not replace the Soviet Union as it did not have the latter's resources and commitment, and it was involved in a deep market-oriented reform. In spite of all the factors described above, the decision to reform was long and convoluted.

Faced with the island's desperate need to reinsert itself in the world capitalist market, raise domestic efficiency, and improve consumption, in 1990 a few Cuban economists began to look at market reform as the lesser of two evils. There was a nonpublicized discussion of the possibility of combining a socialist framework with market mechanisms—which the Cubans rushed to clarify were not exclusive of capitalism. In August 1990 I held conversations in Havana with small academic groups of economists and other social scientists, who gave me the impression that the debate among them was not on whether to use market tools, but to what degree they should be employed and how to avoid their potentially negative consequences. Some of my counterparts argued that (1) if market mechanisms were ignored or repressed, they would emerge anyway, as the black market had demonstrated; (2) the satisfaction of urgent basic needs of the population should be more important than the desire to curtail profiteering by a small group who could actually help meet those needs; and (3) if the state was unable to satisfy such needs, a regulated market or private activity should be allowed to fulfill it. In the fall of 1990 midlevel technicians were calling for privatization of personal services, which the state was unable to provide, and the reintroduction of free peasant markets, production bonuses, and other mechanisms abolished or greatly reduced under the RP (sources for this chapter, unless specified, are Mesa-Lago 1993a, 1993b, 1993c, 1994b, 1994c).

Open-minded Cuban economists and technicians, nevertheless, harbored reservations about market mechanisms, largely resulting from their observation of adverse consequences of market reforms in the Soviet Union and Eastern Europe. They saw the private sector as capable of playing positive roles (elimination of the state monopoly, competition to improve state efficiency) but feared a snowball effect as the sector demanded increasing inputs, accumulated wealth, and challenged the state. The disappearance or sharp reduction of the safety net was their major preoccupation: (1) high unemployment that would create serious political and social problems, (2) significant inequalities that would break the cement that kept the Cuban people together, (3) price increases that would sharply reduce consumption of low-income groups, and (4) erosion of social services.

At that time, the stumbling block to a market-oriented reform in Cuba was Castro's stern opposition even to the type of reform implemented in China and Vietnam, countries that have managed to combine economic progress with political control. In several speeches he systematically rejected privatization of small enterprises, contracts between state farms and factories with families and groups of workers, free peasant markets, self-employed street vendors, and tiny producers. Conversely, he promised that the Revolution would more progressively socialize, battle against the remaining private farmers, and solve all economic problems through the state, an approach that had repeatedly failed before. Castro's speeches in 1990–92 showed disdain for those weak in supporting the Revolution, aversion to any market reform, readiness to smash those who opposed him, and a disposition to die entrenched in his ideas, taking the whole nation with him. He attacked individuals and groups inside Cuba whom he called "skeptical," "disaffected," "critical," "defeatists," and "cowards." He accused economic reformers of being "imperialist puppets," "political snipers," "pseudo-revolutionaries," "fifth columnists," and "traitors," and he threatened them with harsh retaliation. Carlos Aldana, the third most important political figure in Cuba, who had shown cautious sympathy for reform, publicly confessed his error (after discussions with Castro—he said) and exhorted others who believed in reform to recant too, a confession that did not prevent his dismissal in the fall of 1992 under accusations of corruption. As late as April 1992 Castro publicly stated:

> [Some] think that the problems [we have] are the result of stupid acts committed by . . . many cadres. . . . There are strategists who are saying what has to be done now. . . . Our people do not understand anything about the market economy. . . . We must engage in an all war against those who ignore the facts. . . . We should not get tired of repeating arguments once, 10 times, 100 times . . . a million times. . . . True revolutionaries never surrender, never sell out, never betray. That is for cowards, traitors and opportunists. None of us want that trash that [capitalists] are offering us. We prefer any sacrifice, any fate to that of capitalism. (Castro 1992a)

And yet the crisis was of such magnitude and depth that already in 1990 Castro had to launch an emergency adjustment program. He also grudgingly accepted the idea that the crisis could be solved with an external approach: a carefully controlled opening to foreign investment and expansion of external tourism, which would provide badly needed hard currency but be restricted to enclaves, without any domestic reforms. The 4th Party Congress, held in 1991, ratified the RP and FP strategies (already a failure), but it approved a more flexible foreign investment policy, while a 1992 constitutional amendment made possible the creation of mixed enterprises, joint ventures, and the like. But these measures were unable to stop the deepening of the crisis and precipitous economic downfall.

In the summer of 1993 four adverse factors convinced Castro of the need to introduce domestic market reforms: (1) a 39% drop in sugar output that cost U.S.$700 million in lost exports; (2) continuous production declines in nonsugar agriculture, mining, and manufacturing; (3) a severe scarcity of fuel that forced the shutting of more factories, further reduction in transportation, and long electricity blackouts; and (4) a huge budget deficit and excess money in circulation, a boom in the black market, and rapid devaluation of the peso, all of which created serious labor disincentives.

At that point a general consensus on the need for the reform was reached among political leaders, technocrats, and economic scholars but with two main differing positions concerning the type, scope, depth, and pace of such reform. The hard-liners led by Castro, who maintain a common front and hold power, favored a "conjectural," "minimalist," and slow-gradual approach: cautiously take the fewest steps needed to halt the economic decline, achieve budget equilibrium, restore the value of the peso, and ensure the continuation of the regime. This group opposed deeper reforms that entailed a danger of the government losing economic power and the unleashing of a potential chain reaction that could provoke a collapse similar to what occurred in the Soviet Union and Eastern Europe. The second position, held by academic economists and technocrats, relatively young (in their forties and fifties) and mostly trained abroad, supported a comprehensive "structural" reform going "to the roots of the problems." They thought the minimalists could temporarily restore the equilibrium and halt the economic downturn but would not be able to hold those gains in the medium and long run. This loose group, which lacked political power, was in favor of a mixed economy but with diverging degrees of state direction; they agreed nevertheless, on the need for an integrated reform program, implemented in sequential stages, with the following main features: (1) termination of the state's overwhelming predominance in ownership of the means of production, in favor of a more balanced combination of state, cooperative, mixed, and private ownership; (2) a shift of allocations from the central plan to a regulated market (with different degrees of government control), competition for capital and other resources, and profitability of enterprises (elimination of state subsidies); (3) a midpoint in distribution (neither egalitarianism nor extreme inequality), which would mean prices of consumer goods largely set by the market above production costs (ending state subsidies), workers properly rewarded according to their skills, effort, and productivity, and social assistance to the needy; and (4) government retention of enough power to promote basic economic and social development and relative equity in distribution. No one in this second group supported a free-market economy (or full restitution of capitalism) but aimed at either a Scandinavian type of social democracy or a Chinese-Vietnamese type of reform, or a more important state role than in the other two countries but still with significant decentralization and reliance on market tools (author's interviews with several Cuban economists in August 1990; González 1993; Lage 1993a; Carranza 1994; Marquetti and Everleny 1994; Monreal and Rua 1994; Casanova and Triana 1995; the most serious and articulated reform proposal was Carranza, Gutiérrez, and Monreal 1995). Castro made fun of both the diversity of ideas within the second group and their skills to conduct the reform: "There are 1,000 political economic schools now . . . and [each] has a plan or a formula for solving our economic problems. . . . But they did not go to Harvard where capitalist economics is taught. They went over there [the Soviet Union and Eastern Europe] . . . and I ask myself: How can we use socialist economics in our situation?" (Castro 1993a).

Yielding to the economic crisis and lacking a viable alternative, beginning in August 1993 Castro introduced several market-oriented reforms, but in a piecemeal fashion, without integration into a cohesive program, and not following a well-thought-out logical sequence: (1) legalization of the possession and circulation of hard currency (including remittances by Cubans living abroad and more flexibility in their visits) and state dollar shops opened to the population; (2) authorization of specific types of self-employment; (3) transformation of state farms into a new type of cooperatives and granting of small land parcels to families; (4) reintroduction of free agricultural markets with a larger scope, as well as artisan markets; (5) fiscal measures to reduce the budget deficit and the monetary overhang, such as new taxes and increased public-utility rates, some cuts in state subsidies and other public expenditures, and a rise in prices of nonessential consumer goods; (6) creation of a so-called convertible peso and opening of foreign exchange agencies; and (7) a new foreign investment law with a broader scope and incentives for foreign capital, as well as creation of free-trade zones. Although these policies were submitted to many regulations, restrictions, and state controls (as well as steps backward in some cases), by 1994–95 they seemed to have halted the economic decline, reduced both the fiscal deficit and excess money in circulation, and attracted some foreign capital.

In the summer of 1994, another wave of emigration to the United States, encouraged by Castro, led to a serious confrontation and the U.S.'s imposition of economic sanctions on Cuba. The difficult situation prompted an impressive public demonstration in Havana against the government, which seemed to give another push to the reform. Furthermore, in 1993–94 several foreign economists of diverse ideological orientations were invited to Cuba and unanimously advised a deepening of the reform, among them Jude Wanniski, one of the founders of "Reaganomics" and Robert Dole's advisor; Professor Santos Mercado, Academic Director of the Cultural Institute Ludwig von Mises (who showed a Milton Friedman video in Havana); Carlos Solchaga, Spain's former Minister of Economics in Felipe Gonzalez's socialist government; and two IMF officials. In 1994 a master program in market economics was opened at the University of Havana in cooperation with Carleton University and ECLAC (Mesa-Lago 1994a; Oppenheimer 1994; Solchaga 1994; *Toronto Globe and Mail,* September 19, 1994).

By mid-1995 the government appeared to have a strong hold on the economic and political situation, and the pace of reform began to slow. To the slowdown contributed the introduction of the "Track II" of the Torricelli Law in 1995 and the enactment of the Helms-Burton Law in 1996, which strengthened the hard-liners in Cuba. In March 1996 Raul Castro (1996) publicly criticized the negative effects of the economic reform, denounced some Cuban academic institutions and scholars favorable to stronger reforms as being "penetrated" ideologically by the enemy, threatened more regulations, higher taxes, and tougher sanctions, and called for an ideological campaign, all of which basically halted the reform process.

1. Policies

A. Ownership

In this stage, the share of state ownership shrank because of expansion of foreign investment, reauthorization of self-employment, transformation of state farms into cooperatives, granting of uncultivated small state plots to families and individuals, and authorization of ownership in real estate as well as some transportation and fishing. Furthermore, the creation of pseudo-private corporations, the reintroduction of free agricultural and artisan markets (see section B below), authorization to open banking accounts in hard currency, and the approval and regulation of free-trade zones (see section F below) reinforced the trend toward nonstate forms of ownership. The new cooperative and private sectors have been granted the right of usufructus (use and exploitation) through contracts for specific or indefinite periods, but not the right of ownership, which is retained by the state (only in real estate and some self-employment activities is full ownership granted). State regulations, restriction, and control over all new nongovernment activities are strong, and so are the sanctions for violations. Finally Cuban citizens are not allowed to own any businesses in manufacturing and commerce, excluding tiny restaurants and self-employed work. The complexity of these new forms of ownership and lack of data prevent an estimation of the state's share in economic branches, except for agriculture.

In July 1992 the 1976 constitution was amended to limit state ownership to the "fundamental" (instead of all) means of production (e.g., land, mines, waters) and to allow (1) transfers of state rights to individuals and businesses (by approval of the Council of Ministries), provided they help economic development and do not conflict with public goals; (2) ownership by mixed enterprises, economic associations (such as joint ventures), and similar entities; and (3) creation of foreign trade enterprises of a quasi-private nature to directly export and import. The president of the National Assembly warned, however, that the amendment was not a retreat or a transition to capitalism ("Constitución de la República de Cuba" 1992).

Cuban quasi-private corporations (*sociedades anónimas*) had existed for years, but they were located abroad, mainly to buy crucial goods. Now they operate inside Cuba, their number and activities have expanded, and they are often authorized to import and export goods and services directly. Legally these are private corporations autonomous from the state; their capital is owned by shareholders who are Cuban citizens, seek partnership with a foreign firm, and earn dividends (Monreal and Rua 1994). In practice, the capital is supplied by the state, independence is a fiction, shareholders are figureheads—usually government officials—and all profits go to the state. Castro has rejected the possibility that Cuban citizens acquire means of production and has asserted that capital and technology cannot be controlled by domestic private sources but only by the state in association with foreign investors (interview with Evans 1992). Carlos Lage (1993a), vice president of the Council of State and the top economic officer, has added that Cuban citizens cannot be associated directly with foreign capital but only through the state; hence there is no privatization, and the government, rather than the Cuban enterprise partner, gets the profits.

The most important domestic change in ownership has been the transformation of state farms into a new type of production cooperative called Basic Units of Cooperative Production (UBPC), and the granting of public uncultivated small parcels of land to groups and individuals. Tantamount to a third agrarian reform, this law and its regulations were enacted in the last quarter of 1993, their unspoken but obvious reason being the failure of both the state farms and the FP. Prior to the UBPCs, there were two other types of cooperatives in Cuba: the CPAs, whose members owned the land, and the cooperatives of credit and services (CCS) without land ownership. In agreement with the government, workers on a state farm, both in sugarcane and in the rest of agriculture, can sign a contract for an indefinite period to become an UBPC, with the following features: (1) usufructus (not ownership) of the land, which is rent free; (2) collective ownership of the former state equipment (for that purpose and further investment, the National Bank gives credit to the UBPCs, with a three-year grace period and 4% annual interest later); (3) obligation to plant certain crops and sell most of them to the state (*acopio*) at prices set in pesos by the government, below the market price; (4) allocation of part of the UBPC land for self-consumption (about 7%); (5) any crop surplus left after meeting *acopio* can be sold at agricultural free markets reintroduced in September 1994 (see section B; individuals were authorized to own trucks for transportation of agricultural products and other goods); (6) UBPC members "elect" their own manager, but there is a powerful government representative and UBPCs are submitted to state auditing; (7) members are paid out of the co-op revenue after all other costs are met (state farm workers have a guaranteed salary); and (8) the UBPC decides how to use any remaining profit (reinvest it or build homes for its members).

The government's goals were that UBPC members would feel like owners and, hence, stay in agriculture, cut production costs, and increase their effort, productivity, and output (to raise their income). The Cuban reform, nevertheless, lacked the three crucial elements of its Chinese counterpart, which, since the late 1970s, have contributed to increasing both agricultural output and economic growth: the cooperative decides what to produce, to whom the crop should be sold, and at a price set by the market. In Cuba UBPC members have an incentive to minimize production sold to the state (paid in pesos and low prices) and maximize their own consumption. If directly selling a surplus to agricultural free markets is obstructed by the *acopio* obligation, UBPC members can turn produce over to middlemen or sell it on the black market. If these alternatives are not feasible, they can simply reduce their labor effort (Mesa-Lago 1994c; La Sociedad 1994b).

The reform also allows the transfer of small noncultivated state parcels (no more than half a hectare) that were isolated and for that reason could not be integrated into UBPCs. Such a transfer is limited to usufructus (not ownership) for an indefinite period to families and individuals (e.g., pensioners, unemployed, state employees cultivating the parcel outside of their labor schedule). The transfer goal is self-consumption, but small surpluses might be sold in the agricultural free markets.

On paper the reform took place rapidly: by the end of 1993 virtually all sugarcane farms had been converted into UBPCs, and, in November of 1994 half of the remaining agricultural state farms followed suit. Data on small plots are very scarce, but, by April 1996, there were close to 12,000 parcels in tobacco alone embracing 25,000 ha. The impact of the reform on the percentage distribution of cultivated land by type of ownership was significant. In 1989, 78% was in state farms, 18.7% in cooperatives (10.2% in CPAs and 8.5% in CCSs), and 3.3% in small private farms. At the end of 1994 only 33.1% was in state farms (nonsugarcane), 61.8% in cooperatives (40.6% in UBPCs, 11.2% in CPAs, and probably 10% in CCSs), and probably 5.1% in small private farms and plots (CEE, *AEC* 1989a; Deere 1995; Alfonso 1996; Rodríguez 1996).

In spite of this dramatic transformation, the government's goals had not been met at least until 1996. According to the Ministry of Sugar, in 1994, 41.2% of UBPCs had problems with no immediate solution, 49.9% of them faced difficulties that could be solved in one year, and only 8.9% were profitable and showed increased output (Alfonso 1995). In 1995, 75% of sugarcane UBPCs and 50% of the remaining UBPCs had losses, and the net outcome of the sector was a deficit because of the sugarcane higher weight ("A Survey of Cuba" 1996). Sugarcane and the rest of agricultural output kept declining in 1994–95 despite the reform; some UBPCs showed a rise in production value in 1994, but through price instead of output increases. In 1995, 52% of the total national loan portfolio (4.2 billion pesos) was given to agriculture, mainly the UBPCs, but there are questions about their ability to repay such loans plus interest after the initial grace period that ended in 1996–97. The UBPCs claimed manpower deficits in 1994, but largely because their members worked 5 out of the 8 hours of the daily labor schedule. From October 1994 to June 1995, *all* cooperatives delivered only 8% of total sales in the free agricultural markets, while state farms supplied 12%, and private producers (that had only 5% of total cultivated land) sold 80% (Pagés 1994; BNC 1995). In mid-1996 the Ministry of Agriculture reported that most UBPCs in Matanzas province were neither meeting their *acopio* obligation nor selling directly to the free agricultural markets, but turning over a good part of their crops to middlemen who paid a higher price than the state and then sold the produce in the free markets at twice the price they paid to the UBPCs (*Nuevo Herald,* July 21, 1996, p. 1B). The government's promise that UBPC members would feel like owners and feel independent has obviously not materialized, because of state control and restrictions on their operations. Three Cuban reformers advocated increased autonomy to UBPCs vis-à-vis the state, significant cuts in *acopio,* and state prices closer to market prices (Carranza, Gutiérrez, and Monreal 1995).

In 1991 the 4th Party Congress reapproved self-employment, submitted to state regulations that were not enacted until September 1993. At that time, 117 self-employed occupations were authorized; later some of them were banned and others added, growing to about 160. Most of them are in services (e.g., taxi drivers, repairers, electricians, masons, carpenters, plumbers, barbers, gardeners, hairdressers, tailors, cooks, domestic servants), but a few are in small-scale manufacturing (shoemakers, smelters) and in primary production (flowers, fish, pets). Prohibited from doing self-employment are state leaders, executives, and employees (the latter except in their free time); university graduates in their own fields; occupations not included in the official lists or that replace state activities (only supplementary activities are allowed); violators of labor discipline; and workers in locations where the state suffers from a labor shortage. Only allowed, therefore, are pensioners, housewives, the unemployed (but if receiving compensation they lose it), and state employees in their free time and with a good labor record.

Self-employed workers must (1) register with the municipal labor authority (the permit is based on the opinion of the local popular council), (2) purchase a license and pay a monthly flat tax, and (3) hire only family members (middlemen and wage earners are banned). Prices of services and goods produced by the self-employed are freely set by the market, but, if such prices or their profits are "excessive," they could be regulated by the government. For that purpose and to pay taxes, the self-employed must keep a record of revenue and expenditures and submit to frequent government inspection. State enterprises can neither buy from the self-employed nor supply them with raw-material inputs, unless the self-employed activities are "useful" to the population (Mesa-Lago 1994c).

Castro (1993c) ardently defended, at the National Assembly meeting at the end of 1993, the state's monopoly on domestic commerce, and he criticized several recently approved self-employed occupations, such as restaurants and taxi driving (which had rapidly proliferated and were successfully competing with similar state services). Against Lage's arguments on the negative impact that withdrawing the legal authorization would have, the Assembly went along with Castro and prohibited those activities. And yet taxi drivers and small restaurants continued to proliferate illegally, because of the government's inability to detect and prevent their operation. Eventually the two occupations were reauthorized. Restaurants were subject to new regulations on self-employment enacted in June 1995 but under stricter limitations: they must (1) have a maximum of twelve chairs and two family employees without pay, (2) be located in the operator's own home, (3) buy supplies only in state dollar shops and free agricultural markets, (4) cannot be managed by university graduates, and (5) cannot advertise or serve certain foodstuffs. Additional regulations, passed in May 1996, forced all self-employed to register again, increased licenses and taxes on restauranteurs several times, and imposed tough fines and imprisonment on violators. Street vendors must be mobile, continuously moving from place to place (MEICE 1995; MF-TSS 1995; for further discussion of self-employment, see section G below).

The 4th Party Congress of 1991 approved a series of informal practices (that had actually begun before) that made the ineffective 1982 investment law more flexible and appealing: it allowed more foreign investors to hold a majority of shares in joint ventures, faster recovery of invested capital, more tax exemptions, and increased facilities for repatriation of profits, salaries, and proceeds from liquidated businesses in hard currency (Evans 1992). After considerable discussion of six drafts of a new foreign investment law, which began in October 1994, the law was unanimously approved by the National Assembly on September 5, 1995, which declared that it was "not inspired by neoliberalism and did not aim at a transition to capitalism." Castro had complained a month before: "Some friends have advised us to say [that foreign investment] is a good thing. The truth is that we took this way because it was the only alternative." When the law was enacted, he added that the opening to foreign capital had brought "a bag of problems, contradictions and daily headaches" and warned that the law does not allow "subordination and dependency on foreign capital"; hence, "nothing is going to get out of hand" (Castro 1995; "Cuba Passes New Foreign Investment Law" 1995).

The main features of the law are the following: (1) all foreign individuals and firms can invest (including Cuban-Americans) in all economic sectors, except in defense, national security, health care, and education; (2) enterprises with 100% foreign capital are allowed, subject to previous approval by the Ministry of Foreign Investment, but additional authorization from the Executive Committee of the Council of Ministers is needed when their capital is more than U.S.$10 million, they are totally foreign, operate public services, or involve capital from a foreign state, and they include a transfer of state property or deal with military enterprises; (3) real estate can be owned by foreigners for homes, offices, and tourist developments, but, if it involves a transfer of state property, it requires a hearing from the corresponding state agency and approval by two ministries; (4) foreign investment cannot be expropriated (except for national interest and previous compensation in hard currency), it is protected by the Cuban government against third-party claims, and legal disputes should be solved by mutual agreement and can be appealed; (5) foreign-investment contracts have a term that can be extended by request and, if not granted, are liquidated and paid in hard currency; (6)

profits, dividends, nonresident employee salaries, and proceeds from liquidation or selling of foreign assets can be freely sent abroad in hard currency;
(7) foreign assets can be sold in hard currency to the state or third parties by
mutual agreement and government authorization; (8) foreign investors can
open branches and bank accounts in Cuba and abroad, take loans in hard currency, and directly export and import; (9) employees of foreign enterprises
should be Cuban nationals or foreign residents (except for executive and
technical jobs) and must be hired, dismissed, and paid by state employment
agencies; (10) taxes payable are 30% on enterprise profits (up to 50% if ex-
ploiting natural resources), 11% on the total wage bill for labor, and 14% for
social security, plus custom duties (in hard currency); all these taxes, however, can be partially or totally exempted (foreigners are always exempted
from personal income tax); and (11) trade zones and industrial parks can be
authorized by the Executive Committee on the Council of Ministries and receive special treatment with the rules for foreign investment (MIECE 1995).

The law legalized some ongoing practices and expanded the rights of foreign investors, but the Executive Committee of the Council of Ministries
must still approve the most important concessions, while various ministries
and state agencies have to authorize regular ones. Furthermore foreign investment contracts have terms that may not be renewed by the government,
the government is responsible for hiring and paying employees of foreign
enterprises, legal disputes can be appealed only to local first-level courts, and
the government "protection" against third-party claims (e.g., U.S. citizens
and expropriated firms suing foreign investors based on the Helms-Burton
Law; see section F below) is vague and ineffective. There is a final irony in
the law: its permitting Cuban exiles to fully own enterprises on the island but
withdrawing that right from its own citizens. This obvious discrimination
was a subject of discussion in the National Assembly, but Castro publicly dismissed it, arguing that Cubans abroad could bring capital, technology, and
markets that nationals do not have (In China about half of industry, in small
and private enterprises, is in the hands of individuals, families, and groups
of workers.) Reportedly a draft granting that right to Cubans was secretly circulating as early as mid-1995, but one year later there was no public ac-
knowledgment of it (most structural reformers supported this, including Carranza, Gutiérrez, and Monreal 1995).

B. Planning

The last five-year plan was between 1986 and 1990, but the sharp economic
decline in 1990 forced the enactment of a national emergency adjustment
program ("The Special Period in Time of Peace"), which replaced the cen-

tral plan and set a list of crucial priorities to be met and cuts to be implemented, the latter steadily expanding in 1991–93. The 4th Party Congress of 1991 granted exceptional powers to the PCC Central Committee, presided over by Castro, to make economic decisions and enact decree laws (in lieu of the National Assembly) during the economic crisis. In 1992 Castro (1992c) argued that the severe crisis and tough adjustment program had not been the result of his domestic economic policies (the RP was politically and economically correct) but provoked by the collapse of the Soviet camp and the tightening of the U.S. embargo. He maintained that the emergency program was preserving Cuba's cherished social services and that the adoption of a market-oriented reform would have brought a worse outcome.

The special period

Until the summer of 1993 the most relevant economic decentralization measure was the expansion of quasi-private corporations that, at least on paper, operated independently from the state. Many of them dealt with foreign trade and tourism (engaging in joint ventures inside and outside Cuba); by mid-1992 there were 88 such corporations in operation, while the Ministry of Foreign Trade directly controlled 68 enterprises. Other corporations were organized in steel, biotechnology, fishing, and tobacco (Evans 1992; Monreal 1993b). But the vice minister of the State Committee for Economic Cooperation cautioned that such a move did not mean "abandoning the idea of a centrally planned economy" ("New Role for CECE" 1992). A more important push toward decentralization was the reforms that began in August 1993: self-employment and UBPCs (explained already), free agricultural and artisan markets (to be discussed in this section), and the expansion of joint ventures (see section F below).

Tourism + foreign trade

The reintroduction of the free peasant markets was the subject of acute debate within the leadership. Structural reformers supported the markets based on the same reasons that led to their creation in 1980, but now aggravated by the crisis: (1) the incentive of higher market prices for producers to increase their output and supply, which would ultimately bring prices down; (2) a tool to combat the booming black market, which charged skyrocketing prices, mostly in dollars; and (3) a state food distribution system in total disarray, severe scarcity of foodstuffs through rationing, and lack of food for high-income workers to purchase (the latter contributed to the loss in value of the peso and disincentives for labor effort). Castro adamantly opposed the reintroduction of the peasant markets in 1991–93, based on a similar rationale as the one he used to abolish them in 1986: (1) high prices in the markets would be out of reach for most of the population, thus creating inequalities; (2) sellers in the markets would make huge profits, use middlemen, and both would get rich; (3) farmers with more capital would start buying other goods, thus expanding inequalities in income and access to all goods; and (4)

food

state farms and UBPCs would try to shift production for the state (*acopio*) to the free markets (because of higher prices); hence the flow of food to the central allocation system would decline, further exacerbating inequalities and creating social tensions. Declining agricultural output in 1994, despite the third agrarian reform, forced Castro to yield to the reformers, but, to avoid losing face, he entrusted his brother Raul to make the public announcement.

Decree law 191 of September 1994 reauthorized the free peasant markets, now rechristened "agricultural markets," which opened on October 1. The decree and its regulations tried to reach a compromise between the two reform factions and prevent or attenuate some of the problems feared by Castro: (1) all agricultural producers (state farms, all co-ops, military enterprises, the Youth Labor Army, recipients of small parcels) are authorized to sell in the markets (thus avoiding the previous restriction to private farmers); (2) producers (particularly state farms and UBPCs) must first meet their monthly *acopio* quota before selling their surpluses in the market (violators would be punished); (3) local governments organize and supervise the markets, which must be self-sufficient; (4) vendors have to pay a license (flat fee for using the market) plus a tax from 5% to 15% of the value of produce, collectable at the outset (before vendors start to sell), and tax revenue should be used by the state to help low-income groups; (5) prices are set by supply and demand; (6) initially goods could be paid for in dollars but soon they were limited to pesos; (7) all foodstuff can be sold except meat (pork is permitted), fresh milk, tobacco, coffee, and cocoa; (8) large producers can select "representatives" from their ranks (e.g., members of a UBPC) to bring the produce to the market (but outside middlemen are still prohibited); and (9) producers are free to use their own vehicles or rent state or private trucks to move the produce to the markets. In spite of these regulations, some of the old flaws have not been corrected; for instance, 80% of foodstuff sold in the markets is from private farmers and only 8% is from UBPCs. The difference is not mainly due to the high proportion of the UBPC crop that must be sold to the state (reportedly 80%), because many of them do not meet their *acopio* obligations; actually they use middlemen to sell in the markets, regardless of the prohibition of the latter and the threat of sanctions (Decreto-Ley 191; Whitefield 1994; Deere 1995; Ritter 1995).

Decree law 192 of October 1994 authorized the creation of artisan and industrial markets, through a national network of some 100 shops and open-air fairs. State manufacturing enterprises can sell surpluses at the markets, once their production commitments with the state are met; self-employed can sell handicrafts provided they are registered. Products can be sold directly in the market, given in consignment for selling, or sold to the shops; prices are set by supply and demand. Sellers must get a license, pay a fee for renting space, and submit a tax to the state. These markets have had less success than the agricultural ones, because of the lack of material inputs for the self-employed, low state output, and strict regulations. Articles sold are relatively few, of low quality, and costly (Decreto-Ley 192, 1994; *Nuevo Herald,* October 7, 1994, p. 3A, and December 2, 1994, p. 2A).

The government has not released data on the size of the "private market" in Cuba; the only information available is scattered figures on the value of sales in the agricultural markets and taxes paid by the registered self-employed; left out are the black market (only very rough estimates), the non-registered self-employed, and other smaller markets like fishing and transportation. From October 1994 to June 1995, 1.3 billion pesos were sold in the agricultural markets that, projected for one year, would be close to 2 billion pesos. The registered self-employed paid 63 million pesos in taxes in the first quarter of 1996, which, projected for the year, would be 190 million; assuming that the average tax on revenue was 20%, the self-employed income was close to 1 billion pesos. The two figures combined account for about 3 billion pesos, equal to 24% of the GDP in 1995. The value of the black market transactions of consumer goods was estimated as 2 billion pesos in 1990 and increased seven times in 1991–92, reaching, therefore, 14 billion pesos in 1992; another big jump occurred in 1993 (Carranza 1993, 1994). No data are available thereafter, but the volume of black market activities may have declined in 1994–95 because of the introduction of state dollar shops, and agricultural and industrial markets. If we add the black market and the non-registered self-employed market to the previous estimate, the size and proportion of GDP of the total private market must be much higher. Data on employment (discussed in section G below) suggest, however, a considerably lower proportion of workers in the nongovernment sector. Although it is impossible to reach a conclusion on the size of the private market, it has undoubtedly grown substantially despite government restrictions and regulations.

Both foreign experts and Cuban economists have noted that, in spite of the official rhetoric, there is no longer a conventional central plan, the adjustment program provides only broad guidelines to confront the crisis, and there is not an integrated cohesive system to coordinate all the new economic policies. Actually the design of that system was postponed allegedly because of the severity and emergency of the crisis (Carranza 1993). The lack of consensus (two main contending schools of thought on the reform style) aggravated the vacuum, leaving Castro free to choose (oppose) in piecemeal fashion those measures he deemed best (worst) according to his views (Mesa-Lago 1994c).

A reorganization in the government administrative structure was introduced by Decree law 147 of April 1994, enacted by the Council of Ministers (just ten days before a session of the National Assembly, an indication of the latter's irrelevance). All "central committees" existing under the former Soviet-style central planning (e.g., prices, material supply, statistics, basic industry) were disbanded and 18 ministries created or reorganized (e.g., economics and planning, foreign investment and economic collaboration, finances and prices, labor and social security, sugar, education and culture, public health), plus a dozen institutions including the National Bank (*Granma*, April 22, 1994, p. 1A). The new administrative structure is typical of Western market economies, but, in a good number of cases, the head of a central committee became the minister in the same field with similar functions; hence the impact of such a change on decentralization is doubtful. The reorganization did not clarify the ranking of the new Ministry of Economics and Planning, and if the elaboration of a national plan (of an indicative type?) was one of its functions. Minister José Luis Rodríguez (one of the key architects of the reform) said in 1996 that the system of material balances (GSP) and the centralized allocation of resources, both typical of the former socialist countries and previously applied in Cuba, had been replaced by financial planning (monetary and fiscal policy as tools of macroeconomic direction) and the system of national accounts (Rodríguez 1996).

In July 1995, at a meeting of the Council of Ministers, Lage stated that "the steps toward decentralization have gone beyond the capacity to assimilate them," and Vice Minister Raul Taladrid added that "we have to go to the pace of society." In March 1996 Raul Castro (1996) criticized the negative effects of the market reform and asserted that in the solution of problems "we have to use the market, but the National Economic Plan and the state must have predominance," and the new institutions "must be strictly regulated, with efficient application of the rules, detection and tough sanctions of the violators." He urged the Party to "establish a unified policy [without any] weaknesses [to] eradicate the problems and control the negative consequences of the economic reform."

C. Financing

The 4th Party Congress ratified the principle of self-financing, especially in enterprises that operate in hard currency (tourism, fishing, biotechnology, nickel), but allowed the continuation of budgetary financing. Between 1989 and 1993 state budget subsidies to cover enterprises with losses more than doubled, from 2.6 to 5.4 billion pesos, a clear indication that self-financing was not expanding. The tough adjustment, nevertheless, reduced the subsidy to 3.4 billion in 1994 and was projected to decline to 2.2 billion in 1995, slightly below the 1989 level (BNC 1995; see also next section).

The crisis and the adjustment program led to a cancellation of most domestic investment projects; hence investment dropped 43% in 1989–91 and further in 1992–93; it slightly increased in 1994–96 but still was extremely low. In the summer of 1996 Lage reported important delays in investment as well as inefficiencies. There are no data on investment distribution in this stage, but the adjustment program originally assigned priorities to sectors crucial for hard-currency earnings and exports, such as oil, tourism, nickel, and biotechnology. Sugar and food were initially neglected, but, as production precipitously declined, more funds were channeled to them, and, in 1995, 54% of loans were given to agriculture (Carranza 1993; Monreal 1993a, 1993b; BNC 1995; Carranza, Gutiérrez and Monreal 1995; *Nuevo Herald,* August 8, 1996, p. 13A).

Hard currency reserves and precious metals decreased from U.S.$102 to U.S.$12 million in 1991–92 and to virtually zero in 1993. The severe scarcity of hard-currency revenue forced a dramatic cut in imports desperately needed to hold production, and the latter also dropped. The increase in the peso supply could not solve the financing problem and aggravated the fiscal disequilibrium. Domestic savings could not tackle the financing needs either, although they helped to reduce circulating cash and inflationary pressures. The huge monetary surplus, severe scarcity of consumer goods, and expansion of the nonstate sector led to a triple of saving deposits at the state Savings Popular Bank, from 2.1 to 6.5 billion pesos between 1989 and 1993; a withdrawal of 600 million pesos in 1994–95 (as the monetary surplus decreased) reduced the savings to 5.9 billion in 1995. Deposits in hard currency earning "market" interest were authorized in September 1995 in all agencies of the National Bank, but no data have been released on their amount. External borrowing was very limited, although in 1995 a loan from U.S.$130 to U.S.$200 million was taken from foreign banks in order to finance an increase in sugar output in 1995–96, but the loan had to be paid in one year with a 14% interest. The vicious cycle could be broken only with significant foreign investment, hence, the enactment of the 1995 law (for more details see section F below).

In 1992 Castro said in an interview that banking reform was not a priority because the government first had to solve the internal financial imbalance. As the imbalance improved, in 1995 a legal draft for banking reform circulated, with several key features, some of which were introduced in 1996. The National Bank would be limited to typical central-bank functions such as money and bond emission, setting the interest rate and foreign exchange rate, control of hard currency, and design of credit policy. The Popular Saving Bank would either continue its operations or merge into a new state Agro-Industrial and Commercial Bank that would handle commercial banking operations to finance productive and trade activities; it would lend with interest to state enterprises, cooperatives, and the private sector. Central financing of state enterprises would end, as all become self-financed, but they could take loans with interest (if unable to repay, those enterprises would be shut down, except for strategic ones). Interest would start to play a role in capital allocation although the government would still assign priorities to key economic sectors. A new state Investment Bank would promote investment by placing securities and stocks in the world capital market through investment funds. In 1994 an International Trade Bank Corporation was established to deal with international trade, and the government approved the operation of the first foreign commercial bank (from Holland) but limited it to foreign investment and trade (they cannot give credit to domestic enterprises). Six other foreign banks (from Canada, France, Holland, and Spain) were in operation in 1995 (Mesa-Lago 1994c; BNC 1995; Carranza et al. 1995).

At the end of 1993, the National Assembly discussed a potential change in currency, but it did not materialize. One year later Cuba introduced a "convertible peso" exchangeable (at a rate of one-to-one) for U.S. dollars and usable in state dollar shops (*Granma,* December 20, 1994, p. 1). At that time, 50 regular pesos were exchanged on the black market for U.S.$1. The government's goal was to strengthen the peso and gradually eliminate the dollar from circulation, but few people voluntarily changed U.S. dollars (which can be used everywhere including the black market) for a "convertible peso" of limited use and considerable lower value than the dollar. After a brief appreciation of the peso on the black market, in August 1995 it stabilized at an exchange rate of 25 to 1 (until 1996). At the end of 1995, the government opened exchange houses in Cuba, which change regular pesos into "convertible pesos" at a rate similar to the black market but do not exchange pesos into hard currency. Some government officials and scholars have acknowledged that the lack of a realistic exchange rate and truly convertible peso are disadvantages for foreign investors and for measuring efficiency of exports, but others have said that such a measure would still take some time (Marquetti and Everleny 1994; Carranza 1994; *Nuevo Herald,* May 12, 1995, p. 1B). Some foreign experts predicted that, in 1996, the government would force foreign tourists and Cubans to change dollars into "convertible pesos" and make the latter mandatory in state dollar shops ("A Survey of Cuba" 1996), but the measure did not pass because of its adverse effects on foreign earnings and tourism.

D. Stability and Prices

The budget deficit further increased in 1990–93, peaking at more than 5 billion pesos in the last year. (The distribution of budget revenue and expenditures changed in 1991, and comparisons with previous years are very difficult.) Total revenue declined 24% between 1989 and 1993, along with its two major sources (which generated 50% of the total): the circulation or turnover tax by 36%, and the enterprise profit tax by 26%; such decreases resulted from the sharp economic decline and growing deficit of state enterprises. In 1991, for the first time, two revenue categories were disaggregated in the state budget: "amortization tax and other levies on enterprises and budgeted units," which combined accounted for 29% of the total. In 1993 two other new revenue categories were disaggregated: "tax on services" (a new tax), and "social security taxes," which jointly accounted for 13% of revenue. These four new revenue sources could not offset the decline in the major two sources and, hence, the net overall decline in budget revenue.

Expenditures diminished only 6% in 1990–93, while revenue dropped 30%, hence expanding the deficit. Subsidies to state enterprise losses jumped 82% and took 37% of total expenditures in 1993 (compared to 19% in 1990), explained by their rapidly growing losses; price subsidies took 25% of expenditures in 1990–92 but decreased to the 1990 proportion in 1993. Social services increased almost 3% in 1990–93, from 26% to 29% of total expenditures, but while the shares of social security and health expanded, those of education and housing contracted; the government was unable to cut the former, particularly the booming pensions. On the other hand, investment, defense, administration, and production expenditures declined 46%, and their combined share of total expenditures shrank from 37% to 23%.

Compounding this problem was the expansion of "monetary-circulation-accumulated liquidity" (a new term replacing "cumulative monetary surplus") by 138% from December 1990 to May 1994, as a result of a twofold increase in monetary supply and the severe scarcity of consumer goods and services (BNC 1995). The only way to reduce the fiscal deficit and excess money was to raise revenue, reduce expenditures (particularly subsidies to state enterprises and to prices, pensions and health care), and control the monetary supply. In October 1993 Lage said that, to put the finances in order, a gradualist approach rather than shock therapy would be applied. In December the National Assembly approved a budget for 1994 (ending four years "without budgetary discipline") and concurred on the need to create new taxes, raise some prices, and reduce or eliminate certain gratuitous services, but it could not agree on specifics. A stumbling block was Castro warning against cuts that would harm low-income families (Mesa-Lago 1994c). In May 1994 the Assembly granted wide space and flexibility to the executive branch to introduce taxes and other stabilization measures.

Law 73 on the Tax System was unanimously approved by the Assembly in August 1994. It introduced numerous taxes and charges, but the wage tax was postponed until the socioeconomic conditions are right. It is incorrect to say that there were neither wage nor income taxes before, but details are scarce and contradictory. According to one source, prior to 1967 there was a "gross salary" from which taxes—including social security—were deducted, hence leaving a "net salary"; after that year the government stopped the accounting of the gross salary and simply paid the net salary. Another source reports that an income tax of 11.9% was created in 1962 (which included social security), but it was abolished with the salary reform of 1980; enterprises continued paying the social security tax but were largely compensated by state subsidies. It has been noted already that, when self-employment was reauthorized in 1993, licenses and taxes were imposed, and similar charges were established with the reintroduction of agricultural markets in 1994.

New taxes created or regulated by the 1994 law and subsequent resolutions were: (1) an enterprise profit tax of 35%, plus 25% for labor and social security on the wage bill; (2) a sales tax replacing the previous "circulation or turnover tax"; (3) real estate taxes on property such as farms, "nonsocial" housing, and uncultivated land; (4) taxes on exploitation of natural resources, for example, mines, forests, and fishing; (5) taxes on harmful consumer goods such as alcohol and tobacco; (6) taxes on cars, other transportation vehicles, and recreation vessels, as well as toll taxes on highways close to tourist centers; (7) taxes on the use of ports, airports, and commercial advertisement in buildings; (8) inheritance taxes up to 60%, according to the amount bequeathed; (9) taxes on hard-currency income from abroad (except remittances from relatives) starting at 10% for less than U.S.\$2,400 annually to a marginal rate of 50% on U.S.\$60,000 and more; (10) import taxes equal to 100% of value, payable on U.S. dollars, by foreign travelers who bring food or gifts (medicine packages above 22 pounds are taxed and no more than two packages per year are allowed); (11) small increases in tariffs on public utilities such as water, sewage, and electricity (exempting low-income families, about 52% of the population) and significant raises in mail and transportation (buses, railroad, air); (12) charges for formerly free services such as school and worker-canteen meals, nonessential health services and medicines, entry to museums, gymnasium, art exhibits, and sports, and school uniforms; and (13) replacing loans for fellowships to secondary and higher-education students. These taxes and charges are being enforced gradually, starting in June 1994; in June 1995 taxes on self-employed were raised substantially (*Granma,* July 18, 1994, p. 1; *Trabajadores,* May 22, 1994, and September 19, 1994; *Nuevo Herald,* August 5, 1994, p. 6A; September 20, 1994, p. 8A; January 19, 1995, p. 8A; May 25, 1995, pp. 1A, 14A).

The above measures generated significant changes in the budget between 1993 and 1995. Revenue rose by almost 23% (although it was still 14% below the 1990 peak), led by a 75% rise in the circulation tax and 15% in the profit tax; these two sources combined increased their share from 50% to 63% of income, but the other new sources (added in 1991–93) saw their share shrink from 50% to 37% and suffered a decrease of 13%. Expenditures declined by almost 13% (18% below the 1990 peak), led by drops of 60% in enterprise subsidies and 12% in investment (minor decreases occurred in administration and production), but social services kept rising at a rate of 4.5% (their combined share of total expenditures growing from 29% to 34%, with all four components expanding), and other minor reductions were made in defense (2%) and price subsidies (1%). The growth in income and deep slashes in expenditures led to a substantial cut in the budget deficit (BNC 1995). According to Cuban scholars the reduction in the monetary surplus in 1994 was mainly accomplished by increased prices and taxes on cigarettes (68.6%) and alcoholic beverages (16.2%), higher tariffs on electricity and transport (7.1%), charges for meals in school and labor centers (3.5%), and increased prices of fuel and public services (4.3%) (Casanova and Triana 1995).

The adjustment program has reduced the fiscal deficit and excess money in circulation, but other painful adjustment measures were still pending in 1996: the halting or reduction in social service expenditures (34% of 1995 expenditures), the dismissal of 500,000 to 800,000 unneeded state workers, the complete elimination of subsidies for enterprises and prices (23% of expenditures), and the introduction of a wage-income tax, a sales tax, and workers' social security contributions. The needed general price reform is not feasible until those tough fiscal measures are implemented.

Although prices of rationed essential consumer goods (particularly foodstuffs) remain largely unchanged, it is widely acknowledged that the rationing package now barely covers family basic food needs for only two weeks (and through long lines). To satisfy food needs in the other two weeks (as well as virtually all other consumer goods), people must either receive hard-currency remittances, be self-employed, be a farmer or co-op member, be employed in jobs connected with tourism or joint ventures, or be involved in the black market, prostitution, or other illegal activities. Having dollars or a substantial peso income permit people to buy those goods in state dollar shops, free agricultural and artisan markets, and the black market. Prices in these markets are several times higher than in the rationed market or are set in dollars. For instance, beef is not available through rationing and in 1994 cost U.S.$5 per pound in state shops; a pound of pork (not available through rationing either) cost U.S.$1 in agricultural markets and U.S.$3.50 in state stores; a bottle of rum cost from 1 to 2 pesos through rationing and U.S.$4.50 in a state store.

E. Development Strategy

The failure of the FP and the collapse of the Soviet camp forced a change in the development strategy, although sugar still remains a key hard-currency earner. In a chain reaction, the termination of Soviet price subsidies and aid, as well as a sharp decline in trade, led to a dramatic cut in Cuban imports, which, in turn, provoked severe scarcities of fuel, chemicals, raw materials, spare parts, fertilizers, fodder, and so on. As a result, 80% of industry was shut down, and nickel, sugar, tobacco, citrus, and fishing output decreased drastically. The island's principal exports plummeted because of lack of inputs and traditional buyers, hence further reducing the country's ability to import. The FP failed because of its unrealistic targets and dearth of key inputs expected from the no-longer-existent Soviet camp. As food domestic production and imports fell, severe shortages ensued, which led to the third agrarian reform, already explained. The sharp cut in Soviet supply of oil (and its selling at world market prices) further aggravated the crisis. The opening to foreign investment and hard-currency remittances from Cubans abroad have become a crucial component of the new development strategy in a desperate search for capital, technology, fuel, and markets to promote a recovery. But high investment risks and U.S. pressures (particularly the Helms-Burton Law) are significant barriers despite Cuba's expanded concessions and incentives to foreign investors. Shifting exports to the world market is also obstructed by Cuba's lack of export diversification and competitiveness, after 30 years of virtual isolation from that market (main source for this section is Mesa-Lago 1994c).

The sugar sector was particularly harmed by the lack of inputs and official neglect; hence production steadily decreased with a low in 1995. In order to increase output, it was vital to import fertilizer, fuel, pesticides, herbicides, and spare parts, and the leadership took a loan from foreign banks payable in one year at a very high interest rate. Although sugar output increased somewhat in 1996, the net profit made after paying principal and interest was very small. Except for spare parts, all inputs bought with the loan were consumed in the 1996 harvest (as most sugar mills are quite old, they will increasingly break down and demand more spare parts). Mechanization of planting, cutting, cleaning, and transporting the sugarcane turned from a blessing to a curse, because of the fuel shortage and breakdown of the equipment. Maintaining and increasing sugar output in the future, therefore, will require similar or higher loans, demanding more effort with higher risks.

Citrus production and yields declined sharply in 1991–93 because of reduced area planted, irrigation, fertilizers, and so forth. Citrus exports to the former Soviet camp virtually stopped, and the shift to the world market is difficult because of the low quality and appearance of the Cuban fruits. Foreign investment from Israel, Chile, and Greece is trying to correct those flaws (Nova 1992; Spreen et al. 1996). The severe shortage of fodder (mostly imported from the Soviet Union) harmed cattle, hog, and poultry raising and the output of eggs and milk (the FP's dreams for liquid fodder vanished). Tobacco production also fell because of the scarcity of inputs and a hurricane in 1993. The dearth of fuel and spare parts for the aging fishing fleet provoked a decline in the fish and seafood caught also.

After a severe drop in nickel output in 1991–94 (combined with declining world prices) Cuba signed a contract with Canada's Sherritt Corp. to restore and expand production in the U.S.-built plants in Moa and Nicaro, the former considerably more technologically advanced than the recently completed Soviet-CMEA plant in Punta Gorda. Output has been restored, and Sherritt has so far resisted the intense U.S. pressure, under the Helms-Burton Law, to withdraw from Cuba. Foreign investment has helped to restore and surpass previous output in existing oil wells but so far has failed to find significant new deposits of profitable crude quality. Construction of the Juraguá nuclear power plant has been paralyzed since 1991; the Russians have given a small credit just to preserve the plant from deterioration, but substantial foreign investment (at least U.S.$800 million in a consortium of Russian and European partners) is needed to complete that plant, and fear of its security is another stumbling block.

Biotechnology does not appear to have fulfilled its initial promise because Cuban products have not been fully tested, the profitability of the industry is questionable, and having lost the principal buyer (the Soviet Union) Cuba has now to compete in a tough world market. The pharmaceutical industry has been harmed by the disappearance of CMEA inputs. Foreign investment in some manufacturing sectors seems to be helping to raise output in steel, cement, and textiles, but previous output levels have not been recovered (BNC 1995). Cigar exports have declined because of a decrease in tobacco-leaf output and a 1992 court ruling in France that prohibited using the best-known Cuban trademarks, but Spanish credit and high world demand and prices for Cuban cigars are helping. Foreign investment in tourism, particularly from Spain, has been crucial in steadily raising the number of hotels, rooms, tourists, and revenue in this stage. The share of defense and internal security in total state budget expenditures continued the decline that began in the previous stage: from 9.6% in 1990 to 6.3% in 1995 (Table III.6). Cuban withdrawal of troops from foreign countries, Soviet halting of weapons exports and withdrawal of most foreign advisors, and the severity of the crisis have caused the decreasing trend.

F. External Sector

The declining trend in total trade transactions that begun in the previous stage turned into a precipitous fall in 1991–94. Trade with Russia declined by 94% between 1990 and 1994 and virtually disappeared with Eastern European countries, while trade volume with market economies decreased by 21% because of Cuba's decline in production and exports. CMEA was disbanded in 1991, all Soviet/Russian economic and military aid terminated in 1992 (leaving 600 incomplete investment projects), Russian supply of oil and oil by-products was cut in half between 1989 and 1994 (hard-currency payments for oil "reexports" ended in 1991), and Russian vessels started to charge hard currency in 1992 for transporting Cuban cargo. After the Soviet-Cuban five-year trade agreement of 1986–90, the two countries have signed annual trade (barter) pacts, basically exchanging oil and its by-products for sugar in the respective following amounts (in million metric tons each): 8.6 and 3.8 in 1991; 1.8 and 1.0 in 1992 (only for the first half of the year); 3.2 and 1.5 in 1993 (by August there was no agreement for the second half of the year, hence provoking the worst fuel shortage under the Revolution); 2.5 and 1.0 in 1994 (by September Russia had completed 60% of deliveries, but Cuba had supplied only 49%, and the rest was postponed until 1995); and 3 and 1 in 1995 (the 1996 trade pact did not specify quantities of both products). In 1993 Russia granted Cuba a credit of U.S.$380 million to continue or finish 12 of the 600 investment projects abandoned, including U.S.$30 million annually to maintain the nuclear power plant, U.S.$50 million to complete the oil refinery at Cienfuegos, and U.S.$80 million to finish the nickel plant at Camarioca. In 1995 the Russians agreed to pay U.S.$200 annually (in fuel, spare parts, etc.) as rent for their intelligence base at Lourdes (Rodríguez 1992c; EFE May 2, 1993; Mesa-Lago 1993a, 1994c, 1995; *Nuevo Herald* May 5, 1995, p. 12A).

The deterioration in the terms of trade against Cuba became worse between 1991 and 1995 as all Soviet/Russian price subsidies ended in 1992 and trade began to be conducted in world market prices. If the 1986–90 quinquennium is used as a base (Table III.22), in 1995–96 Cuba lost U.S.$10 billion in Russian price subsidies (but see below) and, instead of U.S.$11.6 billion in trade credits and loans, received only U.S.$580 million. Increasing world sugar prices in 1992–95 (from U.S. 9 cents to U.S. 13 cents per pound) and declining oil prices in 1991–94 (from U.S.$18.30 to U.S.$15.45 per barrel; Table III.19) helped Cuba avoid a more precipitous decline of the sugar/oil ratio (but oil prices increased in 1995–96 while sugar prices fell in 1996). Estimates, based on the annual average world prices of oil and sugar, indicate that Cuba received a small Russian subsidy in the barter operation (in millions of U.S. dollars): 424 in 1991 (when generous subsidies were still paid), 45 in 1992, 57 in 1993, 20 in 1994, and 78 in 1995 (this subsidy may have resulted, however, from the use of a base price different than the annual price average).

Russia took responsibility for all Cuban debt owed to the former republics of the Soviet Union and has unsuccessfully tried to negotiate its payment with Cuba. Most Eastern European countries have conditioned their resumption of trade with Cuba to an agreement on debt payment. A problem in these negotiations (in addition to Cuba's lack of resources) is either the disappearance of a currency (the "transferable ruble" used in CMEA, the East German mark) or its significant devaluation (the ruble/U.S. dollar exchange ratio deteriorated from 1.78 in 1990 to 5,500 in 1996). Since 1986 Cuba has not paid any principal and interest on its hard-currency debt with the Club of Paris either, resulting in a growing amount of that debt.

In order to get oil not supplied by Russia, Cuba signed barter pacts with a couple of former Soviet Union republics (as well as Iraq), but data are not available on those deals. Similar approaches were tried temporarily with Venezuela and Colombia, but Cuba's lack of resources ended those deals. In 1994 the Mexican oil consortium Mexpetrol entered a joint venture with Cuba to supply 3.25 million tons of oil annually that would be refined in the Cienfuegos plant adapted to Mexican crude (it was not explain how that refinery would process both Mexican and Russian crude); part of the refined oil would be kept by Cuba and the rest exported. The Mexican crisis of 1995 forced a suspension of that deal (Mesa-Lago 1995).

China and Cuba signed a trade (barter) agreement for 1991–95, which set annual total transactions at U.S.$500 million, 13% below the volume of 1990. Actually trade steadily declined to U.S.$260 million in 1995, for an annual average of U.S.$318 million, less than two-thirds of the agreed-upon volume. The reason for the decline was the decrease in Cuba's sugar output and exports that led to a nondelivery of 500,000 tons to China in 1994, one-half of the committed amount (that year Cuba owed more than one million tons in sugar exports to China and Russia). China has supplied bikes, rice, and machinery, and all transactions have been in world market prices. At the end of 1995 Castro visited China, but no information was released on any potential agreement for 1996–2000 (Mesa-Lago 1994c; CIA 1995; *Nuevo Herald*, February 22, 1995, p. 1B, June 13, 1995, p. 13A, November 29, 1995, p. 1B).

A decree law in August 1993 legalized the remittance, possession, and circulation of hard currency in Cuba, the use of it to buy goods (mainly imported) in state dollar shops, and eventually open bank accounts. In addition, the number of Cuban exiles allowed to visit the island (and Cubans to visit relatives in the United States) was considerably increased by more flexibility in granting visas; visitors can bring hard currency and gifts into the island to spend themselves and for their relatives and friends. (U.S. government policies on both dollar remittances and travel by Cuban-Americans changed various times in 1993–96; U.S. restrictions, however, are usually overcome by using third countries.) The amount of foreign remittances is difficult to assess as is how much of them are spent in state stores or go to the black market and the self-employed. The prohibition on Cubans owning and managing businesses, combined with restrictions on self-employment and sanctions, make it very difficult to invest such remittances in legal activities, hence limiting the amount and stimulating consumption. The high prices of goods sold in state stores (100% profit), lack of managerial flexibility to fix such prices to get rid of unwanted stocks, and absence of competition and incentives to increase domestic supplies have limited both the number of people who can buy in the stores and their sale volume and have made the struggle against the black market less effective (Marquetti and Everleny 1994).

Foreign investment increased between 1991 and 1995, although its exact amount is the subject of debate. Cubans emphasize the following advantages for foreign investors: (1) up to 100% in enterprise shares, (2) rapid recovery of investment (e.g., 3 to 4 years in tourism), (3) total exemption from taxes on personal income and discretional exemption from profit tax and custom duties, (4) protection against Cuban government expropriation and third-party claims, and (5) highly skilled manpower, low wages, and peaceful labor relations, including a ban on strikes and government dismissal of troublesome workers (Monreal and Rua 1994). However, foreign experts have noted the following disadvantages: (1) no ownership of factories and installations; (2) excessive regulations and red tape, including approval by the Executive Committee of the Council of Ministers and two or three other ministries or agencies, depending on the type of investment; (3) the need to import virtually all raw materials and semiprocessed products, as they are not available domestically; (4) production for hard-currency exports only and prohibitions on selling to the domestic market; (5) obsolescence of Cuba's industrial plant and machinery, lack of spare parts, and frequent breakdown of equipment; (6) inability to hire, promote, and pay workers directly (in hard currency), hence poor labor incentives; (7) corruption, bribery, and commission seeking by Cuban officials; and (8) high risks due to U.S. legislation and pressures, and Cuba's vague, poor protection against claims of expropriated owners, as well as occasional cancellation of business by the Cuban government (Evans 1992; Mesa-Lago 1994c; Pérez-López 1995c).

Four foreign publications have included Cuba among the worst countries in the world concerning foreign investment risks and economic freedoms: (1) the Economist Intelligence Unit ranked Cuba 116th among 129 countries in terms of investment safety; (2) the Heritage Foundation placed Cuba 100th among 101 countries in terms of economic freedoms; (3) Euromoney considered Cuba the worst country among 167 based on several economic indicators; and (4) Freedom House ranked Cuba 79th among 84 countries concerning economic freedoms (Mesa-Lago 1994c; *Transition* 1995; Messick 1996).

The toughening of the U.S. embargo has made foreign investment and trade with Cuba riskier (the U.N. General Assembly approved, by a large majority of votes, five nonbinding resolutions between 1992 and 1996, asking the United States to lift the embargo). The 1992 Torricelli Law prohibits U.S. subsidiaries abroad from investing in or trading with Cuba and sanctions ships that carry Cuban cargo, prohibiting them from entering U.S. ports. In August 1994 after the raft exodus, President Clinton tightened the regulations for travel and sending remittances to Cuba; these rules became more flexible in October 1995 but were toughened again in February 1996 after two civilian airplanes were shot down by the Cuban air force. The Helms-Burton Law, enacted in March 1996, introduced new tougher prohibitions and sanctions: (1) the U.S. embargo becomes permanent, it does not need to be annually reinstated as before; (2) the United States will oppose Cuba's entrance into international financial organizations (IMF, World Bank, IDB, OAS) until a democratically elected government is in power in Cuba; (3) U.S. aid to Russia will be reduced by the U.S.$200 million paid for rental of the Lourdes base; (4) the United States will suspend aid to any government that provides economic aid, trade subsidies, or debt-equity swaps to Cuba; (5) the United States prohibits imports of Cuban goods or products that contain any substance produced in Cuba through other countries (especially Canada and Mexico); (6) the banning of family travel and remittances to Cuba will continue until its government allows full operation of small businesses by Cuban citizens; (7) U.S. citizens (including naturalized Cubans) can sue in U.S. courts individuals or firms that "traffic" with property confiscated by the Cuban government ("traffic" includes possession, sales, transfers, distribution, management, use, and holding interest in such property), but the right to sue has been suspended every six months by President Clinton since 1996;

(8) a three-month period is given to those who have "trafficked" to withdraw and be liable for the higher amount between a certified claim and the fair market value of such property, plus interest since confiscation, and court and attorney fees (if there is not a withdrawal, the liability increases threefold); and (9) U.S. entry visas will be denied to "traffickers," their spouses, and minor children ("Cuban Liberty and Democratic Act" 1996).The law prompted threats of retaliation by the European Union, Canada, Mexico, and other countries, but they have had a chilling effect on new investment in Cuba, although only a few foreign firms have withdrawn.

The foreign investment law of 1995 gave power to the Council of Ministers to authorize free-trade zones and industrial parks, with special status concerning customs, exchange rates, taxes, labor, investment, and foreign trade. A decree approving and regulating these new institutions was enacted in June 1996. Free-trade zones are scheduled to open in the ports of Mariel, Cienfuegos, and Wajay and possibly in the ports of Santiago de Cuba and Nuevitas.

G. Labor and Employment

All the RP labor goals and programs failed and were discarded in this stage: the labor surplus expanded tremendously rather than being reduced; instead of rising (through tighter control of work quotas), labor productivity precipitously fell as many enterprises were shut down, but most of their workers kept receiving wages; the revival of unpaid voluntary labor and military mobilization became absurd in view of the growing manpower surplus; construction brigades and contingents were quietly disbanded because of the shortage of construction materials and budget cuts in housing; moral stimulation was rapidly replaced, once again, by material incentives, to a greater extent than ever before under the Revolution; the praised "integral system of enterprise improvement" went into oblivion; and corruption and crime rapidly grew because of the severe scarcity of consumer goods, foreign investment, and tourism and the expanding nongovernment sector.

The manpower surplus expanded between 1990 and 1995 because of an increase in the labor supply and contraction in its demand: (1) more than 50,000 soldiers and military personnel returned from Africa and elsewhere (at a time when the defense budget was trimmed), 15,000 civilian workers and at least 6,000 students with fellowships were repatriated from Russia and Eastern Europe after the collapse of socialism, and thousands of "internationalist" civilian workers and military advisors came back from several countries, as pro-socialist governments ended in them; (2) 300,000 new workers entered the labor force between 1991 and 1995; (3) the collapse of socialism in the Soviet Union and Eastern Europe with its outcome of fewer imports and exports, lack of inputs, and abandonment of 600 investment projects led to widespread shutdowns in industry and mining, almost a standstill in transportation, sharp reductions in energy and water services, a virtual halt in construction, and dramatic cuts in commerce and entertainment; and (4) the adjustment program trimmed the state bureaucracy (11,600 jobs were lost by the administrative reorganization of 1995 alone), cut subsidies to state enterprises (59% to 69% of them were nonprofitable), and reduced state expenditures by 18% and investment by 59% (Mesa-Lago 1993c; Carranza 1994; BNC 1995; *Miami Herald,* January 22, 1995, p. 3A; *Trabajadores,* February 21, 1995; *Nuevo Herald,* January 26, 1995, p. 3A).

It was estimated that, in 1992, from 525,000 to 906,000 workers were affected by the crisis or from 10.4% to 19.3% of the labor force (Mesa-Lago 1993c). This estimate was confirmed in March 1995 by the secretary general of the CTC, Pedro Ross Leal, who said that from 500,000 to 800,000 workers in the state sector were not needed and should be "rationalized" or "voluntarily relocated" (*Miami Herald,* March 26, 1995, p. 20A; *New York Times,* May 13, 1995, pp. 1, 4).

The government tried to cope with the labor surplus in four ways: (1) easing workers' retirement, (2) allowing mothers to stay at home for longer periods to take care of their children, (3) relocating unneeded workers paying them unemployment compensation, and (4) generating new jobs in areas like the foreign investment sector, self-employment, and agriculture. (Mesa-Lago 1993c). Liberalizing retirement increased the cost of pensions, which took 12.4% of the budget in 1995. Relocation requires the availability of productive jobs elsewhere, which are difficult to find, and unemployment compensation is very costly (see section H below). Creation of new jobs, particularly in the nongovernment sector, is the only viable alternative but has been obstructed by the restrictions on self-employment and reluctance to allow Cubans to own or manage small and medium business (foreign investment has created a relative small number of new jobs).

A rough estimate of the size of employment in the nongovernment sector at the end of 1995 is based on the following figures: (1) 208,500 registered self-employed plus a conservative estimate of 190,000 nonregistered; (2) 217,857 private farmers and members of all cooperatives (421,362 according to another estimate); and (3) 53,000 workers in the foreign investment sector (these figures exclude the artisan and black markets). The total of 669,357 workers (872,862 if the higher figure in agriculture is used), compared with labor force estimates of 4,088,000 and 4,483,600, indicates that from 16.4% to 19.5% of the labor force is in the nongovernment sector (Casanova and Triana 1995; Alfonso 1996; Rodríguez 1996; *Trabajadores,*

April 22, 1996, p. 5; ECLAC 1997). A Cuban estimate of the size of the nongovernment sector in 1994 was 750,000 workers or 16.7%–18.3% of the labor force (Alvarez and Casanova 1994). The nongovernment sector is, therefore, very small and incapable, under current conditions, of doubling its size to absorb the 500,00 to 800,000 workers not needed in the state sector. (In section B the peso value of the nongovernment sector in 1995, excluding the black market, was estimated as 24% of GDP, bigger than its percentage of the labor force; such a discrepancy may be the result of flaws in these estimates or an indication of the considerably higher productivity and income in this sector.)

The above figures, nevertheless, overestimate the number of *net* jobs created in the nongovernment sector. In agriculture the only additional jobs are in the small plots given out under the third agrarian reform (and part of them are not replacing state jobs), because the UBPCs did not add jobs as their members were previously employed in state farms. Furthermore, Raul Castro (1996) has warned that unneeded workers cannot be absorbed in agriculture because this sector needs to increase productivity. In foreign investment, except for tourism, many of the new joint ventures have simply inherited state workers and, in some cases, have downsized them. Self-employment, therefore, was the only sector growing (until 1995) but had to increase its size by twofold (including the nonregistered) to absorb all the state labor surplus. In 1996 only 46% of the self-employed were previously unemployed, but the remaning 54% were retired workers and housewives who certainly did not reduce unemployment but increased the labor surplus (Rodríguez 1996; *Nuevo Herald,* November 30, 1994, p. 5A).

Some dismissals began in February 1995; in March Castro announced that 500,000 workers would be "rationalized" that year, and in May CTC chief Ross reported that 80,926 workers had been "rationalized" already: 74% of them were shifted to new state jobs (not specifying which) and 26% were at home receiving a subsidy or had gone to work as self-employed (ECLAC 1997 estimated those receiving subsidies alone at 31.5% in 1995). The trade unions, in meetings throughout Cuba, accepted the need for rationalization but asked that cuts be done gradually to avoid harmful effects on the workers. Castro, the Minister of Labor, and the CTC chief clarified that indeed the "rationalization" would be gradual, with a careful study of which workers were needed and which were redundant, and securing job creation first (*Trabajadores,* November 29, 1993, p. 2; *Nuevo Herald,* March 26, 1995, p. 20A, April 19, 1995, p. 1B, May 2, 1995, p. 1A; *New York Times,* May 13, 1995, pp. 1, 4).

Cuban structuralist reformers and foreign advisors recommended much more flexibility in self-employment, authorizing Cubans to own or manage small businesses, university graduates to exercise their professions, self-employed to hire nonfamily wage earners, and middlemen to operate legally. All of these steps were considered essential to creating jobs for those dismissed; otherwise the elimination of the labor surplus would not be feasible (Carranza 1994; Carranza, Gutiérrez, and Monreal 1995; Solchaga 1995). None of these suggestions, however, were accepted by the hard-liners, who fear losing more economic power. Conversely, Decree 186 of March 1994 established sanctions (fines from 500 to 1,500 pesos and confiscation of goods) for the following violations of self-employment rules: lack of registration and license, performing a banned occupation, selling in a nonauthorized location, hiring wage earners, being a middleman, charging "excessive" prices, providing false data on earnings, and cheating on taxes. In the first half of 1995, sanctions for 5 million pesos were imposed on 6,800 self-employed. In March 1996 Raul Castro (1996) criticized the "many negative flaws" of self-employment such as stimulation of crime, enrichment, tax avoiding (about 40%), and organization of groups independent from the state that are "receptive to the enemy's work." He asked for more severe punishment for violators as well as higher taxes. A joint resolution of the Ministries of Labor-Social Security and Finances-Prices, enacted in May 1996, imposed new restrictions, forced a reregistration of all self-employed in June, and raised licenses and monthly fees by as much as 300% (taxi drivers) and 650% (small restaurants). The number of registered self-employed plummeted from 208,500 to 127,407 in 1995–97; hence the massive labor dismissals were postponed several times and had not taken place by the end of 1997 (*Miami Herald,* August 3, 1995, p. 19A; *Trabajadores,* July 3, 1995, May 27, 1996, p. 2; Alfonso 1996; ECLAC 1997).

The government's reluctance to give more labor power to joint ventures and other foreign investment enterprises explains why, in spite of high expectations, the 1995 foreign investment law kept the system of hiring, promoting, and paying workers through a state agency, instead of allowing the foreign enterprises to do it directly. This means that the enterprise pays wages in dollars to the government and the latter pays a similar amount to the Cuban employees, but in pesos, at 4% of the U.S. dollar value in the black market and the state exchange agencies. (This clause in the law was strongly opposed by foreign investors who wanted to do these functions directly.) To somewhat counteract this exploitation, the law allowed foreign enterprises to create a stimulation fund based on their profits. In addition, in some foreign sectors (such as tourism), a small proportion of the salary is paid in dollars, but this practice has been criticized because it expands inequalities and the workers may conclude that a "capitalist enterprise treats workers better than state enterprises [hence, the former] is not as bad as we have told." This is "a source of admiration that may weaken the nationalist-socialist feelings" of the people (R. Castro 1996).

Fraud, corruption, and crime have escalated in this stage. Managers and workers of state enterprises steal goods for their own consumption and to sell on the black market or as inputs to the self-employed. About 30% of food produced in the state sector never reaches the consumers, and stealing from crops is frequent; police and military attempts in 1994 to control this problem were unsuccessful. Prostitutes of both sexes (called *Jineteras*) have flourished, particularly connected with tourism; there have been occasional raids against them (in 1994 and 1996), but the government normally closes its eyes because "erotic tourism" is a good source of hard-currency earnings. Self-employment, the black market, and middlemen are also the target of government campaigns and punishment. Corruption by Cuban officials who get commissions and gifts from foreign enterprises have been the subject of scandals and imprisonment. A meeting of the Council of Ministers and heads of hard-currency enterprises held in August 1995 denounced these problems and threatened severe sanctions. Top officials of the two finest national museums in Havana stole valuable art pieces that were later sold in Europe and the United States, and the Cuban government warned Sotheby's and other auction companies about stolen art. In the main state dollar shop in Havana, U.S.$52,000 worth of goods vanished in 1995, and in one of the big hotels the entire kitchen staff was fired for theft. Even the famous ice cream parlor "Coppelia" was prohibited from selling in hard currency because their employees took ice cream reserved to be sold in pesos, shifted it to hard-currency buyers, changed the dollars on the black market, and pocketed the difference (*Wall Street Journal,* March 22, 1994, p. 11A; *Nuevo Herald,* March 8, 1994, p. 1B, April 7, 1994, p. 3A; "A Survey of Cuba" 1996; R. Castro 1996).

Decree law 149 of May 1994 mandated confiscation of all goods and income acquired by people through illegitimate means or simply "disproportionate" to their normal income. This sanction is applied retroactively and can be initiated by a denouncement; confiscation is done first, and the defendant must prove in ten days that the goods and money in his or her possession were legally acquired, and there is no right to appeal the decision. The police checks income from wages or other legal sources to assess if they are sufficient to buy the goods or justify the defendant's bank deposits. Two decree laws enacted in June 1994 changed the Penal Code to raise prison sentences by ten years (to a maximum of thirty years) for serious corruption crimes; self-employed who hire wage earners or use illegal inputs are sentenced from six months to three years in prison, and tax evasion results in as long as eight years in prison and 5,000 pesos in fines. In the second half of

1994 thousands were under investigation or convicted, ɛ
confiscated (Castro 1993b; *Gaceta Oficial,* May 5, 199
bajadores, July 4, 1994; *Nuevo Herald,* May 6, 1994, ɪ
1994, p. 3A, May 13, 1994, p. 3A, July 8, 1994, p. 9A,
p. 8A).

H. Distribution and Social Services

The search for egalitarianism under the RP was completely reversed in this
stage, as Castro acknowledged at the end of 1993:

> One of the things for which the Revolution can be reproached is that it
> brought too much equality. . . . This has to be rectified because it wasn't
> working and it works even less in a situation of poverty. The more poverty
> there is, the less egalitarianism works. . . . The changes [we have introduced]
> were inevitable and we have to make some more which [will] foster indi-
> vidualism, selfishness . . . and generate alienating effects. (Castro 1993b)

The trade union newspaper rushed to declare that "egalitarianism went
too far, beyond the nation's economic capacity" (*Trabajadores,* November
22, 1993, p. 2), and the Party newspaper acknowledged that "it has become
evident that there is a process of unequal redistribution of income" (*Granma,*
January 4, 1995, p. 4). Inequality has expanded because a minority of the
population receives dollar remittances, food, and medicine packages from
relatives abroad; the self-employed and farmers earn several times the average wage in the state sector; middlemen and truck owners make big profits
in the agricultural markets; black-marketeers enrich themselves; and employees in tourism, foreign enterprises, and strategic sectors (tobacco, energy, mining, docks) earn part of their salaries or a bonus in dollars or receive
packages of goods (the government paid U.S.$3 million for these bonuses in
1994). This minority, albeit a rapidly growing one, can buy all kinds of consumer goods in state dollar shops and agricultural, artisan, and black markets
or receive them from relatives (*Juventud Rebelde,* June 21, 1993; *Trabajadores,* March 27, 1995; *Miami Herald,* March 26, 1995, pp. 1A, 20A; Ritter 1995). The elite preserves its privileges such as access to special stores,
good housing and vacation homes, cars with plenty of gas, and travel abroad.
The well-being of the majority of the population has severely deteriorated
because the rationing system provides food for only half a month and virtually no other consumer goods (rationing, therefore, has ceased to be an equalizer). The majority's real wages and pensions have decreased sharply, and
they have little or no access to buy food and consumer goods in the free mar-

s and state dollar shops because the exchange rate of pesos for one dollar deteriorated from 8 to 25 between 1990 and 1996, they do not receive remittances and packages from abroad, university graduates cannot exercise their professions as self-employed (executives, managers, and cadres are banned completely from being self-employed), and the price of food in agricultural markets is several times the rationing price. Blacks have been harmed more than whites, because close to half of the Cuban population is black, but only 3% of the Cuban-American population of South Florida is of that race; hence Afro-Cubans receive a tiny proportion of total remittances. Occupational income and status have reversed: physicians, engineers, and university professors, who used to be at the top of the ladder, are now at the bottom, and hence many of them have become taxi drivers or plumbers or work in tourist hotels (Mesa-Lago 1994c, 1998).

A comparison of the share of social services in total budget expenditures is blocked by the change in methodology. In the old system current and capital expenditures were included, and the share increased from 43.7% to 44.9% between 1990 and 1995 (Table III.6). In the new system only current expenditures are shown (investment is separate and not desegregated by spending categories) and increased from 25.4% to 34.4% (BNC 1995). A comparison of both sets of data suggests that investment and other state allocations to social services have shrunk from 18.3% to 10.5%. The government has so far succeeded in maintaining and even raising current expenditures in social services, both in budget share and nominal pesos (an increase from 3.9 billion to 4.4 billion pesos), but the real value of that amount has shrunk because of rising inflation and the booming monetary surplus. Furthermore, as the economy dramatically shrank and social expenditures increased, the latter's proportional burden on both the state budget and the national product has grown to intolerable levels. Cutting free social services, however, is an explosive political issue, as it is charging the population for those services. A closer look at the composition of the budget reveals, nevertheless, a different pattern among the four main social services: social security (pensions, paid leaves, and social welfare cash payments) increased 35% between 1990 and 1995 and health care 17.6%, but housing declined 17.3% and education 8.7% (BNC 1995).

Despite the crisis, social security entitlement conditions were liberalized in this stage: (1) retirement was made easier for workers whose labor history was incomplete and could not document 25 years of service (this aimed at reducing the labor surplus but it increased pension costs); (2) the time required to collect the first pension (from the time of application for retirement) was reduced to one month in 1992; (3) also in 1992, welfare monthly minimum benefits were increased (but not minimum pensions); and (4) retirement for disability became laxer; hence disability pensions rose from 25.9% to 37.3% of total pensions between 1990 and 1995, a very high proportion. It is not surprising, therefore, that the number of pensioners grew by almost 9% in 1990–93 (no data are available thereafter, but the above analysis suggests a bigger expansion by 1995), while social security costs (including health care) jumped from 9.3% to 16.9% of GSP in 1990–93 (from 17.9% to 19.8% of GDP), certainly the highest in Latin America and among the highest in the world (Table III.34; Mesa-Lago 1993c, 1996; Alfonso 1996).

Adding to social security costs was the creation of unemployment compensation to cope with dismissals resulting from the huge labor surplus. According to the "rationalization" rules (gradually introduced in 1992–95 in a piecemeal, confusing manner), (1) workers waiting for reassignment are paid their full wage during the first month and 60% thereafter until a job is found (with a three-year limit), (2) workers who refuse reassignment are dismissed and paid one full month's wage, and (3) young unemployed graduates have the option of retraining, continuing their studies, or waiting for a job (a monthly subsidy is paid to them). In 1992 I estimated that 114,000 to 496,000 unemployed ("dislocated") workers and graduate students collected from 149 to 667 million pesos in unemployment compensation, tantamount to 0.7% to 5.1% of GSP (the range is due to three different estimates) without taking into account costs of retraining and reassignment (Mesa-Lago 1993c). In 1994 the cost of the subsidy was estimated from 9.7% to 16.2% of GDP (ECLAC 1997). When the 500,000 to 800,000 workers are "rationalized," those costs will boom.

The high and growing costs of social security have led to a heated debate on imposing contributions on the workers (enterprise contributions were increased from 10% to 14% in 1995). The tax law authorized such contributions, but they were deferred and had not been implemented by the end of 1997. Castro has explained the delay based on the crisis and the need to change the workers' mentality, but he said that the contribution would range from 5% to 7% (*Time,* February 20, 1995, p. 59).

Health-care current expenditures increased in this stage, but investment in physical plant and equipment was halted, except for the family doctor program: in 1992 there were 12,000 units built, and 67% of the population was covered, at an estimated cost of 465 million pesos or close to half of the total health-care budget in that year. Furthermore, the annual salaries of 12,000 physicians and nurses added 75 million pesos annually or 7.7% of the 1992 budget, without taking into account costs like supplies and utilities. Few will question the value of this program, but its costs are exorbitant, particularly in view of the high health standards Cuba had achieved at the end of the 1980s and the severity of the crisis in the 1990s (Mesa-Lago 1993c). Another indi-

cation of waste was excessive hospital infrastructure: hospital bed occupancy further decreased from 73.9% to 71.3% between 1989 and 1993, while
the average length of stay rose from 9.9 to 10.4 days (CEE, *BEC* 1990; MIN-
SAP 1994). If the latter had been cut—according to international norms of
efficiency—to 6 days, hospital occupancy would have dropped to 41%. The
ratio of physicians per 10,000 inhabitants, which was 36.4 in 1990 (the highest in Latin America), jumped to 49.1 in 1994 (Table III.30); the glut of physicians was aggravated by the return of thousands who were working abroad
(such a glut partly explains the creation of the family doctor program in the
1980s and its continuation in this stage). Contrasting with the above largesse,
the water and sewage system badly deteriorated. In 1994 six advisors from
the Spanish cooperation agency found that only 40% of water was potable in
Cuba because of a lack of chlorine and calcium hypochlorite as well as breaks
in water pumps (*El País,* May 1, 1994, pp. 10–11). In 1995, at a UNICEF
meeting in Havana, MINSAP and the Institute of Hydraulics Resources reported that the bad state of water and sewage network, and poor water treatment, did not permit the control of bacteria and water contamination (author's interview with MINSAP official).

The collapse of the Soviet camp and CMEA led to a halt or sharp decrease
in the supply of (1) medicine and raw materials required to produce 85% of
all drugs consumed in Cuba, resulting in the lack of 300 medicines (including antibiotics, anesthetics, asthma medicine for one million asthmatics, and
insulin); (2) sutures, X-ray plates, surgical gloves, thermometers, spare parts
for equipment, insecticides (needed to control mosquitoes and epidemics
such as dengue and malaria), and soap and raw materials to produce it (crucial to maintain hygiene); (3) fuel and spare parts for garbage pickup trucks
(the number of operating trucks declined from 200 to 99 in Havana, and in-
frequent pickups have resulted in garbage piling up and proliferation of rats);
and (4) adequate condoms, which, combined with the increase in tourism and
prostitution, raise the risks of venereal diseases. Food shortages have reintroduced the specter of malnutrition-based diseases. Cuba's splendid physical infrastructure and health-care personnel is now largely useless because
of the shortage of medicine and other crucial supplies, and the government's
current survival strategy cannot truly solve that problem: (1) target medicine
and food to the most vulnerable population groups; (2) use of traditional and
herbal medicine, acupuncture, and organic substitutes; (3) diagnosis done by
clinical examination rather than tests; (4) treatment of patients at home (saving transportation and reducing hospital admissions, but worsening the underutilization of services); and (5) detecting diseases through the family doctor, who lacks the medicine to cure most illnesses (Barret 1993; Feinsilver
1993; Mesa-Lago 1993c).

Castro (1992c) has claimed that, in spite of the adjustment, no schools have been closed, they do not lack essential utensils, and student meals have not been eliminated. In fact, there are grave shortages of books, paper, pencil, and chalk in schools, which have forced campaigns to collect some of them at homes or ask for donations abroad. Very few books are imported, and 30% of raw material used in domestic production of paper is wood pulp, which was imported at very low prices from Soviet Union and Eastern Europe but now must be bought in the world market in hard currency. In addition, 25% to 30% of paper output is wasted because of obsolete technology and poor quality control. Furthermore, there are charges for previously free school meals, many students cannot attend school or arrive late because of lack of transportation, and loans instead of fellowships are given to secondary and higher education students. Many textbooks and curricula should be drastically reviewed (e.g., Marxist economics, still taught in 1995), but there are few resources and strong ideological resistance. In 1994 a master's degree in market economics was introduced at the University of Havana (in collaboration with Carleton University and ECLAC), but only a dozen students are enrolled annually. The scarcity of hard currency prevents students from being sent to study abroad. The government has relaxed the rules to allow Cuban scientists to go for training and research in developed market economies and arranges contracts for technicians to work abroad and share their earnings with the state.

Prior to the crisis, emphasis was placed on formal as opposed to vocational education, a priority inconsistent with economic needs that became more incongruous because of rising unemployment. In 1989–90, 76% of students who had completed elementary school were enrolled in secondary, pre-university, or higher education, while only 24% were enrolled in technical-professional (20.3%), special (3%), and vocational (0.5%) schools. In 1991–92 the Ministry of Education decided that 60% of students would go to polytechnics (vocational schools) and only 40% to pre-university schools; 43 of the latter were being converted into vocational schools in 1992, and 50 others were planned to follow suit in 1993. Secondary schools in the countryside are being transformed into housing for agricultural workers because of declining enrollment. In May 1994 the Minister of Education reported that 21,000 teachers had quit in 1993 (7% of the total) in search of better jobs and payment in dollars (CCE, *AEC* 1989a; Mesa-Lago 1993c; *Proceso,* July 18, 1994, p. 55; *Trabajadores,* November 28, 1994; *Miami Herald,* March 26, 1995, p. 20A).

Housing expenditures have been severely cut and, beginning in 1990, there was a dramatic decline in housing construction except for labor camps in the countryside (natural materials such as clay and plant fibers have replaced cement, steel, and wood); construction brigades and contingents have virtually disappeared. Because of the lack of construction materials or their poor quality, many houses and apartment buildings have collapsed or are propped up or have been demolished because of dangerous conditions; inhabitants of demolished buildings are sent to government shelters, sometimes for years (*Granma,* January 4, 1995, p. 5; *Trabajadores,* March 6, 1995; *Nuevo Herald,* March 7, 1995, p. 1B, March 13, 1995, p. 2B).

There was no change in population policy in this stage, but, because of the crisis, the birth rate declined from 17.6 to 13.4 per 1,000 between 1990 and 1994. Furthermore, in the summer of 1994, the government encouraged a new exodus to the United States, this time by rudimentary rafters, that totaled 35,000 people. The exodus ended with a U.S.-Cuban immigration agreement that includes the granting of 20,000 visas annually. For those reasons, the population growth rate slowed from 1.1% to 0.5% between 1990 and 1994 (Table III.30).

2. Performance

A. Growth

Evaluation of performance in this stage is the most difficult under the Revolution because of lack of data. The publication of the statistical yearbook was halted in 1989, and that was true of other sources such as the statistical bulletin. The National Bank annual report resumed publication, in abridged form in 1995, for the year 1994 (BNC 1995) but replaced the methodology of the material product system (MPS) by the system of national accounts (SNA), changed the composition of the state budget, and provided physical output data for only sugar, nickel, and oil. The scarce data available on production came occasionally from Cuban scholars, Castro's speeches, and top economic officials. In 1998, when this book was in production, the statistical yearbook resumed publication and provided data for 1990–96 (ONE 1998). Some figures from this source have been incorporated at the last minute (particularly in part V), but a thorough updating of this chapter was not possible.

Cuban scholars have estimated that GSP declined 45% between 1989 and 1993 (−47% per capita) at an annual rate of −13.6% or −14.5 per capita (Table III.3). No more data on GSP have been published thereafter because, according to the Minister of Economics and Planning and the National Bank, the MPS "used in the no longer existing socialist countries of Eastern Europe" has been replaced by the SNA (GDP) "used in almost all countries in the world" (BNC 1995; Rodríguez 1996). But no information has been published on how GDP is currently calculated in constant prices of 1981 (still with the same controversial base, after 15 years), how the 1985–93 GSP series was converted into GDP, what the deflator is and how it is estimated, and how the value of goods and services in the nongovernment sector (particularly in the informal and illegal areas) has been measured. If there were questions on the reliability of the MPS series when relatively abundant data were published, much more doubts exist now on the new GDP series.

The official GDP series in 1981 constant prices for 1985–95 (ONE 1995; BNC 1995) compared with the GSP series, also in constant prices, for 1985–93 (Table III.3) shows the following: (1) GDP is, on average, 25% smaller than GSP, therefore confirming my contention (see the footnote in chapter 3) that the upward-bias distortion caused by double counting was larger than the downward-distortion created by excluding the value of nonproductive services (the gap between GSP and GDP gradually decreased between 1986 and 1993); (2) the annual average GSP decline during the RP (1986–90) averaged 0.6% (1.6% per capita), but the annual decline in GDP in the same period was bigger, 1.3% (2.3% per capita); hence the deterioration caused by the RP was twice as bad than reported before; and (3) the annual average GSP decline in 1991–93 was 16.9%, but the GDP decline in the same period was smaller: 12.4% (11.7%, according to ECLAC 1997). The last two points suggest statistical manipulation: GDP between 1986 and 1990 has been reduced in order to attenuate the fall of GDP in 1991–93. Finally, the annual average decline of GDP in constant prices in 1990–93 from a nonofficial Cuban source (Terrero 1994) was 18.7%, bigger than the GSP decline of 16.9% and much bigger than the official GDP decline of 12.4% (Table III.4).

According to official data GDP grew by 0.7% or zero per capita in 1994, 2.5% or 1.9% per capita in 1995, and 7.8% or 7.1% per capita in 1996. The rate for the last year is questionable (Mesa-Lago 1998), but, even if a 7.1% per capita rate is maintained in the future (which is highly improbable), it would take seven years to recover the GDP per capita peak of 1985 (2,004 pesos), which was meager to begin with. Based on a still quite high annual rate of 5%, it would take ten years to recover the 1985 peak. Furthermore, GDP per capita in 1995 was 1,190 pesos, which at the arbitrary official exchange with the dollar (one to one) was the lowest in Latin America, only above that of Haiti. At the informal market exchange rate (state exchange agencies and black market) of 25 pesos per U.S.$1 in 1995, GDP per capita in that year was equal to U.S.$47.24.

Average annual sugar output between 1991 and 1995 was 5.25 million tons, 2.34 million tons less than between 1986 and 1990 and the worst five-year average under the Revolution. Output in 1993 was 3.3 million tons, 60% less than in 1990 and 55% less than in 1952; hence 1993 was the worst crop under the Revolution and in the previous fifty years. Output increased to 4.44 million tons in 1996 but at the cost of taking a one-year U.S.$200 million loan at 14% interest; after paying it, the net gain over 1995 was U.S.$42 million. In 1996 output declined to 4.25 million tons, making it even more difficult to pay a bigger foreign loan to finance that year's harvest. The industrial yield in 1995 was 9.91, which suggests that the downward trend in yield since 1959 continued unabated (Table III.11; Mesa-Lago 1998).

Overall performance in agriculture was very poor. The FAO index of agricultural output per capita (1979–81=100) was 99.5 in 1990 and 66.6 in 1994, a 33% decline, possibly taking Cuba back to the 1963 level (FAO 1970–95). The combined output of agriculture, forestry, hunting, and fishing fell by 54% between 1990 and 1994 (BNC 1995). Heads of cattle declined 6.3% in 1990–93 and in per capita terms from 0.45 to 0.41; and milk output shrank 57% from 924 to 398 thousand metric tons between 1989 and 1994, back to the 1970 level. Between 1989 and 1993 heads of pigs declined 57% from 1,292 to 558, and poultry 48% from 27,904 to 14,367 heads. Egg production dropped 38%, from 2,523 to 1,561 million units between 1989 and 1994, back to the level of the late 1960s. The output of another four agricultural products (key for exports and domestic consumption) decreased (in thousand metric tons) between 1989 and 1994: tobacco from 42 to 17, citrus from 825 to 505, rice from 532 to 226, and beans from 14 to 11. Fish and seafood caught declined 21% in 1986–89 and a further 51% between 1989 and 1994, from 244 to 88 thousand metric tons between 1986 and 1994 (−64%) (Tables III.10, III.12).

Mining production plunged 20.7% between 1989 and 1994 (BNC 1995). Nickel output sank 34.5% (from 41,100 to 26,900 tons), back to the mid-1960s level; the 1994 target of 106,500 tons was unfulfilled by three-fourths. The Moa mine was modernized by Sherritt Corp., which allowed the government to set the output target for 1995 at 43,000 tons, almost back to the 1988 level, and was fulfilled (Tables III.10, III.13). After a decline of 21% in 1991, oil output steadily rose and reached a record 1,298,800 metric tons in 1994, an impressive jump of 94% over 1990; the target for 1995 was 1,400,800 tons and was slightly surpassed, but it met less than one-fifth of domestic consumption needs (Table III.21; Mesa-Lago 1998).

Reportedly, manufacturing output fell 28% between 1990 and 1994, less than one could expect in view of the shutdown of 80% of factories (BNC 1995). The major lines in heavy industry suffered sharp output decreases between 1989 and 1994: cement 71% (from 3,759 to 1,085 metric tons), electricity 21% (from 15,240 to 11,967 Mkwh), and steel output in 1995 (201,000 tons), which was half the 1986 peak. Fertilizers decreased 81% (from 898 to 170 thousand tons), textiles 78% between 1988 and 1994 (from 260 to 56 thousand tons), and cigars 40% between 1989 and 1995 (from 308 to 186 thousand tons) (Table III.10). Electricity, gas, and water shrank 23% between 1990 and 1994 and construction 75%.

Services as a whole (for the first time reported including all its components) shrank 26% between 1989 and 1994. The worst declines were 40.5% in trade, restaurants, and hotels, and 41% in transport, warehousing, and communications, while 18% in finance, real estate, and business, and only 3.5% in community, social, and personal services—helped by growing social services and expanding self-employment (BNC 1995). The tourist sector continued to expand in this stage: the number of foreign tourists increased 89%, from 327,000 to 617,000 between 1990 and 1994, and the number of rooms by 27%. "Gross revenue" jumped by 249%, but "net revenue" (profit) rose 87% (from 150 to 280 million pesos), as the percentage of the latter over the former dropped from 62% to 33% because of increasing costs of inputs. Foreign tourism accounted for 29% of "trade, restaurants, and hotels"; hence, the decline in the remaining 71% (particularly trade) had to be much worse than the average decline of 40.5% for that line. The target for tourists in 1995 was initially set at 2 million and subsequently reduced to 1.5 and 1 million; the actual number was 742,000 tourists or 26% less than the third target. The target for the number of rooms for 1995 was 50,000 vis-à-vis 24,200 in reality or less than half (Table III.15; BNC 1995). The hotel occupancy rate was 43.8% in 1993 and increased to 46% in 1994, considerably lower than the rates of 68% in the Dominican Republic and 66% in Puerto Rico (La Sociedad 1993a; ECLAC 1997).

Evaluation of investment is complicated by the change in the 1990s in both measuring of the national product and the composition of the budget. According to the MPS method, gross investment decreased 71% between 1989 and 1994, from 4.5 to 1.3 billion pesos, and averaged 11.4% of GSP in 1991–93, the lowest under the Revolution. The new budget shows a smaller investment decline of 59%, from 4.4 to 1.8 billion pesos between 1990 and 1995. Based on the new series of GDP, the gross domestic investment percentage dropped from 25% in 1990 to 5% in 1994; the annual average was 23.7% between 1986 and 1990 and 7.9% in 1991–94 (Table III.7; BNC 1995). The significant decrease in investment must adversely affect future economic growth. No data are available for this stage for investment efficiency, although it must have dived sharply for reasons explained earlier.

B. Inflation

Cuba stopped publishing inflation data after 1988 (the CEE, *AEC* 1989a excluded those data); the GSP series for 1989–93 and the GDP series for 1989–

95 are available only in constant pesos, and the lack of similar series in current pesos was a serious obstacle to estimating the induced inflation rate. I managed to estimate the latter between 1990 and 1995 as follows: 3.5% in 1990, −6.8% in 1991, 3.3% in 1992, 19.7% in 1993, 25.7% in 1994, and 11.2% in 1995, for an annual average rate of 9.4% in the period (Mesa-Lago 1998). According to ECLAC (1997) the annual inflation rates were somewhat lower and averaged 8.7% in the period. These are the highest inflation rates under the Revolution.

The cumulative monetary surplus jumped 121% in 1990–93, from 4,164 to 11,045 million pesos. In 1993 the cumulative surplus was almost equal to the population income; on an annual per capita base it was 1,004 pesos, about one-half the average annual wage, and 2.6 times the per capita of 1970, when money virtually lost all its value. The adjustment program reduced the monetary surplus by 16% in 1993–95 (from 11,045 to 9,253 million pesos), a significant cut, but in 1996 the surplus grew by 3.7%. That increase was caused by the halting of the most painful adjustment measures such as introduction of wage and sales taxes, dismissal of 500,000 to 800,000 workers, and elimination of state subsidies, combined with growing social service expenditures (Table III.5; BNC 1995; Mesa-Lago 1998; ONE 1998).

The reduction of the monetary overhang by 10% in 1994 is in conflict with an increase in the inflation rate of 25.7% that year, and a cut in the fiscal deficit by 72% (from 5.1 to 1.4 billion pesos or from 33.5% to 7.4% of GDP in 1993–94). Is it possible that increasing prices in agricultural and black markets, state dollar shops, and self-employed activities accounted for the jump in inflation? The answer is no, because this entire sector is rather small, and the agricultural markets did not start to operate until October 1994. Another discrepancy results from the black market exchange rate of pesos to U.S.$1: although it widely fluctuated in 1994, its annual average was 79, an increase of 14.5 % over 69 in 1993. There were more consistent improvements in 1995: the fiscal deficit was further cut by 30% to 1 billion pesos (3.7% of GDP), the monetary overhang was reduced by 7.2% (42% of GDP), the peso-dollar exchange on the black market fluctuated but averaged 25 (for a 68% decline below 1993), and the inflation rate was reduced from 25.7% to 11% (Mesa-Lago 1998).

C. Diversification

The three available series on the percentage distribution of GSP by economic activity ended in 1988–89 (Table III.8). But in 1995, the BNC published a new series on the percentage distribution of GDP by economic activities for 1989–94 (Table III.9). The difference between these two series is that GSP excludes nonproductive services, while GDP includes them. I argued above that (1) the exclusion of such services from GSP artificially inflated the proportions of other sectors, (2) two of the three available series appeared to manipulate taxes to give the impression of a much higher and growing industrial sector, and (3) the most dynamic sector in the economy was services instead of industry. Table III.9 ratifies my three points. The share of industry/GSP that was 35.9% in the first series (1988), 46.6% in the second (1989), and 55.3% in the third (1989) dropped dramatically to 27.9% of GDP in 1989 and was virtually stagnant until it increased to 29.5% in 1994. The share of agriculture was considerably smaller too, as it decreased from 16% of GSP to 9.8% of GDP in 1989 and declined to 6.8% in 1994. The shares of construction and transportation-communication diminished less in 1989 and also showed a descending trend thereafter. The share of commerce, which was 31.3% of GSP in the first series (1988) and drastically declined to 19.7% in the second series (1989) and to 11.3% in the third series (1989), jumped to 26.3% of GDP in 1989 and, after an increase to 27% in 1992, declined in 1993–94. Finally the share of *productive* services in GSP was 0.7% in the three series but catapulted to 22.2% as a percentage of GDP in 1989 (because of the addition of nonproductive services) and grew to 32.4% in 1994 (much higher than industry). Another series on the composition of GDP by economic activity for 1988–94, elaborated by ECLAC (1997), is also shown in Table III.9 (column 5, contrasted with the BNC series in column 4). The ECLAC series further reduced the share of industry in 1994, from 29.5% (BNC) to 26.2%, and the shares of other activities were also smaller except services, which increased from 32.4% (BNC) to 39.7%. Because of a lack of data we cannot assess sugar dependency.

D. Trade Balance and External Dependency

Overall trade dependency cannot be estimated after 1989 because of the discontinuation of the GSP series. Nevertheless, the fall in total trade transactions was 75% between 1990 and 1994 (76% in exports and 74% in imports), while the decrease in GSP/GDP ranged from 35% to 45%, hence probably resulting in a reduction of trade dependency in this stage. The decrease in exports was the result not only of a fall in volume (sugar, nickel, citrus, tobacco) but also of the termination of Soviet price subsidies and the shift to lower world market prices. Because of the fall in total transactions, the trade deficit diminished by 68%, from 2,740 to 642 million pesos between 1989 and 1994 (Table III.16). And yet the cut in the deficit cannot be assessed as positive because of the disastrous effects that the decline in exports and imports had on the Cuban economy.

Trade dependency on the Soviet Union/Russia dropped from 68% of total transactions in 1990 to 15.5% in 1994, and trade with Eastern Europe virtually disappeared. The dramatic decrease in trade with Russia was due to not only a cut in transactions but also the disappearance of price subsidies and the exclusion of trade with the former republics of the Soviet Union. Some Cuban officials have hailed this as a positive effect of the crisis, because it would lead to more diversified trade partners, but most Cuban leaders have pinpointed the precipitous trade decline with the former Soviet camp as a major cause of the crisis. The Russian share of Cuba's total trade deficit decreased from 75.8% to 17% between 1990 and 1994 because of the sharp decline in trade between the two countries (Table III.20). But, in the past, Cuba's huge deficits with the Soviet Union (2.3 billion pesos at its peak in 1985) were automatically covered with Soviet loans, which were not repaid. The terms of trade badly deteriorated against Cuba, because of the loss of Soviet price subsidies to sugar and nickel, as trade was conducted at world market prices.

Russian supply of crude oil sank 61%, from 7.8 million tons in 1987 to 3 million tons in 1995, while the total supply of crude oil and oil by-products decreased 52%. Furthermore, since 1991 oil has been exchanged for sugar, both at world market prices, and "oil reexports" terminated. In 1994 Cuba's domestic oil production was 1.3 million tons, and Russian oil imports were 2.5 million tons, a total of 3.8 million tons or 52% of the island's average annual consumption between 1985 and 1989 (7.3 million tons) excluding "oil reexports" (Table III.21). Although Cuba has reduced its oil consumption dramatically, it must have imported oil from other countries, but the shortage of fuel is still abysmal.

If the 1986–90 quinquennium is taken as a base, Cuba lost U.S.$21.7 billion between 1991 and 1995 (U.S.$4.4 billion annually) in Russian economic aid (Table III.22). Cuba's debt to Russia (which absorbed the total island's debt with all former republics of the Soviet Union) was 15.5 billion rubles in 1989, which was equal to U.S.$25.6 billion at the official exchange rate in 1990, but only U.S.$8.67 billion at the commercial exchange rate. Because of the devaluation of the ruble vis-à-vis the U.S. dollar, in 1995 the debt had been reduced to U.S.$3 million. However, based on the peso/ruble exchange rate, the debt was 18.2 billion pesos in 1990, similar to Cuba's total GDP that year. In spite of years of negotiations, both countries had not agreed, by the end of 1996, on an exchange rate for Cuba's repayment of its debt. Cuba's debt with Eastern Europe ranged from U.S.$1.3 to U.S.$2.5 billion in 1990 (or 1.5 billion pesos), and, as in the case of Russia, Cuba has neither paid nor signed agreements to pay this debt, a stumbling block for resuming trade with those nations (Table III.23).

Cuba's total transactions with China decreased 53%, from U.S.$578 to U.S.$268 million between 1990 and 1994, but the Chinese share of the island's total trade rose slightly from 7.8% to 8.2% in the same period because of the decline in Cuba's total transactions (CIA 1995; Table III.16). In 1994 Cuba's combined total trade with Russia and China was 25%; adding another 1% with the former Soviet republics and Eastern Europe, that left 74% for market economies. In 1990 Cuba's trade with market economies was 24% but accounted for U.S.$3 billion, while the 74% share in 1994 accounted for U.S.$2.4 billion. The decline in volume was due to the decrease in Cuba's major exports and lack of credit to buy in hard currency. The trade proportion with market economies suggests significant trade diversification, but the trade volume shows Cuba's incapacity even to sustain, much less increase, commerce in the world market. A significant obstacle to achieving the latter is the island's debt in hard-currency: U.S.$6.2 billion in 1989. Cuba suspended payment of that debt in 1986 and ten years later had been unable to reach an agreement with the Club of Paris. The hard currency debt, therefore, kept growing to U.S.$9.08 billion in 1994 and U.S.$9.16 billion in 1995 (Table III.23; BNC 1995).

Export concentration of sugar decreased from 80% to 57% between 1990 and 1994, because of a 78% fall in sugar-export value, due to a 50% decline in output and the loss of Soviet price subsidies (from 42 to 12 cents per pound). As the sugar share in exports diminished between 1990 and 1994, the share of nickel rose from 7% to 15%, that of tobacco from 1% to 4%, and other products from 12% to 24% (Table III.17). The logical conclusion, based on those export shares alone, is that Cuba has been, at last, successful in diversifying exports. And yet the absolute value of nickel and all nonsugar exports decreased between 1990 and 1994 (because of a fall in production and declining world market prices of nickel) as follows: nickel 50%, other exports 61%, citrus 47%, tobacco 20%, fish 12%, and medical products 10% (CIA 1995; ECLAC 1997). With a further decline of sugar output and exports in 1995, the diversification illusion should have intensified, but the sad reality is that Cuban exports have decreased by 76% including all its components. Biotechnical and medical exports, which seemed to have a great future, accounted for less than 5.8% of total transactions in 1994 and 2.8% in 1995; they do not have the potential to grow in the immediate future (Carranza, Gutiérrez, and Monreal 1995; ECLAC 1997).

The composition of imports changed significantly between 1990 and 1994: the fuel share increased from 27% to 39%, foodstuffs from 12% to 23%, and manufactures from 14% to 23% (the latter two mostly for tourism and state dollar shops); conversely, machinery and transportation dropped from 37% to 6% as Cuba faced a severe fuel shortage and most of its industry and transportation was paralyzed. Raw-material and chemical shares changed little (Table III.18).

E. Unemployment

There are several estimates of the labor force and a confusing terminology for those affected by the crisis: "displaced," "dislocated," "rationalized," "relocated," "unemployed," "equivalent unemployed." Furthermore, it is not always clear whether figures refer to the state civilian sector alone or the entire labor force. Two estimates of the labor force "dislocated" by enterprise shutdowns in 1992 showed either a low of 10.4% with one-fifth of them collecting unemployment compensation or a high of 18% with one-half collecting compensation (Mesa-Lago 1993c). The Cuban Institute of Independent Economists calculated that 26.7% of the labor force was "unemployed" in 1995–96, probably combining open unemployed and those not needed in the state sector (ICEI 1996). According to Lage (1996) only 8% of the labor force was unemployed in 1995, but that was probably open unemployment alone. The first series on open unemployment and "equivalent unemployment" (adding the former to those who were receiving unemployment compensation) was estimated by ECLAC (1997) for 1990–96 and is partly reproduced in Table III.26. In 1994 the open unemployment rate was 6.7%, but "equivalent unemployment" (not needed workers mainly in the state sector) jumped to 33.3%. The 500,000 to 800,000 workers not needed in the state sector were tantamount to 16.4% to 19.5% of the labor force, a gross underestimation of "equivalent unemployment" based on ECLAC estimates. In 1996 from 95,680 to 104,000 registered self-employed were previously unemployed (from 2.1% to 2.3% of the labor force), and 12% of the state civilian labor force was part-time workers who could not find full time jobs (Rodríguez 1996; *Trabajadores,* June 3, 1996, pp. 5, 10). All the above estimates indicate that more than one-third of the labor force either are openly unemployed, receive unemployment compensation, are part-time workers who cannot find full-time jobs, or are unneeded workers in the state sector. The strongest statement on unemployment under the Revolution has been made by Raul Castro: "Hundreds of thousands of state workers are unemployed or their labor has been reduced, and there has been growing unemployment among dozens of thousands of young people who finish their [educational] careers and cannot find jobs. This has had a traumatic effect on the youth and thousands of them have left the country" (R. Castro 1996).

There are no figures after 1989 on the composition of the labor force by occupational groups, women in the labor force, and labor productivity. However, there are data on the composition of the *employed* labor force by eco-

nomic activity for 1989 and 1994 (Table III.24), which
sector had a low of 21.9% in 1989 but rose to 28.2%
1970 proportion), the secondary sector steadily declin
and 23.2% in 1994 (consistent with the decrease in th
GDP), and the tertiary sector declined to 42.9% (from 4
if the nonspecified state sector (probably members of tl
security) are added, the service sector would increase to ____ ... Summariz-
ing, the agricultural share rose significantly, the secondary share shrank, and
the tertiary share probably increased.

F. Equality

No data on income distribution are available in this stage, but the information analyzed earlier showed that inequalities in income distribution, consumer goods, and services have significantly expanded, a fact acknowledged
by Cuban leaders. Access to education and health care continues to be fairly
equal—except for the elite and medicines—but the quality of these social
services have deteriorated badly.

Although no data have been published in this stage on the total wage bill
in the state sector, it must have shrunk: in 1990 total state expenditures on
salaries and wages was 9.2 billion pesos, and it declined 10% to 8.3 billion
pesos in 1994, including subsidies to UBPC that were introduced in the last
quarter of 1993 (BNC 1995). The average nominal wage in the state sector
decreased in 1990–93, and, although it was raised in 1994–95 because of
the high rate of inflation, it dove 39% in real terms between 1991 and 1995
(Table III.28). Conversely, incomes of the self-employed, private farmers,
and black market speculators have boomed, and the income gap expanded
tremendously as the examples below illustrate.

In 1995, based on an annual average exchange rate of 32 pesos per U.S.$1
in Havana's state agencies and on the black market, various occupations had
the following monthly dollar incomes: average wage earner, U.S.$6; retiree
with minimum pension, U.S.$3; teacher, U.S.$8 to U.S.$9; surgeon, top en-
gineer, and university professor, U.S.$11 to U.S.$12; worker receiving a dollar bonus (without taking his or her wage into account), U.S.$19 to U.S.$28;
bartender in tourist hotel (tips or bonus only) and self-employer hairdresser,
U.S.$93; tourist taxi driver, U.S.$100 to U.S.$467; private farmer, U.S.$187
to U.S.$311; prostitute working the tourist areas, U.S.$373; relative receiving dollar remittances from abroad (without other income), U.S.$280 to
U.S.$934; and owner of small restaurant, U.S.$2,500 to U.S.$5,000 (Mesa-
Lago 1998). The extreme ratio between the highest income earner and the
average wage was 829:1 in 1995; the maximum wage differential in 1987

Wages

4.5:1, indicating a significant expansion in income inequality. Cuban scholars have confirmed that conclusion; they have estimated that, in 1995, the lowest-income worker in the informal economy made in a day the monthly average wage of a state worker (Carranza, Gutiérrez, and Montreal 1995). This explains the shift of Cuban professionals to working as self-employed, even in manual jobs. Furthermore, in the same year, 54% of the population had savings, but they were heavily concentrated in a minority and with a tendency to increase: 65% of the accounts had deposits up to 200 pesos (3% of total savings), 22% had deposits from 201 to 2,000 pesos (15% of total savings), 11% had deposits from 2,001 to 10,000 pesos (44% of total savings), and 2% had deposits above 10,001—some above 100,000 (38% of total savings) (BNC 1995). On the other hand, mendacity is back, as acknowledged by the 9th Plenum of the National Commission on Social Prevention and Care held in Havana in mid-1995, which decided to impose strong sanctions on parents of children who are beggars and ask money and goods from tourists (*Nuevo Herald,* June 29, 1995, p. 1B).

Rationing expanded to virtually all consumer goods in 1991–94, and out of 20 products, the quotas of 17 had been cut or shifted from free distribution to rationing. A total of 28 food products and 180 consumer goods that were "free" became rationed. The situation deteriorated further in 1993–94 when rationing provided only half of the monthly food minimum requirements (Table III.29). In 1994 the average wage earner could buy in state stores or in the agricultural or black markets, with his or her full monthly salary (without taking into account housing, rationed food, utilities, and transportation expenses), *either* 1 to 5 pounds of beef, 3 to 6 pounds of chicken, 1 to 12 pounds of powdered milk, 2 to 4 liters of oil, 1½ to 4 cans of tomato puree, one pound of coffee, 7 to 12 liters of gasoline, one tube of toothpaste, 5 pounds of detergent, 1 tube of insect spray, ⅓ of a pair of jeans, or ½ of a T-shirt (author's interviews with Cuban visitors to the United States and letters from Cuba; Mesa-Lago 1993c; *Nuevo Herald,* numerous issues 1994; ICEI 1996).

G. Social Indicators

No official statistics on illiteracy rate and enrollment in primary and secondary education are available after 1990. But UNESCO (1996) estimates that the illiteracy rate declined from 6% to 5.3% in 1990–92 (Table III.33). According to ECLAC (1997), enrollment in secondary education dropped 18% in 1990–92; the corresponding student cohort might have declined, but less than enrollment; hence the enrollment ratio might have decreased from 90% to 80% in 1990–92. The number of students enrolled in higher education dove from 242,000 in 1989 to 198,500 in 1992 and 122,300 1995 (because of lack of job opportunities); as the student cohort was either stagnant or declined slightly, the enrollment ratio probably sank from 21 in 1990 to 18 in 1992 and to 12 in 1995. The Minister of Education José Gómez Izquierdo gave a teacher abandonment rate of 7% in 1993, an increase from 5% in 1992; and in 1995 the 9th Plenum of the National Commission for Social Prevention and Care reported increasing student abandonment of elementary and secondary education (Table III.33; *Nuevo Herald,* September 6, 1994, p. 9A, June 30, 1995, p. 1B; *Proceso,* July 18, 1994, p. 55; Casanova and Triana 1995).

Infant mortality (per 1,000 infants born alive) declined from 10.7 to 9.4 in 1990–93 and rose slightly to 9.9 in 1994; however, PAHO estimated that the actual rate for 1992 was 14 instead of the official 10.2. The crude mortality rate rose from 6.8 to 7.2 per 1,000 between 1990 and 1994, because of population aging as well as an increase in mortality rates in the population age 60 and older from 48% to 53% between 1989 and 1993. Daily calories per capita dropped from 2,845 to 1,670 in the same period, and infants with low weight at birth increased from 7.3% to 9%, while mortality of pregnant women increased from 26.1 to 36.2 in 1988–91. Principal causes of death per 100,000 inhabitants rose between 1989 and 1993 as follows: heart diseases from 168.0 to 199.6, malignant tumors from 113.6 to 128.5, brain/vascular diseases from 57 to 68.3, accidents from 45 to 51 (mainly due to bikes), and respiratory diseases from 3.8 to 10.7 (Table III.30; MINSAP 1994; *El País,* based on MINSAP, 5-1-94: 10-11; Mesa-Lago 1998).

Between 1989 and 1994, (1) morbidity rates per 100,000 inhabitants increased for six diseases (acute diarrhea, chicken pox, hepatitis, typhoid, tuberculosis, and syphilis, because of water and food contamination and lack of vaccines and condoms); (2) the rates remained basically unchanged for five diseases (polio, diphtheria, tetanus, and measles—all virtually without reported cases and continuing to be controlled by immunization —and acute respiratory disease); and (3) rates declined for two diseases (gonorrhea, which increased again in 1994, and malaria). Between 1989 and 1993 the mortality rate for acute diarrhea rose from 2.7% to 6.8% (Table III.31; MINSAP 1994). An epidemic of optic neuritis blinded 45,584 people in 1993, caused—according to PAHO—by an intake lower than 50% of recommended doses of protein, thiamine, vitamins A and E, oils, and other nutrients, which resulted in severe nutritional deficiencies and loss of weight (Gay et al. 1994).

Extreme differences in health standards and services among Cuban provinces remained significant: 6.6 and 11.6 in infant mortality, 48.6 and 70.2 mortality among age 65 and over, 18.3 and 55.9 mortality among pregnant women, 1.6 and 11.2 deaths due to acute diarrhea, 7.4 and 21.2 deaths due to infectious/parasite diseases, 13.1 and 5.7 hospital beds per 1,000 inhabitants, and 84 and 28.4 physicians per 1,000 inhabitants. The best provinces were Havana City, Villa Clara, and Sancti Spiritus, while the worst were Guantanamo, Granma, and the Isle of Youth (MINSAP 1994).

No data on social security coverage are available in this stage, but the number of pensioners increased 9% in 1990–93, while the population growth rate declined from 1.1% to 0.5% and the number of employed declined. As a result, the active-passive ratio further fell from 4.2 to 3.7 and is projected to fall to 2.8 in 2010, one of the lowest in Latin America. Cuba's percentage wage contribution is about one-fourth that in other countries of the region with a similar level of social security (only 14% is paid by enterprises in Cuba since 1995 and 10% before), and expenditures over GDP are the highest; therefore the deficit of the system in 1993 was equal to 173% of its revenue (Table III.34). Since there are no reserves, the future of Cuban social security is in serious jeopardy. Pensioners are probably the population group most harmed by the crisis: their minimum pension has not been raised, and the value of their pensions in 1995 was equal to U.S.$3 monthly (the lowest of all income groups), and half of it goes to pay housing, electricity, and water. They cannot stand in long lines to buy scarce goods or use bikes to go to a physician, the severe scarcity of medicine affects them badly, and state nursing homes have little food and medicine available (Mesa-Lago 1993c, 1996).

The housing shortage, which was quite bad before the crisis, worsened in 1991–93 as investment in public housing was drastically cut (R. Castro 1996). The number of public dwellings constructed in the civilian sector dwindled by 25% in 1990–93 (by 56% in 1989–92); total units built per 1,000 inhabitants (excluding private without certificate of habitability) decreased from 3.7 in 1989 to 1.8 in 1992 and then rose to 2.4 (still back to the 1980 level) (Table III.35). Furthermore, deterioration of the housing stock has been aggravated: in 1995 out of 556,000 dwellings in Havana, 16% had to be demolished, 24% were in bad need of repair, 49% were from "fair to bad," and only 11% were in "good shape" (*Trabajadores,* March 6, 1995). For all the above reasons, the housing deficit must have surpassed the one million mark in the early 1990s.

Crime and alcoholism have increased in this stage, as discussed earlier. In 1995 a study published in Cuba estimated that alcoholism was responsible for two-thirds of all deaths in traffic accidents, half of all assassinations, and one-fourth of all suicides—the last accounted for 22.5 per 100,000 inhabitants and exhibited a raising trend (*Tribuna de La Habana,* March 12, 1995). The city of Havana, which was one of the safest in Latin America, has become dangerous because of violent robberies to get desperately needed food and consumer goods.

After several market-oriented reforms were implemented, particularly in 1993–95, the process has seemed to be halted or considerably slowed since 1996. The least relatively painful adjustment measures have already been taken, and more daring steps are required, but they confront ideological and sociopolitical barriers. The hard-liners feel that they have halted the economic decline and promoted a recovery, albeit a weak one, as well as achieving some fiscal and political stability; they fear that further market reforms will harm the lowest-income groups, reduce their economic power, and prompt a growing independent nonstate sector that could challenge the regime. The structuralist reformers have been significantly impaired by the harsh attack of Vice President Raul Castro in 1996 and their demotion from academic positions of influence. The final part of this book will analyze the feasibility of the current system and prospects for further reform.

Tables to Part III

Table III.1

Summary of Socioeconomic Policies by Stages in Cuba, 1959–1995

Economic Policies	*Liquidation of Capitalism and Market Erosion (1959–60)*	*Orthodox (Stalinist) Central Planning Model (1961–63)*	*Debate on Alternative Socialist Models (1964–66)*	
			Pro-Soviet	*Guevarist*
Ownership	Mostly private but increasing collectivization reaching momentum in late 1960.	Collectivization of social services (1961), co-ops become state farms (1962), private agriculture further reduced (1963).	No significant change, but this group is cautious about further collectivization.	No significant change, but this group favors further collectivization.
Planning and market	Indicative (not applied), JUCEPLAN and central agencies established.	Central planning (Stalinist model) introduced; 1962–65 plan.	When central planning fails, debate on alternatives follows. Applied in 1/3 of economy	Applied in 2/3 of economy
Degree of centralization	Low but growing	High but ineffective	Supports decentralization and market tools	Supports complete centralization
Allocation	Market	Physical, rationing begins	Mixed	Physical
Directive indicators	Profit	Gross output	Mixed, including profit	Gross output
Incentives	Mostly individual and material.	Introduction of moral and collective incentives	Predominantly material and individual	Preference for moral and collective in long run
Financing	Mixture of private (declining) and budgetary in state sector (expanding).	Budgetary except in small private sector	Self-financing but adulterated	Budgetary
	Emphasis on consumption; disregard of investment.	Restriction in consumption to increase investment.	More emphasis on capital efficiency.	More emphasis on capital accumulation.
Stability and prices	Demand grows faster than supply, depleting stocks, increasing state expenditures, only partly offset by higher tax revenue, money in circulation	To avoid inflationary spiral, prices—mainly fixed by the state—are frozen, state subsidies begin, rationing is introduced, the black market and the queue appear.	Favors the use of prices, turnover taxes, and selected market tools to achieve equilibrium. State subsidies to consumer goods and enterprises grow, gratuitous services	Not explicit

Adoption and Radicalization of Guevarist Model (1966–70)	Soviet (Pre-Gorbachev) Economic Reform Model (1971–85)	Rectification Process and Move Away from Market (1986–90)	Collapse of Soviet Block, Domestic Economic Crisis, and Move to the Market (1991 on)
Elimination of private plots in state farms (1967), collectivization of small businesses (1968), state ownership almost complete.	Reduction of private farms and expansion of co-ops but free peasant markets and small expansion of private services. Foreign investment allowed but under tight restrictions.	Acceleration in elimination of private farms, abolition of peasant markets and virtually all private sector activities.	Constitution amended to permit private property; joint ventures expand (new foreign investment law); state farms become new type of co-ops; self-employment and free agricultural markets reauthorized.
Long-run central macro-plan substituted by short-run sectorial plans.	Central plan reintroduced with some market tools (SDPE).	Decentralization and market halted (except for small foreign sector).	Planning virtually disappears; emergency adjustment program (Special Period) begins; lack of an integrated cohesive model.
High but personalistic rather than through central plan.	Some decentralization toward enterprise administrators.	Recentralization but with less role of the plan.	Growing decentralization first in foreign sector, later in domestic sector.
Virtually physical	Physical and partly by markets	Renewed emphasis on physical and rationing.	Rationing expands to all consumer goods and quotas decline, but market allocation rapidly increases.
Gross output	Profit, gross output, and others	Gross output	Priorities set for crucial sectors
Gradual substitution of material by moral incentives.	Reintroduction of material incentives, decline of moral stimulation.	Reemphasis on moral incentives and decline in material.	Return to material incentives, possession and circulation of dollar authorized.
Budgetary throughout	Mostly budgetary but increasing self-financing although adulterated.	Stagnation in expansion of self-financing.	Increase in self-financing particularly in foreign sector, tourism, and other key lines.
Priority to increase capital accumulation but disregarding its efficiency.	Renewed emphasis on capital efficiency at least in theory.	Some priorities on investment to improve its efficiency but personalized decision on allocation.	Domestic investment declines sharply; emphasis on hard currency activities. Banking reform announced.
State budget is discontinued, prices are kept frozen and become useless, state subsidies expand, surplus money in circulation grows, and money is increasingly worthless.	State budget reintroduced; attempt to achieve fiscal equilibrium and reduce excess money in circulation by increasing prices, reducing gratuities and state subsidies; money	Huge and increasing budget deficits; monetary surplus expands significantly again.	Budget deficit and monetary surplus peak in 1993. Inflation sharply increases, black market booms, value of peso declines dramatically. Adjustment measures

(*continued*)

Table III.1
(Continued)

Economic Policies	Liquidation of Capitalism and Market Erosion (1959–60)	Orthodox (Stalinist) Central Planning Model (1961–63)	Debate on Alternative Socialist Models (1964–66)	
			Pro-Soviet	Guevarist
	rapidly grows. Prices mostly set by market, but state fixing expands.		continue expanding, prices become increasingly distorted, excess money in circulation increases.	
Development strategy	Import-substitution industrialization and agricultural diversification; sugarcane land reduced; machinery and equipment ordered from socialist camp.		Return to sugar as major engine of (1965–70) sets increasing output in 1970); additional plans to expand other sectors.	
External sector	Raising state controls on foreign trade; Soviet-Cuban 5-year trade pact; the Soviet Union grants credits, takes part of U.S. sugar quota, and supplies most oil by end of 1960.	State monopoly of foreign trade; shift in trade from U.S. to Soviet Union and socialist countries; Soviet aid expands; U.S. embargo and beginning of Cuba's isolation in the Western Hemisphere. Exchange rate fixed by gov't par with dollar until 1971.	More freedom of enterprises to trade with partners abroad. Soviet-Cuban trade agreement (1965–70); the Soviet Union increases buying of sugar at a higher price and (together with CMEA) grants aid to modernize sugar industry; OAS imposes trade embargo.	State monopoly on foreign trade.
Labor	State interference and control starts.	Control of unions completed and their objectives changed, strikes banned.	Tightened labor discipline and empowered managers.	
Employment	Expansion in state sector, rural migration reduces seasonal unemployment.	Stable employment in state farms, growth of military and service sector (but not industry), labor surplus kept in payroll.	Continuation of previous employment policies; transfer of urban labor surplus to agriculture.	

Adoption and Radicalization of Guevarist Model (1966–70)	Soviet (Pre-Gorbachev) Economic Reform Model (1971–85)	Rectification Process and Move Away from Market (1986–90)	Collapse of Soviet Block, Domestic Economic Crisis, and Move to the Market (1991 on)
	recuperates part of its value.		began and produce some results: cuts in deficit, monetary surplus, and inflation; peso appreciates.
development; Sugar Plan targets (10 million tons cattle, nickel, fishing, and	Sugar continues its predominance but with more balance among sectors; sugar output increases through modernization and mechanization; and other plans to develop nickel, citrus, tourism, biotechnology, etc. In 1986–90 Food Program is launched to achieve self sufficiency.		FP failure and collapse of Soviet camp force a new strategy based on foreign investment (new law 1995), remittances from Cuban exiles, and hard-currency exports. Sugar output halved, 80% of industry is shut, but tourism grows and nickel output recovers.
State monopoly of trade. Soviet Union keeps aid and trade despite conflicts with Cuba but in 1967 reduces oil supply; Castro retaliates but later supports Soviet invasion of Czechoslovakia; Cuba's quarrel with China leads to cut in trade.	Cuba enters CMEA and signs numerous economic and trade agreements with the Soviet Union, which sharply increases aid and trade, but trade deficit escalates. Cuba becomes indebted to the West, gets rescheduling but fresh loans stop and share of trade dramatically declines. Peso appreciates in gov't-fixed exchange rate with dollar.	Trade with the Soviet Union and Eastern Europe begins to decline; Soviet aid stagnant and decline in price subsidies. Trade and fresh credit in hard currency stop. Gov't fixes peso exchange rate with dollar at par (policy continues through 1990s).	Soviet and EE aid and subsidies end; Soviet trade and oil supply decline sharply; CMEA dissolves. Russian-Cuban annual oil for sugar barter. Attempt to shift trade to world market limited by lack of export diversification and competitiveness. Foreign investment small and harmed by high risks and U.S. laws and pressure.
Trade unions gradually replaced by Vanguard Workers.	Revival of trade unions but failed attempt at democratization.	Labor discipline tightened	No official change in labor policy but growing self-employment and informal economy reduces state sector.
Full employment achieved at the cost of underemployment, attempt to curtail bureaucracy.	Appearance of unemployment leads to new policy to export or retire the surplus, or employ it in private sector.	Open unemployment grows in spite of few dismissals.	Labor surplus and open unemployment increase rapidly and unemployment compensation expands as part of the state economy is shut down. Non-gov't sector cannot absorb public labor surplus.

(*continued*)

Table III.1
(Continued)

Economic Policies	*Liquidation of Capitalism and Market Erosion (1959–60)*	*Orthodox (Stalinist) Central Planning Model (1961–63)*	*Debate on Alternative Socialist Models (1964–66)*	
			Pro-Soviet	*Guevarist*
Productivity	Neglected	More emphasis	To be increased through work quotas and wage scales.	To be increased mostly by raising worker's conscience.
Work quotas and wage scales	Wages begin to be controlled by state.	Introduction of work quotas and wage scales.	System virtually completed but weak application in agriculture.	
Distribution and social services	Income of poor rise by agrarian and urban reforms, cut in utility rates, expansion of free social services (mainly in rural), and increases in minimum wages and pensions.	Wealthier emigrate or lose capital, midsized farmers wiped out, "labor aristocracy" income cut, rationing is equalizer also.	Distribution according to work; caution about further expansion of free social services; defense of wage differences.	Goal is distribution according to needs; egalitarianism, new Man; expansion of free social services, and redution of monetary wage.

Adoption and Radicalization of Guevarist Model (1966–70)	Soviet (Pre-Gorbachev) Economic Reform Model (1971–85)	Rectification Process and Move Away from Market (1986–90)	Collapse of Soviet Block, Domestic Economic Crisis, and Move to the Market (1991 on)
Huge labor mobilizations and peaking absenteeism harm productivity.	Elimination of voluntary labor; steps to increase productivity.	Reemphasis in labor mobilization; sharp decline in productivity.	Labor mobilization ends, decline in productivity in state sector.
Enforcement and connection between quotas and scales weakens.	Reenforcement of work quotas and wage scales.	Work quotas tightened, wages cut except lowest bracket.	System of work quotas and wages becomes irrelevant due to huge labor surplus.
Elimination of production bonuses and overtime payments, reduction of wage differences, expansion of free social services and rationing, egalitarianism.	Wage differentials defended; bonuses, overtime, peasant markets reintroduced, a new enterprise incentive fund created, free social services curtailed.	Elimination or reduction of bonuses, overtime, peasant markets, private construction, self-employment; expansion of rationing.	Inequality expands because of dollar remittances, earnings of self-employed and in agricultural and black markets, erosion of rationing as egalitarian tool. Free social services harmed by shortages and peso devaluation.

Table III.2

The Process of State Collectivization of Means of Production in Cuba, 1959–1988 (Rough Estimates, Percentage)

Sector	1959	1961	1963	1968	1977	1988
Agriculture	0	37	70	74	79	97[a]
Industry	0	85	95	100	100	100
Construction	10–20	80	98	100	100	100
Transportation	15–20	92	95	98	98	99
Retail trade	0	52	75	100	100	100
Wholesale and foreign trade	5–10	100	100	100	100	100
Banking	5–10	100	100	100	100	100
Education	80	100	100	100	100	100

Sources: Mesa-Lago 1981; Castro 1989.

Note: Figures in the table refer to property, not to production. In 1976 the output of the private sector represented about 4% of national output (excluding trade) with the following shares by economic sector: 25% in agriculture, less than 7% in transportation, and less than 1% in communication. [a]78% in state farms and 18.7% in cooperatives (similar to Soviet *kolkhozi*) tightly controlled by the state; in 1977 only 0.4% of agricultural land was under cooperatives.

Table III.3

Basic Macroeconomic Indicators of Cuba, 1959–1993

Year	GSP Rate[a] (Percentage) Absolute	Per Capita	Gross Domestic Investment (Percentage of GSP)	Annual Inflation Rate[b] (Percentage)	State Budget Balance[c] (Percentage of GSP)	Official Exchange Rate[d] (Pesos per U.S.$)
1959						1.00
1960						1.00
1961						1.00
1962			11.1		0.0	1.00
1963	−1.1	−3.7	12.4	10.2	0.0	1.00
1964	7.3	4.7	11.0	8.5	0.0	1.00
1965	4.0	1.5	12.4	−1.7	0.0	1.00
1966	−0.0	−2.0	13.6	1.7		1.00
1967			14.3			1.00
1968	1.6	−0.1	12.5			1.00
1969	−1.3	−2.9	12.4			1.00
1970			9.6			1.00
1971	6.9	5.1	10.8			1.00
1972	15.8	13.7	10.6			0.92
1973	15.0	13.1	12.4			0.84
1974	12.7	11.4	12.8			0.83
1975	17.6	16.1	16.3			0.83
1976	3.3	1.9	17.9	−0.5		0.82
1977	5.8	4.6	18.7	−3.4		0.79
1978	7.3	6.4	15.9	3.8		0.75
1979	1.5	0.8	15.4	1.7		0.72
1980	−0.5	0.1[e]	15.6	4.2		0.71
1981	16.0	15.4	15.3	8.5	0.0	0.78
1982	3.9	2.9	13.0	0.4	−0.7	0.83
1983	4.9	3.9	14.0	0.4	3.2	0.86
1984	7.2	6.2	15.3	−0.1	−0.3	0.92
1985	4.6	3.5	15.9	−1.0	−0.9	0.93
1986	1.2	0.1	16.3	−2.8	−0.7	1.00
1987	−3.8	−4.7	14.8	0.2	−2.4	1.00
1988	2.2	1.1	15.7	0.5	−4.4	1.00
1989	1.1	0.1	16.9		−6.0	1.00
1990	−3.6	−4.7			−7.5	1.00
1991	−24.0	−24.9	10.5		−18.9	1.00

(continued)

Table III.3
(Continued)

Year	GSP Rate[a] (Percentage) Absolute	Per Capita	Gross Domestic Investment (Percentage of GSP)	Annual Inflation Rate[b] (Percentage)	State Budget Balance[c] (Percentage of GSP)	Official Exchange Rate[d] (Pesos per V. S.$)
1992	−15.0	−15.9	11.7		−28.7	1.00
1993	−11.7	−12.6	12.0		−33.7	1.00

Sources: Based on JUCEPLAN, *BE* 1966–71, and *AEC* 1972–74; CEE, *AEC* 1975–89, and *CeC* 1989; BNC, *IE* 1982–89, BNC-CEE, *CQER* 1982–89; Carranza, 1993; Carranza, Gutierrez, and Montreal 1995; Mesa-Lago 1997; ECLAC 1997.

[a]There are five series that cannot be connected, and only 1959–61 is GDP; the other four are in Global Social Product (GSP): 1962–66 in constant prices with unknown valuation method; 1967–69 is available only in current prices, also with an unknown method; 1970–76 is in current prices with "complete circulation" method; 1975–89 is in constant prices with "enterprise exit" method; and 1990–93 is in constant prices with an unknown method. [b]1963–66 in 1965 prices; 1976–89 in 1981 prices. The annual average inflation rate (based on GDP) averaged 9.4% in 1990–95 (Mesa-Lago 1997) or 8.7% (ECLAC 1997). [c]The budget was not published in 1966–77. Estimates for 1990–93 are based on GSP in constant prices. ECLAC gives the following in GDP at constant prices 1990, −21.4%, 1991, −29.7%, and 1993, −30.4%. [d]Unilaterally set by the Cuban government. [e]Due to a negative population growth rate (the exodus of more than 100,000).

Table III.4
Other Estimates of Annual Economic Growth and Inflation in Cuba, 1960–1995

1. Economic Growth Rates (Absolute, Constant Prices)

Period	Cuba				Pérez-López[c]		Mesa-Lago/Pérez-López NMP[d]			Zimbalist/Brundenius GDP[e]		ECLAC GDP
	Official GSP[a]	Rodríguez TMP[b]	Terrero GDP	BNC GDP	GSP	GDP	I	II	III	I	II	
1960–70	2.8	3.7								5.4	7.1	
1961–65	5.2	2.7								3.6	3.8	
1966–70	0.4	4.8			0.0	1.1				6.6	6.7	
1971–75	7.5	7.0			6.5	6.4				4.0	3.6	
1976–80	3.5	3.5			2.2	2.7	−0.3	1.5	2.9	7.9	5.4	
1981–85	7.3	6.7					3.9	4.4	4.5			
1986–90	−0.6	−0.5	0.4	−1.3			−1.5	−2.4	−6.2			
1991–94	−16.9		−18.7	−9.1								
1962–85	4.8						1.2	2.0	2.0	5.5	5.2	
1976–85	5.4											
1986–93/94	−6.7		−9.2	−5.2								
1990–95	1.9											
1960–93												−5.5

2. Inflation (GSP) (Percentage)

	Mesa-Lago/ Pérez-López[f]	Cuba Official[g]	Author GDP[h]	ECLAC GDP
1963–65	5.7			
1966–70	1.3			
1971–75	6.1			
1976–80	1.12	1.16		
1981–85	1.66	1.64		
1986–88	−0.80	−0.70	−1.18	
1990–95			13.78	8.7
1976–88	0.98	0.92		
1986–95			7.80	

Sources: Segment 1: GSP official 1960–75 from BNC, *IE* 1982; 1976–89 from CEE, *AEC* 1977–89; and 1990–93 from Carranza 1993, Carranza et al. 1995. TMP from Rodriguez 1988, 1989. GDP 1987–93 from Terrero 1994. GDP 1986–94 from BNC 1995; Pérez-López 1995; Mesa-Lago and Pérez-López 1992; Zimbalist and Brudenius 1989; ECLAC 1997. Segment 2 from Mesa-Lago and Pérez-López 1985a, 1985c; CEE, *AEC* 1988; ECLAC 1997.

GSP = Global Social Product (excludes value of nonproductive services but induces double counting of productive material consumption).

TMP = Total Material Product (also excludes value of commerce, transportation, and productive services).

NMP = Net Material Product (should eliminate double counting of productive material consumption).

GDP = Estimated Gross Domestic Product.

[a]1960–70 and 1971–75 are from the BNC (disaggregation for 1961–65 and 1966–70 is author's rough estimate based on Cuban data); the BNC does not show how the series in constant prices for 1967–70 was done and is connected with the 1960–66 series. Estimates for 1960–70 are done by the author assuming that all different series can be connected, which is not the case. [b]Based on 1965 prices, methodology not explained; estimates end in 1988. [c]Based on an index of physical output of goods and services derived from official Cuban data, confirmed using estimated factor-cost prices and value-added weights; estimates available only for 1965–82. [d]Recalculation of official GSP series deflating its trade-balance component with three international deflators; 1986–87 instead of 1986–90. [e]Based on two different industrial indices. [f]1963–65 in 1965 prices; 1966–75 base year unknown; 1976–88 in 1981 prices. [g]From GSP deflators, 1981 prices. [h]1986–89 based on GDP in constant prices from BNC 1995 and GDP at current prices from ILO 1996; 1990–95 based on fiscal deficit in current pesos from BNC 1995, deficit as percentage of GDP in current prices from ECLAC 1996 and author's estimate of GDP at current prices.

Table III.6

Percentage Distribution of State Budget Revenue (by Source) and Expenditures in Cuba, 1962–1995

	1962	1963	1964	1965	1978	1979	1980	1981	1982
Revenues (million pesos)	1,854	2,094	2,399	2,536	9,169	9,414	9,534	11,201	9,413
State contributions							98.8	98.9	98.7
Circulation tax									
Profits									
Difference in foreign trade price									
Others									
Nonstate sector taxes							0.2	0.2	0.1
Population taxes							1.0	0.9	1.2
Total							100.0	100.0	100.0
Expenditures (million pesos)	1,854	2,094	2,399	2,536	9,160	9,409	9,531	11,197	9,834
Financing production	32.9	41.6	29.8	34.6	44.0	41.3	41.7	41.7	32.3
Social services	35.7	33.7	31.5	32.8	32.9	35.3	36.5	33.0	41.3
Education & health	30.7	29.1	26.1	27.4	16.7	17.9	18.9	16.5	20.7
Social security welfare, culture					12.6	13.2	13.8	12.8	15.7
Housing and community	5.0	4.6	5.4	5.4	3.6	4.2	3.8	3.7	4.9
Public administration	10.5	6.9	6.0	5.4	5.9	5.5	5.1	6.0	6.3
Defense and security	13.3	10.2	9.2	8.4	8.6	8.9	5.4	7.5	9.4
Other activities	6.3	6.1	6.2	7.2	4.4	4.8	4.7	6.8	5.5
Reserve	1.3	1.4	17.2	12.4	4.4	4.1	3.5	4.9	5.0
Total	100.0	100.0	100.0	100.0	100.0	100.0	100.0	100.0	100.0
Balance (million pesos)	0	0	0	0	9	5	3	4	−421

Sources: Based on preliminary annual budgets published in *Gaceta Oficial* and *Granma* and final budgets published in BNC, *IE* 1982–89; BNC-CEE, *CQEC*, 1982–89. 1990–94 from BNC 1995; 1995 from Ley de Presupuesto del Estado 1995. Different figures for 1986–90 are given by Pérez-López 1992.

[a]Changes in distribution of income and expenditures began in 1991, and categories are not comparable, except for 1995.
[b]Preliminary.

1983	1984	1985	1986	1987	1988	1989	1990	1991[a]	1992[a]	1993[a]	1994[a,b]	1995[b]
10,496	11,472	11,311	11,699	11,272	11,385	12,501	13,524	10,949	10,179	9,516	12,757	11,683
98.4	98.3	98.2	98.2	98.2	97.9	97.7	97.8					94.7
		45.0	44.2	44.7	41.1	37.1		36.3	36.7	34.8	40.0	49.6
		13.2	12.7	12.5	15.1	8.3		9.7	16.5	14.7	14.6	13.8
			8.2	10.6	9.5	11.2						$\Big\{$ 31.3
			31.8	30.7	31.2	30.3						
0.1	0.2	0.2	0.4	0.3	0.5	0.6	0.6					1.9
1.5	1.5	1.6	1.4	1.5	1.6	1.7	1.6					3.4
100.0	100.0	100.0	100.0	100.0	100.0	100.0	100.0	100.0	100.0	100.0	100.0	100.0
10,300		11,295	11,887	11,881	12,532	13,904	15,482	14,714	15,048	14,566	14,178	12,683
40.3	36.7	39.5	37.2	38.5	37.6	36.8	37.7					35.3
39.7	42.3	41.8	44.0	44.2	45.5	44.8	43.7					44.9
19.4	20.3	20.3	22.6	22.9	22.8	21.5	20.4					20.0
14.8	15.5	15.7	15.4	15.6	16.4	17.0	17.3					21.6
5.5	6.5	5.8	6.0	5.7	6.3	6.3	6.0					3.3
5.4	5.8	5.1	5.4	4.8	4.5	3.9	3.5					3.1
9.9	11.6	10.6	10.7	10.4	10.2	10.2	9.6					6.3
4.8	3.6	3.0	2.7	2.1	2.2	2.2	1.7					5.4
6.4					3.0	2.1	3.8					5.0
100.0	100.0	100.0	100.0	100.0	100.0	100.0	100.0	100.0	100.0	100.0	100.0	100.0
196	222	16	−188	−609	−1,147	−1,403	−1,958	−3,765	−4,869	−5,051	−1,421	−1,000

Table III.5

Monetary Surplus of the Population in Cuba, 1962–1994 (Million Pesos at Current Prices)

Year	Population			Cumulative Monetary Surplus[a]	Percent Surplus/ Income	Surplus per Capita
	Income	*Expenditures*	*Difference*			
1962	2,629	2,436	193	2,387	90.8	326
1965	3,472	3,474	−2	2,530	72.9	320
1967	3,890	3,611	279	2,914	74.9	355
1970	4,016	3,347	669	3,339	83.1	388
1975	5,489	5,564	−75	2,013	36.6	215
1976	5,813	5,772	40	2,053	35.3	216
1977	6,060	5,990	70	2,123	35.0	221
1978	6,464	6,415	49	2,172	33.6	224
1979	6,644	6,634	10	2,182	32.8	224
1980	6,766	6,855	−89	2,093	30.9	216
1981	8,053	7,606	447	2,540	31.5	260
1982	8,583	8,465	118	2,658	31.0	270
1983	9,155	9,086	69	2,727	29.8	274
1984	9,926	9,722	204	2,931	29.5	292
1985	10,315	10,149	166	3,097	30.0	305
1986	10,761	10,671	90	3,187	29.6	311
1987	10,653	10,656	−3	3,184	29.9	307
1988	11,388	10,937	451	3,635	31.9	347
1989	11,825	11,296	529	4,164	35.2	393
1990	11,928	11,104	824	4,988	41.8	466
1991	11,622	10,046	1,576	6,564	56.5	608
1992	11,539	9,741	1,798	8,362	72.5	767
1993	11,450	8,767	2,683	11,045	96.5	1,004
1994	11,340	12,440	−1,100	9,945	87.7	904

Sources: 1962–89 based on Martínez Fagundo 1989 and CEE, *AEC* 1986–89. 1990–94 based on BNC 1995 and ONE 1998.

[a]Cumulative excess liquidity.

Table III.7

Estimates of Investment in Cuba, 1958–1994 (Millions of Pesos at Current Prices)

Year	GSP	Gross Investment[a]	Budget Investment Expenditures	Gross Investment over GSP		Gross Investment over GDP	
				Annual	Quinquenium	Annual	Quinquenium
1958[b]						17.6	17.7
1962	5.2	572		11.1			
1963	5.6	696		12.4	11.7		
1964	6.5	772		11.0			
1965	6.8	842		12.4			
1966	6.8	930		13.6			
1967	7.2	1,032		14.3			
1968	7.3	918		12.5	12.5		
1969	7.2	896		12.4			
1970	8.4	800		9.6			
1971	8.9	964		10.8		15.1	
1972	10.3	1,094		10.6		15.0	
1973	11.9	1,475		12.4	12.6	17.4	17.7
1974	13.4	1,712		12.8		18.5	
1975	14.0	2,304		16.3		22.6	
1976	14.4	2,588		17.9		25.0	
1977	14.7	2,766		18.7		22.5	
1978	16.4	2,624		15.9	16.7	21.5	25.5
1979	16.9	2,606		15.4		21.3	
1980	17.6	2,739		15.6		19.3	
1981	22.1	3,386		15.3			
1982	23.1	2,996		13.0			
1983	14.3	3,409		14.0	14.7		
1984	26.3	3,989		15.3			
1985	26.9	4,289		15.9			
1986	26.5	4,333		16.3		23.6	
1987	25.5	3,807		14.8		21.7	
1988	26.3	4,097		15.7	15.9	23.0	23.7
1989	26.6	4,511	3,060	16.9		25.0	
1990			4,398			25.0	
1991		2,090	3,625	10.5[c]		14.9	
1992		1,989	3,239	11.7[c]	11.4	6.9	7.9
1993		1,800	2,038	12.0[c]		4.8	
1994		1,304	2,683			5.1	

Sources: Gross Investment/GSP based on JUCEPLAN, *BE* 1966–71, and *AEC* 1972–74; CEE, *AEC* 1975–89; Marquetti 1994; ONE 1995. Gross Investment/GDP from Mesa-Lago and Pérez-López 1985c; ECLAC 1997. Budget investment expenditures from BNC 1995.

[a]State civil sector. [b]Gross fixed investment as percentage of GDP in constant 1950 pesos; average for 1956–58 (BNC 1957–59; ECLAC 1957). [c]Based on GSP at constant prices.

Table III.8
Percentage Distribution of GSP by Economic Activity in Cuba, 1962–1989

1. Old Series: Enterprise Prices, Excludes Indirect Taxes[a]

	1962	1970	1975	1976	1977	1978	1979	1980	1981	1982	1983	1984	1985	1986	1987	1988	1989
GSP	100.0	100.0	100.0	100.0	100.0	100.0	100.0	100.0	100.0	100.0	100.0	100.0	100.0	100.0	100.0	100.0	
Agriculture	17.8	14.7	11.8	12.1	12.3	11.7	11.7	11.6	16.0	14.8	13.9	13.9	13.9	14.8	15.6	15.7	
Industry	48.2	47.9	37.6	37.7	37.3	36.5	36.0	35.6	34.9	34.8	34.8	35.9	36.1	37.1	36.1	35.9	
Construction	7.2	5.2	8.9	9.1	9.8	9.5	9.2	8.9	8.1	7.8	8.2	8.9	8.8	8.8	8.1	8.6	
Transport	5.6	9.4	7.1	7.2	7.4	7.1	7.2	8.1	7.3	7.0	6.9	6.7	6.6	6.6	6.8	6.8	
Communication	0.9	0.8	0.6	0.6	0.6	0.7	0.7	0.8	0.8	0.8	0.8	0.9	0.9	1.0	1.0	1.0	
Trade	20.3	22.0	33.8	33.2	32.4	34.3	34.7	33.6	32.6	34.4	34.9	33.2	33.2	30.9	31.5	31.3	
Other	0.2	0.1	0.2	0.1	0.2	0.2	0.5	0.4	0.3	0.4	0.5	0.5	0.5	0.9	0.9	0.7	

2. New Series: Producer Prices, Indirect Taxes[b]

	1975	1976	1977	1978	1979	1980	1981	1982	1983	1984	1985	1986	1987	1988	1989
GSP	100.0	100.0	100.0	100.0	100.0	100.0	100.0	100.0	100.0	100.0	100.0	100.0	100.0	100.0	100.0
Agriculture	11.8	12.1	12.3	11.7	12.0	12.7	16.2	15.1	14.2	14.1	14.2	15.1	15.9	16.1	16.1
Industry	47.8	48.5	47.3	45.9	44.6	44.0	42.9	43.7	43.5	45.0	45.8	47.2	46.7	46.7	46.6
Construction	8.9	9.1	9.9	9.5	9.2	8.9	8.1	7.8	8.2	8.9	8.8	8.9	8.2	8.6	9.0
Transport	7.2	7.2	7.4	7.1	7.2	8.1	7.3	7.0	6.9	6.7	6.7	6.7	7.0	6.9	6.9
Communication	0.6	0.6	0.6	0.7	0.8	0.9	0.8	0.8	0.8	0.9	0.9	1.0	1.0	1.1	1.0
Trade	23.5	22.3	22.3	24.8	23.8	24.9	24.3	25.1	25.9	23.8	23.1	20.2	20.3	19.9	19.7
Other	0.2	0.2	0.2	0.3	0.4	0.5	0.4	0.5	0.5	0.6	0.5	0.9	0.9	0.7	0.7

3. New Series: Distributing Taxes among Each Sector[c]

	1975	1976	1977	1978	1979	1980	1981	1982	1983	1984	1985	1986	1987	1988	1989
GSP	100.0	100.0	100.0	100.0	100.0	100.0	100.0	100.0	100.0	100.0	100.0	100.0	100.0	100.0	100.0
Agriculture	12.0	12.2	12.4	11.9	11.9	12.8	16.2	15.0	14.1	14.1	14.1	15.0	15.8	15.8	15.9
Industry	48.7	49.3	48.2	49.8	51.3	50.7	50.5	53.5	53.7	54.3	55.1	56.3	55.5	55.3	55.3
Construction	8.9	9.1	9.9	9.5	9.2	8.9	8.1	7.8	8.2	8.8	8.8	8.8	8.1	8.5	9.1
Transport	7.1	7.2	7.4	7.1	7.2	8.1	7.3	7.0	6.9	6.7	6.6	6.7	6.8	6.8	6.7
Communication	0.6	0.6	0.6	0.6	0.7	0.8	0.8	0.8	0.8	0.9	0.9	1.0	1.0	1.0	1.0
Trade	22.5	21.4	21.3	20.8	18.3	18.3	16.7	15.4	15.8	14.6	14.0	11.4	11.9	11.8	11.3
Other	0.2	0.2	0.2	0.3	0.4	0.4	0.4	0.5	0.5	0.6	0.5	0.9	0.9	0.7	0.7

Sources: Based on JUCEPLAN, *CEC* 1968; *AEC* 1973–74; CEE, *AEC* 1975–89.

[a]The original distribution was published in *CEC* 1968, *AEC* 1973, 1978, and 1979. It was discontinued until *AEC* 1985, which reintroduced it with minor modifications. [b]This series began in *AEC* 1980, replacing the old one. It continued in successive issues of *AEC*. In *AEC* 1985 it was revised, increasing somewhat the agricultural share and reducing the industrial share proportionally. [c]This series began to be published in *AEC* 1980 and continued annually, including *AEC* 1985, when the explantion of the three series was given for the first time. A more elaborated explanation was published in *AEC* 1987.

Table III.10

Physical Output of Principal Products in Cuba, 1958–1994 (Thousand Metric Tons Unless Specified)

Product	1958	1960	1965	1970	1975	1976	1977	1978	1979	1980
Sugar	5,862	5,943	6,156	8,353	6,314	6,155	6,485	7,350	7,992	6,665
Tobacco	51	45	43	32	42	52	43	41	33	8
Citrus fruits	111	73	160[a]	93	170	186	226	282	285	444
Coffee	30	42	24	20	20	27	17	15	26	24
Eggs (MU)	315	430	920	1,509	1,851	1,829	1,846	1,924	2,018	2,326
Rice	253	323	50	366	447	451	456	457	425	478
Beans	23	37	11	2	3	2	3	4	4	10
Pork	37	38	48	15	43	52	58	61	60	58
Milk	765	767	575	380	591	682	722	783	791	889
Fish	22	31	40	106	143	193	184	211	155	186
Nickel	18	13	28	37	37	37	37	35	32	38
Salt	68	59	106	89	157	151	129	130	122	131
Electricity (Mkwh)	2,589	2,981	3,387	4,888	6,583	7,192	7,707	8,481	9,403	9,895
Steel		63	36	140	298	250	330	324	313	292
Cement	736	813	801	742	2,083	2,501	2,656	2,711	2,613	2,840
Fertilizers		438[c]	860[d]	577	749	798	863	946	873	1,059
Textiles (Mm^2)		116[c]	96	78	144	139	152	156	151	159
Shoes (M)	20	14	16	16	23	21	15	18	16	15
Soap		34[c]	37	33	41	43	35	38	34	38
Refrigerators (TU)	0	0	12	6	50	44	46	45	55	25
Radios (TU)	0	0	82	19	113	92	120	121	143	200
Cigars (MU)	628	591[e]	657	364	383	359	352	354	295	166

Sources: Based on JUCEPLAN, *BE* 1966–71, *AEC* 1972–74; CEE, *AEC* 1975–89; 1992–94 from Terrero 1994; JUCE-PLAN 1994; BNC 1995; Marquetti 1996; Spreen et al. 1996; ECLAC 1997; ONE 1998.

M = millions, T = thousands, U = units, m^2 = square meters. kwh = kilowatts/hour.

[a]1966. [b]1995. [c]1963. [d]1969. [e]1959.

1981	1982	1983	1984	1985	1986	1987	1988	1989	1992	1993	1994
7,359	8,210	7,109	8,207	8,004	7,255	7,117	7,415	8,121	7,030	4,280	4,000
55	45	30	45	45	46	39	39	42	25	20	17
471	530	631	600	747	786	886	981	825	787	644	505
22	29	18	23	24	23	26	29	29			15[b]
2,360	2,247	2,493	2,557	2,524	2,518	2,495	2,460	2,523	2,331	1,512	1,561
461	520	518	555	524	576	466	489	532	358	177	226
8	12	13	12	11	14	12	15	14	10	9	11
68	71	73	86	95	100	106	105	110	59	79	86
926	929	948	943	929	926	940	918	924	400	300	398
164	195	198	200	220	244	214	232	192	109	94	88
40	38	39	33	34	35	36	44	46	32	30	27
161	198	180	184	221	266	230	200	206	172	136	159
10,559	11,069	11,551	12,292	12,199	13,167	13,593	14,542	15,420	11,538	11,004	11,967
371	290	352	325	401	412	402	320	314	160	98	147
3,292	3,163	3,231	3,347	3,182	3,305	3,535	3,566	3,759	1,134	1,049	1,085
1,067	1,026	1,082	1,036	1,160	1,045	996	840	898	178	94	136
172	153	170	172	205	221	258	260	220	66	51	56
19	16	17	15	16	16	17	16	12	5	4	3
41	32	42	45	39	44	36	32	37	17	4	6
41	18	16	24	26	17	5	7	9	3	0	0
256	239	273	253	236	237	227	153	173	12	24	14
230	358	333	302	366	340	279	270	308	295	208	186

Table III.9

Percentage Distribution of GSP and GDP by Economic Activity in Cuba, 1988–1994

Economic Activity	GSP[a] 1988 (1)	1989 (2)	1989 (3)	GDP[b] 1988 (4)	1989 (4)	1989 (5)	1990 (4)	1990 (5)	1991 (4)	1991 (5)	1992 (4)	1992 (5)	1993 (4)	1993 (5)	1994 (4)	1994 (5)
Agriculture[c]	15.7	16.1	15.9	9.3	9.8	9.2	9.2	8.6	7.9	7.2	8.0	7.2	7.2	6.5	6.8	6.1
Industry[d]	35.9	46.6	55.3	26.6	27.9	26.1	27.3	25.5	27.7	25.5	26.6	24.0	27.7	24.7	29.5	26.2
Construction	8.6	9.0	9.1	5.8	6.9	6.4	7.9	7.4	6.4	5.9	4.0	3.6	3.0	2.7	3.0	2.7
Transport & communications	7.8	7.9	7.7	6.6	6.9	6.5	6.3	5.9	6.2	5.8	6.1	5.5	5.8	5.1	5.5	4.9
Commerce[e]	31.3	19.7	11.3	25.3	26.3	24.6	26.0	24.3	25.9	23.9	27.0	24.4	23.0	20.5	22.8	20.4
Services[f]	0.7	0.7	0.7	26.4	22.2	27.2	23.3	28.3	25.9	31.7	28.3	35.2	33.3	40.5	32.4	39.7
Total	100.0	100.0	100.0	100.0	100.0	100.0	100.0	100.0	100.0	100.0	100.0	100.0	100.0	100.0	100.0	100.0

Source: GSP from table III.8; GDP from BNC 1995; ECLAC 1997.

[a](1) first series, (2) second series, and (3) third series of GSP from table III.8. [b](4) GDP series from BNC. (5) GDP series from ECLAC. [c]Includes forestry and fishing. [d]Includes mining, manufacturing, and electricity, gas, and water. [e]Includes restaurants and hotels. [f]Includes financing, real estate, business, and social and personal services.

Table III.11
Sugar Dependency, Industrial Prodution, and Yields in Cuba, 1958–1995

Year	Sugar Dependency			Sugar Output (Thousand Tons)		Industrial Yields[b]		Effective Grinding Days
	Output[a]/GSP	Exports/GSP	Exports/GDP	Annual	Quinquenium	Annual	Quinquenium	
1958			22.2	5,826.6		12.82		84
1959				6,038.6		12.57		89
1960				5,942.9	5,991	12.51	12.5	88
1961				6,785.5		12.66		104
1962	11.4	8.4		4,882.1		13.31		76
1963	9.8	8.4		3,882.5	5,254	12.36	12.5	68
1964	10.4	9.3		4,474.5		12.03		82
1965	13.8	8.8		6,156.2		12.15		105
1966	10.1	7.4		4,537.4		12.32		76
1967	12.9	8.3		6,236.1		12.26		101
1968	11.9	6.8		5,164.5	5,787	12.19	11.7	87
1969	12.8	7.0		4,459.4		11.02		86
1970	15.1	9.7		8,537.6		10.71		143
1971	12.5	7.4	10.2	5,924.8		11.49		101
1972	9.4	5.5	7.8	4,324.8		9.93		91
1973	8.9	7.3	10.2	5,252.7	5,548	11.07	11.4	92
1974	8.2	14.4	21.1	5,924.9		11.95		95
1975	8.5	19.1	26.1	6,314.4		12.44		99

(continued)

Table III.11
(Continued)

Year	Sugar Dependency Output[a]/GSP	Sugar Dependency Exports/GSP	Sugar Dependency Exports/GDP	Sugar Output (Thousand Tons) Annual	Sugar Output (Thousand Tons) Quinquenium	Industrial Yields[b] Annual	Industrial Yields[b] Quinquenium	Effective Grinding Days
1976	8.3	16.6	22.6	6,155.7		11.84		99
1977	9.0	16.6	22.5	6,484.9		11.55		104
1978	9.0	18.3	24.4	7,350.5	6,929	10.96	11.2	119
1979	9.0	17.8	24.6	7,991.8		10.94		128
1980	8.2	18.9	23.3	6,665.2		10.82		109
1981	11.5	15.0		7,358.9		11.08		114
1982	11.0	16.5		8,210.1		11.17		124
1983	9.9	16.8		7,108.6	7,777	10.35	11.0	113
1984	10.4	15.8		8,206.6		10.47		126
1985	10.2	16.6		8,003.9		11.99		103
1986	10.1	15.5		7,254.6		10.62		104
1987	10.1	15.7		7,116.8		10.64		99
1988	10.5	15.7		7,415.4	7,582	10.85	10.7	100
1989	10.2	14.9		8,121.0		10.83		109
1990				8,004.0		10.70		110
1991				7,623.0		10.59		105
1992				7,030.0		10.57		97
1993				4,280.0	5,247	9.85	10.0	69
1994				4,000.0		9.25		80
1995				3,300.0		9.91		60

Sources: Dependency from Mesa-Lago and Pérez-López 1985c updated with CEE, *AEC* 1982–89. The rest from Mesa-Lago 1981 updated with CEE, *AEC* 1979–89; Castro 1993a; Lage 1996.

[a]Output value in industrial plus agricultural sectors. [b]Proportion of sugar obtained in the mills in relation to the weight of the cut cane. Thus, in 1958, 12.82 tons of sugar were produced out of 100 tons of sugarcane at 96 degrees of polarization.

Table III.12

Livestock, Poultry, and Fishing Production in Cuba, 1958–1993 (Livestock and Poultry in Thousand Heads, Fishing in Thousand Tons)

	Cattle				Fishing	
Year	Total	Per Capita	Pigs[a]	Poultry[a]	Total	Per 100 Inhabitants
1958	5,700	0.84	1,780		22.0	0.32
1961	5,776	0.80	827	15,380	30.4	0.43
1962	5,975	0.82	1,358	18,600	35.4	0.48
1963	6,378	0.85	1,539	19,500	35.6	0.47
1964	6,611	0.86	1,746	21,900	36.4	0.47
1965	6,700	0.85	1,810	21,400	40.4	0.51
1966	6,774	0.84	298	11,016	43.5	0.54
1967	6,800[b]	0.83	343	12,468	63.4	0.77
1968			276	12,436	65.2	0.78
1969			318	13,526	79.8	0.94
1970	5,738[c]	0.67	280	13,581	106.4	1.23
1971			320	13,346	126.1	1.44
1972			377	16,435	139.7	1.56
1973	5,486	0.60	382	15,873	150.2	1.65
1974			489	18,328	165.2	1.79
1975	5,622	0.60	599	18,130	143.5	1.53
1976			673	19,946	194.0	2.04
1977			662	19,686	184.4	1.92
1978	5,274	0.54	698	22,376	211.1	2.18
1979			715	24,866	153.8	1.57
1980	5,057	0.52	765	24,616	186.4	1.92
1981	5,096	0.52	840	23,989	164.5	1.69
1982	5,108	0.52	853	23,052	195.2	1.98
1983	5,099	0.51	911	25,744	198.4	1.99
1984	5,115	0.51	1,009	26,734	199.6	1.98
1985	5,020	0.49	1,038	25,859	219.9	2.16
1986	5,007	0.49	1,100	25,678	244.6	2.39
1987	4,984	0.48	1,093	25,959	214.4	2.07
1988	4,926	0.47	1,168	27,308	231.6	2.21
1989	4,920	0.46	1,292	27,904	192.0	1.82
1990	4,803	0.45			188.2	1.76
1991	4,735	0.44	1,142	20,428		
1992	4,609	0.43	658	16,799	109.5	1.00
1993	4,583	0.41	558	14,367	93.4	0.85

Sources: Mesa-Lago 1981, updated with CEE, *AEC* 1979–89; Terrero 1994; Marquetti 1996; ECLAC 1997; ONE 1998.

[a]1961–65, all; since 1966 state and private sector only. [b]Another higher figure is 7.1 million. [c]Goal was 8 million heads.

Table III.13
Planned and Actual Nickel Production in Cuba, 1981–1994 (Thousand Tons)

Year	Remodeling Nicaro[a] (René RamosLatour)	Remodeling Moa[a] (Pedro Soto Alba)	Construction of New Plants Punta Gorda[b] (Che Guevara)	Construction of New Plants Camariocas-Moa[c] (CMEA 1)	Total	Actual Output Nicaro + Moa	Actual Output Punta Gorda	Actual Output CMEA 1	Actual Output Total
1981	20.0	19	0	0	39.0	39	0	0	39
1982	22.5	19	0	0	41.5	36	0	0	36
1983	22.5	24	0	0	46.5	39	0	0	39
1984	22.5	24	23	0	69.5	33	0	0	33
1985	22.5	24	23	0	69.5	34	0	0	34
1986	22.5	24	30	30	106.5	35	0	0	35
1987	22.5	24	30	30	106.5	35	1	0	37
1988	22.5	24	30	30	106.5	36	8	0	44
1989	22.5	24	30	30	106.5	36	10	0	47
1990	22.5	24	30	30	106.5	36	6	0	41
1991	22.5	24	30	30	106.5			0	34
1992	22.5	24	30	30	106.5			0	32
1993	22.5	24	30	30	106.5			0	30
1994	22.5	24	30	30	106.5			0	27

Sources: Mesa-Lago 1993b; Hernández 1992; La Sociedad 1993a; Terrero 1994; BNC 1995; ECLAC 1995; BNC 1995.

[a]Overhauling and expansion of existing plants (Nicaro 1943; Moa 1958); agreed with Soviet Union in 1973 at a cost of 160 million rubles. Ore extraction is done through leaching with water plus acid: ammonium carbonate in Nicaro and sulfuric acid in Moa. By 1983 combined production of the two plants was planned to be 46,500 tons, but it was 39,000 and then declined to 35–36,000 because of technical problems. In 1992 UNDP announced a donation to improve efficiency in Moa. [b]Construction of new plant began in 1976 with 600 million rubles support from Soviet Union, Czechoslovakia, Bulgaria, and Poland. It uses the same old technology as Nicaro. Stage one (11,000 tons) was to become operational in 1984 and stage two (12,000 tons) in 1985; plans were postponed with new target of 15,000 for 1989, but at most 10,000 were produced. Two-thirds of output should go to Soviet Union. This plant was shut down in August 1990 because of oil shortage and technical problems, but it was reopened in 1991 or 1992. [c]Construction of new plant began in 1984 with 400 million rubles support from Soviet Union, Czechoslovakia, GDR, Bulgaria, Rumania, and Hungary. It uses the same technology as Nicaro. About half of the output should go to Soviet Union and one-fourth to other CMEA partners. It was scheduled to begin operation in 1990 and then postponed to 1993 or 1995. About 65% of this plant is completed; it requires $70 million to be finished.

Table III.14

Comparison between Planned Targets and Actual Performance in Five-year Plans in Cuba, 1980, 1985, and 1990

	1980			1985			1990		
	Planned	*Actual*	*Percentage*	*Planned*	*Actual*	*Percentage*	*Planned*	*Actual*[a]	*Percentage*
Macro-indicators (percentage annual):									
GSP	6.0	3.5	-42	5.0	7.3	46	5.0	0.2	-96
Investment/GSP	15.0	13.3	-11	15.5	18.1	17	23.1	16.8	-27
Labor productivity	7.0	4.2	-40	3.0	5.1	70	3.5	-2.5	-171
Exports		6.5		7.0	8.7	24	5.0	-2.4	-148
Imports		8.5		6.5	11.7	80	1.5	0.3	-80
Output (thousand metric tons):									
Sugar	8–8,700	6,665	-20	9.5–10,000	8,004	-18	9,560	8,121	-15
Tobacco	60	8	-87	50	45	-10	70	42	-40
Citrus	550	444	-19	1,000	747	-25	1,400	825	-41
Coffee		24		29	24	-17	36	29	-19
Eggs (million units)	2,000	2,326	16	2,300	2,524	10	2,610	2,523	-3
Rice	600	478	-20	635	524	-17	620	532	-14
Beans		10		35	11	-68		14	
Pork	80	58	-28	80	95	18	120	110	-8
Milk	1,000	889	-11	1,005	929	-8	1,250	924	-24
Fish	350	186	-47	320	220	-31	248	192	-22
Oil		274			868		2,000	718	-64
Nickel	100	38	-62	70	34	-50	106	46	-56

(continued)

Table III.14
(Continued)

	1980 Planned	1980 Actual	1980 Percentage	1985 Planned	1985 Actual	1985 Percentage	1990 Planned	1990 Actual[a]	1990 Percentage
Salt		131		600	221	−63		206	
Electricity (million kwh)	9,000	9,895	10	15,840	12,199	−23	15,660	15,240	−3
Steel	440	292	−34	1,900	401	−78	600	314	−48
Cement	5,000	2,840	−43	4,900	3,182	−35		3,759	
Fertilizers		1,059		1,300	1,160	−11	1,530	3,898	−41
Textiles (million m²)	270	159	−41	325	205	−37	335	220	−34
Shoes (million)	35	15	−57	29	16	−45	25	13	−48
Beer (thousand hectoliters)		1,002		3,675	2,736	−25	4,150	3,333	−20
Refrigerators (thousand units)	100	25	−75		26			9	
Radios (thousand units)	300	200	−33	500	236	−53		173	
Social indicators:									
Infant mortality (per 1,000)	24	19.6	−18		16.5		15	10.7[b]	−26
Enrollment higher education (percentage)		20		39	21	−46	35	21[b]	−34
Housing (thousand units)[c]	150	82	−45	299	110	−45	185	100[d]	−46

Sources: Planned targets from Mesa-Lago 1982; Pérez-López 1986. Actual performance from Tables III.3, III.7, III.10, III.13, III.16, III.21, III.30, III.33, III.35; Rodríguez 1982; *Economía y Desarrollo*, various issues; CEE, *AEC* 1988, 1989.
[a]1989. [b]1990. [c]Only houses built by the state for civilians. [d]Estimate.

Table III.15

International Tourism in Cuba, 1957–1995

Year	Foreign Visitors (Thousands)		Tourist pole Rooms[c]	Tourist Revenue (Million Pesos)[d]		Percentage of GSP	
	All[a]	Tourists[b]		Gross	Net	Gross	Net
1957	272			62.1			
1960	86						
1971	2						
1975	40	34					
1979	191	83		87.6		0.11	
1980	130	101		39.6		0.10	
1981	106	94	14,303	43.6		0.08	
1985	172	168	16,003	100.4	60.2	0.37	0.22
1988	247	242	16,946	152.9	91.7	0.58	0.34
1989	276	270	17,600	168.0	100.8	0.62	0.59
1990		327	18,950[e]	243.4	150.0	0.98	0.59
1991		418	20,300[e]	387.4	240.0		
1992		455	21,650[e]	567.0	340.0		
1993		544	23,000	720.0	240.0		
1994		617	24,000	850.0	280.0[e]		
1995 (goals)[f]		1,500–2,000	50,000	1,000–1,200			

Sources: Lage 1992; La Sociedad 1993b; Carranza 1993; Castro 1993a; Mesa-Lago 1993b; Terrero 1994; BNC 1995; Ministerio de Turismo 1995; BNC 1995; ECLAC 1997.

[a]Another series ("all visitors") available for 1982–86 gives slightly higher figures. All visitors are those in transit or spending one or two days only, while tourists are those staying longer. [b]Another series ("tourists INTUR") available for 1974–86 gives lower figures. Scattered figures are higher than the series in the table, e.g., 309,200 in 1988. [c]"Locations that have most demand from foreign tourism"; another series gives figures twice as high; probably includes rooms that do not meet international tourism standards. [d]The 1979–81 series might be net income. Other series give higher and lower figures than those in the table. [e]Estimate. In 1993 only 18,000 "rooms reserved for international tourists" were reported. [f]Goals for 1995 were originally set in 1991; they were reduced in 1993 to on million tourists, 30,000 rooms, and 900 million pesos in gross revenue. ECLAC figures for 1995 are 742,000 tourists, 24,200 rooms and 1.1 million in gross revenue. The two million tourists goal has been postponed to 2000, but in 1997 there were only 1.17 million, hence it may not be met.

Table III.16

Trade Merchandise: Balance and Dependency in Cuba, 1959–1994

Year	Merchandise Trade (Million Pesos)				Trade Balance		Trade Dependency (Percentage of GSP in Current Prices)		
	Exports (f.o.b.)	Imports (c.i.f.)	Total Transactions	Trade Balance[a]	Total (Million U.S.$)[b]	Per Capita (U.S.$)	Exports	Imports	Total Transactions
1959	636.0	674.8	1,310.8	−38.8	−38.8	−5.5			
1960	608.3	579.9	1,188.2	28.4	28.4	4.0			
1961	626.4	638.7	1,265.1	−12.3	−12.3	−1.7			
1962	522.3	759.3	1,281.6	−237.0	−237.0	−32.4	10.1	14.7	24.8
1963	545.1	867.3	1,412.4	−322.2	−322.2	−42.9	9.7	15.4	25.1
1964	714.3	1,018.8	1,733.1	−304.5	−304.5	−39.5	10.9	15.5	26.4
1965	690.6	866.2	1,556.8	−175.6	−175.6	−22.2	10.2	12.8	23.0
1966	597.8	925.5	1,523.3	−327.7	−327.7	−40.6	8.8	13.5	22.3
1967	705.0	999.1	1,704.1	−294.1	−294.1	−35.8	9.8	13.8	23.6
1968	651.4	1,102.3	1,753.7	−450.9	−450.9	−54.0	8.9	14.8	23.7
1969	666.7	1,221.7	1,888.4	−555.0	−555.0	−65.4	9.2	16.9	26.1
1970	1,049.5	1,311.0	2,360.5	−261.5	−261.5	−30.4	12.3	15.3	27.6
1971	861.2	1,386.6	2,248.7	−526.3	−571.4	−65.2	9.6	15.6	25.2
1972	770.9	1,189.8	1,960.7	−418.9	−454.8	−50.8	7.4	11.5	18.9
1973	1,153.0	1,462.6	2,615.6	−309.6	−379.9	−41.7	9.7	12.3	22.0
1974	2,236.5	2,225.9	4,462.4	10.6	12.8	1.4	16.7	16.5	33.2
1975	2,952.2	3,113.1	6,065.3	−160.9	−194.1	−20.7	18.7–21.2	19.6–22.4	38.3–43.6
1976	2,692.3	3,179.7	5,872.0	−487.4	−594.4	−62.6	17.0–19.1	20.0–22.6	37.0–41.7

Year									
1977	2,918.4	3,461.6	6,380.0	−543.2	−684.1	−71.2	19.9	23.6	43.5
1978	3,440.1	3,573.8	7,013.9	−133.7	−177.8	−18.4	21.1	21.9	43.0
1979	3,499.2	3,687.5	7,186.7	−188.3	−259.7	−26.6	20.6	21.7	42.3
1980	3,966.7	4,627.0	8,593.7	−660.3	−931.3	−96.1	22.5	26.3	48.8
1981	4,233.8	5,114.0	9,337.8	−890.2	−1,139.8	−116.9	19.0	23.1	42.1
1982	4,933.2	5,530.6	10,463.8	−597.4	−717.2	−72.8	21.3	24.0	45.3
1983	5,534.9	6,222.1	11,757.0	−687.2	−797.2	−80.2	22.7	25.6	48.3
1984	5,476.5	7,227.5	12,704.0	−1,751.0	−1,903.2	−189.5	21.0	27.8	48.8
1985	5,991.5	8,035.0	14,026.5	−2,043.5	−2,197.3	−219.5	22.2	29.8	52.0
1986	5,321.5	7,596.1	12,917.6	−2,274.6	−2,715.2	−265.0	20.1	28.6	48.7
1987	5,401.0	7,611.5	13,012.5	−2,210.5	−2,210.5	−213.4	21.1	29.8	50.9
1988	5,518.3	7,579.4	13,097.7	−2,061.1	−2,061.1	−196.9	21.0	28.0	49.9
1989	5,399.9	8,139.8	13,539.7	−2,739.9	−2,739.2	−259.0	20.2	30.5	50.7
1990	5,414.9	7,416.5	12,831.4	−2,001.6	−2,001.6	−187.2			
1991	2,979.5	4,233.8	7,213.3	−1,254.3	−1,254.3	−116.1			
1992	1,779.4	2,134.9	4,094.3	−535.5	−535.5	−49.1			
1993	1,136.5	2,036.8	3,173.3	−900.3	−900.3	−81.7			
1994[c]	1,314.2	1,956.1	3,270.3	−641.9	−641.9	−58.0			

Sources: CEE, *AEC* 1989; BNC 1995. Trade dependency from Mesa-Lago 1994c.

[a]Cumulative Trade Deficit 1959–94: in pesos, −26,958 million; in U.S.$ −29,568 million. [b]Based on Cuba's official exchange rate unilaterally set since 1971. [c]Preliminary. ECLAC (1997) gives 2,111 imports in 1993, total 3,425, deficit 797.

Table III.17
Percentage Distribution of Exports by Major Products in Cuba, 1959–1994

Year	Sugar	Minerals	Tobacco	Total	Oil Re-Exports	Non-oil Others[a]	Sugar over Nonfuel Exports
					Others		
1959	75	3	9	13			
1960	78	4	10	8			
1961	85	6	6	3			
1962	83	7	5	5			
1963	87	6	4	3			
1964	88	5	4	3			
1965	86	6	5	3			
1966	85	7	4	4			
1967	86	8	4	2			
1968	77	12	6	5			
1969	76	13	6	5			
1970	77	17	3	3			
1971	76	16	4	4			
1972	74	15	5	6			
1973	75	14	5	6			
1974	87	6	3	4			
1975	89.9	5	2	3	0.1	2.9	90.1

Year							
1976	87.0	6	2	5			
1977	83.6	7	2	8	2.3	5.7	85.5
1978	86.7	5	2	2	1.3	0.7	87.8
1979	86.1	4	2	8	1.6	6.4	87.5
1980	83.7	4.9	0.9	10.5	4.2	6.3	87.6
1981	79.1	7.9	1.3	11.7	4.2	7.5	82.7
1982	77.2	6.1	2.1	14.6	5.5	9.1	81.7
1983	74.0	5.4	1.9	18.7	9.3	9.4	81.5
1984	75.2	5.5	1.0	18.3	10.0	8.3	83.4
1985	74.5	5.1	1.5	18.9	9.5	9.4	82.3
1986	77.0	5.9	1.5	15.6	4.6	11.0	80.7
1987	74.3	6.1	1.7	17.9	6.5	11.4	79.4
1988	74.6	8.2	1.8	15.4	3.4	12.0	77.2
1989	73.2	9.2	1.6	16.0	3.9	12.1	76.2
1990	79.7	7.2	1.3	11.8	1.0	10.8	80.5
1991	75.8	7.6	2.4	14.2	0.7	13.5	76.3
1992	68.6	12.1	4.1	15.2	0.0	15.2	68.6
1993	66.2	12.4	4.8	16.6	0.0	16.6	66.2
1994	56.9	14.9	4.2	24.0	0.0	24.0	56.9

Sources: 1959–89 based on JUCEPLAN, *BE* 1966–71 and *AEC* 1972–74; CEE, *AEC* 1975–89; ECLAC, *Survey* 1989; 1990–94 from BNC 1995 and ECLAC 1997.

[a]Mainly citrus and fishing products, as well as medical products since 1989.

Table III.18

Percentage Distribution of Imports by Major Products in Cuba, 1958–1994

Year	Food and Fats	Raw Materials	Fuel and Minerals	Chemicals	Manufacturers	Machinery and Transportation	Total
1958	21	7	11	6	24	31	100
1970	22	6	9	9	18	36	100
1975	20	6	10	8	25	31	100
1977	18	4	15	5	16	42	100
1978	18	4	19	6	17	36	100
1979	17	4	21	6	18	34	100
1980	17	4	20	6	17	36	100
1981	16	4	23	6	17	34	100
1982	16	3	27	6	17	31	100
1983	13	3	30	7	16	31	100
1984	12	3	31	6	17	31	100
1985	12	4	33	5	16	30	100
1986	10	4	33	6	16	31	100
1987	11	4	35	6	14	31	100
1988	11	4	34	6	14	32	100
1989	13	4	32	6	14	31	100
1990	12	4	27	6	14	37	100
1991	20	3	30	7	9	31	100
1992	25	2	36	9	9	19	100
1993	26	3	37	10	12	12	100
1994	23	2	39	7	23	6	100

Sources: Based on CEE, *AEC* 1982–89; 1990–94 from BNC 1995.

Table III.19

Comparison of Export/Import Prices in Soviet-Cuban Market and World Market, 1960–1994

Year	Raw Sugar (Cents per Pound)					Nickel Sulfide (Cents per Pound)					Crude Oil (Pesos/Dollar per Barrel)				
	Soviet		World	Ratios[a]		Soviet		World	Ratios[a]		Soviet		World	Ratios[a]	
	Pesos	U.S.$	U.S.$	Pesos	U.S.$	Pesos	U.S.$	U.S.$	Pesos	U.S.$	Pesos	U.S.$	U.S.$	Pesos	U.S.$
1960	3.2	3.2	3.1	1.03	1.03			0.74			1.74	1.74	1.92	0.91	0.91
1965	6.1	6.1	2.1	2.90	2.90	0.56	0.56	0.79	0.70	0.70	1.79	1.79	1.80	0.99	0.99
1970	6.1	6.1	3.8	1.60	1.60	2.84	2.84	1.29	2.20	2.20	1.75	1.75	1.80	0.97	0.97
1975	21.9	26.4	20.4	1.07	1.29	2.26	2.73	2.05	1.10	1.33	4.83	5.85	11.53	0.42	0.50
1980	33.7	47.5	28.2	1.20	1.68	2.26	3.19	2.96	0.76	1.08	10.87	20.67	28.67	0.38	0.72
1981	27.5	35.2	16.6	1.65	2.12	4.90	6.27	2.70	1.81	2.32	13.87	17.75	32.50	0.43	0.55
1982	29.8	35.7	8.4	3.54	4.25	4.90	5.88	2.19	2.24	2.68	17.21	20.65	33.47	0.51	0.62
1983	39.6	45.9	8.5	4.65	5.40	4.90	5.68	2.12	2.31	2.68	20.42	23.69	29.31	0.70	0.81
1984	39.3	44.4	5.2	7.55	8.53	4.92	5.56	2.16	2.28	2.57	23.80	26.90	28.47	0.83	0.94
1985	44.7	48.7	4.1	10.90	11.87	4.92	5.36	2.22	2.21	2.41	26.19	28.55	26.98	0.97	1.05
1986	39.3	47.5	6.1	6.44	7.67	4.93	5.96	1.76	2.80	3.38	26.38	31.92	13.82	1.91	2.31
1987	38.6	38.6	6.8	5.67	5.67	4.94	4.94	2.21	2.24	2.24	26.56	26.56	17.79	1.49	1.49
1988	41.8	41.8	10.2	4.09	4.09	4.94[b]	4.94[b]	6.25	0.79	0.79	26.55	26.55	14.15	1.88	1.88
1989	41.8[b]	41.8[b]	12.8	3.26	3.26	4.94[b]	4.94[b]	6.04	0.82	0.82	26.55[b]	26.55[b]	17.19	1.54	1.54
1990	41.8[b]	41.8[b]	12.5	3.34	3.34	4.94[b]	4.94[b]	4.02	1.23	1.23	26.55[b]	26.55[b]	22.05	1.20	1.20
1991	9.0	9.0	9.0	1.00	1.00	3.70	3.70	3.70	1.00	1.00	18.30	18.30	18.30	1.00	1.00
1992	9.1	9.1	9.1	1.00	1.00	3.18	3.18	3.18	1.00	1.00	18.22	18.22	18.22	1.00	1.00
1993	10.0	10.0	10.0	1.00	1.00	2.41	2.41	2.41	1.00	1.00	16.13	16.13	16.13	1.00	1.00
1994	12.1	12.1	12.1	1.00	1.00	2.87	2.87	2.87	1.00	1.00	15.47	15.47	15.47	1.00	1.00

Sources: Mesa-Lago and Gil 1989; Mesa-Lago 1993a.

[a] Ratio of Soviet-paid prices (in pesos and converted to U.S. dollars) over world market prices (in U.S. dollars). [b] Estimate assuming price remained constant.

Table III.20
Trade Concentration with Main Commercial Partner (Soviet Union) in Cuba, 1959–1994 (Million Pesos)

Year	Soviet-Cuban Trade			Percentage of Total Cuban Transactions with		Soviet-Cuban Trade Balance			Percentage of Soviet Deficit over Cuba's total Trade Deficit
	Exports (f.o.b.)	Imports (c.i.f.)	Total Transactions	Soviet Union	CMEA	Million Pesos	Million U.S.$	Without Soviet Trade Subsidies	
1959	12.9	0.01	12.9	1.0	1.0	12.9	12.9	12.9[a]	0[b]
1960	103.5	80.2	183.7	15.5	17.1	23.3	23.3	23.3[a]	0[c]
1961	303.7	262.6	566.3	44.8	57.0	41.1	41.1	37.3[a]	0[b]
1962	221.9	411.4	633.3	49.4	67.0	-189.5	-189.5	-191.9[a]	80.0
1963	163.9	460.9	624.8	44.2	63.3	-297.0	-297.0	-294.8[a]	92.2
1964	275.0	410.0	685.0	39.5	51.8	-135.0	-135.0	-135.3[a]	44.3
1965	322.5	428.4	750.9	48.2	61.5	-105.9	-105.9	-115.2[a]	60.3
1966	274.0	521.2	795.2	52.2	67.3	-247.2	-247.2	-255.0[a]	75.4
1967	366.1	582.0	948.1	55.6	68.4	-215.9	-215.9	-432.9	73.4
1968	289.6	671.8	961.4	54.8	68.3	-382.9	-382.9	-538.2	84.8
1969	233.0	657.9	890.9	47.2	62.0	-424.9	-424.9	-491.9	76.6
1970	529.0	690.6	1,219.6	51.7	64.0	-161.6	-161.6	-371.6	61.8
1971	303.7	730.8	1,034.5	46.0	59.5	-427.1	-439.9	-538.9	81.2
1972	224.1	714.4	938.5	47.9	60.2	-479.3	-523.4	-536.4	117.0
1973	476.7	811.0	1,287.7	49.2	61.7	-334.3	-410.2	-605.2	108.0
1974	811.2	1,024.9	1,836.1	41.1	52.9	-213.7	-275.8	-341.8	213.7[c]
1975	1,611.9	1,250.2	2,912.1	48.0	56.0	411.7	496.6	-273.4	0[b]

1976	1,638.3	1,490.2	3,128.5	53.3	63.5	148.1	180.6	−1,246.4	0[b]
1977	2,065.8	1,858.3	3,924.1	61.5	71.6	207.5	261.3	−1,719.7	0[b]
1978	2,495.5	2,327.7	4,823.2	68.8	79.2	167.8	223.1	−2,457.9	0[b]
1979	2,370.0	2,513.4	4,883.4	68.0	79.1	−143.4	−197.8	−2,898.8	76.2
1980	2,253.5	2,903.7	5,157.2	60.0	71.7	−650.2	−916.8	−3,354.6	98.5
1981	2,357.5	3,234.0	5,591.5	59.9	74.0	−876.5	−1,121.9	−3,839.9	98.5
1982	3,289.6	3,774.0	7,034.0	67.2	81.5	−454.8	−545.8	−4,327.8	76.1
1983	3,881.1	4,245.3	8,127.1	69.1	83.1	−363.5	−421.7	−4,412.7	52.9
1984	3,952.2	4,782.4	8,734.6	68.8	82.6	−830.2	−935.1	−5,156.1	48.0
1985	4,481.6	5,418.9	9,900.5	70.5	83.0	−937.3	−1,021.6		45.9
1986	3,935.8	5,337.6	9,273.4	71.7	84.4	−1,401.8	−1,696.2		61.6
1987	3,867.5	5,495.5	9,363.0	72.0	86.6	−1,628.0	−1,628.0		73.6
1988	3,683.1	5,364.4	9,047.5	69.1	83.7	−1,681.3	−1,681.3		81.6
1989	3,231.2	5,522.4	8,753.6	64.7	78.9	−2,291.2	−2,291.2		83.6
1990	3,597.0	5,114.4	8,711.4	67.9		−1,517.4	−1,517.4		75.8
1991[d]	1,794.7	2,633.6	4,428.3	61.4		−838.9	−838.9		66.9
1992[d]	191.0	566.0	757.0	18.5		−375.0	−375.0		70.0
1993[d]	311.5	399.1	710.0	22.4		−87.6	−87.6		9.7
1994[d]	200.0	309.0	509.0	15.5		−109.0	−109.0		17.0

Sources: Based on JUCEPLAN *BE* 1970 and *AEC* 1972–74; CEE, *AEC* 1975–89; Mesa-Lago and Gil 1989; Rodríguez 1992c, and Marquetti 1996b for 1990–94.

[a]Only sugar subsidies. [b]There was a deficit in the total trade balance. [c]There was a surplus in the total trade balance. [d]Russia and other independent republics of CIS in 1991–93, Russia alone in 1994.

Table III.21

Dependency on Crude Oil Imports in Cuba, 1963–1994 *(Thousands Metric Tons)*

	Crude Oil						Percentage Distribution of Supply			Soviet Supply of Crude Oil and Oil Products
Year	Domestic Production	Imports	Total Supply	Consumption	Difference[a]	"Re-Exports"[b]	Domestically Produced	Imported from the Soviet Union	Imported from Other Countries[c]	
1963	31	3,709	3,740			0	0.8			4,078[c]
1964	37	3,469	3,506			0	1.0			4,562[c]
1965	57	3,480	3,537			0	1.6			4,588[c]
1966	69	3,826	3,895			0	1.8			5,048[c]
1967	116	3,713	3,829			0	3.0	96.3	0.7	5,097[c]
1968	197	3,851	4,048			0	4.9	93.8	1.3	5,225
1969	206	4,156	4,362			0	4.7	92.3	3.0	5,681
1970	159	4,261	4,420	4,308	112	0	3.6	94.1	2.3	6,016
1971	120	4,757	4,877	4,350	527	0	2.5	95.6	1.9	6,817
1972	112	4,749	4,861	4,746	115	0	2.1	95.5	2.4	6,671
1973	138	5,243	5,381	5,345	36	0	2.6	96.7	0.7	7,154
1974	168	5,875	6,043	5,561	482	0	2.8	94.9	2.3	7,766
1975	226	5,797	6,023	5,976	47	0	3.7	94.7	1.6	7,748
1976	235	5,783	6,018	6,129	(111)	0	3.9	95.5	0.6	8,231
1977	256	6,201	6,457	6,324	133	162	4.0	95.6	0.4	9,236

1978	288	6,359	6,647	6,359	288	85	4.3	95.2	0.5	9,623
1979	288	6,131	6,419	6,376	43	0	4.5	95.2	0.3	9,875
1980	274	6,025	6,298	6,344	(46)	0	4.3	93.7	2.0	10,564
1981	259	6,355	6,608	6,473	135	0	3.8	95.6	0.6	11,089
1982	541	6,247	6,788	6,710	78	0	8.0	91.2	0.8	11,688
1983	742	6,861	7,603	6,784	819	781	9.8	89.3	0.9	12,410
1984	770	7,235	8,005	6,781	1,224	1,298	9.6	90.3	0.0	12,485
1985	868	8,046	8,914	6,847	2,067	1,891	9.7	88.7	1.6	13,093
1986	938	7,366	8,034	6,925	1,109	1,390	11.6	91.4	0.0	13,069
1987	894	7,894	8,788	7,290	1,498	1,220	10.2	89.3	0.5	13,467
1988	717			7,991			7.8	92.2	0.0	13,248
1989	718									13,300
1990	671									10,150
1991	527					0				8,600
1992	882					0				6,900
1993	1,107					0				6,800
1994	1,299					0				6,500

Sources: 1963–89 from Mesa-Lago and Gil 1989, updated with CEE, *AEC* 1984–89, *Compendio . . . Energía* 1989; 1990–94 from *BEC* 1990, Carranza 1993, and BNC 1995; total 1992–94 (last column) from ECLAC 1995.

[a]Difference between total supply and consumption. [b]Other exports include fuel oil, which might have been manufactured from crude oil imports. [c]Unspecified.

Table III.22

Soviet Economic Aid to Cuba and Estimates of Cuba's Trade Gain/Losses with the Soviet Union, 1960–1990 (Million U.S.$)

A. Soviet Economic Aid to Cuba

Period	Repayable Loans (Debt)			Nonrepayable Price Subsidies[a]	Total Aid	Percentage Distribution		Percentage Growth	
	Trade Deficit	Development	Subtotal			Loans (Debt)	Subsidies (Grants)	Loans (Debt)	Subsidies (Grants)
1960–70	2,083	344	2,427	1,131	3,558	68.2	31.8		
1971–75	1,649	749	2,398	1,143	3,451	67.8	32.2	97[b]	101[b]
1976–80	1,115	1,872	2,987	11,228	14,215	21.0	79.0	24	882
1981–85	4,046	2,266	6,312	15,760	22,072	28.6	71.4	111	40
1986–90	8,205[c]	3,400	11,605	10,128	21,733	53.4	46.6	83	−36
Total	17,098[d]	8,631[d]	25,729	39,390	65,119	39.5	60.5		

B. Cuba's Trade Gain/Losses with the Soviet Union

Year[e]	Sugar Exports			Nickel Exports			Oil Imports			Total
	Soviet Prices	World Prices[f]	Gain/ Loss	Soviet Prices	World Prices	Gain/ Loss	Soviet Prices	World Prices	Gain/ Loss	
1986	4,081	523	3,558	236	70	166	1,763	763	−1,000	2,724
1987	3,240	570	2,670	200	90	110	1,561	1,045	−516	2,264
1988	3,138	765	2,373	200[g]	254	−54	1,496	796	−700	1,619
1989	3,138[g]	960	2,178	200[g]	245	−45	1,476	977	−499	1,634
1990	3,138[g]	938	2,200	200[g]	163	37	1,476	1,126	350	1,887
Total	16,735	3,756	12,979	1,036	822	214	7,772	4,707	−3,065	10,128

Source: Mesa-Lago 1993a.

Note: Excludes military aid, which has been reported as $13.4 billion in 1960–85. [a]Subsidies to sugar and nickel exports and petroleum imports are all estimated in comparison with world market prices. In 1960–85 the table includes an insignificant negative subsidy to grains. Excludes additional revenue in hard currency obtained by Cuba in the 1980s by "re-exporting" subsidized Soviet oil "imports." [b]Over the estimated average for 1966–70. [c]Includes estimates for 1989–90. According to a former Cuban trade official, the initial credit for the period was set as 2.5 billion rubles ($4 billion) as in 1981–85, but it was insufficient and later was increased by the equal amount. [d]According to a Cuban source, the distribution of the debt by source in 1990 was: 62% trade deficits since 1972, 35% development loans since 1972, and 3% debt accumulated until 1972. Such distribution is close to the debt distribution in the table: 66% trade deficits and 34% development loans. [e]In 1987–90 the Cuban exchange rate of the peso and the dollar was par; the rate in 1986 was $1.21 per one peso, hence increasing the totals for the period in dollars by $1 million. [f]In the case of sugar, comparison of the Soviet price with preferential prices set in bilateral agreements would result in lower subsidies than compared with world prices. [g]Unchanged value of exports and Soviet prices are assumed.

Table III.23
Total Disbursed External Debt of Cuba, 1980–1994

1. Hard Currency Debt (million U.S.$)

	1980	1982	1983	1984	1985	1986	1987	1988	1989	1991	1993	1994
Total disbursed debt	3,226	2,669	2,790	2,989	3,621	4,985	6,094	6,606	6,165	6,377	8,785	9,083
Percentage distribution	100.0	100.0	100.0	100.0	100.0	100.0	100.0	100.0	100.0	100.0	100.0	100.0
Official bilateral	42.0	47.8	47.8	52.8	50.2	41.8	43.6	44.0	45.7	45.7	46.1	44.0
Official multilateral	0.3	0.7	0.9	0.6	0.6	0.5	0.4	0.4	1.0	0.0	5.0	5.5
Creditors (suppliers)	0.8	1.8	3.5	7.7	12.0	22.6	22.4	22.7	22.8	21.0	21.2	22.7
Financial institutions	56.9	49.7	47.8	38.9	37.2	35.1	33.6	31.9	29.8	33.3	27.4	27.5
Other credits	0.0	0.0	0.0	0.0	0.0	0.0	0.0	0.7	0.7	0.0	0.3	0.3
Debt service			319.0	403.0								
Relations (percentage)												
Total debt/GSP	18.3	11.6	11.5	11.4	13.4	18.8	23.8	25.1	22.9	33.5[a]	68.8[a]	70.6[a]
Debt service/exports	28.1	63.4	20.2	28.8	41.8	67.9						

2. Nonconvertible Currency Debt and Total Debt: 1989–90

	Rubles (Millions)	U.S.$ (Millions) Rates			Million Pesos 1990
		Official Nov. 1989 = 1.58	Official Nov. 1990 = 1.78	Commercial Nov. 1990 = 0.56	
Soviet Union (Nov. 1989)	15,490	24,474	27,572	8,674	18,222
Eastern Europe		2,277	2,464	1,329	1,511
Czechoslovakia	460	727	819	258	511
Bulgaria	300	474	534	168	333
Hungary	170	268	303	95	189
Germany	2,000[b]	808	808	808	478
Subtotal		26,751	30,036	10,003	19,733
Hard currency (Dec, 1989)		6,165	6,687	6,165	6,687
Total		32,916	36,723	16,168	26,420

Sources: Segment 1 1980–91 from ECLAC *Survey* 1989 Rodríguez 1992d; 1993–94 from BNC 1995. Segment 2 from Mesa-Lago 1993a; debt in pesos from Rodríguez 1992d.
[a]As a percentage of constant (1981) GDP (BNC 1995). [b]German Democratic Republic marks.

Table III.24

Percentage Distribution of the Labor Force by Occupational Group and Economic Activity in Cuba, Selected Years between 1956 and 1994

1. Distribution of Labor Force by Occupational Groups: 1989

	Thousands	*Percentage*
Total Labor Force	4,728.2	100.0
Military Sector	574.3	12.2
Civil Sector	3,870.2	81.8
State	3,641.1	77.0
Non-state	229.1	4.8
Private farmers	123.1	2.6
Members co-ops	64.5	1.4
Self-employed[a]	25.2	0.5
Private salaried	16.3	0.3
Unemployed	283.7	6.0

2. Percentage Distribution of Civil Sector by Occupational Groups: 1956/57–1988

	1970	*1979*	*1981*	*1985*	*1989*
State	86.3	93.6	93.4	93.1	94.1
Non-state	13.7	6.4	6.6	6.9	5.9
Agricultural co-op members	0.0	0.0	0.9	2.1	1.6
Private farmers	11.0	4.9	3.5	3.2	3.2
Private salaried	1.5	0.4	0.7	0.4	0.4
Self-employed[a]	1.2	0.8	1.3	1.2	0.7
Family workers		0.3	0.2		
Without co-ops	13.7	6.4	5.7	4.7	4.3
Total	100.0	100.0	100.0	100.0	100.0

3. Percentage Distribution of Labor Force by Economic Activity: 1956/57–1991

	1956–57	*1970*	*1979*	*1981*	*1990*[b]	*1994*[b]
Primary: Agriculture, fishing, and forestry	38.8	30.0	21.9	22.3	21.9	28.2
Secondary	21.2	26.3	27.8	27.8	25.5	23.2
Industry and mining	17.4	20.3	20.0	18.9	17.4	18.1
Construction	3.8	6.0	7.8	8.9	8.1	5.1

(*continued*)

Table III.24
(Continued)

	1956–57	*1970*	*1979*	*1981*	*1990*[b]	*1994*[b]
Tertiary	36.0	41.3	42.9	46.3	40.1	42.9
Transport and communication	4.8	6.1	6.2	7.0	8.9	4.5
Commerce	12.2	11.6	8.1	8.6	5.4	7.9
Services[c]	19.0	23.6	28.6	30.7	25.8	24.7
Nonspecified	4.0	2.4	7.4	3.6	12.5	5.7
Total	100.0	100.0	100.0	100.0	100.0	100.0

Sources: Gutiérrez 1958; JUCEPLAN, *Censo 1970* 1973; CEE, *Encuesta* 1981; ONC 1983; and CEE, *AEC* 1986–89. Military sector and unemployed from Mesa-Lago 1993d. Years 1989 and 1994 are author's calculations based on ECLAC 1997.

[a]Fisherman, taxi drivers, cargo porters, personal services. [b]Employed labor force, excludes unemployed (whose economic activity is not available). In agriculture the state and public sectors were added; self-employed were included in tertiary sector, which is where virtually all work; non-specified workers in noncivilian state sector are probably in the armed forces, and they could be added to services. [c]Non-productive sphere in 1970–81.

Table III.25

Women in the Labor Force in Cuba, Selected Years between 1953 and 1989

1. Percentage of Females in Labor Force and Civil Sector

Year	Labor Force	Civil Sector
1956–57	12.6	
1970	18.3	23.0
1979	27.4	31.2
1981	31.4	33.8
1988		38.2

2. Percentage Distribution of Females by Economic Activity (Labor Force)

	1953	1970	1979	1981
Primary	5.7	7.9	10.7	10.2
Secondary	19.5	21.3	19.2	20.8
Industry	19.1	20.7	16.4	17.7
Construction	0.4	0.6	2.8	3.1
Tertiary	74.3	67.5	70.1	65.4
Transportation & Communications	1.7	2.3	3.3	4.0
Commerce	7.9	23.7	11.7	12.2
Services	64.7	41.5	55.1	49.2
Others	0.5	3.3	0.0	3.6
Total	100.0	100.0	100.0	100.0

3. Percentage of Participation of Females by Type of Work (Civil Sector)[a]

	1975	1978	1985	1989
Administration	74.7	76.9	83.9	90.1
Services	51.6	56.1	62.2	64.1
Technicians	49.1	51.5	55.8	54.8
Executives	15.3	17.6	25.4	33.7
Blue-collars	13.2	13.3	18.3	19.4

Sources: ONCDE 1953; Gutiérrez 1958; JUCEPLAN, *Censo 1970* 1973; CEE, *Encuesta* 1981; ONC 1983; JUCEPLAN, *BE* 1972; CE, *AEC* 1986–89.

[a]Percentage of female workers in each category.

Table III.26

Open (National) Unemployment Rates in Cuba, 1959–1995 (Thousands)

				Rates (Percentage)	
Year	Labor Force	Open Unemployed	Equivalent Unemployment[a]	Open Unemployment	Equivalent Unemployment
1959	2,257	307		13.6[b]	
1960	2,276	269		11.8	
1963	2,431	198		8.1	
1965	2,490	163		6.5	
1970	2,638	35		1.3	
1975	3,031	135		4.5	
1979	3,458	187[c]		5.4	
1981	3,618	199[d]		5.5	
1988	4,621	277[e]		6.0	
1989	4,728	372		7.9	
1990	4,742	348	512	7.3	10.8
1991	4,737	362	910	7.7	19.2[f]
1994	4,496	301	1,497	6.7	33.3
1995	4,550	305	1,433	7.9	31.5

Sources: Gutiérrez 1958; ONCDE 1959–61; JUCEPLAN *Censo 1970;* Mesa-Lago 1981, 1993d; CEE *Encuesta* 1981c; ONC 1983; Brundenius 1984; CEE, *AEC* 1988; 1989–95 from ECLAC 1997.

[a]Open unemployed and those receiving unemployment subsidy (ECLAC 1997). [b]The one-year survey taken in 1956–57 gave a rate of 16.4%. [c]Calculated subtracting the employed population (3,270,341) from the labor force. [d]Sum of unemployed (121,700) and those searching jobs for the first time (76,900). [e]The percentage of unemployment is given by Rodríguez and the labor force by CEE; the number of unemployed is derived from those two figures. [f]The author conservatively estimated this figure for 1992 from 10% to 18% (Mesa-Lago 1993d).

Table III.27

Crude Estimates of Income Distribution in Cuba, 1958–1986 (Percentage)

			Personal Income					
	Family Income					1978[b]		
Quintiles	1958	1962	1953	1962	1973[a]	Low	High	1986[c]
0–20	5.7	9.5	2.1	6.2	7.8	7.8	11.0	11.3
21–40	8.9	12.2	4.4	11.0	12.5	12.4	13.8	14.7
41–60	12.5	13.5	11.1	16.3	19.2	19.7	16.5	17.0
61–80	18.3	18.3	24.5	25.1	26.0	26.7	22.7	23.2
81–100	54.6	46.5	57.9	41.4	34.5	33.4	36.0	33.8
Total	100.0	100.0	100.0	100.0	100.0	100.0	100.0	100.0

Sources: Family income from MacEwan 1981; personal income from Brundenius 1979, 1984, and Zimbalist and Brundenius 1989.

[a]Excludes private sector. [b]Includes private sector. [c]The authors do not clarify if the private sector is included or excluded.

Table III.28
Estimation of Real Wage Index in Cuba, 1975–1995

Year	Annual Average Nominal Wage (Pesos)	Annual Inflation Rate[a]	Price-Index[a] (1980 = 100)	Real Annual Wage (1980 Pesos)	Real Wage Index[b] (1980 = 100)
1975	1,616.0	-0.5	98.6	1,627.2	91.72
1976	1,651.0	-3.4	98.1	1,623.9	91.54
1977	1,656.0	3.8	94.7	1,591.4	89.71
1978	1,680.0	1.7	98.3	1,692.2	95.39
1979	1,721.0	4.2	100.0	1,774.0	100.00
1980	1,774.0	8.5	108.5	1,875.6	105.73
1981	2,035.0	0.4	108.9	1,939.7	109.34
1982	2,113.0	0.4	109.4	1,974.0	111.28
1983	2,159.0	-0.1	109.3	2,041.0	115.05
1984	2,230.0	-1.0	108.2	2,082.0	117.36
1985	2,252.0	-2.8	105.1	2,144.8	120.90
1986	2,255.0	0.2	105.3	2,095.9	118.14
1987	2,208.0	0.5	105.9	2,117.6	119.37
1988	2,242.0	0.2	106.1	2,130.3	120.09[c]
1989	2,260.0	3.5	109.8	2,062.3	116.25[c]
1990	2,264.4	-6.8	102.3	2,169.4	122.29[c]
1991	2,220.0	3.1	105.5	2,074.6	116.94[c]
1992	2,188.8	19.9	126.5	1,723.6	97.16[c]
1993	2,180.4	25.7	159.0	1,401.4	79.00[c]
1994	2,228.4	11.2	176.8	1,330.1	74.98[c]
1995	2,352.0				

Sources: Nominal wages from CEE, *AEC 1989,* and ECLAC 1997; inflation from Table III.3 and Mesa-Lago 1997; rest are author's calculations.

[a]GSP deflator for 1976–88, GDP deflator for 1989–95; technically the two series can not be connected. [b]Because we lack the consumer price index, the GSP/GDP deflator was used. Since 1990, nevertheless, the informal market has expanded considerably, and prices escalated in it; the share of the informal market has been estimated at about 50% in consumer goods. [c]ECLAC (1997) has calculated an index based on 1990 = 100: 1989, 103.8; 1990, 100.0; 1991, 96.4; 1992, 86.2; 1993, 77.2; 1994, 59.5; and 1996, 56.1.

Table III.29

Monthly Per Capita Quotas of Selected Rationed Consumer Goods in Havana, Cuba, 1962–1994 (Pounds)

	1962	1969	1971–72	1979[a]	1991–94[b]
Meat[c]	3	3	3	2.5	0.75[d]
Fish	1	2	4	Free[e]	0.67[e]
Rice	6	4	3–6	5	5[m]
Beans	1.5	1.5	1.5–3	1.25	0.62[g]
Tubers	14	9			
Fats	2	1	2	1.5	1.5[d]
Eggs (units)	5	15	15–24	Free	20[h]
Butter	0.125	0.125	Free	Free	[d]
Coffee	1	0.375	0.375	0.375	0.25
Milk (canned)[i]	6	2	3	3	3
Sugar	Free	6	6–4[f]	4[f]	4[f]
Bread	Free	15		Free	5[j]
Cigarettes (package)	Free	4	4	4	4
Gasoline (gallon)	Free			10	7[k]
Detergent (medium package)	1	1		0.5	0.25[d]
Soap (cake)	2	2.5		1.5	1[l]
Toilet paper (roll)	Free	1		1	1[d]
Toothpaste (small tube)	1	1		0.33	0.25
Cigars (units)	Free	2	4	4	4
Beer (bottle)	Free	1	Free	Free	24[m]

Sources: Mesa-Lago 1981, 1993d; interviews with Cuban visitors to the United States in 1994–95.

[a]Also free in 1979 were macaroni, spaghetti, butter, and yogurt; cakes and vegetables (according to season); and bread (after 4 P.M.). [b]June; since September 1990, 28 food products and 180 consumer goods have been reintroduced into the list of rationed commodities. [c]Beef; if not available, chicken is provided—only in this way. In 1991 the chicken meat ration was 1.5 pounds, and in 1992 it was 0.75; at the end of the year it was not available. [d]Not available in practice in 1994. [e]Small fish. Seafood has not been available for more than two decades. [f]White sugar, cut to 3 in 1994, plus 3 of crude sugar. [g]Black, red, and white beans; black are seldom available; reduced to 0.5 in mid-1992. [h]Subsequently cut to 16, 8, and 3 (1993). [i]Children under 7 have a daily ration of one liter of fresh milk. Adults over 65 receive 6 cans of condensed or evaporated milk monthly but not always (eliminated in 1994). [j]One small roll daily since 1994. [k]Cut to 5 in 1992 and all together at the end of 1992. [l]Bath soap; washing soap has not been supplied for as long as four months. At the end of 1992 the quota was cut in half. [m]Per family, not available at all in 1994.

Table III.30
Demographic and Health Indicators in Cuba, 1958–1994

Year	Population[a] (Thousands)	Growth Rate (Percentage)	Birth Rate	Net Migration	Doctors per 10,000 Inhabitants	Hospital Beds per 1,000 Inhabitants	Mortality Rates (per 1,000) General	Mortality Rates (per 1,000) Infant	Life Expectancy[b] (Years at Birth)
1958	6,824	1.8	26.1	−4,449	9.2	4.2	6.3	33.4	
1959	6,977	2.2	27.7	−12,345			6.4	34.7	
1960	7,077	1.4	30.1	−62,379			6.1	35.9	64.0
1961	7,191	1.6	32.5	−67,468			6.4	37.6	
1962	7,318	1.6	34.3	−66,264	5.4		7.1	41.5	65.3
1963	7,512	2.6	35.1	−12,201	8.9		6.7	37.1	
1964	7,713	2.6	35.0	−12,791	8.6		6.3	37.4	
1965	7,907	2.5	34.3	−18,003	7.9	5.3	6.4	37.8	67.2
1966	8,064	2.0	33.1	−53,409	8.7		6.4	37.2	
1967	8,215	1.9	31.7	−51,972	8.0		6.3	36.4	
1968	8,353	1.7	30.4	−56,755	7.5		6.5	38.2	68.4
1969	8,489	1.6	29.2	−49,776	7.1		6.6	46.7	
1970	8,613	1.5	27.7	−56,404	7.1	5.0	6.3	38.7	70.0
1971	8,769	1.8	29.5	−49,631	7.1		6.2	37.4	
1972	8,951	2.1	28.0	−16,856	7.3	4.6	5.5	27.4	
1973	9,118	1.9	25.0	−7,073	7.7	4.4	5.7	28.9	70.9
1974	9,232	1.3	21.9	−3,893	8.8	4.3	5.6	29.0	
1975	9,366	1.5	20.7	−2,891	10.0	4.2	5.4	27.3	

388

Year										
1976	9,493	1.4	19.8	−2,891	11.2	4.2	5.5	22.9		
1977	9,601	1.1	17.5	−968	14.8	4.1	5.8	24.8	73.0	73.0
1978	9,686	0.9	15.4	−3,462	14.8	4.1	5.7	22.4		
1979	9,754	0.7	14.8	−16,270	15.4	4.2	5.6	19.4		
1980	9,694	−0.6c	14.1	−141,742	15.7	4.3	5.7	19.6		
1981	9,753	0.6	14.0	−18,928	16.6	4.4	5.9	18.5		
1982	9,848	1.0	16.3	−8,234	17.1	4.5	5.8	17.3	74.3	73.9
1983	9,946	1.0	16.7	−9,533	18.9	4.6	5.9	16.8		
1984	10,043	1.0	16.6	−9,007	20.4	4.7d	6.0	15.0		
1985	10,153	1.1	18.0	−8,164	22.5	4.7d	6.4	16.5	74.5	
1986	10,246	1.0	16.3	−9,635	24.9	4.7d	6.2	13.6		
1987	10,356	1.0	17.4	−4,114	27.1	4.8d	6.3	13.3	74.7	74.6
1988	10,469	1.1	18.1	−7,521	29.8	5.0d	6.5	11.9		
1989	10,577	1.0	17.6	−9,279	32.8	5.1d	6.4	11.1		
1990	10,694	1.1	17.6	−5,352	36.4	5.3d	6.8	10.7		
1991	10,800	1.0	16.3	−3,737	39.8		6.7	10.7		
1992	10,909	1.0	14.5	−5,604	43.3		7.0	10.2		
1993	11,019	0.9	13.9	−3,303	46.7	5.2d	7.2	9.4	75.4	75.3
1994	11,069	0.5c	13.4	−47,844	49.1		7.2	9.9		

Sources: JUCEPLAN, *AEC,* 1972–74; CEE, *AEC* 1975–89; O. Castro 1992; MINSAP 1994; *Estadísticas* 1994; ECLAC 1986–96. Life expectancy by quinquenia from United Nations 1995; years 1960, 1965, and 1970 from Díaz-Briquets 1982; biannual averages 1977–78/1987–88 from CEE, *AEC* 1983–89. and "*Estadísticas* 1994"; 1993 from UNDP 1996.

aEnd of the year. bFive-year averages from United Nations, two-year averages from Cuba. cThe rate declined sharply due to a massive emigration. dReal beds.

Table III.31

Rates of Contagious Diseases in Cuba, 1958–1994 (Reported Cases per 100,000 Inhabitants)

Year	Acute Diarrhea	Acute Respiratory	Chicken Pox	Diphtheria	Hepatitis	Malaria	Measles	Polio	Syphilis	Gonorrhea	Tetanus	Tuberculosis	Typhoid
1958				2.4		2.0	2.9	1.6	0.7			18.0	5.1
1959				4.7		2.1	10.7	4.3	0.7		4.1	27.6	13.0
1960				8.1		19.0	5.0	4.3	8.3		4.6	27.1	17.5
1961				19.1	5.0	46.6	0.4	4.9	6.9			37.8	13.7
1962				19.4	51.1	49.8	22.5	0.7	11.4		9.0	38.6	14.2
1963				12.8	64.4	11.5	94.0	—	23.4		6.0	38.3	5.8
1964				8.6	70.6	8.4	28.9	—	25.1		5.5	52.6	15.6
1965	5,707		118.6	8.2	115.8	1.7	121.6	—	30.4	8.9	6.7	65.0	3.1
1966	5,876		138.3	4.6	115.1	0.5	136.4	—	26.3		6.1	36.5	2.2
1967	6,165		208.2	5.5	139.6	0.6	165.9	—	13.1		5.4	37.2	2.4
1968	6,319			1.6	208.6		145.5	—	6.7		3.9	41.0	12.0
1969	6,419		104.6	0.6	85.3		132.2	—	7.1		3.5	43.3	5.5
1970	7,694	10,162	150.1	0.1	102.6		105.2	—	7.8	2.6	2.6	30.8	5.0
1971	7,879		76.3	—a	151.9	0.1	129.7		11.1		2.0	17.9	4.8
1972	8,038	12,549	65.4	—	114.5	0.4	59.9		24.3	8.4	1.7	14.3	5.1
1973	8,286	14,219	93.0	—	133.6	0.1	78.3		48.9	9.7	1.1	15.4	3.5
1974	7,317	15,596	178.4	—	205.9	0.4	150.9		50.6	35.3	1.0	15.4	3.7
1975	6,876	15,520	161.7	—	217.0	0.9	113.4		47.6	47.2	0.7	14.2	4.0

1976	6,346	17,267	261.4	—	145.8	1.9	157.2	—	41.1	66.1	0.6	13.5	4.3
1977	7,358	19,348	144.3	—	123.2	1.8	263.3	—	39.2	86.4	0.6	13.1	4.7
1978	6,920	23,594	113.5	—	172.6	1.6	194.4	—	44.2	105.9	0.4	13.1	3.8
1979	6,951	21,906	94.8	—	225.8	3.2	77.3	—	43.6	141.6	0.3	11.6	1.8
1980	6,839	21,980	200.7	—	208.3	3.1	39.1	—	44.7	169.4	0.3	11.6	1.0
1981	7,836	27,595	425.1	—	147.2	5.9	190.1	—	36.9	201.8	0.2	8.6	1.8
1982	8,732	27,441	191.5	—	208.4	3.4	238.8	—	38.5	238.9	0.2	8.5	1.3
1983	8,527	33,000	291.1	—	101.2	3.0	33.2	—	44.3	294.3	0.2	7.7	0.6
1984	8,777	31,810	351.0	—	78.4	4.0	34.0	—	53.2	355.6	0.1	7.1	0.6
1985	10,487	38,160	820.8	—	209.2	4.5	28.5	—	62.6	359.6	0.1	6.7	0.6
1986	9,824	35,816	373.2	—	300.4	4.0	32.5	—	71.4	340.0	0.1	6.4	0.7
1987	11,436	35,452	374.9	—	238.3	2.8	8.3	—	84.2	352.7	0.1	6.2	0.7
1988	9,939	40,308	415.3	—	165.7	7.9	1.2	—	82.3	371.3	—	6.0	0.9
1989	8,842	36,804	365.6	—	106.1	7.2	0.1	—	82.1	381.3	0.1	5.5	0.5
1990	9,991	44,272	353.4	—	124.6	4.3	0.2	—	86.1	334.0	—	5.1	0.6
1992	10,112	40,368	965.9	—	295.4[b]	0.1	0.1	—	101.7	240.8	—	5.8	0.5
1993	10,242	35,449	397.4	—	149.5	0.1	—	—	91.2	227.4	—	7.2	0.2
1994	10,380	35,310	381.2	—	163.7	0.2	—	—	105.5	312.5	—	11.7	0.7

Sources: Mesa-Lago 1981; CEE, *AEC* 1975–89; MINSAP 1994; "Estadísticas 1994," 1995; ONE 1998.

[a]—No cases reported or negligible rates. [b]324.7 in 1991.

Table III.32

Access to Potable Water and Sanitation Service in Cuba, 1953–1981
(Percentage of Dwellings[a])

Year[b]	Percentage Urban Population			Percentage Rural Population		
		Sanitation			Sanitation	
	Water	Toilet	All[c]	Water	Toilet	All[c]
1953	81.8	61.7	95.1	15.0	7.9	45.9
1970	87.8	64.2	93.3	24.0	6.0	61.4
1981	89.9	67.5	95.8	32.9	7.5	79.8

Sources: Census figures for 1953, 1970, and 1981 from ONCDE 1955, JUCEPLAN 1973, and ONC 1983. No further data have been published in Cuba after 1981; CEE statistical yearbooks have never provided statistics on this indicator.

Note: No data available on sewerage but only on sanitation services. [a]The 1953 census did not provide data on population (the 1970 and 1981 censuses did) but only dwellings, which were used in the table to standardize the comparison. Differences between dwelling and population percentages (in 1970 and 1981) were insignificant in water; percentages of population were slightly smaller than dwellings in sanitation. [b]The three censuses are not strictly comparable because 1953 had different categories than 1970 and 1981 (which have the same). The categories used were standardized as follows. *Water:* included were internal piped from aqueduct, internal piped from cistern and well (it is not clear whether the latter was included or not with cistern in 1953), and external piped; excluded were cistern/well nonpiped, aqueduct external nonpiped, and river, spring, and other unidentified sources. *Sanitation:* toilet (either internal or external, exclusive or common use), latrine, black hole (this was not a separate category in 1953, but was in 1970 and 1981); excluded was "without sanitation" (same in three census). There was an "undeclared" category in 1953 (3.6% urban and 2.4% rural) and 1970 (0.3% and 0.4%) but not in 1981; in order to standardize the figures, this category was excluded to estimate the percentage distribution in 1953 and 1970. Other data published by international and regional organizations (UNDP, PAHO, ECLAC) were inconsistent with census data, and neither provided definitions nor sources: therefore, the author decided to exclude them (PAHO 1994 published in the same book two completely different figures for urban water access in 1992: 83% and 100%, and for rural: 78% and 91%). [c]Includes toilet, latrine, and black hole.

Table III.33

Illiteracy Rates and Percentage of Age Group Enrolled by Educational Level in Cuba, 1953–1992

	Illiteracy Rates (Percentage)[a]				Enrollment in Education (Percentage)[b]		
	Cuba			UNESCO			
Year	National	Urban	Rural	National	Elementary	Secondary	Higher
1953	23.6	11.6	41.7	22.1			
1960				21.0[c]	110	14	3
1961	3.9[c]						
1965					129	25	4
1970	12.9	7.1	21.5		121	25	5
1971					126	25	5
1972					130	28	7
1973					126	33	8
1974					128	41	9
1975					124	54	11
1976					121	66	14
1977					118	75	16
1978					115	80	18
1979	4.0	2.3	7.1		112	83	19
1980					108	80	20
1981	1.9[d]				108	81	20
1982					111	78	19
1983					111	81	20
1984					106	83	20
1985				7.6	104	85	21
1986					105	88	23
1987					104	88	23
1990				6.0[e]	100	90	21
1992				5.3	100	80	18

Sources: Cuban illiteracy rates from ONCDE 1953; JUCEPLAN, *Censo 1970* 1973; CEE, *Encuesta* 1979; ONC 1983. UNESCO 1980, 1993, 1996. Enrollment from ECLAC, *Yearbook* 1980–89; 1990 from UNDP 1994; 1992, author's estimates based on ECLAC 1997.

[a]Cuban data change the age group and hence are not comparable through time. The 1953, 1961, and 1970 percentages are for 10 years and older, while the 1979 and 1981 percentages are 10 to 49 (excluding the older group with highest literacy rates). Furthermore, the number of illiterates reportedly was cut in half between 1979 and 1981 from 236,622 to 115,374. The column by UNESCO estimates national percentages for 15 and older for 1953, 1985, and 1990, allowing for a proper comparison, both in Cuba and with the other two countries (in 1953 percentages [15+] were 11.1% in urban and 40% in rural). [b]Limits of age for educational levels are: elementary 6–11 years, secondary 12–17 (12–18 in 1971–74), and higher 20–24. Elementary enrollment goes over 100% because of a mismatch between population and education ages. [c]Author's projection for 1958 (10 years and older) based on 1943 and 1953 censuses. [d]The percentage 10 and older increases to 3.8% according to UNESCO. [e]The same percentage can be estimated (15+) based on Cuban rates of 5% for males and 7% for females ("Indicadores" 1994) and gender composition of population.

Table III.35

Dwellings Built (by Builder) and Housing Deficit in Cuba, 1959–1993

| | State | | | | Population | | |
	Total[a]	Civilian	Military	Cooperatives	Habitable	No Certificate Habitability	Total
Year							
1959–63[b]		17,089		0			
1964		7,088		0			
1965		5,040		0			
1966		6,271		0			
1967		10,257		0			
1968		6,458		0			
1969		4,817		0			
1970		4,004		0			
1971		5,014		0			
1972		16,807		0			
1973		20,710		0			
1974		18,522		0			
1975		18,602		0			
1976		15,342		0			
1977		20,024		0			
1978		17,072		0			
1979		14,523		0			
1980		15,462		0	4,916		
1981	20,453	18,247	2,206	610	6,655	32,858	39,513
1982	23,851	21,211	2,640	1,384	8,499	31,014	39,513
1983	27,674	24,090	3,584	2,766	10,519	28,994	39,513
1984	26,246	22,829	3,417	2,564	13,591	29,979	43,570
1985	27,265	24,195	3,070	2,053	11,852	33,267	45,119
1986	25,833	23,132	2,701	2,709	10,792	34,281	45,073
1987	23,768	21,760	2,008	4,800	9,564	30,539	40,535
1988	25,168			3,127	7,364		
1989	26,380			2,899	8,394		
1990	22,516			1,654	12,162		
1991	16,696			688	8,821		
1992	12,334			429	7,267		
1993	16,933			1,993	8,202		

Sources: Based on Mesa-Lago 1981; JUCEPLAN, *BE* 1966–71; and *SEC* 1972–74; CEE, *AEC* 1975–89; 1990–93 from ECLAC 1997.

[a]After 1989 a new series of housing for physicians is added starting in 1986, which has been excluded.
[b]Annual average. [c]Includes military.

Totals			Units Built per 1,000 Inhabitants			
All	*Minus Military*	*Minus No Certificate Habitability*	*State Civilian*	*Private Habitable*	*All Minus No Certificate*	*Housing Deficit*
			2.4			
			0.9			655,000
			0.6			
			0.8			
			1.2			
			0.8			
			0.6			
			0.6			755,000
			0.6			
			1.9			
			2.3			
			2.0			
			2.0			
			1.6			
			2.1			
			1.7			
			1.5			
		20,378	1.6	0.5		
60,576	58,370	25,512	1.9	0.7	2.8	877,000
64,748	62,108	31,094	2.5	0.9	3.4	
69,953	66,369	37,375	2.4	1.0	4.1	
72,380	68,963	38,984	2.3	1.4	4.2	
74,437	71,367	38,100	2.4	1.2	4.0	880,000
73,615	70,914	36,633	2.2	1.0	3.8	
69,107	67,099	35,560	2.1	0.9	3.7	
				0.7		
				0.8		
		36,326[c]		1.1	3.4	
		26,205[c]		0.8	2.4	
		20,030[c]		0.7	1.8	
		27,128[c]		0.7	2.4	

Table III.34

Social Security Population Coverage and Costs in Cuba, 1958–1993

| | Percentage of Population Covered | | | | Cost of Social Security[c] | | |
Year	Total[a]	Labor Force[b]	Thousand Pensioners	Ratio of Active Worker per Pensioner	Percentage GSP	Percentage GDP	Deficit financed by State (Percentage of Revenue)[d]
1958	4.2	62.6	154	14.7		6.0	
1970	100.0	88.7	363	7.2	7.4		30.9
1979	100.0	89.6	671	5.2	6.4		41.1
1981	100.0	93.0			5.9	11.7	57.0
1989	100.0	94.1	1,072		7.5	17.9	62.6
1990	100.0		1,102	4.2	9.3		
1993	100.0		1,200	3.7	16.9	19.8	173.4

Sources: Mesa-Lago 1993d; ILO 1996; and author's calculations based on BNC 1995.

[a]Health-care coverage; since 1970 based on law not on statistics (1989 based on ILO data). [b]Pension coverage, author's estimate based on civilian labor force; it is assumed that the military sector is also insured. [c]Includes social security and health care. [d]Years correspond to 1974, 1978, 1985, 1989, and 1993.

Part IV

COSTA RICA
The Mixed Model

1

Introduction

1. Summary of Socioeconomic Conditions at the End of the 1930s

In the 1930s Costa Rica was an agrarian country almost exclusively dependent on the exports of coffee and bananas, with a tiny industrial sector. The precariousness of this dependency on agricultural products was manifested during the Great Depression, which caused a plunge in world prices of coffee and banana. Costa Rica's economy was hit hard by the ensuing decline in the value of exports, which, in turn, reduced its capacity to import. Fiscal revenue plummeted, as it had been highly dependent on export and import taxes. Although Costa Rican standards of living at the time were relatively high compared to the rest of Central America, the country was still generally poor, and the depression worsened the situation. Unemployment and underemployment were widespread; housing was often inadequate and lacked basic hygienic conditions; and malnutrition and endemic diseases afflicted a significant segment of the population. Before World War II Costa Rica ranked below nine Latin American nations in three per capita consumption indicators: total calories, grams of daily protein, and annual consumption of milk (Bell 1971).

The deteriorating socioeconomic conditions led to labor unrest as well as increased social tensions and fostered the growth of the Communist Party (founded in 1931), which was strongest in the severely afflicted banana zones (the most important labor group in the rural sector was the banana workers, but urban labor was dispersed and poorly organized). The crisis challenged Costa Rica's leaders, who for the most part were followers of nineteenth-century liberalism, espousing such values as a commitment to free enterprise (with the support of the coffee oligarchy), universal suffrage, freedom of expression, and separation of church and state. These leaders, who in 1932 organized the National Republican Party (PRN, with a conservative ideology), had governed Costa Rica during the 1930s and chose a physician, Dr. Rafael Angel Calderón Guardia, as their candidate for the 1940 election.

2. Periodization of Mixed-Model Policies between 1940 and 1994

This part studies three stages in the economy of Costa Rica between 1940 and 1994. In each of them there is a brief discussion of the main economic and social policies, followed by an evaluation of performance (except in the first stage; see below). The first stage covers the antecedents and development of Costa Rica's dominant political party, the National Liberation Party (PLN), and its economic and social development model. It includes the administrations of the pioneer reformers Rafael Angel Calderón Guardia (1940–44) and Teodoro Picado (1944–48), José Figueres's junta government (1948–49), and the administrations of Otilio Ulate (1949–53) and Figueres (1953–58).

The second stage, which deals with the consolidation, expansion, and crisis of the model, is divided into two substages. The first encompasses the administrations of Mario Echandi Jiménez (1958–62), Francisco Orlich (1962–66), and José Joaquín Trejos Fernández (1966–70), when the emphasis was on Costa Rica's integration into the Central American Common Market and the elaboration of the import-substitution-industrialization (ISI) strategy. The second includes the administrations of José Figueres (1970–74), Daniel Oduber (1974–78), and Rodrigo Carazo Odio (1978–82), when the state clearly became more interventionist under Figueres and Oduber, although there was a brief neoconservative challenge to the PLN model under Carazo. However, as the Carazo coalition weakened, and the international economic situation worsened, the ISI strategy ran its course and confronted a severe crisis.

The third and final stage covers the administrations of Luis Alberto Monge (1982–86), Oscar Arias Sánchez (1986–90), and Rafael Angel Calderón Fournier (1990–94). During this stage the harsh economic crisis and the dictates of international financial institutions prompted a move toward stabilization and structural adjustment. The national debate over key aspects of the model intensified with the increasing economic liberalization.

Tables IV.1 and IV.2 summarize these stages and substages: the establishment of the foundations of the model (1948–58), the consolidation, expansion, and crisis of the model (1958–82), and the adjustment, restructuring, and recovery (1982–94). Table IV.1 shows which parties controlled the executive and legislative branches during each administration; despite shifts in party control of the presidency, the National Liberation Party (PLN) has dominated the Legislative Assembly since its formation in 1950 for all but two administrations. Table IV.2 summarizes the major policies and their shifts in the three stages.

A technical note on periodization and statistics is necessary. Presidential elections in Costa Rica take place on the first Sunday in February, and the president enters office on May 8, serving for four years (except in the first administration of José Figueres). In the evaluation of performance in this part, an election year shall normally be included under the previous administration for two reasons: the effects of the incumbent administration's performance can carry over into that year, and there are often delays in the implementation of policy changes by the new administration (This is not a problem, however, in the analysis of policy; thus an election year should normally be discussed in two consecutive stages). But the year 1982, economically the worst after World War II and a year in which the administration changed, will be included in the evaluation of performance in two stages. Some indicators for 1982 (GDP growth, unemployment, inflation) are relevant for the analysis of the performance of the consecutive administrations of Rodrigo Carazo and Alberto Monge (i.e., in discussing the results of the crisis under the former and economic improvement under the latter). Finally, most of the statistical series in the tables of this part begin in 1960, in the middle of the Mario Echandi's administration. His policies and those of his predecessors will be discussed, as well as overall economic performance, but the analysis of statistical data must begin in 1960.

2

Establishing the Foundations of the Model

1940–1958

1. Calderón's Socioeconomic Reforms and the Crisis: 1940–1948

Calderón (1940–44) was elected president and took power in May 1940, but the PRN maintained a majority in the Legislative Assembly. A believer in social Christian principles and social reform, Calderón broke with the more conservative sectors of the PRN and responded to the crisis by initiating a reform process that would lay the foundations of a welfare state.

In 1942 the constitution was amended to include the Social Guarantees, which stated basic principles to be interpreted by the Legislative Assembly and the courts. The government should guarantee the establishment of cooperatives, labor courts, a social security system, a minimum wage, safe conditions in the workplace, collective bargaining, and preferential access of Costa Ricans to the job market. The new constitutional social principles required legal implementation; thus in 1943 a Labor Code was enacted that regulated many of the guarantees related to labor relations. The code ordered the creation of a Labor Ministry, made collective bargaining mandatory in disputes between management and labor, granted workers the right to organize trade unions, established a minimum wage and an eight-hour workday, protected workers against arbitrary dismissal, established labor courts to mediate labor conflicts, and made provisions for the establishment of cooperatives (Bell 1971; Franco and León 1984).

Two important reforms took place in agriculture and industry. A land law facilitated access to state and private uncultivated land to numerous squatters provided that they farm it and that the state compensate the landowners. The land distribution brought uncultivated land into production, with mini-

402

mal bureaucratic effort, and increased the number of independent farmers, essential to the strength of Costa Rican democracy (Bell 1971; Bird 1984). A Law of New Industries, enacted in 1940, promoted industrialization and economic diversity; it offered incentives to use domestic products as well as tariff protection and tax exemptions on the imports of machinery, tools, and raw materials (Cruz and Botey 1987).

The social security law was enacted in 1941, and the Costa Rican Social Insurance Fund (CCSS) was charged with the administration of the system, which began to operate in 1943. The system is financed through mandatory contributions (established on wages and income) paid by workers, employers, and the state. Coverage became compulsory for all persons under 60 years of age working in industry, agriculture, or domestic service, as well as self-employed artisans working at home. The social security system protected workers against occupational accidents, common sicknesses, old age, disability, and death (survivors) and called for the creation of hospitals and clinics (Bell 1971; Ameringer 1982).

Other legislation protected tenants in rented housing from eviction, froze rents, and created low-cost housing cooperatives. The National Bank of Costa Rica (founded in 1914 as a state bank) began to offer credits and technical assistance to agricultural cooperatives and to finance programs for the construction of low-cost housing. The University of Costa Rica was founded in 1940 to teach those who could not study abroad, and thus train the professionals needed for national development (Bell 1971; Bird 1984).

The success of Calderón's social programs was initially helped by a relatively sound fiscal situation inherited from a previous austere administration. However, Costa Rica's economy, which in the second half of the 1930s began to recover from the Great Depression, slid back into a recession with the onslaught of World War II. The halt of European imports led to shortages of capital, intermediate, and consumer goods, including foodstuffs, which fueled severe inflation. The government intervened to regulate prices and create employment by initiating public works projects (such as construction of the Pan American highway), but the economy and living standards continued to deteriorate. Out of three main sources of fiscal revenue—customs duties, export taxes, and receipts from the liquor monopoly—only the last was not adversely affected by the wartime conditions. In 1939–42 the colón lost about half of its buying power, and by 1944 the foreign trade deficit (which had begun in 1934) worsened as the country imported almost twice as much as it exported. Foreign borrowing also escalated in the first half of the 1940s to pay for the new socioeconomic programs.

Some of Calderón's reforms were not succesfull, and others promted opposition from some sectors of the population, particularly the oligarchy. The

Labor Code met with immediate opposition from employers, who began to dismiss workers before the bill was signed into law, arguing that the code created a financial burden that made it difficult to maintain employment. Calderón's programs targeted the country's poor, but the urban middle-income sectors enjoyed relatively few benefits from them. The Law of New Industries did foster expansion in some industries (e.g., textiles, shoes, soap, beer, paint, nails, wiring, glass); nevertheless, industrial output did not grow significantly, and industries that suffered from the wartime cut in imports were not assisted. Internal limitations on credit and a 1941 measure permitting the duty-free import of some U.S. products had negative effects. Allegations of corruption (favoritism in appointing government officials and awarding state contracts) and fiscal mismanagement also hurt Calderón's credibility. These problems partially offset the overall positive effects of the reform and had negative political repercussions. The economic crisis helped to cement and mount opposition (including by businessmen) and weakened the *Calderonistas* (Bell 1971; Bird 1984; Botey and Cruz 1987; Doryan 1990).

In 1942 some members of the oligarchy began plotting Calderón's overthrow and even approached the leader of the Communist Party for his cooperation. But the World War II alliance of the United States and the Soviet Union, coupled with Calderón's impressive social reforms, facilitated instead a coalition between the Communist Party (which changed its name to the Popular Vanguard Party to improve its image) and Calderón's conservative PRN. The coalition candidate Teodoro Picado (hand-picked by Calderón) was elected president in 1944 and assumed office in May, while the PRN maintained a majority in Congress.

Picado's (1944–48) first task was to reestablish an image of fiscal integrity and stability. He thus initiated administrative reforms to foster more effective control and distribution of state revenues, including the creation of the Comptroller's Office and the Budget Office. These efforts, however, did little to sway the opposition, and government attempts to raise fiscal revenue were unsuccessful. The end of World War II brought an increase in the prices of coffee and other agricultural products, but the economic situation in Costa Rica did not improve significantly. Overall, during the administrations of Calderón and Picado, the persistent balance of payments deficit plus the high cost of the social programs led to growing inflation and a fiscal deficit, despite government measures to control these problems (Bell 1971).

Support for *Calderonistas* remained strong among the masses, but the growing opposition became increasingly organized and powerful. As early as 1940, a middle-of-the-road social democratic movement appeared and founded a Center for the Study of National Problems, made up by a group of law-school graduates who rejected both the old liberalism and communism. They supported social reform and an expansion in government planning and intervention in the economy, without curtailing the democracy process. Major projects of the center included negotiating more favorable contracts with foreign companies (particularly for bananas), utilizing foreign credit for development projects instead of financing the fiscal deficit, diversifying agriculture to counter the dependency on coffee and bananas, and stimulating industrial development. Center members were particularly irritated by Calderón's close ties with the Catholic Church and alliance with the communists. Thus, they directed their criticism against Calderón rather than his reforms, often accusing him of dictatorial tendencies (Doryan 1990).

By February 1944 a Democratic Action Party (DAP) was organized but with a more conservative stand than the center's. Both were in favor of democracy and reform, but although the DAP accepted the state's regulating the economy, it overwhelmingly endorsed capitalism, while the center supported a stronger role for the government in a mixed economy to ensure economic and social development. In 1945 both groups joined to organize the Social Democratic Party (PSD, the predecessor of the National Liberation Party [PLN]). One of the organizers of the PSD was José Figueres, among Calderón's most visible and vocal critics. He was a landowner who opposed communism and favored social policies to improve poor living conditions, which he saw as a fertile ground for the growth of communism.

The PSD had small importance in politics at the time of its founding, but it had a well-defined economic and social program. It saw the need to increase and diversify production, protect private property, foster cooperatives, and promote a more just distribution of wealth. The PSD also advocated the creation of autonomous institutions, that is, public agencies independent and decentralized from the central government (to avoid the Executive's control) to guide, regulate, and perform almost every function in the social and economic spheres (Rovira 1988a).

In 1941 former president León Cortes deserted the National Republican Party over disagreement with Calderón's reforms and organized the right-wing Democrat Party. Another conservative party was the National Union Party (PUN) founded in 1901. In 1945 these two conservative parties joined the social-democratic PSD to back Otilio Ulate Blanco, a newspaper publisher, as presidential candidate in opposition to Calderón Guardia, who ran again as the PRN's presidential candidate in the 1948 elections. Ulate won the elections, but the government accused the opposition of fraud and annulled the election results. Figueres immediately led a revolt and was victorious in six weeks. Ulate and Figueres then signed a pact, agreeing to establish a junta headed by Figueres to rule for 18 months beginning May 8, 1948.

2. Figueres's First Administration under the Junta: 1948–1949

The junta held elections for a constitutional assembly and oversaw the drafting of a new constitution (enacted in 1949), which forged a new state and style of development. The constitution merged nineteenth-century liberal and socialist principles, sponsoring a predominantly market but planned economy, with a better distribution of wealth and within a democratic system. While the constitution endorsed enlarged roles for the central government and the public sector, it attempted to decentralize decision making by strengthening the Legislative Assembly, curtailing the authority of the president, establishing autonomous institutions, and creating the Supreme Electoral Tribunal to guarantee free and fair elections.

In the financial arena Figueres took a series of important measures: he levied a 10% across-the-board tax on private assets valued at more than 50,000 colones (about U.S.$10,000); negotiated with the banana-exporting United Fruit Company an agreement that imposed a 15% profit tax on it and increased property taxes; and nationalized (in June 1948) Costa Rica's banking system. The state banks not only would handle the current and savings accounts but also, according to government plans, would administer and direct public financial resources to agriculture, industry, and commerce. In line with the PSD's stand that development should be led by the state, the government was therefore able to allocate credit to those economic branches it sought to stimulate. Although the national banking system operated fairly independently from the Legislative Assembly, the executive branch maintained its influence through the appointment of members to the banking Board of Directors (Sojo 1984).

According to the constitution, the new autonomous institutions were to enjoy administrative, political, and financial autonomy so that the president had no power over the appointment of their directors and other personnel. These institutions laid the base for a state economic bureaucracy, crucial for the modernization of the Costa Rican economy and the expansion of a decentralized public sector. Two crucial autonomous institutions, established by the junta, are explained below.

Prior to the establishment of the junta, the Economic and Trade Ministry was in charge of setting and enforcing price ceilings for various products including milk, eggs, sugar, and meat. In 1949 the National Production Council (CNP) was established as a semi-autonomous regulatory agency (becoming fully autonomous in 1956) to stabilize agricultural prices in the domestic market, stimulate production through price subsidies, and act as intermediary between farmers and consumers. The CNP set minimum prices for agricultural products of popular consumption (such as rice, corn, beans, sorghum), guaranteed minimal profits to farmers and protected them from large oscillations in prices, and sought to block the rise of monopolies and oligopolies. To prevent price fluctuations caused by shortages or surpluses, the CNP built warehouses to store agricultural commodities and provide for orderly year-round marketing. The CNP also became the principal source of credit for farmers producing for the domestic market (Corrales 1984).

The Institute for the Defense of Coffee had been founded in 1933 by coffee producers, processors, and representatives of the state to counter the negative effects of the Great Depression on world coffee prices and production. Under the junta, the institute was converted into an autonomous institution, the National Coffee Office, whose principal function was to regulate the prices coffee processors paid to small producers. To secure energy sources for industrial development, the Costa Rican Electricity Institute (ICE) was established in 1949 and eventually absorbed various foreign-owned enterprises dealing in energy and telephone and telegraph services.

Figueres continued the incentives provided by the Law of New Industries of 1940, granting duty exemptions for the import of equipment for industries that produced a commodity using 75% of native raw materials. He also launched an extensive public works program and stimulated construction in housing, electrical plants, a cement factory, and a milk-processing facility. Figueres neither challenged nor changed Calderón's social reforms and increased salaries and wages for public employees and workers in sugar-cane and coffee plantations. He felt that such increases would foster demand, fuel economic growth (stimulate agricultural and industrial production), raise living standards, and enhance government revenues (Rovira 1988a).

Figueres and the educated members of the PSD (professionals, professors, students, intellectuals) considered education a cornerstone of democracy and social mobility. Consequently, major changes were introduced in the 1949 constitution to bolster Costa Rican education. Because there had been little centralization and unity throughout the education system, an effort was made to integrate the public system by creating the Superior Council of Education (to oversee public education) and incorporating secondary schools into the Ministry of Education (which previously administered only elementary education). Secondary education was instituted to complement compulsory primary education (making both levels free and state-financed). The state supplied food and clothing to poor students and organized an adult-education program to fight illiteracy. In addition, the University of Costa Rica was strengthened by guaranteeing its autonomy and adequate financing, and the Ministry of Education granted university scholarships for needy students (Waggoner and Waggoner 1971; Aguilar 1990).

In addition to laying the foundations for a new socioeconomic system in Costa Rica, the junta brought profound changes in the country's politics and balance of power. One of Figueres's first steps was to abolish the army. The oligarchy, particularly the coffee barons, wanted to regain political control and eliminate the socioeconomic reforms. Figueres, however, had no intention of restoring the oligarchies to power and abolishing Calderón's reforms. The nationalization of the banks and the tax on private assets were a blow to private bankers and merchants (particularly importers) who depended on bank loans. Credit would now be directed toward general development, favoring small as well as large producers and the diversification of the agricultural sector (reducing the hegemony of the coffee exporters). Figueres's reforms marked the political decline of the old oligarchy and granted new power to emerging social sectors: farmers, industrialists, and intellectuals of the middle class who began to enter the political arena. But the most prominent new social actors were the civil servants who directed the strategy to develop and modernize the private sector and the nation (Doryan 1990).

3. Ulate's Interregnum: 1949–1953

Based on the 1948 agreement, Figueres returned power to Otilio Ulate on November 8, 1949. Ulate's party (PUN) controlled 33 seats in the Legislative Assembly out of a total of 45, and hence it had a majority. Ulate was a conservative, and so he did not institute any far-reaching economic reforms, but he was successful in attaining his triple goal of stabilizing the economy, government finances, and the national currency (the colón) vis-à-vis the dollar. Increased world prices for coffee and bananas helped to expand exports, trade, and economic growth, making it easier for Ulate to reschedule debt payments with external creditors. Fiscal income heavily depended on indirect taxes, in particular import and consumer taxes; hence the economic expansion led to an increase in government revenue (in spite of which public expenditures were reduced). The budgetary deficits of 1940–48 turned into surpluses, and by 1950 the nation's financial situation was basically sound. Still, most Costa Ricans remained poor, but Ulate did not take any measures to improve them. He did not attempt, however, to alter the social welfare programs of Calderón and Figueres because of wide popular support for those programs (Rovira 1988a).

The Central Bank was founded in 1950 as a logical culmination to Figueres's nationalization of the banking system; this bank, whose director is appointed by the president, fixes interest rates for other national banks, decides on the allocation of public investments, administers foreign reserves, and determines the exchange rate. A sound financial situation and favorable coffee prices allowed Ulate to proceed with a few construction projects, such as a larger airport, a dam, and a power plant. The Ministry of Agriculture introduced measures to raise coffee output in response to the dramatic increase in world prices for it.

The growing value of exports fueled a domestic demand for imports and foreign exchange. Ulate was committed to a strong currency and was opposed to devaluation; thus he favored importers and the traditional economic elite and designed other methods to stabilize the colón and bolster its internal purchasing power. To dampen the demand for imports, in 1950 the Legislative Assembly passed the Law of Control of Transactions. Foreign exchange surcharges, which enhanced government finances, were established for the sale of dollars according to import categories; in 1951 the surcharges were replaced with increased customs tariffs. Continuously growing export earnings and foreign reserves permitted a relaxation of import controls. A 1952 Law for the Import of Capital Goods extended credit to enterprises for importing capital goods in order to expand domestic production. (This law did not succeed at first because of lack of interest from many businessmen but later became more effective and industry-oriented with the help of World Bank resources during the administrations of Figueres and Echandi.) The 1952 Law of Free Foreign Exchange for Exports stimulated some enterprises that produced for export, particularly nontraditional products (e.g., furniture, tomatoes, canned tuna). Part of the dollars earned from exports could be converted in colones at a higher free exchange rate. During Ulate's term, the official exchange rate of 5.60 colones per dollar was maintained, and the free-market exchange rate fell from 8.72 in 1950 to 6.65 in 1953. In view of the instability created by World War II, the Central Bank maintained a fixed official exchange rate (to protect the colón's external value) for the next three decades, with a few devaluations (Rovira 1988a).

4. Figueres's Second Administration: 1953–1958

In 1951 the National Liberation Party (PLN) was founded on the ideological legacy of the Social Democratic Party and the policies of the Figueres junta: representative democracy, a mixed economy (predominantly market but with government guidance), and a welfare state. The PLN (which continuously dominated the Legislative Assembly for 25 years) was responsible for extending the role of government and the public sector until the end of the 1970s. Because of the varying backgrounds of its founders, with different views on the degrees of state-directed capitalist development, the PLN has often lacked ideological unity. In the long run, the party has evolved with the exercise of political power and has shown considerable pragmatism (Ameringer 1982).

Figueres was chosen as the PLN's candidate for the presidential elections in 1953, which he won by a landslide, beating Ulate's PUN candidate, and the PLN obtained a majority of 30 out of 45 seats in the Legislative Assembly. Figueres's main concerns in his second administration were to increase the country's purchasing power to bolster domestic demand, establish and stimulate nontraditional productive sectors to respond to such demand, and raise taxes to finance state-supported economic and social programs. Figueres's administration was a controversial one: supporters claim that his presidency strengthened the foundation for a new order in Costa Rica, while critics charge that his expensive policies brought inflation and economic instability (Bird 1984; Rovira 1988a).

The Costa Rican economy enjoyed rapid economic growth under the Ulate and Figueres administrations largely based on the expansion of traditional exports stimulated by high coffee prices. Figueres further stimulated the economy with his ambitious public works program for the construction of roads, highways, and bridges to integrate the country. The Costa Rican Electrical Institute (ICE) received a great impetus, and the first state hydroelectric plant was inaugurated in 1958. Internal demand was bolstered through expansion of employment and an increase in salaries.

Figueres raised the share of profits that the United Fruit Company paid to the state from 15% to 35%. He also increased the general income tax, hence affecting enterprises with major profits such as the coffee industry, which had benefited from higher world prices. Still, indirect taxes, particularly import taxes, continued to generate the bulk of government revenue, an average of 48% between 1946 and 1958 versus 13% from direct taxes. In the mid-1950s the value of exports declined (as a result of bad coffee harvests due to flooding) as did economic growth and fiscal revenue, hence worsening the budget deficit. To maintain internal demand growth, Figueres tried to expand domestic credit. But, despite government pressure, the Central Bank refused to continue financing the fiscal deficit and pursued a restrictive monetary policy to counter inflation (Bird 1984; Rovira 1988a; Céspedes et al. 1990).

Costa Rica was still an agro-exporting country, its economy highly dependent on the exports of coffee and bananas, which in 1951 accounted for 89% of the value of total exports. Coffee prices in the world market were high during Figueres's second administration, 1953–57 (U.S.$1.48 per kg in 1956 compared to U.S.$0.66 in 1949); thus the government stimulated production through national bank credit for coffee growers. These loans were used for fertilizers, planting better coffee varieties, and developing new cultivation and processing techniques. Another target of Figueres's was agricultural diversification. Attention was given to the production of basic grains for internal consumption (rice, beans, corn), milk and meat, sugarcane, cotton, and fishing. Banking credit was increased to cattle ranching and other import-substitution incentives provided to key agricultural products such as rice, corn, and beans.

Industry grew, but it was still small: less than 11% of the economically active population worked in the industrial sector in 1951 while 55% worked in agriculture. Costa Rica therefore had to import many manufactured and capital goods, as well as some raw materials and foodstuffs. While not dismissing foreign investment, Figueres wanted to promote national industries that would utilize domestic raw materials, create new jobs, and replace imports or generate exports. Therefore the government provided credit to those industries, and in 1954 new custom tariffs granted low duties to raw-material and fixed-capital-goods imports and imposed higher levies on imported products that competed with national industries. With the desire to further stimulate industry, Costa Rica took part in the talks that began in 1951 sponsored by the UN Economic Commission for Latin America (ECLAC) on the economic integration of Central America. Still, the effort to promote the industrial sector was smaller than that to promote the agricultural sector, in part because of favorable economic conditions for agriculture such as high coffee prices (Rovira 1988a; Doryan 1990).

In 1954 the National Institute of Housing and Urban Affairs (INVU) was founded as an autonomous institution to continue and expand the program of public housing initiated in the 1940s. INVU was charged with the formulation and execution of national housing programs, regulation of low-cost construction projects, and assistance to housing built by cooperatives and nonprofit institutions. INVU also contributed to creating jobs and giving impetus to construction firms. In 1955 the Ministry of Labor and Social Security was established to offer services for unemployment, family allowances, alcoholism, and national emergencies. Reflecting the PLN's notion of education as a door toward upward social mobility, income distribution, and democracy, Figueres also increased expenditures to expand the public school system. He raised the minimum wage and overall salaries and created new jobs through the growth of the public and private sectors. Finally he successfully renegotiated the contract with the United Fruit Company to raise their workers' wages and transfer (free of charge) all its housing projects, schools, and medical facilities to the government (Pascua and Valverde 1987).

3

Consolidation, Expansion, and Crisis of the Model

1958–1982

This stage is divided into two substages. The first (1958–70) deals with the implementation of the ISI model and agricultural diversification under Echandi, Orlich, and Trejos. A major catalyst for these policies was Costa Rica's entry into the Central American Common Market. In the second substage (1970–82) there was an increase in state intervention in the economy (the "state entrepreneur") and social matters under Figueres and Oduber, with a brief neoconservative challenge by Carazo. The policy analysis will be done by topic (e.g., ownership) within each substage, explaining the various measures taken by successive administrations; the evaluation of performance will similarly be done by substage instead of by administration.

1. Industrial and Agricultural Diversification: 1958–1970

There were three administrations during this substage. In only one did the PLN control the presidency, but it steadily dominated the legislative branch. The opposition parties, therefore, faced severe limitations to enacting the laws they wanted, as the Legislative Assembly is the strongest branch of the Costa Rican government: it makes and repeals all laws. Also, the 1949 constitution had considerably weakened the presidency, particularly through the creation of autonomous institutions.

The constitutional prohibition of reelection, the absence of PLN leaders of Figueres's stature, and some economic problems (inflation and slowdown in growth) contributed to the defeat of the PLN candidate in the 1958 election. The PUN candidate (supported by Ulate) was Mario Echandi Jiménez, a representative of the old agro-exporting elite; he was elected president, but the PLN kept 20 seats in the Legislative Assembly (versus the PUN's 10, out of 45 seats) and maintained considerable influence in the autonomous institutions. In the next election, Francisco José Orlich, a prominent PLN leader and strong ally of Figueres, was elected and took power in 1962; furthermore, the PLN won a majority of 29 seats in the Legislative Assembly against 9 by the PUN, and the total number of seats in the Legislative Assembly was increased from 45 to 57. Driven by their opposition to the PLN, Calderón's party (PRN) and Ulate's party (PUN) joined forces in 1965 to form the National Unification Party (PufN), but there were differences between the two parties in the coalition: the PRN espoused an extensive social agenda while the PUfN represented the conservative interests of the agro-exporting upper class (because of its dependence on its leader, the PUfN would disappear after Ulate died in 1973). José Joaquín Trejos Fernández, the coalition candidate, won the election and became president in 1966; the coalition, nevertheless, would disintegrate after losing the next two elections. Again, the PLN continued to hold a majority in the Legislative Assembly (29 out of 57 seats, versus 26 by the PufN) and thus was able to block Trejos's reversing prior key policies (Rovira 1988a).

A. Policies

i. Ownership

In 1961 the Legislative Assembly approved the Land and Colonization Law and, in 1962, established the Land and Colonization Institute (ITCO) as an autonomous agency to enforce and administer the law. Its purposes were to improve the distribution of farmland, increase agricultural productivity, mediate in land disputes, and improve farmers' living standards. The law specified the conditions and priorities under which private land might be expropriated, as well as compensation. The ITCO first focused on colonization schemes, designed to settle a substantial number of peasants on virgin lands owned by the state (not on privately owned land); by 1968 a total of 11 colonization projects were initiated, benefiting 1,222 peasants. The ITCO provided land titles and other ownership guarantees to the settled families and promoted the development of cooperatives among them. These programs helped reduce tensions in the agricultural sector and stimulate production of some agricultural products for the internal market (beans, corn) as well as some export products (bananas). However, the ITCO was forced to abandon its colonization program in 1968 because of financial difficulties (and inaccessible locations) and spent 1967–69 concentrating on the solution of squatter conflicts that had emerged on public and private lands (IDB 1968; Seligson 1977; Fernández 1988; Rovira 1988a).

ii. Planning and Financing

Two new public institutions were created by Echandi in 1960–61: the Ministry of Industries (mandated by the Industrial Protection and Development Law of 1959 mainly through the PLN leadership) and the semi-autonomous National Service of Aqueducts and Sewers (SNAA) (Rovira 1988a; see also section iii below). Orlich, in line with the PLN philosophy, did expand the state sector with the establishment of three new institutions in 1963: (1) the Board of Port Administration and Economic Development of the Atlantic Region (JAPDEVA) to promote development in the most underdeveloped region of Costa Rica, playing an intermediary role for the injection of financial resources into the region and modernization of the port facilities at Limón; (2) the Costa Rican Petroleum Refinery (RECOPE) as the only oil refinery in the country (85% private and 15% public), empowered with exclusive rights to import, refine, and distribute oil; and (3) the National Planning Office (OFIPLAN).

OFIPLAN was the most important institution created by Orlich; its director was appointed by him and subordinated to the presidency. Its functions were to collect and systematize information and to elaborate national strategies and plans (annual, medium, and long term) for socioeconomic development. The first four-year plan (1965–68) set two investment priorities: economic infrastructure (transport, energy, and telecommunications), which received 58% of total investment, and social services (education, housing, and health), which were allocated 37% of the funds. The plan's target was an annual GDP growth rate of 6.5%, based on promotion of traditional exports, accelerated industrialization, and agricultural expansion, as well as improved income distribution and a better regional and urban-rural balance. The second four-year plan (1969–72, elaborated by OFIPLAN under Trejos, but whose major impact would occur under Figueres) called for a rapid expansion of public investment with a continued focus on industrial development; a higher priority was assigned to economic infrastructure (62% of total investment) than social services (31%) (ECLAC 1964a; IDB 1968, 1969; Aguilar et al. 1987; Fernández 1988).

To counter adverse economic conditions during Echandi's administration (resulting from a decrease in coffee prices and banana exports), the Legislative Assembly enacted the Law of Economic Promotion, a key cornerstone of Echandi's policies to strengthen the traditional agricultural sector, particularly coffee (and, hence, the traditional agricultural elite), as well as industries facing difficulties. The law provided financial aid as follows: deferred payments for coffee firms, bank credits to the rural sector (partly to promote the establishment of agricultural cooperatives) and to "family industries," and bank loans to agricultural and industrial debtors in financial trouble. Echandi also resorted to external financing to circumvent the fiscal restrictions imposed by the Central Bank, mostly to protect the agricultural sector from the impact of external fluctuations (Rovira 1988a; Céspedes et al. 1990). Under Orlich, public expenditures in general administration, infrastructure, and social services grew 29% in 1963–66 to meet the targets of investment plans. In addition, banks increased credits for the private sector, particularly agriculture and industry, which fueled an increased demand for foreign exchange, worsened the balance of payments deficit, and depleted international reserves (ECLAC 1966a).

iii. Stability and Prices

Financial difficulties mounted as the current account surplus for the public sector fell, affecting central government finance. Orlich's expansionary policies caused budgetary deficits for the central government and autonomous institutions, making necessary a stabilization policy to control public expenditures and demand. Orlich sought alternate sources of fiscal income, including a sales tax passed in 1964 to help pay for the fiscal needs of industrialization, administrative improvements in collecting income taxes, and a 1966 law allowing an annual issuance of bonds by the executive branch to help finance public investment (Rovira 1988a).

The Trejos administration inherited disequilibria in the state budget and the balance of payments, as well as a depletion of international reserves. An economic conservative, Trejos opposed the growth of the state unless necessary and (like Ulate) set as his priority a balanced fiscal budget, emphasizing austerity in the public sector through reductions in public investment, credit, public works, and imports. In pursuit of those goals, the Central Bank limited the use of foreign reserves for imports, increased the rediscount rate, set ceilings on bank loans, and kept cash reserves high, all of which restricted both the money in circulation and total means of payment. In 1967 a temporary income tax, land tax surcharges, and a general 5% sales tax were imposed, both to dampen demand for imports of consumer goods and to recover lost fiscal income due to the duty exemptions granted by previous administrations. Despite these measures, government expenditures kept a steady upward trend. A revival of public investment in 1969 and a greater flow of private investment contributed to increase capital formation (offsetting previous investment cutbacks). Most investment projects were financed with external funds, such as highways, the Limón dock, a drinking-water supply system for the San José metropolitan area, and hydroelectric projects. However, bank credit for personal use and for consumption purposes was restricted in 1969 to cut imports and household expenditures and lessen the deterioration in the balance of payments (ECLAC 1966a, 1968a, 1969a).

iv. Development Strategy

The three administrations in this substage continued to target agriculture as the cornerstone of their development strategy; hence public and private investment in and national-banking credit to this sector continued to expand. Echandi joined the Legislative Assembly to pass the Law of Economic Promotion directed toward traditional agriculture and industry. Orlich acted to protect, modernize, and raise yields of the coffee sector, continuing Figueres's policy of improving the coffee farms by planting better varieties and stimulating the use of fertilizers. He also provided technical and credit assistance to those producers harmed by the Irazu Volcano eruptions in 1963–64. Orlich also fostered the organization of coffee cooperatives and the establishment of the Federation of Coffee Cooperatives in 1962, which led to a further decline in the economic power of the agro-exporting group. Finally, in 1962 Costa Rica was a signatory to the International Coffee Agreement between producing and consumer countries to avoid excessive fluctuations in the world price of that product (Rovira 1988a).

Until 1956 the Banana Company of Costa Rica, a subsidiary of the United Fruit Company, had absolute control over foreign production; thereafter three other foreign corporations began operations in the Atlantic region: the Standard Fruit Company in 1956, and the Banana Development Company (BANDECO) and the Banana Company of the Atlantic (COBAL) in 1965. The 1965–68 plan placed a high priority on an increase in banana production by national growers; under Orlich, the national banking system granted more than U.S.$9 million credit to domestic producers. The PLN policies fostered new plantations of disease-resistant species, adoption of up-to-date marketing, and a three-year program (launched in 1967) to expand the area sowed. Finally, banana companies began to offer guaranteed prices to independent producers. These changes led to a dramatic rise in the production and export of bananas, and national growers began to play a more significant role, soon reaching an area sowed similar to that of foreign corporations (ECLAC 1969a; Rovira 1988a).

The Agro-Industrial Sugar Cane League (LAICA) was established by the government in 1965, combining its own interests with those of the sugar growers and industry. National-bank credit was directed to the promotion of sugar, livestock, cotton, and tropical fruits; the 1965–68 plan gave high priority to all of these activities, using World Bank credit. The government also promoted a vigorous expansion of production of rice, beans, corn, sorghum, and sesame to help the country become self-sufficient in basic foodstuffs.

The PLN had been discussing an industrialization strategy since its inception: a draft of an industrial law was elaborated during Figueres's first administration. The endorsed ISI strategy was based on state stimuli and protection to national industry, facilitating the necessary imports of equipment and inputs (under low or no tariffs), and banning or imposing high tariffs on imports of manufactured goods that competed with domestic production. The logic of ISI was that, as industrialization advanced, the nation would be able to cut industrial imports, become more self-sufficient (less vulnerable to external influence), integrate the various stages of industrial production, improve the terms of trade, increase the value added, stimulate production of domestic raw materials, provide new jobs, foster economic growth, and improve income distribution and living standards. The implementation of the ISI strategy was postponed because of high coffee and banana prices in the world market during most of the 1950s, but these conditions changed at the end of that decade: coffee prices dropped, and Guatemala and El Salvador began an active process of industrialization. In 1958 several members of the PLN (which controlled the Assembly) reactivated their efforts for an industrialization strategy based on the use of local raw materials. The Chamber of Industries, nevertheless, supported a less nationalistic project that—with Echandi's cooperation—resulted in the enactment of the Industrial Protection and Development Law in 1959.

This law marked a new period for industrialization in Costa Rica because it was the first law to significantly stimulate investment in that sector, and a key component of the PLN's strategy to diversify production. ISI protectionist policies tripled the customs tariff on manufactures competitive with domestic production; exempted duties by 99% on imports of industrial machinery and equipment, as well as raw materials necessary for production and exports; granted partial exemptions on property and municipal taxes, as well as a 100% exemption in taxes over invested capital and profits for an initial period, followed by a 50% exemption after that period; exempted export and income taxes on reinvested profits; exempted manufactured exports from tax and custom duties; and provided lines of credit for domestic industry and exporting of manufactures. The newly created Ministry of Industry (1960) was put in charge of the industrialization strategy (Fernández 1988; Rovira 1988a).

Significant impetus to industrialization was given by Costa Rica's entry into the Central American Common Market (CACM) in 1962. This organization provided income tax exemptions and deductions for certain types of capital expenditures. Exemptions from custom duties varied from 50% to 100% and were granted for 3 to 10 years depending on the classification of the industries (existing or new) and into which categories they fell, for example, producers of industrial raw materials, capital goods, or consumer goods (Andic 1983; Rovira 1988a).

The development strategy also sponsored an ambitious public-works program under the three administrations but particularly under Orlich's, when the Ministry of Public Works and Transportation completed an ambitious road plan. The development and modernization of the infrastructure (e.g., roads and transportation) was a pillar of the industrialization strategy.

v. External Sector

In contrast to Figueres's support of regional economic integration, Echandi had a negative attitude concerning Costa Rica's joining CACM, whose purpose was to increase the size of national markets and assure the free movement of goods among its members. Although Echandi continued to participate in the talks overseen by ECLAC on that issue, in 1960 he refused to sign the General Treaty of Central American Economic Integration. There was much pressure from the agrarian and importing elites, who felt that the integration process might reduce their power and harm their interests through the emergence of new elites in other sectors. As soon as he took office in 1962, Orlich officially announced his willingness to abide by the General Treaty, and Costa Rica began to participate as a full member in 1963. The Common Market Agreement established a free-trade area in Central America with Common External Tariffs (CET) for the rest of the world, consisting of ad valorem and specific duties. CACM countries were also exempted from duties on imports of raw materials, intermediate inputs, and capital goods coming from outside the region. I have also mentioned other income tax exemptions and deductions for certain types of capital expenditures (Andic 1983).

The implementation of ISI policies and entry into CACM resulted in an expansion of Costa Rican foreign trade as well as in a worsening of its balance of payments because of an increase in the demand for foreign exchange and imports (as well as the foreign debt) coupled with a decline in world prices of coffee (1961–62 and 1966–68) and bananas (1964–71). Corrective measures included restrictions on the use of foreign reserves for imports, taxation of certain imports, and attempts to stabilize coffee prices in the world market. Exchange-rate policies diverged according to changes in the administration.

The General Plan for Economic Equilibrium elaborated by Echandi in

1961 sought to combat a decline in GDP that year by targeting the external sector. While Costa Rica experimented with a multiple exchange rate in 1960–61, in 1961 the colón was devalued from its official exchange rate of 5.615 colones/U.S.$1 to a 6.625 rate, equal to the free-market rate; hence both rates were unified (see Table IV.3). The plan also increased customs duties on luxury imports, created export taxes for some items, increased these taxes for other items, and repealed the Law of Free Foreign Exchange for Exports of 1952. Trejos resisted pressure to devalue the colón, and in December 1966 the country returned to exchange surcharges (which were revoked in 1969). A dual foreign exchange system was introduced from mid-1967 to 1969, also aimed at cutting imports of consumer goods. The fixed official exchange rate (6.625 colones/U.S.$1) was used for imports of Central American goods, while a higher, "free" exchange rate was applied for imports from the rest of the world, except for essential commodities. Until 1969 a few enterprises were allowed to sell on the free market some of the foreign exchange generated by their exports (Table IV.3; Fernández 1988; Rovira 1988a).

vi. Labor and Employment

A key labor policy was the fixing of minimum wages, through different systems for the private sector (except for workers in banana companies) and the public sector. The National Wage Council was responsible for settling minimum wages (every two years) for each branch of economic activity in the private sector. The Council was composed of nine members with equal representation from the state, employers and workers. Minimum wages were expected to insure for the worker and his family adequate food, housing, clothing, children education, and any other basic needs for families with the lowest purchasing power. The capacity to pay such wages in various economic branches was taken into account and their profit-making ability safeguarded. Wages in the public sector were set based on seniority and increases in the price index—if it rose at least 4% annually (ECLAC 1974a).

High economic growth enjoyed under the three administrations of this substage allowed for steady increases in wages, while the expansion of agriculture, industry and the public sector provided many new jobs. In 1968–69, demands for salary increases by civil servants were granted: the huge increase in expenditures on public education in 1968–69 was due, almost entirely, to higher salaries for primary school teachers (ECLAC 1969a).

vii. Distribution and Social Services

Neither Echandi nor Trejos attempted to reverse the social policies of the PLN governments, and public expenditures in social services continued to grow strongly, especially under Orlich, who strengthened the welfare state. There was an increase in planning in social services (the establishment of INA and ITCO). In the 1960s the Organization of American States and the UN Children's Fund (UNICEF) sent technical experts to advise Costa Rica on the development of social services; the latter also helped in establishing community centers and in offering scholarships to social workers and students (Pascua and Valverde 1987).

A constitutional amendment was approved in 1961 mandating the universalization of social security coverage (in both health and pensions) within a decade. Thereafter the CCSS gradually extended its coverage to most industrial, commercial, and construction workers, as well as to dependents of the insured, but it raised salary ceilings for inclusion, thus preventing the incorporation of middle- and high-income salaried employees. In 1963 the Office of Social Welfare was established under the Ministry of Labor to provide more family services (such as day care for working mothers and family subsidies) and to design programs to improve living standards in communities (Mesa-Lago 1985; Pascua and Valverde 1987).

In 1961 the government launched an adult education program to combat illiteracy as well as an educational reform to reorganize and improve this sector, further define and diversify the curriculum (to better accommodate the students' interests), and improve the range and quality of education. The Office for Educational Planning was established in 1964, under the Ministry of Public Education of OFIPLAN; its principal task was to organize and analyze pertinent data and to conduct studies for educational planning and development. In 1965 the National Institute for Training (INA) was established as an autonomous institution to train apprentices and workers required by the industrialization process. The INA's major source of revenue was a 1% payroll tax paid by the employers, thus charging them for the training cost of the labor they would eventually require (González 1987; Pascua and Valverde 1987; Rovira 1988a; Aguilar 1990).

The Trejos administration developed an ambitious public-housing program for which expenditures increased greatly; a sales tax generated much of the income needed for the INVU's housing program.

B. Performance

i. Growth

Annual real GDP growth in 1961–70 averaged an impressive 6.1% during the stage but only 2.7 per capita because of Costa Rica's extremely high population growth rate—an annual average of 3.4% in the substage. The leading sector in growth was industry. Gross fixed capital formation averaged 17.7% in the stage, increasing from 16.1% to 19.5% between 1960 and 1970 (Table IV.3).

The Echandi administration faced most difficulties (GDP fell 0.8% in 1961 or 4.6% per capita, while the industrial product declined 5.2%; see Tables IV.3, IV.6), mainly because of a decline of prices for traditional exports. International coffee prices declined from U.S.$0.67 per pound in 1956 to U.S.$0.33 in 1963; prices of cacao and bananas also decreased, and the value of exports stagnated during his administration (Table IV.10). The value of coffee exports fell 21% from U.S.$50.5 million to U.S.$40 million in 1958–59, while banana exports dropped 28% in value from U.S.$26.5 million to U.S.$19.1 million (these exports recovered somewhat in 1960–61). The ensuing drop in international reserves and the growth in imports combined with a decline in export value aggravated the trade deficit (there was a growing fiscal deficit also) despite substantial loans granted by the United States and the Export Import Bank. Only exports of beef and nontraditional exports experienced steady growth due to favorable prices and the Law of Free Foreign Exchange for Exports (Céspedes et al. 1990; Doryan 1990).

Echandi's Law of Economic Promotion helped improve somewhat the economic situation in the agricultural sector through expanded credit, but critics charged that the law's impact was insignificant for industrial development and diversification of production. Also, in 1960 the rapid expansion of internal credit brought the first devaluation of the colón. The 1961 General Plan for Economic Equilibrium was also implemented to counter the economic downturn, but the plan led to a general rise in the cost of living, which particularly affected workers. However, these measures did increase economic growth (the GDP rate in 1962 was 8.1%) and bolster the traditional exporting sector (such as coffee) while penalizing the importers, which saw their gains drop as demand for imports fell by 3% in 1961 (Rovira 1988a; Table IV.3).

The Orlich and Trejos administrations were marked by dynamic economic growth, fueled by high public spending, a strong flow of private investment into agriculture and industry, and an increase in exports. The average annual GDP growth rate between 1963 and 1970 was a robust 6.7% (3.5% per capita), amply surpassing the average annual population growth rate of 3.2%, one of the highest in Latin America (Table IV.3). Economic expansion during the 1960s was in large part based on exports and trade with CACM. This buoyancy of external demand was the main force behind the rise in income and employment levels, along with the increase in public and private investment in industrialization and the banana sector (Céspedes et al. 1990).

Gross fixed capital formation averaged an impressive 17.7% between

1960 and 1970, and there were no significant differences in the averages of the three administrations (Table IV.3). Under Trejos, restrictive policies impeded a fulfillment of the targets of the 1965–68 plan, although they were too high to begin with. Thus, public investment fell short of the target set forth by the plan, in part because of the government's strained fiscal conditions and, to a lesser degree, because of the limits placed on construction by existing technical and administrative capacities (ECLAC 1966a).

ii. Inflation

The annual rate of inflation between 1961 and 1970 averaged 2.3%, low by Latin American levels. The rate increased from 2.4% in 1961 to 4.7% in 1970 but fluctuated significantly: it increased in 1961–64, decreased in 1965–67, and rose in 1968–70 (Table IV.3).

Essential data are missing for part of the Echandi administration to attempt an evaluation of its performance in this area. Orlich basically continued the PLN policies established by the Figueres junta and his first administration of promoting economic growth through increased public expenditures and a less restrained monetary policy. Orlich faced three adverse economic conditions: declining world market prices of coffee in 1962–63 and bananas in 1963–66, although coffee prices increased in 1964–65 (Table IV.10); the 1963–64 eruptions of the Irazu volcano, which seriously harmed the coffee crops (coffee output fell 13% in 1964; Table IV.5) and reduced overall agricultural production; and the fiscal debts of the past two administrations (Figueres's liberal spending and Echandi's easy credit to counter the sharp drop in coffee prices). On the positive side, there were major inflows of foreign capital (primarily from the United States) into the industrial sector, and loans from the Alliance for Progress (these capital inflows were prompted by Costa Rica's entry into CACM and the ensuing development of industrialization and markets) (Rovira 1988a).

The Orlich administration was the first to have a substantial external debt, not only to sustain public investment but also to finance the budget deficit of the central government, which was 4% of GDP in 1966. The rapid extension of domestic credit for the public sector during his administration led not only to a cut in credit for the private sector (the share of net credit to the private sector from the national banking system declined from 88% to 83% in 1963–66; BCCR 1986) but also to a decrease in international reserves. Orlich did attempt to control public expenditures and increase government revenue (the consumption tax), but salary raises for public employees and subsidies to autonomous agencies offset those measures. Inflation, therefore, increased from 2.7% to 3.3% in 1962–64 but was reduced to virtually zero in the following year (Céspedes et al. 1990).

The disequilibria in the state budget and the balance of payments were the prime concern in Trejos's economic policy, which endorsed austerity to reduce the growth rate of the public sector. Confronting a PLN-controlled Legislative Assembly, Trejos managed to avoid implementing all public expenditures authorized by the budget, and he had some success in increasing fiscal revenue and savings. The budget deficit declined from 4.7% to 1.6% of GDP in 1967–70 (Table IV.3). Inflation, however, rose from 0.2% to 4.1% in 1966–68. The inflexibility of government expenditures was compounded by greater costs of social services (health, social security, etc.), as well as public utility rates kept by autonomous institutions below real costs, hence making it difficult for Trejos to restrict public expenditures, even when faced with the financial crisis. The inflation rate was cut to 2.6% in 1969 by means of restricted monetary circulation (ECLAC 1966a, 1969a; IDB 1968; BCCR 1986).

Another factor that complicated matters was the change in the tax structure of the government. Because of the economic integration and industrialization processes, import duties, the largest single source of revenue, declined because of tax exemptions for needed imports granted under the Industrial Protection and Development Law and lower customs tariffs for CACM. The decline in the share of taxes on foreign trade limited the chances of tapping resources to meet growing economic and social needs. Overall, the inelasticity of the tax system hindered the generation of tax revenue sufficient to cover current government expenditures. Attempts to improve the taxation system did make it possible for the public sector to increase its activities in line with economic growth. By the end of the 1960s, revenue from sales taxes increased, as did revenue from certain direct taxes, especially those on the profits of banana companies. Tax revenue also increased because of the expansion of national income, a greater degree of administrative control, and the issue of more government bonds in 1968–69. The improved situation helped to reduce inflation in 1969 (ECLAC 1969a).

The national debt grew rapidly, and the interest payable on it was beginning to be a heavy burden on the government's resources. Toward the end of his administration, Trejos had moderate success in decreasing the portion of government expenditures covered by external funds through the issue of more government bonds (ECLAC 1969a; Table IV.13).

Macroeconomic management before the 1970s was relatively simple. Confronting an external disturbance, the government resorted to increases in internal and external indebtedness. Although public revenue rose, it did not keep pace with rising public expenditures, and there were continuing government deficits. The compensatory financing meant that public investment came to depend increasingly on external financial resources. Ample access to external credit temporarily relieved the shortage of funds for public-sector programs and facilitated the adjustment of the balance of payments when international prices or exports fell, without provoking an excessive reduction in employment and consumption. As soon as inflationary pressures and balance-of-payment problems became evident, the authorities would reverse their policies, and the Central Bank would restrict credit and the money supply. With these simple instruments and the objective of keeping a fixed exchange rate, the authorities were successful in maintaining relative economic stability, despite external disturbances. However, the result was a sharp rise in total debt servicing and more strains on the balance of payments (Céspedes et al. 1990).

iii. Diversification

The share of the industrial sector in GDP increased significantly between 1960 and 1970, while the shares of construction and transportation-communications were almost stagnant, the share of agriculture declined slightly, and the shares of commerce, finance, and other services decreased (Table IV.4).

The performance of the autonomous institutions was a mixed one. While they helped achieve economic and social goals in nonpolitical ways, at times their autonomy hampered their effectiveness by minimizing their accountability and coordination. Rovira (1988a) claims that OFIPLAN's authority was limited by its inability to obligate the different autonomous institutions and public enterprises to comply with its directions, and thus planning was not fully effective. Also, the CNP's subsidized prices aided agriculture but benefited the large producers more than the peasants. Eventually the CNP became an agro-business in its own right, participating in the market by buying and selling agricultural products, to the dismay of the private sector (Ameringer 1982).

The aforementioned programs to stimulate agricultural production, especially in regard to such export products as coffee and bananas, were successful throughout the 1960s despite lower world coffee prices in the early 1960s and banana prices in the second half of the decade. The production of certain crops for domestic consumption and for export, such as coffee, were affected by the Irazu eruptions of 1963–64 and the resulting floods. However, agricultural production recovered in 1965, and coffee production expanded from 57 million kilograms in 1965 to 81 million kilograms in 1970. Fueled by the government programs and foreign investment, banana production soared from 348 million kilograms in 1960 to 959 million kilograms in 1970. Production of beef and sugarcane also increased (70% and 115%, respectively) as a result of special government programs to foster their development. The policies of the CNP (e.g., support prices) also helped to increase production of rice and corn, but bean output declined (Table IV.5). The agricultural sector expanded an annual average of 5.2% between 1960 and

1964 and 7.7% between 1965 and 1969 (BCCR 1986; ECLAC 1980b), but still below the economic growth rate; hence the agricultural share of GDP decreased slightly from 25.2% to 24.1% between 1960 and 1970 because of the phenomenal development of industry. The agricultural sector became considerably more diversified, as the coffee share in total output decreased and those of other products such as bananas, sugar, and beef expanded.

The most important development in the 1960s regarding Costa Rica's economy was the growth of the industrial sector. With increased credit resources plus Costa Rica's entry into CACM and the resulting market expansion for Costa Rican manufactures, investment increased much faster in industry than in any other sector as well as GDP. Existing industries were expanded, and plants of new industrial branches were established. The industrial sector grew at an annual rate of 6.3% between 1960 and 1964 and 11.5% between 1965 and 1969, and increased its share of GDP from 15.1% in 1960 to 20.5% in 1970 (Table IV.4; BCCR 1986; ECLAC 1980b).

Industrial growth was accompanied by a change in the structure of industrial production as traditional industries (foodstuffs, beverages, shoes, and other leather products) became less important in relation to the production of intermediate and finished goods, such as fertilizers, cattle fodder, vegetable extracts, chemicals (e.g., insecticides and ammonia), petroleum derivatives, rubber products (e.g., tires and inner tubes), nonmetallic minerals, rolled iron products, clothing, textiles, cement, pharmaceutical products, batteries, machinery, and electrical appliances. Still, much of the industry was producing consumer goods that required simple skills and relatively little sophisticated technology to manufacture (ECLAC 1966a, 1969a; Franco and León 1984).

While there is no doubt that the import-substitution policies of the Industrial Protection and Development Law of 1959 and CACM helped stimulate significant economic growth, they ironically stimulated imports and also laid the foundations for inefficient industries that were heavily dependent on imported inputs and that needed to be protected in order to stay competitive. There was also initial reluctance in Costa Rica on entering CACM because of fears that the costs and benefits of economic integration would not be shared equally, as Costa Rica would have to subsidize its industry and be inundated by cheap consumer products from its neighbors. Some also claimed that higher wages and social programs placed Costa Rica at a disadvantage with the other countries, where wages and social overhead were low (Ameringer 1982).

Another factor that stimulated industrial growth was the increasing inflow of foreign capital. Industry particularly required domestic public funds to create the technical and social conditions needed for investment (e.g., infrastructure), but additional resources for the development of economic infrastructure were obtained from the economic integration fund established with contributions from the U.S. government and the Central American countries. This increased supply of funds made it possible to finance the imports of raw materials and of intermediate and capital goods needed for industrial development. Although the PLN beginning with the second Figueres administration was cautious on external investment, the 1960s saw the emergence of many economic institutions, including the Alliance for Progress, which led to an inflow of U.S. capital into Costa Rica and particularly in the industrial sector (whereas before most of foreign investment had been in agriculture, especially bananas). It has been calculated that between 1960 and 1970, domestic investment in industry was U.S.$218 million, while investment by multinational corporations reached U.S.$281 million (ECLAC 1965a; Franco and León 1984).

iv. Trade Balance and External Dependency

Economic expansion was also tied to the expansion in Costa Rica's trade, expansion related to increased exports of traditional products such as coffee and bananas as well as manufactures. Table IV.7 shows Costa Rica's tremendous growth in foreign trade after joining CACM. Between 1964 and 1970, Costa Rica's exports grew at an annual average rate of 13.9%. However, imports also expanded in the same period at the annual average growth rate of 14.8% as incentives were introduced to encourage the import of necessary inputs for the industrialization process (a corresponding increased demand for foreign exchange maintained pressure on the international reserves). Costa Rica's growth in trade after 1963 also brought an increase in the country's dependency on trade. The share of trade transactions in current prices as a percentage of GDP was 47% in 1960 and rose to 62% in 1970; it is not available at constant prices (Table IV.7). As trade with the rest of Central America expanded, the U.S. share in Costa Rican trade fell from 51% in 1963 to 38% in 1970 (Table IV.11).

The composition of exports changed notably between 1960 and 1970 (Table IV.8). The coffee share in total value of exports steadily decreased from 53% to 31.6%. The banana share widely fluctuated during the period but increased from 23.6% to 29.3%, helped by stable world prices (Table IV.10). Efforts to promote beef and sugar production succeeded in making them important exports, contributing to the diversification of the productive structure and making Costa Rica less vulnerable to price swings in coffee and bananas. The beef share in total exports increased from 5% to 7.8% between 1960 and 1970, and that of sugar from 2.2% to 6.8% between 1960 and 1966, but declined to 4.7% in 1970. The share of "other" exports increased dramatically after Costa Rica's entry into CACM in 1963, from 9.5% to 27.6% between 1963 and 1968, but declined to 25.6% in 1970. While much of the growth in exports was based on traditional exports (coffee, bananas), industrial exports increased 24 times between 1961 and 1970: from U.S.$2.2 million to U.S.$53.5 million (Table IV.6).

The industrial boom and increased investment in infrastructure led to an increase in imports of raw materials as well as capital and technological goods: machinery and equipment for cement plants, petroleum refineries, tire plants, power stations, and construction equipment. As a result, the share of machinery and transportation in the total value of imports rose from 26% to 29% between 1960 and 1970. Vigorous economic growth also fostered the import of consumer goods, mostly from Central America; thus, the share of "other manufactures" maintained a steady average in the range of 54% to 58% between 1960 and 1970. But while in the 1950s it was necessary to import most manufactured goods, the domestic industrial expansion reduced imports of some of those goods (as they began to be produced domestically), although other types of manufactures increased. Imports of food and beverages declined from 13% to 10% in the period (Table IV.9; ECLAC 1965a, 1966a; Naranjo 1980).

The growth of imports led to a growing deterioration in the merchandise trade balance: imports grew from U.S.$110.4 million to U.S.$316.7 million between 1960 and 1970, and the merchandise trade deficit expanded from U.S.$26.1 million to U.S.$85.5 million in the same period (Table IV.7). Concern over the growing trade deficit led Trejos to impose some import restrictions at the beginning of his term (consumption and sales taxes, multiple exchange rates). These measures (coupled with the increased value of exports) briefly improved the trade balance, but imports were later stimulated by increased investment, a reduction in stocks, a stable exchange rate, and a higher degree of liquidity that stimulated consumption (ECLAC, 1966a, 1969a).

Financing of the trade deficit was partly done with external borrowing; hence Costa Rica's disbursed external debt grew, between 1960 and 1970, from U.S.$158 to U.S.$354 million in real terms or from U.S.$128 to U.S.$204 in per capita terms. As a percentage of GDP the debt jumped from 8.6% to 13.6%, but as a percentage of exports the debt rose considerably less: from 40.3% to 48.2%. The external debt grew at a lower rate under Trejos than under Orlich (Table IV.13).

v. Unemployment

Although statistics are not available, unemployment most have remained low because of job growth in industry, agriculture, and the public sector. The female participation rate in the labor force increased slightly from 15% to 15.9% (Table IV.15).

vi. Equality

The expansion of the domestic market was supported by the policy of increased wages. Labor conditions improved in Costa Rica as real wages grew beginning in the 1950s and throughout the 1960s (Sojo 1989). Available data on income distribution are contradictory. Between 1961 and 1971, family income of the wealthiest quintiles declined (by 11.6 percentage points) but that of the poorest quintile also decreased albeit slightly (0.5 points); the middle-income quintiles, particularly those at the upper level, were those who increased (12.1 points). Conversely the Gini coefficient improved from 0.50 to 0.43 in the same period (Table IV.18).

Union activity in Costa Rica had been legalized under Calderón. The relatively open political climate since the Figueres junta allowed for disagreements and confrontations between the government and trade unions, generally within certain unwritten limits (interest-group conflicts normally did not escalate beyond a certain point). Some co-optation by the state did occur in an attempt to limit the powers of trade unions; the latter, however, were generally weak in Costa Rica (except in the banana sector) and union activity was not significant during this stage. With state support, especially from the PLN and Figueres, cooperatives became popular in Costa Rica. They offered a way for launching or maintaining expensive projects that an individual could not fund, and profits were distributed more widely than in a private enterprise. With ample credit available, cooperative banks, grocery stores, coffee and sugarcane producers, and processors flourished (Anderson 1991).

vii. Social Indicators

Social indicators improved significantly during this substage as neither Echandi nor Trejos challenged the continuation of the welfare programs. The combination of social improvement and economic growth (plus access to external credit, political stability, and adequate performance of public institutions) probably led to a decrease in poverty incidence, but statistics are not available.

Considerable public resources were needed to finance social security (health and pension programs) and other public services. The social security system had been fairly stagnant in the 1950s, covering a small portion of the labor force in the urban areas, and mostly civil servants and white-collar employees in public and private enterprises. Expansion was incremental and largely limited to those areas that had been previously covered. The constitutional amendment of 1961, however, mandated the universalization of social security coverage, which led to more state intervention and growth of the CCSS: the percentage of the general population covered by social security increased from 15% to 47% between 1960 and 1970, while the economically active population covered rose from 25% to 38% (Rosenberg 1979; Mesa-Lago 1985; Table IV.25).

Several health indicators for Costa Rica attest to a significant improvement between 1960 and 1970: the rate of doctors per 10,000 inhabitants increased from 3.7 to 6.1; the general mortality rate (per 1,000 inhabitants) fell steadily from 8.9 to 6.6; the infant mortality rate (per 1,000) fluctuated more but also showed a declining trend from 74.3 to 61.5; and life expectancy at birth climbed continuously from 61.6 to 67.1 years (Table IV.21). There were declines, between 1961 and 1970, in the rates (per 100,000 inhabitants) of diphtheria, malaria, typhoid, polio, and tuberculosis; but the rates of hepatitis, measles, and syphilis fluctuated, showing an increasing trend (Table IV.22). Coverage of potable water in the urban areas became universal, while in rural areas increased from 36.4% to 53.6% between 1960 and 1969 (Table IV.23).

Education improved in the urban sector in the 1940s and 1950s, but the education gap between the rural and urban sectors widened because of a lack of adequate services. Increased government expenditures in education after 1960 led to dramatic improvements in primary education in the rural sector, and secondary and higher education in the urban sector. The Educational Reform of 1963 and the establishment of the Office for Education Planning significantly improved the quality of education in Costa Rica, reflected by indications of improved student performance (e.g., better grades). In 1963 the illiteracy rate was 14.3%, and we lack data for 1970. Between 1960 and 1970 there were increases in enrollment in primary (93% to 110%), secondary (20% to 28%), and higher education (5% to 9%) (García 1977; González 1987; Table IV.24).

Trejos paid particular attention to the housing sector. In 1966, 476 housing units were built under the INVU program, and another 1,286 units were completed in 1967 (IDB 1968). Dwelling units built per 1,000 inhabitants probably declined under Orlich but increased from 2.3 to 3.0 under Trejos (Table IV.26).

2. The State Entrepreneur: 1970–1982

This substage was first dominated by the PLN, which controlled the executive and legislative branches for two consecutive administrations (1970–78), but a coalition of opposition parties won the presidency and, for the first time in 25 years, also won and maintained a majority in the Legislative Assembly (1978–82).

Figueres was again elected president in February 1970 and thus returned the executive power to the PLN, which also kept control of the Legislative Assembly with 32 out of 57 seats, while the National Unification Party (NUfP) held 22 seats. The PLN retained the executive branch with the election of Daniel Oduber in 1974 and also kept control of the legislative branch with 27 seats, while the NufP had 16. Oduber, one of the authors of the 1959 industrialization law, was a leader of the *político-empresarios* (politicians who became entrepreneurs and favored an increased economic role for the state), and he worked to consolidate the *estado empresario* (state entrepreneur) in Costa Rica. On the other hand, Figueres and Orlich were entrepreneurs who became political leaders—*empresarios-políticos.* Both groups operated within the PLN, although with some differences, and believed that the state should increasingly play a role as capitalist-entrepreneur in the economy, along with its other regular functions, in order to diversify the economy and limit the excessive influence of external capital (Sojo 1984).

By 1978 the NUfP was in severe decline as an opposition party to the PLN, in part because of its refusal to join the Coalition Unity (CU), which was supporting the candidacy of Rodrigo Carazo Odio. The latter left the PLN in 1970 and for the 1974 elections organized the Democratic Renovation Party, made up largely of younger PLN members dissatisfied with the domination by the "old guard" and perceived corruption in the PLN. Carazo put together the CU coalition, which, in addition to his own party, also included the new Republican Calderonist Party (founded by Calderón's son, with a conservative orientation), the Christian Democratic Party, and the Popular Union Party supported by the conservative oligarchy. This was the first time a major neoconservative force was organized and questioned the hegemonic role of the state. But the coalition was made up by heterogenous social forces whose only common motivation for alliance was their anti-PLN stance. They agreed on the need to both transform the economy and reduce the state's role in it, but they could not reach a consensus on the means to bring about those changes. They shared few other common economic objectives and, after winning the 1978 election, the parties of the coalition maintained their separate identities. Such disunity created contradictions and prevented the elaboration of a coherent package of economic policies. However, the coalition endorsed an end to public credit and subsidies to the agricultural and industrial sectors and the strengthening of the private financial sector. This philosophy provoked opposition from the *político-empresarios* and the protected agricultural and industrial sectors (Ameringer 1982; Trejos 1985; Rovira 1988a).

A. Policies

i. Ownership

Private ownership remained predominant in the economy, but the creation of the Costa Rican Development Corporation (CODESA) in 1972 strengthened the interventionist role of the state. CODESA was a financial support agency whose objectives included the promotion of new productive activities; the modernization, rationalization, and expansion of existing state and private enterprises; and the integration of the various sectors and regions of the country, all within a policy aimed at promoting and diversifying exports and substituting imports (ISI). CODESA entered joint ventures with private national and foreign investors (the state controlling two-thirds of the stocks and the private sector one-third) and provided technical assistance and loans to such mixed enterprises. Some of them, once consolidated, would be sold to the private sector. The objective of this policy was to strengthen the private sector, although with a stronger role of the public sector. Almost all operations were financed by the Central Bank. With Oduber's strong support, CODESA began full operation in 1976 and geared large investments to activities such as cement, sugar, and cotton (ECLAC 1972a; Sojo 1984; Rovira 1988b).

Citing higher oil prices and financial difficulties, the state gained 65% ownership of the Costa Rican Petroleum Refinery (RECOPE) in 1973 and fully nationalized it in the following year. In 1975 RECOPE was given exclusive rights to import, refine, and distribute oil; other companies that distributed oil and gasoline were nationalized (Sojo 1984).

Land distribution continued to be a priority for the PLN. Under Figueres, the ITCO embarked on a massive four-year titling program (1971–75), whose goal was to provide titles for approximately 660,000 hectares of national reserve lands (about 55% of the untitled farm land in Costa Rica) to 27,000 small-to-medium-sized farmers. After these four years, with cost recovery provided by the program, the remaining untitled farm land in the country would then be subject to the titling program. Oduber supported a more active agrarian reform. With new sources of financing and an enlarged staff, ITCO increased its number of projects from 11 to 38 between 1972 and 1976. In the last year, ITCO was transformed into the Institute of Agrarian Development (IDA) in charge of agricultural investment projects but with the main function of buying, selling, and renting land for a better distribution. The IDA was also put in charge of managing all resources of the Aluminum Corporation of America (ALCOA), which had failed to mine bauxite because of the low quality of Costa Rica's ore (unexploited land was to be turned over by the IDA to agrarian use). In 1977 and 1979 IDA launched two other major titling programs on national lands and pumped new funds into them (the 1979 program alone granted 36,469 titles). A more aggressive stand was also taken on the expropriation of private land, including part of that owned by the United Fruit Company (Seligson 1977, 1982; Sojo 1984).

ii. Planning

Planning and power became more centralized in the 1970s as the executive branch exerted more control over the previously autonomous institutions. Their independence from the central government began to lose ground with the 1968 and 1974 constitutional reforms that removed political autonomy (restricting it to administrative matters) and empowered the president to name the directors of the institutions (the executive branch thus gained more power over the Central Bank). Oduber also tried to enhance the coordination of the institutions and make state action more coherent. A number of sectoral planning offices were established, and the autonomous institutions had to submit their investment budgets to OFIPLAN for approval; eventually the Budgetary Authority was created in 1979 to exert control over those budgets (ECLAC 1975a; Sojo 1984; Reuben 1988; Rovira 1988a; Céspedes et al. 1990).

Like the previous plans, the Economic and Social Development Plan for 1972–78 reflected the PLN model of development. The plan objectives included expansion and diversification of output (to reduce economic dependence on a few agricultural commodities), an increase in employment, regional development, and a rise in the savings and investment ratios. Through easier access to credit and technical assistance, the plan expected to further raise agricultural production and the productivity of small farmers and cooperatives. It also called for the expansion of manufacturing exports to countries outside CACM and the continuous building of the infrastructure necessary for the productive sectors (IDB 1972).

Mirroring the conservative philosophy of Carazo and his CU coalition, the National Development Plan for 1979–82 was different from the previous plans. The new plan still emphasized the interaction of economic and social policies to generate both economic growth and expansion and improvement of social services. But the plan called for a reduction in the size of the state (e.g., public employment), privatization of productive sectors (to improve their efficiency), a cautious monetary and credit policy (to avoid inflationary pressures), and the adjustment of interest rates according to international rates (Murillo Rojas 1981; Fernández 1988).

iii. Financing

Figueres's third administration pursued an anticyclical policy to maintain economic growth and employment by compensating for the 1971 fall in export prices through increased public expenditure, financed with domestic funds (through government bonds and tax revenue) and external resources. He therefore reversed Trejos's restrictive credit policy and raised ceilings on certain bank loans. But the expansionist credit trend of the early 1970s had to operate under different conditions during Figueres's third term. The contraction of the external sector highlighted the government's financial vulnerability and forced it to obtain credit from the Central Bank in order to maintain a high liquidity in the economy. Some changes in the credit control system were implemented in 1971 to make the national banking policy more flexible and prevent excessive resources from being channeled into low-priority activities. The changes included the replacement of the bank's traditional portfolio ceilings by a specific distribution structure of loans. A group of private financial institutions was established in 1972, and the exclusive right of the national banks to tap savings deposits and grant loans to private enterprises and individuals was extended to financial intermediaries to fuel private-sector financing. Terms and interest rates were still regulated by the state, however, and thus the changes reflected the government's desire to extend control into the private financial sphere (ECLAC 1970a–72a, 1974a; Andic 1983; Sojo 1984).

In view of growing public expenditures and difficulties faced by previous administrations in generating tax revenue, Figueres enacted the important tax reform of March 1972 to increase tax revenue and dampen excessive demand for imports. A general sales tax rate of 5% was approved, and selective consumption taxes began to distinguish between essential and nonessential goods (the classification and respective rates could be altered to preserve flexibility). Thus, in addition to the elimination of foreign-exchange surcharges, the government could impose taxes of up to 50% on the taxable value of nonessential or luxury goods. The personal income tax rates became more progressive to distribute the tax burden more evenly, although larger deductions (e.g., as for dependents) were allowed. The old tax scale comprising 30 income strata (rates ranging from 1% to 30%) was compressed into a scale of 12 income strata (rates ranging from 5% to 50%). Tax rates on the profits of enterprises (including profits remitted abroad) became more progressive as well. The taxation changes also aimed at improving the efficiency in tax collection and management (ECLAC 1971a, 1974a; Andic 1983).

Rising world coffee prices, more efficient tax control, and the growth of imports led to increases in tax revenue, but the tax system was again reformed in June 1976 to generate resources for higher education. The corporate income tax rate was raised, a 3% tax on net assets of bearer shares of corporations was introduced, and sales of real estate values above 2 million colones were subjected to a progressive tax. There was also an increase in the rate of the selective consumption tax on certain imports, as well as temporary surcharges on imports, to provide resources for an export promotion fund; the surcharges were imposed mainly on luxury goods and goods competing with those domestically produced (Andic 1983).

iv. Stability and Prices

The economy grew well under the expansionary policies until 1974, when the full impact of the 1973 oil crisis was felt and Oduber was forced to take measures to counter those negative effects. Government consumption and investment was increased to stimulate the economy and prevent increases in unemployment. To reverse the deterioration in the balance of payments and avoid pressure on foreign reserves, import surcharges were established, and the government restricted credit for the purchase of nonessential consumer goods. Banks raised interest rates and brought them into line with the higher international rates in order to attract funds, avoid capital flight, and stimulate savings. Banks were also allowed to receive deposits in foreign currency, and the government regulated the sale of dollars to the public, restricting foreign travel. A more moderate policy of expanding credit and the means of payment was adopted, and coffee bonds were issued to absorb domestic liquidity.

Price increases for some essential products were restricted, but the CNP raised price subsidies for basic grains (rice, beans, corn) paid to producers in order to stimulate production. Other measures included the maintenance of adequate external supplies of mass-consumption products and the provision of incentives (technical assistance, new credit programs, favorable interest rates) to sustain and fuel the productive sectors—especially manufacturers and producers of staple grains—and continue the promotion of nontraditional exports. For example, the government granted more exemptions for industry, including yielding custom duties, eliminating ceilings on credits for exports, and financing export sales with subsidized interest rates (ECLAC 1974a).

Credit policy under Oduber continued to support production and redistribution. Immediately after the oil-shock-induced economic crisis, the monetary authorities were faced with the dilemma of preventing more excess liquidity or maintaining the level of financing for productive activities to counter the effects of the crisis. The latter option was chosen in 1975, increasing money supply and domestic credit by 20% and 40%, respectively (a recovery in international reserves also rose liquidity). In 1976–77, however, the monetary authorities had to enact measures to absorb excess liquidity, such as raising the interest rates and minimum reserve requirements on savings and time deposits, reducing the ceilings on credit and rediscount lines, and increasing interest rates on loans to the coffee sector (to stimulate the self-financing of producers in the expectation of continued high world coffee prices). The Central Bank also issued three-year bonds for a stabilization fund and suspended the authorization granted to national banks in 1975 to arrange foreign loans directly (ECLAC 1975a–77a).

In the first half of his administration, Carazo's stabilization plan sought to liberalize the economy and strengthen the private sector by reducing state controls and intervention. The government decreased price controls on some products of general consumption and liberalized other prices. Taxes on imports of durable consumer goods were reduced to discourage smuggling. In 1978 the authorities initiated reforms to liberalize the financial system. Claiming that the subsidized rates for the promotion of certain activities led to inefficiency in the allocation of resources, Carazo had the Central Bank raise interest rates on loans and deposits of national banks, and adjust them according to the trends of the international financial markets, on the basis of the LIBOR rate. (However, sugarcane cooperatives, small agricultural and industrial producers, handicraft workers, forestry, cheap housing, and rural self-managed community enterprises continued to enjoy some preferential rates.) These financial reforms aimed at increasing investment and attracting more savings by domestic financial intermediaries, so that credit could be expanded on the basis of such savings rather than by lowering the discount rate. And yet, the ensuing rise in the cost of credit and the negative reaction of producers (e.g., industrialists, cattle ranchers, agricultural producers) forced Carazo, after only three months, to lower interest rates and reduce import duties on agricultural inputs (ECLAC 1978a; Trejos 1985).

Foreign investment was encouraged with the suppression in 1978 of the registering of foreign capital. Practically no restrictions were placed on the operations of nonbanking financial institutions in public and private sectors, with the exception of the receipt of current-account deposits. Interest rates were liberalized, and the institutions were authorized to engage in operations previously restricted to the banking system, such as financing exports and imports. It was hoped that these measures would encourage inflows of foreign capital (liberalized interest rates also seemed to ensure a better adaptation to changing international financial conditions) (ECLAC 1978a).

In 1978–79 coffee prices plummeted (Table IV.10), the country faced the second increase in oil prices, and political turmoil in Nicaragua obstructed trade within CACM. To counter the growth of inflation in 1979, the government restricted wage increases (intensifying labor conflicts), froze the agricultural support prices at the level of the previous year, granted subsidies to the electricity sector (ICE) and collective passenger transport (to offset raising fuel prices), temporarily cut the growth rate of public spending, and began a moderate money-supply policy. A substantial change was made in the structure of banking liabilities, greatly increasing time deposits at the expense of sight deposits and further decreasing liquidity (ECLAC 1979a).

As output and employment fell and economic conditions deteriorated, the aforementioned measures were countered by expansion through fiscal means. Certain prices were freed, the domestic price of gasoline was raised, and tariffs were also increased for public utilities such as electricity. There was strong opposition from the industrial sector to an attempt to reform the income and property taxes, and rejection by the Legislative Assembly prevented the government from generating additional resources.

In order to bolster the weakened external sector without jeopardizing economic growth, the government decided to increase external indebtedness. Negotiations were initiated with the IMF in order to strengthen Costa Rica's position in the international financial markets and open new sources of revenue. In March 1980 the government signed an agreement with the IMF concerning a stabilization program covered by a stand-by agreement for U.S.$60 million. Under this agreement, the government formulated a two-year stabilization plan to minimize the expansion of domestic demand, reduce the fiscal deficit, limit new external indebtedness of the public sector, and reduce imports. This policy was to be applied mainly through the establishment of higher taxes (some selective consumer taxes were raised, but the above mentioned tax reform failed to pass), the restriction of credit from the banking system to reduce government expenditure, and an official devaluation of the colón (ECLAC 1980a).

Prime lending rates consequently rose but with a much greater coverage. In 1979 preferential rates in the agricultural sector were mainly given to rural autonomous community enterprises, sugarcane cooperatives, and small producers. In 1980 such preferential rates were granted to larger producers, especially for the replanting of banana plantations affected by disease and the improvement of coffee plantations, as well as to many other crops. Interest rates on deposits continued to rise but maintained certain stability: in addition to LIBOR, other factors taken into consideration included the prevailing rates in the U.S. financial market, the domestic rate of inflation, and the supply and demand for funds in the domestic market. This new system attempted to avoid capital flight by setting interest rates at more attractive and competitive levels (ECLAC 1980a).

The weakening of the external situation and fall in international reserves meant that the targets of the stabilization agreement with the IMF could not be met. Domestic credit to the public sector expanded more than the amount set in the plan, and the stabilization program failed to reduce the fiscal deficit (although domestic demand was curbed). The tax reform was not passed, and there was no official devaluation of the colón. The agreement was suspended after three months, which caused further conflicts within the coalition (ECLAC 1981a; Andic 1983).

In September 1980 Carazo announced a package of measures to cope with the crisis. Imports of certain goods were prohibited and surcharges applied to others, a fund for export promotion was established, and a de facto devaluation was carried out. After arduous negotiations with the IMF, a second, more rigorous and extensive agreement was signed in June 1981; it called for the reduction of the public sector (mainly through privatization of CODESA's enterprises), further liberalization of interest rates and the financial system, elimination of protectionism, and maintenance of the floating of the colón. To curb inflation and minimize fiscal imbalances, the monetary authorities set limitations on the growth of domestic credit to the government (and also freed up more credit for the private sector), established minimum values for net international reserves, and placed more restrictions on the state external indebtedness. The government also agreed to liberalize prices and reduce subsidies to reflect the production costs of state enterprises; consequently, many public utility rates were raised, particularly those on energy and fuels. In October 1981 the government prohibited the import of the majority of capital goods, and in November the colón was officially devalued (Trejos 1985).

In spite of these measures, the economic crisis and the financial situation worsened in 1981 as tax revenue stagnated and private investment fell because of economic uncertainty. Debate intensified over the stabilization measures, and the Legislative Assembly approved a freeze on prices of energy in mid-1981, which aggravated the financial position of the public sector. These developments, along with a Supreme Court decision that the devaluation of colón was unconstitutional, contributed to the suspension of the second agreement with the IMF in November 1981. Thus, Carazo was forced to suspend payments on the public external debt with private and multilateral creditors as he could not comply with the requirements of the stabilization program. In July 1981 the government announced to its creditor banks that it would pay only the interest on the debt, and two months later it declared the temporary suspension of all payments, including interest. In January 1982 Carazo broke off negotiations with the IMF, charging that it wanted to impose conditions that would produce social regression to an intolerable degree (Trejos 1985).

v. Development Strategy

Figueres's and Oduber's administrations remained faithful to the PLN strategy for economic development, with expansionary fiscal and credit policies, and the elaboration of plans and programs that fostered increased state intervention in infrastructure, agriculture, industry, trade, and social development. The state acted as intermediary, stabilizer, and financier to guide and promote development either directly or through private enterprises. While Carazo challenged some aspects of this strategy, many of his policies remained within this general framework, though disunity and external factors induced conflicts and numerous policy shifts.

The two PLN administrations continued their efforts to strengthen the country's economic development through investment, much of it carried out by public-sector agencies (especially by Oduber's creation of CODESA): the ICE completed hydroelectric and electrical programs in the rural areas and expanded the telecommunications system; the water and sewerage agency (SNAA) implemented sanitary improvements; and there was public construction of roads, new port facilities on the Pacific coast, and modernization of port facilities at Limón. External loans were procured for new investments in agriculture, industry, and tourism. Carazo did not deviate from the upward trend in public investment in construction (especially road projects), energy, and communications (ECLAC 1970a–79a).

The two PLN administrations also continued the development of the agricultural sector. Figueres launched an eight-year program to improve agricultural productivity of basic grains, tropical fruits, dairy products, and pig raising through easier access to credit and technical assistance, as well as a program of improvement of coffee plantations. He also continued the training and inspection program through which technology and improved seeds were provided to farmers. In 1975 Oduber initiated the National Basic Grains Program to achieve self-sufficiency in the production of these crops (partly because the elimination of regional tariffs in CACM had induced dependence on imported grains such as beans and corn), reduce imports, and increase income in the rural sector. As incentives, the CNP established minimum buying prices above the level of world market prices for corn, beans, sorghum, and rice and provided credit at low interest rates to promote cultivation of these crops as well as technical assistance to improve farming techniques. The grains program was linked to the settlements program carried out on 75,000 acres of land acquired from banana companies, where the planting of corn, beans, and rice was promoted. Limitations of the storage network were tackled through the construction of new silos. In 1977 Oduber launched a project of planting African oil palm in the Pacific areas not suitable for growing basic grains, promoted by CODESA jointly with private capital (ECLAC 1972a–77a).

Figueres and Oduber continued to support the development and diversification of industrial activities, particularly through CODESA. It emphasized a more intensive use of local raw materials, the establishment of new industries in less developed areas, and the promotion of activities with export potential both to CACM and outside of the region.

The 1972 Export Promotion Act aimed at promoting nontraditional exports through tax drawbacks, tax credit certificates, the simplification of formalities for recovering indirect taxes on imported articles, and the deduction from income tax payments of external expenditure associated with the promotion of nontraditional exports (ECLAC 1972a).

From the beginning, the Carazo administration made clear its intention of encouraging market forces to achieve a more efficient allocation of resources and to correct the monetary and fiscal disequilibria that had plagued the economy for years. The goals of Carazo's economic strategy were to increase productivity (particularly in the public sector and agriculture), eliminate pockets of poverty by encouraging labor-intensive sectors (e.g., construction), cut public spending and change its sectoral composition, reduce industrial protection by halting subsidized credit and decreasing tariff protection (especially on durable consumer goods), and liberalize interest rates to limit Central Bank financing and, along with cuts in fiscal spending, curb demand pressures on domestic prices and the balance of payments (ECLAC 1978a; Rovira 1988b). A new element in the industrial policy introduced by Carazo was the reduction, in 1979, of duty rates on a number of tariff items to increase efficiency in production. Both CODESA (with the establishment of a special branch) and the Ministry of Economic Affairs tried to stimulate agro-industrial development as a means of increasing domestic consumption, production, and exports to nontraditional markets.

Despite efforts to liberalize and diversify the economic structure of the country, Carazo's coalition and the Legislative Assembly lacked unity and direction, thus harming confidence in the government's development strategy. The ensuing economic crisis further intensified the conflicts and made more evident the lack of a coherent strategy.

vi. External Sector

The exchange-rate policy of the Figueres and Oduber administrations remained unaltered: maintaining a stable, fixed official exchange rate with a few devaluations when necessary (Table IV.3). Because of a reduction in international reserves caused by a worseingn trade balance in 1970–71, Figueres did experiment with a dual foreign exchange rate in 1971–73 to restrict demand for imports, especially of nonessential goods: the official rate, which remained unchanged for essential transactions related to economic development, and the free-market rate for other operations; the former was lower than the latter. A system of foreign exchange surcharges was introduced on the official rate whereby imports were grouped in various categories. In early 1972 the Central Bank eliminated all surcharges but simultaneously restricted the use of the official rate to fewer, preferential import categories. In September 1972 Central American imports were subjected to the same dual exchange rate, while exports to the region were promoted by granting them a more favorable exchange rate. The preferential official rate continued to have a decisive effect, as it was applied to almost 80% of all transactions in value terms. But in October 1972 the number of categories of imports that had the preferential rate were drastically cut since the balance of payments and international reserves did not improve (ECLAC 1972a, 1974a).

The new restrictions to get foreign exchange at the official rate made imports more expensive and also raised the production costs of export industries that relied on imported inputs. To offset the higher production costs and ensure the competitiveness of such exporters in Central America, the producers (particularly of nontraditional and agricultural products) were authorized to liquidate, on the free market, 50% of foreign exchange obtained from exports (the free-market rate was 30% higher than the official rate). The free-market rate was suspended by Figueres in 1973, and, after the devaluations of 1974–75, Oduber maintained a single fixed exchange rate for the rest of his administration, because of a rise in international reserves (Table IV.3).

To confront external disturbances, authorities restricted imports but also promoted exports. Under Figueres and Oduber, the emphasis on export promotion, which led to an increase in the exports of manufactures, was based on various credit and fiscal measures. The national banking system supported an increase in the working capital of export enterprises. Based on the 1972 Law for the Promotion of Exports, the Center for the Promotion of Exports and Investment (CENPRO) provided subsidies to exports (CATs, CIEXs). Tax rebate certificates (CATs) were introduced in 1973 and were awarded by the Central Bank to firms exporting nontraditional goods to countries outside CACM; CATs provided a 15% tax credit on the f.o.b. value of such exports and were negotiable on the open market. Export increase certificates (CIEX) stimulated exports by granting exemptions equivalent to as much as 10% of the annual value of increased exports. Other incentives were reductions in export taxes, and a 100% exemption from import duties on machinery and equipment for enterprises set up to export their entire production. In 1976 these measures were supplemented by the establishment of an Export Promotion Fund, which granted medium- and long-term credit insurance to expand exports and develop import substitutes. The fund was financed with new temporary import surcharges, which transferred to imports the value of tax exemptions granted by CATs and CIEXs (ECLAC 1976a; Andic 1983; Rovira 1988b; Colburn and Saballos 1988).

In spite of its central importance in such a small economy, foreign exchange policy had traditionally been subject to considerations unrelated to the country competitiveness. Critics of such a policy argued that the oil shocks, world inflation, increasing interest rates, and the recession in the world economy made it necessary to adopt a more flexible exchange policy. Nevertheless, the traditional policy was kept by Carazo: by 1978 the overvaluation of the colón was obvious, but he refused to devalue it and instead pursued external financing to prop up the exchange rate. As the increasing cost of imports aggravated the external imbalance, Carazo adopted the following measures: he (1) instituted multiple exchange rates to curtail demand for foreign exchange; (2) authorized a parallel currency market, which already existed informally, to which 50% of the purchases of foreign exchange for import and export earnings were directed; (3) gave the Central Bank only 50% of the necessary exchange for imports, forcing it to purchase the rest on the free market; (4) prohibited imports of certain articles to restrict external purchases; (5) increased surcharges on imports of manufactured consumer goods, capital goods, and construction materials; and (6) mandated prior deposits for such imports, with the exception of those from Central America, which, nevertheless, had to use the parallel currency market for 50% of each transaction. As the administration adamantly opposed devaluation, the management of the exchange rate in 1980–81 became chaotic—the gap between the free exchange rate and the overvalued official rate expanded rapidly. At the end of 1980, the pressure on the colón made it unavoidable to adopt a floating exchange rate, which led to a huge currency devaluation. This delayed action took place at the time when the country's international reserves were running out, and its foreign borrowing capacity was zero (ECLAC 1980a; Trejos 1985; Céspedes et al. 1990).

In March 1981 the government introduced an interbank rate, to be administered by the Central Bank, as a third rate for foreign exchange. At that time there were at least four different exchange rates: the official rate, two set by the Central Bank, and the parallel market rate, obviously violating the 1981 IMF agreement, which endorsed a rigorous stabilization program including the modification of the exchange policy. In mid-1981 the parallel market rate was transferred to the street, and the Supreme Court declared that the 1980 executive decision to float the colón was unconstitutional, as it lay in purview of the Legislative Assembly. The assembly finally agreed to officially devaluate the colón in November 1981, but only to half the parallel market rate. The official rate was fixed at 20 colones per dollar, the parallel market rate at 40, and the Central Bank rate at 35 (the last applicable to all transactions except exports). The decision to float the colón led to huge devaluations: 154% in 1981 and 72% in 1982, and the exchange rate increased from 8.6 to 37.4 colones per dollar in 1982 (Table IV.3; ECLAC 1981a; Trejos 1985).

During this substage the external debt increased significantly. Under Figueres and Oduber, indebtedness rose to counter the effects of the oil shocks and to meet the aggregate demand that grew with more state intervention. Carazo also increased the external debt to alleviate the effects of the crisis, but his chaotic policies, inability to comply with basic IMF requirements, and the worsening crisis forced him to suspend payments on the debt in 1981.

vii. Labor and Employment

As in the 1960s, increased government activity in the 1970s generated a surge in public employment. In the 1960s unemployment had generally decreased, and it was stagnant in the 1970s because of the growth of industry, combined with the expansion of the public sector. The slowdown and decline in growth in 1980–82, however, resulted in increasing unemployment despite government efforts.

Strong economic growth in the 1970s allowed for wage increases, including the government bureaucracy, which accounted for a large part of the expansion in public expenditures. In previous decades, the combination of price stability and economic growth did not make wage policy a top priority; biannual adjustments in minimum wages were sufficient, but two-digit inflation in 1973–75 and 1980–82 forced a change in wage policy. Under the PLN, wage policy aimed at progressive redistribution in an attempt to reduce inequalities and was implemented as follows: rises in real wages similar to gains in productivity (to avoid cost-push inflation), compensation to the lowest wage earners for increases in the cost of living, and a gradual narrowing of wage gaps among different groups of workers. The big upsurge of inflation in 1974 and strong trade union pressure led Figueres to grant significant wage increases to compensate for the fall in purchasing power; in addition, minimum wages began to be revised annually instead of biannually. Oduber continued the policy of differential wage increases by income levels and economic sectors, consistent with his redistribution objective: the biggest increments went to agricultural workers, whose average wage was the lowest; and within each economic activity, the largest increases went to the lowest income strata. Wage increases under Oduber slightly exceeded those of consumer prices, except for public employees, who got most favorable treatment. Carazo maintained the policy of wage raises to protect the purchasing power of workers; with the jump of inflation in 1980, minimum wages were adjusted twice a year, and major wage increases were granted to public employees (ECLAC 1974a–80a; Pollack and Uthoff 1987).

viii. Distribution and Social Services

In the 1970s Figueres and Oduber supported state intervention in social matters to make the mass of the population beneficiaries of the growth process, promote better access to social services, and improve distribution and living standards. The government extended health-care coverage to the urban and rural populations through various steps. In 1971 the CCSS eliminated salary ceilings, which were barriers to coverage, and made affiliation in and contributions to the social security system mandatory for all blue- and white-collar workers. Agricultural workers, the self-employed, domestic servants, and pensioners, as well as their dependents, were later incorporated into the CCSS. In 1973 all hospitals under the Ministry of Health were transferred to the CCSS (which was entrusted with hospital care for the entire population), and they were provided enough resources to achieve universal coverage, for example, the rapid construction of health facilities and training of health personnel. The CCSS concentrated on curative medicine, while the Ministry of Health focused on preventive medicine and expansion of primary health care to the most remote rural areas (beginning in 1973) as well as to urban marginal groups (starting in 1976). Worker protection against common sickness, maternity, old age, disability, and death was thus entrusted to the CCSS, except for a few programs that remained in the Ministry of Health and coverage of occupational hazards, performed by the National Insurance Institute (Rosenberg 1979; Mesa-Lago 1985).

A key policy for improving income distribution was Figueres's creation in 1970 of the Institute of Social Assistance (IMAS) to "combat extreme misery." Initially IMAS was to deal with slums and squatter communities, but it later expanded its functions to other matters related to extreme poverty, such as providing meals for school children and housing for poor families. In 1975 Oduber founded the Family Allowance Program administered by the Ministry of Labor and Social Security. This program, which in 1975 received revenue from an increased sales tax and a 2% payroll tax, was designed to transfer resources from urban to rural areas in order to raise the standard of living of the rural population through the provision of electricity, roads, potable water, health clinics, food rations, and improvements in housing. Services offered by Family Allowances included a program to increase the nutritional level (49% of Costa Rican families in 1971 still received less than 90% of the required daily calorie intake); a noncontributory pension scheme, providing minimum pensions and health care to the dispossessed who did not qualify for insurance coverage (thus financing the CCSS and Ministry of Health programs for the poor); and a policy of cash allowances based on family size and income, for families who earned no more than 2.25 times the lowest minimum wage paid in the metropolitan area of San José (ECLAC 1975a; IDB 1977; Ameringer 1982; Andic 1983; Pascua and Valverde 1987; Mesa-Lago 1989).

Previous reforms in the educational system generally had been partial; Figueres decided to deal with all levels and aspects of the educational system as a whole (from kindergarten to the university), arguing that the effectiveness of a reform could be jeopardized if its targets were compartmentalized. The National Educational Development Plan for 1972–79 was elaborated to accomplish that goal and accounted for much of the expenditures of the two PLN administrations. It tried to improve education, cope with quantitative and qualitative manpower requirements, raise the average level of schooling of the population 15 years of age or older, and bring children into the school system at an earlier age. The plan made compulsory a nine-year basic education (expanding the length of time in school), included the community (parents) in the process, improved methods for assisting students (to decrease number of dropouts and repeaters), increased the availability of education in the rural sector through better distribution of resources, improved adult education (encouraging a return to schooling), made basic materials and services (e.g., libraries) available to all education centers, and built new schools. There was also a tremendous expansion of higher education: only one university existed in 1970, but throughout the decade there was a proliferation of new state institutes and universities (the Costa Rican Technological Institute, the National Autonomous University, and the Distance Learning State University). Also, the first private university, the Central American Autonomous University, was authorized to operate (González 1987; Aguilar 1990).

The three administrations, especially Oduber's, devoted considerable expenditures to housing (in part through IMAS), but, in the midst of the economic crisis under Carazo, the housing sector suffered, as resources originally intended for it were used for other purposes (Sojo 1989).

B. Performance

i. Growth

The annual real GDP growth rate between 1971 and 1982 averaged 4.9%, a slowdown compared with the 1961–70 rate of 6.1%; in per capita terms the rate averaged 2.1% (versus 2.7%) in spite of a slowdown of the average population growth rate from 3.4% to 2.8%. Nevertheless growth during the

Figueres-Oduber expansionist administrations averaged 6.4% (3.6% per capita) higher than the average for 1961–70, while during Carazo's administration, there was a average annual decline of 1% (−3.8% per capita) (Table IV.3).

Under Figueres GDP growth averaged 7.1% annually (1971–74) and 4.4% per capita (Table IV.3). The main causes were the growth in agriculture (bananas), manufacturing, construction, transport, and communications, as well as the continued expansion of the external sector and participation in CACM. The public sector enlarged its share in capital formation, industrialization continued to contribute to economic development, and private investment rose in bananas, livestock for export, coffee, and manufactures. GDP growth under Oduber slowed down to 5.7% and 2.8% per capita (still the latter was higher than the average rate in 1961–70). In 1975 growth slowed down to 2.1% (−0.4% per capita) because of the first oil shock and Oduber's stabilization policy. GDP growth recovered to an average 6.9% in 1976–78 (3.9% per capita; Table IV.3). The economic recovery was due to the combined effect of the expansion of public expenditures (increased to compensate for the economic slowdown but offset by restrictive measures), a recovery in trade due to a more dynamic world economy, very high world prices for coffee, and increasing international reserves (Table IV.10). The tax reform of 1976 was successful in providing increased income for the government, while the redistributive social policies and the promotion programs in staple grains stimulated the economic recovery.

GDP declined by an average rate of 1% under Carazo (−3.8% per capita). GDP was stagnant in 1980 and declined by 4.8% annually in 1981–82 (−7.6% per capita; Table IV.3). At the beginning of the 1980s, the Carazo administration was confronted with the second oil crisis, a world recession, high international prices for imports, stagnation in demand for exports, a decline in coffee prices, worsening terms of trade, growing international interest rates, and a 43% decrease in international reserves (in 1979). His chaotic policies and adjustment measures, combined with the halt in international lending and his failure to honor the IMF agreement, were additional causes of the severe crisis.

During the entire substage, domestic investment was very dynamic. Gross fixed capital formation averaged 22.6% of GDP between 1971 and 1978, compared to 17.7% between 1960 and 1970 (Table IV.3). This high rate continued under Carazo with a peak of 26.2% in 1979, partly due to increased capital expenditures for the modernization of the railroads, the completion of a hydroelectric plant, and the expansion of the telecommunications system (investment later declined to 20.3% because of the economic crisis). The high levels of capital formation attest to the building of the industrial base, particularly investment in fixed capital goods. Public investment increased dramatically: in the 1960s, it represented about one-fifth of total investment, but by the end of the 1970s it jumped to one-third. Private investment concentrated on the purchase of machinery and equipment, while public investment was primarily geared to infrastructure (construction, electricity). The share of infrastructure in public investment was 63% in 1967–70, 56% in 1975–78, and 71% in 1979. In the 1970s an increasing share of public investment went to CODESA subsidiaries; the share of public enterprises in total investment increased from less than 10% at the end of the 1960s to more than 20% at the beginning of the 1980s, which critics charged diminished the efficiency in distribution of capital (Andic 1983).

ii. Inflation

The annual rate of inflation between 1971 and 1982 averaged almost 20%, contrasted with 2.4% between 1961 and 1970. Under Figueres it averaged 13% and exhibited an increasing trend; Oduber reduced the rate to an average of less than 8%, but Carazo confronted the worst inflation in the nation's history: an annual average of close to 39% (Table IV.3). Costa Rica's small and open economy has always been significantly affected by international factors: the demand and international prices for its major exports (e.g., the coffee boom of 1976–77), participation in CACM (which began to decline in the 1970s), external credit, and oil prices (e.g, the oil shock of 1973). In the 1950s and 1960s economic growth was compatible with a certain degree of external instability in Costa Rica. Government moderate intervention in the economy, a rapid extension of internal and external credit, the relatively small size of the public sector, a cautious approach to fiscal and monetary policy, and the strong leadership of the Central Bank all allowed for stable prices and exchange rates, despite external vulnerabilities. After the oil crisis, however, the government's macroeconomic instruments were no longer adequate to maintain stability, and the need for substantial adjustment became apparent. The amount of credit demanded was greater than in the past, and a substantial increase in external debt was insufficient to prevent Costa Rica's first important inflationary experience (Lizano 1990).

At the beginning of Figueres's administration, there was an effort to contain consumption in order to provide the needed resources for economic expansion, for example, import restrictions, tax increases, and changes in credit policy. And yet demand continued to be dynamic, fueled by an expansionary credit policy (in part to finance the fiscal deficit), wage increases and external loans, and increased public expenditures, all of which generated growing liquidity. The tax reform of 1972 (as well as taxes on the profits of banana companies, export taxes, and import duties) contributed to enhancing government revenues, but most was used for more public spending, although the state deficit was reduced. Figueres also reversed Trejos's efforts to lessen government dependence on external credit; hence the fiscal deficit was increasingly financed by foreign borrowing. Inflation rapidly escalated to 15% in 1973 (Table IV.3; ECLAC 1970a, 1971a, 1974a).

The Oduber administration was hit by the first international oil crisis, and the inflation rate peaked at 30% in 1974 (Table IV.3); the greatest price increases were in fuel. The coffee boom, the moderate stabilization policy (limiting price increases on some essential products, restricting monetary and credit measures, issuing of coffee bonds, etc.), and external borrowing managed to reduce inflation to 17.4% in 1975 and 3.5% in 1977 and cut the budget deficit, without sacrificing economic growth or diminishing the expansionary fiscal policy. The coffee bonanza made it possible to tackle the excess demand with increased imports and expand credit to counter the loss in international reserves, instead of fueling an increase in prices. This adjustment with indebtedness could not be successfully repeated thereafter because instead of paying the debt used for the adjustment, once conditions improved under the coffee bonanza, the Oduber administration continued increasing external indebtedness as well as the size and intervention of the public sector (expanding public investment and imports). The international banks also facilitated access to ample credit with low interest rates (Céspedes et al. 1990).

The central government budget deficit as a percentage of GDP grew from an average 2.9% in 1972–74 to 3.4% in 1975–78 and 4.5% in 1979–82 (the peak in the deficit was 7.4% in 1980). Public expenditures grew rapidly to meet the requirements of economic growth (particularly regarding the infrastructure) and social welfare. Consumption taxes continued to contribute the most to public revenue (because of rate increases) while the share of direct-tax in revenue stagnated (Pollack and Uthoff 1985). Differential and selective wage increases stimulated consumption, production, and imports (ECLAC 1977a; Andic 1983).

More credit was made available to the public sector during the three administrations. The distribution of net credit of the national banking system in 1971 was 13.5% to the public sector and 86.5% to the private sector; by 1982 these shares were 43.4% and 56.6%, respectively (BCCR 1986). The growth of the public sector meant increased competition for resources and limited financing for the private sector, which contributed to some stagnation in production (Trejos 1985). Not only did the public share of domestic credit increase but there was also greater external indebtedness (in part to cover increased fuel prices). Under Figueres the disbursed external debt increased 81%, under Oduber it grew almost 300%, and under Carazo it grew 72% (Table IV.13; see section iv below).

In Carazo's administration the importance of and dependence on external borrowing became crucial. In the 1950s and 1960s foreign loans went principally to the nation's infrastructure and long-term investments of a social nature. Prior to Oduber there was increasing reliance on short-term foreign debt to alleviate the crises caused by external factors, but when economic conditions improved there was a slowdown in indebtedness (e.g., under Trejos). The situation changed under Oduber because the oil shock and his ambitious expansionary policies accelerated indebtedness. Beginning in the mid-1970s, external funds were used not to alleviate foreign-induced crises but to sustain domestic aggregate demand. Faced with a decrease in income and restrictions in the capacity to import during the crisis, Carazo first considered decreasing spending, an action opposed by many sectors, and his ultimate decision was to increase internal and external financing and postpone adjustments in spending (Vargas 1980; Céspedes et al. 1990).

Carazo's efforts to reduce certain controls in the financial system initially stimulated an increase in savings and time deposits. The raising of interest rates attracted savings to the banking system, but these rates were higher than government bond yields, hence diminishing their appeal and harming government finances. The increase in interest rates and the restrictive monetary and credit policies did reduce the expansion of the money supply and domestic demand in 1978–80. However, Carazo did not fully implement his financial reforms, and his monetary and credit policies failed to reduce the fiscal deficit. The restricted liquidity also slowed the growth of the industrial and agricultural sectors and raised their production costs. When the economic crisis hit, credit was at first increased, but a growing share of it went to finance the expanding fiscal deficit, limiting banking credit for the private sector, while international reserves declined. There were also increases in fuel prices and support prices to basic grains. This situation led to a steady increase in the inflation rate from 6% in 1978 to 9% in 1979 and 18% in 1980 (Table IV.3). In 1981 the government launched a restrictive monetary and credit policy in order to reduce demand and external indebtedness, preserve international reserves, and minimize economic imbalances. However, these measures, particularly the reduced credit, further contributed to economic stagnation. Real interest rates became negative (they were 50% below the inflation rate in 1981), which prompted a capital flight. The stabilization measures failed, and the authorities resumed the expansion of domestic credit to sustain public spending, but the resulting inflation cut international reserves further (by 10% in 1981). In 1981 inflation jumped to 37% and escalated to 90% the following year. Current expenditures increased faster than current revenues; thus the government budget deficit grew from 5% of GDP in 1978 to 6.8% in 1979 and 7.4% in 1980 (Table IV.3; ECLAC 1979a, 1981a; Vagas 1980).

The economic crisis reached a climax in 1981–82. The amount of fiscal deficit that external creditors were willing to finance hit a limit (half of Costa Rica's external debt was with commercial banks whose loans had shorter maturities and higher interest rates than loans from international agencies), and Carazo's moratorium on debt service brought the international cutoff of lending. Certainly external factors played a crucial role in the crisis, but they were compounded by Carazo's inconsistent and chaotic policies on exchange rates, subsidies, credit, fiscal, and monetary matters (Céspedes et al. 1990).

There were also cumulative structural factors and policies, although experts differ on the degree that such factors contributed to the crisis (Trejos 1985; Céspedes et al. 1990). A growing dependence of the public sector on external credit has been mentioned. This was largely due to the tremendous growth in the public sector, associated with government services, electricity, roads, telecommunications, water, and transportation. The number of public institutions rose from 65 at the beginning of the 1950s to 185 in 1980, and most autonomous institutions suffered deficit (Andic 1983). Increases in the size, economic role, and spending of the public sector were not exclusive of Carazo's administration but accumulated over time.

The pluralistic political system and the increasing power of diverse interest groups generated growing pressures on the economy. Lizano (1990) argues that political parties, trade unions, bureaucratic organizations, and business groups created economic distortions through demands for higher wages, greater protection, more subsidies, lower interest rates, fixed or favorable exchange rates, and price controls. While these groups used the state for their advantage and benefit, they created distortions in market size, prices for domestic and imported goods and services, and so forth, which in turn promoted widespread inefficiency. For instance, when the economic crisis intensified and Carazo decided to cut government spending, he faced the opposition of many of those groups: the Chamber of Industries (heavily dependent on foreign inputs) pressured against restricting imports, the agricultural sector clamored to protect their subsidies, and public employees kept enjoying annual automatic pay increases mandated by law. All this made it impossible for the president to reduce public spending (Vargas 1980).

The extensive and expanding network of social protection also contributed to pressure on the government: social insurance, health care, education, family allowances, low-cost housing, protection of the dispossessed, and transfers to consumers from the CNP (Trejos 1985). Protectionist measures connected with the ISI strategy (e.g., the effective tariff rates under Oduber were high, with estimates ranging from 101% to 164%) distorted the efficient distribution of resources, impeded competition, fostered a dependence on imports, and did not stimulate investment in technological innovation that would have improved the comparative advantage of the country (Andic 1983). Industrial production had been geared mostly to the internal market and CACM, leaving the task of generating foreign exchange to the primary sector, whose agricultural exports were restricted by demand and price rigidities in the international market. The CNP, with privileged access to Central Bank credit to subsidize grain prices, provoked a deficit and the Central Bank absorbed some of its losses. Tax exemptions and reductions on imports and the maintenance of a fixed exchange rate fostered overvaluation of the colón, thus reducing the competitiveness of the export sector while encouraging imports and further indebtedness through external borrowing. In the experimentations with multiple exchange rates, exports were always granted the lower and less favorable official exchange rate, to help import substitution but to the detriment of exports. In addition, the three devaluations effected between 1961 and 1979 were not intended to stimulate exports, but rather they stemmed from intentions, explicit or implicit, to curtail imports. In summary, the rigid structure of the protectionist strategy of development created an environment that was less responsive but at the same time more susceptible to external factors (Céspedes et al. 1990).

iii. Diversification

Between 1970 and 1979 the industrial sector grew almost three times more rapidly than the agricultural sector: an annual average of 8.4% versus 3.1%. The real growth of the annual industrial product averaged 10.5% between 1970 and 1974 and 6.5% between 1975 and 1979 (BCCR 1986; ECLAC 1980b). The share of the industrial sector in GDP increased from 20.9% in 1971 to 24.5% in 1978 but stagnated thereafter (Table IV.4). Industrial exports surged from U.S.$58.6 million in 1971 to U.S.$456.7 million in 1980 (Table IV.6).

The policies of CODESA under Figueres and particularly Oduber (as well as fiscal and credit incentives such as the CATs and CIEXs) led to a strengthening of domestic production and some industrial diversification. Activities were directed toward the production or processing of raw materials and foodstuffs (African oil palm, sugar, salt, cocoa, dairy products, cotton), manufactures for direct consumption (e.g., textiles, toys, footwear, cement and other building materials), intermediate and capital goods (like metal manufactures and machinery, aluminum products, and metal spare parts and molds), and chemicals (e.g., sulphur, fertilizers, distilling of anhydrous alcohol for fueling engines, and pharmaceuticals). However, there was stagnation or decline in the production of petroleum products and paper and paperboard. Thus, considerable progress was made in the expansion of output of intermediate and capital goods, although the bulk of industrial investment continued to be in the manufacture of consumer goods (ECLAC 1977a, 1980a, 1981a).

However, industry began to be negatively affected by several factors: increased costs in energy, transport, and imports (highlighting industry's overwhelming dependence on imports); a slowing and eventual decline of per capita income under Carazo; and a fall in exports of manufactures due to reduced trade with CACM. The loss of industrial dynamism under Carazo was also due to the reversal of measures to promote industrial development (for instance, lower tariffs for manufactured consumer goods that increased competition from imports); the suspension of export credits during part of 1979, which reduced exports as they became more expensive; higher taxes on certain consumer goods, which dampened demand; the imposition of additional surcharges on imports; and the establishment of prior deposits to guarantee payment, which made the import of raw materials and intermediate inputs for industry more costly. The industrial lines most affected by the increased cost of inputs (parts, equipment) were the metal manufactures, machinery, and nonmetallic minerals (for the latter, a slump in construction was also a factor). Tanning, foodstuffs/beverages, and motor-vehicle assembly industries were negatively affected by more expensive imports of tanning materials, glass containers, and components and parts, respectively. The fall of domestic demand and contraction of CACM also hit the chemicals, wood products, and canned food industries. The annual growth rate of the industrial products sector slowed from 8.2% in 1978 to 2.7% in 1979 and 0.8% in 1980; it declined 0.5% in 1981 and 11.4% in 1982. The industrial share of GDP stabilized at about 24.5% between 1978 and 1982, in the midst of the crisis (Tables IV.4, IV.6; ECLAC 1977a–82a).

The growth of CODESA during the Oduber administration was partly the result of the president's support but also because it was subject neither to state controls (such as authorization of its budget) nor to the need to generate profits as in the private sector. CODESA's growth highlighted the emergence of the "state entrepreneur" under which the state became both an arbiter (through intervention in the economy) and a competitor of the private sector (particularly in sugar and cement). The original intention was to create and strengthen enterprises with state intervention to overcome initial barriers and then transfer such enterprises to the private sector, but some of those enterprises became the permanent property of CODESA, and none were profitable. In 1974–76 CODESA directed 96% of its resources toward its own projects while only 4% went to the private sector (Doryan 1990). CODESA also competed against the private sector for available credit: in 1978, 60% of public investment went to CODESA; by 1983 it received half of all domestic credit for the public sector and 18% of the total credit of the national banking system, and yet CODESA enterprises contributed an insignificant 1.8% of GDP and employed only 0.3% of the labor force (Céspedes et al., 1990; Doryan 1990). Because of all these reasons, some experts believe that CODESA not only was a failure but also hindered the development of the private sector (Franco and León 1984).

These problems led to a rift during the Oduber administration. Private enterprises, especially the Chamber of Industries, disputed the interventionist role of CODESA as an invasion into areas traditionally reserved for the private sector. Oduber became infuriated at the opposition, and in 1976, after placing CODESA under complete executive control, he cut the latter's support to the private sector in order to speed up its development. Since the forging of the alliance between the state and private sectors (based on the import substitution strategy), this was the first major rift between the two sectors. These events helped defeat the PLN in the 1978 elections (Sojo 1984; Rovira 1988b; Céspedes et al. 1990).

The agricultural product annual growth average declined from 6.5% between 1960 and 1969 to 3.1% between 1970 and 1979 (BCCR 1986; ECLAC *Yearbook* 1980b). The share of agriculture in GDP continued a downward trend, from 23.6% of GDP in 1971 to 18.0% in 1980, although it increased to 19.9% in 1982 (Table IV.4). Reasons for the decline in agricultural output were growing inflation, higher cost of inputs and credit, drought under Oduber, and excessive rainfall under Carazo. Agriculture had also relied on the use of extensive production techniques, which seemed to approach a level of exhaustion in the 1970s (Andic 1983). Agricultural activity was adversely affected by the rise in the cost of main inputs, mostly imported, under Carazo. Although monetary authorities maintained preferential interest rates for small producers and launched a program to encourage coffee and sugarcane plantings, the banking system was inadequate to meet the credit needs. Credits granted to agriculture by the banking system decreased in real terms in 1978 in part because of the rise in interest rates and the restricted liquidity of the traditional banking system. Medium-sized and larger producers had to resort to the more expensive credit terms of financial institutions outside the national banking system, whose higher interest rates evolved similarly to those on international markets. Furthermore, increases in the support prices for grains were insufficient to compensate for rising prices of inputs such as fertilizer, insecticides, and other chemical products. Thus, external factors and Carazo's credit policy contributed to the stagnation of this sector (ECLAC 1979a–80a).

Agricultural expansion was still based on export crops such as coffee and bananas, which remained predominant. Because of special government programs, coffee productivity per unit area became among the highest in the world. While increasing banana prices stimulated production, output stagnated under Carazo because of disease, labor conflicts, and replacement of banana plantations with the cultivation of the African oil palm in the Pacific (Tables IV.5, IV.10). Beef production increased 27% between 1971 and 1981, because of improvements in beef prices and increases in export quotas to the United States. As in the early 1960s, high cocoa prices stimulated cultivation of this crop, especially in the second half of the 1970s, but production plunged 49% in 1980 because of disease. Sugar production increased 20% between 1971 and 1981, also benefiting from favorable prices. Drought conditions fostered the cultivation of sorghum, a drought-resistant crop. Increases in the output of rice, corn, and beans were largely due to the National Basic Grains Program of 1975. Self-sufficiency was achieved in basic grains (except beans) by 1976, although corn production fell 26% the next year (Table IV.5; ECLAC 1975a–78a).

iv. Trade Balance and External Dependency

Favorable prices for export commodities and industrial expansion stimulated growth in trade. Total transactions increased 342% between 1971 and 1980 but declined in 1981–82; exports rose 344% and imports 340% between 1971 and 1980 but decreased in 1981–82 (Table IV.7). Trade dependency, based on total transactions at current/constant prices, was almost stagnant between 1971 and 1980 but jumped from 64% of GDP in 1980 to 91% in 1981 because of the decline of GDP in that year, thus making the country more vulnerable to external factors (Table IV.7; BCCR 1986).

Prices for the traditional export commodities, coffee, and bananas, dropped significantly in 1971 but recovered in 1972 and grew thereafter. International coffee prices fell from 50.5 U.S. cents/pound in 1970 to 44.7 U.S. cents/pound in 1971 but grew until 1977 to an all-time high of U.S.$2.29/pound. International prices for bananas fell from 7.53 U.S. cents/pound in 1970 to 6.37 U.S. cents/pound in 1971, but recovered in 1972 and kept growing for the rest of the decade; banana prices grew at an annual average 9.7% between 1972 and 1982. Beef prices increased under the three administrations, from U.S.$0.43/pound in 1971 to U.S.$0.92/pound in 1979; these prices fell in 1980–81 but rose to U.S.$0.99/pound in 1982 (Table IV.10).

While the expansion of trade continued to rely on traditional exports, the 1972 Law for the Promotion of Exports and Industrial Development led to increased diversification. Between 1971 and 1982, the share of coffee in total exports was virtually stagnant (although it reached 40.6% in 1977 because of booming world prices and declined to 27.5% in 1982), the share of bananas decreased from 29% to 25%, and the share of other exports increased from 29% to 39% (Table IV.8). Nontraditional exports increased their share of exports from 8.5% to 18.5% in the period. The main industrial exports included fertilizers, pharmaceutical products, clothing, insecticides and fungicides, synthetic fabrics, plastic articles, galvanized metal sheets, refrigerators and freezers, tires and inner tubes, and dressed leather (ECLAC 1977a; Colburn and Saballos 1988).

Figueres's fiscal and foreign exchange measures had some success in temporarily changing the composition of imports: fewer consumer goods and more imports of raw materials and capital goods. The dual and foreign exchange surcharge systems also slowed the growth of imports in 1972; an additional factor later was the higher prices of fuels and raw materials. The temporary exchange surcharges, however, raised production costs and made exports to CACM less competitive. The unification of the exchange rates (which became necessary because of the deterioration in the balance of payments) further increased domestic production costs and the price of exports. Still, the fixed official exchange rate was very stable under Figueres and Oduber, with the only major devaluations taking place in 1974 and 1975 (Table IV.3; ECLAC 1974a–75a).

Between 1971 and 1982 there was a reduction in the import shares of foodstuffs from 10% to 7%, while manufactures declined from 54% to 49% between 1971 and 1979 but then increased to 56% in 1982 (the latter was quite high despite the industrialization effort). Although imports of capital goods (machinery and equipment for industry, agriculture and transport) increased, the corresponding share was stagnant at 30% between 1971 and 1979 but declined thereafter to 15% in 1982 because of the crisis. As Costa Rica is totally dependent on oil imports (Table IV.12), the country's economy was substantially affected by the oil crises of the 1970s: fuels increased their import share from 4% to 20% between 1971 and 1982, reducing resources for other imports (Table IV.9).

Despite occasional measures to restrict imports, they grew under Figueres and Oduber because of high export earnings, vigorous economic growth, and expanded consumption. Particularly under the Oduber's recovery, plentiful international reserves and industrial needs stimulated imports. The increases in import volumes and prices were reflected in large and increasing trade deficits, from U.S.$92 million in 1972 to U.S.$279 million in 1974. Trade deficit levels were lower in 1975–77, in large part because of the coffee boom. The external imbalance worsened dramatically in 1978–80 under Carazo, as tariffs were cut on imports of durable consumer goods, fuel prices rose because of the second oil crisis, export commodity prices fell, production stagnated, and trade with CACM decreased. The 1969 war between El Salvador and Honduras, earthquakes in Nicaragua and Guatemala, and the political turmoil in Nicaragua and El Salvador provoked a steady decline of Costa Rican trade with CACM (Table IV.11). But the country continued to expand its imports, relying increasingly on foreign credit to finance both the domestic and external disequilibria; thus, the merchandise trade deficit steadily rose in 1978–80, reaching a peak of U.S.$539 million in 1980. However, foreign loans were insufficient to finance the increase in imports, and the servicing of the debt reduced international reserves. The limits of the import substitution policies became increasingly evident: high dependency on imports, especially capital goods, plus inefficient industries. This crisis brought imports down in 1981–82, and the trade deficit reached a low of U.S.$19 million in the last year (Table IV.7).

The U.S. share in total transactions continued its decline from 36.3% to 34.7% between 1971 and 1982, while that of CACM decreased from 21.5% to 15.9% in the same period (because of the decline in CACM after 1969); the share of the other trade partners, therefore, took almost half of total transactions, increasing trade partner diversification (Table IV.11).

The real total external debt rose by 863% between 1971 and 1982 (from U.S.$418 million to U.S.$4,026 million); the debt burden increased in that period: from 16% to 139% of GDP, from 57% to 309% of the export value of goods and services, and from U.S.$235 to U.S.$1,673 per capita (Table IV.13).

v. Unemployment

Steady economic growth under the Figueres and Oduber administrations had a favorable effect on employment growth. Figures are not available for 1970–75, but the unemployment rate was a moderate 6.3% in 1976 and further declined to 4.5% in 1978 (Table IV.16), although there was substantial underemployment in both urban and rural sectors. Industry, construction, trade activities, and nontraditional agriculture continued to absorb labor. However, there was a decrease in the proportion of those employed in agriculture and a high growth rate for employment in modern nonagricultural activities. The agricultural share of the labor force declined from 49% in 1963 to 36% in 1973 and 27% in 1980. Conversely, the combined share of industry, mining, and construction rose from 19% in 1973 to 24% in 1980 (Table IV.14). A decrease in the availability of uncultivated land and expanded differences in urban and rural salaries fostered increased migration from the rural to the urban sector.

The expansion of employment in the service sector, which includes government services, was remarkable. The public sector absorbed about 20% of the work force during the Carazo administration and became the second largest employer after the agricultural sector (but contributing to fiscal disequilibrium). The service sector increased its share in the labor force from

17.2% in 1963 to 22.7% in 1973 and 22.9% in 1980 (if transportation and commerce are added, the shares were 31%, 38%, and 48%, respectively) (Table IV.14). However, these figures do not represent the total picture, since part of the employment in other sectors (construction, electricity, gas, water) are in the public sector. The expansion in the state sector was crucial in the PLN strategy to decrease unemployment by expanding public employment. The creation of numerous autonomous institutions and expansion of social services contributed to that goal; employment in the public sector was also attractive because salaries were generally higher than those in the private sector. The percentage of women in the labor force increased from 16.3% in 1963 to 19.3% in 1973 and 24.8% in 1980, and the participation rate rose from 16% to almost 21% between 1970 and 1980 (Table IV.15).

The open unemployment rate rose to 4.9% in 1979, reaching 8.7% in 1981 and 9.4% in 1982 during the two worst years of the crisis. The urban unemployment rate in those two years was higher than both the national and the rural rate (Table IV.16). In 1979–82 the traditional-rural and informal-urban sectors increased their participation within the employed population from 27.7% to 29.2% and from 14.5% to 15.2%, respectively. These figures suggest a concentration of workers in lower income strata and the growth of underemployment and the informal sector, because of income reduction and higher formal unemployment (Pollack and Uthoff 1987).

Labor productivity grew well in the 1960s, particularly in industry and agriculture. The high rate of productivity growth in industry was due to the ambitious investments in infrastructure and improvements in technology. In agriculture it resulted from increased mechanization and acreage, implementation of advanced techniques (e.g., fertilizers, better seeds especially in coffee), and transfers of workers from rural occupations of a low productivity to modern occupations of higher productivity. Labor productivity slowed after 1974 because of the impact of increased oil prices; it declined especially in industry and the public sector, in the latter due also to increased public employment under Oduber (Andic 1983).

Union activity increased particularly in the agrarian sector because of the deterioration of income among landless wage laborers. They began to unionize in 1978 in different regions of the country, eventually organizing 14 unions. In the early 1980s, under Carazo, strikes in banana plantations paralyzed production (Anderson 1991). The concentration of workers in the public sector facilitated their unionization: in 1975, 62% of unionized workers were in the public sector (Sojo 1984). Public employees have been among the most active in political parties, particularly in the PLN, thus exerting influence through political activism and powerful unions. One reason for the growth in expenditures in education was the political influence exerted by teachers unions, probably the most powerful pressure group in Costa Rica (Aguilar 1990).

Labor conflicts in both the private and public sectors under Carazo reached levels not seen since the 1930s. The number of strikes and lockouts rose from 14 to 61 in 1978–80 (they declined in 1981 and 1982 to 6 and 14, respectively), taking place in the urban centers and the Atlantic port of Limón. The number of workers involved in strikes and lockouts increased from 8,303 (1.5% of total employment in 1973) to 25,671 (3.6% of total employment) in 1979, and the number of workdays lost in 1980 reached a record 427,350 (ILO 1982a). Much of the conflict arose from increased unemployment and a fall in real wages, as well as popular discontent with Carazo's efforts to liberalize the economy.

vi. Equality

The two series on income distribution in Costa Rica are apparently not comparable, and we do not have an entire series for the 1971–82 substage (Table IV.18). In the series on family income, there was a worsening in distribution between 1971 and 1983, while in the series on heads of household there was a worsening also, although less accentuated, between 1979 and 1982. On the other hand, a comparison (not technically correct) of 1971 (first series) with 1979 (second series) indicates an improvement: the income of the wealthiest quintile declined significantly, while the income of the poorest quintile increased, but, as between 1961 and 1971, the middle-income sectors were those having the biggest increase.

Data on poverty incidence, nevertheless, consistently show an improvement, at least until before the crisis (Table IV.20). The series of Sauna-Trejos and PREALC exhibit a dramatic decline of poverty—and to a less extent indigency or extreme poverty—between 1971 and 1977 (prior to the crisis), both at the national level and in urban and rural areas, regardless of whether individual or family income are used. The ECLAC series on household income between 1970 and 1981 (hence including the first year of the crisis) shows only a slight decline of poverty at the national level and in rural areas, but stagnation or a small deterioration in indigency and urban poverty.

Real wages declined in 1973–75 with increased inflation but recovered steadily for the rest of the decade: there was an increase of 20 percentage points in the mean wage between 1973 and 1980. Oduber's stabilization program, which included extraordinary adjustments of minimum wages, successfully restored purchasing power. Because of the redistributive nature of this adjustment, agricultural workers benefited the most (Andic 1983). Carazo tried to maintain the real minimum wage by adjusting it to inflation (in 1978–80), but as the inflation worsened in 1981–82 real average and minimum wages plummeted by 29 and 14 percentage points, respectively (Table IV.20). The crisis affected more workers in the private than in the public sector, and there was increased participation in the labor force of low-paid and less-qualified workers, such as manual workers or service personnel in agriculture and industry (Pollack 1987). However, among salary workers, the effect was felt more in the public sector; the drop in public salaries declined more and recovered less than the salaries in the private sector (Sojo 1989).

The first ITCO titling program failed to achieve the goal of 27,000 titles set out in the 1971–75 period: by 1976 only 14,764 titles were granted. The ITCO's preoccupation with other titling efforts (e.g., in private lands and on Indian reservations), conflicts among prospective title holders, and disputes with third parties over land ownership limited the program's success. However, by 1979 ITCO (now IDA) had accomplished 76% of the goal by granting 20,462 titles. For the second titling program of 1979, by 1981 17,113 of 36,469 titles had been granted. Overall, the two ITCO/IDA titling programs improved farm production, stimulated the planting of permanent crops, reduced land concentration, and increased the use of credit and technical assistance, the latter less successfully (Seligson 1982). As international prices for coffee dropped, the income of small and medium-sized producers did not cover production costs, and many became indebted and risked losing their land. Credit also became increasingly scarce, expensive and difficult to repay. The deteriorating situation of the small producers adversely affected landless wage laborers employed by them.

Social welfare policy (see next section) narrowed the gap between urban and rural areas and improved income distribution. The Family Allowance Program reduced poverty as indicated by (1) the quadrupling of the number of beneficiaries of the nutrition program in 1975–77, (2) an increase of health stations in rural areas from 140 to 220, with the number of people receiving medical attention rising from 360,000 to 660,000, and (3) the doubling of beneficiaries in the noncontributory (welfare) pension program (IDB 1977). The redistributive effect of social spending also became of major importance in view of the increasingly regressive tax structure. Costa Rica became a model of growth with equity: with the appropriate government tools, benefits of economic growth were widely spread and more equity attained (Mesa-Lago and Díaz-Briquets 1988; Sojo 1989; Céspedes et al. 1990).

vii. Social Indicators

The share of social expenditures in total central government expenditures steadily rose from 55.4% to 69.5% between 1972 and 1982 (the index of *real* social expenditures of the central government steadily increased from 35.3

to 100 between 1972 and 1980 but declined to 73.7 in 1982). Within the area of social expenditures, the share of social security and health care kept growing between 1972 and 1982, but the share of education declined, and that of housing increased slightly (Table IV.17). The dramatic improvement in social indicators in the 1970s reflected the rapid expansion of the infrastructure and social services funded by public spending, supported by steady economic growth and access to external financing. But the crisis of the early 1980s adversely affected many social services, although some health indicators continued improving.

Table IV.21 shows the continued improvement in health care between 1971 and 1982. The number of doctors per 10,000 inhabitants exhibited an upward trend, from 6.2 to 8.3 (although the number of hospital beds per 1,000 inhabitants continued to decline, from 4.1 to 2.9); the general mortality rate (per 1,000) dropped from 5.9 to 3.8 and the infant mortality rate (per 1,000) from 56.5 to 18.9; and life expectancy rose from 67.6 to 73.5 years. The Program of Family Allowances was successful in reducing the level of malnutrition due to insufficient protein and calorie intake from 53% in 1975 to 46% in 1978 and 34% in 1982 (Ministry of Health 1985). The percentage of the urban population with sewerage services increased from 22% in 1969 to 40% in 1973 and 92% in 1979. Coverage of water services expanded in the rural sector from 54% in 1969 to 66% in 1973 and 68% in 1979 (Table IV.23).

The extension of population coverage and the better quality of health care combined with preventive medicine changed the national pathological profile away from "diseases of underdevelopment" (such as malnutrition, digestive, respiratory, and contagious) toward "diseases of development" (such as cardiovascular and cancer) (Mesa-Lago 1992). A comparison of average rates of contagious diseases between 1971 and 1982 shows significant reductions in the rates of diphtheria and polio (the rates for both diseases being zero or negligible by 1976), measles (despite a dramatic increase in 1979), tetanus, tuberculosis, and typhoid. However, hepatitis, malaria and syphilis did not show a clear trend (Table IV.22).

The aforementioned improvements also reflect the success of the policy of extending social security to the whole population. In the 1970s the CCSS continued to extend coverage, and by 1980 practically all the population received health coverage, about three-fourths by social insurance and the remaining one-fourth through social-welfare and public-health programs. In 1971, 52% of the total population and 42% of the economically active population were covered under social security; these rates increased to 84% and 75% in 1979, respectively, although both rates declined during the crisis of 1980–82 to 68% and 64%, respectively (Table IV.25).

Primary and secondary education services increased remarkably during this substage. The number of elementary schools rose from 2,856 to 3,482 between 1971 and 1981, while the number of secondary schools jumped from 142 to 261, and the public system of higher education grew from one to four universities (Aguilar 1990; Fischel 1988). Enrollment in elementary education continued to be universal in the 1970s, while enrollments in secondary and higher education between 1971 and 1978 increased from 30% to 53% and from 12% to 24%, respectively (Table IV.24). The crisis and cut in social expenditures reversed some of the previous trends; thus in 1982 secondary enrollment had dropped to 46% and higher education enrollment to 21%. The National Training Institute and the Technological Institute were instrumental in providing skilled labor for industry (ECLAC 1977a; Rovira 1988b).

The number of houses built by the government increased under Figueres and peaked in 1976 under Oduber, but public spending constraints during the crisis badly harmed the provision of housing, which recorded lower indices in 1981–82. Compared to the 1,989 units built by INVU in 1978, only 52 were completed in 1982 (Sojo 1989). Housing units built by 1,000 inhabitants steadily increased from 3.0 in 1970 to 6.7 in 1974 (6.6 in 1976) but declined thereafter to 3.5 in 1982 (Table IV.26).

4

Stabilization, Adjustment, and Restructuring

1982–1994

Because of widespread dissatisfaction with Carazo and his CU coalition, Luis Alberto Monge of the PLN was elected president in February 1982; the PLN also won 33 out of 57 seats in the Legislative Assembly versus 18 seats by the CU. Such an ample legislative majority was vital for the PLN to pass the necessary reforms to stabilize and reactivate the economy. In the 1986 elections, the PLN's candidate, Oscar Arias, also won the presidency by a comfortable margin and controlled 29 out of the 57 seats versus 25 by the opposition. The PLN control of the executive and legislative powers for two consecutive terms were tempered by a drastically deteriorated economic situation compared to previous decades: the severe economic-financial crisis, combined with the conditions imposed by international organizations to obtain external financing, made necessary a program of structural adjustment. The state could no longer depend on traditional instruments (planning, ownership, public investment, credit, fiscal deficit, external borrowing) to stimulate economic growth and provide employment and social services to the population, and yet those social gains had to be saved as essential elements of Costa Rica's model.

In 1983 Rafael Angel Calderón Fournier (the son of Calderón Guardia) organized a center-right Social Christian Unity Party (PUSC) constituted by four parties including the Calderón-led Republican Calderonista Party (PRC). In the 1986 election, Calderón lost the presidency but gained 25 seats and the PUSC coalition became the second largest party in the Assembly. He then led the PUSC to victory in the 1990 election and also won a majority in the National Assembly. Throughout the electoral campaign, Calderón identified with the legacy of his father, and took a populist stand. He won considerable backing from the poor with promises to support agriculture (to attain self-sufficiency and reduce the need to import certain foodstuffs) and to provide food and free housing to them. The PUSC was to the right of the PLN and represented many conservative views of the business elite (e.g., reducing overall state intervention in the economy and the dominance of national banks). Like Carazo, Calderón had to reconcile diverse ideologies within the PUSC regarding the degree and type of government role in the economy, ranging from the very conservative to those in favor of continued state support in some areas, such as agriculture (Daremblum 1990; LAN 1990a).

The three administrations, although of diverse ideology, did not differ significantly on policy that was aimed at: reducing the public sector and expanding the private economy; reforming taxes (to increase government revenue) and cutting expenditures (to reduce the fiscal deficit, stabilize the economy, and decrease inflation); shifting credit from the public to the private sector and deregulating private banking and liberalizing prices and the interest rate; abandoning the ISI for an export-promotion development strategy; opening up the economy to world trade (reducing import tariffs), unifying the exchange rate, and gradually shifting it from state control to market-setting; renegotiating the external debt and accepting a structural-adjustment program from international financial organizations; launching programs to reduce unemployment and adjust wages; and applying compensatory policies to counter the adverse effects of structural adjustment. Calderón, however, accelerated the path of some liberalization policies, unsuccessfully attempted to privatize public utilities and some social services, and cut educational and housing expenses but was able to reform pension programs.

1. Policies

A. Ownership

Under Monge, and especially Arias and Calderón, there was a tilt in economic policy toward economic liberalization and the market, which led to increased privatization. The financial difficulties of CODESA enterprises (particularly in cement, fertilizer, metal manufactures, and machinery) had contributed to the deficit of that institution. As a condition of structural adjustment agreements with international financial agencies (to reduce fiscal expenditures and the public sector), the government had to sell off most of the CODESA enterprises to both the private sector and cooperatives. The PLN had opposed the selling of CODESA enterprises during the Carazo administration but eventually was forced to undertake that action because of the severity of the crisis and external pressure. In January 1985 Monge's government signed an agreement with the Agency for International Development (USAID) through which U.S.$140 million were allocated to the dismantling of CODESA. That loan was to help cancel CODESA's massive debt—a major obstacle to economic stabilization agreements—with the Central Bank and improve the finances of the enterprises to make them more attractive to potential buyers. The Arias administration continued the sale of the CODESA subsidiaries, which closed its agro-industry branch, and sold its cement subsidiaries. By 1990 out of the 40 CODESA enterprises, 23 had been liquidated or were in the process of liquidation, and 12 had been sold or were being sold. Calderón's government privatized the last 2 of 40 CODESA enterprises: a major cement producer (CEMPASA) in 1993 and a fertilizer company (FERTICA) in 1994 (ECLAC 1982a, 1993a, 1994a; Trejos 1985; Céspedes et al. 1990; Lizano 1990; Salazar 1990).

Although Monge and Arias gave private banks greater scope to participate in local business, the privatization of the nationalized banking system was delayed by internal political debate. Calderón unsuccessfully tried to privatize public services and expand private banking. In 1991 he established the bipartisan Commission for State Reform (COREC II), which elaborated several proposals of constitutional amendment such as the "Law of Public Sector Democratization," which advocated transfer of public services to private organizations, and the "Law of Public Works Concessions," which promoted privatization of construction of the infrastructure. Calderón's attempts to negotiate reform through this partisan commission, outside of the Legislative Assembly, were not successful because of the PLN's withdrawal from the commission in 1992. Additionally, plans to privatize INS (insurance) and ICE (electricity) met with stiff resistance from public-sector employees, who frequently striked and paralyzed operations (Daremblum 1991; IDB 1994a).

B. Planning

There were two main stages in the Monge administration. The first ran from May 1982 to September 1983, when a final agreement with the international financial community was reached on the external debt; its two major objectives were to stabilize the economy and halt the deterioration in social conditions. The administration launched a structural adjustment program, to halt inflation and set the basis for a recovery, but combined it with compensatory social policies. The emergency stabilization policy was concentrated in four areas: (1) stabilization and eventual unification of the exchange rate, (2) reestablishment of relations with international financial organizations to renegotiate the external public debt and obtain continued financial and technical assistance, (3) improvement of public finances (reducing public expenditures while increasing revenues), and (4) a fair distribution of the social cost of the stabilization program among the population. The major economic goals were to control inflation and stop the devaluation of the colón and to bolster confidence in the economy by increasing investment and halting capital flight. Monge's second stage ran from 1983 to the end of his administration in 1986; its central objectives were to maintain and consolidate the stability that had been accomplished in the first stage, as well as to reactivate the economy (Trejos 1985; Rovira 1988b; Céspedes et al. 1990).

As part of the Monge (and Arias) policy, there was a decline of control or change in functions of some state agencies (CNP, Central Bank, Ministry of Trade) in order to liberalize the economy and strengthen the private sector, but new state agencies were created (Ministry of Exports, CNI, COREC) to implement the new policies. Monge's 1982–86 plan also introduced a new strategy for development, targeting agriculture to achieve food self-sufficiency and increase exports (see section E below). A management and planning subsystem was created for coordinating the activities of autonomous institutions and entities as a culmination of a trend that began in the 1970s toward greater central government control. A 1985 law mandated that such institutions submit their budgets to both the General Comptroller and the central Budgetary Authority. The latter could solicit reductions in the budgets from the Comptroller so that these expenses could be adjusted according to the National Plan of Development. The law also limited central government access to credit from the national banking system (based on expenditures of the previous year) and prohibited the use of external credit to cover current expenditures of autonomous institutions. Quarterly reports to the Legislative Assembly on the internal credit received by the central government and autonomous institutions became mandatory (Trejos 1985).

Criticizing the "excessive expenditures" of the Arias administration, Calderón's economic program focused on reducing the deficit of both the public sector and the balance of payments. Although not radically shifting economic policy, such a program did accelerate the process of liberalization by implementing policies proposed but not enforced by the previous two administrations. Calderón entered into negotiations with the IMF for an adjustment loan specifically oriented at reducing the size and role of the state, through cuts in public employment and spending, and decreasing the functions of the national development banks. The agreement was eventually signed with the IMF in 1991; its main economic targets were virtual elimination of the fiscal deficit, reduction of the foreign-trade deficit to one-third its level, replenishing the country's international reserves, and cutting the inflation rate by half. The government agreed to curb domestic demand by restricting credit and implementing a more disciplined fiscal policy that would boost tax receipts and cut public spending (ECLAC 1991a; Castro and González 1992; Hansen-Kuhn 1993).

C. Financing

The three administrations introduced tax reforms to create or raise taxes, increase fiscal revenue, reduce inflation, cut the public deficit, simplify and expedite collection, impose tougher sanctions on evaders, and eliminate exemptions. In 1983 Monge raised social security wage contributions, introduced import surcharges, imposed additional surcharges on exports, and passed a tax reform that increased both sale taxes (from 8% to 10%) and consumption taxes and established a temporary surcharge on income tax (to expand the tax base and increase revenues). Under Arias a tax bill approved in November 1987 generated several new sources of revenue: taxes on luxury goods and automobile ownership, higher real estate tax rates, and broader sales tax coverage. In order to improve the efficiency of the tax system, an important reform of both personal and corporate income tax was implemented in April 1988 that lowered marginal income tax rates, reduced the number of deductions, and eliminated a large number of individuals from the tax rolls (ECLAC 1987a; Céspedes et al. 1990; IDB 1990).

Calderón took several steps to restructure the tax system and increase tax revenues. In 1991 numerous exemptions were eliminated, harsher penalties for tax evasion established, and the tax on banana exports was increased. Administrative reform simplified the tax system, streamlined procedures for tax collection through court action, and adopted measures to speed up tax collection. These provisions boosted receipts. In 1991 the Legislative Assembly broadened the sales tax to include electricity and telephone services, as well as petroleum sales: monthly electricity rates were increased by 1.8% and basic telephone rates by 10%, and the prices of oil derivatives produced by RECOPE were raised by 13% above cost. In addition, there was a temporary increase of the sales tax rate from 10% to 13%. Several public utility rates were again raised in 1992, aimed at meeting the expected growth of service demand: water by 18%, electricity rates by 24%, and new telephone services by 25% and the basic rate by 50%. Finally, higher taxes were imposed on pensions paid to teachers (ECLAC 1990–92a; Daremblum 1991; Castro and González 1992; IDB 1992, 1994).

The three administrations also had steady policies to reduce domestic and external credit to the public sector and shift it to the private sector. Policies on the interest rate varied. Under Monge interest rates were set by the Central Bank, but it gradually reducing its role, Arias allowed private banks to fix rates, and Calderón raised them. Under Monge, credit was allocated by the Central Bank based on profitability and soundness of recipients; Arias subsequently established credit ceilings to private banks, then dropped and reintroduced them; and Calderón froze credit for one year. Monge began deregulation of private banks; Arias expanded their operation but regulated them when problems arose; and Calderón failed to allow private banks to receive savings deposits. These policies are discussed in more detail next.

Monge introduced notable changes in monetary and credit policies to gradually eliminate controls on interest rates and credit allocation to channel the latter to the private sector. Interest rates were set by the Central Bank, but it gradually reduced its role. In 1982 the interest rate on bank deposits was raised by 25% and lending rates by 28% to increase savings. Many producers objected to the increase, arguing that the resulting rise of production costs was greater than the increase in prices of their goods and services. As a result, the monetary authorities maintained preferential lines of credit for certain priority activities, such as agriculture. The Central Bank also assumed the financial cost of excess reserves so that commercial banks would not cancel or restrict their lending operations. In 1983 the decline in the inflation rate and more confidence in the monetary system allowed a gradual reduction of interest rates; in 1984, however, the Central Bank increased the interest rate charged to commercial banks to reduce liquidity in the economy. In 1983 the money supply was increased by a percentage similar to the combined growth rates of prices and production (the expansion in credit to the private sector had much to do with the increase in money supply). Later the rate of growth of the means of payment was brought down, financial savings were increased, the speed of monetary circulation was slowed, and credit policy became easier.

As part of an agreement with USAID, efforts were made by Monge in 1984 to reduce the direct participation of the Central Bank in domestic financing, deregulate the private banks, and thus expand the operations of the private financial system. New legislation enacted that year allowed the Central Bank to give loans in foreign currency to private banks and permitted the rediscounting of funds to private banks and their access to other credit programs on an equal basis with the nationalized banking system. Savings were also encouraged by the sale of bonds, as an additional means of stabilization. In 1985 the Central Bank began to allocate credit based on the profitability and financial soundness of each activity instead of judging which economic sectors should be stimulated (ECLAC 1984a; Céspedes et al. 1990; Lizano 1990).

Arias's monetary policy had three main objectives: to reduce inflation, promote savings, and foster the integration of the financial system. Restriction of state financing continued, and government setting of interest rates was further reduced to enhance the role of the market. In 1987 the government authorized commercial banks to freely determine interest rates on loans and deposits in the national currency (partly as a result of this, real interest rates throughout most of the banking system became positive). The Central Bank, therefore, decided to no longer set interest rates. The credit liberalization program continued under Arias. In 1986 quarterly credit ceilings were set on national banks. In 1987 the Central Bank eliminated all credit-allocating categories and overall credit ceilings and reduced advance deposit requirements for imports from 100% to 10%. Credit ceilings were replaced by the more frequent use of open market operations, by changes in reserve requirements on deposits, and by discount rates. As the inflation rate increased in 1987, however, the Central Bank attempted to reduce liquidity in the economy by paying more competitive interest rates and increasing previous deposits for importers from 10% to 50%. In order to control credit expansion, overall ceilings were reinstated in 1988, and a limit was set on the amount of credit that could be granted to commercial activities and consumers. Bank regulations were thus strengthened, and provisions to increase solvency and efficiency of state-owned banks were instituted (ECLAC 1986a; Céspedes et al. 1990).

A significant increase in inflation in 1990–91 moved Calderón to enforce a more restrictive monetary policy. In September 1990 the Central Bank froze credit to the private sector for the rest of the year. In order to absorb the excess liquidity coming in from external funds in 1991, the Central Bank entered into operations on the open market, sharply increased reserve requirements on deposits, and raised interest rates substantially (Daremblum 1990; IDB 1992a; IMF *IFSY* 1994). Calderón took measures that focused on reducing private-sector credit expansion, which had risen at an annualized rate of 39% during the first half of 1993. The authorities tightened monetary policy by sharply raising reserve requirements. In addition, they raised interest rates on Central Bank and government securities and quickened the pace of daily exchange-rate devaluations. The Central Bank added liquidity to the system by engaging in net purchases of its open bond markets in an attempt to keep interest rates from rising even further (IDB 1994a).

The Central Bank, in line with the financial reform promoted by Calderón, approved private banks to receive savings for periods of less than 30 days. This measure was supported by the financial sector and private banks, which affirmed that it would have a favorable impact on banks, both state and private, by increasing the amount of loans available. However, strong opposition by the PLN in the Legislative Assembly and its pullout from COREC II forced the government to suspend those measures. Critics charged that the policy of allowing short-term accounts in private banks was a direct attack on the nationalized banking system in place since 1949 (Castro and González 1992).

D. Stability and Prices

The three administrations pursued similar policies of adjustment and price liberalization, although Calderón accelerated the process. In order to cut the fiscal deficit, taxes were raised (as seen in the previous section), and public expenditures were cut, for example, credit, public investment, and employment, and there was wage control, and reductions in housing, higher-education, and transport expenditures. Prices of fuel and tariffs on public utilities (transport, electricity, water, telephone) were raised. Subsidies to prices of consumer goods were cut also. Price regulatory agencies (CNP, Ministry of Trade) began to reduce their role, as prices were liberalized.

According to conditions set by international agreements, Monge was committed to cutting the deficit of the public sector (that is, central government, public institutions, state enterprises, Central Bank) by one-half in 1982–83. We have seen that the public sector's access to credit was restricted, in order for the private sector to increase its share, and that taxes were raised. Prices for fuel and some public utilities were increased in 1982, aimed at restoring the financial equilibrium of the corresponding agencies: fuel prices by 92%, public transport fares by 100%, and electricity rates by 200%. Capital expenditures were cut, and some road works were canceled. Strong consumer pressure in 1983 caused by widespread price increases the year before, however, led the government to expand control of prices: the number of products subject to price control was enlarged, authorization for price increases were limited, administrative mechanisms for ensuring compliance with ceiling prices were strengthened, and price increments planned for some public utilities were deferred or reconsidered. Additional measures were taken in 1984 to stabilize the economy, reduce public spending, and enhance revenues. There were rises in some taxes as well as in rates for electricity, water, and telephone services (9%, 70%, and 70% increases, respectively). In the public sector, salary raises for public employees were restricted, hiring freezes and incentives for voluntary retirement were passed, and budgets were cut. Arias also increased prices for gasoline and electricity rates in 1987, along with certain taxes (ECLAC 1983a; Trejos 1985; Rovira 1988b).

There was increasing debate over the role of the National Production Council (CNP). As a condition for external financing, the IMF and other international agencies stipulated that the CNP's deficit should be reduced and its policy of intervention in the markets should be phased out. The CNP bought certain grains (e.g., beans) from producers at prices higher than producer equilibrium prices, and then the Trade Ministry sold them to consumers at prices lower than equilibrium prices (there was often disagreement between the two offices regarding the prices set). The basic grains thus had a minimum support price above the equilibrium market price. The PLN's logic was that the fixing of minimum and maximum prices stimulated both production and demand. Critics charged that the policy of subsidizing agricultural prices for producers of basic grains distorted the system by generating costly overproduction and raising costs, especially in the case of rice and corn (ECLAC 1984a; Corrales 1984).

Monge reduced the subsidies paid to producers of basic grains and increased consumer prices, in order to cut CNP financial losses. Arias cut subsidies to agricultural products and other forms of state price fixing and transformed the CNP into the enforcing agency of the new policy to make agriculture more efficient. The CNP stopped buying rice and sorghum, allowing prices to be set by domestic and external markets; prices of other basic grains continued to be readjusted, at both the producer and consumer levels, and hence consumer prices for wheat, beans, and corn were raised (Céspedes et al. 1990). The Trade Ministry also set price ceilings (instead of minimum prices paid to producers) that were often below equilibrium prices (such as in milk, meat, eggs, sugar, coffee); this action created an excess demand over supply. Consumers often had to pay prices for some goods higher than comparable prices in other countries (such as for milk, basic grains, coffee, sugar); the state did this to allow certain productive activities to survive. However, the fixing of price ceilings, lower than equilibrium prices, had a serious negative impact on the production and consumption of rice, eggs, coffee, and milk. "Mixed" prices were also used (prices fixed according to usually higher internal and lower international prices), although they generated high cost in animal feeding (Corrales 1984).

Calderón's key targets of the stabilization program included reduction of the public sector to 0.5% of GDP within a year, a cut in public employment by 5%, limiting real salary growth to 15%, decreasing inflation to 15%, and diminishing the trade balance deficit to 3.5% of GDP (Castro and González 1992). To cut public expenditures in 1990–91, a freeze was imposed on the creation of new jobs in the central government, 2,800 public employees were dismissed, wage increases limited, and investment in some state enterprises reduced. By December 1992 the government eliminated subsidies to nontraditional exports, as part of the agreement with the IMF to continue the move toward free trade and reduction of the fiscal deficit. This move was opposed by exporters of nontraditional products, which are extremely important to the Costa Rican economy: in 1991 they earned more than the traditional exports of coffee, bananas, and sugar. On the revenue side Calderón rose taxes, increased rates of public utilities (water, electricity, and phones), and introduced custom duty reforms (Scott 1991b; Taylor 1992a).

The April 1991 IMF agreement had barely been signed when an earthquake struck Costa Rica, killing 62 people and causing massive damage to the port of Limón and other infrastructure. Although there was an urgent need to provide emergency relief and repair damaged roads, bridges, and port facilities, the IMF insisted that the government continue its planned reduction of spending. Deep cuts throughout the rest of 1991 followed in housing, higher education, and transportation. Low harvest yields in 1991 and higher prices for basic grains in 1992 led the government to reconsider its earlier measures to reduce agricultural subsidies and maintain minimum prices for grains (Castro and González 1992; Hansen-Kuhn 1993).

The adjustment measures and austere economic program, along with the accumulation of international reserves during 1991, laid the base for the progress of stabilization efforts in 1992. A rise in domestic demand during 1992 exerted only minimal pressure on prices thanks to an increase in imports. Even so, inflation was higher than expected (ECLAC 1992a). The liberalization of prices begun in late 1992 for basic consumer products (such as milk, basic grains, coffee, sugar) threatened many small businesses, such as neighborhood grocery stores and their suppliers. As a result of the liberalization, prices of only 6 out of the 82 articles of the "basic basket" remained regulated by the government: rice, beans, eggs, milk, butter, and poultry feed (Castro and González 1992). The rapid slackening in price rises in 1993 brought inflation down to the lowest level in 15 years, less than half the figure for the previous year, and marked a major advance in the stabilization process.

E. Development Strategy

The three administrations moved away from import substitution toward export promotion and opening to world trade. Agriculture was one of Monge's main concerns, as production was lagging because of the crisis and a drought. His 1982–86 plan was called "Return to the Land" and targeted agricultural and agro-industrial sectors to promote production, self-sufficiency in food, and exports. The plan also called for better organization, modernization through improved technology, increased productivity, a fair price system, more credit for the sector, employment generation, and a fair distribution of income. To facilitate plan implementation, the public agricultural sector was restructured, the planning system strengthened, and the Ministry of Agriculture reorganized to increase its regional presence and avoid duplication of functions (MIDEPLAN 1983; Villasuso 1987).

Support measures to the plan included a Program to Increase Agricultural Production (PIPA), a national dairy development program, an irrigation and drainage system, and a project to improve livestock production and animal health. The Program for the Improvement of Coffee Production also helped to achieve record coffee harvests. Another project was to restore the competitiveness of banana production in external markets (which had been impaired by disease, a drop in prices, and strikes) through lower export taxes, price subsidies, and assistance with disease control. In search of new alternatives for sugarcane, alcohol production was attempted, but it faced low international prices. Cocoa-sown area was expanded and production bolstered. The government also acquired the land of a transnational banana company moving out of Costa Rica to promote the cultivation of African oil palm and livestock raising. Finally, a policy of farm credit and insurance for the most important food crops was launched (ECLAC 1985a).

Price adjustments of sugar, black beans, corn, tortillas, milk, coffee, and butter sought to stimulate and then stabilize production, thus favoring both producers and consumers. In 1982–83 there were price increases of 100% for producers of rice, beans, and sorghum and smaller increases for producers of corn and eggs. Those rises were more moderate in 1984–85 as a result of the fall in inflation and the stability of import prices. Monge tried to patch up the differences between the state and the private sectors by reducing the role of the "state entrepreneur" (dismantling CODESA) and reexamining the traditional ISI development strategy. In the early 1980s, the limits to such a strategy were evident: substantial dependence on imports and external financing, tremendous growth of the public sector, and domestic and external disequilibria.

Under Monge and Arias, a new development strategy was pursued based on elimination of or cuts in subsidies and other forms of state intervention, promotion of traditional and nontraditional exports (specially outside CACM), increased economic liberalization (e.g., relaxation of domestic financial regulations), and openings to the world market (for instance, to imports through a gradual reduction of tariffs and surcharges to achieve higher efficiency). A debate unfolded on the new strategy as it harmed several important groups; for instance, the reduction of agricultural subsidies would harm the production of staple grains, and lower tariff protection would adversely affect the emerging industrial sector (Bulmer-Thomas 1988).

Calderón sought to expand the export-promotion strategy (both of industrial and agricultural goods) begun under Monge and Arias. Export-assembly plants (*maquiladoras*) continued to receive incentives such as preferential interest rates, exemption from income taxes, and export incentive bonds (CATs). The last, available to exporters of agriculture and industrial products, were worth up to 12% of the value of nontraditional exports sold and could be used by recipients to reduce their income taxes or sold for cash. Over 70% of the export-oriented factories produced textiles, although investment had been growing in electronics. Calderón also introduced a new agricultural policy to reorient production even more toward exports. Credit and guaranteed prices for grain and bean production for the domestic market were cut, and restrictions on grain imports, which competed with domestic production, were lifted. The colón was devalued to make agricultural exports cheaper and more competitive in world markets. Incentives for exports included the elimination of export taxes and import duties on farm inputs, income tax exemptions of production for export, preferential interest rates, special access to foreign exchange, and CATs. This greater opening to imports through a steep reduction in tariffs aimed at increasing domestic efficiency (Hansen-Kuhn 1993).

Critics of Calderón's development strategy claimed that ownership in both the agricultural and industrial nontraditional sectors had been heavily concentrated in foreign investors, who also took a large share of the incentives and benefits provided by the government. The reduced economic role of the state and the opening of the economy to the outside world was seen by many "neostructuralists" and PLN hard-liners as detrimental to local control over economic development efforts (Castro and González 1992; Hansen-Kuhn 1993).

F. External Sector

The three administrations took steps to gradually liberalize the foreign exchange rate: Monge introduced gradual devaluations, unified the three rates, and adopted the crawling peg; Arias continued the policy of gradual devaluations; and Calderón abandoned the crawling peg and adopted a floating policy. There were steady policies as well on the negotiations over the external debt with international financial organization and foreign commercial bank and government creditors: Monge signed agreements with IMF, the World Bank (SAL I), IDB, USAID, and foreign private banks; Arias began the policy of equity swaps and signed agreements with IMF and the World Bank (SAL II); and Calderón signed agreements with foreign commercial banks, the Club of Paris, IMF, World Bank (SAL III), and IDB. Finally, foreign trade policies were fairly consistent in favor of external openings to imports and promotion of exports: Monge created new public agencies and provided incentives to promote exports, reformed tariffs, and established free-trade zones; Arias reduced import tariffs and import surcharges and led Costa Rica's entrance into GATT; and Calderón joined the Central American effort to increase trade, signed an agreement with Mexico (with the ultimate goal of joining NAFTA), and further reduced import tariffs and eliminated import surcharges.

Monge tried to stabilize the foreign exchange rate with two objectives: to reduce the disparities between the various exchange rates (the free, the official, and the interbank rates), and to lessen the erratic fluctuations that the exchange rate had experienced in the past. The number of operations undertaken under the official exchange rate was diminished, hence it lost importance; for instance, the percentage of foreign exchange that exporters had to sell to the Central Bank at the official rate was decreased from 15% to 5%. In August 1982 the foreign exchange market was centralized under the Central Bank, ending the sharp variations in the exchange rates. The Central Bank also set prices for the dollar, which led to a gradual devaluation of the colón. Thereafter, the free (parallel) exchange rate, the principal source of trouble as it led to speculation and put pressure on the official exchange rate, began to decline. In the meantime, the interbank rate remained stable.

At the beginning of 1983, the only two effective exchange rates left were the interbank and the free one, both managed by the Central Bank. In June of that year the monetary authorities decided to increase the interbank exchange rate by 1 colón and reduce the free rate by the same amount. The aim of this measure was to encourage exports (net payments for 98% of exports was made at the interbank exchange rate), discourage imports, and decrease disparities between the two rates to advance more rapidly toward their unification (one of the IMF conditions under the stabilization program). Finally, in November single exchange rates for purchases and sales were set, thus successfully unifying the foreign exchange market. Additionally, in 1983 the Regulations for the Application of the Exchange Regime were also modified, to bestow preferential treatment in the authorization of foreign exchange on enterprises exporting goods whose domestic production content exceeded 35% or whose annual sales amounted to over 1 million colones (ECLAC 1983a; Trejos 1985; Céspedes et al. 1990).

Afterwards (including under Arias) the Central Bank continued to slowly and periodically adjust the exchange rate (applying a crawling peg policy), taking into account three factors: the difference between internal inflation and the inflation levels of Costa Rica's major trade partners, the country's trade deficit, and the offer of and demand for foreign exchange. Arias increased devaluations because of growing imports and decreasing international foreign reserves.

In order to realign relative prices, the Calderón government undertook an 8% real devaluation of the colón. In 1991 the administration decided to slow down the pace of the crawling peg and to place a temporary freeze on commodity prices and public rates and charges. As part of a strategy toward free trade, under agreements with the IMF and IDB, the Central Bank moved in February 1992 to liberalize foreign exchange controls. The Central Bank abandoned the crawling peg and adopted a floating exchange rate. The bank would intervene only as necessary to prevent destabilizing fluctuations in the exchange market. As part of that policy, the capital account was deregulated to allow for transactions in foreign-exchange-denominated assets (Castro and González 1992; IDB 1992). During the first half of 1993, faced with active domestic demand, the government's stabilization of prices coincided with a virtually constant exchange rate due to the strengthening of the colón as a result of the inflow of external resources attracted by the relatively high interest rates. Faster growth of liquidity due to expanding domestic credit and fears of a decline in international reserves led to the adoption of compulsory bank reserves, which caused a rise in interest rates on loans and faster devaluation vis-à-vis the dollar. Despite these stabilization and structural adjustment reforms, the current account deficit continued to widen, and credit expanded beyond growth of the money supply in 1993 (ECLAC 1993c; IDB 1994a).

Communication with the international financial community over the external debt, which had deteriorated during the final years of the Carazo administration, was reopened by Monge to renegotiate it. In June 1982 the government began partial payments of interests to private bank creditors, thus improving relations with the international financial community (Céspedes et al. 1990). Conditions for external loans included reduction of tariffs, privatization of some state-owned enterprises, lifting of price controls, and application of a "prudent" wage policy. A contingency agreement for one year was signed with the IMF in December 1982 whereby the latter granted a standby loan of U.S.$100 million to support efforts to stabilize the exchange rate and meet external financial commitments. A second credit line of U.S.$20 million was set to offset the decline in exports due to the fall in international prices. The agreement established a stabilization program with fiscal, monetary, and foreign exchange objectives: to reduce inflation, maintain a flexible exchange rate, normalize payments on the external debt and limit external indebtedness, reduce the fiscal deficit, promote exports and reduce protectionism, and compensate for the adverse effects of adjustment on employment and economic activity. The agreement with the IMF opened the door to an accord with other creditors (Trejos 1985).

As most of the agreement conditions were successfully met, Monge's government was allowed to obtain a rollover credit to finance imports, which supplemented the country's resources to meet delinquent interest payments. In January 1983 a consolidation agreement reached with creditor governments (Club of Paris) resulted in postponement of payments on the debt and interests, and in more flexible clauses of loans from international financial agencies geared to accelerate procedures and disbursements for new loans (Trejos 1985; Rovira 1988b).

The Monge administration initiated the structural adjustment process with the assistance of a structural adjustment loan (SAL I) granted in 1984 by the World Bank for U.S.$300 million. Two conditions of the agreement were a reduction of and greater efficiency in public spending, partly through the sale of CODESA enterprises, and the adoption of a new tariff policy to create a more efficient, expanded export sector capable of generating foreign exchange to meet the country's external obligations. The World Bank lent an additional U.S.$80 million in 1985–86 to support the structural adjustment program. Other agreements were signed with the Inter-American Development ment Bank (IDB) for a U.S.$60 million loan to stimulate production, and with USAID for U.S.$65 million to deregulate private banks and expand their operations. A stand-by arrangement was signed in 1985 with the IMF to help consolidate the stabilization process, whose major objectives were reductions in the fiscal and balance of payments deficit, as well as inflation. The reduction in the fiscal deficit called for further increases on taxes and public utility rates, curbs on public expenditures, and a reduction in the budget deficit of autonomous institutions. Domestic credit for the public sector was to be reduced but compensated for by greater external financing. A new agreement signed in May 1985 with private banks provided U.S.$75 million in credit and postponed payment of the principal on this loan (ECLAC 1984a; Céspedes et al. 1990).

In 1986 Arias began the conversion of the external debt (debt-equity swaps successfully used in Chile) by which part of the external debt in foreign currency was exchanged for bonds in domestic currency to be used in local investment projects (such as in nontraditional exports, tourism, or the protection of the environment). This scheme was designed to take advantage of the international discount rates on the Costa Rican external debt. In February 1987 U.S.$60 million worth of debt conversion was approved by the Central Bank, and, in April 1988, U.S.$129 million was approved (Céspedes et al. 1990).

In October 1987 Arias signed an agreement with the World Bank concerning the second phase of the country's structural adjustment (SAL II), which granted a credit of U.S.$100 million in exchange for a commitment to reduce public employment by 5,000 employees over three years. A stand-by arrangement with the IMF was also signed that year calling for a reduction of the public-sector deficit to 3% of GDP in 1988, a periodic adjustment of the exchange rate according to the differential between domestic and external inflation rates, and the maintenance of a flexible interest rate policy. In May 1989 the IMF approved an agreement to reduce the external debt under the Brady Plan, which led to elimination of arrears on the debt, and in October 1989 Costa Rica and the external commercial bank creditors agreed on rescheduling the U.S.$1.8 billion debt (ECLAC 1987a; Céspedes et al. 1990; IDB 1991).

In May 1990 Costa Rica's external debt creditors signed an agreement with the Calderón government to buy back 64% of the foreign debt owed to commercial banks, at 16% face value. As a result, the commercial bank debt was reduced by U.S.$1 billion, and thus Costa Rica's external indebtedness decreased in 1990. Most of the foreign debt left was then owed to the IMF and the World Bank (LAN 1990b; IDB 1990, 1992).

The drop in international interest rates was one of the main reasons why interest payments had a less significant impact on the current account balance; other factors included the renegotiation of the external debt with commercial banks and the signing of a new agreement with the Club of Paris. As a result, interest payments dropped from about U.S.$325 to U.S.$224 million. The interest-rate spread in foreign currency brought in a considerable amount of private short-term capital from abroad. In addition, the agreement with the IMF made it possible to release funds from the second stage of the World Bank's Structural Adjustment Loan (SAL II) as well as get access to IDB loan resources. The capital account consequently showed a net surplus, which, combined with the reduction in the current account deficit, led to an increase in Costa Rica's international reserves (ECLAC 1991a).

In late 1992 Costa Rica and the World Bank finally negotiated the details of SAL III, a continuation of the structural adjustment initiated under Monge and continued by Arias. This new U.S.$300 million disbursement package plus a U.S.$1 billion IDB energy loan (for hydroelectric and geothermal energy projects that could eventually permit Costa Rica to sell electricity to Mexico and Central and South America) generated criticism of new foreign debt obligations. Proponents of the new loans argued that most were low-interest, medium- and long-term multilateral credits, with generous grace periods. Critics pointed to new record debt levels, many unfulfilled macroeconomic targets, and slackening growth as structural problems that require fewer disparities in the distribution of export earnings between national and international economies (Edelman and Monge 1993).

During the first half of 1993, progress was made in managing foreign debt operations through the elimination of about U.S.$60 million in arrears to Club of Paris members. The latter recommended further rescheduling of loan payments on the country's previously rescheduled obligations, but not on other outstanding foreign debt. After the rescheduling, however, the Costa

Rican government again experienced difficulties in complying with its debt service obligations to Club of Paris members and by the end of 1993 had about U.S.$31 million in arrears. In spite of these problems, Costa Rica obtained Eurobond financing for an electricity project in 1994; this type of financing, which carries lower interest rates than suppliers' credits, had been closed to Costa Rica since 1981 (IDB 1994a).

A stand-by arrangement of U.S.$30 million was approved by the IMF in 1993, which called for inflation of no more than 12%, an accumulation of at least U.S.$90 million in international reserves of the Central Bank, and a public-sector deficit not to exceed 1% of GDP. Although the government complied with most of those conditions in 1994, delays in the ratifying of loan agreements by the Legislative Assembly caused lower than expected disbursements of multilateral credits for the year (IDB 1994a).

It was clear in 1983 that economic recovery based on domestic demand was valid as a short-term measure, but only a structural adjustment policy would create the basis for a more solid and permanent recovery. There was consensus in the two PLN administrations that the economic recovery should focus on export promotion as a central element, but there were disagreements over the degree of involvement of the international financial agencies in the design of economic policy and on how to achieve export promotion. Both Monge and Arias sought to stimulate exports to reactivate the economy, because trade imbalances and external debt regulations prompted a need for foreign exchange (Trejos 1985).

The quest for new external markets and export promotion for nontraditional products, especially manufactures, became the responsibilities of a new Ministry of Exports (MINEX) created in 1983 to promote exports to markets outside of CACM and to coordinate policies of the different export-promoting organizations (such as the Export and Investment Promotion Center). MINEX also implemented policies to reduce or eliminate tariffs on exports to other markets and to simplify the procedures for exporting or seeking credit for exporting.

Also in 1983, barter regulations were established to rationalize import priorities and to permit the export of some production surpluses. The export promotion policy was intensified in 1984, especially for nontraditional exports outside CACM. Preferential interest rates were established for certain services linked to exports, export taxes (including those on bananas) were reduced, a 100% exemption on income tax from profits derived from exporting nontraditional exports to third markets was allowed, and inputs for the manufacture of exports were exempted from customs duties. Other measures aimed at promoting nontraditional exports included moderate and controlled devaluations, and decreasing the proportion of exchange that exporters were required to sell to the Central Bank at the official exchange rate (ECLAC 1984a; Trejos 1985; Lizano 1990).

A National Investment Council was set up in 1985 to approve export programs and contracts, consult with state agencies on the benefits of and conditions for export contracts, coordinate the application of export policy, and advise the Central Bank on the granting of tax-credit certificates (CATs, CIEXs) for increases in exports. In the same year "export contracts" were introduced (i.e., agreements between private applicants and the Costa Rican government that offer incentives to attract foreign investment) with the following features: they stipulate the tax benefits to which enterprises exporting nontraditional goods are entitled, simplify export procedures, allow for special customs tariffs and bank credit with preferential interest rates, and provide preferential access to CATs and CIEXs. The government also took measures to improve administrative functions regarding CATs (ECLAC 1985a; Colburn and Saballos 1988; Rovira 1988b; Lizano 1990).

The promotion of new products, such as ornamental plants and flowers, played an important role in the expansion of nontraditional exports. These efforts received support from two agencies set up with funds from external and domestic sources: the National Investment Council and the Coalition of Initiatives for Development (CINDE).

In keeping with the trade liberalization policy agreed with international financial organizations, reductions in import surcharges were decreed. A new tariff schedule became effective, under Monge, in January 1986 offering lower nominal protection and greater flexibility for modifying tariffs; it eliminated all specific tariffs and included only ad valorem rates. Under Arias, all tariff rates exceeding the 40% maximum were reduced by 10%, and an additional 10% in 1988. Finally, Costa Rica joined GATT at the end of 1989 (IDB 1990a).

Monge and Arias promoted the establishment of duty-free trade zones (for *maquiladoras*) and free ports, as well as cross-border subcontracting, to boost confidence and incentives in the industrial sector. Costa Rica thus strengthened and improved the administration of the drawback schemes, under which firms can reclaim duty paid on intermediate imports, provided that the finished product is exported. A free-trade zone was set up under private administration and public supervision. With the liberalization of custom controls in 1984, slightly more than 100 *maquiladoras* entered the country in 1984–85; 70% of them were involved in textiles and the remainder in electronics, metal manufactures and machinery, and other industries (Rovira 1988b, Lizano 1990; Céspedes et al. 1990).

The growing globalization of markets and formation of regional economic blocks led the Central American nations to renew efforts of economic cooperation and integration. In 1991 the Central American presidents re-formed the Organization of Central American States (ODECA), establishing the basis for a new legal and institutional system of regional economic inte-gration. Signed by all the members of CACM, except Panama, the System of Central American Integration (SICA) aimed at reorganizing the common market by 1994. The implementation of proposed price bands related to the trade of basic grains and other agricultural products, however, was key to Costa Rica's objections to joining SICA. Meanwhile, Guatemala, El Sal-vador, and Honduras continued with integration plans and established a free-trade zone among themselves. In 1993 Calderón rejoined discussions with SICA in order to lower trade barriers and harmonize economic policies within the region. As a result of these negotiations, Costa Rica lowered the minimum on import tariffs from 10% to 5% in 1994 and eliminated import surcharges (Castro and González 1992; IDB 1994a).

The government also placed a high priority on gaining better access to larger markets, in particular NAFTA. In August 1992, the Calderón admin-istration signed a bilateral trade agreement with Mexico in hope of develop-ing connections with the emerging regional economic block. Under the free-trade agreement, 85% of import tariffs (covering 40% of trade) would drop to zero by early 1995; the remaining 15% will fall to zero over a five to ten-year period. The agreement also included the elimination of nontariff trade barriers, preferential tariffs in certain products, an investment pact, cooper-ation in aviation, ecology, housing, quality control, refinery personnel train-ing, and grain commercialization. In keeping with these and other efforts at trade liberalization, the most import tariffs were lowered from a maximum of 27% to 20% in 1993 (Castro and González 1992; IDB 1994a).

G. Labor and Employment

The three administrations supported policies to reduce open unemployment (particularly that of Monge, who faced the highest rates in the nation's his-tory), freeze public employment, and adjust wages (Monge and Arias used different techniques). Monge was under the strongest labor pressure and con-flicts, which receded under Arias and Calderón (except for election years). Calderón tried to undermine union power by supporting "solidarist" associ-ations, and his attempt to modify labor legislation, following ILO requests, was defeated by the Legislative Assembly at the end of his term.

As part of Monge's plan to counter the negative impact on jobs of both the economic crisis and adjustment, the Ministry of Labor implemented an emergency program to create employment (6,000 jobs in 1983) and granted minimum compensation of up to three months to the unemployed who had worked in public services. But Monge also tried to reduce the growth of public employment (through a public hiring freeze in 1984–86) and encouraged the retirement of central-government employees older than 65. Finally he adopted measures to bail out enterprises in financial trouble (particularly in manufacturing) because of difficulties paying domestic and foreign debts, devaluations, and weakening of internal demand. Such measures included assistance in restructuring internal and external debts and a program of cooperation between the government and the Chamber of Industries to grant credit and technical assistance to enterprises that either generated foreign exchange or a minimum number of jobs or produced basic consumer goods (ECLAC 1982a; Trejos 1985; Rovira 1988b). Arias basically followed the previous policies, and reduction of unemployment took off pressure on this front.

At the end of 1990, Calderón launched a Labor Mobility Plan to alleviate the negative impact of the reduction in public employment, attempting to relocate 2,000 public employees to the private sector through various incentives, such as small loans and benefits. The plan objectives were only partially achieved, because many of the dismissed workers filed suits and were reinstated in their jobs. In March 1991 the plan became a voluntary retirement program with attractive financial incentives designed to ease the transition to private employment (ECLAC 1991a; Castro and González 1992; IDB 1992).

Monge intended to maintain real wages, but his policy came into conflict with the 1982–83 stabilization program. And yet, the hardening of the trade unions' bargaining position and the need to stimulate domestic demand led to wage adjustments, albeit restrictive at first. A basic consumer basket composed of 16 goods and subject to price control came into operation in 1983, but the list of goods in the basket was soon enlarged. A sliding wage scale (increasing wages twice a year) was set according to the absolute variation in prices of the basic consumer goods in the basket. In addition, a single salary scale with 73 categories was established for the public sector, while the National Wage Council (made up by representatives of the government, workers, and employers) was strengthened to facilitate agreements on minimum wage adjustment. Several wage increases were granted to the public and private sectors, but they were limited in the former because of agreements with international agencies. In practice, wage adjustment exceeded price increases at least in the private sector (ECLAC 1983a; Céspedes et al. 1990).

In May 1986 the Arias administration changed the wage-adjustment policy for the private sector, substituting the consumer price index (CPI) for the absolute increases in the basic consumer basket, and in 1987 the public sector began to use this system also. This policy blocked mean wage adjustments exceeding price increases, but the urban minimum wage did surpass it (Céspedes et al. 1990). In 1991 Calderón adopted a more austere adjustment policy: mean real wages were cut by 4% and the urban minimum wage by 9%. Real mean wages were increased in 1992 and particularly in 1993–94, while the minimum wage rose somewhat in 1990 but was drastically cut in 1992–94 (Table IV.20).

Compared to 1979–80 under Carazo (when strikes and lockouts peaked at 61 in 1980), labor conflicts under Monge fell somewhat (down to 10 in 1985), but 1986 was an election year, and labor conflicts rose to 23 strikes and lockouts with a record number of workers involved (4.4% of the labor force), which largely explains Monge's more flexible wage adjustment that year. The number of lost workdays, however, was the lowest since 1975 except for 1984 (ILO *Yearbook* 1983–94). In 1984 strikes in the banana sector forced a transnational corporation on the Pacific to shut down, which had a negative effect on banana output and resulted in lost jobs. The number of labor conflicts was not greater because of divisions within trade unions (organized labor was considerably weakened by the ideological split that the leftist Popular Vanguard Party suffered in 1982), as well as the positive effects of Monge's social policies and ensuing economic recuperation, which improved living conditions for workers. The generally equal manner in which the crisis affected the population also helped preserve social stability, as well as the fact that indices of health and nutrition did not deteriorate. Dissatisfaction among peasant unions continued, nevertheless, as evidenced by an increase in land takeovers (ECLAC 1983a).

Labor conflicts declined during the first year of the Arias administration (down to 7) but slowly rose in the next two years and reached 40 in the election year of 1990, but yet there were no significant increases in wages. Data on labor conflicts under Calderón are available only for 1991–92 and show a decline to 19 (ILO *Yearbook* 1994). Under Calderón many firms in the free-trade zones and *maquiladoras* established "solidarist" associations for their employees, funded with monthly contributions from both employers and employees. Employers' contributions go to a fund administered by the solidarist association at the enterprise and offer severance payments, as well as savings-and-loan plans, consumer goods at lower prices, access to health services, housing and recreation, supplementary pensions, and cheap credit for microenterprise programs. If workers try to organize a union, the employer threatens to manage the fund directly instead of leaving it to the workers.

In 1991 the Freedom of Association Committee of the ILO investigated claims made by Costa Rican trade unions that the solidarist associations were being used to undermine the unions. (The ILO had repeatedly accused Costa Rica of failing to amend labor legislation enacted almost 50 years ago that is considered unfair to unions.) In 1993 the ILO's complaint was taken up by the principal trade union federation in the United States (the AFL-CIO), and the U.S. Department of Commerce threatened to withdraw the Most Favored Nation trading privileges to Costa Rica. Such a move would have devastated the economy, as about half of all exports go to the United States. A draft bill amending the labor legislation and bringing it into line with minimum international requirements was submitted to the Legislative Assembly at the end of Calderón's administration, but it could not get the necessary two-thirds majority (Hansen-Kuhn 1993).

H. Distribution and Social Services

Monge and Arias established a social compensation program for the poor, intervened in some social institutions to reduce their deficit, paid the state debt to the CCSS, strengthening its noncontributory programs' protection of the most vulnerable groups, gave priority to public housing for the poor, and increased educational expenses, almost recovering the 1980 level. After two years without paying state contribution to the CCSS, Calderón's administration signed a payment agreement and reformed the CCSS and pension programs; a new integrated health-care approach was agreed upon by the CCSS and MINSA but not implemented; housing programs under Calderón were paralyzed by lack of funds, and educational expenses declined.

Monge's plan to attenuate the social costs of both the crisis and structural adjustment centered on the Social Compensation Plan, which targeted the poorest sectors of the population. Introduced in January 1983, it was composed of five programs: wage policy, employment generation (these were discussed in the previous section), distribution of foodstuffs to extremely poor families, social housing, and land distribution for the rural sector. IMAS and the CNP, with external assistance, implemented the program to redistribute food supplies, which assisted 42,000 families in 1984. The INVU and IMAS put into effect the housing program, which by September 1983 had met 6,000 requests for houses or lots. In 1984 Monge moved to invest more in social stability after a previous focus on economic stability (Trejos 1985; Rovira 1988b; Doryan 1990).

Under Monge and Arias, central government intervention in the decision making of some social institutions (e.g., INVU, IDA, JAPDEVA) increased in order to reduce their budgetary deficits through administrative and fiscal reforms. Intervention procedures included the establishment of commissions of "experts"; a review of the strategies, methods, and procedures used by the institutions; the development of an administrative restructuring plan; and the creation of administrative controls and technical bodies to implement the new guidelines. These procedures addressed financial difficulties, deficiencies in the provision of services, user discontent, and alleged administrative irregularities (Sojo 1989).

The social security and health systems played an important role in mollifying social costs during the crisis. Beginning in the mid-1970s the CCSS provided free coverage of curative health care as well as welfare minimum pensions to the dispossessed (noncontributory programs). When the crisis hit, population coverage of the CCSS under contributory programs diminished, but those left without protection became eligible for the CCSS noncontributory (welfare) programs. Furthermore, the Ministry of Health's primary health-care program for urban and rural marginal groups was maintained. Family Allowance funds increasingly financed those two programs for the poor and low-income groups. The real investment yield of CCSS funds declined at an annual rate of 18.4% between 1980 and 1984, but stabilization and better policies led to a positive rate of 2.7% in 1985–87. The government's debt to the CCSS (which rapidly grew under Carazo) began to be paid under Monge and Arias through signed payment agreements. The average real pension paid by the CCSS, which had declined by one-half during the crisis, was increased and by 1987 surpassed the 1980 level; the noncontributory pension was cut in half between 1979 and 1990. With the assistance of the World Bank and USAID, the CCSS also improved its financing system and introduced emergency programs to cut unnecessary expenses. In order to improve the efficiency and quality of health care, as well as cut its costs, the CCSS began several collaborative programs with the private sector with positive results (Mesa-Lago 1989, 1992, 1993).

Under Calderón the government did not pay its contribution to the CCSS as an employer and third party (including the subsidy for health-care treatment of indigents); in 1992 alone the state debt was U.S.$57 million and was declining in real terms because of inflation. The average real pension paid by the CCSS decreased again in 1989–92. Conversely, the government financed 86% of the cost of pensions in the twenty independent pension funds for public employees, which had only 20% of the nation's total pensioners. Private employers evaded their obligations to the CCSS by 38%, and the real CCSS investment yield in 1992 slowed to 0.4% because of excessive concentration on government bonds, which had a negative yield. In 1992 there was a reform of the CCSS that included an increase in the retirement age, a rise in wage contributions, measures to reduce evasion and payment delays, and cuts in expenditures. Out of the twenty independent public pension funds, fourteen were eliminated and merged with the CCSS and six maintained (including those for teachers and the judiciary), but all new public employees must now enter the CCSS. The CCSS's collaboration with the private sector in health care expanded under Calderón. At the end of 1993 the state renegotiated its debt to the CCSS, indexing it to inflation and paying a real interest rate (Mesa-Lago 1994b; Sojo 1994).

In 1993, after three years of negotiation under Calderón, the CCSS and MINSA approved a reform of health care with the following characteristics: (1) the ministry would be the "rector" of the system with the responsibilities of direction, regulation, and supervision; (2) all the ministry facilities, equipment, and personnel would be transferred to the CCSS; (3) there would be a process of administrative decentralization and regionalization; and (4) the ministry's priorities would be health promotion, the environment, and infant nutrition, while the CCSS would provide preventive and curative care to both the insured and the poor, with an emphasis in increasing the participation of the private sector. The plan, however, had not been implemented by the end of 1994 (Saenz 1994).

There was no significant change in educational policy in this stage. State expenditures on education increased between 1983 and 1989, almost recovering the 1980 level, but a decline occurred during Calderón's early years.

The Arias administration placed a particular priority on providing housing because, under Carazo, the growing housing deficit resulted in strong social demands. The state had neglected the low-income groups, many of which did not have the ability to pay for housing. Furthermore, in the midst of the fiscal crises under Carazo and Monge, a large amount of resources originally intended for housing was used for other purposes. The crux of Arias's restructuring of the housing sector was a new financial system under a central budget that administered all the resources; for that purpose the National Home Financing System was established at the end of 1986 under the management of the Home Mortgage Bank (BANHVI). Two special funds were created: the National Housing Fund (FONAVI), whose purpose was to provide financing at the lowest possible cost, and the Housing Subsidy Fund (FOSUVI) for low-income families, a permanent fund that operated a system of housing subsidies for the neediest and granted family housing credit as a long-term loan to enhance a family's creditworthiness. The financing established by law for FOSUVI represented a considerable reallocation of public funds, including 3% from the national budget (Sojo 1989).

The Calderón administration's promise to continue the housing programs begun under Arias met with severe financial constraints. The debt accumulated by the housing institute (INVU) blocked its access to funds from the housing bank (BANHVI). Additionally, bureaucratic tensions between INVU and the Commission for Housing Evaluation (CEV) contributed to the slowing of disbursements for housing. The two special housing funds created under the Arias administration met with different obstacles. FONAVI's short-term focus and limited financing led it to quickly run out of funds. Calderón's campaign promise to openly award housing bonds altered FOSUVI's original permanent financing structure as it quickly disbursed limited funds in an effort to reach official housing targets. Because of these constraints, the housing institutions became virtually paralyzed in 1991 (Sojo 1994).

2. Performance

A. Growth

The annual real GDP growth rate between 1983 and 1994 averaged 4.4%, slightly below the 1971–82 rate of 4.9%, and considerably lower than the 1961–70 rate of 6.1%. In per capita terms the rate averaged 1.8% vis-à-vis 2.1 in the previous stage and 2.7% in the first stage; a further decline in the population growth rate to 2.4%, from the previous rates of 2.8% and 3.4%, helped this indicator. Growth during the two PLN administrations averaged 4.3% (1.7% per capita), slightly higher under Arias than under Monge; the Calderón administration's rate was 4.6% (2.2% per capita), the highest in this stage (Table IV.3).

In 1982, at the end of the Carazo and beginning of the Monge administrations, the economy entered the worst economic crisis in recent history because of low export prices, the economic contraction of CACM, and the lack of external financing: GDP per capita dropped a record 10%, unemployment peaked at 9.4%, the inflation rate reached 90%, and average real wages declined 18 percentage points; gross fixed capital formation decreased 6 percentage points in 1979–82 (Tables IV.3, IV.16, IV.20). The dramatic devaluation of the colón failed to stimulate exports because of inflation, the high imports basis of domestic industry, and taxes on exports.

GDP per capita increased 0.2% in 1983 and 5.4% in 1984; after a decline in 1985, growth recovered to 2.7% in 1986. Monge's successful renegotiation of the external debt resulted in an inflow of U.S.$700 million in external loans and returned confidence to investors. International coffee prices recovered, and the devaluation of the colón gave a boost to exports; however, export volume did not increase as much as production did because of limits in export agreement quotas, for example, in coffee, bananas, and sugarcane (Villasuso 1987). Monge's monetary and credit policies increased credit to the private sector (in 1982 and 1985), which, after 1983, ended the capital flight and built up private capital formation. The strength of private investment was the main factor in some recovery of gross domestic investment in

1984. However, gross fixed capital formation averaged 19% of GDP in this stage, much less than in the previous 12 years (Table IV.3).

Industrial growth averaged 5.4% under Monge, with a jump of 10.4% in 1984. The Development Plan helped cushion the impact of the crisis on the rural sector, and the price stabilization policy helped maintain agricultural output. The Farm Productivity Incentives Program, combined with the tax policy, increased the domestic demand by incorporation of technology without forcing production costs up very much. The agricultural sector began to recover in 1983, in part because of a record coffee crop stimulated by the Program for the Improvement of Coffee Production. In that year coffee production rose 8%, and there was another increase of 10% in 1984; output also rose in rice, corn, beef, and sugarcane (Table IV.5). Agricultural output fell in 1985, in part because of a decrease in banana production due to a drop in prices, diseases, and strikes in 1983–84. But annual average agricultural production increased at a rate of 3.3% under Monge.

Under Arias, GDP per capita growth slowed to 2% in 1987 and 0.7% in 1988, increased to 3% in 1989, and slowed to 1.1% in 1990. Continued renegotiation of the foreign debt led to another inflow of loans (but less than under Monge), and lower international rates reduced the burden of debt servicing. After a boom in 1986, world coffee prices declined in 1987–90 but were compensated for by rising prices of bananas and beef; the value of exports steadily increased as did the purchasing power of exports. Gross investment averaged 20.4% under Arias (higher than under Monge) and exhibited an increasing trend; credit to the private sector grew from 51.5% to 55.2% of total credit in 1987–89 (Tables IV.3, IV.5, IV.7, IV.10, IV.13).

Industrial growth stabilized at an annual rate of 3.6% (lower than under Monge, but the latter was built upon a 12% decline in industrial output in 1981–82). Agricultural output growth averaged 4.6% under Arias, much higher than under Monge. Coffee production reached record levels in 1988–89. Banana production slowly recovered and by 1990 exceeded the previous output peak; this increase was fueled by record international banana prices in 1988–90. Livestock production and exports rose but faced a critical situation because of a decline in international prices, a sluggish domestic market, and restrictive credit policy. Sugarcane production increased but ran into problems of overproduction, low international prices, and a fall in external demand due to the substitution of corn syrup for sugar in the United States. Production was also harmed by a rise in costs of inputs and labor, scarcity of credit, and increased interest rates; these encouraged the transformation of sugar surplus into alcohol for export. The output of rice, corn, and beans increased to meet national requirements (Tables IV.5–6, IV.10). The liberalization of the CNP had some success in reducing its losses, although opposition from producers was firm. Under Arias, however, Costa Rica began to import foods that it had previously produced (Anderson 1991).

Under Calderón, GDP per capita declined by 0.1% in 1991 (Table IV.3). This fall in economic activity reflected financial instability due to an increase in inflation and the consequences of the adjustment program (fiscal measures and tighter monetary policy). The surcharge on imports, the increases in fuel prices, and the sales tax all pushed up production costs. These factors, in addition to high interest rates, discouraged investment: gross fixed capital formation fell from 22.5% of GDP in 1990 to 19.7% in 1991. Economic performance improved considerably in 1992–93 as GDP per capita increased to 3% and 3.7%, respectively, but slowed to 2.1% in 1994. Calderón's continued renegotiation of the foreign debt led to U.S.$1.5 billion in new loans and a substantial reduction of the old debt. International prices of coffee declined, but those of bananas increased, and the purchasing power of exports rose in 1991–93. Gross investment increased from 19.7% to 22.1% in 1991–93, but decreased to 19.8% in 1994, and the 1991–94 average was almost 21%, the highest in this stage (Table IV.3; ECLAC 1990a–91a).

Industry grew at an average rate of 5% and agriculture at a 3% rate (the lowest in this stage). Coffee output increased in 1991 but declined in 1992–93 (because of decreased yields and a labor shortage), and world prices decreased in 1991–93; banana production and prices rose, sugar and beans output increased, but production of rice and corn declined. There was a healthy expansion in services (finance, trade, and tourism) and the external sector, and investment rose in industry and nontraditional agriculture. The fastest growing sectors were service activities, where the boom in tourism had a particularly positive impact on transportation and communications. The steep rise in exports and imports increased total transactions, while the liberalization of the financial market, the inflow of external resources, and the economy's considerable liquidity gave a boost to financial services (Tables IV.5–6; ECLAC 1992a–95a).

B. Inflation

The annual rate of inflation between 1983 and 1994 averaged 18.2%, a slight decline vis-à-vis the 1971–82 rate of 19.8%. The rate actually increased from an average of 17.9% under Monge to 18.3% under Arias and 18.4% under Calderón (Table IV.3). Monge's stabilization policies were successful in steadily reducing inflation from 90% in 1982 to 33% in 1983, and to 12% in 1984 and 1986; there was an increase of 15% in 1985 (Table IV.3). The conditions set by the IMF and the World Bank agreements in 1985 were largely met, especially the goal of keeping the public deficit below 4.5% of GDP.

The negotiations with the international financial community were instrumental in receiving financial and technical aid for the stabilization program. Declining but still high inflation in 1983 was the outcome of indirect taxes, price adjustments for essential consumer goods (in agriculture, agro-industry and manufacturing) and other goods regulated by the government, increases of rates for utilities (e.g., electricity), and the effect of wage adjustments upon costs. The most significant price increases in nonregulated services were in medical care, education, transport, entertainment, and other personal services. Inflation rates further declined in 1984–86 because of tightening of price controls, stabilization of the exchange rate (speculation ceased), and gradual devaluations (ECLAC 1984a).

The program was fairly successful in lowering the fiscal deficit in 1982, because of a 93% increase in government income (sales, income, and social security taxes and tariffs) rather than a decrease in government spending, although several public works (particularly roads) were canceled and credit was restricted. The main step to raising public revenue by 61% in 1983 was a surcharge on corporate income. Taxes on international trade were maintained, and revenue from them rapidly increased. Fiscal discipline eased in 1983, and the central government's deficit rose to 2% of GDP that year. Political pressure to increase public expenditures to compensate for the social costs of the crisis, wage increases, and a rise in public debt servicing made it impossible to reduce the public-sector deficit, despite the significant tax effort. Also, some public works were reinstated in 1983–84, such as public building and port and road construction. However, the growth of public expenditures moderated. The government deficit fell to 0.7% of GDP in 1984 and 1.3% in 1985 but then increased to 4.5% of GDP in 1986. The low deficit in 1984–85 was the result of increasing fiscal revenue, a freeze in public employment and wages, and cuts in capital expenditures. Fiscal discipline was not maintained in 1986 since it was an election year; thus salary adjustments for public employees were greater than planned, and fuel prices were not increased. The Arias administration inherited a sizable fiscal deficit (Table IV.3; ECLAC 1982a–84a; Trejos 1985; Céspedes et al. 1990).

Under Arias the inflation rate increased from 11.8% in 1986 to almost 20.8% in 1988, declined to 16.5% in 1989, and rose again to 19% in 1990. The increasing trend in inflation was the result of the removal of price controls and subsidies, increases in public utility rates, expansion of credit, devaluation of the colón, new taxes, an increase in minimum urban wages, adjustment of pensions, and raising expenditures in education and housing. Central government finances remained weak under Arias as revenue growth slowed in 1986–89. However, the deficit was reduced in 1987 to 2.9% and eliminated in 1988, but it increased to 2.1% in 1989 and 3.2% in 1990 (Table

IV.3). The improvement in the balance of payments allowed for continued government expenditures, although with continued reduction in public investment projects. The introduction of tax incentives for nontraditional exports, the reduction of the export tax on bananas, and the lowering of import tariffs all helped lower the tax burden. Tax revenue slightly increased its share in the revenue of the central government in 1985–88, but the share of taxes on foreign trade fell from 34% to 29% (again indicating increased economic liberalization).

Inflation under Calderón continued to increase: from 19% in 1990 to 28.7% in 1991; it remained high at 21.8% in 1992 but declined sharply to 9.8% in 1993 and rose again to 13.5% in 1994. The annual average inflation under Calderón was 18.4%, the highest in this stage (Table IV.3). The high inflation rate in 1991 was fueled by a significant devaluation of the colón, increases in public utility rates, the temporary import surcharge, and a buildup of international reserves. Given the high level of liquidity, the frequent small devaluations of the currency instituted throughout the first seven months of 1991 pushed up domestic prices. The resulting inflation, temporarily checked by a temporary freeze on commodity prices and public utility rates and charges, as well as a cut in real wages, again picked up speed in late 1991. Still, the fiscal deficit was cut from 3.2% of GDP in 1990 to 1.4% in 1991. Fiscal revenue increased because of new and/or raised taxes and public utility rates, as well as surpluses in many state enterprises. Expenditures were controlled by savings in not paying state contributions to the CCSS and a decline in education and housing spending, as well as by a freeze in public employment; these gains compensated for the U.S.$100 million spent to repair the damage caused by the 1991 earthquake (ECLAC 1991a; Scott 1991a; IDB 1992).

The liberalization of the exchange rate in February 1992, the reduction of tariffs, and the elimination of advance deposit requirements and surcharges on imports attracted a considerable amount of external resources. Since a floating exchange rate was in effect, the inflow of external capital set the stage for a revaluation of the local currency, which contributed to the reduction in inflation to 21.8% that year. Such a decline showed that, thanks to the import-driven increase in supply, the rise in domestic demand during 1992 placed only minimal pressure on prices. Even so, inflation was higher than expected, in view of the virtually stable nominal exchange rate, because of sharp rises in public-sector rates and higher prices for basic grains owing to the relaxation of government controls. The 9.8% inflation rate in 1993 was considerably better than the government's target of 12%. This significant fall in inflation was principally due to a relatively low public-sector deficit and low price increases on tradable goods, as the real effective exchange rate appreciated. Containment of the demand for credit by the public sector was also important in the maintenance of sound stabilization policies that relieved pressure on interest rates and inflation (IDB 1994a).

The fiscal deficit increased to 1.9% in 1992 and remained at the same level in 1993 (still below the average during the previous two administrations). Fiscal revenue grew from increased taxes, elimination of exemptions, and the surpluses of state enterprises (due to sharp adjustments in prices and rates charged by RECOPE and ICE, as well as reductions in CNP losses due to the privatization of retail food stores). But in 1993 the government began to pay its accumulated debt to the CCSS, and there were increases in real wages in 1992–93. In 1994 there was an increase in both the inflation rate (13.5%) and the fiscal deficit (6.5%). Being an election year, there was also an increase in public expenditures (Table IV.3; ECLAC 1994c; IDB 1994a).

C. Diversification

Between 1983 and 1987 some minor changes occurred in the composition of GDP by economic activity: agriculture continued its decline (interrupted during the crisis) from 20.1% to 18.7%, while industry resumed its increase from 24.5% to 25.4% (higher than the precrisis level); commerce and finance increased from 29.2% to 30.9% (back to the 1979 level); other services decreased from 14.9% to 13.6%; and other sectors remained basically unchanged. Between 1988 and 1994 there was another shift: all activities shares declined slightly or were stagnant, except transportation-communication and commerce-finance, and the latter only slightly (Table IV.4). A comparison of the 1980–84 and 1985–92 GDP shares is more illustrative: agriculture increased 1.1 percentage points, industry grew 2.2, and exports of goods and services rose by 1.9 (BCCR 1989b–92b; ECLAC 1980b–95b).

The most dynamic sectors were transportation and communication, which are related to trade and tourism, as well as exports, responding to the new outward-oriented development strategy. The agricultural share was sluggish, despite government support to agriculture, the growth rate of this sector (which almost doubled the 1971–82 rate), and increases in output of key crops (bananas, sugar, beans) at considerably higher rates than between 1971 and 1982, as well as recovery of coffee output. But the data hide the fact that about half of exports are agricultural products. The industrial share increased (partly because of the expansion of *maquiladoras*) but at a lower rate than between 1971 and 1982, because of the shift away from ISI to export promotion focused on agriculture. The construction sector continued its deterioration (in spite of a brief increase in 1984–85) because of a soft market for commercial building due to high interest rates and reduced public investment. But tourism (and housing under Arias) increased its importance (IDB 1994a).

D. Trade Balance and External Dependency

As a result of the opening to world trade and the outward-oriented strategy, trade transactions increased 182% between 1983 and 1994, at a lower rate than in the previous stage but vigorously pulling the country out of the crisis. Overall trade dependency rose from 74% to 84% of GDP in current/constant prices (Table IV.7; BCCR 1989b–92b; IDB 1994a; ECLAC 1995b).

International prices of coffee increased 33% in 1983–86 but declined 59% thereafter and in 1993 were down to the 1974 level. Such a decline was offset, between 1983 and 1993, by a 61% increase in banana prices and 24% in beef prices. Therefore, the purchasing power of exports more than doubled in the stage, but the cost of imports also increased, and the terms of trade (after an improvement in 1986 due to booming coffee prices) were the same in 1983 and 1993. But there was a big jump in world coffee prices in 1994, as well as a rise in banana prices, and the terms of trade improved substantially in that year (Table IV.10). The value of exports increased 183% between 1983 and 1994, but that of imports rose 206%, and the trade deficit jumped sevenfold (Table IV.7).

Exports became much more diversified in this stage, responding to the new strategy that encouraged nontraditional exports and the devaluation of the colón, which made exports more competitive (the decline in coffee prices between 1987 and 1993 was another factor, but it was compensated for by increases in banana prices). The shares of various exports changed as follows: coffee shrank from 27% to 10% (after a peak of 36% in 1986), bananas decreased from 29% to 26% (after a low of 19% in 1988), beef declined from 3.8% to 3.2% and sugar from 3% to 1%, but "others" (nontraditional exports) jumped from 36% to 60%, an expansion more than twice that achieved between 1971 and 1982. Among these exports were fish and seafood, cement, plastic, furniture, ornamental plants and flowers, processed vegetables, fruits, juices, vegetable oils, and nuts. Exports of textiles were very successful because of the expansion of *maquiladoras* (Table IV.8; ECLAC 1984a; Colburn 1988; IDB 1990; Salazar 1990).

The composition of imports reversed some previous trends. The share of food and beverages, which had declined in the 1960s and 1970s, continued shrinking from 8% to 4% between 1983 and 1987 but rose thereafter and reached 8% in 1993, compared with 13% in 1960. The government policy of reaching self-sufficiency in food was countered by increased imports of luxury foodstuffs and alcoholic beverages, aid by decontrol of the exchange rate, the economic recovery and expanding credit to the private sector, lifting or sharp reduction of import surcharges and tariffs, elimination of subsidies to agriculture (which made some imports cheaper), and expanding domestic demand fueled by increased employment and wages. Conversely the share of fuel imports that had increased fivefold between 1971 and 1982 decreased from 19% to 9% between 1983 and 1993 because of declining world prices (especially after the Persian Gulf War) and less domestic demand. The share of machinery and transportation, which had declined by half between 1971 and 1982 (particularly during the crisis), rose back to 30% in 1987 but declined again to 26% in 1993. Finally, the share of manufactures, which had been stagnant around 56% since 1960, declined to 49% in 1990 (the lowest on record) but rose again to 55% in 1993. This declining trend can be generally explained by the devaluation of the colón, which made imports of manufactures much more expensive, as well as by Calderón's restrictive policies in 1990 to curtail imports: reintroduction of an import surcharge and a hike in deposits on imports (Table IV.9; ECLAC 1990a–91a; IDB 1992–94).

The trade deficit, which was at a record low in 1982 (U.S.$18.6 million) because of the crisis and the drastic cut in imports, slowly increased and accelerated in the 1990s, responding to trade openings and elimination and reduction of barriers to imports. The deficit reached a historical record of U.S.$822 million in 1993; in per capita terms, however, the deficit was U.S.$251, similar to that in 1980, prior to the crisis (Table IV.7).

The U.S. trade share in Costa Rica's total transactions increased from 35% to 55% in the stage (a historical peak of 57.4% was reached in 1992), while the CACM trade share steadily decreased from 17% to 6%, and the "other" partners' share shrank from 48% to 39%. U.S. financial aid to Costa Rica, the expansion of the U.S. trade quota and incentives under the Caribbean Basin Initiative, and domestic resistance to regional integration led to more trade dependency on the United States, in spite of the government's efforts to diversify trade partners (Table IV.11)

The successful negotiation of Costa Rica's external debt throughout the entire stage brought the following benefits: U.S.$1.8 billion was first rescheduled, and later there was a U.S.$1 billion reduction in the debt with commercial banks; the Club of Paris and other creditors eliminated arrears, and part of the debt was converted into equity and domestic currency obligations; the proportion of the debt owed to private lenders declined from 34.4% to 18.9% between 1982 and 1990 while the proportion owed to international agencies (with more flexible terms) increased from 65.6% to 81.1%; and the nation received more than U.S.$2 billion in fresh credit from international lending agencies, most of it for development projects, for example, U.S.$1 billion from IDB for energy sources (IDB 1990a–94a; ECLAC

1992b; LAN 1990b). In current prices, the debt was U.S.$4.2 billion in 1983 and U.S.$3.8 billion in 1994, but, in real terms, it declined 38% from U.S.$4.5 billion to U.S.$2.8 billion. As a percentage of GDP the debt dropped from 135% to 49%; as a proportion of exports it decreased from 375% to 125%; and in per capita terms it declined from U.S.$1,808 to U.S.$842 (Table IV.13).

E. Unemployment

Monge's emergency employment program and bailout of enterprises, which began in 1983, helped to reduce open unemployment, particularly urban unemployment, but the economic recovery after 1984 was the major factor in creating jobs. Monge's efforts in 1985 to slow public employment as part of its program to limit government expenditures were only partially successful, as he was not able to implement a hiring freeze: in 1985, 11,000 jobs were created in the public sector in contrast to 16,000 in 1984 (Céspedes et al. 1990). The national unemployment rate declined from 9.4% in 1982 to 3.8% in 1989; the urban rate decreased even more, from 9.9% to 3.7%, while the rural rate shrank from 9.6% to 3.8% (the rates in 1989, under Arias, were the lowest in record). All rates, particularly urban, grew again in 1990–91 but declined in 1992–93: in the last year, 4.1% national, 4.0% urban, and 4.2% rural (Table IV.16). Calderón's dismissal of public employees at the beginning of his administration (although part of them were reinstated) and the slowdown in growth in these years due to his adjustment program were the causes of rising unemployment, while the strong recovery in 1992–93 led to an increase in jobs and the lowest unemployment rates since 1970, except for 1989. At the beginning of 1993, about 8,400 employees were cut from the public sector. The breakdown of the total employee relocation was 60% through voluntary relocation without incentives, 28% through the national budget (retirement, dismissal, resignation), 9% through forced relocation, and only 3% with incentives (Castro and González 1992; IDB 1994a).

The low rates in unemployment between 1989 and 1993 are even more remarkable when considering that women continued to join the labor force: in 1980, 25% of the labor force were women, 26% in 1985, and 30% in 1993. Many women found jobs in expanding services, but the greatest gains in women's sectoral percentage of employment were in manufacturing, probably in *maquilas* (Table IV.15; Tardanico 1995).

The composition of the labor force by labor activity between 1984 and 1993 showed a continuing decline in the primary sector (from 31% to 23%) but increases in the secondary (from 20% to 26%) and tertiary sectors (from 38% to 50%) as well as a decrease in the share of unemployed and nonspecified occupations (from 11% to 1%). Released labor in agriculture and the unemployed found jobs during the recovery, mostly in services (particularly in commerce and tourism) and in industry and construction (Table IV.14). The expansion of informal activities in some of those lines partly explained the increase in employment.

F. Equality

The distribution of family income worsened between 1971 and 1983 (one year after the worst point in the crisis) and improved only slightly between 1983 and 1988 (after six years of recovery): the wealthiest quintile's share of income declined by 3.2 percentage points; 3 points of that went to the middle-income strata (mostly to the upper group), and only 0.2 accrued to the poorest quintile. The Gini coefficient slightly improved from 0.47 to 0.43 in that period. Data on salaried heads of household show a gloomier picture between 1982 (the worst of the crisis) and 1988: the wealthiest quintile share increased by 7.2 percentage points, while the share of the middle strata declined 5.1, and that of the poorest quintile decreased 2.1. There was a very minor improvement in 1990 as the wealthiest quintile lost 2 percentage points, which went to the middle strata, mostly to the upper group, but the poorest decile was stagnant (Table IV.18).

Poverty incidence (based on individuals and families) markedly improved between 1983 and 1986 based on two different sources. Sauma and Trejos (1990) estimate that the national poverty incidence among individuals declined from 35% to 20%, while indigence decreased from 17% to 11% (the decrease was more noted in rural than urban areas); poverty incidence among families—normally lower than among individuals—declined from 30% to 17% while indigence decreased from 14% to 10% (again the reduction was bigger in rural than in urban areas). PREALC (1992) reports a decline in poverty incidence among individuals in 1983–86 from 40% to 29% (from 19% to 16% in indigence) and among families a decrease from 34% to 25% (from 16% to 14% in indigence). However, ECLAC (1994e) has estimated that between 1981 (prior to the crisis) and 1992 (after one decade of recovery), the national incidence of poverty among households increased from 22% to 25% while indigence worsened from 6% to 10%; however, urban poverty rose from 16% to 25%, but rural poverty decreased from 28% to 25%; while indigence increased in both areas. ECLAC actually showed, between 1988 and 1990, a slight reduction in the national incidence of poverty (1 percentage point) and rural incidence (3 points) but an increase between 1990 and 1992 (1 point more at the national level and no change in rural areas). In 1992–94, however, there were declines in all indicators: the rate of national poverty was 21 in 1994 versus 24 in 1970, but national indigence was 8 versus 6. The annual household survey of 1993, according to Trejos (1994), showed a decrease in the proportion of national households from 22% in 1992 to 17% in 1993; in the urban sector the decline was from 13% to 9% and in the rural sector from 30% to 26% (Table IV.19).

The index of mean real wages increased from 70.8 in 1982 to 98 in 1986. Under Monge, wage adjustments were consistently above increases in inflation, and minimum wages were readjusted disproportionally, thus protecting the purchasing power of the lowest income strata (Sojo 1989). The index shows a decline under Arias from 98 to 85 in 1986–89 (as he based wage adjustment on the consumer price index), and a further decline to 82.5 in 1991 under Calderón (due to his wage freeze), but an increase to 98.4 in 1994, still below the 1980 level. Conversely the index of the urban minimum wage shows steady increases from 85.9 in 1982 to 120.5 in 1990 (approved by Arias but implemented by Calderón), but a decline to 112.8 in 1994 under Calderón: 8 points below the 1990 peak but 12.8 points above the 1980 level (Table IV.20).

Sauma and Trejos (1990) have noted that the recovery was not equally distributed. Generally speaking, the increase in poverty appears to have been concentrated in groups slightly above the poverty threshold, primarily in urban areas. In terms of income levels, middle-income families and lower-income families in the urban sector were most hard hit by the crisis. Salaried workers, especially professional and public employees, suffered the worst losses. By 1986 average real income for lower- and middle-income groups in the urban sector had not regained their 1977 levels, although the greatest decrease in the magnitude and incidence of poverty took place in the urban sector (Sojo 1989). While the average real income in the rural sector did improve above 1977 levels (due in part to Monge's efforts to reactivate agriculture), this improvement was concentrated among the richer groups. Income rose for workers in the agro-export sector under the policy of export promotion, especially nontraditional agricultural products. Some workers that had migrated from the rural areas to the urban sectors returned to their farms and towns. Increased inflation under Arias also hindered income recovery (Sojo 1989; Sauma and Trejos 1990; Lizano 1990).

Anderson (1991) claims that peasants thought that the Institute of Agrarian Development (IDA, formerly the ITCO) had achieved only minimal success in distributing lands (funding for the IDA suffered with the economic crisis). Between 1961 and 1983 about 16,000 peasants received land, but there was no marked increase in land distribution thereafter. While Costa Rica does have a higher percentage of small farms than other Central American countries, some studies estimate landlessness peasants at 46% in 1980 and 60% in 1985, partly caused by steady population growth. For some time there have also been signs of a slow tendency toward land concentration, because of the expansion of export-oriented agriculture.

Finally, the tax system became increasingly regressive with more reliance on indirect taxes (e.g., sales tax) than on direct taxes on income and property: in 1980 indirect taxes accounted for 77% of the tax structure and direct taxes for 23%, but in 1989 these shares were 81% and 19%, respectively (Carciofi, Centragolo, and Barris 1993; MIDEPLAN 1988; Pollack and Uthoff 1985). Critics of Calderón charge that his policies widened the gulf between rich and poor and were harsher on the poorer sectors, for example, because of decreases in buying power due to inflation, cuts in the minimum urban wage, and regressive sales tax (Daremblum 1991). But the above data on income distribution do not show any significant improvement under the PLN administrations, while data on poverty incidence are contradictory (significant decreases estimated by Sauma and Trejos and PREALC, but increases by ECLAC).

G. Social Indicators

Monge's adjustment was compensated for by increases in real social expenditures; their index (1980 = 100) had declined to 73.7 in 1982 but increased to 125.3 in 1986. Arias increased social expenditures slightly to 127.2 in 1990: 72% above the 1982 level. Calderón accelerated those increases to 158.4 in 1993. The share of social expenditures in total central government expenditures declined in 1983–85 but recovered somewhat thereafter in the stage; allocation of social expenditures by sector was not even (Table IV.17). According to Sojo (1989), although there was a decline in social expenditures in some sectors due to the crisis, there was no dismantling of the welfare institutions, whose considerable redistributive effect persisted. Furthermore, financial stabilization to deal with deficits in the social institutions was basically achieved through rationalizing spending, giving preference to administrative reform, revenue enhancement, and the restructuring of services.

The share of social security expenditures in total central government expenditures declined slightly under the two PLN administrations, but as a percentage of GDP it increased from 6.6% in 1982 to 9.5% in 1990 (Tables IV.17, IV.21). This was largely the result of both Monge and Arias paying state contributions to social security. The CCSS countered the effects of the economic crisis by raising the percentage contributions and reducing expenditures through adjustment programs (the real average pension for indigents declined during the decade, but the deficit of the sickness-maternity program turned into a surplus). Under Monge and Arias, the CCSS tried to reduce health-care costs, raise efficiency, and improve the quality of services by increasingly relying on the private sector and decentralizing its services, for example, by providing diagnostic services and drugs to doctors hired by private enterprises, as well as support services to health-care programs managed by cooperatives and other arrangements (Mesa-Lago 1992). After the decline in CCSS coverage in 1980–82, during the crisis, the percentage of the population covered by health care increased under Monge and Arias from 69% to 86% between 1983 and 1990, while the percentage of the economically active population covered increased from 65% to 67% in the same period (Table IV.25). Even if some of the poor—mainly in remote areas—were not covered by the CCSS curative medicine program, practically all of them were reached by the preventive and primary health-care services of the Ministry of Health; thus, in effect, the population achieved universal health coverage (Mesa-Lago 1992). Health-care coverage kept increasing between 1990 and 1994, under Calderón, from 85.6% to 86.2% of the population and from 67% to 77.3% of the EAP. As a result of continuing growth in coverage, the expenditures for sickness, maternity, disability, old age, and death reached 9.4% of GDP in 1993 (Table IV.25; Mesa-Lago 1994b). In 1990–92, however, the Calderón administration did not pay the state's contributions to the CCSS, hence provoking a difficult financial situation; in 1993 an agreement was reached, and the state's debt was acknowledged and adjusted to inflation.

The share of central government expenditures on health care declined under Monge (except for 1984) but increased under Arias; and yet, if the share of GDP is used, there was an increasing trend under the two administrations (Tables IV.17, IV.25). There was no deterioration in health indicators during the two PLN administrations. On the one hand, hospital beds per 1,000 inhabitants decreased from 2.9 in 1982 to 2.2 in 1990, but this was largely because of improving efficiency; on the other hand, the number of physicians increased from 8.3 per 10,000 to 10.1 in 1982–84 but declined to 9.8 in 1990. The infant mortality rate fell from 18.9 per 1,000 in 1982 to 14.8 in 1990 (the general mortality rate was stable), and life expectancy rose from 73.5 to 75.2 years in the same period (Table IV.21). Rates of contagious diseases per 100,000 inhabitants declined for measles (except in 1987), tetanus (except in 1990), and tuberculosis, while virtually no cases were reported for diphtheria, polio, and typhoid (Table IV.22). However, there were increases for hepatitis and malaria (since 1984), probably due to a significant increase in refugee immigrants from other Central American countries (due to war in El Salvador and Nicaragua) that had lower health standards. Under Calderón the decline in hospital beds per 1,000 apparently was reversed from 2.2 to 2.5, and physicians per 10,000 rose from 9.8 to 10.8; the infant mortality rate further decreased from 14.8 to 13.0, while life expectancy rose from 75.2 to 76.3. Diphtheria, polio, and tetanus continued under control, while hepatitis probably declined, but tuberculosis, measles, and malaria increased. The population growth rate declined from 2.7% to 2.3% between 1983 and 1994 (Tables IV.21–22). Access of the urban population to sewerage became universal by 1983, while the rural population's access to potable water increased from 82% to 86% between 1983 and 1989 and to sewerage from 87% to 94% (Table IV.23).

The share of central government expenditures on education kept decreasing from 22.6% to 19.0% between 1982 and 1990, under Monge and Arias, but rose to 22.3% in 1993 under Calderón (still 6 percentage points under the 1977 level; Table IV.17). The quality of education deteriorated in the stage: there was an increase in dropout rates, the infrastructure deteriorated, and hiring of teachers was insufficient. The illiteracy rate declined from 7.4% to 7.2% between 1984 and 1990, but secondary enrollment declined from 46% to 40% in 1982–85 and increased to 42% in 1990, (still below the 1978–79 level); enrollment in higher education increased from 21% to 27% between 1982 and 1989. During the worst year of the crisis, the children of middle- and higher-income families were in general the ones able to continue attending universities (Sojo 1989; Aguilar 1990; Sauma and Trejos 1990). Data for the Calderón administration are scarce but indicate a continuous decline in illiteracy and increases in enrollment in secondary (47%) and higher (28%) education (Table IV.24).

As a percentage of central government expenditures, the housing allocation increased from 2.9% to 7.4% between 1982 and 1986 (under Monge), declined to 1.1% in 1990 (after increases to 9.1% and 3.5% in 1987 and 1989, respectively, under Arias), and further decreased to 0.3% in 1993 under Calderón (Table IV.17). Dwelling units built per 1,000 inhabitants under the Monge administration averaged 3.8 vis-à-vis an average of 5.2 between 1971 and 1982 (Table IV.26). However, according to Sojo (1989), 46,462 dwellings were built from May 1986 to September 1988, under Arias, which would be equivalent to 5.6 dwellings built per 1,000 inhabitants in those years.

Costa Rica is often presented as a successful model of gradualist structural adjustment combined with an export promotion strategy and a compensatory package to alleviate the social costs of the transition. Despite the remarkably positive outcomes, the model has been criticized by factions from both sides of the ideological spectrum. On the one hand, neoconservatives have called for faster and deeper reforms and noted Calderón's retreat or failure on some key issues (somewhat reminiscent of the Carazo administration) under pressure from unions and students: privatization of state monopolies (such as oil refineries, electricity, and insurance), a greater role for private banking, dismissal of public employees, and elimination of subsidies to some enterprises and goods. The neoconservatives also have noted that the inflation rate is still high and that there is a growing trade deficit. On the other hand, critics from the left have pinpointed the significant influence of international financial agencies (like the IMF and the World Bank), growing trade dependency on the United States, more unequal income distribution and growing poverty (at least in the 1990s), an industrial growth rate lower than that in the 1960s and 1970s, an even more sluggish agricultural growth (which only slightly exceeds population growth), and cuts in social expenditures that have led to deterioration in housing and education. These issues will be discussed in the final part of this book.

Tables to Part IV

Table IV.1

Governments and Economic-Policy Periods in Costa Rica, 1948–1994

Period	President	Ideology	Party	Control Legislative Assembly
Establishing the foundations of the model				
1948–49	Figueres (Junta)	Center	Social Democrat Party (PSD)	
1949–53	Ulate	Center-Right	National Union Party (PUN)	PUN
1953–58	Figueres	Center	National Liberation Party (PLN)	PLN
Consolidation, expansion, and crisis of the model				
Industrial and agricultural diversification				
1958–62	Echandi	Center-Right	PUN	PLN
1962–66	Orlich	Center	PLN	PLN
1966–70	Trejos	Center-Right	National Unification Party (coalition of PRN and PUN)	PLN
State Entrepreneur				
1970–74	Figueres	Center	PLN	PLN
1974–78	Oduber	Center	PLN	PLN
1978–82	Carazo	Center-Right	Coalition against PLN	Coalition
Adjustment, restructuring, and recovery				
1982–86	Monge	Center-Right	PLN	PLN
1986–90	Arias	Center-Right	PLN	PLN
1990–94	Calderón Fournier	Right-Center	Social Christian Unity Party (PUSC)	Coalition

Table IV.2

Summary of Socioeconomic Policies in Costa Rica, 1948–1994

Economic Policies	Consolidation, Expansion, and Crisis of the Model (1958–82)			Adjustment, Restructuring, and Recovery (1982–94)
	Establishment of the Foundations of the Model (1948–58)	Industrial and Agricultural Diversification (1958–70)	State Entrepreneur and Crisis (1970–82)	
Ownership	Under Figueres banks nationalized; government allocates credit to branches it sought to stimulate; Electricity Institute (ICE) created in 1949, began absorption of foreign enterprises in energy and communications and built state hydroelectric plant. United Fruit transferred schools, clinics, and housing- to government. Airport and other public facilities built. Ulate halts process.	Continued development of autonomous institutions (regional development, aqueducts, oil refinery). Agrarian Reform (1962) to improve land distribution, productivity, and living standards; private land expropriation, resettlement in state land; but the latter abandoned.	CODESA created in 1974 as a state agency to finance and promote modernization and diversification of production; first with mixed capital (two-thirds by state), but eventually the government competes with the private sector. Nationalization of oil and part of United Fruitland; massive titling programs in agriculture (using state land).	Growing economic privatization through sale of CODESA enterprises and process of deregulation and increasing functions of private banks. Calderón's plans to privatize banking, public services, the INS, and ICE failed because of PLN opposition.
Planning and market	Figueres (Junta) introduces indicative planning and creates autonomous institutions to facilitate state intervention in economy and decentralize executive power: National Production Council (CNP), Institute for Defense of Coffee, ICE, etc. Ulate establishes Central Bank but halts state- intervention process. Figueres founds Institute of Housing.	OFIPLAN (1963) put in charge of economic planning; the 1965–68 and 1969–72 plans called for rapid expansion of public investment in economic infrastructure, transport, energy, communications (for industrial development), development of Atlantic Region, and social services.	Planning became more centralized as autonomous institutions lost independence and OFIPLAN had to approve their budgets; 1972–78 plan targeted output (agriculture, industry) expansion, and diversification and increase in employment and investment; 1979–82 plan called for decreases in size/role of state, privatization, and more cautious fiscal and monetary policies.	Some state agencies reduce their economic role, as the private sector and the role of the market are strengthened, but new institutions are created to implement new policies. Autonomous institutions become less independent as their budgets are more centrally controlled: Plan for 1982–86 targets agriculture to ensure food self-sufficiency and increase exports.

(continued)

Table IV.2
(Continued)

Economic Policies	Establishment of the Foundations of the Model (1948–58)	Consolidation, Expansion, and Crisis of the Model (1958–82)		Adjustment, Restructuring, and Recovery (1982–94)
		Industrial and Agricultural Diversification (1958–70)	State Entrepreneur and Crisis (1970–82)	
		Increased Budgetary Imbalances Due to Expansionary Fiscal and Credit Policies		
Financing	National banks and CNP provide credit for coffee, banana and grain growers, industry, etc.; 10% tax on private assets and increases in income tax and levies on United Fruit Co. enhance government revenue; Central Bank founded in 1950.	Revenue from import duties cut because of entry into CACM. Sales tax, improved collection of income taxes, bond emission, and external financing were raised to counter declines in tariff revenue and export prices, and to sustain public investment.	Progressive 1972 tax reform increased tax collection, but there was growing reliance on external funds to finance the fiscal deficit; some liberalization of the financial sector occurred under Carazo (interest rates increased), but these measures raised the cost of credit for productive sectors.	Three administrations introduce tax reforms to simplify collection, impose tougher penalties for evasion, and create or raise taxes. Domestic and international credit to public sector reduced and shifted to private sector. Increasing liberalizatoion of financial system and private banks. Interest rate liberalized, but Central Bank still controls it to curtail excessive liquidity. Credit also controlled through ceilings and frozen one year to private sector to reduce inflation.
Stability and prices	Under Figueres, CNP stabilizes agricultural prices and provides subsidies; Ministry of Economy & Trade also controls prices. Ulate takes conservative fiscal stand aimed at domestic and external equilibria, settlement with	Economic growth and moderate inflation. Orlich's expansionary policies (increase in public expenditures and credit) and insufficient gov't revenue (through raised taxes, bonds, and foreign borrowing) led to a budgetary deficit.	Inflation stabilized in 1975–76 by price restrictions, increases in interest rates, and more moderate credit policy; was kept low in 1976–79 but exploded with the crisis of 1980–82; Carazo's stabilization programs failed to counter economic deterioration	Adjustment under Monge stabilizes economy; prices on public utilities and fuel raised to reduce deficits; subsidies to agricultural prices cut by both Monge and Arias. Calderón further pushes price liberalization of consumer goods and cuts in public expenditures (jobs, investment, credit, and social services).

	Outward Development with Increased State Intervention	Inward Development with Increased State Intervention	Outward Development with Declining State Intervention
Development strategy	creditors, and stabilization of colón. Under Figueres, development and diversification of agriculture, especially for export (technical improvement of coffee cultivation, production of basic grains, diversification into sugar, beef, etc.); expenditures on public works and development of energy sources; some import substitution industrialization (ISI); credits to agriculture and (to less extend) to industry; new custom tariffs to protect domestic industry. After 1958, decline in coffee and banana world market prices leads to new strategy to avoid stagnation.	Trejos tried to balance the budget through restriction of public credit, expenditures, and money supply, as well as new taxes, but gov't expenditures and investment kept growing. Agriculture is the cornerstone of development strategy under three presidents: government supports agroexports (coffee, bananas, sugar, cattle, cotton, fruits) through credit, investment, new domestic producers and land, technical improvement, price stabilization, and foreign investment, thus dramatically increasing both export and production-crops for domestic consumption. ISI began with the 1959 industrial law and entry into CACM; it was nationalistic (use of domestic capital, labor, and raw materials) and protectionistic (through tax exemptions and credits to domestic industry and increases in tariffs to competitive imports).	and increased inflation; two agreements with IMF failed. Demographic explosion, closing of agriculture frontier, limited industrial capacity to create jobs (end of 1st stage of industrialization), and CACM lead to new phase. Under PLN, continued expansion of state role with creation of CODESA: programs to increase agricultural output and productivity (self-sufficiency in grains) and develop/diversify industry (promotion of industrial exports). Carazo's goals were to reduce protection to industry, increase efficiency, and raise agricultural production, nontraditional exports, and markets; but his lack of steadiness in implementing such goals led to failure.	Monge and Arias new strategy focuses on agriculture (increase in domestic output and exports); new programs created; reduction of "state entrepreneur," questioning of ISI, reduction of subsidies, opening up to world trade. Calderón reorients production even more to exports (with tax incentives) and eliminates guaranteed prices to producers and restrictions on imports of grains, to increase competition and domestic efficiency.

(continued)

Table IV.2
(Continued)

Economic Policies	Establishment of the Foundations of the Model (1948–58)	Consolidation, Expansion, and Crisis of the Model (1958–82)		Adjustment, Restructuring, and Recovery (1982–94)
		Industrial and Agricultural Diversification (1958–70)	State Entrepreneur and Crisis (1970–82)	
		Continued Emphasis on Agricultural Exports and Tremendous Expansion of Industrial Exports		
External sector	Stimulation of agricultural exports based on higher world prices; fixed exchange rate maintained with occasional devaluations; exemption on low custom duties for imports geared to domestic industry. Attempt to increase trade with Central America.	ISI policies and entry into CACM in 1963 led to trade expansion but stimulated imports and, coupled with decline in value of coffee prices, aggravated trade imbalance. Corrective measures were restriction on use of foreign exchange, taxes on imports, and attempts to stabilize coffee prices.	Law of exports promotion of 1972 (tax rebate certificates) and Fund established (1976). Increases in import volumes and prices (oil shocks) worsen trade deficit; external debt increased considerably under Oduber/Carazo to finance fiscal deficit; public-debt servide suspended in 1981. Fixed exchange rate under Figueres (but dual rates); Oduber made minor devaluations in 1974–75, thereafter the rate was fixed (overvaluation); Carazo opposed devaluation (and introduced multiple exchange rates) until forced to make huge devaluations in 1981–82. Agreement with IMF fails.	The three administrations followed fairly consistent policies. The exchange rate was stabilized and unified; a crawling peg was introduced by Monge and abandoned by Calderón in favor of a floating rate. The foreign debt was successfully negotiated with international financial agencies (including SAL I, SAL II, and SAL III), foreign commercial banks, and governments. Opening to world trade included a gradual reduction of import tariffs, entry in GATT, an effort to revive the CACM, and a trade agreement with Mexico.

Labor and employment	Economic growth and new jobs allow for decreases in unemployment and increases in wages/salaries; growth of public sector employment, particularly in autonomous institutes.	Economic growth and industrialization generated wage increases and expansion in private and public employment. Government set minimum wages and established a national training institute.	Under Figueres/Oduber, the expansion of the public sector and jobs, combined with growth and relatively low inflation, permitted continued wage increases and unemployment decreases; however, wages, unemployment, and labor conflicts worsened with double-digit inflation and economic crisis of 1980–82. Wage adjustments changed from every other year to annual and then twice a year.	Sliding wage scale implemented by Monge, based on basket of consumer goods, increases wages; Arias shifts to consumer price index as a base for wage adjustments; Calderón reduces wages in first year but increases them in 1992–93. Monge launches emergency employment program and unemployment compensation. Calderón unsuccessfully tries to introduce a plan to shift public employees to private sector.
Distribution and social services	Social reforms of 1940–44 strengthened under Figueres; Ministry of Labor and Social Security founded (1955); public housing construction; adult education program to fight illiteracy; free secondary education expanded; public education integrated under the Superior Council of Education; University strengthened. Ulate halts social reforms but doesn't reverse them.	Expansion of public expenditures on social services: social security health-care coverage extended to almost all of population; ambitious poverty programs under Figueres/Oduber (creating new autonomous institute); improvements in income distribution; plan to reduce urban-rural inequalities; programs and reforms to extend and raise the quality of all levels of education; and housing programs. The crisis of 1981–82 hurt most social programs (although health indicators continue to improve) and worsened distribution.		Monge's social programs counter effects of crisis with emphasis on the poor; social security and health programs protect the poor during the crisis; increased state control of social institutions to reduce their deficits. Real wages decline during the crisis but recover in the '90s. Arias gives priority to public housing, but Calderón halts it. Calderón did not pay state contributions to CCSS in 1991–92 but reached an agreement in 1993; reform of CCSS in 1993; new approach on health care but not implemented; housing program paralyzed for lack of funds.

Table IV.3

Basic Macroeconomic Indicators of Costa Rica, 1960–1994

Year	GDP Rate[a] (Percentage) Absolute	Per Capita	Gross Fixed Capital Formation[b] (Percentage of GDP)	Annual Inflation Rate[c] (Percentage)	Central Gov't Budget Balance (Percentage of GDP)[d]	Official Exchange Rate (Colones per U.S. $)[e]
1960			16.1	0.8		5.615
1961	−0.8	−4.6	17.2	2.4		5.952
1962	8.1	4.3	18.5	2.7		6.625
1963	4.8	1.2	18.2	2.9		6.625
1964	4.1	0.5	16.4	3.3		6.625
1965	9.8	6.3	18.6	−0.7		6.625
1966	7.9	4.9	17.2	0.2	−4.0	6.625
1967	5.7	2.6	18.0	1.2	−4.7	6.625
1968	8.5	5.5	17.2	4.1		6.625
1969	5.5	2.4	18.1	2.6		6.625
1970	7.5	4.7	19.5	4.7	−1.6	6.625
1971	6.8	4.1	22.1	3.1	−4.0	6.626
1972	8.2	5.6	21.9	4.6	−4.3	6.635
1973	7.7	5.1	22.2	15.2	−3.7	6.647
1974	5.5	3.0	24.0	30.1	−0.7	7.930
1975	2.1	−0.4	22.0	17.4	−2.2	8.570
1976	5.5	2.6	23.4	3.5	−3.4	8.570
1977	8.9	5.8	22.4	4.2	−3.1	8.570
1978	6.3	3.2	23.0	6.0	−5.0	8.570
1979	4.9	1.9	26.2	9.2	−6.8	8.570
1980	0.8	−2.1	23.9	18.1	−7.4	8.570
1981	−2.3	−5.1	24.1	37.1	−2.9	21.763
1982	−7.3	−10.0	20.3	90.1	−0.9	37.407
1983	2.9	0.2	18.3	32.6	−2.0	41.094
1984	8.0	5.4	20.0	12.0	−0.7	44.533
1985	0.7	−1.9[f]	19.3	15.1	−1.3	50.453
1986	5.5	2.7	18.7	11.8	−4.5	55.986
1987	4.8	2.0	19.8	16.8	−2.9	62.776
1988	3.4	0.7	18.9	20.8	0.0	75.805
1989	5.6	3.0	20.5	16.5	−2.1	81.504
1990	3.6	1.1	22.5	19.0	−3.2	91.579
1991	2.2	−0.2	19.7	28.7	−1.4	122.430
1992	5.4	3.0	20.8	21.8	−1.9	134.510
1993	6.1	3.7	22.1	9.0		

Sources: IMF, *IFSY* 1979, 1990, 1992, 1994 and *IFS,* March 1993 and August 1995.

[a]1985 prices. [b]Current prices. [c]San José. [d]Current prices. [e]Annual averages. [f]The reported population growth rate was 4.2% because two series, not strictly comparable, were merged. It was decided instead to use an average of 2.6%.

Table IV.4
Percentage Distribution of GDP by Economic Activity in Costa Rica, 1960–1993

	Including Other Services						Excluding Other Services				
Year	Agriculture	Industry[a]	Construction	Transportation and Communications	Commerce and Finance	Other Services[b]	Agriculture	Industry[a]	Construction	Transportation and Communications	Commerce and Finance
1960	25.2	15.1	4.5	4.6	34.0	16.6	30.2	18.1	5.4	5.5	40.8
1961	26.4	14.5	5.1	4.5	33.1	16.4	31.6	17.3	6.1	5.4	39.6
1962	25.9	14.4	5.3	4.3	33.8	16.3	30.9	17.2	6.3	5.1	40.4
1963	24.6	15.5	5.1	4.2	34.0	16.5	29.5	18.6	6.1	5.0	40.8
1964	24.7	16.6	4.4	4.3	33.4	16.6	29.6	19.9	5.3	5.2	40.0
1965	22.9	18.2	4.7	4.2	33.5	16.5	27.4	21.8	5.6	5.0	40.1
1966	23.2	18.5	4.3	4.2	33.5	16.3	27.7	22.1	5.1	5.0	40.0
1967	23.7	18.8	4.4	4.4	33.1	15.7	28.1	22.3	5.2	5.2	39.2
1968	23.8	19.7	4.4	4.5	32.7	14.9	28.0	23.1	5.2	5.3	38.4
1969	24.9	20.1	4.2	4.6	31.2	15.0	29.3	23.7	4.9	5.4	36.7
1970	24.1	20.5	4.1	4.4	31.8	15.0	28.4	24.1	4.8	5.2	37.5
1971	23.6	20.9	4.5	4.6	31.3	15.1	27.8	24.6	5.3	5.4	36.9
1972	23.0	21.3	5.2	4.8	30.9	14.9	27.0	25.0	6.0	5.6	36.3
1973	22.6	21.7	4.9	5.1	31.1	14.6	26.5	25.4	5.7	6.0	36.4
1974	21.0	23.1	5.0	5.6	30.3	15.0	24.7	27.2	5.9	6.6	35.6
1975	21.2	23.3	5.2	5.8	29.6	14.9	24.9	27.4	6.1	6.8	34.8
1976	20.2	23.4	5.9	5.8	30.0	14.6	23.7	27.5	6.9	6.8	35.1
1977	19.0	24.2	5.6	6.0	31.0	14.2	22.1	28.2	6.5	7.0	36.1
1978	19.0	24.5	5.6	6.3	30.6	14.0	22.1	28.5	6.5	7.3	35.6
1979	18.2	24.1	6.4	6.7	30.6	14.0	21.2	28.0	7.4	7.8	35.6

(continued)

Table IV.4
(Continued)

Year	Including Other Services						Excluding Other Services				
	Agriculture	Industry[a]	Construction	Transportation and Communications	Commerce and Finance	Other Services[b]	Agriculture	Industry[a]	Construction	Transportation and Communications	Commerce and Finance
1980	18.0	24.3	6.3	7.0	30.1	14.3	21.0	28.3	7.4	8.2	35.1
1981	19.3	24.9	5.0	7.1	28.9	14.7	22.7	29.2	5.9	8.3	33.9
1982	19.9	24.3	3.7	7.6	29.2	15.4	23.5	28.7	4.3	9.0	34.5
1983	20.1	24.5	3.7	7.5	29.2	14.9	23.6	28.8	4.4	8.8	34.4
1984	20.5	24.8	4.3	7.2	29.1	14.0	23.8	28.9	5.0	8.4	33.9
1985	19.2	24.9	4.5	7.3	30.0	14.1	22.4	29.0	5.2	8.5	34.9
1986	19.0	25.2	4.4	7.3	30.5	13.6	22.0	29.2	5.1	8.4	35.3
1987	18.7	25.4	4.2	7.5	30.9	13.3	21.6	29.3	4.8	8.7	35.6
1988	19.2	25.2	4.1	8.1	30.0	13.4	22.2	29.1	4.7	9.4	34.6
1989	19.5	24.7	4.3	8.4	30.0	13.1	22.4	28.4	5.0	9.7	34.5
1990	19.3	24.6	4.1	8.6	30.4	13.0	22.2	28.3	4.7	9.9	34.9
1991	19.8	24.6	3.5	8.8	30.3	13.0	22.8	28.3	4.0	10.1	34.8
1992	19.3	25.3	3.5	9.2	30.4	12.3	22.0	28.8	4.0	10.5	34.7
1993	18.7	25.0	3.9	9.6	30.9	11.9	21.2	28.4	4.4	10.9	35.1

Sources: 1960–72 from BCCR 1986; 1972–90 and 1992–93 from ECLAC *Yearbook* 1980b–95b and BCCR 1989b–92b.

Note: 1966 constant prices. [a]Manufacturing, mining, electricity, gas, and water. [b]Public administration; community, social, and personal services.

Table IV.5

Physical Output of Principal Agricultural Products in Costa Rica, 1960–1993
(Millions of Kilograms)

Year	Coffee	Bananas	Beef	Sugarcane	Cacao	Rice	Corn	Beans
1960	56.7	348.3	69.3	833.3	12.1	47.4	49.1	17.5
1961	63.6	310.0	70.3	1,069.7	10.6	47.8	51.9	16.4
1962	62.7	372.6	71.6	1,085.8	12.6	57.6	56.8	17.1
1963	63.4	346.3	74.7	1,258.1	10.7	48.1	59.0	20.9
1964	55.4	380.4	78.0	1,330.4	10.2	40.6	61.2	17.5
1965	57.3	406.0	78.6	1,397.2	7.6	48.7	77.3	21.0
1966	69.8	451.2	80.7	1,664.4	8.5	50.1	77.5	17.0
1967	78.3	466.0	87.3	1,645.2	8.2	56.3	84.8	15.8
1968	77.5	650.7	94.1	1,726.7	6.1	61.4	81.6	11.1
1969	84.1	794.6	118.5	1,792.2	9.8	51.1	76.7	15.3
1970	80.6	958.7	111.0	2,134.8	4.2	55.6	71.3	12.0
1971	87.7	1,027.6	116.1	2,098.0	4.4	68.7	70.1	8.9
1972	88.8	1,186.1	115.7	2,301.4	7.1	62.7	75.9	14.2
1973	92.6	1,289.4	116.4	2,341.3	5.6	81.6	65.5	11.0
1974	91.2	1,151.3	127.7	2,192.6	5.9	62.2	60.5	13.7
1975	85.3	1,220.7	128.9	2,323.9	6.6	112.1	67.8	14.6
1976	81.8	1,187.2	125.0	2,291.6	5.8	169.4	114.0	16.2
1977	87.2	1,124.7	134.1	2,519.4	7.7	175.9	84.7	14.1
1978	98.5	1,183.0	146.0	2,578.7	10.4	197.8	62.3	14.0
1979	98.6	1,154.3	137.3	2,615.1	10.4	219.6	72.9	11.3
1980	106.4	1,107.5	118.5	2,516.5	5.3	230.6	75.3	11.5
1981	113.1	1,141.3	147.6	2,521.0	5.0	222.5	82.8	12.3
1982	115.1	1,153.3	119.6	2,446.2	3.5	146.2	82.3	16.3
1983	124.0	1,155.3	97.8	2,543.5	2.2	246.8	94.1	14.4
1984	136.9	1,160.6	124.6	2,935.8	4.1	223.0	103.0	20.8
1985	124.0	1,002.4	107.0	2,950.5	4.7	224.0	119.0	22.9
1986	120.0	1,096.2	128.0	2,802.0	4.5	200.0	134.0	29.0
1987	145.0	1,145.0	124.0	2,675.0	4.4	152.0	104.0	32.0
1988	158.0	1,222.0	112.0	2,796.0	4.0	172.0	88.0	27.0
1989	158.0	1,424.0		2,511.0	4.0	204.0	81.0	22.0
1990	153.0	1,598.0		2,756.0	4.0	190.0	66.0	32.0
1991	162.0	1,713.0		2,948.0	3.0	183.0	57.0	36.0
1992	149.0	1,921.0		3,158.0	2.0	208.0	42.0	37.0
1993	148.0	1,928.0		2,987.0		170.0	34.0	33.0

Sources: 1960–85 from BCCR 1986; 1986–89 and 1993 from ECLAC *Yearbook* 1989b–95b, *Survey* 1988a–92a, and MIDEPLAN 1988.

Table IV.6

Statistics on Industrial Sector of Costa Rica, 1960–1992

Year	Annual Growth Industrial Product[a] (Percentage)	Annual Growth GDP[a] (Percentage)	Employment Industry (Thousands)	Exports (Current Million U.S.$)
1960	4.4	6.1		
1961	−5.2	−1.0		2.2
1962	7.7	8.1		2.4
1963	13.4	4.8	43,125	5.2
1964	11.4	4.1		15.9
1965	20.3	9.8		19.4
1966	10.1	7.9		27.4
1967	6.6	5.7		29.8
1968	13.5	8.4		40.2
1969	7.1	5.6		42.1
1970	9.4	7.5		53.5
1971	8.1	6.8		58.6
1972	10.5	8.2		64.5
1973	10.2	7.7		87.0
1974	12.7	5.5		130.6
1975	3.2	2.1		136.6
1976	5.8	5.5	90,451	173.0
1977	12.7	8.9	104,129	207.7
1978	8.2	6.3	105,475	224.1
1979	2.7	4.9	117,027	269.1
1980	0.8	0.8	117,860	456.7
1981	−0.5	−2.3	112,070	
1982	−11.4	−7.3	115,810	359.7
1983	1.8	2.9	127,140	346.4
1984	10.4	8.0	128,030	393.4
1985	2.0	0.7	131,230	361.9
1986	7.3	5.5	146,583	375.4
1987	5.5	4.8	159,360	440.2
1988	2.2	3.4	157,220	464.6
1989	3.6	5.6	184,460	663.4
1990	3.1	3.6	183,010	680.6
1991	1.5	2.2	188,740	730.1
1992		5.4	197,150	846.8

Sources: Growth from BCCR 1986, 1989b–92b. Employment and exports from OFIPLAN 1982, UN, *ITSY* 1982–1995, and ILO *Yearbook* 1976–94.

[a]1966 prices.

Table IV.7

Trade Merchandise: Balance and Dependency in Costa Rica, 1960–1994

(Millions of U.S.$)

Year	Exports (f.o.b.)	Imports (c.i.f.)	Total Transactions	Trade Balance		Trade Dependency (Percentage of GDP in Current Prices)		
				Total	Per Capita (U.S.$)	Exports	Imports	Total Transactions
1960	84.3	110.4	194.7	−26.1	−20.9	21.2	26.1	47.3
1961	84.2	107.2	191.4	−23.0	−17.7	20.9	25.1	46.0
1962	93.0	113.4	206.4	−20.4	−15.1	22.7	26.0	48.7
1963	95.0	123.9	218.9	−28.9	−20.8	22.1	27.1	49.2
1964	113.9	138.6	252.5	−24.7	−17.2	24.4	28.6	53.0
1965	111.8	178.2	290.0	−66.4	−44.6	22.6	33.2	55.8
1966	135.5	178.5	314.0	−43.0	−27.9	24.8	30.8	55.6
1967	143.8	190.7	334.5	−46.9	−29.5	24.9	31.2	56.1
1968	170.8	213.9	384.7	−43.1	−26.4	27.8	32.5	60.3
1969	189.7	245.1	434.8	−55.4	−32.8	26.6	32.0	58.6
1970	231.2	316.7	547.9	−85.5	−49.4	27.8	34.6	62.4
1971	225.4	349.7	575.1	−124.3	−69.1	26.8	37.1	63.9
1972	280.9	372.8	653.7	−91.9	−49.9	30.2	36.6	66.8
1973	344.5	455.3	799.8	−110.8	−59.3	30.8	36.9	67.7
1974	440.3	719.7	1,160.0	−279.4	−145.5	33.1	48.1	81.2
1975	493.3	694.0	1,187.3	−200.7	−102.4	30.1	38.5	68.6
1976	592.9	770.4	1,363.3	−177.5	−88.3	28.9	34.9	63.8
1977	828.2	1,021.4	1,849.6	−193.2	−93.3	30.9	36.3	67.2

(continued)

513

Table IV.7
(Continued)

Year	Exports (f.o.b.)	Imports (c.i.f.)	Total Transactions	Trade Balance Total	Per Capita (U.S.$)	Exports	Imports	Total Transactions
						Trade Dependency (Percentage of GDP in Current Prices)		
1978	864.9	1,165.7	2,030.6	−300.8	−141.9	28.2	36.0	64.2
1979	934.4	1,396.8	2,331.2	−462.4	−213.1	26.9	37.2	64.1
1980	1,007.7	1,540.4	2,542.1	−538.7	−239.4	26.5	36.8	63.3
1981	1,008.1	1,208.5	2,216.6	−200.4	−88.3	43.3	48.2	91.4
1982	870.4	889.0	1,759.4	−18.6	−8.0	45.1	42.2	87.2
1983	872.6	987.8	1,860.4	−115.2	−47.2	36.0	36.8	72.8
1984	1,006.4	1,093.7	2,100.1	−87.3	−35.8	34.4	34.0	68.4
1985	976.0	1,098.2	2,074.2	−122.2	−49.1	30.7	32.5	63.2
1986	1,120.5	1,147.5	2,268.0	−27.0	−9.9	31.3	30.5	61.8
1987	1,158.3	1,382.5	2,540.8	−224.2	−80.6	31.7	35.8	67.5
1988	1,245.7	1,409.8	2,655.5	−164.1	−57.6	34.2	36.0	70.2
1989	1,414.6	1,717.4	3,132.0	−302.8	−103.7	35.0	38.8	73.8
1990	1,448.2	1,989.7	3,437.9	−541.5	−179.6	34.4	42.1	76.5
1991	1,597.7	1,876.6	3,474.3	−278.9	−90.3	38.6	40.5	79.1
1992	1,833.8	2,457.8	4,291.6	−624.0	−197.4	38.7	43.6	82.3
1993	2,085.3	2,907.0	4,992.3	−821.7	−251.4	38.3	45.2	83.5
1994	2,215.3	3,025.1	5,240.4	−809.8	−244.4	39.3	44.2	83.5

Sources: BCCR 1986, 1989b–92b; ECLAC 1995b and IMF *IFSY*, 1990–94 and *IFS* August 1995.

Table IV.8

Percentage Distribution of Exports by Major Products in Costa Rica,
1960–1993

Year	Coffee	Bananas	Cocoa	Beef	Sugar	Other
1960	52.9	23.6	6.9	5.0	2.2	9.4
1961	53.5	24.8	5.8	3.3	3.9	8.7
1962	52.2	29.0	5.4	3.0	3.2	7.2
1963	47.8	27.2	4.6	5.3	5.6	9.5
1964	42.2	24.9	3.7	5.3	4.8	19.1
1965	41.7	25.5	2.1	2.9	4.5	23.3
1966	38.8	21.9	2.4	4.0	6.8	26.1
1967	38.1	21.9	2.4	6.0	6.1	25.5
1968	32.4	25.5	2.0	7.0	5.5	27.6
1969	29.4	27.8	4.0	8.0	5.1	25.7
1970	31.6	29.3	1.0	7.8	4.7	25.6
1971	26.3	28.6	0.8	9.1	6.0	29.2
1972	27.7	29.7	1.2	10.1	4.8	26.5
1973	27.3	26.5	1.5	9.2	6.5	29.0
1974	28.3	22.5	1.8	7.8	5.8	33.8
1975	20.1	29.3	1.4	6.5	10.0	32.7
1976	27.5	24.9	1.5	6.8	4.3	35.0
1977	40.6	18.1	2.6	5.3	2.0	31.4
1978	34.2	18.7	2.7	6.6	1.9	35.9
1979	33.8	20.8	2.3	8.7	2.0	32.4
1980	24.0	20.8	1.4	6.9	4.1	42.8
1981	23.8	22.7	0.8	7.3	4.3	41.1
1982	27.5	24.9	0.6	6.1	1.7	39.2
1983	27.3	29.0	0.4	3.8	3.1	36.4
1984	28.1	26.6	0.7	4.6	4.0	36.0
1985	33.6	22.9	0.8	5.7	1.5	35.5
1986	36.0	22.5	0.8	6.1	0.7	33.9
1987	30.2	20.7	0.1	5.6	1.4	42.0
1988	26.8	18.7	0.1	4.7	1.1	48.6
1989	21.5	21.3	0.1	3.9	1.2	52.0
1990	17.8	23.1	0.1	3.6	1.8	53.6
1991	17.7	26.9	0.0	4.0	1.7	49.7
1992	11.1	26.5	0.0	2.4	1.5	58.5
1993	9.8	26.2	0.0	3.2	1.2	59.6

Sources: 1960–86 from UN 1961–90; 1986–93 from BCCR 1990c–91c and 1993.

Table IV.9

Percentage Distribution of Imports by Major Products in Costa Rica, 1960–1993

Year	Food and Beverages[a]	Non-Food Agricultural Products and Minerals	Fuels	Machinery and Transportation	Other Manufactures	Other
1960	13	1	6	26	54	0
1961	11	2	7	25	56	0
1962	9	2	7	26	56	0
1963	9	2	6	27	56	0
1964	10	2	6	27	56	0
1965	8	2	5	29	56	0
1966	9	2	5	29	55	0
1967	10	3	5	28	54	0
1968	11	3	5	23	58	0
1969	9	3	4	28	56	0
1970	10	3	4	29	54	0
1971	10	2	4	30	54	0
1972	8	2	5	31	54	0
1973	8	3	6	29	54	0
1974	10	2	9	25	54	0
1975	9	2	10	27	52	0
1976	7	2	9	30	53	0
1977	6	1	9	31	53	0
1978	6	1	9	30	53	1
1979	6	2	13	30	49	0
1980	7	2	15	24	52	0
1981	7	2	16	23	53	0
1982	7	3	20	15	56	0
1983	8	3	19	16	55	0
1984	7	3	15	21	54	0
1985	6	2	16	23	53	0
1986	7	3	8	29	53	0
1987	4	2	10	30	54	0
1988	5	2	12	28	52	1
1989	8	4	4	28	57	0
1990	8	5	10	28	49	0
1991	9	4	17	20	50	0
1992	8	3	17	23	49	0
1993	8	2	9	26	55	0

Sources: 1960–85 from UN 1960–90; 1986–93 from WB *WDR* 1988b–95.

Note: The World Bank has the same series for various years, but the figures are not strictly comparable with those of the U.N. and BCCR. [a]Data for 1960–70 includes tobacco.

Table IV.10

World Prices of Principal Export Products and Purchasing Power of Exports in Costa Rica, 1960–1994

Year	Average Annual Prices (U.S. Cents/Pound) Coffee[a] (New York)	Bananas	Beef (New York)	Purchasing Power of Exports (1970 = 100)	(1980 = 100)	Terms of Trade (1980 = 100)
1960	33.81	9.15	32.90	41		
1961	31.87	8.89	32.55			
1962	31.09	8.44	33.19			
1963	33.22	8.09	31.11			
1964	43.51	7.77	28.71			
1965	41.04	7.25	29.61	52		
1966	38.19	6.99	35.44			
1967	37.08	7.15	35.70			
1968	37.36	6.93	36.04			
1969	38.53	7.24	38.93			
1970	50.53	7.53	41.32	100		
1971	44.66	6.37	42.51			
1972	50.40	7.33	49.76			
1973	62.16	7.48	63.67			
1974	67.95	8.35	53.19			
1975	72.48	11.15	45.01	107		
1976	141.96	11.73	52.38	135		
1977	229.09	12.38	50.90	173		
1978	155.00	13.00	71.30	152		
1979	169.50	14.78	91.70	155		
1980	150.71	17.01	86.76	142	100	100
1981	115.82	18.20	86.39	135		
1982	125.62	17.00	98.61	111	95	94
1983	127.94	19.47	95.62		87	88
1984	141.24	17.04	97.19		104	90
1985	133.47	17.15	89.75		95	89
1986	170.28	17.32	76.67		116	106
1987	107.32	17.11	81.42		116	97
1988	115.11	21.73	81.59		120	88
1989	91.30	24.80	87.17		131	84
1990	89.15	24.60	94.32		123	73
1991	85.03	25.46	90.47		161	91
1992	63.66	21.69	90.13		185	87
1993	69.90	31.40	118.70		211	88
1994	135.90	34.40	108.10		228	95

Sources: Prices from IMF *IFSY* 1990–94 and ECLAC *Preliminary* 1994c. Purchasing power: base year 1970 from ECLAC *Yearbook* 1983; base year 1980 and terms of trade from ECLAC *Preliminary* 1985c–94c.

[a]After 1989, prices are for other mild coffees (New York) instead of all coffees; the two series are not comparable.

Table IV.11

***Trade Concentration with Main Commercial Partner (U.S.) in Costa Rica,
1960–1993***

Year	Percentage of Trade with U.S.			Percentage of Total Transactions with CACM[a]	Percentage with Rest
	Total Transactions	Exports	Imports		
1960	50.9	55.9	47.0	3.2	45.9
1961	50.9	56.3	46.6	3.3	45.8
1962	48.8	51.5	46.5	2.4	48.8
1963	50.9	55.2	47.7	3.7	45.4
1964	49.4	53.3	46.2	9.2	41.4
1965	44.0	50.4	39.9	11.4	44.6
1966	42.5	47.0	39.0	15.7	41.8
1967	42.5	47.4	38.9	18.5	39.0
1968	42.2	47.6	37.8	22.2	35.6
1969	41.2	49.3	35.0	20.5	38.3
1970	37.5	41.2	34.8	21.0	41.5
1971	36.3	41.9	32.6	21.5	42.2
1972	36.1	40.3	33.0	20.4	43.5
1973	34.4	33.4	35.1	19.3	46.3
1974	33.7	32.3	34.5	18.8	47.5
1975	37.6	42.0	34.5	18.7	43.7
1976	36.8	39.7	34.6	19.5	43.7
1977	32.5	31.0	33.6	18.5	49.0
1978	31.7	31.0	32.2	18.8	49.5
1979	33.1	37.1	30.4	16.6	50.3
1980	32.9	33.1	32.7	19.3	47.8
1981	32.9	32.5	33.3	17.6	49.5
1982	34.7	33.5	35.8	15.9	49.4
1983	34.8	31.4	37.9	17.1	48.1
1984	36.6	37.0	36.2	14.7	48.7
1985	35.9	37.4	34.6	11.4	52.7
1986	38.7	41.7	35.7	9.1	52.2
1987	40.1	43.7	37.1	8.9	51.0
1988	41.5	44.4	38.9	9.2	49.3
1989	43.2	45.7	41.2	7.0	49.8
1990	42.7	45.7	40.6	8.1	49.2
1991	45.7	48.3	43.5	9.2	45.1
1992	57.4	51.8	62.1	4.9	37.7
1993	55.0	56.3	53.8	5.7	39.3

Sources: IMF *DTA* 1960–77, *DTY* 1978–79, *DISY* 1980–94.

[a]El Salvador, Guatemala, Honduras, Nicaragua.

Table IV.12

Dependency on Crude Oil Imports in Costa Rica, 1972–1987
(Thousand Barrels)

Year	Imports[a]	Domestic Production	Total Supply	Dependency on Imports (Percentage)
1972	2,694	0	2,694	100.0
1973	3,195	0	3,195	100.0
1974	2,737	0	2,737	100.0
1975	1,995	0	1,995	100.0
1976	1,845	0	1,845	100.0
1977	2,377	0	2,377	100.0
1978	3,377	0	3,377	100.0
1979	2,927	0	2,927	100.0
1980	3,483	0	3,483	100.0
1981	3,430	0	3,430	100.0
1982	3,334	0	3,334	100.0
1983	3,352	0	3,352	100.0
1984	3,250	0	3,250	100.0
1985	3,065	0	3,065	100.0
1986	4,724	0	4,724	100.0
1987	4,585	0	4,585	100.0

Source: IDB 1975–89; IDB has not published data after 1987.

[a]Costa Rica also imports a considerable amount of refined oil; between 1975 and 1980 the latter equaled imports of crude oil, but between 1980 and 1987 refined oil imports declined from 3.5 to 1.8 million barrels. Virtually all crude imports are refined domestically.

Table IV.13
Total Disbursed External Debt of Costa Rica, 1960–1994
(Million U.S. Current Dollars)

Year	Current	Real (1985 = 100)	Public	Private	GDP	Export Goods and Services	Real Debt per Capita (U.S.$)
	Disbursed External Debt[a]		Percentage Distribution		Debt as Percentage of		
1960	44	158			8.6	40.3	127.8
1966	103	327			15.9	63.7	212.3
1967	110	340			15.7	62.4	214.2
1968	118	347			15.2	54.1	212.2
1969	125	348			14.6	54.4	206.5
1970	134	354			13.6	48.2	204.4
1971	167	418			15.5	56.9	235.0
1972	207	494			16.7	54.5	270.7
1973	249	558			16.3	52.3	298.1
1974	303	623			18.2	54.2	324.8
1975	421	787			21.5	70.6	400.5
1976	536	944			22.2	75.5	466.9
1977	735	1,213			23.9	76.8	582.1
1978	1,678	2,578	56.4	43.6	47.6	167.4	1,199.6
1979	2,109	2,979	61.7	38.3	52.3	194.1	1,345.5
1980	2,735	3,538	61.8	38.2	56.6	213.8	1,552.4
1981	3,286	3,880	66.7	33.3	125.2	289.4	1,656.7
1982	3,627	4,026	65.6	34.4	139.1	308.6	1,673.3
1983	4,181	4,467	75.1	24.9	135.4	375.2	1,808.5
1984	3,990	4,098	79.7	20.3	108.5	315.5	1,616.6
1985	4,401	4,401	80.2	19.8	111.4	362.7	1,665.8
1986	4,575	4,452	79.0	21.0	102.8	328.0	1,639.2
1987	4,723	4,450	78.4	21.6	103.5	326.9	1,594.4
1988	4,470	4,088	78.0	22.0	96.5	283.7	1,426.4
1989	4,485	4,101	77.9	22.1	87.4	258.7	1,394.4
1990	3,924	3,311	81.1	18.9	66.0	192.4	1,098.2
1991	3,992	3,215			71.7	186.5	1,041.1
1992	3,992	3,149			61.6	163.1	996.2
1993	3,827	2,944			53.5	139.6	909.5
1994	3,818	2,788			49.2	125.1	841.5

Sources: Disbursed external debt and distribution 1960–94 from IDB 1976–93 and ECLAC *Preliminary* 1994, 1996. Real debt calculated from U.S. GNP deflator (IMF *ISFY,* 1990, 1994). GDP and exports from IMF, *IFSY,* 1990, 1991, 1994 (converted to dollars using official exchange rate). Per capita calculated with population from Table IV.21.

[a]1960–1977 is disbursed external public debt.

Table IV.14

Percentage Distribution of the Labor Force by Economic Activity in Costa Rica, 1963–1993

Economic Activities	1963	1973	1980	1984	1987	1989	1990	1991	1992	1993
Agriculture	49.2	36.4	26.9	31.0	27.5	25.9	25.3	25.5	23.8	22.6
Mining	0.2	0.3	⎱ 16.2	0.2	0.2	0.1	0.2	0.1	0.1	0.2
Industry	11.5	11.9		13.2	17.2	18.6	18.0	18.7	18.8	18.0
Electricity, gas, water	1.1[a]	1.0		1.1	1.2	1.2	1.2	1.1	1.2	1.4
Construction	5.9	6.7	7.9	5.2	6.0	6.3	6.6	6.3	6.1	6.2
Commerce	9.8	11.5	18.0	10.9	15.8	15.7	15.7	15.6	16.6	17.8
Transportation, storage, and communication[a]	3.7	4.3	6.5	2.5	4.0	3.6	4.0	4.3	4.6	4.7
Financial services	⎱ 17.2	2.3	⎱ 22.9[b]	2.6	2.8	3.3	3.3	3.7	3.5	4.2
Services		20.4		21.9	23.2	23.5	24.2	23.7	23.8	23.7
Nonspecified, unemployed, other[c]	1.4	5.2	1.6	11.4	2.1	1.8	1.5	1.0	1.5	1.2
Total	100.0	100.0	100.0	100.0	100.0	100.0	100.0	100.0	100.0	100.0

Source: ILO 1975–94.

[a]Includes sanitary services. [b]Includes electricity, gas, water. [c]Unemployed not included in 1963.

Table IV.15

Percentage of Women in the Labor Force and Women's Participation Rates in Costa Rica, 1960–1993

Year	Percentage of Labor Force	Participation Rate[a] (Percentage)
1960		15.0
1965	16.3[b]	
1970		15.9
1975	19.3[c]	
1980	24.8	20.7
1985	26.1	20.6
1990	28.5	
1991	29.9	
1993	29.9	21.9[d]

Sources: Percentage 1960–85 from ILO *Retrospective* 1990; 1990–93 from ILO *YBLS* 1992 and 1994. Rates from ECLAC *Yearbook* 1992, 1995.

[a]Economically active female population aged 10 years and over as a percentage of the total population aged 10 years and over. [b]1963. [c]1973. [d]1992. ECLAC gives 37% in urban areas and 28% in rural areas.

Table IV.16

Open Unemployment Rates in Costa Rica,
1963–1993 (Percentage of Labor Force)

Year	National	Urban	Rural
1963	6.9		
1970		3.5	
1976	6.3	5.4	5.8
1977	4.6	5.1	4.1
1978	4.5	5.8	3.6
1979	4.9	5.3	4.2
1980	5.9	6.0	5.9
1981	8.7	9.1	8.4
1982	9.4	9.9	8.3
1983	9.0	8.5	9.6
1984	5.0	6.6	9.2
1985	6.8	6.7	7.0
1986	6.2	6.7	5.6
1987	5.6	5.9	5.3
1988	5.5	6.3	4.7
1989	3.8	3.7	3.8
1990	4.6	5.4	4.1
1991	5.5	6.0	5.2
1992	4.1	4.3	3.8
1993	4.1	4.0	4.2

Sources: National: DGEC 1966 and ILO *YBLS* 1976–94. Urban: 1970–93, ECLAC *Yearbook* 1980b–95b. Rural from Rottenberg 1993 and ECLAC *Survey* 1980a–95a.

Table IV.17

Percentage Distribution of Central Government Expenditures by Social Programs in Costa Rica, 1972–1993

Year	Social Security[a]	Health Care[b]	Education	Housing, etc.	Subtotals Social[c]	Nonsocial	Total
1972	23.1	3.5	26.7	2.1	55.4	44.6	100.0
1973	23.6	2.9	25.7	5.2	57.4	42.6	100.0
1974	22.2	3.9	27.0	2.4	55.5	44.5	100.0
1975	25.1	4.3	27.3	1.7	58.4	41.6	100.0
1976	24.9	4.5	26.2	1.1	56.7	43.3	100.0
1977	23.5	3.3	28.5	2.1	57.4	42.6	100.0
1978	29.7	3.8	25.7	2.0	61.2	38.8	100.0
1979	30.2	2.4	24.8	2.6	60.0	40.0	100.0
1980	30.8	5.0	24.6	2.2	62.6	37.4	100.0
1981	36.0	4.0	23.7	2.3	66.0	34.0	100.0
1982	37.7	6.3	22.6	2.9	69.5	30.5	100.0
1983	34.1	2.8	19.4	2.7	59.0	41.0	100.0
1984	30.0	5.7	18.4	5.8	59.9	40.1	100.0
1985	35.3	2.2	18.8	1.8	58.1	41.9	100.0
1986	36.9	1.7	16.2	7.4	62.2	37.8	100.0
1987	28.8	2.3	22.1	9.1	62.3	37.7	100.0
1988	34.0	4.0	18.6	1.5	58.1	41.9	100.0
1989	35.7	4.8	17.0	3.5	61.0	39.0	100.0
1990	35.0	5.0	19.0	1.1	60.1	39.9	100.0
1991	37.9	6.4	19.1	0.7	64.1	35.9	100.0
1992	36.8	6.3	23.9	0.3	67.3	32.7	100.0
1993	33.3	5.7	22.3	0.3	61.6	38.4	100.0

Source: Author's calculations based on IMF 1980a–94a.

[a]CCSS sickness-maternity and pension programs, plus civil servant pensions, and INS. [b]Rest of health-care and sanitation programs: MINSA, ICAA, etc. [c]Sum of colums 1–4.

Table IV.18

Income Distribution in Costa Rica, 1961–1990 (Deciles)

Deciles	Family Income				Income Head of Household-Salaried Employee				
	1961	*1971*	*1983*	*1988*	*1979*	*1982*	*1985*	*1988*	*1990*
First	2.6	2.1	1.5	1.6	2.2	2.1	1.7	1.2	1.1
Second	3.4	3.3	3.0	3.1	4.0	3.9	3.1	2.7	2.8
Third	3.8	4.2	4.1	4.3	4.9	5.5	5.3	3.9	4.3
Fourth	4.0	5.1	5.2	5.5	6.0	6.0	5.8	5.3	5.2
Fifth	4.4	6.2	6.3	6.6	7.3	7.9	6.1	6.3	6.4
Sixth	5.4	7.5	7.5	8.1	8.3	8.5	8.1	7.7	8.1
Seventh	7.1	9.3	9.2	9.8	9.5	10.4	10.0	9.5	10.1
Eighth	9.3	11.7	11.4	12.5	12.1	11.8	12.8	12.3	12.9
Ninth	14.0	16.2	15.1	16.8	17.3	16.0	17.4	17.0	17.2
Tenth	46.0	34.4	36.7	31.7	28.4	27.9	29.7	34.1	31.9
Total	100.0	100.0	100.0	100.0	100.0	100.0	100.0	100.0	100.0
Gini						0.328		0.364	0.345
coefficient[a]	0.50	0.43	0.47	0.43		0.355		0.358	0.351

Sources: Family income: 1961 from ECLAC *Survey* 1968a; 1971 from Céspedes 1973; 1983 from Trejos and Elizalde 1985; 1988 from Baldares 1988. Income head of household: 1979 from Altimar 1984; 1982–90 from ECLAC 1993d. Baldares's help was crucial in putting this table together. Gini from Baldares and ECLAC 1994e.

Note: All national. The two series are not technically comparable. [a]Family income national; heads of household urban and rural.

Table IV.19
Poverty Incidence in Costa Rica, 1970–1993

	Individuals				Households			
	National				National			
Year	Poverty	Indigency[a]	Urban	Rural	Poverty	Indigency[a]	Urban	Rural
PREALC								
1971	46	22	35	54	39	17	28	46
1977	29	16	17	39	25	14	14	34
1983	40	19	30	50	34	16	25	44
1986	29	16	19	37	25	14	16	32
Sauma & Trejos								
1971	30	8	19	39	25	9	14	33
1977	16	8	10	21	13	7	8	17
1983	35	17	26	42	30	14	23	37
1986	20	11	12	25	17	10	11	22

	Households					
	National		Urban		Rural	
Year	Poverty	Indigency	Poverty	Indigency	Poverty	Indigency
ECLAC						
1970	24	6	15	5	30	7
1981	22	6	16	5	28	8
1988	25	8	21	6	28	10
1990	24	10	22	7	25	12
1992	25	10	25	8	25	12
1994	21	8	18	6	23	10
Trejos						
1988	22		11		30	
1990	20		10		29	
1992	22		13		30	
1993	17	9	9	4	26	14

Sources: Sauma and Trejos 1990 and World Bank 1990; PREALC 1992; ECLAC 1994e, 1997; Trejos 1994.
[a]Extreme poverty in PREALC.

Table IV.20
Real Wages Indices in Costa Rica, 1973–1994

	1980 = 100[a]	
Year	*Mean*	*Urban Minimum*
1973	80.0	
1974	72.2	
1975	73.9	
1976	82.5	
1977	87.0	
1978	94.7	96.0
1979	99.2	98.5
1980	100.0	100.0
1981	88.3	90.4
1982	70.8	85.9
1983	78.5	99.3
1984	84.7	104.4
1985	92.2	112.2
1986	98.0	118.7
1987	88.5	117.9
1988	84.5	114.6
1989	85.1	119.4
1990	86.5	120.5
1991	82.5	111.8
1992	85.9	111.5
1993	94.7	112.5
1994	98.4	112.8

Sources: ECLAC Preliminary 1986–95 and *Survey* 1981, 1992.

[a]The figures for 1973–79 were calculated from a series in *Survey 1981* with an original base year of 1973. The two series are not strictly comparable.

Table IV.21
Demographic and Health Indicators in Costa Rica, 1960–1994

Year	Population (Thousands)	Growth Rate (Percentage)	Doctors per 10,000 Inhabitants	Hospital Beds per 1,000 Inhabitants	Mortality Rates (per 1,000) General	Mortality Rates (per 1,000) Infant	Life Expectancy (Years at Birth)
1960	1,236		3.7	4.5	8.9	74.3	61.6
1961	1,298	5.0					
1962	1,347	3.8					
1963	1,395	3.6	4.7				
1964	1,445	3.6		4.5	8.5	82.5	64.3
1965	1,495	3.5	4.9	4.2	7.8	75.0	64.9
1966	1,540	3.0	5.1		7.4	69.9	65.7
1967	1,587	3.1	5.4	3.5	7.1	62.3	66.1
1968	1,635	3.0	5.4	3.9	6.5	59.7	66.6
1969	1,685	3.1	5.5	4.2	6.9	67.1	67.1
1970	1,732	2.8	6.1	4.0	6.6	61.5	67.6
1971	1,779	2.7	6.2	4.1	5.9	56.5	68.1
1972	1,825	2.6		4.0	5.9	54.4	68.6
1973	1,872	2.6	7.0	3.9	5.1	44.8	69.2
1974	1,918	2.5		3.8	5.0	37.6	69.7
1975	1,965	2.5	6.6	3.8	4.9	37.1	70.3
1976	2,022	2.9	6.6	3.6	4.6	33.2	70.8
1977	2,084	3.1		3.5	4.3	27.8	71.3
1978	2,149	3.1	7.1	3.5	4.1	22.3	71.9
1979	2,214	3.0	7.2	3.4	4.2	22.1	72.4
1980	2,279	2.9		3.0	4.1	19.1	

(continued)

Table IV.21
Demographic and Health Indicators in Costa Rica, 1960–1994

Year	Population (Thousands)	Growth Rate (Percentage)	Doctors per 10,000 Inhabitants	Hospital Beds per 1,000 Inhabitants	Mortality Rates (per 1,000) General	Mortality Rates (per 1,000) Infant	Life Expectancy (Years at Birth)
1981	2,342	2.8			3.8	18.0	73.0
1982	2,406	2.7	8.3	2.9	3.8	18.9	73.5
1983	2,470	2.7		2.3	3.8	18.6	73.8
1984	2,535	2.6	10.1	2.9	3.9	19.0	74.0
1985	2,642	2.6[a]		2.6	4.0	17.7	74.2
1986	2,716	2.8		2.5	3.8	17.8	74.4
1987	2,791	2.8	9.5	2.4	3.8	17.4	74.6
1988	2,866	2.7		2.3	3.8	15.5	74.8
1989	2,941	2.6		2.2		14.7	75.0
1990	3,015	2.5	9.8	2.2	3.9	14.8	75.2
1991	3,088	2.4	10.0			13.9	75.6
1992	3,161	2.4	10.2		4.0	13.7	75.7
1993	3,237	2.4	10.2		4.0	13.7	75.8
1994	3,313[b]	2.3	10.8	2.5		13.0	76.3

Sources: Population 1960–69 from BCCR 1960–85, and 1970–90 from CELADE 1984–91. Doctors from WHO 1967–78 with scattered figures from PAHO 1961–90, ECLAC, *Yearbook* 1980b–95b, and MIDEPLAN 1997; hospital beds from Mesa-Lago 1992 and ECLAC, *Yearbook* 1977b–95b, WHO 1964–90, and PAHO 1964–94; mortality rates for 1960 from ECLAC, *Yearbook* 1976; the rest from WHO 1966–81, PAHO 1990, and Durán 1994; life expectancy from World Bank, *World Tables* 1985a–91a and *Social Indicators* 1991–95; and Durán 1994. Figures for 1990 on mortality rates and life expectancy from Quiros Coronado 1991; other data from MINSA 1995.
[a]The rate would be 4.2, which is unnaturally high because two population series were combined, which are not strictly comparable; instead we used the average rate of 2.6%. [b]Author's estimate based on the average growth rate for 1991–93.

Table IV.22

Rates of Contagious Diseases in Costa Rica, 1961–1992
(Reported Cases per 100,000 Inhabitants)

Year	Diphtheria	Hepatitis	Malaria	Measles	Polio	Syphilis	Tetanus	Tuberculosis	Typhoid
1961	12.4	32.2	136.6[a]	89.6	2.8	48.7		40.2	8.1
1962	4.8	17.2	124.3[a]	233.7	3.9	94.2		47.3	4.6
1963	6.5	50.9	91.1[a]	283.2	1.3	95.8		42.2	6.3
1964	6.8	50.1	87.2[a]	222.6	0.7	84.4		36.1	5.6
1965	2.8	37.9	172.0	133.4	1.0	42.9	3.0	38.3	3.5
1966	1.5	—[b]	197.7	92.6	0.6	48.9	3.2	36.8	6.7
1967	2.1	—	277.9	239.2	0.4	60.6	3.3	36.6	5.4
1968	1.3	55.9	69.3	6.9	0.2	41.4	1.7	27.3	4.3
1969	3.1	54.7	40.8	391.6	6.2	64.7	5.7	22.9	6.8
1970	3.2	30.7	20.5	266.1	1.3	56.1	5.0	23.1	3.5
1971	5.7	79.6	14.5	200.8	0.1	83.8	4.0	22.7	3.1
1972	2.7	117.3	8.6	248.5	2.7	96.5	4.4	21.4	3.2
1973	1.3	103.1	8.6	110.1	0.2	103.3	4.3	22.2	2.2
1974	0.5	77.9	8.9	26.6	—	102.2	3.4	23.1	2.3
1975	0.3	36.8	14.7	36.0	—	74.7	2.3	29.9	1.4
1976	—	44.5	24.0	82.5	—	151.8	2.6	26.4	2.5
1977	—	45.8	10.5	95.3	—	195.5	2.1	22.2	0.9
1978	—	43.3	14.8	16.4	—	119.5	1.9	20.6	0.8
1979	—	38.5	14.1	295.4	—	99.9	1.0	26.1	2.6
1980	—	71.1	16.7	44.6	—	85.4	0.4	19.6	0.2
1981	—	c	7.2	7.5	—	c	0.5	28.0	
1982	—		4.6	7.2	—		0.7	17.3	0.2
1983	—		9.9	1.6	—		0.3	17.6	
1984	—		22.4	0.4	—		0.3	12.8	
1985	—	95.0	27.8	0.1	—		0.2	13.9	0.3
1987	—		31.6	138.6	—		0.3	7.9	c
1988	—	94.3				59.9	0.1		
1990	—	85.1	38.2	2.5	—		5.4	1.6	
1991	—	39.7	106.0	205.3	—		2.0		
1992	—		225.0		—		0.1	6.5	

Sources: PAHO, *Health Conditions* 1961–94; and *Health Statistics* 1992.

[a]Confirmed cases. [b]No cases reported or negligible rates. [c]PAHO ceased or interrrupted the publication of this series on rates of contagious diseases.

Table IV.23

Access to Potable Water and Sewerage Service in Costa Rica, 1960–1991

Year	Percentage of Urban Population		Percentage of Rural Population	
	Water[a]	Sewerage[b]	Water[a]	Sewerage[c]
1960	97.9	28.7	36.4	
1964	96.6	29.7	42.8	
1969	100.0	21.7	53.6	
1973	100.0	40.1	66.0	
1977	100.0	42.2	62.7	4.0
1979	99.9	43.0	64.0	
1980	100.0	92.0	68.0	82.0
1983	100.0	100.0	82.0	87.0
1985	100.0	99.0	83.0	89.5
1988	100.0	100.0	84.0	92.9
1989	100.0	100.0	85.5	94.3
1991	100.0	100.0		

Sources: ECLAC, *Yearbook* 1983b, 1988b; PAHO 1973–90. 1991 from UNDP 1994.

[a]Piped water at home but could also include easy access to pipe water outside the home. [b]Sewerage (*alcantarillado*), but since 1980 probably includes other means ot excreta disposal. [c]From 1980 on probably piped water and other sources of access to potable water.

Table IV.24

Illiteracy Rates and Percentage of Age Group Enrolled by Educational Level in Costa Rica, 1953–1993

	Illiteracy Rates[a] (Percentage)				Enrollment in Education[b] (Percentage)		
	Costa Rica			UNESCO			
Year	National	Urban	Rural	National	Elementary	Secondary	Higher
1953	20.6						
1963	14.3	5.2	19.7		93	20	5
1965					105	24	5
1970					110	28	9
1971					110	30	12
1972					112	33	12
1973	10.2	4.4	14.7	11.6	113	39	13
1974					110	42	16
1975					107	43	17
1976					109	43	18
1977					110	44	19
1978					105	46	24
1979					108	48	24
1980					106	47	23
1981					105	47	22
1982					101	46	21
1983					100	44	20
1984	6.9	3.1	10.2	7.4	98	41	22
1985					98	40	23
1986					98	41	23
1987					98	41	25
1988					100	41	24
1989					100	41	27
1990				7.2	101	42	27
1991					102	43	28
1992	5.7				105	46	
1993					105	47	

Sources: ECLAC, *Yearbook* 1980b–95b; UNESCO 1994.

[a]Percentages for 1953, 1963, 1973, and 1984 are from population census, based on 10 years and older. UNESCO is based on 15 years and older with the following percentages by urban/rural areas in 1973: 4.9% and 17.6%. The population base for 1992 is unknown, but it is probably 15 years and older. [b]Elementary is 6–11 years (rates go over 100% due to mismatch between population and education ages), secondary is 12–16; and higher is 20–24.

Table IV.25

Social Security Population Coverage and Costs in Costa Rica, 1960–1994

| | Population Covered by CSS (Percentage) | | | Expenditures of Social Security as Percentage of GDP | | | | |
| | Health Care | | Pensions | CCSS Sickness, | Rest | Total | CCSS: Sickness-Maternity | |
Year	Total[a]	EAP[a]	EAP	Maternity	Health[b]	Health	and Pensions	Total[c]
1960	15.0	25.0	5.9					
1961	17.0	27.0						
1962	20.0	28.0						
1963	22.0	29.0						
1964	23.0	30.0						
1965	30.0	31.0	16.8					
1966	34.0	31.0						
1967	37.0	32.0						
1968	42.0	35.0						
1969	46.0	38.0						
1970	47.2	38.3	23.6	2.0	2.9	5.1	2.3	
1971	51.5	42.2		2.3			2.7	
1972	53.8	44.7		2.6			3.1	
1973	58.4	48.9		2.6				
1974	60.3	50.1		2.7				
1975	59.6	50.1	45.4	3.1			3.9	
1976	61.2	51.2		3.4			4.3	
1977	74.0	63.3		3.9			4.6	
1978	82.2	71.7		4.6			5.4	7.2
1979	84.3	74.9		5.2			6.1	8.3
1980	75.7	67.8	50.8	5.5	2.5	8.0	6.5	9.0
1981	71.7	65.6		4.9	1.9	6.8	5.8	7.7
1982	68.0	63.5		4.0	1.7	5.7	4.9	6.6
1983	69.3	64.7		4.2	2.0	6.2	5.5	7.5
1984	83.9	67.9		4.4	1.9	6.3	5.8	7.7
1985	81.4	65.3		4.6	2.0	6.6	6.2	8.2
1986	81.1	65.4		4.4	2.5	6.9		
1987	82.2	66.1		4.4	2.4	6.8		
1988	83.0	66.6	44.8	4.9	2.0	6.9		
1989	85.4	67.5	45.8	5.5	2.0	7.5		
1990	85.6	67.0	46.2	5.8	1.8	7.6	7.7	9.5
1991	58.9	66.4	45.9	5.4	1.7	7.1	7.4	9.1
1992	86.2	69.0	47.5	5.2	1.5	6.2	7.0	8.5
1993	86.2	71.0	48.9	5.7	1.8	7.5	7.6	9.4
1994	86.2	77.3	49.3	5.6	1.8	7.4	7.5	9.3

Sources: CCSS, *Memoria* 1975–90; *Anuario* 1991–95; Mesa-Lago 1989, 1990, 1992, 1994b; Jaramillo 1993; IDB 1994; Durán and González 1994; MS 1995.

[a]The figures refer to contributors; actual coverage of health care was virtually universal in 1994 (if the Ministry of Health combined with private coverage were added). [b]Ministry of Health, the National Insurance Institute (INS) monetary expenditures on occupational hazards, the Costa Rican Institute of Aquaduct and Sewerage (ICAA), university and municipal services. [c]Total of Rest Health and CCSS columns.

Table IV.26

Government Expenditures in Housing and Dwellings Built in Costa Rica, 1960–1991

Year	Central Government Expenditures in Housing		Dwellings Built[a]	Units built per 1,000 Inhabitants
	Percentage of Expenditures	Real Index (1980 = 100)		
1960	2.3			
1961	2.1			
1962	2.0			
1963				
1964	0.6		3,858	2.7
1965	0.7		4,003	2.7
1966	0.7		3,500	2.3
1967	0.6		3,952	2.5
1968	1.5		4,724	2.9
1969			4,354	2.6
1970			5,188	3.0
1971			7,010	3.9
1972	2.1		7,601	4.2
1973	5.2		9,921	5.3
1974	2.4		12,784	6.7
1975	1.7		11,918	6.1
1976	1.1		13,279	6.6
1977	2.1		11,163	5.4
1978	2.0		12,208	5.7
1979	2.6		12,229	5.5
1980	2.2		12,439	5.5
1981	2.3		10,473	4.5
1982	2.9		8,317	3.5
1983	2.7		8,180	3.3
1984	5.8		11,311	4.5
1985	1.8		9,470	3.6
1986	7.4		15,487[b]	5.6[b]
1987	9.1			
1988	1.5			
1989	3.5			
1990	1.1			
1991	0.7			

Sources: Expenditures: 1960–68 from *SALA* 1974; the rest from Table IV.17. Dwellings from U.N., *Construction* 1964–85.

[a]Dwelling constructions authorized (i.e., a permit had been issued). [b]According to Sojo (1989), 46,462 dwellings were built from May 1986 to September 1989; the figure is an annual average.

Part V

COMPARISONS OF POLICIES AND PERFORMANCE

1

Comparison of Policies

This part is divided into two chapters. This first chapter summarizes, compares, and analyzes similarities and differences in the policies of the three country models (including the roles of the state and the market, continuity in economic policy, economic organization, development strategies, overall goals and outcomes, and social costs) and deals with some fundamental policy questions raised in the introductory part of this book, such as whether it was feasible to avoid or reduce the adverse effects of the models by applying different policies, compatibility versus trade-offs of policies, and the impact of the crisis of the 1980s and the nature of the recovery. The second chapter evaluates the indicators of performance comparatively and selects those suitable for the final ranking based on their reliability and comparability, elaborates and applies three techniques to measure and rank performance of the three models, briefly deals with nonsystemic factors that might have affected the outcomes, and assesses the feasibility of the three models in the short and medium terms.

Table V.1 summarizes the policies of the three countries in the various stages and their overall outcome during the period of observation. In Costa Rica and Cuba it starts in 1953 and 1959, respectively, and in Chile in 1973. The period closes in 1994 in Chile and Costa Rica (the end of the Alywin and Calderón Jr. administrations, respectively, for which we have statistical series), but the table adds the administrations of Eduardo Frei Jr. (Chile) and José Figueres Jr. (Costa Rica), which ended in early 2000 and 1998, respectively. The purpose of this addition is only to update the information on the political leader and party in power between 1994 and 1998, as the corresponding parts lack data on specific policies and performance related to those two administrations (a brief summary of events in 1994–97 will be given at the end of this part). For Cuba the period ends in 1996, when the reform process appeared to be halted; statistical series in part 3 usually end in 1994 or earlier, and there is some information on developments until 1996. The policy stages shown in Table V.1 are those analyzed in the three preceding parts, and the political leader (as well as party in Costa Rica) is identified in each stage. Economic policies in the table are summarized and clustered in two sections: economic organization and development strategies. In the former I include the prevalent ideology and main policies on ownership, the role of the state versus the market, and monetary and fiscal labor and social measures; in the latter I distinguish between "outward" and "inward" development strategies and state priorities assigned to various sectors such as industry, agriculture, and so forth. The last column of the table summarizes the overall outcome in each stage: crisis, recession, recovery, and high growth.

1. The Double Role of the State, the Market, and Continuity in Economic Policy

The economic role of the state may be assessed in two ways: its power to implement and change policies, and its degree of intervention and functioning in the economy (e.g., production, delivery of services, regulation). In a comparative study of ninety developing countries (including six case studies from Latin America) in search of the causes of success in human development, Lindenberg (1993) found that the state was neither weak and passive nor immense and coercive. The government had a solid institutional infrastructure to make policy work. Concerning economic functions, he discovered that the state was an active promoter and regulator rather than the overly dominant producer and provider.

In both roles the Cuban state has been the most powerful. An authoritarian socialist government has ruled that country throughout the entire period of observation, with one single political party (the communist) and no opposition allowed; hence, the government has been totally free to design, implement, and change policy. The state collectivized almost all means of production and has performed virtually all major economic functions, leaving only a tiny state-controlled private sector and market (although growing in the 1990s). In Chile the state's power to forge policy has been second in strength only to that in Cuba because there was an authoritarian military government between 1973 and 1990, which, for most of the period, banned or tightly controlled political parties, trade unions, and the news media. Not confronting an institutionalized opposition, the government was relatively free to decide and implement policy, although much less than in Cuba. Conversely, the Chilean state has played a subsidiary role performing the least economic functions among the three countries, as the private sector and the market have expanded (at least until 1990). Finally, in Costa Rica the government has been the weakest of the three countries in its power to implement policies because of the existence of a pluralistic democracy and full civic freedoms throughout the period. Yet Costa Rica's state has been the second most effective among the three countries in performing important economic functions, although declining in this respect since the mid-1980s and, particularly, in the 1990s.

Ironically, the two extreme opposite models justified their political regime and economic policy with a similar argument. Pinochet blamed the state for all previous economic and social problems and professed that the market would solve them. Contrarily, Castro attributed all prerevolutionary evils to the market and claimed that the state would correct them. Both leaders justified the authoritarian nature of their governments as needed to implement the drastic changes required (regardless of antagonistic ideologies they called their changes a "revolution"). Figueres and his PLN successors also proclaimed a revolution but conducted it through democratic means and a mixture of market and state roles.

Continuity in economic policy has not always been positively correlated with the state's strong, steady political control. Costa Rica has had the most stable policies despite eleven presidents and eight changes of the political party in power. It should be recalled, however, that the dominant party (PLN) has controlled both the Executive and the Legislative Assembly since 1953, except for eight years when the conservative opposition in full power was unsuccessful in changing the model. The opposition's failure can be explained by three factors: a powerful civil service bureaucracy installed by and sympathetic to the PLN, a strong consensus between the government and the majority of the entrepreneurial elite and the trade unions, and widespread popular support for the PLN's social policies. It was only when the state entrepreneur competed with the private sector and later the crisis forced adjustment policies that the consensus began to erode and a strong opposition party with a neoconservative program successfully organized and took power. Structural adjustment policies between 1983 and 1994 were fairly similar, however, in spite of three presidents and two parties in power, although they intensified during the neoconservative government. The country second in policy continuity has been Chile: Pinochet applied steady market-oriented policies during his tenure with only a brief partial reversal in 1983 (when the crisis threatened the survival of the neoconservative model) and minor corrections between 1976 and 1981 and 1984 and 1990 (to improve the model's performance). The military regime's electoral defeat in 1990 by a democratic coalition (the *Concertación* of Christian Democrats and moderate Socialists) did not bring down its model, which basically continued although with adjustments to infuse more equity in it. Surprisingly, Cuba, which has been ruled by Castro since 1959 (for four decades) and which has maintained a socialist system since 1960, is the country that has experimented with the most policy changes: seven in economic organization and four in development strategy. The Maximum Leader's tight political economic control and his ideological beliefs have resulted in frequent policy changes (conventional Soviet-style in 1961–63 and between 1971 and 1985, strongly antimarket between 1966 and 1970 and 1986 and 1990). Only the severe crisis of the 1990s has forced a timid, piecemeal and hesitant market-oriented policy, which appears stagnant since 1995–96. Continuity in policy should be beneficial for performance in the long run, unless such a policy is inadequate, but then it would probably be corrected. Lindenberg's (1993) study found that a key factor of success in human development was the implementation of consistent, stable policies over a long period of time.

Cuba's frequent changes of policy in opposite directions averaged less than six years in economic organization (four years if the longest 1971–85 stage is excluded), with a similar average in development strategy. Such instability did not allow enough time for a given policy to fully develop and bear fruit. The strong concentration of political power in the leader's hands, the centrally planned nature of the economy, very little discussion at the top, and virtually no feedback or accountability from below explained not only the feasibility of such changes but also the fact they were implemented on the national level instead of being tested first on a small scale. Errors in policy, therefore, had disastrous effects. The steady policies of Costa Rica and Chile, both market economies, probably played a role in their positive outcomes in the long run. But in Costa Rica a pluralistic democracy, changes in the party in power, and influence from below (particularly in election years) contributed to moderation and gradualism, hence mollifying both the process of change and the magnitude of policy errors and their adverse effects on the population. Conversely, in Chile, the authoritarian government (not constrained by opposition) applied drastic policies and committed serious errors that brought deleterious effects to the economy and the people.

2. General Goals, Economic Organization, Development Strategies, Overall Outcome, and Social Costs

A. General Goals

The goals and approaches of the three models represent two extremes in the debate between growth and equity (Chile and Cuba respectively), and a middle-of-the-road position (Costa Rica) similar to Drèze and Sen's stand. These two authors, nevertheless, included the three countries in their so-called support-led security approach, although pinpointing differences among them.

Contrary to the traditional interventionist role of military governments in Latin America, Pinochet supported a state with drastically reduced economic functions. The objective of his coup was to halt the growing process of socialization under Allende, but he lacked an economic program, and the vacuum was filled by the "Chicago Boys"' neoconservative ideology, in a odd marriage of political authoritarianism and economic liberalization. The priority goals of the economic model were to expand investment, the capital market, and growth within a stable, largely free, competitive market system based on private ownership of the means of production. Once such goals were achieved, a "trickle-down" effect would generate more jobs, higher wages, and societal welfare. The state would create a friendly environment for and support the market forces and would play a subsidiary role in the economy only when the market was unable to perform a needed function. In the social arena distribution would be determined by market forces with the government limited to attenuating the worst effects of the market (inequality is essential to fostering wealth, and the drive for equality dampens the effort of most productive individuals in society). A radical and fast reform ("shock therapy") was applied to correct the previous distortions created by state intervention and introduce the new model with a stable, healthier base. Policy errors and the drastic structural adjustment led to two economic crises and forced some corrections in the initial conception of the state role, thus increasing the state's regulatory powers over the market and, since the 1990s, its social functions.

In dramatic contrast with Chile, the Cuban model's goals were to forge a collectivized economy with full employment, egalitarianism, and free delivery of most social services; economic growth was also a target but usually subordinated to the social goals. The transformation of societal values would result in a "perk-up" effect generating high economic growth, external independence, and increased societal welfare. Castro's vision of the future was closer to the Chinese models under Mao than to the conventional Soviet model. He reluctantly applied the latter in two stages (forced by crises and enticed by abundant and generous Soviet economic aid), and he is even more unwillingly introducing a timid market-oriented reform in the current stage (compelled by the collapse of the Soviet camp and the severity of the crisis). The conflict between the leader's ideology and the economic reality of an island economy dependent on sugar and foreign trade generated zig-zag policies in both economic organization and development strategy. Castro pursued grandiose targets within short-run stages such as transforming Cuba into the most industrialized per capita country in Latin America, producing

10 million tons of sugar and then increasing output to 20 million tons, creating an unselfish "New Man" motivated by nonmaterial stimuli, making the island self-sufficient in food, and so forth. As a target failed in a given stage and provoked economic disarray, Castro had to temporarily retrench, apply more conventional policies, and pursue modest goals in the next stage until he felt strong enough to launch a new grand program, and so on in a vicious cycle.

The Costa Rican model's goals were to develop a mixed economy (predominantly private but with significant and growing state economic functions) that would foster growth with equity. Unlike those in the other two countries, the Costa Rican leaders believed that the two sectors could be blended in a beneficial manner, and growth and distribution achieved simultaneously. The state should promote and protect development, largely relying on the private sector but directly intervening in strategic areas (e.g., banking, public utilities, infrastructure, energy, some productive lines)—a mixed base that would generate growing employment and salaries and societal welfare. The state should correct the negative effects of the market through provision of universal social services (including the poor), income redistribution, and social safety nets. The model was very successful for about three decades, but it entered a crisis in 1981–83, forcing the structural adjustment and the reversal of many economic policies; this was done, nevertheless, within the democratic system, in a gradualist fashion, minimizing social costs in the transition, and maintaining social achievements albeit reforming them to cut costs. The same party (PLN) that implemented the model managed its reform in the 1980s, something that had been impossible in three previous conservative opposition administrations. At the start of the 1990s, nevertheless, a stronger party with a neoconservative program took power and pushed the model closer to the market.

B. Economic Organization

Key elements in the economic organization of the Chilean model were steadily applied until 1990, such as monetarism, stabilization, budgetary equilibrium, privatization (only temporarily halted during the crisis of 1981–83), and the increasing role of the market vis-à-vis the state (which was briefly allowed to intervene in 1983 to save the model). Adjustment policies brought the first crisis and were pushed even during the boom of 1984–90 and at the beginning of the first democratic government, the last to correct the increase in expenditures launched by the military regime in a futile attempt to win the elections of 1989–90. But other policies were changed when they faltered or provoked a crisis. For instance, it was believed in the first stage that monetarism adjustment alone would eliminate inflation; when it failed to do so, the exchange rate was used in the second stage as the key stabilization tool. Fixing the exchange rate in 1979–81, however, overvalued the peso and exports, contributing to a trade imbalance. Deregulation of the financial market and suspension of credit controls stimulated the growing indebtedness of the private sector in the first two stages. These two errors, combined with other factors, provoked the second crisis, which was much more severe that the first one. In the third stage there were several devaluations, and the government temporarily intervened with banks and enterprises to block their bankruptcy. Corrections in the fourth stage included investing the state with regulatory powers over the economic conglomerates, the financial system, and the privatized pension funds to avoid a repetition of the same debacle. In the fifth stage, the democratic government launched a tax reform to improve income distribution and generate fiscal revenue to finance social programs geared to the correction of the problems created in the previous four stages.

There have been seven changes in Cuban economic organization throughout the period of observation: a mixed economy, the application of the Stalinist model of central planning, a debate over alternative models of socialist organization (when the Stalinist model did not work), the adoption of antimarket egalitarian policies, a shift to the timid Soviet model of economic reform (when the New Man did not come through), the return to antimarket policies, and the shift to market-oriented reform. Although some policies changed back and forward throughout the period, others were steadily applied and expanded at least until the 1990s. Examples of the latter were *Cuba* collectivization of the means of production, concentration of decision making in a small group at the top, expansion of social services, preservation of virtual full employment, and progressive redistribution. Changing policies were, for example, the use of labor mobilization (and voluntary free labor) versus output quotas and wage scales, "moral" versus material incentives, suppression of markets (e.g., in agriculture) versus allowing them, and authorization versus prohibition or harassment of the self-employed. The first set in each antagonistic pair of policies was predominant in antimarket stages, whereas the second set prevailed in the more conventional policy stages. These constant changes created considerable instability and confusion and harmed economic performance. In the current stage, the first set of policies (linked to the market) has advanced more than ever before under the Revolution but is still subject to criticism and setbacks.

Until the structural reform took place in Costa Rica, most policies on economic organization were steadily implemented: incentives and protection to private enterprises in the key development lines selected by the government, as well as increasing public ownership of means of production (the state and private sectors did not conflict until the "state-entrepreneur" stage); indicative planning combined with decentralized autonomous institutions until the end of the 1970s when they became more centralized; generation of fiscal revenue to finance public programs (investment, credit, subsidies to prices of consumer goods, social services) through taxes but increasingly through bond emission and, particularly, foreign borrowing; control of the foreign exchange rate sometimes fixed and overvalued, alternatively with dual and multiple rates, and with occasional devaluations; high import tariffs (for protectionist and fiscal-revenue purposes) and exemptions or low tariffs for imports geared to industrialization and agricultural diversification; increases in jobs (in the expanding state bureaucracy and private sector); and extension in the coverage of social services. The expansionist policies, nevertheless, often led to fiscal deficit and inflation, while imports frequently grew more than exports, creating trade deficits. Three conservative governments tried to cope with these disequilibria by temporarily raising fiscal revenue, cutting expenditures, controlling prices and imports, and the like, but the following PLN administration returned to conventional policies. At the start of the 1980s foreign indebtedness reached a high point (aggravated by the adverse effects of the two oil shocks) and, combined with internal-external disequilibria and the overvalued currency, forced a suspension of debt service. The weak Carazo administration (made up by heterogenous groups with conflicting interests) shifted policies several times and was unable to cope with the crisis. Carazo resisted devaluation until a massive one was inevitable at the end of his term, his stabilization program did not work (except for a reduction in the fiscal and trade deficit), inflation and unemployment escalated to record heights, GDP and real wages plummeted, and poverty and income distribution worsened, hence aggravating the crisis. The magnitude of the crisis (the worst since the Great Depression) led to the victory of two successive PLN administrations, which, empowered by a strong electoral mandate, initiated the structural adjustment program, later expanded by Calderón's neoconservative administration: reduction in the size of the state; growing privatization of public enterprises; deregulation; price and interest liberalization; cuts in credit, subsidies, and other public expenditures; unification and gradual adjustment of the exchange rate to the market; gradual reduction of import tariffs; and renegotiation of the foreign debt with international agencies and foreign banks. The structural adjustment program did not apply shock therapy like Chile had (and the crisis was not as severe as in Cuba) but took a gradualist approach. For instance, import tariffs were not cut as drastically and rapidly, and privatization has moved more slowly than in Chile.

C. Development Strategies

Chile's development strategy has been even more consistent and steady than its economic organization policy. The movement against ISI and state protectionism (inward development strategy) began in the first stage, although the government had not designed a precise strategy yet and the economy was fairly closed albeit starting to open. In the second stage, ISI was definitely abandoned and replaced by a clear strategy to promote nontraditional exports and open up the economy to foreign trade and capital (outward development). This strategy was strengthened in the next three stages with additions such as providing incentives to traditional agricultural producers and exporters (fourth stage) and involving the state more in the development of the infrastructure and modernization of production (fifth stage). In contrast with the economic organization, it appears that the development strategy did not incur serious errors and was steadily successful. And yet the government's drastic and rapid reduction of tariffs to raise domestic competition provoked the bankruptcy of a good part of the nation's industry and allowed a phenomenal inflow of imported manufactures, which, combined with easy credit, were among the causes for the second crisis.

There have been at least four changes in Cuba's development strategies, which overlap the shifts in economic organization. On three occasions both policies failed simultaneously, hence compounding the resulting crisis: 1963, 1970, and 1990. The first three development strategies were: an inward development model based on ISI and agricultural diversification (1959–63), an outward model fundamentally based on gigantic sugar crops and exports (1964–70), and a more balanced outward model still mainly relying on sugar exports but with mechanization and combined with other exports and tourism (1971–90); a variation of the third strategy, during the Rectification Process (1986–90), pursued self-sufficiency in food. In all these strategies Cuba had a closed economy, heavily depended on Soviet (and to a less extent CMEA) trade and aid, and had little relations with the world capitalist market. Such isolation was mainly the result (by order of importance) of the island's lack of sufficient and diversified exports, Soviet generous price subsidies to Cuban exports and imports, and the U.S. embargo. When the socialist camp collapsed, Cuba began its fourth strategy: outward development but this time with an open economy. It faces the extremely difficult task of reintegrating the island into the world capitalist market (the only one left after the CMEA market disappeared), still with the type of export concentration and heavy dependency on foreign trade that existed at the beginning of the Revolution, aggravated by more than three decades of isolation, protectionism, and lack of competitiveness in exports, as well as the tightening of the U.S. embargo.

Costa Rica's development strategy in the initial stage was outward-oriented and relied on exports of coffee and bananas but with state support to diversification and modernization, and the start of an industrialization policy. It was replaced in the second stage by an inward strategy, also state-supported and protected, based on ISI but reinforcing the goals of agricultural diversification for both domestic consumption and exports. This strategy was energized, during the "state-entrepreneur" stage, by Costa Rica's entrance into the CACM and the creation of CODESA, which promoted industrial exports. Carazo failed in his attempt to change the development strategy applied in the previous two decades, but the crisis eventually led to the shift to outward development supported by three consecutive administrations and based on nontraditional exports, openings to world trade and capital, reduction of subsidies to industry, and increases in competition and efficiency.

D. Overall Outcomes

Although a thorough analysis of performance will be conducted in the second part of this chapter, here I make a brief comparison of the overall outcome of the three models. Chilean policies led to two crises. The first crisis occurred in the first stage as a result of the adjustment program: inflation, the fiscal deficit, and the trade deficit decreased, gross investment and the external debt stagnated, but GDP and real wages declined and unemployment rose. A recovery took place in the second stage: with continued adjustment, inflation and the fiscal deficit kept falling but GDP and gross investment increased, as did real wages while unemployment diminished, but the trade deficit and the external debt grew. The second crisis, in the third stage, was worse than the first: GDP and gross investment plummeted, while inflation and the fiscal and trade deficit rose again (the external debt kept growing), real wages sank, and unemployment reached a historical peak. The recovery began in the fourth stage, and steady growth continued in the fifth: in both stages GDP and gross investment jumped (the latter reached a record in 1993), inflation decreased (except in 1989–90 because of the spending policy in these election years), the fiscal deficit abated (again, except in 1989–90) and became a surplus in the 1990s, the trade deficit turned into a growing surplus (until 1988, when the surplus diminished and became a deficit again in 1993), the external debt dwindled and stabilized, unemployment dropped (the lowest historical rate), and real wages almost recovered the previous peak.

After a brief recovery at the start of the Revolution (first stage, on which almost no data are available), Cuba suffered three crises in the period. The first, in the second stage, was a result of the double failure in economic organization and development strategy: GSP and gross investment probably declined, inflation peaked in 1963, and the trade deficit increased, but unemployment diminished. There was a mild recovery in the third stage (1964–65): GSP rose although gross investment was stagnant, inflation decreased, the trade deficit stagnated, and unemployment kept its downward trend. The second crisis (worse than the first) occurred in the idealistic fourth stage, which ended in double failure again: GSP and gross investment shrank, and the trade deficit swelled but unemployment sank to a record low. The fifth stage (the longest, most steady, with Soviet conventional policies) saw a recovery: GSP grew (except for 1980) as did gross investment, inflation subsided (except in 1981), but the trade deficit, external debt, and unemployment increased (the last for the first time). The antimarket policies of the sixth stage led to a recession: GSP decreased, while the fiscal and trade deficit and the external debt continuously rose, and unemployment further increased. The failure of the previous policy, the collapse of the Soviet camp, and the tightening of the U.S. embargo provoked the worst crisis of the Revolution (1990–93, with a mild recovery in 1994–96): GSP/GDP and gross investment plummeted (the worst decline among the three countries), inflation and the fiscal deficit peaked in 1993 but declined thereafter with the adjustment program, the hard-currency external debt kept increasing and unemployment reached record levels, but the trade deficit was reduced, although it rose again later, and the trade volume shrank dramatically.

Costa Rica enjoyed steady growth (GDP, gross investment) in the first three stages (especially in the 1960s and 1970s) with real wages probably rising and declining unemployment, but the trade deficit and external debt steadily expanded, while inflation oscillated, and the fiscal deficit increased most of the time. The worsening domestic and external disequilibria, combined with the adjustment and the absence of a strong leadership, led to the 1981–83 crisis: GDP and gross investment declined (although not so much as in Chile and considerably less than in Cuba in their worst crises), inflation peaked in 1982 as did unemployment, while real wages sharply decreased, and the external debt kept expanding, but the adjustment managed to reduce both the fiscal and the trade deficit. A recovery occurred in the third stage (from 1984 until 1994), resulting from the gradualist adjustment policies combined with a shift in development strategy and a social safety net: GDP and gross investment rose (except in 1991), inflation was cut although not to the precrisis level, the fiscal deficit was kept under control (except in 1986 and 1994), the trade deficit first stagnated but then increased, the external debt was substantially cut down, and real wages almost recovered the precrisis level while unemployment declined down to traditional rates. A recession nevertheless occurred in 1995–96.

E. Social Costs

Social costs of the Chilean model have been high and unequally shared. While capital enjoyed state support and incentives (e.g., elimination of taxes on property and capital gains, tax reduction on enterprise profits, low sale prices of public enterprises, access to cheap foreign credit), the burden of the shock therapy during the long transition was basically placed on labor and the lowest-income groups who suffered record-high unemployment, sharp decline in real wages, and cuts in social services. Allegedly to avoid coalitions against the market, the government banned unions, collective bargaining, and strikes until 1979, thereafter gradually restoring them albeit under tight rules. And yet, despite the government's stand in favor of competition and a free market, huge economic conglomerates flourished, and supply and demand were not allowed to set the price of labor but was fixed by the state. Keynesian tools were used to attenuate the harmful effects of the model, which threatened its own existence, such as massive emergency job-creation programs when unemployment reached close to 30% of the labor force and prompted the first public demonstrations against the regime. Social assistance in health care and pensions for the poor were provided by the state (a continuation of precoup policies), and the severely reduced public social expenditures were targeted to maximize their effects, for instance, on infant-maternal care. But none of these palliatives impeded the long transition (about one decade) and the worsening of poverty and inequality; eventually, however, unemployment declined and real wages increased—the latter still without recovering their previous level. Improvement on those two social indicators, combined with the impressive performance on growth and stability in the fourth stage, moved the victorious democratic opposition to preserve the model but with corrections to alleviate poverty, attenuate extreme income inequalities, and improve social services.

At the end of the 1980s Cuba's impressive achievements in the social arena (employment, education, health care, social security, income distribution, but not housing) ranked among the best in both Latin America and the socialist world. Those accomplishments responded to the Cuban model's goals and were feasible by means of total state control on the allocation of resources and the phenomenal Soviet aid, which came basically free. But such social gains were not without economic costs: full employment led to overstaffing and low labor productivity, egalitarianism harmed incentives and labor effort, and social expenditures took a high and rapidly increasing share of the national product. When the socialist camp collapsed and the Cuban economy suffered a dramatic decline, the burden of the social services became heavier and difficult to sustain. Furthermore, the drastic cut in imports, decrease in export value, and lack of hard currency have harmed domestic output, provoked the shutdown of many enterprises, and led to an increase in unemployment and erosion of social services. The government's tough adjustment program of the 1990s (which has lasted so far eight years) has tried to protect some of the social gains but with only partial success and the threat of further deterioration.

The foundations of Costa Rica's social policies were established in the 1940s, consolidated during Figueres's first two administrations and continuously extended thereafter. Economic growth helped to reduce unemployment to very low levels, and adjustment of wages led to their steady increase until the crisis. A widespread social welfare net was developed in Costa Rica throughout four decades before the crisis: universal free enrollment in elementary education (incorporating rural areas) and enlargement of free secondary enrollment; universal access to health care through fairly integrated services of social insurance and the Ministry of Health (providing free care to the poor); high coverage of the labor force with pensions (integrating social insurance and assistance programs); low-cost subsidized housing; and antipoverty programs, which preceded the social safety nets that became internationally widespread in the second half of the 1980s. The welfare net compensated for some deterioration in income distribution (which favored middle-income instead of the lowest-income groups) even prior to the crisis and operated as a cushion to protect a good part of the population against the crisis and the structural adjustment (the transition was the shortest in the three countries: about four years). With the recovery, unemployment declined and real wages increased to recover previous levels, while poverty was cut. But the reduction in social expenditures (particularly under Calderón) affected social programs and worsened distribution. In spite of the grave crisis of 1981–83 and some deterioration in the social arena, by the mid-1990s Costa Rica stood at the top of Latin America on most social indicators.

3. Analysis of Some Crucial Policy Issues

This section deals with three crucial questions related to policy and raised in the first part: (1) would it have been feasible to avoid or reduce economic and social costs of the models by changing some of their policies; (2) were all policies compatible and mutually reinforcing or did they confront trade-offs among them; and (3) what were the causes and effects of the regional crisis of the 1980s and the nature of the recovery.

A. Was It Feasible to Avoid or Reduce Economic-Social Costs by Changing Policies?

Staunch partisans of Chile's neoconservative model have asserted that its negative economic and social effects were inherent to it but temporary and unavoidable: the bitter medicine had to be swallowed to cure the sickness (Büchi 1992, 1993; Fontaine 1993). One academic supporter acknowledged errors (some of which could have been avoided or attenuated), but still the model was better than what Chile had before (Harberger 1985). Critical scholars have argued that some adverse effects were inherent to the model and others an outcome of specific policies (Ffrech-Davis 1982) or that such effects were rather a result of the extreme variant applied in Chile than the model itself (Sheahan 1987). Still another view is that many of the adverse effects could have been averted or at least mollified by avoiding significant policy errors (Ramos 1986). The latter interpretation is supported by both enlightened neoconservatives and, indirectly, by the two democratic governments that basically continued with the model although with some corrections. According to this view, policy errors were caused by various reasons, an important one being the ideologues' blindness and prejudices, for example, excessive faith in the market, a rigid stand against state interventionism, belief in automatic market adjustment, and disregard of distributional and social welfare issues. In other cases, policies were in flagrant conflict with key principles of the model but were implemented for other reasons.

For instance, the first monetarist policy was too narrow, focusing on emission control and adjustment to control inflation. It was only after inflation remained quite high, although declining, that the government resorted to other techniques such as the exchange rate. The fixing of the latter in 1979–81 contradicted the free-market principles, and yet it was set and allowed to stay at that level too long (despite the overvaluation of the peso and its negative effects on foreign trade) because of the monetarists' faith that it would automatically reduce domestic inflation to the level of international inflation, as well as their serious concern that a peso devaluation would tarnish the image of the "economic miracle" of the second half of the 1970s. The first assumption proved to be wrong, and the ensuing massive devaluation cast doubt on such a miracle. Avoidance of those two policy errors could have alleviated or perhaps averted the crises. The neoconservatives also believed in an automatic market correction by means of recessions and hence let the economic deterioration go too far, until the government was forced to change the economic team (albeit briefly) by one that took moderate interventionist measures to halt the crisis. A faster state action could have ameliorated the crisis, reduced the transition period, and/or accelerated the recovery. The overly drastic and rapid cut in import tariffs (in pursue of competition and against the excessive protectionism of the past) badly harmed domestic industry; a more gradual approach might have enabled adaptation by part of the domestic producers and reduced widespread bankruptcy. In the brief interlude of 1983, tariffs were temporarily raised to curtail the trade deficit. Fast liberalization of financial markets and suspension of state control of credit led to extensive indebtedness of the private sector (mainly by economic conglomerates that flourished, concentrated financial assets, and had access to cheap foreign capital, because of absence of state controls), which later compelled the government to absorb such debt and apply regulatory measures. If the anti-interventionist mentality had not prevailed and controls had not been abolished, such a serious problem probably would not have occurred. State fixing (freezing) of wages in the initial stages contradicted market principles but was done anyway because of the conviction that it would stop cost-push inflation, and yet the latter was resilient largely because of drastic and fast price liberalization. Wage adjustment was introduced later when real wages and purchasing power had already declined sharply and severely curtailed aggregate demand, production, and welfare. The two emergency employment programs were reluctantly launched when unemployment reached historical records (17% in 1975 and 26% in 1982); less radical policies might have averted such a high rate of unemployment. Social safety nets targeted to the poor would have helped the very high percentage of the population that fell under the poverty line, but such a program was not introduced until the 1990s. The privatization of pensions was proclaimed as a key tool for increasing the rate of national saving, but there is no proof of that assumption (actually data suggest the opposite), while extension of coverage to the self-employed was neglected. The use of fiscal funds to help the self-employed (as well as the poor) instead of to consolidate the private pension system at great cost would have had progressive instead of regressive redistributional effects and would have improved the welfare of the lowest-income groups.

As has been noted, the Costa Rican model incurred fewer large-scale errors, while its policies were more gradualistic in their implementation than the Chilean model. That is not to say, nevertheless, that there were not policy mistakes. The increasing role of the state, both in productive and service activities, led to public monopolies in banking, insurance, public utilities (water and sewerage, transportation, telecommunications), energy, and cement, as well as quasi monopolies in health care and pensions. The creation of CODESA (without state controls or an obligation to generate profits) has-tened the expansion of the state into the productive sphere and its eventual competition with the private sector, which ruptured the crucial state-private alliance. These policies, combined with state protectionism, provoked lack of competition, inefficiencies, losses, and growing state subsidies, which contributed to the fiscal deficit (in spite of that costly state support, CODESA generated a tiny percentage of GDP and employment). A more moderate policy in this area would have reduced the problems that led to the crisis of the 1980s and the reversal of previous policy. For instance, private activities should have been allowed to compete with autonomous institutions and public enterprises in order to improve efficiency and quality of service. CODESA's initial task was to promote new industries in strategic lines not tackled by the private sector and, once those enterprises had been consoli-dated, to sell them to private corporations. And yet, that wise policy was never implemented; thus such state enterprises became permanent and had an edge over the private sector in the competition for public credit. Protec-tionism (for both private and state enterprises) might have been adequate in a reasonable degree and for an initial period, but not so excessively and for such a long time; such a policy resulted in heavy tariffs on foreign imports, lack of technological innovation, high production costs, poor competitive-ness in foregn markets, and costly fiscal subsidies. As opposed to other Latin American countries that pushed the ISI strategy at the cost of agricultural de-cline, Costa Rica promoted development on the two fronts (including do-mestic consumption and exports of agricultural products). The industrial-ization strategy, however, had the handicap of a very small population and market, which impeded large-scale production. A small domestic market has not been an obstacle for success in some East Asian countries, however, but their production is mainly geared for export, and they have had the initial "ad-vantage" of considerably lower labor costs than in Costa Rica. Monopolies or oligopolies, compounded by high labor costs and excessive protection of the ISI, raised production costs, therefore limiting industrial goods to sup-plying part of the small domestic market (and the CACM while it was active) as they were not competitive in the world market. Furthermore, the ISI be-came increasingly dependent on imports of machinery and other inputs; hence it not only failed to generate a trade surplus but also contributed to the trade deficit. A more open and competitive economy with less protection (as well as a careful selection of only a few industrial lines), combined with a more active nontraditional-export promotion policy, might have given a bet-ter chance of success to the industrialization policy, improved the trade bal-ance, and reduced fiscal costs.

Although there was remarkable continuity in most Costa Rican policies, stabilization was not one of them: a few moderate adjustment programs were initiated (usually by conservative governments) but typically dropped at the first sign of trouble; much more consistent was the expansionist path that led to a rising fiscal deficit, inflation, and external borrowing. Even more erratic was the foreign exchange policy (e.g., dual and multiple rates, which were occasionally unified, fixed rates for long periods followed by devaluations and, eventually, by the crawling peg and floating); the fixed rate between 1975 and 1980 led to the same negative effects as in Chile and a massive devaluation. More stable and continuous stabilization and foreign-exchange-rate policies, together with a more moderate expansion, could have averted or alleviated key flaws of the model and the severity of the crisis. The social welfare policy was undoubtedly positive, but the proliferation of institutions and programs was inefficient and very costly, imposed a heavy burden on the payroll (the third highest in the region), and was not always well targeted. A better coordination, administration, and targeting of such programs would have produced even better results at lower costs. The policy reversal since 1982 has been geared to correct the previous flaws of the model and has been successful on most fronts but not on some important ones.

Castro has occasionally acknowledged policy errors (in 1964, 1970, 1986, 1992), but the official view is that Cuba's economic problems are not a result of its model or policies but of external factors such as the U.S. embargo, the collapse of the Soviet camp, and adverse world prices. In the above analysis of Chile and Costa Rica, it was argued that avoidance of errors or use of better policies (without a change in the model) could have averted or mollified adverse effects and crises. The collapse of the Soviet camp, as well as the severe economic problems faced by Cuba throughout its socialist history, particularly in the 1990s, make that argument more difficult to sustain in this country. China and Vietnam, nevertheless, could be presented as successful reforms of socialist economies, but they have labeled their models "socialist market," that is, a mixed economy in which the market plays a significant and increasing role, although the state is still predominant and the guiding force, with strong regulatory powers over the private sector. One could contend that such a model is different from both the conventional socialist model of central planning and the Castroite idealistic version alternatively applied in Cuba until the start of the 1990s. Furthermore, Cuba is not, even in the current stage, applying the Chinese model, which has been rejected as unsuitable for the island. It is exacting, therefore, to maintain that changes in Cuban policies (without switching the model) could have avoided or reduced adverse effects and crises. As I do not want to avoid such a discussion, nevertheless, the following paragraphs identify Cuba's five most significant policy errors.

The most serious policy mistake (at least until the 1990s) was the virtual collectivization of all means of production: in 1990 only a tiny percentage of agriculture was in private hands but submitted to tight state control, and more than 50,000 small business were nationalized in 1968. The state was unable to organize the overwhelming majority of its enterprises, farms, and agencies in an efficient manner. For instance, in spite of the enormous capital investment in the state farms, they had a very low productivity (which compelled their conversion into cooperatives in 1993, but under state control), while the small private farms (in spite of their tiny size and forced sales of produce to the state) were labor intensive and much more productive. The state was unable to supply the services offered by the small businesses shut down in 1968, or those provided by self-employed workers who suffered from criticism and enormous restrictions during the short periods in which they were authorized to function (self-employment was reauthorized in 1993 but limited to certain occupations and under tight controls and heavy taxes). Relatively free peasant markets were permitted to operate—although criticized—in the first half of the 1980s but, despite their success, were shut down in 1986, to be reopened in 1994 after considerable resistance. The consistent elimination of the private sector (even on a small scale) provoked adverse effects on production and services, but the government obstinately continued this policy (mainly for ideological and political-control reasons) until the grave crisis of the 1990s. The application of a Chinese mixed approach in ownership of the means of production (in agriculture, industry, services) would have generated much better results.

The second major policy flaw was the emphasis on egalitarianism; although it was more strongly pursued in some stages (1966–70 and 1980–86) than in others (1971–85), it was fairly constant until the 1990s. This policy created disincentives for labor efforts, aggravated by guaranteed jobs and worthless currency, particularly during the antimarket stages when priority was given to moral incentives. Despite these adverse effects, this policy was continued mainly because of ideological causes until the 1990s, when inequalities have expanded significantly and rapidly. A more moderate policy in distribution would have avoided many of the problems.

The third policy error was to secure full employment regardless of labor productivity (despite official rhetorical concern about the latter in some stages), through artificial job creation or overstaffing of state enterprises, farms, agencies, and the armed forces, which actually transformed open unemployment into underemployment or disguised unemployment. Although there were several campaigns to eliminate, reduce, or rationalize "surplus labor," "redundant workers," and the bureaucracy, the unnecessary manpower always found ways to stay on the state payroll. This policy resulted in high production costs, fiscal subsidies to enterprises, and a perverse demonstration effect as lazy workers were seldom dismissed. But with the crisis of the 1990s such a policy is no longer feasible; hence about one-third of the labor force is either unemployed or receiving some type of unemployment compensation, and from 11% to 18% is officially earmarked for dismissal, but the government cannot proceed because of the lack of jobs in the private sector (mainly due to the leaders' reluctance to expand it). A mixed economy with a strong private sector and more emphasis on labor productivity in the state sector, combined with a reasonable unemployment compensation program, would have created productive jobs, reduced disincentives and fiscal subsidies, cut down costs, and provided minimum welfare protection.

The fourth policy error relates to universal free social services, which were successful although very costly and indirectly subsidized by Soviet aid until 1990 and hence now badly harmed by the crisis; some features of that policy, nevertheless, were faulted even before the 1990s. One of those defects was the gratuitous nature of most social services, logical for the lowest-income groups but not for those in higher income brackets; such financial deficiency led to increasing costs and deficits (e.g., in the pension program), which have become untenable with the crisis. Another flaw of the social policy was its generosity and liberality in entitlement conditions, which further augmented costs; for instance, retirement ages were set at 55/60 years for women/men although Cuba has one of the two highest longevities in the region; another example was the creation of the costly family physician program, when the island had already achieved one of the highest health standards in both Latin America and the socialist world; and a third case was the continuous, expensive investment in reducing infant mortality in spite of Cuba's having the lowest rate in the region. The largesse in those social areas contrasted with the grave deficiencies suffered in others such as housing, food, and clothing. A more balanced, better financed, less extravagant, and better targeted social policy would have achieved similar goals, at less cost, and a surplus to be used in other crucial areas of need.

Last but not least, Cuba's initial strategy of fast industrialization suffered from similar problems confronted by Chile (before 1974) and Costa Rica, exacerbated by the complete state monopoly, closed economy, rapidity of the program goals, complications in receiving the machinery from the Soviet Union, and lack of sufficient resources. Although Cuba later developed some important industrial lines (electricity, nickel, cement, textiles, steel, fertilizers, pharmaceutics, biotechnology), it failed to do so in an efficient manner, and virtually all the output was mostly for domestic consumption and part (mainly nickel) exported to the Soviet Union and, to a less extent, to Eastern Europe (Cuban industrial goods were not competitive in the world market).

Furthermore, Cuban industry was heavily dependent on imported fuel, machinery and spare parts, chemicals, raw materials, and other inputs from CMEA, and, as in the other two countries, the industrialization process had a negative effect on the trade balance. When the Soviet camp collapsed, so did most of Cuban industry: 80% of the plants were shut down for lack of fuel, inputs, and buyers (only foreign investment from industrialized capitalist countries has helped in the 1990s to restore production and exports, mainly of nickel). The second development strategy, huge sugar crops, was ill-conceived and ended in failure because of excessively ambitious goals, disorganization, delay in the reception and installation of imported machinery, inefficient cane cutters transferred from cities, and other problems. The third strategy was more reasonable, balanced, and lasting than the other two, but, except for tourism, it also depended on Soviet and CMEA imports and exports and hence had to be changed after the disappearance of the socialist partners. (The food program to achieve self-sufficiency in the short run, launched during the Rectification Process, did not have any chance of success because of its bad timing and excessively ambitious goals). The current strategy is the most logical but confronts serious obstacles described already; one pillar of this strategy, tourism, heavily depends on foreign capital and imported goods, which absorb most of its earnings. The time (twelve years) and resources lost with the first two development strategies would have been saved if Cuba had pursued more realistic and balanced policies as in the second and, particularly, third strategies. A final important point: if instead of launching the antimarket Rectification Process between 1986 and 1990, Cuba had continued its move toward the market (1971–85), the country would have advanced in the path of reform (in the same direction of the Soviet Union and Eastern Europe) and probably have made it easier to confront the collapse of socialism and the need for reintegration in the world market in the 1990s.

B. Compatibility of Policies Versus Trade-offs

Previous studies on Chile and Cuba have argued that socioeconomic policies cannot always be pursued simultaneously, at least in the short run, because they may not be mutually compatible but generate discrepant effects or compete for scarce resources (Mesa-Lago 1981; Ramos 1986). Often governments try conflicting policies at the same time, because of ignorance or little awareness of their inner contradictions or trade-offs among them. This section analyzes two examples of this problem in the three countries.

The first example is the potential conflict between growth and equity or the trade-off between the goals to increase national savings and investment to foster growth and productivity versus the goals of job creation, redistribution, and provision of social services to the population. Prior to Pinochet, Chile was a typical case of pursuing the second set of goals at the cost of reducing the first; the neoconservatives radically reversed those priorities. And yet, in spite of the incentives provided by the latter to capital, gross domestic investment as a percentage of GDP either was stagnant or declined until the late 1980s (except in 1974). Furthermore, because of tough adjustments and crises, there was a significant increase in unemployment, income inequality, and poverty, as well as a deterioration in social services. There was an attempt, nevertheless, to ameliorate some of these problems through emergency employment programs and targeting health expenditures, but, in spite of some isolated successes (acceleration in the reduction of infant mortality), the overall social balance was negative through most of the Pinochet's period. The first democratic government has so far achieved the double goal of raising both domestic gross investment and improving social services, but it cannot be proved that such an outcome was due to only its own policies. Unlike Pinochet's neoconservative model, for more than three decades Cuba placed top priority on the social goals: full employment, egalitarianism, and free universal provision of social services. As has been noted, the social success was achieved at significant economic cost, and it was largely feasible because of enormous Soviet aid; otherwise gross investment and economic growth would have suffered even more. The Cuban government attempted to promote growth but had a poor record because of the subordination of such targets to the social goals and the ill-conceived zig-zagging economic policies it practiced. In the 1990s the government is trying to save some social services, but they have badly deteriorated because of the severe crisis, while inequality has expanded and unemployment has grown. Costa Rica was able to successfully pursue both sets of goals for more than two decades, until the crisis: gross investment was the highest among the three countries, unemployment declined, income distribution improved (although favoring the growing middle-income sector), and population coverage in social services steadily increased. This dual success was possible because of the expansionist policies promoted by the state and its concern for social issues, but (since the 1970s) with increasing fiscal deficit and external borrowing. The crisis forced some sacrifices, particularly during the brief transition period under the gradualist structural adjustment, but in the late 1980s and the first half of the 1990s Costa Rica still combined high gross investment and social achievements, although income distribution was not back to the precrisis situation particularly for the lowest-income groups.

The second example deals with trade-offs between price-liberalization versus price-control and rationing, and their effects on inflation, protection of low-income groups, and emergence of the black market. In the first stage of Chilean neoconservatism there was an attempt to liberalize prices and eliminate inflation simultaneously. Because official prices had been controlled for about two years during the previous Allende administration (provoking scarcity in the legal market but a growing black market), the rapid price liberalization under Pinochet fueled inflation. The government tried to control it with tough adjustment policies and wage fixing but aggravated the crisis and harmed low-income groups. Cuba faced a situation similar to Chile's under Allende, but considerably worse and with divergent polices. In the second stage, the expanding gap between supply and demand (caused by growing income and stagnant or declining production) raised the specter of an inflationary spiral. To protect low-income groups, prices of consumer goods were maintained unchanged for at least two decades, and rationing was imposed and steadily extended (a painful but fairly egalitarian measure according to the official view). And yet, because of poor production and scarcity of consumer goods (which made it impossible to guarantee rations for all), as well as very low official prices, long lines formed in front of state stores, and the black market grew tremendously in spite of the government's efforts. Between 1971 and 1985, the leadership shifted policy (in order to fight the black market and provide incentives to labor): it slightly raised prices of selected consumer goods and opened a relatively free agricultural market as well as a "parallel" state market with dual prices (one unchanged for rationed goods and another largely set by supply and demand). These markets, however, charged prices many times higher than the corresponding rationed prices, thus creating the inequalities that the government initially wanted to avert (that was one reason for the launching in 1986 of the doomed, antimarket Rectification Process). Under the timid market reform of the 1990s, prices of utilities and selected consumer goods have been raised, thus expanding inequalities, but Cuba has not yet liberalized most prices, and rationing continues. In Costa Rica the government fixed prices of fuel, public utilities, and some agricultural products (to protect low-income groups) and was able to subsidize such prices for many years while fiscal resources were abundant. There was no need to introduce rationing because domestic output of agricultural products increased and, although state subsidies had an adverse effect on the fiscal balance, inflation was fairly controlled. The crisis of the 1980s changed that situation and forced a gradual liberalization of prices, first of fuel and public utilities, and later of some consumer goods (with some negative effects on the lowest-income groups). The gradual and partial price liberalization, combined with other measures, permitted a reduction of inflation and social costs, but a complete liberalization of prices had not been achieved by mid-1990s.

C. The Impact of the Crisis of the 1980s and the Nature of the Recovery

The crisis of the 1980s badly harmed almost all countries in Latin America and the Caribbean, including Chile and Costa Rica, but not Cuba where the crisis was postponed until the 1990s. The two major causes of the regional crisis were: the fall in export value of raw materials (because of the world economic recession and decreased demand for such goods) combined with the increase in prices of oil and other imports, and the heavy burden of the external debt aggravated by swelling interest rates and the halting of commercial-bank loans to developing countries.

At the time of the crisis, Costa Rica's economy was the most open and dependent on trade among the three countries (about 90%), but its exports were the most diversified: about 50% of exports were coffee and bananas; the price of the former dropped 32% in 1979–81 and continued to be low in 1982–83, while the price of bananas was stagnant in 1980–82, and the price of other exports decreased. Furthermore, because of the big jump in oil prices and heavy dependency on fuel imports, the latter's share in total imports jumped from 9% to 20% between 1978 and 1982. The total value of Costa Rica's exports fell by 13 percentage points in 1980–83, and similar decreases were suffered in the purchasing power of its exports and terms of trade. In the same period, the real external debt rose 50% and reached its highest level ever in 1983; as a percentage of GDP the total debt jumped from 57% to 139%, while the debt service as a percentage of the value of export goods and services augmented from 214% to 375%. In 1983 credits and loans to Costa Rica were drastically cut, hence aggravating the crisis. The recovery was helped by increasing prices of coffee and declining prices of oil; thus by 1994 the purchasing power of Costa Rican exports was 2.6 times that of 1983, although the terms of trade were still slightly below the 1980 level. The renegotiation of the foreign debt combined with more flexible terms reduced the debt's real value by one-third between 1983 and 1994 and the burden of its servicing on the value of export goods and services by two-thirds (Tables IV.8–10, IV.13).

At the time of the crisis, Chile dependency on foreign trade was about 43% or less than half of Costa Rica's, but its export concentration on copper alone was 47% of total exports, similar to the combined proportion of coffee and bananas in Costa Rica. Prices of copper dropped 32% in 1980–82 and continued at very low levels until 1986; prices of other exports such as iron and fish meal also declined. Because of the dis-industrialization process in Chile and less dependency on oil imports, the adverse impact of the external oil shocks was not as intense as in Costa Rica, but still the share of fuel imports in total imports increased from 17% to 21% between 1978 and 1983. The value of Chilean exports decreased 21% in 1980–82 and continued its decline until 1985; the purchasing value of exports and the terms of trade diminished, in 1980–82/83, 18 and 16 percentage points respectively. The real external debt grew by 33% in 1980–82; as a percentage of GDP the debt rose from 43% to 115% between 1980 and 1985, and the servicing of such debt as a percentage of export goods and services jumped from 186% to 435%. The twofold increase in copper prices between 1984 and 1989 and rising prices of other exports (the purchasing power of exports increased 2.4 times between 1982 and 1992), combined with a decrease in oil prices (which reduced the corresponding import share from 21% to 9% between 1983 and 1993), helped the process of recovery. Debt-equity swaps and payment of the external debt cut the debt by one-third between 1984 and 1991, and its proportion of GDP from 127% to 44% between 1985 and 1993 and the burden of its servicing on export goods and services from 435% to 208% (Tables II.7–10, II.12–13).

At the start of the 1980s, Cuba's dependency on foreign trade was 49%, similar to Chile's and about half of Costa Rica's, but its export concentration on sugar was 84%, almost twice that of Chile's on copper and Costa Rica's on coffee and bananas combined. The island's dependency on oil imports was also the highest, and its total external debt (combining that with the Soviet Union, Eastern Europe, and in hard currency) in per capita terms was probably similar to Chile's although smaller than Costa Rica's. In contrast with the other two countries, nevertheless, Cuba was protected by the Soviet Union from the two major causes of the regional crisis. About 60% of the island's trade transactions were with the Soviet Union, which heavily subsidized the price of Cuba's most important exports (sugar and nickel) as well as the most significant import (oil). In 1985/86 the Soviet price, in relation to the world price, was 7.7 times higher on sugar and 3.38 times on nickel, but 38% lower in oil in 1982 (the Soviet Union also paid Cuba, in hard currency, for the oil committed for import but not consumed). The value of Cuban exports, therefore, jumped 51% between 1980 and 1985, and the purchasing power of exports and the terms of trade improved significantly, the opposite of what happened in the other two countries. The island's trade deficit with the Soviet Union increased rapidly and often absorbed 100% of the total trade deficit, but it was automatically financed with annual Soviet loans. Cumulative Soviet economic aid to Cuba between 1960 and 1990 was equivalent to U.S.$65 billion, but 60% of it was in nonrepayable price subsidies and only 40% in repayable loans and under very generous terms. Out of Cuba's total external debt in 1989, 74% was with the Soviet Union and 7% with other CMEA members, leaving only 19% in hard currency; the Cubans paid virtually nothing on the major part of the debt; hence 81% of the total debt was free. In the second half of the 1980s the Soviet Union reduced price subsidies to Cuba and increased the debt share of total economic aid, but still the amount of such aid was enormous and Cuba paid only a tiny amount in interest. Cuba's suspension of the service on the hard currency debt in 1986, however, has halted any fresh credit from industrialized countries since then, and the value of such debt has gradually risen. In the 1990s Russia ended all aid to Cuba and the CMEA disappeared; trade with Russia is now conducted basically at world market prices and has been drastically reduced (there is very little trade with Eastern Europe); hence the Cuban crisis occurred in the 1990s when the Soviet umbrella vanished, and very little credit has been available in hard currency (Tables III.16–23).

2
Comparison of Performance

This chapter deals with five topics: methodological problems in the comparison of performance; analysis of the individual indicators of performance; ranking of the performance of three models; the potential role of nonsystemic factors in performance; and viability of the models in the short and medium terms.

1. Methodological Problems in the Comparison of Performance

Three methodological problems confronted in the comparison of performance have been: different time periods in the operation of the models; data availability, reliability, and comparability; and the nonquantifiable nature of nonsystemic factors that might affect performance.

A. Different Time Periods in the Operation of the Models and the Indicators

The most important problem is that the Costa Rican and Cuban models began at the end of the 1950s but the Chilean model in 1974; hence performance will be measured for 35 or 36 years in the first two countries but only for 20 or 21 in the third. This is not an obstacle in the evaluation of absolute performance (e.g., export concentration or infant mortality in 1993), but it is for measuring relative improvement during the period of operation of the three models. For instance, when comparing the reduction in infant mortality, the starting and ending years of observation for both Costa Rica and Cuba are 1960 and 1993, but for Chile are 1973 and 1993; in the 14 years between 1960 and 1973 such indicator changed (improved) and the comparison could be distorted. This problem will be tackled with comparisons of all indicators in the three countries between 1960 and 1993 and 1973 and 1993, in order to determine if there are significant differences in the evaluation of relative improvement.

Despite the effort to have equal spans of time in all statistical series in the three countries, this has not been possible in a minority of cases because of lack of data or noncomparable figures. The total number of tables in each country is 26 in Chile and Costa Rica, and 35 in Cuba; such a difference is the result of specific tables that were needed for policy analysis in Cuba. A minority of the tables deal with policy issues or data unsuitable as indicators of performance: 27% in Costa Rica, 31% in Chile, and 46% in Cuba. Again, the peculiarities and lack of some key indicators in Cuba were the reasons for the need for extra tables for that country. A total of 23 tables have been selected as potential indicators of performance (Table V.2): 61% of those tables cover the period from 1958/63 to 1993/94 in the three countries; another 22% of the tables start in different years but end in 1993/94 and are also comparable; and the remaining 17% of the tables start and end in disparate years, thus making the comparison very difficult or impossible. Cuba is the country with the biggest statistical lacunae and different time periods measuring performance: it lacks data on one table (poverty), ends the series in 1981 in two tables (women in the labor force, and access to water/sewerage) and in 1986/89 in two other tables (income distribution and social security coverage), and starts the data in 1985 in another table (GDP composition).

B. Data Availability, Reliability, and Comparability

There are no major problems in the availability, reliability, and comparability of statistics of Chile and Costa Rica. In the latter, the democratic nature of the regime and openness of information facilitated the generation of abundant and reliable data, although there were different and not necessarily comparable estimates in some indicators such as income distribution and poverty incidence. Even in the toughest years of Pinochet's authoritarian government, critical scholars and experts of ECLAC (whose headquarters are in Santiago) scrutinized the official data and in some cases produced alternative figures, for instance, on inflation, open unemployment, and real wages. Conversely, Cuban authoritarianism, total state centralized generation and control of data, and lack of any critical economic scholars who could publicly assess such statistics made them sparse and in many cases unreliable (Mesa-Lago 1969, 1981, 1988b). Even ECLAC had to take the official figures without evaluation, as the alternative was a halt in the supply of data (an exception is ECLAC 1997d).

Cuba has never published statistics on crucial indicators such as income distribution, real wages, social security coverage, total external debt, and poverty incidence; what is available on the first four indicators are estimates elaborated by foreign scholars. In other indicators such as open unemployment, literacy, and access to potable water, the available data basically come from the censuses of 1970 and 1981, the only ones taken in the four decades of the Revolution; occasional figures have been released by Cuban officials but without any elaboration on how they were calculated. (A series on unemployment for 1989–96 has been calculated by ECLAC, and intermittent estimates on illiteracy are done by UNESCO.) Comparisons of data from the censuses of 1970 and 1981 with the previous census of 1953 are often extremely difficult because of changes in the definitions and categories (e.g., access to potable water and sanitation) or because the statistics exclude a crucial part of the population (e.g., in literacy, those 49 years and older—a cohort that concentrates the highest number of illiterates). The essential source of Cuban statistics, the yearbook *Anuario Estadístico de Cuba,* stopped publication in 1989 and did not resume publication until mid-1998, too late to be used in this chapter. The Cuban National Bank reinstated its annual economic report (after a five-year hiatus) in 1995, but it provides only a tiny fraction of the data that appeared in the *Anuario.*

Finally is the quandary of measuring the national product, growth rate, and income per capita. Until the early 1990s Cuba used the Soviet-style "material product system" (MPS), which estimates the "global social product" (GSP); both are significantly different from the "system of national accounts" (SNA), which calculates GDP (and GNP) in market economies (and now virtually all over the world). GSP excludes the value of "nonmaterial services" (e.g., all social services, defense, bureaucracy) and, in this sense, is smaller than GDP, which includes those services. Conversely, GSP does not use the "value-added" method of the SNA and, hence, is usually "inflated" by the double (or triple, quadruple, etc.) counting of the same item in subsequent stages of the productive process; in this other sense, therefore, GSP is larger than GDP. The net result of those two opposite distortions has been the subject of debate, but scattered evidence (reinforced by the new official 1985–93 series of GDP when contrasted with the GSP series in the same period) shows that GSP is considerably bigger than GDP; hence the underestimation of GSP for the exclusion of services was less important than its overestimation due to double counting. The conversion of GSP into GDP has been made public only for 1974 (with full information supplied on the method and data used in the conversion) and for some years in the 1970s and between 1985 and 1996 (but without disclosing any information on the conversion). Furthermore, between 1961 and 1993 Cuba changed the MPS methodology for estimating GSP at least five times, and, hence, there are divergent series for that period that cannot be connected. Additional problems are the lack of a continuous series on the GDP deflator (the consumer price index has never been published) and that the base year for the fragmented periods available was shifted at least twice. There is a consistent series for 1976–88 based on constant prices, but the method for calculating it has never been revealed. Compounding that vacuum, 1981 has been officially used in Cuba for more than two decades as the base year for estimating economic growth rates in constant prices, but critics have shown that 1981 was an anomalous year in terms of inflation and the growth rate itself (16%), and yet Cuban technicians have kept using the same base year, casting doubts on the reliability of the series in constant prices. Finally, the Cuban peso is not exchangeable in the world market, and its exchange rate to the U.S. dollar and other hard currencies is arbitrarily fixed by the government. For instance, in 1997 the official rate between the peso and the dollar was par, but in the government exchange houses and the black market it was traded at 19 or 20 to 1 (Mesa-Lago 1981, 1988b, 1998; Mesa-Lago and Pérez-López 1985a, 1985b, 1992). All these differences and problems make it technically impossible or very difficult to compare the Cuban real national product, growth rate, per capita income, and inflation rate with those of Chile and Costa Rica.

C. The Unquantifiable Nature of Nonsystemic Factors

It cannot be assumed that the performance of the three countries is the exclusive result of the model itself or its policies, because nonsystemic factors may play a role in the outcome, such as differences in levels of development and natural endowment. Part I showed that the three countries are very similar on those factors, but that there were still some minor differences such as agricultural land per capita (lowest in Costa Rica and highest in Chile) and population growth (lowest in Cuba and highest in Costa Rica). Others are random factors or "acts of God" like earthquakes (in Chile and Costa Rica) and hurricanes (in Cuba), but these have not been significant in the long run although they may have caused severe damage in one or two years during the period of observation. A unique advantage enjoyed by Costa Rica is the lack of military expenditures because its armed forces were abolished in 1948, an action that permitted this country to devote more resources to growth and social services than the other two. Perhaps the most important exogenous factor is foreign power action (in positive or negative ways) on the economies of the three countries. Chile and Costa Rica have received significant U.S. economic aid, while Cuba has endured a U.S. embargo since 1961. A counteracting factor in Cuba (until 1990) was the enormous and generous economic aid provided by the Soviet Union (the highest granted by that country to any of its partners within CMEA), but that aid was lost in the 1990s when the Soviet camp collapsed, and the U.S. embargo was tightened. These non-systemic factors cannot be quantified and controlled to measure their potential impact on performance in the three countries, but they will be discussed in section 4.

2. Analysis of the Indicators of Performance

In this section I compare and evaluate 23 indicators of performance (in 23 tables), which later will be divided into four clusters: (1) domestic macroeconomic, (2) external economic, (3) distribution and employment, and (4) social standards (Table V.2). Data for the 23 tables come from the three country table sets, which have standardized as much as possible the years of comparison; specific problems in the indicators will be discussed in the corresponding table. Based on the reliability and comparability of each indicator, it will be decided whether it is suitable or not for the final ranking of performance (the last column of Table V.2 indicates which indicators will be included and excluded).

A. GDP/GSP Rates of Growth

Table V.3 estimates annual average growth rates of GDP for Chile and Costa Rica and GSP for Cuba between 1961 and 1993, in both absolute and per capita terms. The upper segment of the table gives the rates in quinquennia, except for Chile, for which 1971–73 and 1974–80 are used in order to show performance under Allende and the first two stages of the neoconservative model under Pinochet, respectively. The bottom segment of the table compares various periods: 1961–80 (prior to the crisis of the 1980s, but 1961–73 in Chile to show the rates prior to the introduction of the neoconservative model), 1974–80 (the same, but starting in 1974 when the Chilean model began), 1981–89 (the period of the regional economic crisis), 1961–90 (excluding the 1990s when the Cuban crisis occurs and democracy returned to Chile), and 1961–93 (the entire period of observation). In Chile the last two periods are actually 1974–90 and 1974–93 in order to cover the neoconservative model but separating the Pinochet years from the democratic years. As explained already, Cuban economic growth rates cannot be technically compared with those of Chile and Costa Rica, and a continuous series for Cuba is not available either (except for 1975–93 but with significant flaws) because of various changes in the method of estimation. These problems raise serious doubts about the validity of this indicator because of its very poor reliability in Cuba and its comparability with the other two countries (the comparison of Chile and Costa Rica is reliable and valid). It is technically improper, therefore, to use economic growth in the final ranking of performance, but, because this is one of the crucial indicators of development, it will be first included and then excluded, to assess its impact on the final ranking. Despite its flaws, Table V.3 is useful at least for showing trends and changes in growth.

In Chile there were fair growth rates between 1961 and 1970, economic stagnation or decline (in per capita) under Allende in 1971–73, fair rates during the first two stages under Pinochet (1974–80, that combined the first crisis and the recovery), negative growth during the second crisis under Pinochet (1981–85), high growth rates during the recovery in the last quinquennium under Pinochet (1986–90), and even higher rates—the highest on record—during the first democratic government (1991–93). In Costa Rica there were high absolute rates (fair per capita rates) during the stage of consolidation and expansion of the model (1961–80), stagnation or negative growth (in per capita) during the crisis (1981–85), and fair absolute rates (low per capita rates) during the recovery (1986–93). In Cuba economic growth was better during pragmatist stages than in idealistic stages (when it was negative): relatively low during the first two stages (1961–65), stagnant or negative (in per capita) under the first idealistic experiment (1966–70), the highest under the Revolution with the return to more pragmatist policies—helped by record sugar prices in the world market (1971–75), from low to medium in the following quinquennium when sugar prices declined (1976–80), high at the end of the Soviet-style economic reform (1981–85), low to negative during the antimarket Rectification Process (1986–90), and dramatically negative during the worst part of the crisis (1991–93).

In the period prior to the crisis (1961–80, 1961–73 in Chile) the highest absolute rate was generated in Costa Rica, followed by Cuba and Chile last (in per capita, Cuba was first and Costa Rica second); the bad performance during the Allende years pulled down the Chilean average in this period. During the crisis (1981–89), both in absolute and per capita terms, the Cuban rate was the highest (as it was protected by the Soviet Union), followed by Chile (which suffered a severe crisis but had a strong recovery) and Costa Rica last (whose recovery was weaker than Chile's). Between 1961 and 1990 (1974 and 1990 in Chile), the period prior to the Cuban crisis and Chile's return to democracy, Costa Rica had the highest absolute rate (second in per capita), followed by Cuba (first in per capita) and Chile last (tied with Costa Rica in per capita). Finally, in the entire period of observation (1961–93, 1974–93 in Chile) the highest absolute rate was registered in Costa Rica (4.7%), closely followed by Chile (4.1%) and Cuba lagging behind (2.6%); in per capita terms, however, Chile was first (2.4%) and Costa Rica second

(1.9%), while Cuba continued to be last (1.2%, half the rate of Chile); the severity of the crisis of the 1990s worsened the position Cuba had before. Furthermore, if the controversial year of 1981 is excluded from the Cuban average of 1961–93, it declines to 2.2% (absolute) and 0.7% (per capita).

Costa Rica shows the most important differences in absolute and per capita economic growth, a result of a very high population growth rate, while the opposite is true in Cuba, which has the lowest population growth. In the entire period 1960–93, the annual average population rate was 1.4% in Cuba, 1.8% in Chile, and 2.9% in Costa Rica; those rates were considerable higher between 1960 and 1979: 1.6%, 1.9%, and 3.3%, respectively; but they declined between 1980 and 1993 to 0.9%, 1.6%, and 2.6% (Tables II.21, III.30, IV.21). The demographic burden of Costa Rica was twice that of Cuba during the entire period and three times between 1980 and 1993; Chilean rates are closer to Cuba, although higher, but the gap also expanded significantly between 1980 and 1993 when Chile's average rate was almost twice that of Cuba. The three principal causes of such differences in population growth appear to be the degree of urbanization (highest in Cuba and lowest in Costa Rica), the huge Cuban emigration (about 10% of the population), and Cuba's significant restrictions in consumption and housing.

The widest range in the variation of growth rates was experienced by Cuba, in both absolute and per capita terms (30.5 and 29.7 percentage points, respectively, between the best and worst quinquennia); the range in Chile was considerably lower (8.3 and 8.2 points, respectively), and the shortest was in Costa Rica (6.6 and 6.3 points, respectively).

B. GNP/GDP Per Capita in U.S. Dollars

As in the previous section, there is not a Cuban series on GNP or GDP per capita in U.S. dollars but only estimates made by international organizations and some scholars. Table V.4 compares two series available for the three countries but only for certain years in Cuba. The first series, from the World Bank, presents GNP per capita in constant prices converted to U.S. dollars in current prices for Chile and Costa Rica between 1965 and 1994 but only between 1965 and 1978 for Cuba; the latter's series was discontinued in 1979 after a critical evaluation published by the World Bank that uncovered its faults (Mesa-Lago and Pérez-López 1985). According to this series, Cuban GNP per capita was about half those of Chile and Costa Rica; the former had somewhat higher GNP per capita than the latter, more in 1994.

The second series, from UNDP, began in 1990 and covers the period 1985–94 for the three countries, estimating GDP per capita based on purchasing power parity rates on U.S. dollars (PPP$). Cuba's figure was 51%

and 66% those of Chile and Costa Rica in 1985, and 34% and 53% in 1994. (The UNDP has not explained how it was able to estimate the Cuban real GNP based on the PPP$ method, without the needed base data, particularly after the end of Cuba's statistical yearbook in 1989.) As in the previous series, Chile's GDP per capita is somewhat higher than Costa Rica's, more so in 1994.

The last column of Table V.4 exhibits Cuban data on GDP per capita in constant 1981 pesos for 1985–94; the conversion to dollars can be done either using the official exchange rate (which is par in the period) or based on the exchange rate in the black market (which depreciated from 6 to 1 in 1985 to 79 to 1 in 1994). Both conversions are unrealistic (the first is too high and the second is too low) but conform with the UNDP series that shows that Cuban GNP/GDP per capita between 1985 and 1994 was considerably lower than those of Chile and Costa Rica. The Cuban government correctly argues that GDP converted to dollars using the "informal market rate" is not accurate because it does not take into account the value of free services and price subsidies granted to the population, which the government has estimated as 50% over the nominal wage (BNC 1996). Applying that adjustment to *both* the par conversion and the black-market conversion, the resulting figures for 1994 would be $1,752 and $22, respectively, still considerably below the other two countries.

Although the UNDP figure for Cuba is questionable, all the data analyzed above are consistent on the lowest Cuban ranking; therefore, the UNDP series for 1985–94 will be included in the final evaluation and ranking of performance.

C. Gross Domestic Investment as Percentage of GDP

Gross domestic investment (GDI) is an important indicator of the potential for future growth assuming that investment is done efficiently. The comparison of GDI faces similar obstacles as in the previous two indicators, because in Cuba it was systematically estimated as a percentage of GSP instead of GDP as done in Chile and Costa Rica. We lack a complete series on Cuba's percentage on GDP to undertake a comprehensive comparison with the other two countries, but Table III.7 showed GDI as a percentage of GDP for selected years, and Table V.5 compares those percentages with the ones based on GSP for 1960–93. Although Cuban figures on GDP do not compose a series as comprehensive and reliable as those of the other two countries, it is considered that the comparison is adequate, and, hence, this indicator will be used in the final ranking of performance.

As expected, Cuban percentages of GDP were consistently higher than those of GSP (because GDP was smaller than GSP), and it can be properly surmised, therefore, that in the two years for which we lack GDP percentages (1965 and 1985) they were higher than GSP percentages. Costa Rica had the highest percentages in most years, except for Chile in 1993 and Cuba in 1975 and 1989. Chile had lower percentages than Cuba in most years between 1960 and 1985, but the opposite was true between 1989 and 1993 (the highest percentage in all years was registered in Chile in 1993 under the democratic government). In the entire period (1958/60–93) Chile's percentage increased 12 percentage points, Costa rose 6 points, and Cuba's decreased 13 points. Cuba had the highest percentage of GDP among the three countries in 1958/60 but the lowest in 1993: in this year the Cuban percentage was one-fifth of Costa Rica's and even less of Chile's. Cuba's bad performance in this indicator is surprising as socialist economies usually had higher investment coefficients than market economies.

D. Inflation Rates

The comparison of inflation rates (Table V.6) encounters the same difficulties in Cuba as in the previous indicators because there is not a continuous, consistent, and reliable series for the entire period: (1) available data are a deflator for *GSP* (*GDP* between 1989 and 1994), and information on its calculation has never been released; (2) there are no official annual rates published for 1961–62, 1967–75, and 1989–93 but estimates by foreign scholars contrasting GSP/GDP in constant and current prices (ECLAC 1997d has elaborated a series for 1989–96); (3) the base year changes from 1965 in 1963–66, to unknown between 1971 and 1976, to 1981 between 1976 and 1988, and presumably 1981 for estimates on the GDP deflator between 1989 and 1994; and (4) 1981, used as a base for 1975–94, was an abnormal year and has not been changed for more than two decades in spite of strong foreign criticism. The series for Chile and Costa Rica are standardized and continuous through the entire period. Serious flaws in Cuban data make it improper to use this indicator in the final evaluation of performance, and yet additional qualitative information gathered in many years of research in Cuba confirms that this country had a very low level of inflation at least until the end of the 1980s; therefore I will proceed as with the first indicator: estimating the final ranking of performance both including and excluding inflation.

Chile has been historically afflicted by inflation and had the highest rates of the three countries throughout the entire period, except for Costa Rica in 1981–83 and 1988. Chile's record highest rates occurred between 1972 and

1976, in the last two years of the Allende administration and the first three years of Pinochet's, without parallel in the other two countries; the Chilean average rate of 1991–93 under the first democratic government, however, was the lowest in any three-year period since 1962. Costa Rica had the lowest inflation of the three countries in the 1960s, and moderate inflation in the 1970s; the highest historical rates surged in the crisis of 1981–83, and thereafter the country has had moderate rates although not as low as in the 1960s and early 1970s. Cuba exhibited the lowest inflation rates of the three countries between 1961 and 1993, because of tight price controls exercised by the government and extensive rationing of consumer goods, but inflationary pressures were not eliminated, queues grew exponentially, and price fixing and state subsidies provoked high fiscal costs. In the 1990s Cuban inflation rates increased substantially and in 1993–94 were higher than those of Chile and Costa Rica, but considerably lower in all five-year averages.

E. Fiscal Balance

The fiscal balance in Chile and Costa Rica is measured as a percentage of GDP, but in Cuba as a percentage of GSP (Table V.7); the latter is not technically comparable with the former. But Cuban GDP has been usually smaller than GSP, and, hence, the corresponding percentages on GDP should be higher. The latter is confirmed by recent data on Cuba's fiscal deficit as percentage of GDP (ECLAC 1997d): its annual average between 1989 and 1993 was −21.3% versus −19% of GSP. Problems with this indicator are not serious enough to preclude its use in the final evaluation of performance.

Cuban official data show a balanced budget between 1960 and 1980, but a growing deficit since 1985 peaking at 33.7% in 1993 (a result of the Rectification Process followed by the crisis). Chile endured a deficit in the period before Pinochet peaking at 24.7% in 1973 (the end of Allende's administration), a surplus in 1980 (also in 1979 and 1981), deficit again in 1985 (the peak between 1982 and 1989) in spite of Pinochet's tough adjustment program, and surpluses in the 1990s under the democratic government. Costa Rica had deficits during the entire period (except in 1983 and 1988, when there were a surplus and a balanced budget, respectively), which peaked in 1980, the year prior to the crisis (this was an outcome of the expansionary policies). In half of the years 1966–89, however, Costa Rica had a better fiscal balance than Chile's, while in the other half it had a worse balance; since 1990 Costa Rica has endured deficit while Chile generated surpluses. In 1993 Cuba had a deficit equal to 33.7% of GSP (30.4% of GDP), Costa Rica a deficit of 1.9% of GDP, and Chile a surplus of 1.8% of GDP.

F. Composition of GDP/GSP by Economic Activity

The problems encountered in Cuba's previous indicators pale when contrasted with those on this indicator: (1) Cuba had three divergent distributions of GSP by economic activity (Table III.8), and the first was selected here because it covered the longest period and was the most reliable; (2) Cuban GSP data cover only 1962–88 versus GDP between 1960 and 1993 in the other two countries, which forces the comparison to end in 1988, but a new series on Cuba's composition of GDP is now available for 1985–95 (Table III.9; see below); and (3) Cuba's GSP excluded the value of the extremely important "nonproductive services" (defense, administration, personal and social services), but they were included in Chile's and Costa Rica's. To show the magnitude of the third problem, Table V.8 exhibits two percentage distributions (columns 1 and 2) for each economic sector. In column 1 those services are included in Chile and Costa Rica, but basically excluded in Cuba, thus creating an upward distortion in the Cuban shares of all other sectors. In column 2 those services are excluded in the three countries, in order to eliminate such distortion and present a comparable distribution of all other sectors. For instance, the share of industry in 1993 in Chilean GDP increases from 30.1% (column 1) to 42.8% (column 2), while in Costa Rica the share rises from 25% to 28.4%, but in Cuban GSP the share is almost identical in both columns.

Based on column 1, the share of agriculture declined in Chile until 1973 and then increased or stagnated partly because of the neoconservative development strategy's emphasis on agriculture and their exports (between 1973 and 1993 such a share increased from 6.8% to 8.5%). In Costa Rica the share steadily diminished until 1980 and then stagnated, partly because of the change—although more gradual—in development strategy (the share decreased from 25.2% to 18.7% between 1960 and 1993, the biggest drop of the three countries). In Cuba the share declined until 1980 and then rose somewhat in the 1980s (it decreased from 17.8% to 15.8% between 1962 and 1988, the smallest decline of the three). The share of industry expanded in Chile until 1973 and declined or stagnated thereafter as a result of the abandonment of the ISI (this share went from 34.5% to 30.1% between 1973 and 1993). The industry share of Costa Rica climbed until 1985 and then stagnated, also because of the shift in development strategy (the share jumped from 15.1% to 25% between 1960 and 1993). And that share in Cuba exhibited some oscillation but sank from 48.2% to 35.9% between 1962 and 1988; such a decrease (12 percentage points) occurred before the crisis forced a shutdown of 80% of industrial plants. The share of commerce in Chile was basically stagnant, except for a decline in 1974–75 due to the crisis; the share of Costa Rica dwindled steadily in the period; and, surprisingly, the share of Cuba was the only one that swelled significantly (from 20.3% to 31.3%), partly because of the impact of foreign trade prices and because most taxes were accounted for in commerce. Finally the share of services was basically stagnant in Chile and declined in Costa Rica (no data are available on that share in Cuban GSP).

Based on column 2 and the year of 1988 (the most recent comparable in all three countries), Costa Rica had the largest agricultural share (22.2%), followed by Cuba (15.8%) and finally Chile (13.4%); conversely in industry Chile led (44.7%), trailed by Cuba (36.2%) and Costa Rica (29.1%); finally the highest share in commerce was that of Costa Rica (34.6%), closely followed by Cuba (31.5%) and Chile lingering behind (24.9%). Costa Rica's commerce share includes finance, which is part of the service sector in the other two countries, hence, explaining part of the difference.

Recent data released on Cuba's percentage distribution of GDP by economic activity is presented at the bottom of Table V.8 for the years 1985–93, allowing us to properly compare (1) the Cuban distributions of GSP and GDP in 1988–89 prior to the crisis, (2) the impact of the Cuban crisis on GDP distribution (contrasting 1989 and 1993), and (3) the GDP distributions of the three countries. Cuba's service sector generated 22.2% of GDP in 1989 (versus 0.7% of "productive" services in GSP in 1988) while industry accounted for 27.9% (compared with 35.9% of GSP), therefore ratifying the enormous distortions created by the MPS and GSP, casting serious doubts on the heralded process of industrialization on the island, and demonstrating that the service sector was the largest and most dynamic. The crisis aggravated the situation, as all sectors of GDP decreased between 1989 and 1993, except services, which jumped from 22.2% to 33.3% as a result of the expansion of the informal sector. A comparison of the GDP distribution in 1993 among the three countries, based in the three clusters—primary (agriculture), secondary (industry and construction) and tertiary (transportation-communication, commerce, and services)—shows that Costa Rica had the biggest primary sector (18.7%), with Chile and Cuba well behind (8.5% and 7.2% respectively); Chile led in the secondary sector (36.3%) with Cuba dragging behind (30.7%) followed closely by Costa Rica (28.9%); and conversely Cuba surpassed by far the other two countries in the tertiary sector (62.1%), with Chile lagging behind (55.2%) closely followed by Costa Rica (52.4%).

The two previous comparisons on the share of industry in GSP (excluding services) and in GDP show that (1) Chile's share was consistently the highest, followed by Cuba and Costa Rica last; (2) the share of Costa Rica increased significantly in the period, while Chile's declined slightly and Cuba's shrank significantly in GSP but rose in GDP; and (3) in 1993 and based on GDP, the highest share was found in Chile (30%), followed by Cuba (28%) and Costa Rica (25%). Because of the various flaws of Cuban GSP, in the final ranking of performance I will rely on the GDP composition in the three countries between 1985 and 1993, focusing on the shares of agriculture and industry. It is assumed that the lower the share of agriculture and the higher the share of industry, the more developed the country is.[1]

G. Export Concentration/Diversification

The three economies are heavily dependent on foreign trade: in 1989, the last year when comparable figures are available, total trade transaction value was 73% of GDP in Costa Rica and 57% in Chile, and 51% of GSP in Cuba. As GDP has proved to be smaller than GSP, the percentage of Cuba should have been higher; furthermore, the crisis of the 1990s has made that country even more dependent on external commerce. Trade dependency of Costa Rica and Chile also increased significantly in the 1990s as they opened even more to world commerce (Tables II.7, III.16, IV.7). This indicator will not be used in the final ranking of performance, as trade dependence could be considered an input rather than an output, and it is unclear whether the degree of external dependence and independence is positive or negative by itself.

If in addition to heavy trade dependency there is substantial export concentration on one major product, the country becomes more vulnerable to oscillations in the world market price of such products: copper in Chile, coffee and bananas in Costa Rica, and sugar in Cuba. Export diversification, on the other hand, reduces such vulnerability because world prices of all exports do not usually decline simultaneously and oscillations in prices of various exports may compensate each other. There are no major problems with data related to this indicator that will be used in the final ranking of performance. It is assumed that the lower the export concentration (the more diversified exports), the more developed the country is (the degree of export concentration/diversification in the three countries is compared in Table V.9).[2]

1. Recently it has been argued that with increasing globalization and free trade, comparative advantages and improvements in technology in agriculture may result in a country's development based on agriculture. Chile is given as an example of having a declining share of industry/GDP and a rising share of agriculture/GDP combined with high economic growth (*The Economist*, October 4, 1997, p. 84). Table V.8 shows, nevertheless, that the share of agriculture decreased in 1975–93 and that of industry declined only slightly.

2. One could argue that export concentration is not a proper indicator of performance because it could generate positive or negative results. For instance, Saudi Arabia's export concentration on oil is very high, but it has led to fast economic growth. And yet petroleum is a scarce, strategic good, as well as a high-price export, but the same is not true of other exports

In Chile export concentration rose in the 1960s and peaked in 1973 (largely influenced by a big jump in world prices of copper that year), but it declined dramatically from 83% in 1973 to 35% in 1993. The percentage of trade generated by other exports (in addition to fish meal and iron ore, which accounted for about 10% of total trade value) jumped more than twofold between 1960 and 1993 (fourfold between 1973 and 1993). Costa Rica's major export in 1960 was coffee, and it generated 53% of total export value, followed by bananas, which contributed 24% (a combined total of 77%). In 1993 the share of coffee had dropped to 10%, and that of bananas was almost stagnant at 26% (both exports totaled 36%, less than half the 1960 proportion). Conversely, the value of other exports (aside from beef, which accounted for 3% in 1993) increased more than three times between 1960 and 1993, from 18% to 61%, placing Costa Rica well ahead of Chile in this indicator. The remarkable improvement in export diversification in Costa Rica and Chile has been mainly the outcome of promotion of nontraditional exports.

Cuba was not able to reduce export concentration between 1960 and 1990, as sugar exports generated 78% and 80% of total export value in those years. Actually export concentration increased substantially in most of the 1960s because of Soviet price subsidies, as well as in the second half of the 1970s and the start of the 1980s helped by both Soviet subsidies and high world market prices. The sugar share decreased in the rest of the 1980s, in spite of rising production and Soviet subsidies, but this was largely an outcome of "oil reexports" that escalated from zero to 10% between 1975 and 1985; these, however were not exports but Soviet hard-currency grants for the difference between committed oil export and actual deliveries. With the termination of Soviet price subsidies and grants, as well as a drastic decline in trade between the two nations, Cuba was forced to sell sugar at world market prices, and the proportion of export value of sugar decreased. Furthermore a sharp drop in total exports, compounded by a 38% fall in sugar production and exports in 1993, contributed to reducing the sugar share to 66%. In 1993 Cuba's next two most important exports, nickel and tobacco, ac-

---

such as sugar, bananas, coffee, and copper. Cuba offers convincing evidence of the negative effects of an overly high degree of export concentration on nonstrategic, relatively abundant goods. In fact, the island's major economic problem throughout this century has been its excessive dependence on sugar (combined with trade partner concentration), and a fundamental cause of Cuba's current crisis has been the loss of Soviet price subsidies on sugar (the shift to lower world market prices) and the poor purchasing power of that export to sustain a minimum level of imports, If Cuba had diversified its exports, its situation now would be much better (something similar could be said about Chile's excessive dependence on copper exports in the past, and even today, although in a considerably less degree; see below).

counted for 17% of total export value (compared with 14% in 1960), but, in absolute terms, the value of those exports decreased vis-à-vis 1989. The share of other nontraditional exports increased from 8% to 17% between 1960 and 1993, but, in absolute terms, their value was considerably smaller in 1993 than in 1989. Even taking at face value the shares of 1993, Cuba was by far the least successful of the three countries in diversifying exports and reducing dependency on one product.

H. Import Composition

There are no major flaws in the data on import composition, and I will include this indicator in the final ranking of performance. Within this indicator I will be focusing in Table V.10 on four types of external dependency on imports: food (also an indicator of self-sufficiency in food), fuel (which can be a major constraint for development when world market prices rise), and machinery and manufactures (indirect indicators of the degree of industrialization). It is assumed that the lower the shares of agricultural and fuel imports, the more self-sufficient the country and less its energy burden, while the higher the share of machinery imports and lower the share of manufactured goods, the more industrialized and developed the country is.

The least dependent country on imported foodstuffs was Chile; its share of total imports shrank from 24% to 5% between 1973 and 1993 (18% to 5% between 1960 and 1993) based on expanded domestic output. The second least dependent country was Costa Rica, whose food share decreased from 13% to 4% between 1960 and 1984 but rose to 8% in 1993, probably because of the decline in output of some products for domestic consumption such as beef, rice, and corn. Cuba was the country most heavily dependent on food imports; its share declined from 21% in 1958 to 10% in the late 1980s but jumped to 26% in 1993 (five times the Chilean share and three times the Costa Rican share), a result of the significant drop in overall agricultural production for domestic consumption due to lack of crucial imports such as fertilizer, pesticides, herbicides, and fuel. It should be recalled that Costa Rica's agricultural land per capita (labor force in agriculture) was 53% that of Chile and 40% of Cuba's (Table I.1), a significant handicap, which has been, nevertheless, overcome.

The three countries are net importers of energy, but the percentage of fuel imports in relation to total energy needs varied significantly in 1987: 66% in Chile, 90% in Cuba, and 100% in Costa Rica (Tables II.12, III.21, IV.12). The last, however, produces significant hydroelectric energy, which reduced the need for fuel imports to 41% of total energy consumption in 1994 (WB *WDR* 1996). Costa Rica, therefore, is the country least dependent on fuel imports; due to rising oil prices, its import share of fuels increased between 1974 and 1982 but declined thereafter, and it was 6% in 1960 and 9% in 1993. Chile's fuel import share was slightly higher than Costa Rica's; it also increased between 1973 and 1983 and declined thereafter, but it rose slightly from 7% in 1973 (the same as in 1960) to 9% in 1993. Cuba was the country most dependent on fuel imports, and its share rose from 11% to 37% between 1958 and 1993. But that nation had the unique advantage among the three countries that prices of oil imports (virtually all coming from the Soviet Union) were subsidized by the Soviets until the mid-1980s. In spite of that subsidy, however, the share of fuel imports increased threefold between 1958 and 1985, and it further rose in the 1990s because of the dramatic decline of Soviet oil imports and elimination of all subsidies (which forced Cuba to pay the world market price for oil even from Russia).

The highest share of machinery imports was that of Chile (the most industrialized country of the three): the share decreased between 1974 and 1984 with the abandonment of the ISI but rose again beginning in the late 1980s; in the entire period the share expanded from 34% in 1973 (40% in 1960) to 44% in 1993. Having a larger industrial base to meet domestic consumption, Chile also had the lowest share of manufactures imports: 27% in 1973 (30% in 1960) but, with the de-industrialization process and opening to domestic imports, that share steadily rose and peaked at 41% in 1987; there was a decrease later, and the share stood at 38% in 1993 (the second largest of the three countries). Cuba is less industrialized than Chile but more than Costa Rica, and, consistently, the island's share of machinery imports was the second largest in 1958 (30%) and had risen to 37% in 1990, but the crisis forced a shutdown of most industry, and the share sank to 12% in 1993 (6% in 1994). An expanding domestic industry, combined with severe restrictions on imports of manufactured goods, cut the corresponding import share of manufactures in Cuba from 30% in 1958 to 20% in the late 1980s; the crisis and lack of hard currency shrank that share further to 18% in 1992. Costa Rica is the least industrialized country of the three and also had the lowest share of import of machinery, which was 26% in 1960 and peaked at 31% in 1977 (in the midst of the industrialization boom); it decreased to 26% in 1993 (back to the 1960 level, about half of Chile's and twice that of Cuba), mainly because of some decline in the importance of industry. The ISI process in Costa Rica was less advanced than in the other two countries, and the share of imported manufactured goods exhibited little change: about 54% throughout most of the period, by far the highest of the three.

I. Trade Partner Concentration

High trade concentration of a developing country with one developed partner (particularly if it is a superpower) usually is a disadvantage, because it weakens the negotiating capacity of the less developed country and increases its vulnerability vis-à-vis the developed partner, which is more powerful to fix quotas of imported goods, prices of exports and imports, and so on; conversely, countries that have more diversified trade partners should be able to reduce that vulnerability. Table V.11 measures the concentration of total trade volume (exports plus imports) of the three countries with their major partner: the United States for Chile and Costa Rica (and Cuba on the eve of the Revolution) and the Soviet Union for Cuba. There are no problems with this indicator, and it will be included in the final ranking of performance. It is assumed that the lower the trade partner concentration (the more diversified the trade partners) the better off the country is.

Throughout the entire period Chile had the least concentration or the most diversified trade partners: its share of trade with the United States dropped from 43% to 12% between 1960 and 1973 (under Allende, because of political conflicts between the two countries); the share then rose under Pinochet and peaked at 27% in 1983 but declined thereafter to 18% in 1993; the other two major partners of Chile in that year were Japan (7.5%) and Germany (2.5%). Costa Rica was second to (but distant from) Chile on trade partner diversification; its share with the United States decreased from 51% to 33% between 1960 and 1980 (as trade with members of the Central American Common Market—CACM—absorbed 19% of total trade, and 48% was with other countries), but it increased to 55% in 1993 (as trade with CACM sharply shrank, and the United States increased its influence through the negotiation of the foreign debt). Cuba is the country with the highest trade partner concentration: in 1958, prior to the Revolution, 68% of trade was with the United States; as the Soviet Union replaced the United States, the Soviet trade share climbed and peaked at 72% in 1987 (plus 15% with CMEA). In the 1990s there was a dramatic fall in trade with Russia (as well as with the former Soviet Republics and Eastern Europe), and trade concentration with that country declined to 22% in 1993. But that significant decline in trade concentration has been one of the major causes of the severe crisis in Cuba.

J. Volume and Balance of Merchandise Trade Per Capita

The ideal indicator here would have been the balance of payments, but, because of the lack of Cuban data for most of the period, I rely on the balance of merchandise trade as a surrogate; the other indicator I use is total trade volume. Both indicators are given in cumulative U.S. dollars per capita (to adjust for the considerably lower population of Costa Rica vis-à-vis the other two countries) and estimated in annual averages to facilitate the comparison with Chile. A major difficulty encountered in both indicators was the conversion of Cuban pesos to U.S. dollars; because of the lack of a market exchange rate for the entire period it was decided to use the official exchange rate, which was considerably overvalued (particularly between 1972 and 1985), hence inflating that country's per capita in U.S. dollars. This makes Cuba look better in trade volume but worse in trade balance; as these distortions should compensate each other, the two indicators will be included in the final ranking of performance. It is assumed that the higher the trade volume per capita and the more positive the trade balance per capita (the lower the deficit or the higher the surplus), the better off the country is.

The top segment of Table V.12 compares the two indicators in specific years (by quinquennium) between 1960 and 1993, while the bottom segment contrasts the cumulative trade volume/balance annual average in various stages (similarly to the indicators on growth and inflation). According to the top segment, until the end of the 1980s trade volume per capita was highest in Cuba, closely followed by Costa Rica (which had the highest in 1970), and Chile had the lowest; but the situation changed dramatically in the 1990s. Thus in 1993 Costa Rica had the highest per capita, closely followed by Chile and Cuba far behind. The bottom segment of the table accords with the previous findings: Chile had the lowest annual average trade volume per capita in all stages except during the boom in 1990–93 when it was tied with Costa Rica; the latter also had the highest average in the entire period (1960–93); and Cuba had the highest average before the regional crisis of the 1980s and the lowest average during its own crisis in the 1990s. The crisis of the 1980s adversely affected Chile and Costa Rica, while Cuba reached the highest average between 1981 and 1989 because it was protected by the Soviet Union (Cuba also had the highest averages between 1974 and the 1980s because of the overvaluation of the peso vis-à-vis the dollar between 1972 and 1985). Conversely, in 1990–93 Cuba's average was the lowest among all countries and stages because of the dramatic decline in trade with Russia and its price subsidies. A comparison of the years 1993 and 1989 (top segment of the table) shows an increase in volume per capita of 45% in Costa Rica and 25% in Chile but a plunge of 78% in Cuba. Between 1960 and 1993, the per capita rose tenfold in Chile (fivefold between 1973 and 1993) and Costa Rica, but less than twofold in Cuba.

Contrasting with the trade volume indicator, Costa Rica and Cuba suffered a trade deficit per capita throughout 1960–93 and in each stage, while Chile enjoyed a surplus most of the time, even more so if the cumulative per capita average is used (bottom segment of Table V.12). Costa Rica's deficit was considerably lower than Cuba's, particularly based on the cumulative figures (except for 1974–80). In 1993 Cuba had a deficit per capita lower than Costa Rica's (higher than Chile's) largely because of the dramatic decline in its trade volume and imports in particular. The Cuban deficit is more striking when one takes into account the substantial Soviet price subsidies granted to Cuban major exports and Soviet oil imports (at least during the first 25 years of the relationship between the two countries); without such subsidies the deficit would have been greater. On the other hand, the over-valuation of the Cuban peso-dollar exchange rate (especially between 1972 and 1985) inflated that country's deficit.

K. External Debt Per Capita

A major obstacle to measuring the debt per capita is the lack of hard data on Cuba's debt to the Soviet Union and other members of CMEA, except for my own estimates, which have also added the hard-currency debt. Another problem is that we have the real debt (in U.S. dollars at 1985 prices) for Chile and Costa Rica but not for Cuba; therefore, we have to make the comparison in current U.S. dollars (available for Cuba). As for the previous indicator, Table V.13 presents the debt per capita, in order to adjust for the lower population of Costa Rica. The noted difficulties are not serious enough to impede this indicator's being used in the final evaluation of performance. It is assumed that the lower the external debt per capita, the lesser the burden on the economy.[3]

In 1958/60 the debt per capita of Cuba (only in hard currency) was the smallest of the three countries: one-fifth of Costa Rica's and one-tenth of Chile; but in 1975 the Cuban debt per capita (including mostly that with the Soviet Union and a small amount in hard currency) had become the highest, about twice that of Chile and 2.6 times that of Costa Rica; in 1985 the debt per capita of the three countries was very similar; finally, in 1990 Cuba's debt per capita (including Soviet Union, CMEA, and hard-currency) was 2.6 times that of Chile and Costa Rica; the last's was the smallest of the three countries.

Costa Rica began to reduce the nominal debt in the 1990s after the agreement signed with its creditors; in real terms the debt per capita was cut by 38% between 1983 and 1994. Chile was a pioneer in debt-equity swaps, which, combined with high economic growth, helped to reduce the real debt by 36% between 1982 and 1993. The Cuban debt with the Soviet Union accounted for only about one-third of total Soviet economic aid (the rest was in price subsidies and grants), given under very generous terms and virtually

---

3. A warning about this indicator: the external debt could improve or make an economy worse depending on whether such resources are well used or not, and the debt is paid back normally over a long period of time. It is impossible to assess here the efficiency of the utilization of debt resources; the role of this indicator is to measure such debt's degree of burden on the economy.

not served; but the debt service is a thorn in trade relations between the two countries. Cuba's debt in hard currency alone was U.S.$10.5 billion in 1995 (close to U.S.$1,000 per capita, similar to that of the other two countries) and increased threefold between 1982 and 1994; it has not been served since 1986 and keeps growing, thus becoming a standing block to receiving new credit from the Club of Paris. The estimated total Cuban debt jumped sixfold between 1975 and 1990, but the portion in nonconvertible currency is impossible to estimate after 1990, although it must have decreased significantly.

L. Income Distribution

Cuba has never published data on income distribution (although until the crisis of the 1990s it probably had the most egalitarian distribution in Latin America), and we have only rough and flawed estimates elaborated by foreign scholars, which end in 1986, before the crisis significantly expanded income inequality. Even the comparison between Chile and Costa Rica, for which data are available, is marred by different measurements (personal and family income) and disparate years for the data. Data gaps in these two countries between 1982 and 1990 impede our assessment of the impact of the crisis and structural adjustment on income distribution, while absence of data after 1990 obstruct an evaluation of the effect of the recovery. All these problems make it inappropriate to use income distribution as one of the indicators for measuring performance.

Table V.14 presents all the figures available for the three countries. Cuba had the most egalitarian distribution: the highest income share in the poorest 40% (which exhibited an increasing trend but stagnant in the poorest decile after 1978) and the lowest income share in the wealthiest decile (slowly declining). Costa Rica had an increasing share of the poorest 40% until 1982 (at the time the crisis exploded), but lower than Cuba's and declining by 1990 (particularly the poorest decile), while the richest decile decreased until 1982 and then rose. Chilean data are on personal income (which tend to show more unequal distribution than family income, as in Costa Rica and Cuba) and are limited to Santiago in 1981–82; they show the lowest income share of the poorest 40% among the three countries which was declining in 1981–82, and the highest income share of the wealthiest decile although steadily declining.

M. Real Wages

The vacuum on income distribution could be partially filled with Table V.15, which presents the real mean-wage index for the three countries. Cuba's series is my own estimation based on the GSP deflator for 1975–88 and the GDP deflator for 1989–95, both based on the year 1981. Because of disparate years in the three countries, the wage index can be used only for the period between 1975/76 and 1994 and will be included in the final ranking of performance.

The highest mean wage in Chile was reached in 1971, but it declined sharply in Allende's last year and decreased further during the first crisis under Pinochet; it grew again before the second crisis, shrank, and began to grow again in the late 1980s and 1990s but without recovering the 1971 level. In Costa Rica the peak was reached in 1980 (before the crisis); it fell to a trough in 1982 and increased slowly thereafter but in 1994 was still slightly below the 1980 level. Cuba's real wage steadily grew and peaked in 1986, then stagnated until 1990, and sharply declined thereafter. Between the peak (reached in 1971, 1980, and 1986, respectively) and the mean wage in 1994 there was a decrease of 30 percentage points in Cuba, 9 in Chile, and less than 2 in Costa Rica. In relation to the base year of 1980, the real mean wage in 1994 was 24.5 points higher in Chile, 1.6 points lower in Costa Rica, and 21 points lower in Cuba. The real minimum wage was cut in half in Chile between 1982 and 1987 and rose thereafter, but in 1993 it was still below the peak; conversely in Costa Rica the minimum wage decreased less than in Chile during the crisis, then grew and peaked in 1990. There are no statistics on the real minimum wage in Cuba, which impedes its use in the final ranking of performance.

N. Poverty Incidence

There are data for Chile and Costa Rica on poverty incidence for 1970–92/ 93,[4] but figures are not always comparable: Costa Rica has a series on percentage of households, while Chile mixes that with percentage of individuals. Furthermore, there are no data for Cuba (not even rough estimates); hence it is impossible to use this indicator to evaluate and rank performance. Table V.16 shows that between 1970 and 1990 the incidence of poverty and indigence increased twofold in Chile, but both had declined significantly by 1992 (particularly indigence). In Costa Rica poverty incidence either was stagnant or had declined between 1970 and 1990, but indigence had risen; by

---

4. Poverty incidence is the percentage of the population below a "poverty line," estimated by a basket that sets the cost of basic food, clothing, shelter, and services. The "indigence line" or "extreme poverty" is calculated on the cost of basic food alone. In this book I have mainly followed the ECLAC methodology for the estimation of both, although in the country cases there are poverty estimates that apply other techniques.

1993 the poverty incidence of Costa Rica was much lower than Chile's, but the indigence incidence was higher.

O. Composition of the Labor Force and Women's Participation

There are Cuban data for four years between 1957 and 1981 on the distribution of the *labor force* by economic activity (from two censuses and two surveys), and estimates for 1989–94 on the distribution of the *employed* labor force. Data on Chile and Costa Rica refer to the labor force during the entire period. Such a difference is not serious enough to exclude this important indicator from the final ranking of performance (see Table V.17). Unlike developed countries, in less developed Latin America (including the three countries of this book) a high share of the labor force in the tertiary sector is an indicator of underemployment due to lack of jobs in the secondary sector. On the other hand, a declining percentage of the labor force in the primary sector (mainly agriculture) and a growing percentage in the secondary sector (mainly industry) are proper indicators of development in the region. It is assumed, therefore, that the lower the proportion of the labor force and employment in the primary sector and the higher the proportion in the secondary sector, the more developed the country is.

The proportion in the primary sector continuously diminished in Costa Rica and exhibited a declining trend in the other two countries but with oscillations and a substantial increase in Cuba in the mid-1990s. Between 1957 and 1963 Costa Rica had the highest proportion in that sector (49%), followed by Cuba (39%), and Chile had the smallest (32%); in 1981/84 all countries had reduced this proportion, but the ranking continued to be the same; in 1990 the ranking was unchanged, but the gap was reduced significantly, thus Costa Rica's proportion further shrank (25.5%), while Cuba's became stagnant (21.9%) and Chile's increased (21.5%) because of the shift in its development strategy; and in 1993/94 the gap expanded again: Costa Rica's proportion further diminished (22.8%), but Cuba's jumped and became the largest (28.2%) because of the expansion of agriculture in the nonstate sector, and Chile's proportion resumed its downward trend and remained the smallest (18.5%).

The proportion in the secondary sector steadily expanded in Costa Rica and oscillated in the other two countries: it declined and then rose in Chile, while it climbed and then abruptly fell in Cuba. Between 1957 and 1963 the gap among the three countries was very small: Chile 22%, Cuba 21%, and Costa Rica 18.5%. In 1981/84 the gap had expanded: Cuba's proportion enlarged significantly (a result of the highest growth rates during the Revolution), while Chile's was stagnant first and decreased later (because of the abandonment of ISI), and Costa Rica's increased slightly in spite of the crisis. In 1990 Costa Rica and Cuba were almost identical, and Chile was last but with a growing proportion again. In 1993/94 there was a significant reversal but still the gap was small: Costa Rica 25.6%, Chile 25.2%, and Cuba 23.2% (because of the crisis and shutdown of industry and cut in public utilities).

The sluggish expansion of the secondary sector (except for Costa Rica) could not generate enough jobs to employ manpower released by agriculture, which had to get jobs in the tertiary sector; therefore, its proportion expanded in all countries but at different rates and in diverse activities. Chile had the biggest tertiary sector in the entire period, which grew from 38% to 57% between 1960 and 1993; it actually peaked in 1985 and stagnated thereafter because of the cut in public employment and some social services (but financing, insurance, and banking grew quickly). Costa Rica was second, steadily increasing from 31% to 50% between 1963 and 1993, as the public bureaucracy and social services expanded in spite of the adjustment. Cuba was third: it grew from 36% to 43% or 48% between 1957 and 1994 (the second percentage results from adding "other state personnel," noncivilian, which must be the armed forces). Because of the crisis in the 1990s in Cuba, the secondary sector has shrunk dramatically, the primary sector has increased, and the tertiary sector has expanded further as informal employment and personal services have grown.

The comparison of the percentage of women who are in the labor force is seriously obstructed by the absence of Cuban information after the census of 1981; hence the most recent data are 13 years old, and, unfortunately, this indicator cannot be included in the final ranking. The last column of Table V.17 shows an increasing percentage of the labor force made up by women in the three countries, but much faster in Cuba than in the other two countries. Between 1980 and 1984 the proportions were 31% in Cuba, 29% in Chile, and 25% in Costa Rica. Data available for the last two countries in 1990–93 indicate that Costa Rica was closing the gap (30%) with Chile (32%). In the 1990s the significant increase of open unemployment in Cuba and substantial surplus labor in the state sector is making it more difficult for women to find jobs; in 1989, 90% of all administrative jobs were performed by women, and the bureaucracy will probably suffer the worst cuts in the future.

P. Open Unemployment Rates

The major difficulty with this indicator is the absence of a continuous complete series for national unemployment and no data at all on urban unemployment in Cuba. Still, a comparison is feasible with national rates, which will be used in the final ranking. Table V.18 shows the trends as well as the years when peaks occurred; urban rates are normally higher than national rates, except in two years in Costa Rica.

The national rate in Chile declined in the early 1970s (the lowest on record was 3.1% in 1972, Allende's second year); it jumped to 14% in 1976 during the first crisis, declined to 10.4% in 1980 as a result of the brief recovery, peaked at 19.6% in 1982 in the midst of the second crisis, and gradually declined thereafter to 4.5% in 1993. The urban rates were much higher and peaked at 16.8% and 22.2% in the first and second crisis, but, adding those under the emergency employment programs, the rates ballooned to 21.9% and 31.3%, respectively. Costa Rica's rates were considerably lower than Chile's; the urban rate was 3.5% in 1970 (6.9% national in 1960) and increased to 6% in 1980 (declined to 5.9% national). It peaked at 9.9% in 1982 (9.4% national) at the worst point of the crisis and declined thereafter to 4% in 1993 (4.1% national). Cuban national rates were higher than in the other two countries until 1965 but reached a record low (possible in Latin America) at 1.3% in 1970, the year of the gigantic mobilization for the sugar harvest; the rate slowly grew to 6% in 1988 (similar to those of Chile and Costa Rica) and 7.3% in 1990, the highest national rate of the three countries, and slowed down to 6.7% in 1994, still the highest of the three. The latter, however, reflects open unemployment, but, if the concept of "equivalent unemployment" developed by ECLAC (1997) is used (adding all those that receive unemployment compensation), the rate jumped to 33% in 1994. Furthermore, from 11% to 18% of the labor force in the state sector is not needed and was expected to be dismissed, an action that had not materialized by the end of 1997.

Q. Illiteracy Rates

The two main problems with this indicator are the different years of observation and the different population cohorts used to measure the rates. Table V.19 has partly standardized the cohort to 15 years and older, based on UNESCO data, but different cohorts are given in other years: 10 years and older in 1953 for all countries (resulting in a higher rate than 15 and older, but allowing an uniform comparison at the start), as well as in 1963 for Costa Rica, and 1958 and 1970 for Cuba; and 10 to 49 years in 1979 for Cuba. Data for 1990 is based on 15 years and older for all countries. As there are standardized rates in the start and end years, this indicator will be included in the final ranking.

In 1953 Chile had the lowest rate (19.8%), closely followed by Costa Rica

(20.6%) and Cuba the highest (23.6%); the rates were steadily reduced to 5.7% in Chile and Costa Rica in 1992, and 6% in Cuba in 1990 (or 5.3% in 1992, which is the author's interpolation based on UNESCO estimates for 1995). The comparison done in 1990 (the latest year available for Cuba), uniformly based on 15 years and older for all countries, shows the following rates: 6% in Cuba, 6.6% in Chile, and 7.2% in Costa Rica; while in 1992 were 5.3% for Cuba and 5.7% for the other two countries. Although the difference among the countries was very small, the closing of the gap in Cuba between 1953/57 and 1990/92 was the most impressive. Data on this country in between those years, however, have often been distorted. For instance, after the literacy campaign of 1961, Cuba claimed a decrease of illiteracy to 3.9% (a 17 percentage-point cut from 21% in 1958), a figure internationally praised, but the 1970 census showed a 12.9% rate, thus proving that the 1961 rate was grossly underestimated. The 1981 Cuban census gave a rate of 1.9% in the 10–49-year-old bracket (excluding the older population who had the highest illiteracy rate), and UNESCO adjusted it to 4% among those 15 and older, but that rate was still too low, as subsequent rates within the same age bracket were higher albeit declining: 7.6 % in 1985, 6% in 1990, and 5.3% in 1992.

R. Educational Enrollment

This indicator faces four minor problems, which do not impede its inclusion in the final ranking of performance (see Table V.20). First are the different ages and school periods at the three levels, both among the countries and within each. Second are estimates of enrollment at the elementary level, often above 100%, due to a mismatch between population and education ages, but it is assumed that when that happens (particularly when the overestimation is quite high) there is universal coverage. Third, data prior to 1961 in Cuba excluded enrollment in private schools and universities, but they were included right after the nationalization of those facilities in April 1961, creating the statistical illusion of a big jump in enrollment that year. Fourth, there are no official rates for 1992 in Cuba, only my estimates based on enrollment at the secondary and higher levels (given by ECLAC 1997d).

There is remarkable similarity among the three countries in their educational enrollment at the elementary level. No data are available for Cuba in 1958, but in 1960 there was apparent universal enrollment (in the second year of the Revolution, thus suggesting that there was close to universal enrollment in 1958), while in 1963 Costa Rica was very close to universal enrollment (93%), and in 1960 Chile had 87%. By 1970 the three countries had indeed reached the goal of universality. Because of such almost identical performance on this indicator, it is not worthwhile to include it in the final evaluation of performance (as the three countries would have virtually identical rankings), but enrollment at the secondary and tertiary levels were indeed different, and, hence, they will be included.

In 1960 Chile had the highest enrollment in secondary education (23%) followed by Costa Rica (20% in 1963) and Cuba dragging behind (14%). And yet, between 1960 and 1965, Cuba increased such enrollment by 11 percentage points to 25% (enrollment was stagnant between 1965 and 1971); part of this was the result of nationalization of private facilities and counting of their students, while part was real expansion in coverage, particularly in the countryside; this means that total secondary enrollment was higher than 14% in 1960, but it is not possible to determine the exact figure. Cuba steadily increased secondary enrollment after 1970 and reached 90% in 1990 (an impressive performance), while Chile followed that year with 74%, and Costa Rica was well behind with 42%. (Actually enrollment in Costa Rica peaked at 48% in 1979, but the crisis and adjustment in the 1980s led to stagnation and decline in such enrollment, and the increase in the 1990s did not recover that peak.) In 1992 secondary enrollment rates in Chile and Costa Rica increased to 75% and 46%, respectively, but sharply decreased to 80% in Cuba because of the crisis, albeit maintaining the highest rate.

In 1960 enrollment in higher education was very similar in the three countries: 5% in Costa Rica, 4% in Chile, and 3% in Cuba (those enrolled in private universities were not taken into account; hence the Cuban figure must have been higher). Contrary to secondary education, enrollment in higher education in 1990 was highest in Costa Rica (27%), followed by Cuba (21%) and Chile (19%). In the last, the reform of higher education under Pinochet (including the closing of some schools) led to a reduction in enrollment from 17% to 10% between 1973 and 1982; enrollment increased thereafter and reached 24% in 1992. In Costa Rica enrollment at this level decreased from 24% to 20% between 1979 and 1983 because of the crisis, but that decline was smaller than in secondary education (because of the constitutional mandate that ensured a given percentage of the state budget to universities, but at the price of a drastic cut at the secondary level); enrollment rose to 28% in 1991 (the highest of all countries). In Cuba there was a drop of university enrollment from 23% to 18% between 1989 and 1993, because the crisis resulted in a lack of jobs for graduates.

S. Infant Mortality and Life Expectancy

There are two types of indicators on health care: those that measure inputs (e.g., physicians per 10,000 inhabitants, hospital beds per 1,000 inhabitants) and those that assess outputs; among the latter those most widely used are infant mortality and life expectancy. Input indicators were analyzed in the policy sections of the country parts but not included in Table V.21. There is no major problem with the infant mortality indicator, so it will be included in the final ranking of performance. We lack a Cuban series on life expectancy with annual data for the period; hence various sources had to be combined to construct such a series: official, United Nations, and a foreign demographer's. All these data, nevertheless, were fairly consistent, and the corresponding indicator was judged to be reliable and will be used in the final ranking of performance.

In 1960 Cuba's infant mortality rate of 35.9 was the lowest (actually it was 33.4 in 1958), while Costa Rica had twice that rate (74.3) and Chile three times Cuba's rate (119.5). In the last two countries the rate steadily diminished after 1960, but in Cuba it escalated at the beginning of the Revolution to 41.5% in 1962, and then it declined to climb again later to a peak of 46.7 in 1969; thereafter the rate steadily decreased. It has been argued that as Cuba developed both its health system and registry for infant deaths, the rate appeared to increase when the increase was actually a result of better reporting. This argument is a valid one but could be equally applied to the other two countries. Furthermore, in Cuba there were factors other than better reporting that could explain the increase in infant mortality: about one-third of the total number of physicians had emigrated by 1961, there was a scarcity of medicine and other crucial health-care goods in the early 1960s, and morbidity rates exhibited a similar trend than mortality (both general and infant). Finally, better coverage could have explained the first increase in infant mortality, but it is doubtful that it could justify the second jump and peak in 1969 (11 years after the Revolution and the new government significantly developed the health-care system). Chile managed to accelerate the reduction in infant mortality between 1975 and 1980, in spite of a drastic cut in the public health-care budget, based on targeting pregnant woman and infants, but other health indicators such as morbidity suffered a deterioration. In 1992 Cuba continued to be lowest in infant mortality (10.2), followed by Costa Rica (13.7) and Chile (13.9), but the gap among the three countries had been dramatically reduced vis-à-vis that in 1960.

As in the previous indicator, in 1960 Cuba was ahead of the other two countries in life expectancy at birth: 64 years compared to 61.6 in Costa Rica and 58.1 in Chile. This indicator displayed a declining trend in all countries, and, in 1992, the rates were almost identical in Cuba (75.7) and Costa Rica (75.4), although Chile lingered behind (72.1). But the gap among the three countries in 1992 had substantially decreased in comparison with that in 1960.

T. Rates of Contagious Diseases

Rates of contagious diseases are fairly good indicators and are comparable, although their reliability in 1960 might be questionable, and recent data are not available on a few diseases in Costa Rica. This indicator complements the previous one, but nine diseases are compared in Table V.22, and we have to make a selection of the ones most relevant for the final evaluation of performance.

For diphtheria, polio, and tetanus the starting rates were not very different—except for diphtheria (Cuba had the lowest rates for two diseases and Chile for one), but they had been virtually eradicated by 1992. Malaria is difficult to compare for two reasons: it is almost nonexistent in Chile mainly because of climatological conditions, and it is endemic in the other two countries, which have extensively fought it through immunization. However, it was virtually eradicated in Cuba, while it was significant and climbing in Costa Rica (largely because of immigration from poorer neighboring countries). These four diseases will therefore be excluded from the final ranking.

The rates of the remaining five diseases show considerable differences among the countries at both the start year (1960) and the end year (1990–92); these are not due to environmental conditions but are largely the result of divergent sanitation and/or immunization policies: (1) hepatitis rose in all three countries but was lowest at both points in Chile, and second lowest at the start but highest at the end in Cuba; (2) measles declined in all countries but was the lowest at both points in Cuba and the highest at both points in Chile; (3) tuberculosis decreased in all countries but was the highest at both points in Chile, while Costa Rica and Cuba were very similar; (4) typhoid exhibited the same trend as tuberculosis and was basically eradicated in Costa Rica and Cuba; and (5) the syphilis trend was diverse: it was the highest in Chile at the start but the lowest at the end, while the opposite was true in Cuba (there is no immunization against this disease, and sanitation conditions are not a significant factor; its rates are mainly a result of more or less sexual contact and use of prophylaxis). These five diseases will be used in the final evaluation of performance.

U. Access to Potable Water and Sewerage and Sanitation

This is more an input than output indicator and encounters three significant obstacles for an adequate comparison: (1) definitions of access to potable water vary among the three countries; for instance, it may be water piped inside of the home exclusively or also include access to piped water outside the home or access to other water sources; (2) sewerage can be confined to that service exclusively or also include sanitation or be limited to sanitation only (e.g., in Cuba); and (3) data for Cuba are limited to three years (with significant differences in categories that had to be carefully standardized) and end in 1981. Hence they are too old and do not take into account the deterioration in both services that occurred during the crisis of the 1990s (figures for Chile are available for 1985–93 and for Costa Rica for 1985–89/91). This indicator, therefore, will be excluded from the final evaluation of performance but will be analyzed in this section (Table V.23).

Access of the urban population to potable water in 1963/64 in Chile and Costa Rica, but 1953 in Cuba, was highest in Costa Rica (97%), followed by Cuba (82%) and Chile quite behind (45%). Data for 1970/73 exhibit the same ranking but some closing of the gap: Costa Rica 100%, Cuba 88%, and Chile 69%. Finally, the last data available for the three countries, in 1980/81, exhibited a change in their ranking and a very significant close in the gap: Costa Rica 100%, Chile 91%, and Cuba 90%. Access of the rural population to potable water was lower than among the urban population, but rankings and trends were similar to the latter: at the start Costa Rica (43%), Cuba (15%), and Chile (11%); and in 1980/81 Costa Rica (68%), Chile (44%), and Cuba (33%).

The second indicator is fairly comparable in Chile and Costa Rica, during the entire period of observation, because in both countries it measures access of the urban population to sewerage, but this is not the case with Cuba, as it assesses sanitation (excreta disposal) in a different, shorter period (1953–81). Costa Rica was systematically ahead of Chile on sewerage access and also led Cuba in sanitation. Standardized Cuban data from the three censuses (Table V.23) show that there was stagnation in urban access to sanitation: 95.1% in 1953 and 95.8% in 1981; furthermore sanitation and potable water services had little, and poor, maintenance in the 1980s and severely deteriorated in the 1990s because of the crisis (which could explain the significant increase in rates of certain diseases such as hepatitis or acute diarrhea). Conversely, data available in 1985–89/93 for the other two countries indicate that Costa Rica was able to maintain universal coverage of potable water in urban areas, as well as expand access from 68% to 86% in rural areas, while reaching universal coverage of sewerage for the urban population. Chile enlarged urban access to water from 67% to 97%, and rural access from 44% to 91%, while it extended urban access to sewerage from 67% to 85%.

V. Social Security Coverage

Two indicators of social security are presented in Table V.24: the percentage of the population covered by health care (sickness-maternity) and the percentage of the labor force covered by pensions (old-age, disability, and survivors). Both indicators suffer from the following flaws: (1) There is no series on health-care coverage of the Chilean population; in addition, the series on labor coverage refers to affiliates instead of active contributors (about one-half of the former) and is inflated because it shows a coverage of 90% (105% in 1995) but excludes the overwhelming majority of the self-employed, who are not insured, as well as the armed forces, who have a separate program. Conversely, the series does not take into account welfare pensions paid to the noninsured destitute (*indigente*). An adjusted figure correcting all these distortions had not been released at the time this book was finished. (2) Cuba has never published statistics on either of the two indicators. Data in the table are the author's estimates based on *legal* coverage and other information, but it is improper to use *legal* coverage in Cuba and *statistical* coverage (even with the explained flaws) in the other two countries. (3) The series on health care in Costa Rica excludes protection of the population by the Ministry of Health (when this protection is added to that of social insurance, virtually all the population is covered), while the series on the part of the labor force protected by pensions refers to the contributory program and excludes noncontributory welfare pensions granted to the noninsured destitute (when the two programs are combined, there is virtually universal coverage). (4) Cuban estimates are scattered and end in 1987 (before the recession of the late 1980s and crisis of the 1990s), while data for the other two countries are available until 1993/94 and show the impact of the crisis of the first half of the 1980s. (5) Data on coverage do not provide information on whether treatment for health care is equal for all or discriminates among groups; for instance, all those covered by social insurance in Costa Rica, both contributors and welfare cases, are treated equally, but in Chile about 71% of those insured are in the public system, whose quality of service is worse than the remaining 29% covered by HMOs (ISAPRES). Among the latter, the package of services and quality of the medical attention is commensurate with the amount of premium paid. I have worked 40 years on social security and have done substantial work in the three countries, but I have been unable to elaborate reliable and comparable data on these two indicators. In spite of their importance, therefore, they will not be included in the final ranking of performance, although are briefly discussed below.

In my opinion, based on the above data and qualitative information gathered through many years of research, coverage on both health care and pensions in the three countries is very similar and virtually universal if all existing protective programs are combined. Table V.24 suggests, however, some differences in the impact of the crisis on social insurance coverage. Before the first crisis in Chile, pension coverage was consistently growing but decreased from a peak of 76% in 1973 to 61% in 1980; during the second, more severe crisis, coverage further dropped to 57%; thereafter coverage steadily increased, but the previous peak was not surpassed until 1990 (17 years later). In Costa Rica population coverage by health care has steadily risen since 1960, peaking at 84% in 1979. In the midst of the crisis (1982) it diminished to 68%, but it went back up, and the previous peak was surpassed in 1989 (10 years latter). The recovery of peak coverage in the pension program, however, took longer (15 years). But in Costa Rica social welfare pensions and other social safety nets, established prior to the crisis, operated as cushions for those who lost coverage during the crisis, which was not the case in Chile. Unfortunately I am unable to trace trends in coverage and the impact of the crisis in Cuba; nevertheless, I analyzed in part 3 the drastic deterioration in real pensions as well as the severe problems suffered by pensioners in terms of access to food, transportation, and medical services.

W. Housing Units Built

Two difficulties are confronted in this indicator: there are no data for 1960 and after 1989 in Costa Rica and for 1960–73 in Chile (except for an annual average between 1960 and 1970); and in Cuba, figures for 1960–79 include the "state civilian sector" and the cooperatives but exclude public dwellings built by the military and by the private sector. To partly cope with the first problem, the comparison will begin in 1965 and use the annual average available for Chile. Concerning the second problem, data on military housing were published in Cuba only between 1981 and 1987, and the number was relatively small; furthermore, in Costa Rica there are no armed forces, and military housing is probably not included in the Chilean series either. Private housing construction in Cuba, particularly after the mid-1960s, became rare because of the lack of construction materials, and it was virtually nonexistent in the 1970s (but boomed between 1980 and 1986). These problems, therefore, do not make the indicator unsuitable for use in the final evaluation of performance.

According to Table V.25, Costa Rica had the highest number of dwelling units built per 1,000 inhabitants during the entire period except for three years (1965, 1970, and 1985, when Chile's was higher); Chile was second except in two years (1975 and 1982, when Cuba's was higher), and Cuba had the lowest number. The number of dwellings built in Costa Rica steadily climbed in the period, except for the years of the crisis (1982–83 and 1985). In Chile the number declined between 1974 and 1979 (as government housing was cut), oscillated between 1980 and 1986, and steadily rose thereafter, reaching a record in 1993 (when the overwhelming majority of houses were built by the private sector). In Cuba government housing declined after 1965 (except for a small rise between 1972 and 1976), there were no houses built by cooperatives until 1981, and very few were constructed by the private sector until the 1980s. There was a significant increase in the first half of the 1980s, mostly by the private sector, and a decline during the crisis.

3. The Ranking of Performance

All of the 20 selected indicators in the previous section are summarized in Table V.26, showing the corresponding scores for the following years: 1960 (start of available data for all countries, and the beginning of the Costa Rican and Cuban models), 1973 (end of Allende's administration and eve of neoconservative model in Chile), 1980 (before the regional crisis began), 1990 (when Chile and Costa Rica were out of the crisis and before a crisis began in Cuba), and 1993 (the last year for which we have standardized data). Based on those scores, three types of rankings will be estimated to evaluate the performance of the three models.

(1) *Absolute* ranking will order the countries from 1 to 3 (1 being the best performance and 3 the worst), based on the indicator scores for 1980 and 1993. The years 1960 and 1973 were excluded from the comparison because of the lack of many Cuban indicators. An example of absolute ranking is infant mortality, which will be based on the corresponding rates in 1980 and 1993; the lowest rate will be ranked 1 and the highest 3. In three indicators (economic growth, inflation, trade volume and balance) annual averages will be used to avoid relying on an abnormal year. Arithmetic averages in each of the four clusters (domestic macroeconomic, external economic, distribution and employment, and social standards) will be calculated, and these will be merged into two clusters (economic and social) and, finally, into a total average for all indicators.

(2) *Relative improvement* ranking will also order the countries from 1 to 3, but comparing the start year (1960 for Chile and Costa Rica, and 1973 for Chile) and the end year of 1993 for all countries, in order to measure the change during the period of operation of the model. For instance, the largest reduction in the infant mortality rate will be ranked 1 and the smallest will be ordered 3. Similar arithmetic averages like those for the absolute ranking will also be estimated.

(3) *Indices* for each of the 20 indicators in all five years of observation will give 1 to the best performance and 100 to the worst. These indices then will be combined into each of the four clusters. Finally, the four cluster indices will be merged into an *index of socioeconomic development* based on

different weights assigned to the clusters, as well as to the merging of the last two clusters.

The ranking of the 20 indicators among the three countries will be done considering that the best performance in each is as follows: (1) the highest economic growth rates per capita; (2) the largest GDP per capita in U.S. dollars; (3) the highest gross domestic investment as percentage of GDP; (4) the lowest inflation rate; (6) the most positive fiscal balance (highest surplus or lowest deficit); (6) the smallest agricultural share in GDP and the biggest industrial share; (7) the smallest export concentration (the most diversified export mix); (8) the smallest import shares of agriculture and fuel, and the biggest import share of machinery-transport; (9) the least trade partner concentration (the most diversified trade partners); (10) the highest trade volume per capita and the most positive trade balance per capita (biggest surplus or lowest deficit); (11) the smallest external debt per capita; (12) the lowest proportion of the labor force in the primary sector (agriculture) and the highest in the secondary sector (industry and construction); (13) the biggest growth in the real mean wage; (14) the lowest national open unemployment rate; (15) the lowest illiteracy rate (15 years and over); (16) the highest enrollment rates in secondary and higher education; (17) the lowest infant mortality; (18) the longest life expectancy; (18) the lowest rates of five contagious diseases; and (20) the highest number of dwelling units built (per 1,000 inhabitants).

Four major problems encountered in these rankings and the way they will be dealt with are subsequently summarized. First, there are only three countries, and the ranking range is quite narrow: from 1 to 3 (from best to worst). The ideal would have been to include all Latin American countries or, at least, a larger sample of them, but this was not possible, as this book shows the enormous difficulties found in gathering reliable and comparative data for the three countries studied. Future research based on this book's approach could expand the number of countries in the comparison and the ranking range. In order to contrast these limited observations with international comparisons, I will show the ranking of the three countries based on the UNDP human development index between 1980 and 1994 and other international rankings. Second, the absolute ranking does not properly show the relative distance among the three countries; in some cases, two countries may have very close scores and yet will be ordered differently. Furthermore, the absolute and relative improvement rankings (1 to 3 in both) are not ideal for averaging and aggregation. These problems are tackled with the third type of indicator, which both expands the ranking spread from 1 to 100 and permits a better aggregation of the indicators. Third, the relative improvement ranking contrasts different periods in Chile (1973–93) versus those in Costa Rica and Cuba (1960–93), a problem that will be dealt with by means of an additional comparison of the three countries in two standardized periods (1960–93 and 1973–93), followed by an analysis of the potential changes in ranking resulting from that exercise. Fourth, the weight issue (compounded by the small number of indicators in the third cluster: 3 versus 5–6 in the other three clusters) will be coped with by using various combinations of weights and a merger of the last two clusters to determine if any significant difference results from diverse weights.

A. Absolute Ranking

Table V.27 shows the ranking of the three countries based on the 20 indicators in the years 1980 and 1993 (the years 1960 and 1973 are excluded from the comparison because of the lack of a large number of indicators for Cuba in the first cluster). First I will assess the ranking of the countries in each of the four clusters in the years 1980 and 1993, based on arithmetic averages of the indicators in each cluster (averaging the components in indicators 6, 8, 10, 12, 16, and 19) for a total of 20 observations (see averages in Table V.28). In 1980 Chile ranked 1 in the first and second clusters, 2 in the third, and 3 in the fourth; Costa Rica ranked 3 in the first cluster, 2 in the second, 3 in the third, and 1 in the fourth; and Cuba ranked 2 in the first cluster, 3 in the second, 1 in the third, and 2 in the fourth. In 1993 Chile continued to be 1 in the first and second clusters, improved to 1 in the third (tied with Costa Rica), and remained 3 in the fourth; Costa Rica improved to 2 in the first cluster, remained at 2 in the second, improved to 1 in the third (tied with Chile), and continued to be at 1 in the fourth; and Cuba deteriorated to 3 in the first cluster, remained at 3 in the second, deteriorated to 3 in the third, and remained at 2 in the fourth. The merging of the two economic clusters (domestic macroeconomic and external economic) leads to the same ranking in both years: Chile, Costa Rica, and Cuba. The merging of the two social clusters (distribution and employment, and social standards) helps to correct for the smaller number of indicators in the third cluster (3) versus the fourth cluster (6) and results in the following ranking: in 1980, Costa Rica, Cuba (almost tied with Costa Rica), and Chile, but in 1990 it changes to Costa Rica, Chile and Cuba. The total average (four clusters) shows the same ranking in both years: Chile, Costa Rica, and Cuba (the gap between the last two expands in 1993).

In summary, Chile performed best (1) in the economic indicators in both years, had the worst (3) performance in the social indicators in 1980, but improved to medium (2) in 1993; Costa Rica had a medium performance in economic indicators and the best in the social indicators in both years; and Cuba had the worst performance in the economic indicators in both years, and medium performance in social indicators in 1980 but the worst in 1993. The timing of the crisis was different: in Chile and Costa Rica it took place in the first half of the 1980s and was more than compensated for by the recovery of the second half of the 1980s and the early 1990s (albeit stronger in Chile than in Costa Rica); in Cuba the crisis occurred in the 1990s, thus the significant deterioration; but notice that Cuba ranked worst also in 1980 long *before* the crisis began in that country. If the two unreliable indicators (1 and 4: economic growth and inflation) are excluded from the rankings, only one change is seen: in 1980 Costa Rica improves from 3 to 2 while Cuba deteriorates from 2 to 3. All other rankings remain the same.

If all the 20 indicators plus the components of a single indicator are counted in Table V.27 (the components of indicators 6, 8, 10, 12, 16, and 19), for a total of 30 observations, the following changes are observed between 1980 and 1993 (Table V.28). Chile's rankings remained unmodified in 16 observations, improved in 11 (1, 3, 8—all, 10—1, 14, 16—1, 19—1, and 20), and deteriorated in only 3 (4, 6—1, and 19—1). Costa Rica's rankings did not change in 12 observations, improved in 11 (1, 4, 5, 6—1, 12—both, 14, 18, and 19—3), and deteriorated in 7 (3, 8—2, 9, 15, 17, and 20). Cuba's rankings continued unchanged in 12 observations, improved in only 5 (6—1, 9, 15, 17, and 19—1), and worsened in 13 (1, 5, 6—1, 8—1, 10—1, 11, 12—both, 14, 16—1, 18, and 19—3). The recovery in Chile has led to improvement of both economic and social indicators, and in Costa Rica to an enhancement in a similar number of indicators as in Chile (more social than economic), while the crisis of the 1990s has adversely affected Cuba equally in economic and social indicators.

B. Relative Improvement Rankings

The scores and rankings of the relative improvement indicators are exhibited in Table V.27, usually measuring the change that occurred between 1973 and 1993 in Chile and between 1960 and 1993 in Costa Rica and Cuba. Differing (shorter, more recent) periods are used for indicators 2, 6, 13, 15, and 16, because of lack of data; indicator 10 is made up of annual averages comparing two periods; and indicators 1 and 4 are excluded because of both their unreliability and the impossibility of doing a comparison between two points in time or period averages (see notes to Table V.27).

Twelve examples of important economic and social indicators scores and rankings are summarized below; years in the comparison are those noted above unless specified, and rankings of the three countries (always in the same order: Chile, Costa Rica, and Cuba) are given within parentheses at the end: (2) GDP per capita increased, between 1985 and 1994, by U.S.$4,038 in Chile, U.S.\$1920 in Costa Rica, and U.S.\$500 in Cuba (ranking: 1, 2, and 3, respectively); (3) gross domestic investment as percentage of GDP rose by 18.3 points in Chile and 6 points in Costa Rica, but declined by 12.8 points in Cuba (1, 2, and 3); (5) the fiscal balance as a percentage of GDP in Chile turned from a deficit to a surplus, gaining 26.5 points, and the deficit was cut by 2.1 points in Costa Rica but expanded (as a percentage of GSP) from zero to 33.7 points in Cuba, the last two countries between 1965 and 1993 (1, 2, and 3); (7) export concentration shrank in all countries, by 48 percentage points in Chile, 43 in Costa Rica, and 12 in Cuba (1, 2, and 3); (8) trade partner concentration increased 6 percentage points in Chile and 4 points in Costa Rica but was cut by 46 points in Cuba (3, 2, and 1); (11) the external debt per capita rose in all countries, by U.S.\$1,038 in Chile, U.S.\$1,265 in Costa Rica, and U.S.\$3,426 in Cuba, the comparison ending in 1990 (1, 2, and 3); (13) real mean wages (all between 1973 and 1993) grew by 55 points in Chile and 22 in Costa Rica but diminished by 14 points in Cuba (1, 2, and 3); (14) the open unemployment rate rose by 1.4 points in Chile but declined by 2.8 points in Costa Rica and 4.1 in Cuba (3, 2, and 1); (15) the illiteracy rate (15 years and older) decreased in all countries between 1970/73 and 1992, by 5.3 points in Chile, 5.9 in Costa Rica, and 7.6 in Cuba (3, 2, and 1); (17) the infant mortality rate fell in all countries, by 52 points in Chile, 61 in Costa Rica, and 26 in Cuba (2, 1, and 3); (18) life expectancy climbed in all countries, by 6.4 years in Chile, 14.1 in Costa Rica, and 11.4 in Cuba (3, 1, and 2); and (20) the number of housing units built per 1,000 increased in all three countries, by 5.2 points in Chile, 2.9 in Costa Rica, and 1.9 in Cuba (1, 2, and 3).

The bottom segment of Table V.28 exhibits the arithmetic averages in the four clusters for the three countries, following the same method as for the absolute indicators. Chile ranks at 1 in the first and second clusters, but 3 in the third and 2 in the fourth (tied with Cuba); Costa Rica is ordered at 2 in the first and second clusters, but at 1 in both the third and fourth; and Cuba ranks at 3 in the first and second clusters and at 2 in the third and fourth (tied with Costa Rica). In merged economic indicators the rank is Chile, Costa Rica, and Cuba, while in the merged social indicators the order is Costa Rica, Cuba, and Chile. The total average of all indicators shows Chile first, virtually tied with Costa Rica, and Cuba lagging behind. These rankings are somewhat similar to the absolute indicators, but there are two important exceptions: Costa Rica closes the gap with Chile in the total average, and Cuba is better than Chile in the social-indicator average (same order as the absolute ranking in 1980). The two unreliable indicators are excluded in the relative improvement ranking; hence there is no change here either.

Important differences between the absolute and relative improvement rankings may occur in the same indicator. For instance, the primary share of the labor force in 1993 was lowest in Chile (18.5%), second highest in Costa Rica (22.8%), and highest in Cuba (28.2%); hence the absolute ranking was 1, 2, and 3 respectively. But the period reduction of that share was the largest in Costa Rica (−26.6), followed by Cuba (−10.6) and Chile (−6.6%); thus the relative ranking was 1, 2, and 3, respectively. The rate of open unemployment in 1993 was lowest in Costa Rica (4.1%), followed by Chile (4.5%), and it was highest in Cuba (6.7%); thus the ranking was 1, 2, and 3. But the period reduction in this rate was the largest in Cuba (−4.1%) followed by Costa Rica (−2.8%), while in Chile there was an increase (1.4%); therefore, the ranking shifted to 1, 2, and 3, respectively. In some relative indicators, the improvement becomes increasingly difficult, as the country is advancing to better levels; this is the case of infant mortality and, to a less extent, life expectancy. In 1993 Cuba had the lowest infant mortality rate (10.2), followed by Costa Rica (13.7) and closely by Chile (13.9), and yet the period reduction in that ratio was most impressive in Costa Rica (−60) and Chile (−52), and least in Cuba (−26), partly because the latter had a considerably lower ratio that the other two countries at the outset (if the Chilean comparison had been done beginning in 1960, instead of 1973, the biggest reduction would have been in that country: −105; see below). The case of life expectancy is different: in 1993 Costa Rica had the highest rate (75.7), very closely followed by Cuba (75.4), and Chile had the lowest (72.1), but Costa Rica's achievement was even more remarkable in this indicator because in 1960 it had a lower life expectancy than Cuba (2.4 years less).

As has been noted, the relative improvement indicator of Chile may be distorted because the model (and the comparison) started in 1973, while the models and base year for the other two countries began in 1960. In half of all the observations (indicators and their components) in which that discrepancy occurs, the shift in the base year from 1973 to 1960 would make Chile look better, while in the other half it would make it look worse. An example of the former is the unemployment rate: it was much higher in 1960 (7.1%) than in 1973 (3.1%); therefore, in 1993 the improvement in such a rate would be better when using the 1960 rate instead of that of 1973 (a reduction of 2.6 points instead of an increase of 1.4 points). The same can be said of other indicators such as trade partner concentration, trade balance, composition of the labor force (both components), educational enrollment, infant mortality, life expectancy, and two contagious diseases. However, the use of the year 1960 would make Chile look worse in gross domestic investment/GDP, because it was higher in 1960 (13.9%) than in 1973 (7.9%); hence the increase in 1993 would be smaller (6.4 points instead of 26.5 points). The same is true of other indicators such as fiscal balance, export concentration, import composition, trade volume, external debt per capita, three contagious diseases, and housing units built. These changes will not necessarily generate a modification in rankings, as will be seen later.

Table V.29 has been constructed to determine what difference in ranking, if any, would result from using the start year 1960 instead of 1973 in Chile. Only the 14 indicators that show a difference are included in the table; the other 6 are excluded either because the period of comparison is the same in all countries or because such a comparison is not feasible. The bottom row in each indicator is based on the period 1973–93 for Chile and 1960–93 for the other two countries (thus reproducing the same scores and rankings of Table V.27), while the upper row shows the Chilean score based on the standardized 1960–93 comparison and the potential change in ranking of all three countries. In spite of changes in the Chilean scores, the ranking remains unmodified in eight indicators: 3, 5, 8 (the two components), 10 (the two), 11, 14, 16 (secondary), and 20; but the ranking changes in seven indicators: 7, 9, 12 (the two), 16 (higher), 17, 18, and 19 (all). The use of the base year 1973 for Chile, therefore, distorts only 7 out of 20 indicators.

Changes in rankings are the following: (7) export concentration: Chile deteriorates from 1 to 2, while Costa Rica improves from 2 to 1; (9) trade partner concentration: Chile improves from 3 to 2, while Costa Rica falls from 2 to 3; (12) labor force composition: in both Chile improves from 3 to 2 while Cuba worsens from 2 to 3; (16) higher educational enrollment: Chile gets better, from 3 to 2, while Cuba falls from 2 to 3; (17) infant mortality: Chile improves from 2 to 1 while Costa Rica declines from 1 to 2; (18) life expectancy: Chile increases from 1 to 3 while Cuba falls from 2 to 3; and (19) contagious diseases: in three Chile deteriorates and in two it improves, while rankings change mostly in Costa Rica and to a lesser extent in Cuba. In summary, Chile improves in six indicators and deteriorates in only two, while Costa Rica improves in three and falls in three, and Cuba deteriorates in five and improves in one. With a shift to the 1960 base, therefore, the Chilean ranking in relative improvement would be even better than in Table V.28, while Cuba's would be worse and Costa Rica's even. A more sophisticated treatment of this problem will be made with the indices in the next section.

C. Indices and Combined Index Ranking

Table V.30 exhibits the indices estimated with data from the comparative Tables V.3–V.25 and the summary Table V.26. The indices assign 100 points to the best performance and 1 to the worst; however, rescaling is used when there are negative signs (indicators 1, 4, and 10—balance), giving zero to the lowest figure. These indices show data for all the available 20 indicators in the same five years as in Table V.26: 1960, 1973, 1980, 1990, and 1993. Figures for indicators 1, 4, and 10 (economic growth, inflation, and trade) are annual averages in the same periods specified in Table V.26.

These indices are superior to the absolute and relative improvement ranking methods in five ways: (1) the spread of the range, which was 1 to 3 in the previous two methods, is expanded here to 1 to 100 (zero to 100 when rescaling), thus better showing the differences in ranking among the three countries; (2) the indices can be more properly combined by clusters and into a single index of economic and social development; (3) different weights can be assigned to the clusters, and the last two (social) clusters combined (to correct for the small number of indicators in cluster 3); (4) the Chilean estimates for 1960, as well as the estimates of the other two countries for 1973, permit two standardized period comparisons of the three two countries, between 1960 and 1993 and 1973 and 1993, and the analysis of any resulting changes in ranking in clusters 1 and 3 (correcting any distortions caused by annual averages in economic growth, inflation and trade); and (5) the two unreliable indicators (growth and inflation) can be excluded, and the potential modification in ranking can be better observed.

The combined indices in each of the four clusters are presented in the top segment of Table V.31. The ranking in 1960 and 1973 for the first cluster is Cuba, Costa Rica, and Chile. Cuba's ranking in the macroeconomic cluster is the best because of a higher growth rate and gross domestic investment plus a lower inflation rate than in the other countries, as well as the absence of the two components in the indicator for GDP composition (available for Chile and Costa Rica) and the exclusion of GDP per capita in U.S. dollars in all countries (which adversely affects Cuba). In the first cluster, therefore, there are three observations missing in Cuba in 1960 and four in 1973 (all these were eliminated from the index of the three countries); and in the remaining three to four indicators (two of which are unreliable) Cuba performs best, and its very high score in cluster 1 pulls up the total average for those two years. These flaws seriously affect the first cluster and total averages in 1960 and 1973, thus making them unreliable for the comparison and ranking. The remaining three clusters, nevertheless, are reliable and suitable for ranking: in 1960 Chile ranks best in the three, Costa Rica second in all except the fourth (3), and Cuba third in all except the fourth (2). In 1973 Costa Rica ranks first in all except the third (3), Chile ranks second except in the third (1), and Cuba ranks third except in the third (2).

The order in 1980 is the same as in the absolute ranking in clusters 2 (Chile, Costa Rica, and Cuba) and 4 (Costa Rica, Cuba, and Chile), but different in clusters 1 (Cuba becomes 1 and Chile 2, and Costa Rica remains 3) and 3 (Costa Rica becomes 1 and Cuba 3, and Chile remains 2). The order in

1993 is the same as in the absolute ranking in the first three clusters (Chile, Costa Rica, and Cuba), but reverses in the fourth cluster (from Costa Rica, Cuba, and Chile to Chile, Costa Rica, and Cuba). The discrepancies in ranking between the absolute and indices methods are probably the result of the more accurate measurement of differences in the latter; potential distortions created by the two unreliable indicators (economic growth and inflation) will be analyzed later, based on Table V.32. The 1993 rankings are unchanged (Chile, Costa Rica, and Cuba) in the two standardized comparisons (1960–93 and 1973–93) for the first two clusters, shown in the last two columns of Table V.31, and the range among the three countries does not change substantially either (the standardized comparisons do not affect clusters 3 and 4).

An attempt to correct the potential distortions created by the smaller number of indicators in cluster 3 is made by merging it with cluster 4 in section 5 of the top half of Table V.31. There are no changes in either the rankings of clusters 3 and 4 (separate or merged) in the years 1960 and 1993 or the ranking of social standards in 1973 and 1980. The merging, nevertheless, generates changes in the ranking of the year 1990: in the third cluster the order is Chile, Cuba, and Costa Rica, in the fourth cluster Cuba, Chile, and Costa Rica, and in the merged cluster Cuba, Chile, and Costa Rica. As noted already, the period standardization does not affect the last two clusters and their merging.

The combination of all four clusters into an "Index of Economic and Social Development" is shown in the bottom half of Table V.31, assigning four different weights: three to the four separate clusters in section A (equal in all, $25+25+20+30$, and $25+25+15+35$) and one to the merged two last clusters in section B ($25+25+50$). The last three weights try to adjust for the small number of indicators in the third cluster. Surprisingly, the ranking of the three countries is the same regardless of the divergent weights and the years of observation. Rankings by year follow: in 1960 Cuba, Costa Rica, and Chile (the problems explained above for this year and 1973 rend the index unreliable); in 1973 Costa Rica, Cuba, and Chile (mainly because of flaws in Cuba's first cluster and the severe crisis in Chile at the end of Allende's administration); in 1980 Chile, Costa Rica, and Cuba (in this year all Cuban indicators for the first cluster are available, and the comparison is meaningful because the crisis had not occurred in any of the three countries); in 1990 Chile, Costa Rica, and Cuba (in this year the first two countries were in the process of recovery, and the severe crisis had not begun in Cuba, although it was hurt somewhat by the recession during the Rectification Process); and in 1993 the same order as in 1990 but with a significant deterioration in the Cuban score (because of the severity of the crisis in that year).

The three countries' ranking scores, regardless of the weights used, are very close in the years 1973 and 1980; this is particularly important in the latter because the comparison is much more accurate than in the former. The reason for such proximity may be the good performance of Cuba in economic growth and inflation, both measured in the period 1981–89, when the crisis hit Chile and Costa Rica. But those two indicators have poor reliability in Cuba, and, when excluded from the comparison, the range between Cuba and Chile grows considerably (Table V.32). The range among the three countries significantly expands in the years 1990 and 1993 but decreases somewhat in the second and third weights in section A and in weight B, and yet the extreme range between Chile and Cuba is still quite significant, especially in 1993. The standardized period comparison does not show any change in the ranking of the three countries, regardless of the weight used: the 1960–93 comparison in Table V.31 shows a slightly narrower range than in the year 1993, while the 1974–93 comparison exhibits a slightly wider range. This is probably a result of excluding the bad performance during the last two years of Allende's administration.

The exclusion of the two unreliable indicators in Table V.32 does not change the ranking of the three countries in 1980, 1990, and 1993 (the most reliable years for the comparison) but systematically modifies the ranking in 1960 (from Cuba, Costa Rica, and Chile to Cuba, Chile, and Costa Rica) and in 1973 (from Costa Rica, Cuba, and Chile to Costa Rica, Chile, and Cuba). The range, nevertheless, is significantly expanded between the best and worst performers regardless of the years and weights. For instance, in 1993, the range between Chile and Cuba based on the first weight in Table V.31 is 32.9 points and increases to 39.9 points in Table V.32; with the second weight it rises from 30.4 to 37.4, and with the fourth weight (B) from 28.7 to 33.7. The two standardized period comparisons in the last two columns of Table V.32 exhibit the same rankings as in 1993, but, unlike Table V.31, the extreme range is virtually the same in all three cases regardless of weights.

D. Summary of Rankings and Comparisons with International Rankings

When combining the four clusters, the three types of rankings (absolute, relative improvement, and indices), despite diverse methods, consistently order the performance of the three countries similarly: (1) the absolute rankings for 1980 and 1993 are Chile, Costa Rica, and Cuba; (2) the relative improvement ranking (1960–93 for Costa Rica and Cuba, and 1974–93 for Chile), is Chile first, almost tied with Costa Rica, and Cuba lagging behind; and (3) the index of economic and social development in 1980, 1990, and

1993 (regardless of different weights), ranks the three countries in the same order: Chile, Costa Rica, and Cuba, albeit in 1980 the range is very narrow and Costa Rica and Cuba are very close. Furthermore, the standardized comparisons (1960–93 and 1973–93) show the same rankings (regardless of weights), and the exclusion of the two unreliable indicators (economic growth and inflation) does not modify such rankings but expands the range between Chile and Cuba.

The rankings based on the four separated clusters are relatively similar but not as consistent as when combined. (1) The absolute ranking shows Chile best in the two economic clusters (in 1980 and 1993) but worst in the social indicators combined in 1980 although second best in 1993; Costa Rica has a medium performance in the two economic clusters and the best performance in the two social clusters combined (in both years); and Cuba has the worst performance in the economic indicators (both years), but a medium ranking in social indicators combined in 1980 and the worst in 1993. (2) The relative improvement ranking is the same for the two economic clusters (Chile, Costa Rica, and Cuba) and for the two social clusters combined (Costa Rica, Cuba, and Chile); separately, in the third cluster Cuba is medium (Chile is worst), and in the fourth cluster two are tied. (3) The indices show different rankings in the four clusters in 1980: in the first Cuba, Chile, and Costa Rica (but when growth and inflation are excluded it changes to Chile, Cuba, and Costa Rica); in the second cluster Chile, Costa Rica, and Cuba; in the third Costa Rica, Chile, and Cuba; and in the fourth Costa Rica, Cuba, and Chile. In the years 1990 and 1993 the ranking is the same in the four clusters: Chile, Costa Rica, and Cuba, and the same is true of the standardized comparisons and the exclusion of the two unreliable indicators (the range expands in the last two types of comparisons).

As already noted, the rankings do not place the three countries either within the Latin American region or in an international context. At least two international rankings included the three countries in comparisons done in the 1960s and 1970s (Index of Social Progress: Estes 1984), and the late 1970s (Physical Quality of Life: ODC 1983), but they are not available for the 1980s and 1990s. Gonzalez (1995) compared the three countries in several years (as recently as 1992), within Latin America and the Caribbean, through a socioeconomic development index, but he did not show the indicators and how they were measured, making it impossible to evaluate them and his rankings.

The only available series covering a long period and published annually that ranks the three countries (within a total number of countries rising from 160 to 175) and explains in detail the methodology and measurement of the indicators is the Human Development Index (HDI) estimated by the UNDP

(1991–97) for the years 1980 to 1994 (Table V.33). Such a series shows a world ranking, exclusively among the three countries, similar to the one in this book: in five years the order is Chile, Costa Rica, and Cuba, and in two it is Costa Rica, Chile, and Cuba (rankings of Chile and Costa Rica are very close). Between 1980/88 and 1994, Chile's world ranking improves from 38 to 30 (mainly during the first democratic government), while Costa Rica's improves from 40 to 33 (28 versus 33 in Chile in 1992, and 31 versus 33 in 1993), but Cuba's deteriorates from 62 to 86. Within the 20 countries of Latin America, the order among the three countries is as follows: Chile first in five out of the seven years, Costa Rica first in two years (almost tied with Chile in one year) and second in the remaining years, and Cuba always last. The rankings among the 20 countries are as follows: Chile and Costa Rica oscillate from 1 to 4, and Cuba from 10 to 12. The HDI is based on three indices with equal weight: "real" GDP per capita in PPP$, literacy and educational enrollment, and life expectancy. I have already expressed reservations on the accuracy of the first index, but it is important to note that the HDI takes heavily into consideration the social indicators on which Cuba had a very good performance until the crisis of the 1990s. The UNDP ranking, therefore, not only confirms the three types of rankings used in this book but also orders the three countries among 175 nations in the world and 20 within Latin America and shows trends that are similar to those detected here.

A Human Suffering Index, available for several years, the most recent at the end of the 1980s (Population Crisis Committee 1992), is based on the arithmetic average of 10 indicators with equal weights (life expectancy, daily calorie supply, clean drinking water, infant immunization, secondary school enrollment, GNP per capita, inflation, communication technology, political freedom, and civil rights). It ranked 141 countries, with Costa Rica at 40, Chile 43, and Cuba 45. Within the 20 Latin American countries the order was Costa Rica 1, Chile 3, and Cuba 5 (Table V.33). Some of the problems detected in this index are: the indicator on GNP per capita is highly questionable (it ranks the three countries equally); a weight of 50% is given to five social indicators, while 20% is assigned to only two economic indicators, and the remaining 30% to three technological and civic-political indicators; and Chile ranked fairly well in civic-political freedoms although the survey was taken during the last years of the military government. In spite of these problems, this index also confirms my own findings.

In part II compared the three models in terms of their economic and political freedoms. I have not assessed such freedoms in this book, but two international indices measure them. The first is Messick (1995), who developed a Freedom Index based on six economic freedom indicators: hold property, earn a living, operate a business, invest one's earnings, trade internationally, and participate in the market; he gave equal weights to the six indicators and ranked 82 countries, ordering them from 1 (best) to 82 (worst). The world ranking of the three countries in 1995 was Chile 22, Costa Rica 43, and Cuba 79. Within 13 Latin American countries for which data were available, the ranking was Chile 2, Costa Rica 6, and Cuba 13 or last (Table V.33). These rankings are also commensurate with my analysis in the policy sections. The second world ranking is the Index of Political Rights and Civil Liberties available for several years, the three most recent, including the three countries, being 1988–89, 1989–90, and 1993–94 (McColm et al. 191, 1992; Karatnycky 1996). The latest survey includes 191 countries and is based on 8 indicators of political rights and 13 of civil liberties, with scores ranging from 1 (best) to 7 (worst). The world ranking of the three countries in the three years is as follows: Costa Rica 6, 7, and 31; Chile 41, 45, and 57; and Cuba 153, 173, and 178. The three countries' fall in the ranking cannot be explained by the addition of 8 countries between the last two surveys; also, unless there was a change in methodology, it is highly questionable that there was such deterioration in Costa Rica and Chile (precisely when democracy was restored in the 1990s). The ranking within Latin America, nevertheless, is fairly consistent: Costa Rica is always 1, Chile improves from 4 to 2, and Cuba stagnates at 20 (Table V.33).

In summary, in virtually all the rankings (this and international ones) Costa Rica ranks either first or second on economic and social performance and first in political and civic freedoms, but second in economic freedoms (more state intervention). Chile ranks first or second in economic and social performance, first in economic freedoms (least state intervention), but second (far behind Costa Rica) in political and civic freedoms (although within Latin America it improves with the return to democracy in the 1990s). Cuba ranks third (lagging behind the other two countries, and among the worst in the world) in economic and social performance (but much better in the latter than in the former, particularly until the crisis), and third in both economic and political-civic freedoms (among the worst countries in the world). Costa Rica was able to achieve a remarkable socioeconomic performance without sacrificing political and civic freedoms, albeit with a moderate curtailment of economic freedoms (enhanced in the late 1980s and 1990s) but reducing social costs of the transition. Chile had the best economic performance and was medium or worst in social performance (better in the 1990s), but at the cost of a significant curtailment of political-civic liberties for 17 years, and with the widest economic freedoms but at a high social cost during the transition. Cuba had the worst economic performance but a medium to best social performance (the latter reversed with the crisis and became the worst in the 1990s) and paid the highest costs in suppression of political-civic and economic freedoms.

4. The Potential Impact of Nonsystemic Factors

Is the performance evaluated in the previous two sections the exclusive result of the *model* or the *system* and its policies, or are there nonsystemic factors that might have influenced such outcomes? The answer to this crucial question is negative, but, as already noted, it is not possible to quantify and control those other factors although they will be analyzed in a qualitative manner and a tentative conclusion reached in this section. In part I there was an attempt to control, as much as possible, some of the nonsystemic factors, but we still detected some advantages and disadvantages in the three countries. Two types of factors will be evaluated in this section: physical and other domestic, and exogenous.

A. Physical and Other Domestic Factors

The three countries are at a similar level of development, a point that has been amply demonstrated by both the analysis and rankings in this book as well as by international comparisons and rankings. We identified, however, certain endogenous differences among the three countries concerning population growth per capita, agricultural land per individual in the labor force, production of domestic fuel, and military expenditures.

Costa Rica has two disadvantages in comparison to the other two countries: the highest population growth rate and the lowest agricultural land per capita in the labor force; Cuba has the advantage of the lowest population growth (quite similar to Chile in the 36 years of observation); and Chile has the benefit of the highest agricultural land per capita (very closely followed by Cuba). In spite of these two handicaps, Costa Rica was capable to achieve a medium level in economic growth, increase agricultural output and exports considerably, and improve its self-sufficiency in foodstuffs, thus reducing the share of imports of those goods. Chile had a better performance than Costa Rica in these three indicators, but it also was better in terms of a lower population growth (almost 40% less) and a much larger agricultural land available (2.5 times more). Furthermore, Costa Rica was able to decrease its export concentration much more than Chile; it is true that the latter's major concentration is on copper, while Costa Rica's is on bananas and coffee, but Chile's diversification of exports has been mainly based on agricultural products. Conversely, Cuba had the poorest performance in all these three indicators despite its two significant advantages: the lowest population growth (half of Costa Rica's) and agricultural land per capita almost twice that of Costa Rica.

Costa Rica has the advantage over the two other countries of more production of hydroelectric energy (94% out of the total), while half of Chile's electrical output is generated by the same source, and only a small fraction of Cuba's. It might be argued that Costa Rica, and to a less extent Chile, enjoy a natural resource that Cuba lacks. Furthermore, the share of fuel imports in the total value of imports was virtually the same in Costa Rica and Chile in 1960 and 1993, but it was about double in Cuba. And yet electricity output per capita in Costa Rica was the smallest of the three countries—Chile and Cuba were very similar—and Cuba enjoyed a huge and cheap supply of fuel from the Soviet Union until the beginning of the 1990s. This factor, therefore, did not seem to play a significant role in performance at least until the 1990s; since then Cuba has been impaired by the drastic cut in supply and elimination of price subsidies from Russia. But one could argue that for 22 years Cuba had an advantage on this factor over the other two countries, and, in spite of the generous subsidies, it was not capable of either developing alternative sources of energy or diversifying its exports in order to generate the hard currency needed to buy fuel abroad.

A domestic factor of considerable importance is the lack of armed forces in Costa Rica and hence of military expenditures, contrasted with large armies and military expenses in Chile and, particularly, in Cuba. The abolition of the army in Costa Rica in 1948 generated a dividend that was invested by the government in the expansion of education, health care, and social security. In 1985 Cuba spent 9.6% of GDP in military expenditures (U.S.$208 per capita), and Chile allocated 7.8% (U.S.$135 per capita), but Costa Rica only 0.7% (U.S.$15 per capita). The shares of GNP substantially decreased in Chile in 1994 (because of the shift to a democratic government, but the per capita was similar) and in Cuba (because of the severity of the crisis and no military involvement abroad, with a dramatic decline in the per capita). Still, in 1990–91 military expenditures as a percentage of combined education and health expenditures were 125% in Cuba and 68% in Chile, but only 5% in Costa Rica (UNDP 1996). One could argue that Cuba was under pressure to spend more on defense because of the potential threat of an U.S. intervention. After all, in 1961 the United States supported (although not with its full might) a small exile invasion that was rapidly defeated by Cuba at the Bay of Pigs. Granted that there has been a possibility for another intervention, it was considerably reduced after the Kennedy-Khrushchev agreement that ended the Missile Crisis of 1962, and it was deterred by the significant costs in human lives for the United States that an armed occupation of Cuba would have provoked. In addition, Cuba defeated the 1961 invasion with very poor military hardware, and the enormous military buildup occurred thereafter. Finally, in the 1990s Cuba has been significantly weakened economically, politically, and socially by the crisis, thus making it more vulnerable to an U.S. intervention, but it has been during this crisis that military expenditures have been cut significantly. Part of the military expenditures resulted from Cuba's direct participation in foreign wars, particularly in Africa, as well as in subversive activities, especially in Latin America. The decline in Cuban military expenditures in the 1990s is partly a result of the withdrawal of Cuban troops abroad and the drastic curtailment or halting of subversion. Last but not least, Cuba received free substantial military aid from the Soviet Union and profited from generous credit, price subsidies, and economic aid in reciprocity for its military collaboration.

The high military expenditures in Chile did not have any justification, as that country was not under any realistic threat of war with or intervention from powerful neighboring countries. In Costa Rica, civil wars in Central America caused both a destabilizing effect and a threat to that country, but the pressure to reestablish the army was unsuccessful. The absence of the military burden, therefore, had a positive influence on Costa Rica's performance, but high military expenditures had a negative effect in the other two countries. And yet, that was largely a policy decision of the Chilean and Cuban governments, which had the option, at least, of reducing considerably their military expenditures. The fact that Chile and Cuba had authoritarian governments, where the armed forces played a crucial role, obviously facilitated the largesse in military expenditures, while the democratic government in Costa Rica was an effective barrier against restoring the armed forces and increasing their expenditures.

Finally, climatological and nature disasters such as earthquakes (in Chile and Costa Rica), hurricanes (in Cuba), and droughts and floods (in all three) have afflicted the three countries in one or two years, but such adverse effects have not substantially harmed performance in the long run, especially considering the long period (21 to 36 years) analyzed in this book.

B. Exogenous Factors: The Role of Foreign Powers

The only exogenous factor that may have affected performance is the role of the superpowers: the United States and the Soviet Union. While Chile and Costa Rica have enjoyed U.S. economic aid and trade (more the latter than the former), the U.S. embargo imposed on Cuba since 1961 has caused negative effects on the island's performance. At the beginning of the 1990s, the Cuban government estimated the cost of the U.S. embargo at about U.S.$30 billion in the 36 years since it was established; by 1998 that estimate had doubled, in only eight years. There is no doubt of the adverse impact of the embargo in Cuba; the questions are in how much degree, in what stage(s), and whether it has been compensated for by other positive factors.

Since the mid-1970s until the beginning of the 1990s Cuba had considerable freedom to trade with European and Latin American countries, as well as with Canada, Japan, and other industrialized nations. In addition, Cuba received more than U.S.$6 billion in credits and loans from many of these countries until 1986, when the government suspended the service of such debt. A major problem that Cuba has faced (as important or more so than the embargo) has been its incapacity to diversify its exports (reduce its significant concentration on sugar) in order to generate hard currency to buy imports and balance its foreign trade. Last but not least, between 1960 and 1990 Cuba received the equivalent of about U.S.$65 billion from the Soviet Union (without counting other credits and aid from the CMEA, Eastern European countries, and China) under very generous conditions. Furthermore, two-thirds of that aid was in nonrepayable donations in the form of price subsidies, and Cuba paid virtually nothing on the one-third extended in credits and loans. Although there is considerable debate on the exact value of the Soviet economic aid, even the most conservative estimates would place it well above Cuba's calculated losses from the U.S. embargo through the end of the 1980s. In the 1990s, nevertheless, there has been a tightening of the U.S. embargo and other measures (the Torricelli Act of 1992 and the Helms-Burton Act of 1996), which, combined with the collapse of the Soviet camp (and loss of all economic aid), has had adverse effects on the Cuban economy. However, Cuba claims that there is a substantial inflow of foreign investment and, until very recently, argued that the Helms-Burton Act had not hurt such capital inflow (this claim was reversed in 1997).

In summary, until the 1990s the U.S. embargo was a negative factor but was more than compensated for by the Soviet aid. But regardless of the magnitude and generosity of such aid, Cuba was unable to reduce its export concentration and generate significant nontraditional exports to obtain hard currency in order to buy needed imports and balance its merchandise trade. Rather than the U.S. embargo, the principal cause of Cuba's bad performance has been its economic system, compounded by multiple shifts and errors in policy.

5. The Medium-Term Viability of the Three Models

This section briefly describes policies and results in some indicators under the administrations of Eduardo Frei Jr. in Chile and José Figueres Jr. in Costa

Rica, both in 1994–97, as well as in Cuba in 1995–97. As explained in part I, the lack of sufficient information on such policies and the 20 indicators has impeded the incorporation of these years into the last policy stage and in the measurement of performance in the three countries. The purpose of this section is to provide basic information to the reader on what has happened in these years and to use it (together with the analysis above) in evaluating the viability of the three models in the near term. The description of policies and outcomes will follow the same order of the country parts, particularly the summary table. Table V.33 exhibits available data for 12 of the 20 indicators of performance between 1993 and 1997, contrasting the latest year used in the previous evaluation and ranking with the new statistics for 1994–97; in a few cases figures for 1993/94 are somewhat different from those reported before, because of revisions in the data or new series; unless specified, comparisons thereafter are made between 1993 and 1997.

A. Chile

President Frei's administration continued the *Concertación* (coalition of Christian Democrats and moderate Socialists) and basically the same policies introduced by Aylwin with some minor changes summarized below (sources for this section are Table V.34; ECLAC 1996a, 1996b, 1996c, 1997c; Arenas de Mesa 1997; Ministry of Finance 1997, 1998; Raczynski 1997).

The privatization process was renewed in some areas: electricity, coal, ports and sea transport, and railroad freight. The size of the state, nevertheless, has been stagnant at 25% of GDP: state productive and social service functions have declined, but its regulatory powers have substantially expanded. There has been an emphasis on better governmental policy coordination through the creation of ministerial committees in several areas (social, modernization, and productive development), and there is a project to demote CORFO as a ministry and merge it, again, with the Ministry of Economics. After a slowdown in GDP in 1994 to 4.1% (2.4% per capita, due to the adjustment), there were high growth rates in 1995–97: 8.5%, 7.2%, and 6.5% (6.6%, 5.6%, and 4.8% per capita, respectively), for 13 years of uninterrupted economic growth. This, combined with some policy fine-tuning, led to steady increases in gross domestic investment from 21.3% to 24.4%; a decline in foreign investment in 1995 (due to the Mexican crisis) was followed by a threefold jump in 1996 (holding in 1997), and total investment kept rising (peaking in 1997). An adjustment policy was applied in 1994; the interest rate was raised above international levels in 1995 (another rise occurred at the start of 1998) to counteract inflationary pressures and attract more foreign capital. Stricter monetary policies were adopted in 1996, and amendments to the tax code led to a decline in tax evasion (new taxes on alcohol, tobacco, and fuels were planned for early 1998). These policies were successful in curbing inflation from 12.% to 6% and maintaining a fiscal surplus (in spite of an increase in expenditures) that averaged 2.3% of GDP in 1995–97.

The development strategy continues to be the same: outward, mainly based on nontraditional exports, and "growth with equity." Chile was invited to join NAFTA in 1994, and, although its membership has been delayed by negotiations in the U.S. Congress, bilateral agreements were signed with Canada and Mexico; Chile also joined the Asian Pacific Economic Cooperation in 1994 and signed agreements with MERCOSUR and the European Union. These steps further diversified Chilean trade partners. The country maintained a 17% average of trade with the United States but saw an increase in trade with East Asia. The value of imports steadily rose (particularly in 1995–97), but, after a 39% jump in export value in 1995, there was stagnation in 1996–97, due to the high value of the peso, a decline in the profitability of the agro-export sector (partly affected by drought), and the decrease in the world price of copper in 1996. The trade deficit per capita in 1993 (U.S.$71) turned into a surplus in 1994–95 (U.S.$37 and U.S.$100) but became a deficit in 1996–97 (U.S.$73 and U.S.$81). Export concentration on copper climbed from 35% to 43%, because of the decline in some agro-exports and an increase in the world price of copper in 1994–95 and 1997. International reserves slightly increased. The external debt per capita, in current U.S. dollars, rose 18% between 1993 and 1997, but it declined in real dollars and as a percentage of GDP and exports. In 1995 insurance companies and mutual funds were allowed to invest abroad, and banks granted a wider range of foreign financial instruments. A project to reduce import tariffs was postponed in 1997 and again in early 1998 because of political opposition.

Labor policies included the expansion in coverage of collective bargaining, the creation of the National Training Fund to improve skills of the work force, and a raise in the real minimum wage. The 1998 budget allocates 70% to social programs. The urban real mean wage increased 16.4% between 1993 and 1997, and the peak of 1971 was finally surpassed. According to the ILO, open national unemployment annual rates in 1993–96 were 4.5%, 5.9%, 4.7%, and 5.4%, still low by international standards. Official data report urban unemployment rates of 6.6% in 1993 and 6.5% in 1997. Poverty reduction policy has focused on investment in human capabilities and targeted needs of communities and vulnerable groups (women, children, ethnic groups, the elderly) instead of subsidizing individuals or families. A National Program for Overcoming Poverty was launched in 1994 but halted in

1996, although the Committee of Social Ministries continues to coordinate poverty programs. National surveys in 1994 and 1996 show that poverty among households has decreased from 23.2% to 19.7%, while indigence has shrunk from 6.2% to 4.2%. Income distribution, however, remains unchanged. Pensions under U.S.$245 were increased by 10% in 1995 and minimum pensions were supposed to be raised by 5% at the end of 1997. The "Tequila Effect" harmed the stock market in 1995 and provoked the first real negative investment yield of AFPs. The yield turned positive again in 1996–97, but much lower than the 1981–94 average, and the "Asian Flu" of late 1997–98 led to another decline in the stock market and negative yields. The Superintendency of AFPs has modified the ceilings for investment in financial instruments, enacted new regulations to increase transparency and efficiency in the capital market, and opened new avenues for investment. In the health sector emphasis on decentralization and efficiency continued; new policies included a clearer distinction between the Ministry of Health, FONASA, and the health services, and a legal draft submitted to Congress eliminates the 2% fiscal subsidy to ISAPREs and transforms FONASA into public insurance system to make it more competitive with the private sector. Infant mortality dwindled from 13.9 to 11.8 between 1992 and 1996, and no data are available on life expectancy and contagious diseases. Reforms in education that began in 1996 have expanded spending and teachers' training programs and strive for better quality and linkages with the productive sector; priority has been assigned to preschool, primary, and secondary education, although resources to higher education have increased too. The illiteracy rate decreased from 5.7% to 4.8% in 1992–95, but no data are available on educational enrollment. A new housing program launched in 1997 targets indigent populations living in camps, and there has been an increase in fiscal resources allocated to housing.

The above analysis shows continuity in policies in 1994–97 and good performance in all indicators except a few: stagnation in export values and faster growing import values, which led to a trade deficit, increased export concentration, a rising national unemployment rate, and no change in income distribution, which is quite unequal. The East Asian crisis has harmed Chile, as 33% of total exports (including 31% of all copper and 59% of all fish meal) are with that region, and the world price of copper declined in 1998. Preliminary figures for 1998 show a slowdown of GDP growth and a deterioration in the trade balance and unemployment, but a decline in inflation. The fall in the stock market appears to be similar to that of 1995, but it might worsen. In 1995 and late 1997 to mid-1998, pension funds experienced real negative yields, raising concerns about the need for new investment options now that most of the privatization has been completed (except for the copper industry). These are important areas that need better policies, particularly a reduction in the extreme inequality between income groups, the improvement in the profitability and competitiveness of agriculture, the further development of new exports and markets (to generate trade surpluses), and the search for new financial instruments in which to invest the rapidly growing pension funds. In spite of these problems and a recession in 1998, the viability of the Chilean model in the medium term appears to be fairly high. If the *Concertación* wins the national elections of 1999, the chances of further improvement of the model will be strengthened, but even the conservative opposition now emphasizes social issues.

B. Costa Rica

Part 4 analyzed policies and performance until 1993 and early 1994, this section will provide new information on both for 1994–97 (sources of this section are Table V.34; ECLAC 1996a, 1996b, 1996c, 1997c; CCSS 1997, 1998; CEFSA 1997; MIDEPLAN 1997; BCCR 1998; Sojo 1997; Mesa-Lago 1998; Trejos 1998).

President José M. Figueres ran the 1994 electoral campaign as a champion of populism and the welfare state built by his father and the PLN. He inherited serious financial problems from the Calderón administration: a significant raise in expenditures in an election year, financed mainly with short-term domestic debt that had to be repaid in 1994; the postponement of the adjustment agreement with the World Bank, which withheld loans, and, as a result, the replacing of domestic with external financing at a higher cost. In spite of the growing fiscal deficit and inflation, the president resisted until late in 1994 any stabilization policies as they ran against his electoral promises. Compounding this problem was his personal style of government (different from his father): technocratic and nonengaging in dialogue with the key affected sectors (far from the traditional consensual approach). Eventually he was compelled to design reforms, but it did not happen until late 1994, and they were delayed in the Legislative Assembly, while the economic situation deteriorated. In 1995 Figueres signed an economic pact with the opposition that facilitated the enactment and implementation of the reforms, and in 1996 he reached an alliance with the business sector and called for "national unity" to face the challenge of globalization, which, he argued, demands a reform of Costa Rican institutions in order to increase domestic and external competitiveness, productivity, and economic growth. The president of the Chamber of Industry was appointed minister of economics, and a prominent professor at the university business school was designated minister of finance. The reforms introduced in 1995–97, however, have not significantly affected social programs, although there is an emphasis to make them more effective and cut costs.

Changes in ownership began in 1995 with the privatization of six agro-export public enterprises and authorizing the private domestic and foreign sectors a higher share in ownership and output of electricity (to reduce fiscal subsidies to the state institute in this sector and raise investment) and opening of the infrastructure sector (e.g., ports) to them. A law enacted in 1996 terminated the state monopoly of banking, and later a law regulated the capital market. Several public agencies were shut down or merged and greater autonomy given to the Central Bank to improve the efficiency and competitiveness of public commercial banks. At the end of 1996, a commission was created to find solutions to the high internal debt, including selling additional public enterprises.

The money supply increased substantially in 1994, and, due to the decreased in external capital inflow, the government resorted to a significant increase in bond emission; this, in turn, increased the interest rate and the cost of servicing the domestic debt, transferred more resources to the public sector, and reduced available credit to the private sector. The failure of a large state bank (Banco Anglo-Costarricense) cost the government dearly too, and there was an increasing dollarization of financial investment. Toward the end of 1994 the government began to control monetary emission and submitted a tax reform package (to raise fiscal revenue) to the legislature, but it was not approved until late 1995. The tax reform included a modernization of tax collection, tougher penalties for evasion, a raise in the sales tax (VAT) and selected consumers taxes, and a unified tax for corporations, but, because of the delay in passing the reform, the government had to resort to temporary taxes until the end of 1995. Restrictions in credit, first to the private sector and then to the public sector, would have an adverse effect on growth; in 1996 credit was made easier by lowering the interest rate, but it still remained higher than the international rate and not very attractive to the private sector. The fiscal deficit jumped in 1994 because revenue declined (due to lesser income from the sales tax and a reduction in import tariffs), while expenditures rose because of the high cost of the debt service, wage increases, the heavy burden of public pensions, and subsidies to cover the losses of state enterprises (electricity, oil refining). Cuts in public jobs and restrictive monetary policy began late in 1994, and the expected big increase in fiscal revenue from the tax reform did not come through; hence the deficit continued in 1995 although at a lower rate than in 1994, forcing more restrictions in credit, money supply, and cuts in public expenditures (a reform of pensions was not approved until 1995 and began in 1996). As revenues were insufficient, there was more domestic borrowing. The fiscal deficit rose in 1996 in spite of increased tax revenue and the adjustment program, because of high costs of the debt service, pensions, and higher education.

Because of the late start of the reforms and delays in their implementation, the above measures were not very successful in improving domestic macroeconomic indicators until 1997. The adjustment program had adverse effects on GDP growth, which steadily decreased from 6.1% in 1993 to −0.6% in 1996 (from 3.7% to −1.8% per capita) but recovered to 3.2% in 1997 (1% per capita). Gross domestic investment/GDP steadily diminished from 22.1% to 18.1% in 1993–96 (the BCCR gives much higher percentages and a recovery in 1997 to the 1994 level). The inflation rate jumped from 9% in 1993 to 22.6% in 1995 but decreased to 13.9% in 1996 and 11.5% in 1997. The fiscal deficit grew from 1.9% in 1993 to 6.9% in 1994, was cut to 4.5% in 1995, increased to 5.3% in 1996, and diminished to 4.4% in 1997.

Contrary to the previous indicators, the external sector improved considerably in this period. There was a significant increase in export value (64%), because of growth of domestic production (bigger in bananas than coffee), combined with rising world prices of coffee in 1993–95 (a fall in 1996–97 but still twice the 1993 price) and slightly of bananas, while sugar production increased and then declined toward the end of the period; in addition, there was a significant expansion of nontraditional exports, mainly manufacturing (except textiles because of the adverse effect of NAFTA). Imports expanded only 20% in 1993–96 (but jumped in 1997 for a 42% increase in the entire period) as the result of controls and decline in domestic demand. The trade deficit was cut in half in 1993–96, but, because of the import jump in 1997, it was cut only 9% in the period (per capita it was cut from U.S.$273 to U.S.$120 but expanded to U.S.$227 in 1997, still below 1993). The terms of trade improved throughout the period. Export concentration on coffee remained low but rose from 10% to 12% between 1993 and 1997, mainly because of the very high world price of coffee and to a less extent bananas. Trade partner concentration with the United States was reduced from 55% to 48% in 1993–94, because of more trade within the CACM, an agreement with Mexico, and expanded markets elsewhere, but it then rose to 54% in 1997. The exchange rate was adjusted in the period based on mini-devaluations. The capital inflow decreased, despite an increase in direct investment, partly because of the postponement and delay in disbursement of World Bank funds and less access to foreign credit (the Mexican crisis had an adverse effect in 1995 too). The total external debt in current U.S. dollars per capita declined in the period 1993–96 but rose somewhat in 1997; in per capita it was U.S.$1182 in 1993 and U.S.$1126 in 1997; there was a decrease in the debt in real dollars as well as a percentage of exports.

Despite the economic deterioration, social indicators either improved, were stagnant, or deteriorated slightly. The national open unemployment rate remained almost unchanged in 1993–94 at 4.1% but rose to 5.2% in 1995 and 6.2% in 1996 (because of the recession); it declined to 5.7% in 1997 with the modest recovery, still higher than in 1993. The government began a program in 1995 to infuse more flexibility in wage setting, particularly in the public sector. Real mean wages (based on 1980) rose from 94.7 to 96.2, still below the 1980 level. According to ECLAC, poverty incidence among households was reduced from 25% to 21% in 1992–94 and indigence incidence from 10% to 8%; recent estimates by Trejos show even better results: cuts of poverty incidence among households from 29.4% to 20.7% between 1992 and 1997 and of indigence from 9.3% to 5.7%. Income distribution, measured by the Gini coefficient in the same period, however, was stagnant in urban areas and deteriorated in rural ones. Several improvements occurred in social security pensions: (1) the incorporation of the teachers' independent fund into the CCSS and the tightening of its entitlement conditions (there was a teachers' strike to defend their privileged system, but the government won it); (2) the adjustment to inflation of the state debt to the CCSS, which had been paying a real yield of 3% since 1993; and (3) better investment practices that led to real positive yields particularly in 1995–97; and (4) a general financial surplus in all CCSS schemes in 1994. An overall reform of social security pensions proposes new increases in the retirement age, calculating pensions according to the working life of the insured, and creation of a mandatory supplementary program administered by both public and private institutions. Figueres endorsed the health reform designed by the Calderón administration and continued its implementation: (1) the Ministry of Health was restructured, and it retained the direction, supervision, and promotion functions, while the CCSS was entrusted with preventive, curative, and rehabilitation care, and part of the ministry personnel was transferred to the CCSS; (2) the CCSS was given financing-buying and provision functions, the former centralized, but the latter decentralized through quasi markets; and (3) in 1997 "management commitment" agreements began being signed with the CCSS to decentralize provision of primary health care, but within the CCSS (EBAIS), not mainly with private entities. The infant mortality rate declined from 13.7 to 11.8 in 1993–96 (no data could be gathered for 1997 on this indicator, and none on life expectancy for 1995–97). The rates of four diseases were considerably reduced between 1993 and 1997: measles, malaria, hepatitis, and cholera. In education, an important change was an amendment to the constitution that mandated that 6% of the state budget be assigned to higher education (an obligation that had adverse effects on secondary and elementary education during recessions); now that percentage is allocated to all education (the three levels). The illiteracy rate decreased from 5.7% to 5.2% in 1992–95; no data could be gathered on educational enrollment and housing units built.

Out of the 13 indicators in Table V.34, Costa Rica improved in 6 (trade partner concentration, trade balance per capita, external debt per capita, urban mean wages, illiteracy, and infant mortality) and deteriorated in 7 (GDP and GDP per capita growth, domestic investment/GDP, inflation, fiscal balance, export concentration, and unemployment). It should be noted, however, that the degree of export concentration of Costa Rica is still the lowest of the three countries, and the unemployment rate is very low and similar to Chile's. Other positive indicators noted above are the increase in trade volume and the reduction in poverty, while a negative indicator is the slight worsening in income distribution (still one of the most equal in the region). The adjustment program resulted in a deterioration of domestic macroeconomic indicators until 1997, but in improvement of external economic indicators, as well as maintenance of social indicators in spite of stagnant and sluggish GDP per capita growth and an increase in inflation. The 1997 indicators of performance (and preliminary data for 1998) show that the adjustment program has been successful in raising economic growth, continuing the reduction in inflation, the fiscal deficit, and unemployment, but investment, the internal debt, and the trade balance still must be improved. The viability of the Costa Rican model is fairly high, similar to Chile's. In order to increase performance and the model's viability, several reforms need to be implemented: a continued reduction of the state as a producer in lines that are unprofitable, consolidation of the opening of the banking system and achievement of more efficiency in the public banking sector, breaking of the state's monopoly over insurance and opening of competition to the private sector, steady diversification of exports and their competitiveness, better allocation of credit between the public and private sectors, merging or at least coordination of multiple state institutions that deal with poverty, better targeting of vulnerable groups, particularly in rural areas as well as in those antipoverty programs that help the poor most (nutrition, primary health care, welfare pensions, training), transfer of fiscal resources from urban to rural education and from formal to vocational schools (free tuition in public universities should be given only to capable students in need), targeting of resources assigned for housing to low-income groups, consolidation and advancement in the health reform, and implementation of the proposed reform of social security pensions. The recommended changes would consolidate a model that has contributed to the economic and social progress of Costa Rica for more than four decades.

In 1998 the opposition (PUSC) won the elections, and Miguel Angel Rodríguez became president in May but failed to gain a majority in the National

Assembly; hence he will have to develop a consensus with the PLN in order to pass legislation. A moderate neoconservative, Rodríguez's ideology is not significantly different than Figueres's, and policy continuity is expected with a tilt to the right. During his electoral campaign, he promised to deepen the reform process and set the following goals: privatization of two large state banks and ending of the state insurance monopoly (INS), fiscal discipline, more opening to foreign investment, development of agriculture, industry, tourism, and fishing, support of small enterprises, gradual entry into the Free Trade Area of the Americas, priority given to education, pension reform (possibly of a mixed type), and improvement of high technology in hospitals (*Nuevo Herald,* Feb. 2, 1998).

C. Cuba

The timid, oscillating, and tightly regulated market-oriented reform appears to have been halted since 1996, an assessment confirmed by Raul Castro's speech critical of the negative effects of the reform in March 1996 (followed by the purge of some academic reformists) and by the 5th Communist Party Congress held in October 1997. Between turning back (an unfeasible option) and moving ahead (as the purged reformists recommended), the Party decided to maintain the status quo, because a further opening of the economy and expansion of the nonstate sector could have threatened the regime's power. The political logic, therefore, prevailed over the economic logic, that is, the positive effects of the reform. The part on Cuba provided full information until 1995 (and some on 1996); here policy and performance in 1996–97 (and some preliminary for 1998) will be summarized (sources for this section are Table V.34; ECLAC 1997c, 1997d; "Palabras de Carlos Lage ante el Congreso" [Lage] 1997; Pérez-López 1997; Rohter 1997; Mesa-Lago 1998; Ministerio 1998; ONE 1998; "Resolución Económica" 1998).

The Party Congress Economic Resolution maintained and strengthened the current system, neither endorsing new reforms nor setting a date for the implementation of those pending. According to the resolution, the reforms are geared to maintain the predominance of state property, which will continue to be an intrinsic element of the socialist system, and its efficiency will be increased above that of other property forms such as cooperative and private. The transition from "excessively centralized planning" to another form (not defined, but based on financial balances) is still in process, but planning will continue to play a fundamental role, and the state will stay the direction of the economy. Although some space has been opened to the market, it will be kept under strict state control and regulation, and the government will correct any distortions created by the market and block unjustifiable profits. Enterprises managed by the armed forces will be extended to other economic branches, and state enterprises should be profitable, except in cases of national or social interest, when they will be subsidized. The majority of UBPCs suffer from inefficiency and must correct their problems and increase output, but within the current system. The partial reform of the banking system approved in May 1997 (it relegated Cuba's National Bank to commercial functions, transferred its central bank functions to a newly created Cuban Central Bank, and established a legal framework for commercial banks and financial institutions under the latter's supervision) was briefly mentioned by the resolution but without specifying when the full banking reform will take place. There was no reference to the needed price reform, but the resolution confirmed that prices should be centrally set, although avoiding monopoly prices (an oxymoron). The Congress stressed the need to move gradually toward a more realistic and adequate foreign exchange rate, but without setting a timetable, and declared that the peso should be strengthened by increasing utput, but without a concrete plan. There will be an adequate balance between economic and moral incentives, the resolution stated, and voluntary labor will be reasserted. Self-employment will continue under current regulations and control (it should be recalled that the increase in licenses by 300% and fees by 650% on the self-employed in 1996 led to a drop of 39% in the number legally registered in 1997). A legal draft granting Cuban citizens the right to manage small and medium-sized businesses, circulating for almost three years, was not mentioned in the resolution (Lage explained that it was not a high government priority and would have to wait), and it also did not say anything about authorizing university graduates to practice their professions as self-employed. Concern was expressed about the existing labor surplus (without alluding to the 500,000 to 800,000 state workers expected to be dismissed in 1995–96), as well as about open unemployment-underemployment and the need to create jobs, but this was said to be a relatively small problem compared with the situation in other Latin-American countries, and no concrete program was suggested (the Congress ignored the ECLAC 1997 estimates of 27% combined open unemployment and equivalent unemployment, as well as its recommendations to expand the private sector to create jobs). The resolution acknowledged that social security is a heavy fiscal burden and that the 1994 tax law had mandated (although postponed) the imposition of a payroll tax on the workers, but it did not stipulate the date of implementation (Lage said it would have to wait until "proper conditions" appear); the resolution did not even mention the wage tax, also included in the 1994 law. The new regulations introduced in May 1997, establishing the right to rent rooms to citizens or foreigners albeit requiring a permit and paying a tax, were equally ignored. Finally, the resolution stated that once "the worst disequilibria are attenuated," but certainly not solved, a new stage will begin with empasis in export diversification, rising labor productivity and enterprise profitability, achieving food self-sufficiency, and so on, but, in the short run, current restrictions will continue. In his closing address to the Congress, President Castro made it clear that he opposes any type of privatization of state enterprises as the Chinese have done, and the Party secretary in Havana declared that Cuba could not follow China's path because of different conditions and the adverse effects such a move would cause for social services.

The Congress set very ambitious targets for the future (a timetable was not given) but failed to come up with concrete, detailed policies: (1) GDP will grow at an annual rate from 4% to 6%; (2) sugar output must increase from 3.2 million in 1997 to 7 million tons (mechanization and fertilizers should be limited and replaced by manual work, animal traction, and natural fertilizer); (3) nickel production will reach 100,000 tons (a 60% jump from 1997 output), tobacco 50,000 tons (a 100% jump from 1995), and the fishing catch sustained; (4) two million tourists and a gross revenue of U.S.$2.6 will be reached (a 100% increase over 1997); (5) oil needs will be met with increasing domestic production, savings, a cut in population consumption, and public transportation mainly through bikes; (6) 50,000 dwellings will be built annually, particularly in the countryside; (7) health care should continue to partly rely on traditional and herbal medicine; (8) state pensions should be supplemented with individual savings accounts and life insurance; and (9) inequalities will be curtailed with taxes.

Policies prior to the halting of the reform, although modest and with reversals, in general produced fair results, but there was a deterioration in 1997–98. The precipitous fall between 1989 and 1993 of GSP/GDP was halted in 1994, and there was an increase of 2.5% of GDP in 1995 (1.9% per capita) and a jump of 7.8% in 1996 (7.1% per capita). ECLAC (1996c) reduced the 1996 official rate to 7% (6.5% per capita) and warned that it "did not have complete information on [Cuba] related to the various areas covered in the annual report, hence the rate was excluded from its analysis." Furthermore, ECLAC noted that "the standard of living of the population continued below the level of 1989." The GDP growth target for 1997 was set at 4% to 5% but actually was 2.5% (1.9% per capita); the main reasons for the poor performance were the failure of the sugar harvest, which was planned to be 5 million tons but which actually reached only 4.25 million tons; external credit affected by the Helms-Burton Act; paralyzation and delays in two-thirds of the supply of inputs for the sugar harvest; the heavy burden of the loan service; the 1996 hurricane, which caused an estimated loss of U.S.$800 million; bad weather in the winter of 1996–97; and pests in 1997 that harmed agriculture. In 1996–97 production of nickel and steel continued to expand, the first surpassing a previous peak, while output of citrus, rice, eggs, fishing, electricity, cement, and fertilizers also increased but still were from 10% to 49% below the 1989 level. The annual average GDP per capita growth rate in 1995–97 was 3.6%; even at that rate it would take 15 years to recover the GDP per capita level that Cuba had in 1985, and even that was a meager one. The targets for 1998 were a 2.5% GDP growth rate and sugar output of 4.5 million tons. Only 3.2 million tons of sugar were produced, the lowest harvest under the Revolution and the worst in sixty years. Lage claimed that the planned growth rate for 1998 would still be achieved through increases in production of nickel and tourism, but world prices of the former declined in 1998, and tourism faces a relatively low occupancy rate (54%) and a high cost of imported inputs (as Cuba has been unable to produce them domestically). The actual GDP growth rate was 1.2% and 0.7% per capita.

Domestic gross investment/GDP reportedly rose from 4.8% to 8.2% in 1993–96, but, in the last year, it was still 33% of the 1990 level. Lage told the Party Congress that investment had been "almost totally interrupted" but had begun again in 1997, and the Resolution stated that new investment projects should not begin unless a feasibility study is done first. Access to external credit is extremely limited: new one-year loans from foreign banks were received in 1996 and 1997 to finance the sugar harvests of 1997–98 (about U.S.$300 million each), at 16% interest, but the cost was quite high, and the net gain from a declining sugar production was lower that the amount of the loan and its interest. Lage and the resolution acknowledged the financial difficulties caused by the crop failure of 1997, including less foreign credit available for 1998. The inflation rate decreased from a peak of 25.7% in 1995 to a reported 0.5% in 1996 (a questionable figure) but increased to 2.9% in 1997. The monetary overhang was dramatically reduced in 1994–95 but increased again in 1996 and was stagnant in 1997: 9.44 billion pesos, 41% of GDP, and more than twice the level of 1989. The fiscal deficit was cut considerably from 33.5% of GDP in 1993 to 2% in 1997.

After its dramatic decline of 79% in 1990–93, the value of exports increased by 73% between 1993 and 1997 (still only 35% of the 1989 level); imports dropped 75% and rose 105% (still 51% of the 1989 level). As imports expanded faster than exports (mainly because of the decline in sugar output), the trade balance per capita deficit jumped 150% in 1994–97 (from U.S.$73 to U.S.$183). There was a significant deterioration in the terms of trade in 1996–97 as the world prices of sugar and nickel dwindled, although the price of oil also declined (the share of oil in total imports was about 27% in 1997, a decline in relation to 1994 but still quite high). Export concentration on sugar decreased from 66% to 52% of total export value between 1993 and 1996, mainly a result of the fall in sugar export quantity and value, and yet although all other export shares increased, their actual value shrank. Trade partner concentration with Russia declined from 22% to 15% in 1993–95, a result of both a dramatic cut in trade volume and an elimination of price subsidies, but rose to 20% in 1996. The improvement in the last two indicators, however, does not mean that Cuba is in a better economic situation now, because of the enormous trade losses it has suffered with the collapse of socialism in the Soviet camp. The debt with Russia has decreased catastrophically in real terms, but Cuba has neither paid any part of it nor even reached an agreement on the sum to be reimbursed, an irritant in trade relations between the two countries. Conversely the hard-currency debt has kept rising, in per capita terms by 17.6% between 1993 and 1997; at the end of 1998 there had not been an agreement with the Club of Paris on that debt, a reason for Cuba's not receiving new loans. There are no hard data on foreign investment in Cuba, but the government has acknowledged that it is stagnant: U.S.$2.1 billion in 1995 and U.S.$2.2 billion in 1998; furthermore, it appears that only one-third of it has been disbursed. An estimate of all Cuba's foreign hard-currency earnings in 1996 was 76% less than in 1989. The exchange rate of pesos to one U.S. dollar in the black market deteriorated from 69 in 1993 to 79 in 1994, but appreciated to 20 in 1997 (state exchange houses established in 1995 pay one or two pesos less than in the black market).

The rate of national open unemployment rose from 6.2% to 7.9% in 1993–95 but reportedly decreased to 6.9% in 1997. ECLAC (1997d) has estimated that the "equivalent unemployment rate" (including open, those receiving compensation, etc.) was 27% in 1996. The dismissal of 500,000 to 800,000 unneeded workers in the state sector had not occurred by mid-1998 because of the lack of jobs in the private sector (in turn caused by the government's resistance to expand it); the cost of unemployment compensation for surplus workers is a heavy fiscal burden. Urban mean real wages (based on 1980) fell from 97.1 to 75 in 1993–95 and rose slightly to 79 in 1997 (based on 1990, they dropped from 77.2 to 58.6 in 1993–96). State budget allocations have increased for pensions and health care, but have been cut for education and housing. Although no data are available on income distribution, several indicators show a significant expansion in inequality: in 1995 the ratio of extreme income inequality was 800 to 1 (compared with 4.5 to 1 in 1987), and 13% of all bank deposit accounts concentrated 93% of the value of all deposits. Rationing has extended to virtually all consumer goods but ceased to be a significant equalizer because the monthly rations cover less than two weeks of the minimum food requirements. The rest has to be bought in state dollar shops or on the agricultural and black markets, at very high prices affordable only by those who earn or receive hard currency. The deterioration in health-care infrastructure and the severe scarcity of food and medicine apparently have not affected the declining infant mortality ratio, which reportedly decreased from 9.4 to 9 in 1993–96 (with an increase to 9.9 in 1994). This indicator, however, is unlikely to increase in several years despite the economic deterioration, because it reflects long-run trends because of its stock nature (Betancourt 1996). But there are signs of deterioration in other health standards, for instance, the rate of contagious diseases in 1993–96 increased 84% for tuberculosis, 62% for gonorrhea, 56% for syphilis, 27% for acute respiratory conditions, and 24% for hepatitis (ONE 1998). The illiteracy rate diminished from 5% to 4.3% in 1993–95, but enrollment in secondary education declined 13% between 1992 and 1996 and 55% in higher education, because of the lack of jobs, difficulties in transportation, and charges for school meals. There are no data available on the number of dwellings built.

Out of the 13 indicators in Table V.34, in 1993–95 Cuba had an improvement in 8, deterioration in 4, and stagnation in 1; but a comparison of 8 indicators available in 1996–97 show deterioration in 6 and improvement in only 2 (the outlook for 1998 is even worse). Although more data and time are needed to reach more solid conclusions, the above comparison suggests that the economic reform, albeit timid, was generating a modest recovery, but the halting of that process has led to a deterioration.

A comparison of each indicator among the three countries in 1994–97 shows that Cuba was the worst in 6 (average GDP absolute and per capita, investment/GDP, export concentration, real wages, and unemployment) but was best in two (illiteracy rate and infant mortality). Cuba was worse than Chile in 10 indicators (average GDP absolute and per capita, investment/GDP, average inflation, fiscal balance, export and trade partner concentration, trade balance per capita, mean wages, and unemployment), and it was worse than Costa Rica in 6 (the same as Chile except inflation, fiscal balance, trade partner concentration, and trade balance per capita). The external debt per capita is not comparable because the Cuban figures exclude the non-hard-currency debt, and the enhancement in some Cuban indicators (trade partner and export concentration) does not mean that the island is better off economically, because of the enormous losses suffered in trade. Furthermore, other indicators not shown in Table V.34 but discussed in the sections above or in part 3 indicate that Cuba is in a worse situation than the other two countries or is suffering a severe deterioration: the lowest real GDP per capita in PPP$, the poorest access to foreign capital/credit, a drastic decrease in trade volume, a sharp decline in educational enrollment, and a worsening in health care. The conclusion is that the Cuban model is the least viable of the three.

In order to improve its viability, Cuban authorities must leave aside their ideological resistance in order to further open up the economy; facilitate the expansion of the private sector; transform the UBPC in real cooperatives, ones that are autonomous and with more incentives to increase production and profitability; allow university graduates to practice their professions as self-employed and authorize Cuban citizens and groups of workers to manage small and medium-sized businesses, hence, creating enough jobs in the nonstate sector to permit the dismissal of unneeded workers in the state sector; coplete the banking reform and implement a comprehensive price reform; create a domestic capital market; allow foreign enterprises and joint ventures to hire, promote, and pay their employees directly; establish a truly convertible peso; introduce a progressive income tax and workers' contributions to social security and reform the pension scheme; and devise a social safety net to protect the most vulnerable groups of the population. Unfortunately the decisions taken in the Party Congress do no augur that such urgently needed reforms will be implemented in the near future; therefore, the probability of a strong, steady recovery in Cuba appears to be very low, particularly after the negative performance of 1997–98.

Tables to Part V

Table V.1

Comparative Summary of Economic Policies and Overall Outcome, by Stages in the Three Countries, 1953–1996

Country	Stage	Political Leader/Party	Economic Organization	Development Strategy	Overall Outcome
Chile	1973–76	Pinochet	Monetarism (emission control), adjustment, privatization, price liberalization, 1st employment program	Movement away from ISI, not clearly defined strategy but reliance on market, decreased protectionism, close economy (begins to open)	1st crisis
	1976–81	Pinochet	Monetarism, opening to foreign capital and trade but control of exchange rate (fixed 1979–81), decreased state role, labor reform, and privatization of social services	ISI abandoned, outward development, promotion of nontraditional exports, open economy, financial liberalization	Recovery (mild)
	1981–83	Pinochet	State intervention (1983) to save model, privatization halted; IMF stabilization program, devaluation, 2d employment program	Continuation of same strategy with more gov't incentives to nontraditional exports	2d crisis (severe)
	1984–90	Pinochet	Corrections, massive privatization, but increased state regulations, adjustment (reduction of social expenditures)	Same, but traditional agricultural producers/exporters receive incentives also, increased foreign ownership, IMF-WB programs	Recovery (strong)
	1990–94	Aylwin	Minor corrections, privatization ends, increased state regulations, tax reform, increase in social expenditures	"Economic growth with equity," which maintains key elements of model but introduces new policies: redistribution, social safety net, infrastructure, and modernization of production	Continuous growth
	1994–96	Frei Jr.[a]			
Cuba	1959–60	Castro	Mixed economy but decreased market role, 1st collectivization (1960)	Inward development, ISI, agricultural diversification, close economy in the 1960s (ties with Soviet Union increased), decline in sugar dependency, but domestic/external disequilibria	Recovery
	1961–63	Castro	Soviet model of central plan, increased state role, continued collectivization		1st crisis
	1964–66	Castro	Central planning fails and debate on alternative socialist models — Pro-Soviet: Moderate / Guevarist: Radical	Outward development based on increasing sugar harvests/exports, close economy, some ISI, sugar plan fails	Recovery (mild)
	1966–70	Castro	Guevanism-Castroism, elimination of material stimuli and market residues, state role increased, but central plan decreased		2d crisis

Country	Period	Leader	Policy orientation	Development strategy	Economic outcome
	1971–85	Castro	Soviet-style mild economic reform, some increased market, return to material stimuli	Continued outward development but more balanced, sugar sector to be self-sufficient, other exports and tourism, close economy (Cuba enters CMEA), growth but increased external disequilibria; food self-sufficiency in 1986–90	Recovery (strong
	1986–90	Castro	Rectification Process, state increased, market and material stimuli decreased		Recession
	1991–96	Castro	Market-oriented reform, state decreased but without losing main control, market increased somewhat, reform stagnant since mid-1995	More emphasis on outward development, opening of the economy to world market trade, investment, technology and tourism but under tight state control	3d crisis (severe) until 1993, mild recovery (1994–96)
Costa Rica	1953–58	Figueres (PLN)	Foundations of model, market economy starts moving to mixed	Outward development (coffee, bananas), but foundation for ISI set	
	1958–62	Echandi (O)	Continued increase of state role in a predominantly market economy, providing growth and progressive distribution. State entrepreneur (1970s)	Inward develpment (ISI), protectionism and incentives, but maintaining state support to traditional agricultural products/exports, state incentives to other crops, expansion of industrial exports (partly based on CACM), state increased role as producer (particularly in 1970s), but increasing internal/external disequilibria and growing indebtedness.	High growth (except 1963–65)
	1962–66	Ortlich (PLN)			
	1966–70	Trejos (O)			
	1970–74	Figueres (PLN)			
	1974–78	Oduber (PLN)			
	1978–82	Carazo (O)[b]	Failed attempt at neo-liberalism and adjustment		Crisis (severe)
	1982–86	Monge (PLN)	Adjustment and restructuring (decreased state role) but with gradualism and social safety net	Outward development, reduction of state subsidies and protection to industry, incentives to exports (mainly agricultural), opening up to world trade	Recovery (modest since 1983)
	1986–90	Arias (PLN)			
	1990–94	Calderón Jr. (O)[b]	Neoliberalism more accentuated (state role decreased), privatization, except for 1½ first years of Figueres		Recession
	1994–96	Figueres Jr. (PLN)[c]			

[a]Frei's period ends at the beginning of 2000. [b]Opposition party (O) has a majority in National Assembly; in the rest, the National Liberation Party (PLN) has a majority. [c]Figueres's period ended in 1998.

Table V.2

***Selection of Indicators for Comparative Evaluation of Performance
in the Three Countries***

Indicators	Time Period[a]	Table Source	Selection for Ranking
Domestic macroeconomic			
1. GDP/GSP growth	1961–93	V.3	Yes[b]
2. GNP/GDP per capita	1965/85–94	V.4	Yes
3. Gross domestic investment	1958/60–93	V.5	Yes
4. Inflation	1961–93	V.6	Yes[b]
5. Fiscal balance	1960–93	V.7	Yes
6. Composition of GDP/GSP	1960/85–93	V.8	Yes
External economic			
7. Export concentration/diversification	1960–93	V.9	Yes
8. Import composition	1958/60–93	V.10	Yes
9. Trade partner concentration	1960–93	V.11	Yes
10. Volume and balance of trade per capita	1960–93	V.12	Yes
11. External debt per capita	1958/60–93	V.13	Yes
Distribution and Employment			
12. Income distribution	1961/67–86/90	V.14	No
13. Real wages	1971/76–94	V.15	Yes
14. Poverty incidence	1970–92/93	V.16	No
15. Composition of labor force and women's participation	1957/63–93	V.17	Yes/No[c]
16. Open unemployment	1960–93/94	V.18	Yes
Social standards			
17. Illiteracy	1953–92	V.19	Yes
18. Educational enrollment	1960/63–92	V.20	Yes
19. Infant mortality and life expectancy	1960–91/92	V.21	Yes
20. Rates of contagious diseases	1958/61–92	V.22	Yes
21. Access to water and sewerage/sanitation	1953/64–91/93	V.23	No
22. Social security coverage	1958/60–89/93	V.24	No
23. Housing units built	1965–93	V.25	Yes

[a]Cuba: starts in 1985 in 8, ends in 1990 in 12, not available in 14, ends in 1981 (for women) in 15 and in 21, and in 1989 in 22. [b]This indicator is not technically comparable among the three countries but, because of its importance, it will be included and excluded from the final evaluation to assess its impact on the overall ranking. [c]The first will be included and the second excluded.

Table V.3

Economic Growth Rates in the Three Countries, 1961–1993 (Average Percentage Annual Rates at Constant Prices)

Years	Chile (GDP)		Costa Rica (GDP)		Cuba (GSP)[a]	
	Absolute	*Per Capita*	*Absolute*	*Per Capita*	*Absolute*	*Per Capita*
1961–65	5.0	2.7	5.2	1.3	3.3[b]	0.8
1966–70	3.4	1.4	7.0	4.0	0.1[b]	−1.7
1971–75[c]	0.7	−1.0	6.0	3.5	13.6	11.9
1976–80[d]	3.7	2.0	5.3	2.3	3.5	2.7
1981–85	−0.1	−1.7	0.4	−2.3	7.3	6.4
1986–90	6.5	4.7	4.6	1.9	−0.6	−1.6
1991–93	8.2	6.5	4.6	2.2	−16.9	−17.8
1961–80[e]	3.4	1.3	5.9	2.8	5.1	3.4
1974–80	3.7	2.0	4.8	2.0	6.7	5.8
1981–89	3.2	1.5	2.4	−0.1	4.1	3.2
1961–90[f]	3.4	1.7	4.8	1.7	4.5[g]	3.4[g]
1961–93[h]	4.1	2.4	4.7	1.9	2.6[g]	1.2[g]

Sources: Tables II.3, III.3, III.4 (and BNC *Informe* 1982), and IV.3.

[a]Global Social Product: excludes the value of nonproductive services but is affected by some double counting of intermediate consumption. [b]The official annual average growth for 1960–70 was given as 2.8%: we disaggregated it into the two five-year period averages based on additional Cuban data. [c]For Chile 1971–73. [d]For Chile 1974–80. [e]For Chile 1961–73. [f]For Chile 1974–89. [g]Excluding the controversial figure for 1981, Cuban averages are 1961–90, 4.1% and 2.6%, and 1961–93, 2.2% and 0.7%. [h]For Chile 1974–93.

Table V.4

GNP/GDP per Capita in the Three Countries, 1965–1993 (U.S. $ per Year)

Year	World Bank: GNP per Capita Constant in Current U.S.$[a]			UNDP GDP: per Capita Constant in PPP $[b]			Cuban Data: GDP per Capita Constant Converted to U.S.$ at Exchange Rate[c]	
	Chile	*Costa Rica*	*Cuba*	*Chile*	*Costa Rica*	*Cuba*	*Official*	*Black Market*
1965	480	380	330					
1970	720	560	530					
1976	1,050	1,040	800[d]					
1978	1,410	1,540	810					
1980	2,150	1,730						
1985	1,410	1,300		4,862	3,760	2,500	2,005	334
1990	1,940	1,900		5,099	4,542	2,200	1,777	222
1994	3,520	2,400		8,900	5,680	3,000	1,168	22

Sources: World Bank from *WBA* 1967–80 and *WDR* 1978–96. UNDP from *HDR* 1990–96. Cuban official GDP and black market estimates based on Mesa-Lago 1998.

[a]The methodology is explained in WB, *WBA*, and *WDR* 1996. [b]Purchasing power parity rates in U.S. dollars; the methodology is explained in UNDP *HDR* 1996. [c]The official exchange peso-dollar is par; the black market exchange rate was 6 in 1985, 8 in 1990, and 79 in 1994. [d]1975.

Table V.5

Gross Domestic Investment as Percentage of GDP in the Three Countries, 1958/60–1993 (Current Prices)

Year	Chile	Costa Rica	Cuba	
			GDP	*GSP*
1960	13.9	16.1	17.6[a]	
1965	15.0	18.6		12.4
1970	16.4	19.5	15.1[b]	10.8[b]
1973	7.9	21.9	17.4	12.4
1975	13.1	22.0	22.6	16.3
1980	21.0	23.9	19.3	15.6
1985	13.7	19.3		15.9
1989	19.1	20.5	25.0	16.9
1990	20.3	22.5	14.9[c]	10.5[c,d]
1993	26.2	22.1	4.8	12.0[d]

Sources: Tables II.3, III.3, III.7, and IV.3.
[a]1958. [b]1971. [c]1991. [d]Constant prices.

Table V.6

Inflation Rates for the Three Countries, 1961–1993 (Percentage)

Years	Chile[a]	Costa Rica[b]	Cuba
1961–65	28.9	2.1	5.5[c]
1966–70	26.0	2.5	1.7[c]
1971–75[d]	169.4	13.7	6.1[e]
1976–80[f]	116.6	8.1	1.1[g]
1981–85	20.4	34.8	1.7[g]
1986–90	20.0	16.9	−0.8[g,h]
1991–93	14.5	19.8	9.1[i]
1961–80[j]	51.4	6.5	2.7
1974–80	116.6	12.3	1.1
1981–89	19.4	26.3	0.7
1961–90[k]	54.9	12.5	1.7
1961–93[l]	46.6	13.2	2.8

Sources: Tables II.3, III.3, III.4, and IV.3.

[a]Gran Santiago. [b]San José. [c]1963–65 and 1966 at 1965 prices. [d]For Chile 1974–80. [e]Base year unknown. [f]For Chile 1974–80. [g]1981 prices. [h]1986–88. [i]1990–94. ECLAC (1997) gives 10% for the same period. [j]For Chile 1961–73. [k]For Chile 1974–89; for Cuba 1961–88. [l]For Chile 1974–93; for Cuba 1961–94 (except 1989 for which no data are available).

Table V.7

Fiscal Balance in the Three Countries, 1960–1993
(Percentage of GDP/GSP)

Year	Chile (GDP)	Costa Rica (GDP)	Cuba (GSP)
1960	−4.6		0.0
1965	−4.1	−4.0[a]	0.0
1970	−2.7	−1.6	
1973	−24.7	−2.2	
1980	3.1	−7.4	0.0[b]
1985	−6.3	−1.3	−0.9
1990	1.4	−3.2	−7.5[c]
1993	1.8	−1.9	−33.7[c]

Sources: Tables II.3, III.3, and IV.3.

[a]1966. [b]1981. [c]Cuba's deficit as percentage of GDP was higher than GSP in 1989–93 and averaged from 19.5% to 21.3% annually compared with 19% over GSP (ECLAC 1997; Mesa-Lago 1997).

Table V.8
Composition of GDP in Chile and Costa Rica and of GSP/GDP in Cuba by Economic Activity, 1960–1993 (Percentage)

Country	Year	Agriculture		Industry[a]		Construction		Transportation and Communications		Commerce		Others[b]	
		(1)	(2)	(1)	(2)	(1)	(2)	(1)	(2)	(1)	(2)	(1)	(2)
Chile[c]	1960	10.6	14.9	31.5	44.4	7.6	10.7	4.2	5.9	17.1	24.1	29.0	0.0
	1965	9.0	12.6	34.0	47.6	7.8	10.9	4.7	6.6	15.9	22.3	28.6	0.0
	1970	8.5	12.1	32.9	46.8	7.5	10.7	4.9	7.0	16.5	23.4	29.7	0.0
	1973	6.8	9.7	34.5	49.4	5.3	7.6	4.9	7.0	18.3	26.3	30.2	0.0
	1975	10.3	15.4	31.7	47.5	5.6	8.4	5.2	7.8	13.9	20.9	33.7	0.0
	1980	8.3	12.1	30.9	45.1	5.3	7.7	5.5	8.0	18.5	27.1	31.5	0.0
	1985	9.6	13.8	31.7	45.7	5.8	8.4	5.6	8.1	16.7	24.0	30.6	0.0
	1988	9.4	13.4	31.3	44.7	5.8	8.1	6.2	8.9	17.4	24.9	30.0	0.0
	1990	9.5	13.7	30.6	44.2	5.7	8.2	7.5	10.8	16.0	23.1	30.8	0.0
	1993	8.5	12.1	30.1	42.8	6.2	8.8	8.3	11.8	17.2	24.5	29.7	0.0
Costa Rica[d]	1960	25.2	30.4	15.1	18.0	4.5	5.0	4.6	4.8	34.0	41.9	16.6	0.0
	1965	22.9	27.4	18.2	21.8	4.7	5.6	4.2	5.0	33.5	39.7	16.5	0.0
	1970	24.1	28.4	20.5	24.1	4.1	4.8	4.4	5.2	31.8	37.4	15.0	0.0
	1975	21.2	24.9	23.3	27.4	5.2	6.1	5.8	6.8	29.6	34.8	14.9	0.0
	1980	18.0	21.0	24.3	28.3	6.3	7.3	7.0	8.2	30.1	35.2	14.3	0.0
	1985	19.3	22.4	24.9	28.9	4.5	5.2	7.3	8.5	30.0	35.0	14.1	0.0
	1988	19.2	22.2	25.2	29.1	4.1	4.7	8.1	9.4	30.0	34.6	13.4	0.0
	1990	19.3	22.2	24.6	28.3	4.1	4.7	8.6	9.9	30.4	34.9	13.0	0.0
	1993	18.7	21.2	25.0	28.4	3.9	4.4	9.6	10.9	30.9	35.1	11.9	0.0

	Cuba GSP[e]											
1962	17.8	17.8	48.2	48.2	7.2	7.2	6.5	6.5	20.3	20.3	0.0	0.0
1965	16.5	16.5	42.5	42.5	7.7	7.7	5.9	5.9	27.6	27.4	0.0	0.0
1970	14.7	14.7	47.9	47.9	5.2	5.2	10.2	10.2	22.0	22.0	0.0	0.0
1975	11.8	11.8	37.6	37.7	8.9	8.9	7.7	7.7	33.8	33.9	0.2	0.0
1980	11.6	11.7	35.6	35.7	8.9	8.9	8.9	8.9	33.6	33.7	0.4	0.0
1985	13.9	14.0	36.1	36.3	8.8	8.8	7.5	7.5	33.2	33.4	0.5	0.0
1988	15.7	15.8	35.9	36.2	8.6	8.6	7.8	7.9	31.3	31.5	0.7	0.0
GDP[f]												
1985	8.8		27.6		6.2		6.2		27.3		23.9	
1989	9.2		26.1		6.4		6.5		24.6		27.2	
1990	8.6		25.5		7.4		5.9		24.3		28.3	
1993	6.5		24.7		2.7		5.1		20.5		40.5	

Sources: Tables II.4, III.8, III.9, and IV.4.

Note: (1) Includes "other" (services) in Chile and Costa Rica but, under GSP in Cuba, excludes them ("nonproductive services"); e.g., administration, finance, defense, personal, and social services. GDP in Cuba (bottom of the table) includes those services too. (2) Excludes services described in (1). [a]Manufacturing, mining, electricity, gas, and water. [b]Public administration, finance, defense, personal, and social services (finance included in Commerce in Costa Rica). [c]1988 prices except 1973 (1973 prices) and 1965, 1975 (1980 prices). [d]1988 prices except 1965, 1975 (1980 prices). [e]1962–88 old GSP series based on enterprise prices excluding taxes to industry; there are two new series that include such taxes. [f]ECLAC Series.

Table V.9

Composition of Exports by Major Products in the Three Countries, 1960–1993 (Percentage)

	Chile				Costa Rica				Cuba				
Year	Copper	Iron Ore	Fish Meal	Other	Coffee	Bananas	Beef	Other	Sugar	Nickel	Tobacco	Oil[a]	Other
1960	71	7	0	22	53	24	5	18	78	4	10	0	8
1965	79	12	0	9	42	26	3	29	86	6	5	0	3
1970	67	6	1	26	32	29	8	31	77	17	3	0	3
1973	83	4	1	12	27	26	9	38	75	14	5	0	6
1975	57	6	2	35	20	29	7	44	90	5	2	0	3
1980	46	3	5	46	24	21	7	47	84	5	1	4	6
1985	46	2	8	44	34	23	6	37	74	5	2	10	9
1989	50	2	6	42	22	21	4	53	73	9	2	4	12
1990	46	4	5	45	18	23	4	55	80	7	1	1	11
1993	35	4[b]	6[b]	48[b]	10	26	3	61	66	12	5	0	17

Sources: Tables II.8, III.17, and IV.8.

[a]"Oil reexports," actually Soviet transfer of hard currency to Cuba when oil committed for exports was not consumed. [b]1992.

Table V.10

Composition of Imports by Major Products in the Three Countries, 1960–1993 (Percentage)

Country	Year	Food and Beverages	Non-Food Agricultural Products and Minerals[a]	Fuel[b]	Machinery and Transportation	Other Manufactures[c]	Other
Chile	1960[d]	18	8	7	40	27	0
	1965[e]	18	8	6	37	30	0
	1970	18	9	7	38	28	0
	1973	24	5	7	34	30	0
	1975	16	4	20	34	26	0
	1980	13	3	18	31	35	0
	1985	8	3	19	32	38	0
	1986	4	3	15	36	40	2
	1987	4	3	12	40	41	0
	1988	4	3	12	41	38	2
	1990	4	2	16	44	33	1
	1991	5	3	15	38	37	2
	1993	5	2	9	44	38	2
Costa Rica	1960	13	1	6	26	54	0
	1965	8	2	5	29	56	0
	1970	10	3	4	29	54	0
	1975	9	2	10	27	52	1
	1980	7	2	15	24	52	0
	1985	6	2	16	23	53	0
	1986	7	3	8	29	53	0
	1987	4	2	10	30	54	0
	1988	5	2	12	28	52	0
	1990	8	5	10	28	49	0
	1993	8	2	9	26	55	0
Cuba	1958	21	7	11	31	30	0
	1965						
	1970	22	6	9	36	27	0
	1975	20	6	10	31	33	0
	1980	17	4	20	36	23	0
	1985	12	4	33	30	21	0
	1986	10	4	33	31	22	0
	1987	10	4	35	31	20	0
	1988	10	4	34	32	20	0
	1990	12	4	27	37	20	0
	1992	25	2	36	19	18	0
	1993	26	3	37	12	22	0

Sources: Tables II.9, III.18, and IV.9.

[a]In Cuba, nonfood agricultural products only. [b]In Cuba, fuels and minerals. [c]In Cuba, manufactured and chemical products. [d]1962. [e]1966.

Table V.11

Trade Concentration with Main Commercial Partner of the Three Countries, 1960–1993 (Percentage)

Year	Chile	Costa Rica	Cuba
1960	42.6	50.9	15.5[a]
1965	34.9	44.0	48.2
1970	24.1	37.5	51.7
1973	12.3	34.4	49.2
1975	18.6	37.6	48.0
1980	21.0	32.9	60.0
1985	23.3	35.9	70.5
1989	19.3	43.2	64.7
1990	18.7	42.7	67.9
1993	18.4	55.0	22.4

Sources: Tables II.11, III.20, and IV.11.

Note: Percentage of total exports and total imports with the U.S. for Chile and Costa Rica and with the Soviet Union for Cuba in their total merchandise trade. [a]In 1958, Cuban trade with the U.S. was 68.4% (CEE, *AEC* 1987).

Table V.12

Volume and Balance of Merchandise Trade per Capita of the Three Countries, 1960–1993 (U.S.$)

Year/Period[a]	Chile		Costa Rica		Cuba[b]	
	Volume	*Balance*	*Volume*	*Balance*	*Volume*	*Balance*
1960	134	−5	158	−21	168	4
1965	144	19	194	−45	197	−22
1970	211	26	316	−49	274	−30
1975[c]	268	−1	604	−102	780	−21
1980	913	−69	1,115	−239	1,248	−96
1985	495	14	785	−49	1,426	−220
1989	1,125	122	1,064	−104	1,280	−259
1993	1,405	−71	1,544	−251	287	−82
1960–73	176	10	247	−36	222	−38
1974–80	523	−7	852	−147	888	−42
1981–89	736	46	869	−53	1,310	−176
1990–93	1,346	73	1,345	−56	442	−172
1960–90	489	22	663	−75	769	−89
1960–93	586	23	752	−89	735	−89
1974–90	684	29	883	−96	1,136	−124
1974–93	798	30	969	−112	1,024	−117

Sources: Author's calculations based on Tables II.7, III.16, and IV.7 for totals, and Tables II.21, III.30, and IV.21 for per capita.

[a]Cumulative trade volume and balance per capita in annual averages. [b]In Cuba, in the official exchange, the peso was par with the U.S. dollar in 1960–71 and 1986–93 but much higher than the dollar in 1972–85; the conversion in the table is done based on the official exchange.

Table V.13

Total External Debt (Disbursed) per Capita of the Three Countries, 1960–1993 (Million of U.S. Current $)

Year	Total Debt (Million U.S.$)			Debt per Capita (U.S.$)		
	Chile	Costa Rica	Cuba	Chile	Costa Rica	Cuba
1960	445	44	48[a]	59	36	7[a]
1965	947	101		111	74	
1970	2,065	134		220	127	
1975[b]	2,812	421	5,310[c]	285	214	564[c]
1980	11,084	2,735		994	1,200	
1985	19,444	4,401	16,700[c]	1,604	1,665	1,664[c]
1989	16,250	4,488	30,639[c]	1,254	1,526	3,414[c]
1990	17,425	3,924	36,723[c,d]	1,323	1,301	3,433[c,d]
1993	19,186	3,827		1,389	1,182	

Sources: Tables II.13, III.23, and IV.13 (also for Cuba CERP 1965 and Mesa-Lago 1981) for total debt; author's estimates of debt per capita based on Tables II.21, III,30, and IV.21.

[a]1958. [b]1973 in Chile. [c]Includes debt in convertible currency and debt with the Soviet Union. [d]Debt with the Soviet Union at official exchange rate of ruble; at commercial rate the total debt was 16,168 and 1,512 per capita.

Table V.14

Decile Distribution of Income in Chile (1967, 1981, 1982, 1989, 1992), Costa Rica (1961, 1971, 1979, 1982, 1990), and Cuba (1962, 1973, 1978, 1986) (Percentage)

Deciles	Chile[a]				Costa Rica[b]					Cuba[a]			
	1967	1981[c]	1982[c]	1990	1961	1971	1979	1982	1990	1962	1973	1978	1986
First	1.5	1.7	1.5		2.6	2.1	2.2	2.1	1.1	2.8	2.9	5.1	5.2
Second	2.5	2.9	2.7		3.4	3.3	4.0	3.9	2.8	4.9	4.9	5.9	6.1
Third	3.3	3.6	3.5		3.8	4.2	4.9	5.5	4.3	5.3	5.4	6.5	7.2
Fourth	4.4	4.6	4.5		4.0	5.1	6.0	6.0	5.2	7.0	7.1	7.3	7.5
Fifth	5.4	5.2	5.6		4.4	6.2	7.3	7.9	6.4	8.5	8.7	8.0	7.8
Sixth	6.9	6.7	6.6		5.4	7.5	8.3	8.5	8.1	9.8	10.5	8.5	9.2
Seventh	8.5	7.5	8.3		7.1	9.3	9.5	10.4	10.1	10.2	12.0	9.9	11.1
Eighth	11.1	9.7	11.0		9.3	11.7	12.1	11.8	12.9	13.7	13.5	12.8	12.1
Ninth	16.3	15.1	17.4		14.0	16.2	17.3	16.0	17.2	15.8	15.1	14.9	13.7
Tenth	40.1	43.9	38.9	37.2	46.0	34.4	28.4	27.9	31.9	22.0	19.9	21.1	20.1
Total	100.0	100.0	100.0	100.0	100.0	100.0	100.0	100.0	100.0	100.0	100.0	100.0	100.0

Sources: Chile from Altimir 1984, Marcel and Solimano 1994; Cuba from Table III.27; Costa Rica from Table IV.18.
[a]Personal income. [b]Family income in 1961–71, head of household 1979–90. [c]Greater Santiago.

Table V.15

Real Wage Indices in the Three Countries, 1971–1994 (1980 = 100)

Country	Years	Mean	Urban Minimum
Chile	1971	133.4	
	1973	79.9	
	1975	69.5	60.9
	1982	108.6	117.2
	1985	93.5	76.4
	1990	104.8	86.8
	1993	118.9	105.8
	1994	124.5	
Costa Rica	1973	80.0	
	1975	73.9	96.0[a]
	1982	70.8	85.9
	1985	92.2	112.2
	1990	86.5	120.5
	1993	94.7	112.5
	1994	98.4	112.8
Cuba	1976	91.7	
	1982	109.3	
	1986	120.9	
	1989	120.1[b]	
	1993	97.1[b]	
	1994	79.0[b]	

Sources: Tables II.19, III.28, and IV.20.

[a]1978. [b]ECLAC (1997) index gives 1989, 103.8; 1993, 77.2; and 1994, 59.5.

Table V.16

Poverty Incidence in Chile and Costa Rica,
1970–1993 (National Rates)

Country	Years	Poverty	Indigence
Chile	1970[a]	17	6
	1976[b]	57	28
	1980[b]	44	14
	1984[b]	48	23
	1986[b]	51	25
	1990[a]	35	12
	1992[a]	28	7
Costa Rica[a]	1970	24	6
	1981	22	6
	1988	22–25[c]	8
	1990	20–24[c]	10
	1993	17	9

Sources: Tables II.18 and IV.19.

Note: No data available for Cuba. [a]Percentage of households.
[b]Percentage of individuals. [c]Two different estimates.

Table V.17

Economic Activities and Women as Percentages of Labor Force in the Three Countries, 1960–1993

| | | Labor Force by Economic Activity | | | | Women in |
Country	Year	Primary[a]	Secondary[b]	Tertiary[c]	Nonspecified[d]	Labor Force
Chile	1960	32.3	22.1	38.5	7.1	22.0[e]
	1970	25.1	25.0	43.8	6.1	23.0
	1980	17.5	22.2	57.2	3.1	29.3
	1985	20.8	18.4	58.0	2.8	30.7
	1990	21.5	22.9	55.5	0.1	30.8
	1993	18.5	25.2	56.2	0.1	32.5
Costa Rica	1963	49.4	18.5	30.7	1.4	16.3
	1973	36.7	19.6	38.5	5.2	19.3
	1984	31.2	19.5	37.9	11.4	24.8
	1990	25.5	25.8	47.2	1.5	28.5
	1993	22.8	25.6	50.4	1.2	29.9
Cuba	1957	38.8	21.2	36.0	4.0	12.6
	1970	30.0	26.3	41.3	2.4	18.3
	1979	21.9	27.8	42.9	7.4	27.4
	1981	22.3	27.8	46.3	3.6	31.4
	1990	21.9	25.5	40.1	12.5	
	1994	28.2	23.2	42.9	5.7	

Sources: Economic activities from Tables II.14, III.24, and IV.14; women from II.15, III.25, and IV.15.

[a]Agriculture, fishing, and mining. [b]Industry, electricity, gas and water, construction (includes mining in Cuba). [c]Transport and communication, commerce, services. [d]Nonspecified and unemployed. [e]1965.

Table V.18

Open Unemployment Rates in the Three Countries, 1960–1993
(Percentage of Labor Force)

Years	National Chile[b]	National Costa Rica	National Cuba	Urban[a] Chile	Urban[a] Costa Rica
1960	7.1	6.9	11.8	7.4	
1965	4.7[c]		6.5	5.4	
1970	3.4		1.3	7.1	3.5
1973	3.1[d]			4.6	
1976	14.0	6.3	4.5	16.8	5.4
1980	10.4	5.9	5.5[e]	11.8	6.0
1982	19.6	9.4		22.1	9.9
1985	12.1	6.8		16.4	6.7
1988	6.3	5.5	6.0	9.1[f]	6.3
1990	5.6	4.6	7.3	8.5[g]	5.4
1993	4.5	4.1	6.7[h]	5.9	4.0

Sources: Tables II.16, III.26, and IV.16.

[a]Not available for Cuba; Santiago for Chile. [b]ILO series except for ODEPLAN in 1960. [c]1967. [d]1972. [e]1981. [f]1989. [g]1991. [h]1994; "equivalent unemployment" was estimated as 33% by ECLAC 1997.

Table V.19

Percentage of Illiteracy in the Three Countries, 1953–1992
(15 Years and Older)

Years	Chile[a]	Costa Rica[b]	Cuba[c]
1953	19.8	20.6	23.6
1958–64	16.4[d]	14.3	21.0
1970–73	11.0[d]	11.6[d]	12.9
1979–82	8.9[d]		4.0
1984–85	7.8[d]	7.4[d]	7.6[d]
1990	6.6[d]	7.2[d]	6.0[d]
1992	5.7[d]	5.7	5.3[d]

Sources: Tables II.24, III.33, and IV.24.

[a]All Chilean rates are 15 years and older. The second figure is in 1964, and the fourth figure is in 1982. [b]Costa Rican rates for 1953 and 1963 are based on 10 years and older; the population bracket for 1992 is unknown but probably is 15 years and older. The second figure is in 1963, the third in 1973, and the fifth in 1984. [c]Cuban rates for 1958 (the author's projection based on 1943 and 1953 census) and 1970 are based on 10 years and older. The rate for 1979 is based on 10 to 49 years, hence excluding the population with a higher degree of illiteracy. The 1992 rate is author's interpolation based on an UNESCO estimate for 1995. [d]UNESCO adjusted figures (standardized as 15 years and older).

Table V.20

Percentage of Age Group Enrolled in Education in the Three Countries, 1960–1992

Year	Chile Elementary	Chile Secondary	Chile Higher Education	Costa Rica Elementary	Costa Rica Secondary	Costa Rica Higher Education	Cuba Elementary	Cuba Secondary	Cuba Higher Education
1960[a]	87	23	4	93	20	5	110	14	3
1965	98	30	6	105	24	5	129	25	4
1970	105	38	10	110	28	9	121	25	5
1973	120	51	17	113	39	13	126	33	8
1975	118	48	16	107	43	17	124	54	11
1980	113	61	11	106	47	23	108	80	20
1985	105	67	16	98	40	23	104	85	21
1990	99	74	19[b]	101	42	27	100	90	21
1992	106	75	24	105	46	28[c]	100	80	18

Sources: Tables II.24, III.33, and IV.24.

Note: Each country had its own age limits, which change according to modifications of their educative systems. Chile 1960–65 had elementary, 7–12 years, secondary, 13–18 years, and higher, 20–24 years; 1970–86 had elementary, 6–13 years, secondary, 14–17 years, and higher, 20–24 years. Costa Rica 1960–65 had elementary, 7–12 years, secondary, 13–17 years, and higher, 20–24 years; 1970–85 had elementary, 6–11 years, secondary, 12–16 years, and higher, 20–24 years. Cuba 1960–65 and 1980–85 had elementary, 6–11 years, secondary, 12–17 years, and higher, 20–24 years; 1970–75 had elementary, 6–11, secondary, 12–18, and higher, 20–24. [a]1963 for Costa Rica. [b]1989. [c]1991.

Table V.21

Infant Mortality and Life Expectancy in the Three Countries, 1960–1992

Year	Infant Mortality[a]			Life Expectancy (Years)		
	Chile	Costa Rica	Cuba	Chile	Costa Rica	Cuba
1960	119.5	74.3	35.9[b]	58.1	61.6	64.0
1965	97.3	75.0	37.8	60.6	64.3	67.2
1970	82.2	61.5	38.7	63.6	67.1	70.0
1973	65.8	44.8	28.9	65.7	68.6	70.9[c]
1975	57.6	37.1	27.3	67.2	69.7	73.0[d]
1980	33.0	19.1	19.6	71.0	72.4	74.3[e]
1985	19.5	17.7	16.5	71.5	74.2	74.5[f]
1989	17.1	14.7	11.1	71.9	75.0	74.7[g]
1990	16.0	14.8	10.7	72.0	75.2	
1992	13.9	13.7	10.2	72.1[h]	75.7	75.4

Sources: Tables II.21, III.30, and IV.21.

[a]Infant deaths under age 1 per 1,000 live births. [b]In 1958 was 33.4. [c]Annual average 1971–75. [d]1977. [e]1983. [f]1986. [g]1987. [h]1991.

Table V.22
Rate of Contagious Diseases in the Three Countries, 1960–1992 (Reported Cases per 100,000 Inhabitants)

Country	Year	Diphtheria	Hepatitis	Malaria	Measles	Polio	Syphilis	Tetanus	Tuberculosis	Typhoid
Chile	1961	34.4	1.1	—[a]	489.6	8.2	—	0.7	—	58.8
	1965	12.7	14.6	—	151.7	2.4	51.8	0.3	—	64.8
	1970	3.4	13.9	—	227.5	2.1	15.1	0.3	86.0	54.9
	1973	5.5	44.4	—	39.1	—	27.2	0.3	82.4	37.3
	1980	2.3	38.8	—	34.6	—	73.8	0.3	76.8	97.9
	1985	1.8	107.6[b]	—	141.1	—	—	0.2	55.0	—
	1990	0.3	66.5	—	14.1	—	30.4[c]	0.2	46.7	39.3
	1992	0.2[d]	38.8	—	15.5[d]	—	—	0.1[d]	39.0	13.8
Costa Rica	1961	12.4	32.2	136.6	89.6	2.8	48.7		40.2	8.1
	1965	2.8	37.9	172.0	133.4	1.0	42.9	3.0	38.3	3.5
	1970	3.2	30.7	20.5	266.1	1.3	56.1	5.0	23.1	3.5
	1975	0.3	36.8	14.7	36.0	—	74.7	2.3	29.9	1.4
	1980	—	71.1	16.7	44.6	—	85.4	0.4	19.6	0.2
	1985	—	95.0	27.8	0.1	—	—	0.2	13.9	0.3
	1990	—	85.1	38.2	2.5	—	59.9[c]	5.4	1.6	
	1992	—	24.0	225.0		—	56.0	0.1	6.5	
Cuba	1958	2.4	5.0[e]	2.0	2.9	1.6	0.7	4.1[f]	18.0	5.1
	1965	8.2	115.8	1.7	121.6	—	30.4	6.7	65.0	3.1
	1970	0.1	102.6	0.1[g]	105.2	—	7.8	2.6	30.8	5.0
	1975	—	217.0	0.9	113.4	—	47.6	0.7	14.2	4.0
	1980	—	208.3	3.1	39.1	—	44.7	0.3	11.6	1.0
	1985	—	209.2	4.5	28.5	—	62.6	0.1	6.7	0.6
	1990	—	124.6	4.3	0.2	—	86.1	—	5.1	0.6
	1992	—	295.4	0.1	0.1	—	101.7	—	5.8	0.5

Sources: Tables II.22, III.31, and IV.22

[a] —, no cases reported or negligible rates. [b] 1984. [c] 1988. [d] 1991. [e] 1961. [f] 1959. [g] 1971.

Table V.23

*Access to Potable Water and Sewerage/Sanitation Service in Urban
and Rural Population of the Three Countries, Selected Years
Between 1953 and 1993 (Percentage)*

| Country | Year | Percentage of Urban Population | | Percentage of Rural Population |
		Water[a]	Sewerage[b]	Water[c]
Chile	1963	44.8	21.3	10.8
	1973	68.6	36.5	34.8
	1980	91.4	67.4	44.2
	1985	95.2	75.1	69.3
	1990	96.1	80.6	81.1
	1993	96.7	85.0	90.7
Costa Rica	1964	96.6	29.7	42.8
	1973	100.0	40.1	66.0
	1980	100.0	92.0	68.0
	1985	100.0	99.0	83.0
	1989	100.0	100.0	85.5
	1991	100.0	100.0	
Cuba	1953	81.8	95.1	15.0
	1970	87.8	93.3	24.0
	1981	89.9	95.8	32.9

Sources: Tables II.23, III.32, and IV.23.

[a]Piped water; in Costa Rica and Cuba include easy access to piped water outside the home. [b]Not clear is sewerage only or "sanitation" including all means of excreta disposal (in Cuba only the latter). [c]Probably piped water and other sources of access to potable water.

Table V.24

Social Security Coverage in the Three Countries, 1960–1993

Year	Percentage of Total Population Covered on Health Care[a]		Percentage of Labor Force Covered in Pensions		
	Costa Rica[b]	Cuba[c]	Chile[d]	Costa Rica[e]	Cuba[f]
1960	15.0	4.2	70.8	5.9	62.6
1965	30.0		73.8	16.8	
1970	47.2	100.0	75.6	23.6	88.7
1975	59.6	100.0	75.9	45.4	
1980	75.7	100.0	61.2	50.8	89.6
1985	81.4	100.0	70.0	44.8	93.0
1989	85.4	100.0	74.3	45.8	94.1
1990	85.9	100.0	79.1	46.2	
1993	86.2	100.0	90.2	48.9	

Sources: Tables II.25, III.34, and IV.25.

[a]Data are not available in Chile for this indicator, but at least all the labor force covered with pensions and their dependents are covered by health care; in addition, noninsureds on a pension who are destitute are covered by the public health system under social welfare. Coverage of the population, therefore, is virtually universal. [b]Excludes health care coverage by the Ministry of Health; if it is included, coverage should be virtually universal. [c]1960 is actually 1958; *legal* coverage since 1970. Cuba has never published statistics on coverage. [d]Affiliates; the percentage of active contributors is about half. On the one hand, the figure is inflated because the bulk of the self-employed are not covered, and the armed forces have a separate program; on the other hand, a welfare pension is granted to the noninsured who are destitute. [e]Excludes noncontributory welfare pensions granted to noninsured who are destitute; if included, coverage would increase significantly. The year 1985 is 1988. [f]Author's estimates based on *legal* coverage since 1970; Cuba has never published data on statistical coverage. The year 1960 is 1958, 1975 is 1979, 1980 is 1981, and 1989 is 1987.

Table V.25

Housing Units Built in the Three Countries,
1965–1989/93 (per 1,000 Inhabitants)

Years	Chile	Costa Rica	Cuba[a]
1965	3.5[b]	2.7	0.6
1970		3.0	0.6
1974	2.0	6.7	2.0
1975	1.6	6.1	2.0
1980	3.9	5.5	2.1
1982	2.1	3.5	2.5
1985	4.2	3.6	2.4
1986–89[c]	5.4	5.6	3.7
1974–89[c]	3.5	5.2	3.5[d]
1990–93[c]	7.2		2.5

Sources: Tables II.26, III.35, and IV.26.

[a]Cuba 1965–79 only state-civilian and cooperative, 1980–93 also include state military and private-habitable (the former was small and the latter nonexistent in 1965–79). [b]Annual average 1965–70. [c]Annual averages. [d]1980–89.

Table V.26
Selection of Indicators for Comparative Evaluation of Performance in the Three Countries, 1960–1993 (Percentage unless Specified)

Indicators	Chile					Costa Rica					Cuba				
	1960	1973	1980	1990	1993[a]	1960	1973	1980	1990	1993[a]	1960	1973	1980	1990	1993[a]
Domestic macroeconomic															
1. GDP/GSP growth per capita[b]	1.3	2.0	1.5	1.7	2.4	2.8	2.0	−0.1	1.7	1.9	3.4	5.8	3.2	3.4	1.2
2. GDP per capita (U.S.$)			4,862[c]	5,099	8,900			3,760[c]	4,542	5,680			2,500[c]	2,200	3,000
3. Gross domestic investment/GDP	13.9	7.9	21.0	20.3	26.2	16.1	21.9	23.9	22.5	22.1	17.6	17.4	19.3	14.9	4.8
4. Inflation rates[b]	51.4	116.6	19.4	54.9	46.6	6.5	12.3	26.3	12.5	13.2	2.7	1.1	0.7	1.7	2.8
5. Fiscal balance	−4.6	−24.7	3.1	1.4	1.8	−4.0[d]	−2.2	−7.4	−3.2	−1.9	0		0	−7.5	−33.7
6. Composition of GDP															
Agriculture	10.6	6.8	8.3	9.5	8.5	25.2	21.2	18.0	19.3	18.7			8.8[c]	8.6	6.5
Industry	31.5	34.5	30.9	30.6	30.1	15.1	23.3	24.3	24.6	25.0			27.6[c]	25.5	24.7
External economic															
7. Export concentration[f]	71	83	46	46	35	53	27	24	18	10	78	75	84	80	66
8. Import composition															
Food & Beverage	18	24	13	4	5	13	9	7	8	8	21	20	17	12	26
Fuel	7	7	18	16	9	6	10	15	10	9	11	10	20	27	37
Machinery & transport	40	34	31	44	44	26	27	24	28	26	31	31	36	37	12
9. Trade partner concentration[f]	43	12	21	19	18	51	34	33	43	55	68	49	60	68	22
10. Merchandise trade (U.S.$ per capita)															
Volume[b,g]	176	523	736	684	798	247	852	869	663	752	222	888	1,310	769	735
Balance[b,g]	10	−7	46	29	30	−36	−147	−53	−75	−89	−38	−42	−176	−89	−89
11. External debt (U.S.$ per capita)	59	285	994	1,323	1,389	36	214	1,665	1,301	1,182	7	564	1,664[c]	3,433	
Distribution and employment															
12. Labor force composition															
Primary	32.3	25.1	17.5	21.5	18.5	49.4	36.7	31.2	25.5	22.8	38.8	30.0	22.3	21.9	28.2
Secondary	22.1	25.0	22.2	22.9	25.2	18.5	19.6	19.5	25.8	25.6	21.2	26.3	27.8	25.5	23.2

13. Real mean wages (1980 = 100)	133	80	100	105	124	80	100	86	98	92[h]	100	120	79
14. Open unemployment	7.1	3.1	10.4	5.6	4.5	6.3[h]	5.9	4.6	4.1	4.5[h]	5.5	7.3	7.7[i]
Social standards													
15. Illiteracy	19.8[j]	11.0	7.8[k]	6.6	5.7	11.6	7.4[k]	7.2	5.7	12.9	7.6[k]	6.0	5.3[l]
16. Educational enrollment													
Secondary	30[d]	51	61	74	75	39	47	42	46	25[d]	80	90	80[l]
Higher	6[d]	17	11	19	24	13	23	27	28	4[d]	20	21	18[l]
17. Infant mortality	119.5	65.8	33.0	16.0	13.9	44.8	19.1	14.8	13.0	35.9	19.6	10.7	10.2
18. Life expectancy	58.1	65.7	71.0	72.0	72.1	68.6	72.4	75.2	75.7	64.0	74.3	74.7[m]	75.4
19. Contagious diseases (× 100,000 inhabitants)													
Hepatitis	1.1	44.4	38.8	66.5	38.8	32.2	71.1	85.1		5.0	208.3	124.6	295.4
Measles	489.6	39.1	34.6	14.1	15.5	36.0	44.6	2.5		2.9	39.1	0.2	0.1
Syphilis	0	27.2	73.8	30.4	48.7	74.7	85.4	59.9		0.7	44.7	86.1	101.7
Tuberculosis	0	82.4	76.8	46.7	39.0	29.9	19.6	1.6	6.5	18.0	14.2	11.6	5.8
Typhoid	58.8	37.3	97.9	39.3	13.8	8.1	0.2	0.3[c]		5.1	1.0	0.6	0.5
20. Housing units built (× 1,000 inhabitants)	3.5[n]	2.0	3.9	5.4[o]	7.2[p]	6.7	5.5	5.6[o]		0.6[n,q]	2.1	3.7[o]	2.5[p]

Sources: Tables V.3–V.15, V.17–V.22, and V.25.

Notes: Data for each year, with few exceptions (the year before or after). [a]Most recent year available, in most cases 1993, in a few either 1992 or 1994. [b]Average annual GDP (GSP for Cuba) per capita. In Chile (1960 = 1961–73, 1973 = 1974–80, 1980 = 1981–89, 1990 = 1981–89, 1990 = 1961–90, and 1993 = 1961–93), and in Costa Rica and Cuba (1960 = 1961–73, 1973 = 1974–80, 1980 = 1981–89, 1990 = 1981–89, 1990 = 1961–90, and 1993 = 1961–93). The same periods apply for inflation rates and merchandise trade. [c]1985. [d]1965. [e]Copper in Chile, coffee in Costa Rica, and sugar in Cuba. [f]Chile and Costa Rica with the United States, Cuba with the Soviet Union/Russia (except 1960 with the U.S.). [g]Cumulative trade volume and balance per capita in annual average. [h]1976. [i]1991, equivalent unemployment was 19%. [j]1953. [k]1984–85 annual average. [l]Author's estimates based on ECLAC 1997. [m]1987. [n]1965; in Chile an annual average for 1960–70. [o]1986–89 annual average. [p]1990–93 annual average. [q]State civilian and cooperatives only.

Table V.27

Absolute and Relative Improvement Rankings of the Three Countries, 1960–1993

	Chile				Costa Rica				Cuba			
	Absolute Rank		Relative		Absolute Rank		Relative		Absolute Rank		Relative	
Indicators	1980	1993	Score	Rank	1980	1993	Score	Rank	1980	1993	Score	Rank
Domestic macroeconomic												
1. GDP/GSP growth per capita[a]	2	1			3	2			1	3		
2. GDP per capita (U.S.$)[b]	1	1	4,038	1	2	2	1,920	2	3	3	500	3
3. Gross domestic investment/GDP	2	3	18.3	1	1	2	6.0	2	3	3	−12.8	3
4. Inflation rates[a]	2	3			3	1			1	1		
5. Fiscal balance	1	1	26.5	1	3	2	−2.1	2	2	3	−33.7	3
6. Composition of GDP[c]												
Agriculture	1	2	0.2	1	3	3	0.7	2	2	1	2.3	3
Industry	1	1	−0.8	1	3	2	0.7	2	2	3	−2.9	3
External economic												
7. Export concentration	2	2	−48	1	1	1	−43	2	3	3	−12	3
8. Import composition												
Food & Beverage	2	1	−19	1	1	2	−5	2	3	3	5	3
Fuel	2	1	2	1	1	1	3	2	3	3	26	3
Machinery & transport	2	1	10	1	3	2	0	2	1	3	−19	3
9. Trade partner concentration	1	1	6	3	2	3	4	2	3	2	−46	1
10. Merchandise trade (U.S.$ per capita)												
Volume[a,d]	3	1	622	3	2	2	722	2	1	3	802	1
Balance[a,d]	1	1	20	1	2	2	−76	2	3	2	−79	3
11. External debt (U.S.$ per capita)	1	2	1,038	1	2	1	1,265	2	2	3	3,426	3

652

Distribution and employment

12. Labor force composition

Primary	1	−6.6	3	1	−26.6	2	3	−10.6	2
Secondary	2	0.2	3	1	7.1	1	3	2.0	2
13. Real mean wages (1980 = 100)^e	1	55	1	2	22	2	3	−14	3
14. Open unemployment	2	1.4	3	2	−2.8	1	3	−4.1	1

Social standards

15. Illiteracy^f	2	−5.3	3	2	−5.9	2	3	−7.6	1
16. Educational enrollment									
Secondary^g	2	24	2	3	22	3	2	66	1
Higher^g	3	7	3	1	23	1	3	14	2
17. Infant mortality	3	−52	1	1	−61	2	1	−26	3
18. Life expectancy	3	6.4	2	1	14.1	1	2	11.4	2
19. Contagious diseases (× 100,000 inhabitants)									
Hepatitis	1	22	1	2	53	2	3	120	3
Measles	3	−25	2	3	−87	1	1	−3	3
Syphilis	2	3	1	3	11	2	3	85	3
Tuberculosis	3	−36	2	2	−39	1	2	−13	3
Typhoid	3	2	3	1	−8	1	2	−4	2
20. Housing units built (× 1,000 inhabitants)	2	5.2	1	2	2.9	2	3	1.9	3

Source: Table V.26.

Note: Absolute for all is based on the years 1980 and 1993 or the most recent year available. Relative is the difference between 1960 and 1993 in Costa Rica and Cuba but between 1974 and 1993 in Chile. ^aAbsolute are annual averages: 1980 (1960–80 for Costa Rica and Cuba but be-tween 1974 and 1993 in Chile). ^bAbsolute are annual averages: 1980 (1960–80 for Costa Rica and Cuba and 1974–80 for Chile) and 1993 (1960–93 for Costa Rica and Cuba, 1974–93 for Chile). ^bRelative is 1985–93. ^cRelative is 1980–93. ^dRelative is 1974–93 annual average compared with 1960–73 average. ^eRelative is 1974–93 annual average compared with 1960–73. ^fRelative is 1973–93. ^gRelative is 1970/73–92. ^gRelative is 1965–92.

Table V.28

Arithmetic Rankings in Absolute and Relative Improvement Indicators in the Three Countries

Absolute Indicators (20)	Chile		Costa Rica		Cuba	
	1980	1993	1980	1993	1980	1993
1. Domestic macroeconomic[a]	10.0	8.5	13.0	12.5	12.0	15.0
2. External economic	8.0	7.0	8.7	8.7	12.3	13.5
3. Distribution and employment	4.5	4.5	5.0	4.5	3.5	9.0
4. Social standards	14.5	13.2	9.2	10.6	10.8	11.2
Merging 1 and 2	18.0	15.5	21.7	21.2	24.3	28.5
Merging 3 and 4	19.0	17.7	14.2	15.1	14.5	20.2
Merging 1, 2, 3, and 4	29.8	33.2	35.9	36.3	38.6	48.7

Absolute Indicators (30) Changes between 1960/73 and 1993	Chile	Costa Rica	Cuba
Unchanged	16	12	12
Improved	11	11	5
Deteriorated	3	7	13

Relative Indicators (20)	Chile	Costa Rica	Cuba
1. Domestic macroeconomic	4.0	8.0	12.0
2. External economic	8.0	10.0	12.0
3. Distribution and employment	7.0	5.0	6.0
4. Social standards	13.3	9.4	13.3
Merging 1 and 2	12.0	18.0	24.0
Merging 3 and 4	20.3	14.4	19.3
Merging 1, 2, 3, and 4	32.3	32.4	43.3

Source: Author's calculation based on Table V.27.

[a]If unreliable indicators 1 and 4 (economic growth and inflation) are excluded, the scores of the countries are 6.0, 7.0, and 10.0 in 1980, and 4.5, 8.5, and 11.0 in 1993.

Table V.29

Changes in Relative Improvement Ranking of the Three Countries Based on Standardized Period

Indicators	Chile Score	Chile Rank	Costa Rica Score	Costa Rica Rank	Cuba Score	Cuba Rank
Domestic macroeconomic						
3. Gross domestic investment/GDP	12.3	1		2		3
	18.3	1	6.0	2	−12.8	3
5. Fiscal balance	6.4	1		2		3
	26.5	1	−2.1	2	−33.7	3
External economic						
7. Export concentration	−36	2		1		3
	−48	1	−43	2	−12	3
8. Import composition						
Food & beverage	−13	1		2		3
	−19	1	−5	2	5	3
Machinery & transport	4	1		2		3
	10	1	0	2	−19	3
9. Trade partner concentration	−25	2		3		1
	6	3	4	2	−46	1
10. Merchandise trade (U.S.$ per capita)						
Volume	586	3		2		1
	622	3	722	2	802	1
Balance	23	1		2		3
	20	1	−76	2	−79	3
11. External debt per capita	1,264	1		1		3
	1,038	1	1,265	2	3,426	3
Distribution and employment						
12. Labor force composition						
Primary	−13.8	2		1		3
	−6.6	3	−26.6	1	−10.6	2
Secondary	3.1	2		1		3
	0.2	3	7.1	1	2.0	2
14. Open unemployment	−2.6	3		2		1
	1.4	3	−2.8	2	−4.1	1
Social standards						
16. Educational enrollment						
Secondary	45	2		3		1
	24	2	22	3	66	1
Higher	20	2		1		3
	7	3	23	1	14	2
17. Infant mortality	−105	1		2		3
	−52	2	−61	1	−26	3
18. Life expectancy	14.1	1		1		3
	6.4	3	14.1	1	11.4	2

(continued)

Table V.29
(Continued)

Indicators	Chile Score	Chile Rank	Costa Rica Score	Costa Rica Rank	Cuba Score	Cuba Rank
19. Contagious diseases (× 100,000 inhabitants)						
Hepatitis	65	2		1		3
	22	1	53	2	120	3
Measles	476	1		2		3
	−25	2	−87	1	−3	3
Syphilis	30	2		1		3
	3	1	11	2	85	3
Tuberculosis	47	3		1		2
	−36	2	−39	1	−13	3
Typhoid	−19	1		2		3
	3	3	−8	1	−4	2
20. Housing units built	3.7	1		2		3
(× 1,000 inhabitants)	5.2	1	2.9	2	1.9	3

Sources: Tables V.26, V.27, and author's calculations based on comparative tables in this chapter.

Note: This table reproduces, in the bottom row for each country, the scores and relative rankings of Table V.27 based on 1974–93 for Chile and 1960–93 for Costa Rica and Cuba, while the row above shows the scores and rankings for Chile in 1960–93 and any resulting change in the rankings of the other two countries. The table includes only those indicators on which a difference occurs; six indicators (1, 2, 4, 6, 13, and 15) were excluded because either the period of comparison was the same in all countries or it was not feasible to do such a comparison.

Table V.30

Indices for Ranking Performance in the Three Countries, 1960–1993

Indicators	Country	1960	1973	1980	1990	1993
Domestic macroeconomic						
1. GDP/GSP growth per capita[a]	Chile	38.2	34.5	48.5	50.0	100.0
	Costa Rica	82.4	34.5	0.0	50.0	79.2
	Cuba	100.0	100.0	100.0	100.0	50.0
2. GDP per capita (U.S.$)	Chile			100.0	100.0	100.0
	Costa Rica			77.3	89.1	63.8
	Cuba			51.4	43.1	33.7
3. Gross domestic investment/GDP	Chile	79.0	36.1	87.9	90.2	100.0
	Costa Rica	91.5	100.0	100.0	100.0	84.4
	Cuba	100.0	79.5	80.8	66.2	18.3
4. Inflation rates	Chile	5.3	0.9	3.6	3.1	6.0
	Costa Rica	41.5	8.9	2.7	13.6	21.2
	Cuba	100.0	100.0	100.0	100.0	100.0
5. Fiscal Balance[a]	Chile	0.0		100.0	100.0	100.0
	Costa Rica	13.0		0.0	48.3	89.6
	Cuba	100.0		70.5	0.0	0.0
6. Composition of GDP						
Agriculture	Chile			100.0	90.5	76.5
	Costa Rica			46.1	44.6	34.8
	Cuba			94.3	100.0	100.0
Industry	Chile			100.0	100.0	100.0
	Costa Rica			78.6	80.4	83.1
	Cuba			89.3	83.3	82.1
External economic						
7. Export concentration	Chile	74.6	32.5	52.2	39.1	28.6
	Costa Rica	100.0	100.0	100.0	100.0	100.0
	Cuba	67.9	36.0	28.6	22.5	15.2
8. Import composition						
Food & beverage	Chile	72.2	37.5	53.8	100.0	100.0
	Costa Rica	100.0	100.0	100.0	50.0	62.5
	Cuba	61.9	45.0	41.2	33.3	19.2
Fuel	Chile	100.0	100.0	83.3	62.5	100.0
	Costa Rica	116.7	70.0	100.0	100.0	100.0
	Cuba	63.6	70.0	75.0	37.0	24.3
Machinery & transport	Chile	100.0	100.0	86.1	100.0	100.0
	Costa Rica	65.0	79.4	66.7	63.6	59.1
	Cuba	77.5	91.2	100.0	84.1	27.3
9. Trade partner concentration	Chile	100.0	100.0	100.0	100.0	100.0
	Costa Rica	84.3	35.3	63.6	44.2	32.7
	Cuba	63.2	24.5	35.0	27.9	81.8

(continued)

Table V.30
(Continued)

Indicators	Country	1960	1973	1980	1990	1993
10. Merchandise trade (U.S.$ per capita)						
Volume	Chile	71.3	58.9	56.2	88.9	100.0
	Costa Rica	100.0	95.9	66.3	86.2	94.2
	Cuba	89.9	100.0	100.0	100.0	92.1
Balance[a]	Chile	100.0	100.0	100.0	100.0	100.0
	Costa Rica	3.9	0.0	55.2	13.5	0.0
	Cuba	0.0	74.9	0.0	0.0	0.4
11. External debt (U.S.$ per capita)	Chile	11.9	75.1	100.0	98.3	85.1
	Costa Rica	19.4	100.0	59.7	100.0	100.0
	Cuba	100.0	37.9	59.7	37.9	34.4[b]
Distribution and employment						
12. Labor force composition						
Primary	Chile	100.0	100.0	100.0	100.0	100.0
	Costa Rica	65.4	68.4	56.1	84.3	81.1
	Cuba	83.2	83.7	78.5	98.2	65.6
Secondary	Chile	100.0	95.1	79.9	88.8	98.4
	Costa Rica	83.7	74.5	70.1	100.0	100.0
	Cuba	95.9	100.0	100.0	98.8	90.6
13. Real mean wages[c]	Chile		100.0	100.0	100.0	100.0
	Costa Rica		100.0	100.0	24.0	38.5
	Cuba		100.0	34.8	97.4	0.0
14. Open unemployment	Chile	97.2	100.0	52.9	82.1	91.1
	Costa Rica	100.0	49.2	93.2	100.0	100.0
	Cuba	58.5	68.9	100.0	63.0	53.2
Social standards						
15. Illiteracy	Chile	100.0	100.0	94.9	90.9	93.0
	Costa Rica	96.1	94.8	100.0	83.3	93.0
	Cuba	83.9	85.3	97.4	100.0	100.0
16. Educational enrollment						
Secondary	Chile	100.0	100.0	76.3	82.2	93.8
	Costa Rica	80.0	76.5	58.8	46.7	57.5
	Cuba	83.3	64.7	100.0	100.0	100.0
Higher	Chile	100.0	100.0	47.8	70.4	85.7
	Costa Rica	83.3	76.5	100.0	100.0	100.0
	Cuba	66.7	47.1	87.0	77.8	64.3
17. Infant mortality	Chile	30.0	43.9	57.9	66.9	73.4
	Costa Rica	48.3	64.5	100.0	72.3	74.5
	Cuba	100.0	100.0	97.4	100.0	100.0
18. Life expectancy	Chile	90.8	92.7	95.6	95.7	95.2
	Costa Rica	96.3	96.8	97.4	100.0	100.0
	Cuba	100.0	100.0	100.0	99.3	99.6

(continued)

Table V.30
(Continued)

Indicators	Country	1960	1973	1980	1990	1993
19. Contagious diseases (× 100,000 inhabitants)						
Hepatitis	Chile	100.0	82.9	100.0	100.0	100.0
	Costa Rica	3.4	100.0	54.6	78.1	45.6[d]
	Cuba	22.0	17.0	18.6	53.4	13.1
Measles	Chile	0.6	92.1	100.0	1.4	0.6
	Costa Rica	3.2	100.0	77.6	8.0	4.0[d]
	Cuba	100.0	31.7	88.5	100.0	100.0
Syphilis	Chile	100.0	100.0	60.6	100.0	100.0[e]
	Costa Rica	0.2	36.4	52.3	50.8	50.8[d]
	Cuba	14.3	57.1	100.0	35.3	29.9
Tuberculosis	Chile	100.0	17.2	15.1	3.4	8.7[e]
	Costa Rica	0.2	47.5	59.2	100.0	89.2
	Cuba	0.6	100.0	100.0	31.4	100.0
Typhoid	Chile	8.7	3.8	0.2	0.8	2.2
	Costa Rica	63.0	100.0	100.0	100.0	100.0[d]
	Cuba	100.0	35.0	20.0	50.0	60.0
20. Housing units built (× 1,000 inhabitants)	Chile	100.0	29.9	70.9	96.4	100.0
	Costa Rica	77.1	100.0	100.0	100.0	77.8[d]
	Cuba	17.1	29.9	38.2	66.1	34.7

Sources: Tables V.3–V.15, V.18–V.22, V.25, and V.26.

Note: Data shown for each year, except indicators 1, 4, and 10, which are annual averages in the periods specified in Table V.26. A value of 100 is given normally to the country with the best performance in each indicator, and 1 to the worst performance. [a]This index was calculated based on data from Table V.26 but rescaled because of negative signs; zero was given to the lowest figure. [b]Because of lack of data for 1993, the figure for 1990 was used: the hard currency debt increased in 1993, but the soft debt with Russia declined. [c]The base for the wage index was changed from 1980 (Table V.26) to 1990 to facilitate the index construction. [d]Because of lack of data for 1992, the 1991 figure was used for diseases as there were declining trends in these and other diseases, except for malaria; in housing the annual average for 1973–89 was used. [e]Because of lack of data for 1992, the latest year available was used in syphilis and tuberculosis, which showed declining trends since the late 1970s.

Table V.31

Combined Indices of Performance and Rankings of the Three Countries, 1960–1993

Cluster	Country	1960	1973	1980	1990	1993	All in 1960–93[a]	All in 1974–93[a]
1. Domestic macroeconomic	Chile	30.6	23.5	73.3	73.1	82.4	82.1	81.7
	Costa Rica	57.1	44.8	40.4	60.6	66.2	68.1	58.5
	Cuba	100.0	59.8	82.4	66.8	48.8	50.0	44.0
2. External economic	Chile	72.6	73.2	80.9	83.9	82.7	80.5	80.5
	Costa Rica	69.9	73.3	74.6	72.9	70.7	69.0	68.8
	Cuba	68.8	50.9	49.1	38.0	40.2	40.8	41.0
3. Distribution and employment	Chile	98.6	99.2	80.9	92.2	96.8	96.8	96.8
	Costa Rica	87.3	73.6	85.4	72.1	76.3	76.3	76.3
	Cuba	74.0	86.9	74.7	86.3	43.8	43.8	43.8
4. Social standards	Chile	80.4	70.9	72.7	77.9	82.3	82.3	82.3
	Costa Rica	68.9	84.9	90.9	82.7	80.3	80.3	80.3
	Cuba	70.6	69.9	82.0	84.7	79.5	79.5	79.5
5. Merging clusters 3 and 4	Chile	85.0	80.4	75.5	82.6	87.1	87.1	87.1
	Costa Rica	73.5	81.1	89.1	79.2	79.0	79.0	79.0
	Cuba	71.4	75.5	79.5	85.2	67.6	67.6	67.6

Index of Economic and Social Development:

A. Weights: Four Clusters (1, 2, 3, and 4)

Total	Chile	70.6	66.7	77.0	81.8	86.0	85.4	85.3
Index 1	Costa Rica	70.8	69.1	72.8	72.1	72.8	73.4	71.0
25 + 25 + 25 + 25	Cuba	78.3	66.9	72.0	69.0	53.1	53.5	52.1
Total	Chile	69.7	65.3	76.6	81.0	85.3	84.7	84.6
Index 2	Costa Rica	69.9	69.7	73.1	72.6	73.0	73.6	71.2
25 + 25 + 20 + 30	Cuba	78.2	66.0	72.4	68.9	54.9	55.3	53.9
Total	Chile	68.7	63.9	76.2	80.3	84.6	84.0	83.9
Index 3	Costa Rica	69.0	70.3	73.4	73.1	73.2	73.8	71.4
25 + 25 + 15 + 35	Cuba	78.0	65.2	72.8	68.8	56.7	57.1	55.6

B. Weights: Three Clusters (1, 2, and 3 and 4)

Total	Chile	68.3	64.4	76.3	80.6	84.8	84.2	84.1
Index 4	Costa Rica	68.5	70.1	73.3	72.9	73.1	73.8	71.3
25 + 25 + 50	Cuba	77.9	65.5	72.6	68.8	56.1	56.5	55.0

Source: Author's calculations based on Table V.30.

[a]In cluster 1 only two indicators change: GDP per capita and inflation; and in cluster 2 only one indicator changes: trade volume and balance. The other two clusters do not change.

Table V.32
Combined Indices for the Three Countries Excluding Economic Growth and Inflation, 1960–1993

Cluster	Country	1960	1973	1980	1990	1993	All in 1960–93[a]	All in 1974–93[a]
1. Domestic Macroeconomic	Chile	39.5	18.0	97.0	96.4	97.1	97.1	97.1
	Costa Rica	52.3	50.0	59.9	75.0	74.2	74.2	74.2
	Cuba	100.0	39.7	73.6	50.3	35.8	35.8	35.8
Weights: Four Clusters (1, 2, 3, and 4)								
Total	Chile	72.8	65.3	82.9	87.6	89.7	89.2	89.2
Index 1	Costa Rica	69.6	70.4	77.7	75.7	74.8	75.0	74.9
25 + 25 + 25 + 25	Cuba	78.3	61.9	69.8	64.8	49.8	50.0	50.0
Total	Chile	71.9	63.9	82.5	86.9	89.0	86.4	88.4
Index 2	Costa Rica	68.7	71.0	78.0	76.2	75.0	75.2	75.1
25 + 25 + 20 + 30	Cuba	78.2	61.0	70.2	64.7	51.6	51.7	51.8
Total	Chile	71.0	62.5	82.1	86.1	88.3	87.7	87.7
Index 3	Costa Rica	67.8	71.6	78.3	76.7	75.2	75.4	75.3
25 + 25 + 15 + 35	Cuba	78.0	60.2	70.6	64.7	53.4	53.5	53.6
Weights: Three Clusters (1, 2, and 3 and 4)								
Total	Chile	70.5	63.0	82.2	86.4	86.5	87.9	88.0
Index 4	Costa Rica	67.3	71.4	78.2	76.5	75.1	75.3	75.2
25 + 25 + 50	Cuba	77.9	60.4	70.4	64.7	52.8	52.9	53.0

Source: Author's calculations based on Tables II.3, III.3, IV.3, V.3, V.26, and V.31.

[a]The exclusion of the two unreliable indicators affect this cluster (not the other three clusters) as well as the combined indices.

Table V.33

World and Latin America Rankings of Performance of the Three Countries,
1980–1995 (the Lower the Ranking Number, the Better the Performance)

		Chile		Costa Rica		Cuba	
		Rank		Rank		Rank	
Index[a]	Number of Countries	World	Latin America[b]	World	Latin America[b]	World	Latin America[b]
Human development index[c]							
1980–88 (1991)	160	38	2	40	3	62	10
1989–90 (1992)	160	36	2	42	3	61	10
1990 (1993)	173	36	2	42	3	75	10
1991–92 (1994)	173	38	3	39	4	89	12
1992 (1995)	174	33	4	28	1	72	11
1993 (1996)	174	33	3	31	1	79	10
1994 (1997)	175	30	1	33	2	86	11
Human suffering index[d]							
End of 1980s (1992)	141	43	2	40	1	45	5
Economic freedom index[e]							
1995 (1996)	82	22	2	43	6	79	13
Political rights and civic freedoms[f]							
1988–89 (1990–91)	165	41	4	6	1	153	20
1989–90 (1991–92)	183	45	2	7	1	173	19
1993–94 (1995–96)	191	57	2	31	1	178	20

Sources: (1) UNDP 1991–97; (2) PCC 1992; (3) Messick 1996; (4) McColm et al. 1991, 1992; Karatnycky 1996.
[a]The first year(s) shown under the index is that of the data or survey, and the second year (within parentheses) is that of publication. [b]There are 20 Latin American countries in all but index 3, where the total is 13. [c]UNDP based on 3 indicators with equal weights (GNP p/c in PPP$, life expectancy, and literacy plus educational enrollment); the 1990 edition ranking is not comparable with the following and was omitted. [d]Population Crisis Committee (PCC) based on 10 indicators with equal weights: life expectancy, daily calorie supply, clean drinking water, infant immunization, secondary school enrollment, GNP per capita, inflation rate, communications technology, political freedom, and civil rights. [e]Messick (Freedom House) based on 6 indicators with equal weights (freedom to: hold property, earn a living, operate a business, invest one's earnings, trade internationally, and participate in the market). [f]Freedom House based on 7 political-right indicators and 13 civil-liberty indicators; points (1 to 7 = best to worst) are assigned to each indicators, and arithmetic averages calculated for each of the 2 indices and the total index.

Table V.34

Selected Indicators for the Three Countries, 1993–1997 (Percentage unless Specified)

Indicator	Chile					Costa Rica					Cuba				
	1993	1994	1995	1996	1997[a]	1993	1994	1995	1996	1997[a]	1993	1994	1995	1996	1997[a]
GDP growth absolute	6.3	4.1	8.5	7.2	6.5	6.1	4.5	2.4	−0.6	3.2	−14.9	0.7	2.5	7.8	2.5
GDP growth per capita	4.6	2.4	6.6	5.6	4.8	3.7	2.1	0.1	−2.8	1.0	−15.1	0.0	1.9	7.1	1.9
Gross domestic investment/GDP	21.3[b]	24.2[b]	23.2[b]	24.4[b]		22.1[c]	19.8[c]	19.2[c]	18.1[c]	[c]	4.8	5.5	7.2	8.2	2.9
Inflation rate[d]	12.2	8.9	8.2	6.6	6.0	9.0[e]	19.9	22.6	13.9	11.5	19.9	25.7	11.2	0.5	2.9
Fiscal balance/GDP	1.8	1.7	2.6	2.3	1.9	−1.9[f]	−6.9[f]	−4.4[f]	−5.3[f]	−4.4[f]	−33.5	−7.4	−3.5	−2.5	−2.0
Export concentration	35	37	41	39	43	10	13	15	13	12	66	57	48	52	
Trade partner concentration	18	17	14	17	19	55[g]	48[g]	50[g]	50[g]	54[g]	22[h]	16[h]	15[h]	20[h]	
Trade balance per capita (U.S.$)	−71	50	100	−73	−81	−273[e,i]	−234[i]	−120[i]	−133[i]	−227[i]	−82	−73	−126	−162	−183
External debt per capita (U.S.$)	1,424[e]	1,488	1,463	1,522	1,681	1,182[j]	1,152[j]	1,235[j]	989[j]	1,126[j]	808[k]	828[k]	956[k]	947[k]	950[k]
Urban mean wages (1980 = 100)	118.9	124.5	129.6	134.9	138.5	94.7	98.1	96.2	95.3	96.3	97.1[l]	79.1[l]	75.0[l]	78.9[l]	79.1
Open national unemployment	4.5	5.9	4.7	5.4		4.1	4.2	5.2	6.2	5.7	6.2[m]	6.7[m]	7.9[m]	7.6[m]	6.9
Illiteracy rate (15+ years)	5.7[n]		4.8[o]			5.7[m]		5.2[o]			5.0[p]		4.3[o]		
Infant mortality	13.9[n]	12.0	11.1	11.8		13.7	13.0	13.2	11.8		9.4	9.9	9.4	9.0	

Sources: BCCH 1996; ECLAC 1996b, 1996c, 1997, 1997c; ILO 1996, 1997c; IMF 1996a, 1996b, 1997; UNDP 1996; World Bank 1996; CCSS 1997; CEFSA 1997; IMF *DTSY* and *DTSQ* December 1997; MIDEPLAN 1997; Ministry of Finance 1997, 1998; Raczinski 1997; BCC 1998; BCCR 1998; Ministerio de Economía 1998; ONE 1998; Sojo 1998; Table III.28.

[a]Some are preliminary estimates. [b]The Ministry of Finance gives different figures for savings/GDP: 20.9%, 21.1%, 23.8%, 20.8%, and 24.3%. [c]BCCR 1998 gives much higher figures: 29.8%, 26.4%, 23.5%, 22.8%, and 26.7%. [d]ECLAC: December–December, except Cuba: ONE 1998 and BCC 1998. [e]Revised figures or new series, somewhat different from the country tables. [f]BCCR 1998 gives different figures: −2.3%, −6.5%, −5.2%, −5.1%, and −3.7%. [g]IMF data; BCCR 1998 gives different figures: 45%, 43%, 42%, 41%, and 43%. [h]The percentage drops in the 1990s, not only because of a decline in trade volume but also because trade with the former republics of the Soviet Union are excluded, hence limiting the data to Russia alone. [i]BCCR gives different figures: −212, −123, −137, −232, and −261. [j]BCCR 1998 gives smaller figures: 970, 977, 957, 821, and 747. [k]Only hard currency debt, excludes debt with Russia and Eastern European countries. [l]With a base in 1990; ECLAC (1997) estimates the index for 1993–96 as follows: 77.2, 59.5, 56.1, and 58.6. [m]Equivalent unemployment rates are 1993, 35.2%; 1994, 33.3%; 1995, 31.5%; and 1996, 27%. [n]1992. [o]UNESCO estimate. [p]Author's interpolation based on 1990 and 1995 figures from UNESCO.

Bibliography

INTRODUCTION

Barro, Robert J., and Xavier Sala-i-Martin. 1995. *Economic Growth.* New York: Mc-Graw-Hill.

Betancourt, Roger R. 1996. "Growth Capabilities and Development: Implications for Transition in Cuba." *Economic Development and Cultural Change* 44, no. 2 (January): 315–31.

Bulmer-Thomas, Victor, ed. 1996. *The New Economic Model in Latin America and Its Impact on Income Distribution and Poverty.* New York: St. Martin's Press.

Collier, David. 1991. "The Comparative Method: Two Decades of Change." In *Comparative Political Dynamics: Global Research Perspectives,* ed. Dankwart A. Rustow and Kenneth Paul Erickson, pp. 60–87. New York: HarperCollins.

Dernberger, Robert F., and Richard S. Eckhaus. 1988. *Financing Asian Development. Vol. 2: China and India.* New York: University Press of America.

Drèze, Jean, and Amartya Sen. 1989. *Hunger and Public Action.* Oxford: Oxford University Press, Clarendon Press.

Eckstein, Alexander, ed. 1971. *Comparison of Economic Systems: Theoretical and Methodological Approaches.* Berkeley: University of California Press.

Ghai, Dharam, ed. 1999. *Social Development and Public Policies: Some Lessons from Successful Experiences.* London: Macmillan.

González, Alfonso. 1995. "Cuba, Puerto Rico y Costa Rica: Desarrollo socio-económico comparativo 1960–90." *Papeles de Geografía* 21:87–100.

Gregory, Paul, and Robert Stuart. 1995. *Comparative Economic Systems.* 5th ed. Boston: Houghton, Mifflin.

Hartlyn, Jonathan, and Samuel Morley, eds. 1986. *Latin American Political Economy: Financial Crisis and Political Change.* Boulder: Westview Press.

Lindenberg, Marc M. 1993. *The Human Development Race: Improving the Quality of Life in Developing Countries.* San Francisco: International Center for Economic Growth.

Maddison, Angus, Deepák Lal, and Hia Myint. 1992. *The Political Economy of Poverty, Equity and Growth: Brazil and Mexico.* New York: Oxford University Press.

Mesa-Lago, Carmelo, and Sergio Diaz-Briquets. 1988. "Estrategias diferentes, países similares: Las consecuencias para el crecimiento y la equidad en Costa Rica y Cuba." *Anuario de Estudios Centroamericanos* 14, nos. 1–2: 5–23.

Montias, John M. 1975. "A Classification of Communist Economic Systems." In *Comparative Socialist Systems: Essays on Politics and Economics,* ed. Carmelo Mesa-Lago and Carl Beck, pp. 39–51. Pittsburgh: University of Pittsburgh Center for International Studies.

Montias, John Michael, Avner Ben-Ner, and Egon Neuberger. 1994. *Comparative Economics.* Langhorne, Penn.: Harwood Academic Publishers.

Neuberger, Egon, and William Duffy. 1976. *Comparative Economics Systems: A Decision Making Approach.* Boston: Allyn and Bacon.

Pryor, Frederic L. 1985. *A Guidebook to the Comparative Study of Economic Systems.* Englewood Cliffs, N.J.: Prentice Hall.

———. 1991. *The Political Economy of Poverty, Equity and Growth: Malawi and Madagascar.* New York: Oxford University Press.

Ramos, Joseph. 1986. *Neoconservative Economics in the Southern Cone of Latin America, 1973–1983.* Baltimore: Johns Hopkins University Press.

Randall, Laura, ed. 1997. *The Political Economy of Latin America in the Postwar Period.* Austin: University of Texas Press.

Rottenberg, Simon, et al. 1993. *The Political Economy of Poverty, Equity and Growth: Costa Rica and Uruguay.* New York: Oxford University Press.

Sala-i-Martin, Xavier. 1997. "I Just Ran Two Million Regressions." *American Economic Review* 87, no. 2 (May): 178–83.

Sheahan, John. 1987. *Patterns of Development in Latin America: Poverty, Repression, and Economic Strategy.* Princeton: Princeton University Press.

Smith, Peter H. 1995. "The Changing Agenda for Social Science Research on Latin America." In *Latin America in Comparative Perspective: New Approaches and Methods of Analysis,* ed. P. H. Smith, pp. 1–29. Boulder: Westview Press.

Srinivasan, T. N. 1993. *Agriculture and Trade in China and India: Policies and Performance since 1950.* San Francisco: International Center for Economic Growth.

Urdinola, Antonio, et al. Forthcoming. *The Political Economy of Poverty, Equity and Growth: Colombia and Peru.* New York: Oxford University Press.

World Bank. 1996. "From Plan to Market." In *World Development Report 1996.* New York: Oxford University Press.

CHILE

Altimir, Oscar. 1984. "Poverty, Income Distribution and Child Welfare in Latin America: A Comparison of Pre- and Post-recession Data." *World Development* 12, no. 3 (March): 261–82.

Arellano, José Pablo. 1983. "De la liberalización a la intervención: El mercado de capitales en Chile, 1974–1983." In *Colección Estudios* 11 (December), pp. 5–50. Santiago: CIEPLAN.

———. 1985. *Políticas sociales y desarrollo: Chile 1924–1984.* Santiago: CIEPLAN.

————. 1987. "La salud en los 80: Análisis desde la economía." In *Notas Técnicas* 100 (August). Santiago: CIEPLAN.

————. 1988. "Crisis y recuperación en Chile en los años 80." In *Colección Estudios* 24 (June), pp. 63–84. Santiago: CIEPLAN.

————. 1989. "La seguridad social en Chile en los 90." In *Colección Estudios* 27 (December), pp. 63–82. Santiago: CIEPLAN.

Arellano, José Pablo, and Manuel Marfán. 1987. "25 años de política fiscal en Chile." In *Colección Estudios* 21 (June), pp. 129–62. Santiago: CIEPLAN.

Arellano, José Pablo, and Joseph Ramos. 1987. "Fuga de capitales en Chile: Magnitud y causas." In *Colección Estudios* 22 (December), pp. 63–76. Santiago: CIEPLAN.

Arrau, Patricio. 1992. "La reforma previsional chilena y su financiamiento durante la transición." In *Colección Estudios* 32 (June), pp. 5–44. Santiago: CIEPLAN.

Arenas de Mesa, Alberto. 1991. "Fuentes y mecanismos alternativos de financiamiento para la salud pública." Reporte Final Ministerio de Salud Pública. Unpublished manuscript. Santiago (November).

————. 1995. "The Gender Effect of the Social Security Reform in Chile: Inequalities and Lessons of Policies." Unpublished manuscript (June).

————. 1997. "Learning from the Privatization of the Social Security Pension System in Chile: Macroeconomic Effects, Lessons and Challenges." Ph.D. dissertation, University of Pittsburgh.

Arenas de Mesa, Alberto, and Mario Marcel. 1993. "Proyecciones de gasto previsional 1992–2038: Un modelo de simulación para los bonos de reconocimiento." Santiago: Dirección de Presupuestos, Ministerio de Hacienda, Documento de Trabajo (February).

Arenas de Mesa, Alberto, and Véronica Montecinos. 1995. "Reinforcing Discrimination against Women: The New Social Security in Chile." Paper presented at the XIX International Congress of the Latin American Studies Association, Washington, D.C. (September).

Arriagada, Patricio. 1989. *Financiamiento de la educación superior en Chile, 1960–1988.* Santiago: FLACSO (July).

Balassa, Bela. 1985. "Policy Experiments in Chile, 1973–1983." In Walton, *The National Economic Policies of Chile,* pp. 203–38.

Banco Central de Chile. 1986. *Indicadores económicos y sociales 1960–1985.* Santiago: Banco Central.

————. 1989. *Indicadores económicos y sociales 1960–1988.* Santiago: Banco Central.

————. 1989–94. *Boletín Mensual.* Santiago.

————. 1991. *Indicadores económicos y sociales regionales.* Santiago: Banco Central.

————. 1994. *Síntesis estadística de Chile 1989–1993.* Santiago: Banco Central.

Bianchi, Andrés. 1994. "Política cambiaria, desarrollo exportador y estabilización en Chile, 1990–92." Washington, D.C.: Banco Interamericano de Desarrollo, Series Monográficas, no. 12.

Bitar, Sergio. 1979. *Transición, socialismo y democracia.* Mexico City: Siglo XXI.

Bitrán, Eduardo, and Raúl E. Sáez. 1994. "Privatization and Regulation in Chile." In Bosworth et al., *The Chilean Economy,* pp. 329–78.

Bitrán, Eduardo, and Eduardo Saavedra. 1993. "Profundización del mercado de capitales". Unpublished manuscript, Santiago: Ministerio de Hacienda (February).

Borzutzky, Silvia. 1991. "The Chicago Boys, Social Security and Welfare." In *The Radical Right and the Welfare State: An International Assessment,* ed. Howard Gleenerster and James Midgley, pp. 79–99. Hertfordshire: Harvester Wheatsheaf.

Bosworth, Barry, Rudiger Dornbusch, and Raúl Labán, eds. 1994. *The Chilean Economy: Policy, Lessons and Challenges.* Washington, D.C.: Brookings Institution.

Brunner, José Joaquín, et al. 1991. "Una política para el desarrollo de la educación superior en la década de los noventa, Informe final de la Comisión de Estudio de la Educación Superior." Santiago: Ministerio de Educación (March).

Büchi, Hernán. 1988. "Hacia una economía exportadora." In *Exportar: Un gran desafío para Chile,* ed. Carlos Cáceres, Felipe Larraín, and G. C. Nicolaides, pp. 247–64. Santiago: Editorial Universitaria.

———. 1992. "Principios orientadores del esquema económico chileno." *Cuadernos Universitarios Serie Debates* 1. Santiago.

———. 1993. *La transformación económica de Chile: Del estatismo a la libertad económica.* Santafé de Bogotá: Grupo Editorial Norma.

Bustamante, Julio. 1988. *Funcionamiento del nuevo sistema de pensiones.* Santiago: ICARE.

Campero, Guillermo, and René Cortázar. 1988. "Actores sociales y la transición a la democracia en Chile." In *Colección Estudios* 25 (December), pp. 115–58. Santiago: CIEPLAN.

Carciofi, Ricardo, Oscar Centrángolo, and Guillermo Barris. 1993. "Reformas tributarias en Chile." Santiago: CEPAL, Serie Reformas de Políticas Públicas, no. 9 (June).

Cartin, Brian. 1995. "Chile: The Effectiveness of the Health Care Reform." University of Pittsburgh.

Castañeda, Tarsicio. 1989. "Innovative Social Policies for Reducing Poverty: Chile in the 1980s." Draft (August). Washington, D.C.: World Bank.

Cauas, Jorge, and Sergio de la Cuadra. 1981. "La política económica de la apertura al exterior en Chile." *Cuadernos de Economía* 54–55 (August-December): 195–230.

Ceron, Irene. 1987. "Oferta exportable de productos agrícolas: Evolución y perspectivas." In *Estudios Públicos* 28 (spring), pp. 123–68. Santiago: CEP.

Ceron, Irene, and Irma Staplefield. 1988. "Esfuerzo interno de ahorro y crecimiento económico: Evolución 1960–1986 y perspectivas a 1995." In *Estudios Públicos* 29 (summer), pp. 205–30. Santiago: CEP.

Cheyre, Hernán. 1986. "Análisis de las reformas tributarias de la década 1974–1983." In *Estudios Públicos* 21 (summer), pp. 141–83. Santiago: CEP.

———. 1988. *La previsión en Chile ayer y hoy.* Santiago: CEP.

Comisión Nacional de Educación Parvularia. 1994. *La atención integral del párvulo en Chile: Una gran tarea realizada bajo el gobierno de Don Patricio Aylwin Azócar 1990–1994.* Santiago.

Corbo, Vittorio. 1985. "Chilean Economic Policy and International Economic Relations since 1970." In Walton, *National Economic Policies of Chile,* pp. 107–44.

Corbo, Vittorio, and Stanley Fischer. 1994. "Lessons from the Chilean Stabilization and Recovery." In Bosworth et al., *The Chilean Economy,* pp. 29–80.

Corporación de Fomento de la Producción. 1993–94. *Chile Economic Report.* New York: CORFO.

Corporación de Investigación, Estudios y Desarrollo de la Seguridad Social. 1992. *12 años de modernización de la seguridad social en Chile: Evaluación crítica y proyecciones.* Santiago: CIEDESS.

Cortázar, René. 1982. "Desempleo, pobreza y distribución: Chile 1970–1981." Santiago: CIEPLAN, Apuntes CIEPLAN 34 (June).

———. 1984. "Restricción externa, desempleo y salarios reales." In *Colección Estudios* 14 (September), pp. 43–59. Santiago: CIEPLAN.

———. 1985. "Distributive Results in Chile, 1973–1982." In Walton, *National Economic Policies of Chile,* pp. 79–105.

———. 1993. *Política laboral en el Chile democrático: Avances y desafíos en los noventa.* Santiago: Ediciones DOLMEN, Colección Economía y Gestión.

Cortázar, René, and Patricio Meller. 1987. "Los dos Chiles o la importancia de revisar las estadísticas oficiales." In *Colección Estudios* 21 (June), pp. 5–21. Santiago: CIEPLAN.

Cortés Douglas, Hernán. 1985. "Stabilization Policies in Chile: Inflation, Unemployment and Depression." In Walton, *National Economic Policies of Chile,* pp. 47–78.

Covarrubias, A. 1991. "El sistema de salud en Chile: Una visión crítica y una solución." Santiago: CPU, Documento de Trabajo, no. 28 (July).

Cox, Cristian. 1985. *Chilean Education in 1985: Institutional Profile.* Santiago: CIDE.

Cruz, José Miguel. 1988. "La fruticultura de exportación: Una experiencia de desarrollo empresarial." In *Colección Estudios* 25 (December), pp. 79–114. Santiago: CIEPLAN.

Dahse, Fernando. 1979. *Mapa de la extrema riqueza.* Santiago: Editorial Aconcagua.

Délano, Manuel, and Hugo Traslaviña. 1989. *La herencia de los Chicago boys.* Santiago: Las Ediciones del Ornitorrinco.

Dirección de Presupuestos. 1993–94. *Estadísticas de las finanzas públicas: 1989–1992 and 1989–1993.* Santiago: Ministerio de Hacienda.

Dornbusch, Rudiger, and Sebastián Edwards. 1994. "Exchange Rate Policy and Trade Strategy." In Bosworth et al., *The Chilean Economy,* pp. 81–116.

ECLAC. 1980a–95a. *Statistical Yearbook for Latin America.* Santiago.

———. 1969b–95b. *Economic Survey for Latin America and the Caribbean.* Santiago.

————. 1989c–95c. *Preliminary Overview of the Economy of Latin America and the Caribbean.* Santiago.

Edwards, Sebastián. 1985. "Economic Growth in Chile, 1973–1982." In Walton, *National Economic Policies of Chile,* 11–46.

Edwards, Sebastián, and Alejandra Cox Edwards. 1987. *Monetarism and Liberalization: The Chilean Experiment.* Cambridge, Mass.: Ballinger.

Ffrench-Davis, Ricardo. 1982. "El experimento monetarista en Chile: Una síntesis crítica." In *Colección Estudios* 9 (December), pp. 5–40. Santiago: CIEPLAN.

————. 1987. "Conversión de pagarés de la deuda externa en Chile." In *Colección Estudios* 22 (December), pp. 41–62. Santiago: CIEPLAN.

————. 1988. "Ajuste, renegociaciones de la deuda y financiamiento externo negativo: Chile, 1982–87." In *Apuntes CIEPLAN* 72 (September). Santiago: CIEPLAN.

————. 1989. "Conflicto entre la deuda y el crecimiento en Chile." In *Colección Estudios* 26 (June), pp. 61–89. Santiago: CIEPLAN.

————. 1991. "Desarrollo económico y equidad en Chile: Herencias y desafíos en el retorno a la democracia." In *Colección Estudios* 31 (March), pp. 31–51. Santiago: CIEPLAN.

Ffrench-Davis, Ricardo, and Oscar Muñoz. 1990. "Desarrollo económico, inestabilidad y desequilibrios políticos en Chile: 1950–1989." In *Colección Estudios* 28 (June), pp. 121–56. Santiago: CIEPLAN.

Ffrench-Davis, Ricardo, and Dagmar Raczynski. 1987. "The Impact of Global Recession and National Policies in Living Standards: Chile, 1973–87." In *Notas Técnicas* 97. Santiago: CIEPLAN.

Fondo de Solidaridad e Inversión Social. 1992a. *Informe FOSIS.* Santiago (August).

————. 1992b. [12 reports of evaluation of various programs, May to November] Santiago.

Fontaine, Arturo. 1988. *Los economistas y el presidente Pinochet.* Santiago: Zig-Zag.

Fontaine, Juan Andrés. 1988. "Los mecanismos de conversión de deuda en Chile." In *Estudios Públicos* 30 (fall). Santiago: CEP.

————. 1993. "Transición económica y política en Chile 1970–1990." In *Estudios Públicos* 50 (fall). Santiago: CEP.

Foxley, Alejandro. 1988. *Experimentos neoliberales en América Latina.* Mexico D.F.: Fondo de Cultura Económica.

————. 1993. *Economía política de la transición: El camino del diálogo.* Santiago: Ediciones DOLMEN, Colección de Economía y Gestión.

Gómez, Sergio, and Jorge Echeñique. 1988. *La agricultura chilena. Las dos caras de la modernización.* Santiago: FLACSO.

Goñi, Juan. 1988. "Deuda externa de Chile." Instituto de Estudios Latinoamericanos, Universidad de Estocolmo, Informe 50 (March).

Guillion, Colin, and Alejandro Bonilla. 1992. "Analysis of a National Private Pension Scheme: The Case of Chile." *International Labor Review* 131, no. 2: 171–95.

Hachette, Dominique. 1988. "El sector industrial chileno: 1974–1987." Santiago, Instituto de Economía, Universidad Católica de Chile, Documento de Trabajo 115 (November).

Hachette, Dominique, and Rolf Luders. 1987. "El proceso de privatización de empresas en Chile durante 1974–1982." Santiago: Facultad de Ciencias Económicas, Universidad Católica de Chile, *Boletín Económico,* no. 22 (June-September).

———. 1993. *Privatization in Chile: An Economic Appraisal.* San Francisco: ICS Press.

Harberger, Arnold C. 1985. "Observations on the Chilean Economy 1973–1983." *Economic Development and Cultural Change* 33, no. 3 (April): 451–61.

Held, G. 1990. "Regulación y supervisión de la banca en la experiencia de la liberalización financiera en Chile: 1974–1988." In *Sistema financiero y asignación de recursos: Experiencias Latinoamericanas y del Caribe,* pp. 21–32. Santiago: CEPAL, PNUD, Grupo Editor Latinoamericano.

Iglesias, Augusto, Rodrigo Acuña, and Claudio Chamorro. 1991. *10 años de historia del sistema de AFP.* Santiago: AFP Habitat.

Instituto Nacional de Estadísticas. 1969–88. *Encuesta de Presupuestos Familiares (Gran Santiago).* Santiago.

———. 1974–94. *Compendio estadístico.* Santiago.

Inter-American Development Bank. 1975–95. *Economic and Social Progress in Latin America.* Washington, D.C.

———. 1994. *Modernizar con todos: Hacia la integración de lo social y lo económico en Chile.* Washington, D.C.: Social Agenda Policy Group (January).

International Labor Office. 1976–92. *Yearbook of Labor Statistics.* Geneva.

International Monetary Fund. 1960–92. *Direction of Trade.* Washington, D.C.

———. 1960–92. *International Financial Statistics Yearbook (IFSY).* Washington, D.C.

Jadresic, Esteban. 1990. "Salarios en el largo plazo: Chile 1960–89." In *Colección Estudios* 29 (September), pp. 9–34. Santiago: CIEPLAN.

Junta Nacional de Jardines Infantiles. 1994. *Memoria 1990–94.* Santiago.

Kast, Miguel. 1984. "Relaciones de la política económica con la administración del Estado de Chile: El Estado empresario y el principio de subsidiariedad." In *Estudios Públicos* 13 (summer), pp. 211–28. Santiago: CEP.

Larraín, Felipe, and Patricio Meller. 1990. "La experiencia socialista populista chilena: La Unidad Popular, 1970–1973." In *Colección Estudios* 30 (December), pp. 151–96. Santiago: CIEPLAN.

Larrañaga, Osvaldo. 1991. "Autonomía y déficit del Banco Central." In *Colección Estudios* 32 (June), pp. 121–57. Santiago: CIEPLAN.

Lavín, Joaquín. 1987. *Chile: Revolución silenciosa.* Santiago: Zig-Zag.

MacDonald, Joan. 1983. "Elementos para una política nacional de vivienda." Santiago: CPU, Documento de Trabajo, no. 281.

———. 1994. "¿Cuantas casas faltan? El déficit a nivel nacional y regional." Santiago: CPU, Documento de Trabajo 16 (June).

Marcel, Mario. 1984. "Gasto social del sector público 1979–83." Santiago: CIEPLAN, Notas Técnicas 66.

———. 1988. "La privatización de empresas públicas en Chile 1985–88." Santiago: CIEPLAN, Notas Técnicas 125.

———. 1989. "Privatización y finanzas públicas: El caso de Chile, 1985–88." In *Colección Estudios* 26 (June), pp. 5–60. Santiago: CIEPLAN.

———. 1991. "El financiamiento del gasto social." In *Colección Estudios* 31 (March), pp. 53–60. Santiago: CIEPLAN.

Marcel, Mario, and Alberto Arenas. 1992. "Social Security Reform in Chile." Washington, D.C.: Inter-American Development Bank, Occasional Papers, no. 5.

Marcel, Mario, and Patricio Meller. 1986. "Empalme de las cuentas nacionales de Chile 1960–1985: Métodos alternativos y resultados." In *Colección Estudios* 20 (December), pp. 121–46. Santiago: CIEPLAN.

Marcel, Mario, and Andrés Solimano. 1994. "Distribution of Income and Economic Adjustment." In Barry Bosworth et al., *The Chilean Economy,* pp. 217–56.

Marfán, Manuel, and Patricio Artiagoitía. 1989. "Estimación del PGB potencial: Chile 1960–1988." In *Colección Estudios* 27 (December), pp. 49–62. Santiago: CIEPLAN.

Marfán, Manuel, and Barry Bosworth. 1994. "Saving, Investment, and Economic Growth." In Barry Bosworth et al., *The Chilean Economy,* pp. 165–200.

Meller, Patricio. 1990. "Revisión del proceso de ajuste chileno de la decada del 80." In *Colección Estudios* 30 (December), pp. 5–54. Santiago: CIEPLAN.

———. 1992a. "Reformas laborales." In Muñoz, *Reformas Económicas en Chile,* pp. 76–90.

———. 1992b. "La apertura comercial chilena: Lecciones de política." In *Colección Estudios* 35 (September), pp. 9–54. Santiago: CIEPLAN.

———. 1993. "Economía política de la apertura comercial chilena." Santiago: CEPAL, Serie reformas de políticas públicas, no. 5 (April).

Meller, Patricio, and Mabel Cabezas. 1987. "Estimación de las elasticidades ingreso y precio de las importaciones chilenas 1974–1987." In *Colección Estudios* 26 (June), pp. 127–70. Santiago: CIEPLAN.

Meller, Patricio, Sergio Lehmann, and Rodrigo Cifuentes. 1993. "Los gobiernos de Aylwin y Pinochet: Comparaciones de indicadores económicos y sociales." In *Apuntes CIEPLAN* 118 (September). Santiago: CIEPLAN.

Mesa-Lago, Carmelo. 1985. *El desarrollo de la seguridad social en América Latina.* Santiago: CEPAL, Estudios e Informes de la CEPAL, no. 34.

———. 1987. "Chile SAL III: Final Report on Pension System." Washington, D.C.: World Bank (August 17).

———. 1988. "Review of Chile SAL III Conditions: Pension System." Washington, D.C.: World Bank (November 28).

———. 1989a. *Ascent to Bankruptcy: Social Security Financing in Latin America.* Pittsburgh: University of Pittsburgh Press.

———. 1989b. "Financiamiento de la atención de la salud en América Latina y el Caribe con focalización en el seguro social." World Bank, Institute of Economic Development, no. 42. Washington, D.C.: World Bank.

————. 1990. *La seguridad social y el sector informal*. Santiago: PREALC, Investigaciones sobre Empleo, no. 32.

————. 1991. "Social Security and Prospects for Equity in Latin America." World Bank Discussion Papers, no. 140. Washington, D.C.: World Bank.

————. 1993. *Aspectos económicos-financieros de la seguridad social en América Latina y el Caribe: Tendencias, problemas y alternativas para el año 2,000*. Santiago: CIEDESS.

————. 1994. *Changing Social Security in Latin America: Toward Alleviating the Costs of Economic Reform*. Boulder: Lynne Rienner.

Ministerio de Educación. 1993. "Educación de calidad para todos: Políticas educacionales." Santiago.

Ministerio de Hacienda. 1990–94. *Exposición sobre el estado de la Hacienda Pública*. Santiago.

Ministerio de Salud. 1994. *La gestión del Ministerio de Salud: Informe del sector salud durante el gobierno del presidente Patricio Aylwin Azócar: Chile 1990–1994*. Santiago.

Ministerio de Vivienda y Urbanismo. 1990. *Memoria 1973–1989*. Santiago (February).

————. 1990–93. *Memoria anual*. Santiago.

Moguillansky, Graciela, and Daniel Titelman. 1993. "Análisis empírico del comportamiento de las exportaciones no cobre en Chile: 1963–1990." Santiago: CEPAL, División de Desarrollo Económico, Documento de Trabajo, no. 17 (May).

Montecinos, Verónica. 1988. "Economics and Power. Chilean Economists in Government: 1958–1985." Ph.D. dissertation, University of Pittsburgh.

————. 1994. "Neo-Liberal Economic Reforms and Women in Chile." In *Women in the Age of Economic Transformation,* ed. Nahid Aslanbeigui, Steven Pressman, and Gale Summerfield, pp. 160–77. London: Routledge.

Muñoz, Oscar. 1986. *Chile y su industrialización: Pasado, crisis y acciones*. Santiago: CIEPLAN.

————. 1988a. "Crisis y reorganización industrial en Chile." Santiago: CIEPLAN, Notas Técnicas 123 (November).

————. 1988b. "El Estado y los empresarios: Experiencias comparadas y sus implicancias para Chile." In *Colección Estudios* 25 (December), pp. 5–53. Santiago: CIEPLAN.

————. 1992. "Privatización de empresas públicas." In Muñoz, *Reformas Económicas en Chile,* pp. 63–75.

————, ed. 1992. *Reformas Económicas en Chile*. Washington, D.C.: Banco Interamericano de Desarrollo, Series Monográficas, no. 7.

————. 1993. *Después de las privatizaciones hacia un Estado regulador*. Santiago: Ediciones CIEPLAN.

Muñoz, Oscar, and Carmen Celedón. 1993. "Chile en transición: Estrategia económica y política." In *Colección Estudios* 37 (June), pp. 101–29. Santiago: CIEPLAN.

Oficina de Planificación Nacional. 1973. *Balances Económicos de Chile, 1960–70*. Santiago.

Ortega, Emiliano. 1987. *Transformaciones agrarias y campesinado. De la participación a la exclusión.* Santiago: CIEPLAN.

Oyarzo, César. 1989. "Evolución de la situación financiera del sector salud en la década del 80." Santiago: ILADES, Serie de Ensayos, E-8 (September).

Pan American Health Organization. 1965–68, 1969–72, 1973–76, 1977–78, 1981–84, and 1990. *Health Conditions in the Americas.* Washington, D.C.

———. 1992. *Health Statistics from the Americas.* Washington, D.C.

———. 1997. *Report on Tuberculosis in Latin America and the Caribbean.* Washington, D.C.

Petras, James, Fernando I. Leiva, and Henry Veltmeyer. 1994. *Democracy and Poverty in Chile: The Limits to Electoral Politics.* Boulder: Westview Press.

Piñera, José. 1991. *El cascabel al gato: La batalla por la reforma previsional.* Santiago: Zig-Zag.

Pizarro, Crisóstomo, Dagmar Raczynski, and Joaquín Vial, eds. 1995. *Políticas económicas y sociales en el Chile democrático.* Santiago: CIEPLAN-UNICEF.

Programa Interdisciplinario de Investigaciones en Educación (PIIE). 1989. *Ruptura y construcción de consensos en la educación chilena.* 2d ed. Santiago: PIIE.

Raczynski, Dagmar. 1994. "Políticas sociales y programas de combate a la pobreza en Chile: Balances y desafíos." In *Colección Estudios* 39 (June), pp. 9–73. Santiago: CIEPLAN.

Raczynski, Dagmar, and César Oyarzo. 1981. "¿Por que cae la tasa de mortalidad infantil en Chile?" In *Colección Estudios* 6 (December), pp. 45–83. Santiago: CIEPLAN.

Raczynski, Dagmar, and Claudia Serrano. 1992. "Abriendo el debate: Descentralización del Estado, mujeres y políticas sociales." In *Políticas sociales, mujeres y gobierno local,* ed. Dagmar Raczynski and Claudia Serrano. Santiago: Ediciones CIEPLAN.

Raczynski, Dagmar, and Pilar Romaguera. 1993. "Chile: Poverty, Adjustment and Social Policies in the 1980's." In *Coping with Austerity: Poverty and Inequality in Latin America,* ed. Nora Lustig, pp. 320–38. Washington, D.C.: Brookings Institution.

Ramos, Joseph. 1986. *Neoconservative Economics in the Southern Cone of Latin America, 1973–1983.* Baltimore: Johns Hopkins University Press.

Rodríguez Grossi, Jorge. 1985. *Distribución del ingreso y gasto social en Chile: 1983.* Santiago: ILADES.

Rozas, Patricio, and Gustavo Marín. 1989. *El "mapa de la extrema riqueza" 10 años después.* Santiago: CESOC, Ediciones Chile América.

Sanfuentes, Andrés. 1986. "Financiamiento a la universidad: Antecedentes y alternativas." In *La educación superior en Chile: Riesgos y oportunidades en los 80,* ed. María José Lemaitre and Iván Lavados, pp. 165–209. Santiago: CPU.

———. 1987. "Chile: Effects of the Adjustment Policies on the Agriculture and Forestry Sector." *CEPAL Review* 33 (December): 115–27.

———. 1990. "Comportamiento universitario y políticas de financiamiento." In *Financiamiento de la educación superior: Antecedentes y desafíos,* ed. C. Lehmann, pp. 125–47. Santiago: CEP.

Sapag, Reinaldo. 1994. "Evolución del sistema de salud en Chile durante 1993." *Análisis Laboral* (March): XXVII–XXIX.

Serrano, Claudia. 1992. "Estado, mujer y políticas sociales en Chile." In *Políticas sociales, mujeres y gobierno local,* ed. Dagmar Raczynski and Claudia Serrano, pp. 195–216. Santiago: Ediciones CIEPLAN.

Sheahan, John. 1987. *Patterns of Development in Latin America: Poverty, Repression, and Economic Strategy.* Princeton: Princeton University Press.

Shinke, Rolf. 1987. "Debt Equity Swaps, Investment and Creditworthiness: The Chilean Example." Ibero-Amerika Institut für Wirtschaftsforschung, Universität Göttingen, Diskussionsbeitrage 43 (September).

Silva, Patricio. 1987. *Estado, neoliberalismo y política agraria en Chile, 1973–1981.* Amsterdam: CEDLA.

Solimano, Andrés. 1988. "Política de remuneraciones en Chile: Experiencia pasada, instrumentos y opciones a futuro." In *Colección Estudios* 25 (December), pp. 159–90. Santiago: CIEPLAN.

———. 1990a. "Inversión privada y ajuste." In *Colección Estudios* 28 (June), pp. 29–55. Santiago: CIEPLAN.

———. 1990b. "Economic Growth, Social Equity and Macroeconomic Stability: Looking at the Challenges for the Chilean Economy in 1990." Mimeo (October).

Staplefield, Irma. 1987. "Oferta exportable de productos pesqueros: Evolución y perspectivas." In *Estudios Públicos* 27 (winter), pp. 181–225. Santiago: CEP.

Superintendencia de Administradoras de Fondos de Pensiones. 1981–94. *Boletín Estadístico.* Santiago.

———. 1994. *El sistema chileno de pensiones.* Santiago.

Superintendencia de Seguridad Social. 1990–94. *Seguridad Social. Estadísticas.* Santiago: SUSESO.

———. 1993. *Costo de la seguridad social chilena. Año 1992.* Santiago: SUSESO.

Tironi, Ernesto. 1989. *¿Es posible reducir la pobreza?* Santiago: Zig-Zag.

United Nations. 1964, 1969, 1972–73, 1976–81, 1991, and 1992. *International Trade Statistics Yearbook.* New York.

Valenzuela, M. 1989. "Reprivatización y capitalismo popular en Chile." In *Estudios Públicos* 33 (summer), pp. 175–217. Santiago: CEP.

Vergara, Pilar. 1990. *Políticas hacia la extrema pobreza en Chile: 1973–1988.* Santiago: FLACSO.

Vial, Joaquín. 1992. "Reformas financieras". In Muñoz, *Reformas Económicas en Chile,* pp. 44–62.

Vial, Joaquín, Andrea Butelmann, and Carmen Celedón. 1990. "Fundamentos de las políticas macroeconómicas del gobierno democrático chileno (1990–1993)." In *Colección Estudios* 30 (December), pp. 55–89. Santiago: CIEPLAN.

Vial, Joaquín, and Rodrigo Valdés. 1991. "Patrones de consumo de cobre: Determinantes del consumo de cobre por sectores en EE.UU." In *Colección Estudios* 32 (June), pp. 81–119. Santiago: CIEPLAN.

Walton, G. M., ed. 1985. *National Economic Policies of Chile.* Greenwich, Conn.: Jai Press.

Wisecarver, Daniel. 1985. "Economic Regulation and Deregulation in Chile, 1973–1983." In Walton, *National Economic Policies of Chile,* pp. 145–202.

World Bank. 1987. *Social Indicators of Development.* Washington, D.C.

———. 1989. *Government Expenditures on Social Sectors in Latin America and the Caribbean.* Washington, D.C.

———. 1989–95. *World Development Report.* Washington, D.C.

World Health Organization (WHO). 1964, 1968, 1973–76, 1980, 1984, 1990. *World Health Statistical Annual (WHSA).* Washington, D.C.

Yáñez, José. 1992. "Reformas tributarias." In Muñoz, *Reformas Económicas en Chile,* pp. 22–43.

CUBA

"Acuerdo del Buró Político." 1993. *Granma,* September 15: 1.

Alfonso, Pablo. 1995. "Panorama de las reformas económicas en Cuba." Paper presented at ASCE meetings, Miami, August 11.

———. 1996. "Apuntes sobre la situación socio-económica de Cuba." Paper presented at ASCE meetings, Miami, August 8.

Alonso, José. 1993. "An Analysis of Decree 141 Regarding Cuban Small-Scale Enterprises." *La Sociedad Económica Bulletin* 35, September 20.

Alvarez, Elena, and Alfonso Casanova. 1994. "The Cuban Economy." Washington, D.C.: Georgetown University, Cuban Studies Project, September 9.

Añé, Lía, and Nélida Pérez. 1989. "El proceso de cooperativización agrícola en Cuba." *Temas de Economía Mundial* 26:105–9.

Anonymous. 1988. "Población y fondo de viviendas: 1971–1985." *Economía y Desarrollo* 8 (March–April): 118–23.

Association for the Study of the Cuban Economy (ASCE). 1992–97. *Cuba in Transition.* Vols. 2–7. Miami: Papers and Proceedings of ASCE Meetings.

Ayala Castro, Héctor. 1982. "Transformación de la propiedad en el período 1964–1980." *Economía y Desarrollo,* no. 68 (May-June): 12–20.

Banco Nacional de Cuba. 1960. *Memoria del Banco Nacional de Cuba 1958–1959.* Havana.

———. 1982–89. *Informe Económico 1982* to *1989.* Havana.

———. 1995. *Economic Report 1994.* Havana (August).

Banco Nacional de Cuba and Comité Estatal de Estadística. 1982–89. *Cuba: Quarterly Economic Report 1982* to *1989.* Havana.

Barrett, Kathleen. 1993. "The Impact of the Collapse of the Soviet Union and the East Bloc on the Cuban Health Care System." Master's thesis, Georgetown University.

Bernardo, Roberto M. 1971. "Managing and Financing the Firm." In Mesa-Lago, *Revolutionary Change in Cuba,* pp. 185–208.

Betancourt, Roger R. 1993. "The Distribution Sector in a CPE: Cuba." In *Cuba in Transition,* ed. G. P. Montalvan, pp. 32–45. 2d ed. Miami: Florida International University Press.

Boletín de Investigaciones Económicas de Cuba (BIEC). 1992. (June): 22.

Boorstein, Edward. 1968. *The Economic Transformation of Cuba.* New York: Monthly Review Press.

Brundenius, Claes. 1979. "Measuring Income Distribution in Pre- and Post-Revolutionary Cuba." *Cuban Studies* 9 (July): 29–44.

———. 1984. *Revolutionary Cuba: The Challenge of Economic Growth with Equity.* Boulder: Westview Press.

Brunner, Heinrich. 1977. *Cuban Sugar Policy from 1963 to 1970.* Pittsburgh: University of Pittsburgh Press.

Cardoso, Eliana, and Ann Helwege. 1992. *Cuba after Communism.* Cambridge: MIT Press.

Carranza, Julio. 1993. "Cuba: Retos de la Economía." *Cuadernos de Nuestra América* 19:131–59.

———. 1994. "Economic Reforms in Cuba." Paper given at University of Pittsburgh, March 15.

Carranza, Julio, Luis Gutiérrez, and Pedro Monreal. 1995. *Cuba la restructuración de la economía: Una propuesta para el debate.* Havana: Editorial de Ciencias Sociales.

Casanova, Alfonso, and Juan Triana. 1995. "La economía cubana en 1994." *Areíto* 5, no. 17 (January): 8–15.

Castro, Fidel. 1989. "Speech on the 30th Anniversary of the Triumph of the Revolution." *Granma Weekly Review,* January 22, 1989: 4.

———. 1992a. "Discurso en la clausura de la plenaria del 6° Congreso de la UJC." *Havana Radio,* April 4, 1992.

———. 1992b. "Discurso en la clausura de la cosecha de la papa en La Habana." *Granma,* May 1, 1992.

———. 1992c. "Discurso en el 39 aniversario del asalto al Cuartel Moncada." *Granma,* September 8: 2–6.

———. 1993a. "Discurso en la clausura del 40 aniverisario del asalto al Cuartel Moncada." *Granma,* July 28: 3–7.

———. 1993b. "Speech at the 5th UNEAC Congress." *Granma,* December 8: 3–4.

———. 1993c. "Castro Address to National Assembly." Havana: Tele Rebelde, December 29.

———. 1995. "Closing Speech at the Youth Festival." Havana Radio, August 6.

———. 1996. "Discurso en la clausura del XVII Congreso de la CTC." *Trabajadores,* May 6: 5.

Castro, Osvaldo. 1992. "Estrategia cubana en el financiamiento de la salud." *Cuba Económica* 2, no. 3 (October-March): 111–17.

Castro, Raúl. 1996. "Informe del Buró Político." *Granma,* March 27: 2–6.

Central Intelligence Agency. 1992. *Cuba Handbook of Trade Statistics, Intelligence Research Paper.* Washington, D.C.: ALA 92-10033 (September).

———. 1993. *Cuba: Handbook of Trade Statistics.* Washington, D.C.: ALA 93-10010 (July).

————. 1994. *Cuba Handbook of Trade Statistics, 1994.* Washington, D.C.: ALA 94-10011 (August).

————. 1995. *Cuba Handbook of Trade Statistics, 1995.* Washington, D.C.: ALA 95-10011 (November).

Comité Estatal de Estadística. 1974a–91a. *Anuario Estadístico de Cuba 1975* to *1989.*

————. 1981a. *Cuba desarrollo económico y social durante el período 1958–1980.* Havana.

————. 1980–90. *Cuba en Cifras, 1979* to *1989.* Havana.

————. 1981b. *Principales características laborales de la población de Cuba: Encuesta demográfica.* Havana.

————. 1981c. *Encuesta demográfica nacional de 1979, metodología y tablas seleccionadas.* Havana.

————. 1986 to 1991. *Boletín Estadístico de Cuba 1985* to *1990.* Havana.

————. 1989. *Compendio Estadístico de Energía.* Havana.

"Constitución de la República de Cuba." 1992. *Granma,* September 22: 3–10.

"Cuba Passes New Foreign Investment Law." 1995. Havana: Reuters, September 5.

Cuban Economic Research Project (CERP). 1963. *Labor Conditions in Communist Cuba.* Coral Gables: University of Miami Press.

————. 1965. *A Study on Cuba.* Coral Gables: University of Miami Press.

Cuban Research Institute (CRI). 1993. *Transition in Cuba: New Challenge for U.S. Policy.* Miami: Florida International University.

Decreto-Ley 191. 1994. *Gaceta Oficial,* September 21.

Decreto-Ley 192. 1994. *Gaceta Oficial,* September 26.

Deere, Carmen Diana. 1995. "The New Agricultural Reforms." *Cuba: Adapting to a New Post-Soviet World. NACLA Report on the Americas* 29, no. 2 (September-October): 13–17.

Díaz-Briquets, Sergio. 1983. *The Health Revolution in Cuba,* pp. 81–112. Austin: University of Texas Press.

————. 1993. "Collision Course: Labor Force and Educational Trends in Cuba." *Cuban Studies* 23:91–112.

Díaz-Briquets, Sergio, and Lisandro Pérez. 1982. "Fertility Decline in Cuba: A Socio-economic Interpretation." *Population and Development Review* 8, no. 3 (September): 513–37.

Domínguez, Jorge. 1993. "The Secrets of Castro's Staying Power." *Foreign Affairs* (spring): 97–107.

Echeverría Vallejo, Oscar. 1992. "Apuntes para una discusión sobre el sistema financiero cubano." *Boletín de Información sobre Economía Cubana* 1, nos. 11–12 (November-December): 10–22.

Eckstein, Susan. 1990. "The Rectification of Errors or the Errors of the Rectification Process in Cuba." *Cuban Studies* 20: 67–85.

————. 1991. "More on the Cuban Rectification Process: Whose Errors?" *Cuban Studies* 21:193–98.

Economic Commission for Latin America and the Caribbean. 1980. *Cuba: Estilo de desarrollo y políticas sociales.* Mexico D.F.: Siglo XXI.

————. 1981a–94a. *Statistical Yearbook for Latin America 1980* to *1994*. Santiago.

————. 1981b–93b. *Economic Survey for Latin America and the Caribbean 1980* to *1992*. Santiago.

————. 1989c–96c. *Preliminary Overview of the Latin American Economy 1989* to *1996*. Santiago.

————. 1995d. *Cuba: Evolución económica durante 1994*. Santiago (May 23).

————. 1997. *La economía cubana: Reformas estructurales y desempeño en los noventa*. Mexico D.F.: Fondo de Cultura Económica.

Economic Intelligence Unit (EIU). 1994. *Cuba: Country Report 4th Quarter 1994*. London: *The Economist*.

"Estadísticas 1994." 1995. *Economics Press Service* 8 (July): 14.

Evans, Garry. 1992. "A Way Out of the Wilderness: The Castro Interview." *Euromoney* (July): 40–44.

Feinsilver, Julie M. 1993. *Healing the Masses: Cuban Health Politics at Home and Abroad*. Berkeley: University of California Press.

Food and Agricultural Organization. 1970–95. *Production Yearbook*. Rome.

Gay, J., A. Yáñez, and Fernando Zacarías. 1994. "Factores dietéticos de la neuropatía epidémica en la Isla de la Juventud, Cuba." *Boletin OPS* (November): 389–98.

Ghai, Dharam, Cristobal Kay, and Peter Leek. 1988. *Labour and Development in Cuba*. London: Macmillan.

Gonzalez, Edward, and David Ronfeldt. 1992. *Cuba Adrift in a Postcommunist World*. Santa Monica: Rand Corporation.

González Gutiérrez, Alfredo. 1993. "Modelos económicos socialistas: Escenarios para Cuba en los años noventa." Havana: INIE.

Gunn, Gillian. 1993. "Prospects for Change in Cuba." In CRI, *Transition in Cuba*, pp. 67–96.

Gutiérrez, Gustavo. 1958. *El empleo el subempleo y el desempleo en Cuba*. Havana: Consejo Nacional de Economía.

Hernández, Gladys. 1992. "La producción y exportación de níquel en Cuba: 1970–1992." *Boletín de Información sobre Economía Cubana* 1, no. 6 (June): 20–23.

"Indicadores socio-económicos." 1994. *Cuba en el mes,* Dossier 4 (January): 175–79.

Instituto Cubano de Economistas Independientes (ICEI). 1996. *ICEI Boletín* 1, no. 1 (January-February).

International Labour Office. 1986. *Economically Active Population 1950–2025*. Geneva.

————. 1996. *The Cost of Social Security 1987–1989*. Geneva.

Interviews. 1993. With Cuban Scholars at International Seminar on Cuba. Ottawa: Carleton University, September 23–24.

Junta Central de Planificación. 1973. *Censo de población y viviendas 1970: Datos fundamentales de la población*. Havana: Instituto del Libro.

————. n.d. *Compendio Estadístico de Cuba (CEC) 1966* to *1968*. Havana.

————. 1968–73. *Boletín Estadístico de Cuba (BEC) 1966* to *1971*. Havana.

————. 1974–76. *Anuario Estadístico de Cuba* (AEC) *1972* to *1974*. Havana.

————. 1994. Figures on agricultural output 1989–92 cited by *El País,* May 1: 10–11.

La Sociedad Económica. 1993a. "Cuban Nickel: Market & Production Outlook." *Bulletin* 26 (January 19).

————. 1993b. "Bridging the Gap: Cuban Tourism in the 1990s." *Bulletin* 29 (April 19).

————. 1993c. "Cuban Non-sugar Agriculture." *Bulletin* 32 (July 30).

————. 1993d. "The Cuban Economy: A Twelve Month Review." *Bulletin* 33, August 23.

————. 1994a. "An Index of Foreign Investment in Cuba." *Bulletin* 43 (September).

————. 1994b. "The Cooperativization of State Farms in Cuba: An Appraisal of the UBPCs." *Bulletin* 44 (November).

Lage, Carlos. 1992. Interview. Havana TV, November 6 and 12, reproduced in *Granma,* November 10 and 14.

————. 1993a "De la forma más justa posible" [Interview]. *Areíto* 4: 13 (May): 4–12.

————. 1993b. Interview. *El Mercurio* (Santiago de Chile), June 13: D-17.

————. 1994. "Discurso de apertura de la XII Feria Internacional de La Habana." Havana Radio, October 31.

————. 1996. "Informe del Ministerio de Economía y Planificación." Havana: EFE, July 23. Summary in *Contrapunto* 7, no. 9 (September 1996): 48–52.

Lataste, Albán. 1968. *Cuba: ¿hacia una nueva economía política del socialismo?* Santiago.

León, Francisco. 1996. "El desafío regional de la inserción internacional cubana." *Socialismo y Participación,* no. 76: 101–10.

Lugo Fonte, Orlando. 1989. "La ANAP: Sus principales tareas." *Cuba Socialista* 9 (May-June): 1–14.

MacEwan, Arthur. 1981 *Revolution and Economic Development in Cuba.* New York: St. Martin's Press.

Marquis, Christopher. 1995. "Cuba Takes a Hard Look at Its Reforms." *Miami Herald,* August 3: 19A.

Marquetti, Hiram, and Omar Everleny. 1994. "La despenalización de la tenencia de divisas en Cuba." Havana (July).

Marris, Katherine. 1992. "Cuba: ¿Qué Pasa?" *Seafood Business* 11, no. 1 (January-February): 30–96.

Martínez Fagundo, Carlos. 1989. "Presencia e influencia de los factores de desequilibrio en las finanzas internas de Cuba." *Economía y Desarrollo* 5 (September-October): 166–90.

Martínez Fernández, Ramón. 1988. "El turismo y su destino." *Economía y Desarrollo* 18 (September-October): 30–37.

Masso, Alfredo. 1992. "Las medidas de ajuste: El caso cubano." *Cuba Económica* 2, no. 3 (October-March): 104–11.

Mesa-Lago, Carmelo. 1971a. *Revolutionary Change in Cuba.* Pittsburgh: University of Pittsburgh Press.

———. 1971. "Economic Policies and Growth." In Mesa-Lago, *Revolutionary Change in Cuba,* pp. 277–338.

———. 1972. *The Labor Force, Employment, Unemployment and Underemployment in Cuba: 1989–1970.* Beverly Hills: Sage Publications.

———. 1978. *Cuba in the 1970s: Pragmatism and Institutionalization.* Albuquerque: University of New Mexico Press.

———. 1981. *The Economy of Socialist Cuba: A Two-Decade Appraisal.* Albuquerque: University of New Mexico Press.

———. 1982. "The Economy: Caution, Frugality and Resilient Ideology." In *Cuba: Internal and International Affairs,* ed. Jorge Domínguez, pp. 113–66. Beverly Hills: Sage.

———. 1986. "Cuba's Centrally Planned Economy: An Equity Trade-off for Growth." In Hartlyn and Morley, *Latin American Political Economy,* pp. 292–318.

———. 1988a. "The Cuban Economy in the 1980s: The Return of Ideology." In Roca, *Socialist Cuba,* pp. 59–100.

———. 1988b. "Cuban Statistics: One More Time." *Cuban Studies* 18:133–45.

———. 1990a. "Cuba's Economic Counter-Reform (*Rectificación*): Causes, Policies and Effects." In *Cuba after Thirty Years: Rectification and the Revolution,* ed. Richard Gillespie, pp. 98–139. London: Frank Cass.

———. 1990b. *Ascent to Bankruptcy: Social Security Financing and Development in Latin America.* Pittsburgh: University of Pittsburgh Press.

———. 1990c. "Countdown in Cuba?" *Hemisfile* 1, no. 2 (March): 6–8.

———. 1990d. "On Rectifying Errors of a Courteous Dissenter." *Cuban Studies* 20:87–108.

———. 1991. "Rectification Round Two: An Answer to Eckstein's Rebuttal." *Cuban Studies* 21: 193–98.

———. 1993a. "The Economic Effects of the Soviet-Eastern European Crisis on Cuba." In Mesa-Lago, *Cuba after the Cold War,* pp. 133–96.

———. 1993b. "Cuba's Economic Policies and Alternatives to Confront the Crisis." In Mesa-Lago, *Cuba after the Cold War:* pp. 197–257.

———. 1993c. "The Social Safety Net in the Two Cuban Transitions." In CRI, *Transition in Cuba,* pp. 601–70.

———. 1994a. *Changing Social Security in Latin America: Toward Alleaviating the Social Costs of Economic Reform:* Boulder: Lynne Rienner.

———. 1994b. *Breve historia económica de Cuba socialista: Políticas, resultados y perspectivas.* Madrid: Alianza Editorial.

———. 1994c. *Are Economic Reforms Propelling Cuba to the Market?* Coral Gables: University of Miami, North-South Center.

———. 1994d. "Cuba: A Unique Case of Anti-Market Reform: The Rectification Process Experience." In *Rebuilding Capitalism: Alternative Roads after Socialism 2nd Dirigisme,* ed. A. Solimano, O. Sunkel, and M. Blejer, pp. 207–38. Ann Arbor: University of Michigan Press.

———. 1995. "Oil Woes." *Hemisfile* 6, no. 2 (March-April): 8–9.

————. 1996. "La seguridad social y la pobreza en Cuba." Buenos Aires: CIEDES-Fundación Konrad Adenauer.

————. 1998. "Assessing Economic and Social Performance in the Cuban Transition of the 1990s." *World Development* 26, no. 5 (May): 857–76.

————, ed. 1971. *Revolutionary Change in Cuba.* Pittsburgh: University of Pittsburgh Press.

————. 1985. *The Crisis of Social Security and Health Care: Latin American Experiences and Lessons.* Pittsburgh: Latin American Monograph Series, University of Pittsburgh.

————. 1993. *Cuba after the Cold War.* Pittsburgh: University of Pittsburgh Press.

Mesa-Lago, Carmelo, and Sergio Diaz-Briquets. 1988. "Estrategias diferentes, países similares: Las consecuencias para el crecimiento y la equidad en Costa Rica y Cuba." *Anuario de Estudios Centroamericanos* 14, nos. 1–2: 5–23.

Mesa-Lago, Carmelo,and Fernando Gil. 1989. "Soviet Economic Relations with Cuba." In *Soviet Relations with Latin America in the 1980s,* ed. Eusebio Mujal-León, pp. 183–228. Boston: Allen & Unwin.

Mesa-Lago, Carmelo, and Roberto E. Hernández. 1971. "Labor Organization and Wages." In Mesa-Lago, *Revolutionary Change in Cuba,* pp. 209–49.

Mesa-Lago, Carmelo, and Jorge Pérez-López. 1985a. *A Study of Cuba's National Product System, Its Conversion to the System of National Accounts, and Estimation of GDP Per Capita and Growth Rates.* Washington, D.C.: World Bank.

————. 1985b. "Estimating Cuban GDP Per Capita in Dollars Using Physical Indicators." *Social Indicators Research* 16: 275–300.

————. 1985c. "Imbroglios on the Cuban Economy: A Reply to Brundenius and Zimbalist." *Comparative Economic Studies* 27, no. 1 (spring): 47–83.

————. 1985d. "The Endless Cuban Economic Saga: A Terminal Rebuttal." *Comparative Economic Studies* 27, no. 4 (winter): 67–82.

————. 1992. "Cuban Economic Growth in Current and Constant Prices, 1975–1988: A Puzzle on the Foreign Trade Component of the Material Product System." *Statistical Abstract for Latin America* 29, part 1: 598–615. Los Angeles: UCLA Latin American Center Publications.

Mesa-Lago, Carmelo, and Luc Zephirin. 1971. "Central Planning." In Mesa-Lago, *Revolutionary Change in Cuba,* pp. 145–84.

Messick, Richard, ed. 1996. *World Survey of Economic Freedom: 1995–96 (A Freedom House Study).* New Brunswick, N.J.: Transaction.

Ministerio de Finanzas y Trabajo-Seguridad Social (MF-TSS). 1995. Resolución no. 4, June 14.

Ministerio de Inversión Extranjera y Colaboración Económica (MIECE). 1995. *Ley de Inversión Extranjera.* Havana: Editora Política.

Ministerio de Salud Pública. 1994. *Anuario Estadístico 1993.* Havana.

Monreal, Pedro. 1993a. "Cuba y América Latina y el Caribe: Apuntes sobre un caso de inserción económica." *Estudios Internacionales* 26, no. 103 (July-September): 500–536.

————. 1993b. "Cuba: To Market, to Market." *Hemisfile* 4, no. 3 (May-June): 10–11.

Monreal, Pedro, and Manuel Rúa. 1994. "Apertura y reforma de la economía cubana: las transformaciones institucionales (1990–1993)." *Cuadernos de Nuestra América* 21 (January-June): 139–58.

"New Role for CECE." 1992. *Cuba Business* (June): 4.

Novoa, Armando. 1992. "Cuba: La agroindustria citrícola." *Boletín de Información sobre Economía Cubana* 1, no. 6 (June): 3–11.

Oficina Nacional de los Censos Demográfico y Electoral (ONCDE). 1955. *Censo de población, vivienda y electoral, 1953.* Havana.

———. 1959–61. *Muestreo sobre empleo, subempleo y desempleo.* Havana.

Oficina Nacional del Censo (ONC). 1983. *Censo de población y viviendas 1981: República de Cuba.* Havana.

Oficina Nacional de Estadística. 1995. *La economía cubana en 1994.* Havana.

Oppenheimer, Andrés. 1994. "Ex-asesor de Reagan da consejo económico a La Habana." *Nuevo Herald,* June 15: 8A.

Pagés, Raisa. 1994. "Delinear el plan de 1995 con el principio de eliminar pérdidas." *Granma,* November 1: 6.

Pan American Health Organization. 1994. *Health Conditions in the Americas 1994.* Washington, D.C.

Pastor, Manuel, and Andrew Zimbalist. 1995. "Cuba's Economic Conundrum." *NACLA's Report on the Americas* 29, no. 2 (September-October): 7–12.

Pérez-López, Jorge F. 1979. "Sugar and Petroleum in Cuban-Soviet Terms of Trade." In *Cuba in the World,* ed. Cole Blasier and Carmelo Mesa-Lago, pp. 273–96. Pittsburgh: University of Pittsburgh Press.

———. 1981. "Energy Production, Imports and Consumption in Revolutionary Cuba." *Latin American Research Review* 16, no. 2: 111–37.

———. 1985. *The 1982 Cuban Joint Venture Law: Context, Assessment and Prospects.* Miami: Institute of Interamerican Studies, University of Miami.

———. 1986a. "The Economics of Cuban Joint Ventures." *Cuban Studies* 16:181–207.

———. 1986b. "Cuban Economy in the 1980s." *Problems of Communism* 35 (September-October): 16–34.

———. 1987a. "Cuban Oil Reexports: Significance and Prospects." *Energy Journal* 8, no. 1: 1–16.

———. 1987b. *"Measuring Cuban Economic Performance.* Austin: University of Texas Press.

———. 1988. "Cuban-Soviet Sugar Trade: Price and Subsidy Issues." *Bulletin of Latin American Research* 7, no. 1: 123–47.

———. 1989. "Sugar and Structural Change in the Cuban Economy." *World Development* 17, no. 10 (October): 1627–46.

———. 1991. *The Economics of Cuban Sugar.* Pittsburgh: University of Pittsburgh Press.

———. 1992a. "The Cuban Economy: Rectification in a Changing World." *Cambridge Journal of Economics* 16:113–26.

———. 1992b. *"The Cuban State Budget: Concepts and Measurement.* Coral

Gables: University of Miami, North-South Center, Research Institute for Cuban Studies.

———. 1992–93. "Cuba's Thrust to Attract Foreign Investment: A Special Labor Regime for Joint Ventures in International Tourism." *Inter-American Law Review* 24, no. 2 (winter): 221–79.

———. 1995a. *Cuba's Second Economy.* New Brunswick, N.J.: Transaction.

———. 1995b. "Castro Tries Survival Strategy." *Transition* 6, no. 3 (March): 11–14.

———. 1995c. "A Critical Look at Cuba's Foreign Investment Program." Paper presented at LASA meetings, Washington, D.C., September 28–30.

———, ed. 1994. *Cuba at the Crossroads.* Gainesville: University Press of Florida.

Pérez-López, Jorge F., and Carmelo Mesa-Lago. 1990. "Cuba: Domestic Counter Reform Leads to Crisis." *Transition* 1, no. 8 (November): 6–8.

Radell, Williard W. 1987. "Comparative Performance of Large Cuban Factories in the 1984 'Zafra.'" *Cuban Studies* 17:141–55.

Rathbone, John Paul. 1992. "Cuba: Current Situation and Short-Term Prospects." *La Sociedad Económica Bulletin* 20:1–8.

Regulations of Hard Currency. 1993. "Decreto Ley No. 40" and "Información del Banco Nacional." *Granma,* August 14: 2.

Regulations of Self-employment. 1993. "Sobre el ejercicio del trabajo por cuenta propia." *Granma,* 9 September: 4–5.

Ritter, Archibald R. M. 1974. *The Economic Development of Revolutionary Cuba: Strategy and Performance.* New York: Praeger.

———. 1990. "The Cuban Economy in the 1990s: External Challenge and Policy Imperatives." *Journal of Interamerican Studies and World Affairs* 32 (fall): 117–49.

———. 1995. "The Dual Currency Bifurcation of Cuba's Economy in the 1990s: Causes Consequences and Cures." *Development Studies Working Papers Series* 9 (May).

Rivero, Nicolás. 1993a. "Thoughts on a Cuban Trade Policy." Paper presented at Cuba Business Seminar, Washington, D.C., April 29.

———. 1993b. "Notes on Cuban Trade Policy in a Transition." Paper presented at Third Annual Meeting of ASCE, Miami, FIU, August 14.

Roca, Sergio G. 1976. *Cuban Economic Policy and Ideology: The Ten Million Ton Harvest.* Beverly Hills: Sage.

———. 1988. *Socialist Cuba: Past Interpretations and Future Challenges,* ed. Sergio Roca. Boulder: Westview Press.

Rodríguez, José Luis. 1982. "La economía cubana entre 1976 y 1980." *Economía y Desarrollo* 66 (January-February): 109–49.

———. 1988. *Crítica a nuestros críticos.* Havana: Editorial Ciencias Sociales.

———. 1989. "El desarrollo económico y social en Cuba: resultados de 30 años de revolución." *Cuba Socialista* 9, no. 3 (May-June): 35–65.

———. 1990a. "Aspectos económicos del proceso de rectificación." *Cuba Socialista* 44 (April-June): 86–101.

————. 1990b. Statistics supplied to the author in Havana (July).

————. 1992a. "Commentary." Paper presented at International Congress on Cuba after the Cold War, University of Pittsburgh, April 27–28.

————. 1992b "Las relaciones económicas entre Cuba y la antigua USSR: 1959–1990." *Boletín de Información sobre Economía Cubana* 1, no. 7 (July 1992): 2–12.

————. 1992c ."Las relaciones económicas entre Cuba y la antigua USSR: 1990–1992." *Boletín de Información sobre Economía Cubana* 1, no. 8 (August 1992): 2–11.

————. 1992d. "La deuda externa cubana: Una evaluación actual." *Boletín de Información sobre Economía Cubana* 1, nos. 11–12 (November-December): 2–10.

————. 1996. *Perspectivas económicas de Cuba 1996.* Davos: World Economic Forum (February 1–6).

Rodríguez, José Luis, and George Carriazo Moreno. 1987. *Erradicación de la pobreza en Cuba.* Havana: Editorial Ciencias Sociales.

"Se resiste para evitar una 'tercera' dependencia" [Interview with Marcos Portal Minister of Basic Industry]. 1993. *Cuba en el Mes,* Dossier no. 4 (January): 123–32.

Solchaga, Carlos. 1994. "La Transición Cubana." *Actualidad Económica.*

————. 1995. "Invertir en Cuba." *Actualidad Económica,* May 8.

Spreen, Thomas H., et al. 1996. *The Citrus Industries in Cuba and Florida.* Gainesville: University of Florida.

"A Survey of Cuba." 1996. *The Economist,* April 6, 1–16.

Svejnar, Jan, and Jorge Pérez-López. 1993. "A Strategy for the Economic Transformation in Cuba Based on the East European Experience." In Mesa-Lago, *Cuba after the Cold War,* pp. 323–53.

Terrero, Ariel. 1994. "Tendencias de un ajuste." *Bohemia* (October 28): 835.

UNESCO. 1980. *Statistical Yearbook 1980.* Maxéville: Imprimerie Jean Lamour.

————. 1993. *Statistical Yearbook 1993.* Maxéville: Imprimerie Jean Lamour.

United Nations Development Program. 1993, 1994, and 1995. *Human Development Report 1993, 1994, 1995.* New York: Oxford University Press.

United Nations Population Division. 1995. *World Population Prospects: The 1994 Revision.* New York.

Whitefield, Mimi. 1994. "Cuba OKs Farm Markets," "Cuba Says Reforms Are Back on Track," and "In Cuba, a Sweet Smell of Success." *Miami Herald,* September 18: 1A, 6A; September 22: 17A; and October 13: 20A.

Zimbalist, Andrew. 1992. "Teetering on the Brink: Cuba's Current Economic and Political Crises." *Journal of Latin American Studies,* no. 24: 407–18.

————. 1993a. "Treading Water: The Cuban Economic and Political Crisis in 1993." Paper presented at Smith College, March.

————. 1993b. "Cuba's Changing Economy and Its Implications." Ottawa: Carleton University, International Symposium on Cuba, September 23–25.

————, ed. 1987. *Cuba's Socialist Economy toward the 1990s.* Boulder: Lynne Rienner.

————, ed. 1988. *Cuban Political Economy: Controversies in Cubanology.* Boulder: Westview Press.

Zimbalist, Andrew, and Claes Brundenius. 1989. *The Cuban Economy: Measurement and Analysis of Socialist Performance.* Baltimore: Johns Hopkins University Press.

Zimbalist, Andrew, and Susan Eckstein. 1987. "Patterns of Cuban Development: The First Twenty-five Years." In Zimbalist, *Cuba's Socialist Economy toward the 1990s,* pp. 7–24.

COSTA RICA

Acuña Ulate, José A. 1993. "Un enfoque económico de los problemas de financiamiento de los servicios de salud." *Revista de Ciencias Administrativas de la Seguridad Social* 1, no. 2 (1993): 21–28.

Acuña Ulate, José A., and Fabio A. Durán V. 1994. *Extensión de la cobertura del seguro de vejez, invalidez y muerte: Diagnóstico y estrategias.* San José: CCSS (May).

Agency for International Development (AID), Bureau for Latin America and the Caribbean. 1992. *Costa Rica: The Effects of Structural Adjustment Measures.* Washington, D.C.

Aguilar, Pilar. 1990. "The Evolution of the Costa Rican Education Profile." In *Education in Central America and the Caribbean,* ed. Colin Brock and Donald Clarkson, pp. 257–78. New York: Routledge.

Aguilar Urbina, Francisco José, et al. 1987. *Historia general de Costa Rica.* Vol. 5. San José: Euroamericana de Ediciones.

Altimir, Oscar. 1984. "Poverty, Income Distribution and Child Welfare in Latin America: A Comparison of Pre- and Post-recession Data." *World Development* 12, no. 3 (March): 261–82.

————. 1993. "Income Distribution and Poverty through Crisis and Adjustment." Santiago: ECLAC, Working Paper no. 15.

Ameringer, Charles D. 1982. *Democracy in Costa Rica.* New York: Praeger.

Anderson, Leslie. 1991. "Mixed Blessings: Disruption and Organization among Peasant Unions in Costa Rica." *Latin American Research Review* 26, no. 1: 111–43.

Andic, Fuat M. 1983. *What Price Equity? A Macroeconomic Evaluation of Government Policies in Costa Rica.* Rio Piedras: Institute of Caribbean Studies, University of Puerto Rico.

————. 1994. "Ingresos familiares en Costa Rica: 1988." San José: Universidad de Costa Rica, Documento de Trabajo.

Baldares, Manuel De Jesús. 1986. *La distribución del ingreso y los sueldos en Costa Rica.* San José: Editorial Costa Rica.

Banco Central de Costa Rica. 1986. *Estadísticas 1950–1985.* San José.

————. 1988. *Datos socio-económicos de Costa Rica 1987.* San José.

————. 1989a. *Cuentas nacionales de Costa Rica 1978–1987.* San José.

———. 1989b–92b. *Anuario Estadístico, Cuentas Nacionales 1984–1988* to *1987–1991*. San José.

———. 1990c–91c. *Anuario Estadístico, Sector Externo 1985–1989* and *1987–1991*. San José.

———. 1991d. *Anuario Estadístico, Cuentas Monetarias 1986–1990*. San José.

Bell, John Patrick. 1971. *Crisis in Costa Rica: The 1948 Revolution*. Austin: University of Texas Press.

Bird, Leonard. 1984. *Costa Rica: The Unarmed Democracy*. London: Sheppard Press.

Botey Sobrado, Ana María, and Vladimir de la Cruz de Lemos. 1987. *Historia general de Costa Rica*. Vol. 4. San José: Euroamericana de Ediciones.

Bulmer-Thomas, Victor. 1988. "The New Model of Development in Costa Rica." In *Central America: Crisis and Possibilities,* ed. Rigoberto García, pp. 177–96. Stockholm: Institute of Latin American Studies.

Bureau for Latin America and the Caribbean. 1992. *Costa Rica: The Effects of Structural Adjustment Measures*. Washington, D.C.: Agency for International Development.

Caja Costarricense de Seguro Social. 1976–95. *Anuario Estadístico 1977 to 1994*. San José.

———. 1975–90. *Memoria Anual*. San José.

———. 1993, 1995. *Costa Rica: Indicadores de seguridad social. 1990–1994* and *1990–1995*. San José.

Camacho Mejía, Edna, and Claudio González Vega. 1992. *Apertura Comercial y Ajuste de las Empresas*. San José: Academia de Centroamérica.

Carciofi, Ricardo, Oscar Centrangolo, and Guillermo Barris. 1993. *Reformas Tributarias en Costa Rica*. Santiago: CEPAL.

Cartin Carranza, Ronald A. 1991. *Sistema de pensiones en América Latina: Diagnóstico y alternativas de reforma, Costa Rica*. Santiago: ECLAC.

Castro Valverde, Carlos, and Mauricio González Oviedo, eds. 1992. *Costa Rica: Balance de la situación*. San José: Centro de Estudios para la Acción Social.

Centro Latinoamericano de Demografía. January 1977, January 1984, January 1991, July 1991. *Boletín Demográfico*. Santiago.

Céspedes, Víctor Hugo. 1973. "Costa Rica: La distribución del ingreso y el consumo de algunos alimentos." San José: Universidad de Costa Rica, Serie Economia y Estadística, no. 45.

Céspedes, Víctor Hugo, et al. 1990. *Costa Rica frente a la crisis: Políticas y resultados*. San José: Academia de Centroamérica.

Chaves A., Luis Arturo, ed. 1992. *Déficit fiscal y ajuste estructural en Centroamérica*. San José: Escuela de Economía de la Universidad Nacional.

Colburn, Forrest D., and Iván Saballos Patiño. 1988. "El impulso a las ventas externas no tradicionales de Costa Rica." *Comercio Exterior* (Mexico) 38, no. 11 (November): 1027–32.

Corrales, Jorge. 1984. *Políticas de precios y de subsidios en Costa Rica*. San José: Academia de Centroamérica.

————, ed. 1993. *Raices institucionales de la política económica costarricense.* San José: CIAPA.

Daremblum, Jaime. 1990. "Costa Rica Needs Lower Taxes and a Leaner State." *Wall Street Journal,* October 5, 1990: A19.

————. 1991. "Costa Rica Risks Missing the Boat on Free Trade." *Wall Street Journal,* December 6, 1991: A15.

Dirección de Desarrollo Social y Asignaciones Familiares (DESAF). 1995. *Reestructuración del FODESAF.* San José (March).

Dirección General de Estadística y Censos-DGEC (Costa Rica). 1966. *Censo de población, 1963.* San José.

————. 1974–75. *Censo de población 1973.* San José.

Doryan Garrón, Eduardo. 1990. *De la abolición del ejército al Premio Nobel de la Paz: Ideas, poder y estrategias de desarrollo durante cuatro décadas de la economía política costarricense.* San José: Editorial de la Universidad de Costa Rica.

Durán V., Fabio. 1993. "Seguridad social y privatización de servicios de salud." *Revista de Ciencias Administrativas de la Seguridad Social* 1, no. 2 (1993): 13–19.

Durán V., Fabio, and Róger González Ch. 1994. "El gasto público en salud durante el período 1980–1993." *Revista de Ciencias Administrativas de la Seguridad Social* 2, no. 2 (1994): 15–23.

Economic Commission for Latin America and the Caribbean. 1964a–95a. *Economic Survey of Latin America 1964* to *1993.* Santiago.

————. 1977b–96b. *Statistical Yearbook for Latin America 1976* to *1995.* Santiago.

————. 1984c–96c. *Preliminary Overview of the Latin American Economy 1983* to *1996.* Santiago.

————. 1993d. "Antecedentes estadísticos de la distribución del ingreso en los ochenta: Costa Rica." Santiago.

————. 1994e–95e. *Panorama social de América Latina 1994, 1995.* Santiago.

Edelman, Marc, and Rodolfo Monge Oviedo. 1993. "Costa Rica: The Non-market Roots of Market Success." *NACLA: Report on the Americas* 26, no. 4 (February): 22–29.

Emling, Shelley. 1992. "Costa Rica Will Liberalize Rules on Foreign Exchange Transactions." *Journal of Commerce,* February 6, 1992.

Fernández, Janina. 1988. *Inestabilidad económica con estabilidad política: El caso singular de Costa Rica 1950–1982.* San José: Editorial de la Universidad de Costa Rica.

Fields, Gary S. 1980. *Poverty, Inequality and Development.* New York: Cambridge University Press.

Fondo de Desarrollo Social y Asignaciones Familiares (FOSEDAF). 1993. *Presupuesto ordinario.* San José: Ministerio del Trabajo y Seguridad Social.

Franco, Rolando, and Arturo León. 1984. "Estilos de desarrollo, papel del estado y estructura social en Costa Rica." *Pensamiento Iberoamericano,* no. 6 (July-December): 65–92.

García, José Fernando. 1977. *Educación y desarrollo en Costa Rica.* Buenos Aires: UNESCO/CEPAL.

González González, Fernando. 1987. *Educación costarricense: Desarrollo histórico del proceso pedagógico costarricense.* San José: Editorial Universidad Estatal a Distancia.

Guardia Quirós, Jorge, et al. 1987. *La política de precios en Costa Rica.* San José: COUNSEL.

Güendel, Ludwig G., and Juan D. Trejos. 1994. *Reformas recientes en el sector salud de Costa Rica.* Santiago: CEPAL, Serie de Reformas de Política Pública, no. 18.

Hansen-Kuhn, Karen. 1993. "Sapping the Economy: Structural Adjustment Policies in Costa Rica." *The Ecologist* 23, no. 5 (September/October): 179–84.

Inter-American Development Bank. 1968–95. *Economic and Social Progress in Latin America 1968 to 1995.* Washington, D.C.

———. 1994a. *A la búsqueda del siglo XXI: Nuevos caminos del desarrollo en Costa Rica.* Washington, D.C. (November).

International Labour Office. 1976–94. *Year Book of Labour Statistics 1975 to 1994.* Geneva.

———. 1990a. *Yearbook of Labour Statistics, Retrospective Edition on Population Censuses 1945–1989.* Geneva.

International Monetary Fund. 1960–77. *Direction of Trade Annual* (DTA) *1960* to *1977.* Washington, D.C.

———. 1978–79. *Direction of Trade Yearbook* (DTY) *1978* to *1979.* Washington, D.C.

———. *Direction of Trade Statistics Yearbook* (DTSY) *1980* to *1994.* Washington, D.C.

———. 1980–94. *Government Finance Statistics Yearbook* (GFSY) *1980* to *1994.* Washington, D.C.

———. 1990–95. *International Financial Statistics Yearbook* (IFSY) *1990* to *1995.* Washington, D.C.

———. 1993, 1995. *International Financial Statistics* (IFS). Washington, D.C. (March and August).

Isuani, Ernesto Aldo. 1994. *Seguridad social y salud en Costa Rica.* San José (March).

Jaramillo, Antillón. 1993. *Salud y seguridad social.* San José: Editorial Universitaria de Costa Rica.

Latin American Newsletters Ltd. (LAN). 1990a. "Agriculture Is the Key for Calderón." *Latin America Economic Report,* February 28, 1990: 12.

———. 1990b. "Debt Deal Finally Signed." *Latin America Economic Report,* May 31, 1990: 12.

Lizano, Eduardo. 1990. *Programa de ajuste estructural en Costa Rica.* San José: Academia de Centroamérica.

Mesa-Lago, Carmelo. 1988. "Análisis económico de los sistemas de pensiones en Costa Rica y recomendaciones de reforma." Washington, D.C.: Development Technologies.

―――. 1989. *Ascent to Bankruptcy: Financing Social Security in Latin America.* Pittsburgh: University of Pittsburgh Press.

―――. 1990. *La seguridad social y el sector informal.* Santiago: PREALC, no. 32.

―――. 1992. *Health Care for the Poor in Latin America and the Caribbean.* Washington, D.C.: Pan American Health Organization.

―――. 1994a. *Changing Social Security: Toward Alleviating the Social Costs of Economic Reform.* Boulder: Lynne Rienner.

―――. 1994b. "Estudio sobre la situación de la seguridad social en la región de México, Centroamérica y el Caribe: Avances, problemas y recomendaciones." Miami: Informe para el BID (December).

Mesa-Lago, Carmelo, and Sergio Díaz-Briquets. 1988. "Estrategias diferentes, países similares: Las consecuencias para el crecimiento y la equidad en Costa Rica y Cuba." *Anuario de Estudios Centroamericanos* 14, nos. 1–2: 5–23.

Ministerio de Educación Pública (MEP). 1992. *Expansión del sistema educativo costarricense, 1992.* San José (October).

―――. 1993. *Costos, gastos e indicadores de la educación pública en Costa Rica.* San José.

Ministerio de Gobernación y Policía (MGP). 1987. *Censo de Población 1984.* San José: Imprenta Nacional.

Ministerio de Planificación Nacional y Política Económica. 1983. *Plan Nacional de Desarrollo 1982–1986: Diagnóstico y estrategia global.* San José.

―――. 1988. *Evolución económica y social de Costa Rica en el año 1987.* San José.

―――. 1992. *El proyecto de reforma del sector salud: Resumen.* San José.

―――. 1994a. *Perfil de la pobreza en Costa Rica.* San José.

―――. 1994b. *Costa Rica: Programas y proyectos estatales para la superación de la pobreza.* San José.

―――. 1995. *Costa Rica, Indicadores básicos 1995.* San José.

Ministerio de Salud (MS). *Salud sin riqueza.* San José.

Mora, Minor, and José M. Valverde. 1993. *Privatización, deterioro e improvisación en el sector salud.* San José: Espacios Consultores Asociados (November).

Morley, Samuel A., and Carole Alvarez. 1992. *Recession and the Growth of Poverty in Costa Rica.* Washington D.C.: IDB.

Murillo Rojas, Luis Antonio. 1981. *Banca y desarrollo económico.* San José: Editorial Universidad Estatal a Distancia.

Naranjo Villalobos, Fernando. 1980. "Análisis y diagnóstico de la situación económica actual." In *Los problemas económicos del desarrollo en Costa Rica,* 137–165. Heredia: Unidad Coordinadora de Investigación y Documentación/ Universidad Estatal a Distancia.

Oficina de Planificación Nacional y Política Económica. 1982. *Evolución Socioeconómica de Costa Rica 1950–1980.* San José.

Pan American Health Organization. 1961–94. *Health Conditions in the Americas 1961–1964* to *1994.* Washington, D.C.

―――. 1992a. *Health Statistics from the Americas.* Washington, D.C.

Pascua, María del Rocío, and Luis Alberto Valverde. 1987. *Bienestar social en Costa*

Rica: Una reseña de su desarrollo. San José: Instituto de Investigaciones Sociales, Universidad de Costa Rica.

Pollack, Molly, and Andras Uthoff. 1985. *Costa Rica: Evolución macroeconómica 1976–1983.* Santiago: Programa Regional del Empleo para América Latina y el Caribe.

Programa Regional del Empleo para América Latina y el Caribe (PREALC). 1992. *Costa Rica: Políticas para pagar el gasto social.* Santiago, no. 366 (August).

Quirós Coronado, Roberto. 1991. *Costa Rica: La atención médica en la seguridad social.* Ottawa: AISS 5th Conferencia Regional Americana.

Riboud, Michelle. 1990. *Costa Rica: El gasto público en los sectores sociales.* Washington, D.C.: World Bank (October).

Rodríguez Céspedes, Ennio. 1986. "Costa Rica: Inflación y crecimiento ante la crisis de deuda externa." *Pensamiento Iberoamericano,* no. 9 (January-June): 179–88.

Rosenberg, Mark B. 1979. "Social Security Policymaking in Costa Rica: A Research Report." *Latin American Research Review* 14, no. 1: 116–33.

Rottenberg, Simon, et al. 1993. *The Political Economy of Poverty, Equity and Growth: Costa Rica and Uruguay.* New York: Oxford University Press.

Rovira Mas, Jorge. 1988a. *Estado y política económica en Costa Rica 1948–1970.* 3d ed. San José: Editorial Porvenir.

———. 1988b. *Costa Rica en los años 80.* 2d ed. San José: Editorial Porvenir.

Saenz, Rocío. 1994. "La reforma de la salud en Costa Rica." Pittsburgh: University of Pittsburgh, unpublished paper.

Salazar X., José Manuel. 1990. "El estado y el ajuste en el sector industrial." In *Políticas económicas en Costa Rica: tomo II,* ed. Claudio González Vega and Edna Camacho Mejía. San José: Academia de Centroamérica.

Sanguinetty, Jorge A. 1988. *La educación general en Costa Rica: La crisis y sus posibles soluciones.* San José: Development Techologies, S.A.

Sauma, Pablo, and Juan Diego Trejos. 1990. *Evolución reciente de la distribución del ingreso en Costa Rica: 1977–1986.* San José: Instituto de Investigaciones en Ciencias Económicas, Universidad de Costa Rica.

Scott, David Clark. 1991a. "Costa Rica Digs Out." *Christian Science Monitor,* September 4, 1991: 10–11.

———. 1991b. "Growth of Alternative Crops Help Pull Economy Ahead." *Christian Science Monitor,* September 4, 1991: 11.

Seligson, Mitchell A. 1977. "Agrarian Policies in Dependent Countries: Costa Rica." *Journal of Interamerican Studies and World Affairs* 19, no. 2 (May): 201–31.

———. 1978. *Agrarian Reform in Costa Rica, 1942–1976: The Evolution of a Program.* Madison: Land Tenure Center, University Of Wisconsin.

———. 1982. "Agrarian Reform in Costa Rica: The Impact of the Title Security Program." *Inter-American Economic Affairs* 35, no. 4 (spring): 31–56.

Sojo, Ana. 1984. *Estado empresario y lucha política en Costa Rica.* San José: Editorial Universitaria Centroamericana.

———. 1989. "Social Policies in Costa Rica." *CEPAL Review,* no. 38 (August): 105–19.

———. 1994. *Política social en Costa Rica: Reformas recientes.* San José: Facultad Latinoamericana de Ciencias Sociales.

Tardanico, Richard. 1996. "From Crisis to Restructuring: The Nexus of Global and National Change in the Costa Rican Labor Market." *Review* (State University of New York Press) 19, no. 2: 155–96.

Taylor Valdes, Mia. 1992a. "Exports and Tourism on the Rise." *Mesoamerica* 11, no. 1 (January 1992): 11–12.

———. 1992b. "Taking Stock of '91." *Mesoamerica* 11, no. 1 (January 1992): 11.

Trejos S., Juan Diego. 1985. *Costa Rica: Economic Crisis and Public Policy, 1978–1984.* Miami: Florida International University.

———. 1990. *Pobreza y política social en Costa Rica.* San José: MIDEPLAN.

———. 1994. "Evolución reciente de la pobreza en Costa Rica." San José: Informe para el BID.

Trejos, Juan Diego, and M. L. Elizalde. 1983. "Costa Rica: La distribución del ingreso y el acceso a los programas de carácter social." San José: Universidad de Costa Rica, Documento de Trabajo, no. 90.

———. 1992. Servicios de salud para indigentes en Costa Rica," and "Pensiones no contributivas en Costa Rica." In *From Platitudes to Practice: Targeting Social Programs in Latin America.* LACTD, Report no. 21. Washington, D.C.: World Bank (September).

United Nations. 1961–95. *International Trade Statistics Yearbook (ITSY) 1960* to *1995.* New York.

———. 1964–85. *Construction Statistical Yearbook.* New York.

United Nations Development Program. 1994. *Human Development Report 1994.* New York: Oxford University Press.

United Nations Educational, Scientific and Cultural Organization. 1993, 1994. *Statistical Yearbook 1993, 1994.* Paris.

Valverde, Jorge. 1994. "Las pensiones y otros beneficios de la seguridad social costarricense." San José: EDNASSS.

Vargas Peralta, Federico. 1980. "El problema fiscal en Costa Rica." In *Los problemas económicos del desarrollo en Costa Rica,* pp. 41–83. Heredia: Unidad Coordinadora de Investigación y Documentación/Universidad Estatal a Distancia.

Villasuso, Juan M. 1987. "Costa Rica: Crisis, Adjustment Policies and Rural Development." *CEPAL Review,* no. 33 (December): 107–13.

Waggoner, George R., and Barbara Ashton Waggoner. 1971. *Education in Central America.* Wichita: University Press of Kansas.

World Bank. 1985a–95a. *World Tables 1984* to *1994.* Washington, D.C.

———. 1988b–95b. *World Development Report* (WDR) *1988* to *1995.* Washington, D.C.

———. 1990. *Costa Rica: El gasto público en los sectores sociales.* Washington, D.C., October.

————. 1991c–95c. *Social Indicators of Development 1990* to *1995*. Washington, D.C.

World Health Organization (WHO). 1967–90. *World Health Statistics Annual 1966* to *1990*. Geneva.

CONCLUSIONS

Banco Central de Chile. 1996. *Boletín Mensual* no. 826 (December).

Banco Central de Costa Rica. 1998. Information gathered by the author, San José (February).

Banco Nacional de Cuba. 1996. *Informe Económico 1995*. Havana (May).

Caja Costarricense de Seguro Social. 1997. *Variables e indicadores socio-demográficos*. San José (April).

————. 1998. *Informe Gestión Corporativa CCSS 1997*. San José (February).

Economic Commission for Latin America and the Caribbean. 1996a, 1996b. *Economic Survey for Latin America and the Caribbean 1994–95* and *1995–96*. Santiago.

————. 1995c, 1996c, 1997c. *Preliminary Overview of the Economy of Latin America and the Caribbean 1995* to *1997*. Santiago.

————. 1996d. *Statistical Yearbook for Latin America 1996*. Santiago.

————. 1997d. *La economía cubana: Reformas estructurales y desempeño en los noventa*. Mexico D.F.: Fondo de Cultura Económica.

Estes, Richard. 1984. *The Social Progress of Nations*. New York: Praeger.

González, Alfonso. 1995. "Cuba, Puerto Rico y Costa Rica: Desarrollo socio-económico comparativo 1960–90." *Papeles de Geografía* 24:87–100.

International Labour Office. 1996, 1997. *Yearbook of Labour Statistics 1996* and *1997*. Geneva.

International Monetary Fund. 1996a, 1997a. *International Financial Statistics Yearbook 1996* and *1997*. Washington, D.C.

————. 1996b, 1997b. *Direction of Trade Statistics Yearbook (DTSY) 1996* and *1997*. Washington, D.C.

————. 1997. *International Financial Statistics (IFS)*. Washington, D.C.

Karatnycky, Adrian, et al. 1996. *Freedom in the World: 1995–1996*. New York: Freedom House.

McColm, Bruce, et al. 1991, 1992. *Freedom in the World 1990–1991* and *1991–1992*. New York: Freedom House.

Mesa-Lago, Carmelo. 1969. "Availability and Reliability of Statistics in Socialist Cuba." *Latin American Research Review* 4, nos. 1–2 (spring and summer 1969): 53–91, 47–81.

————. 1981. *The Economy of Socialist Cuba: A Two Decade Appraisal*. Albuquerque: University of New Mexico Press

————. 1988. "Cuban Statistics: One More Time." *Cuban Studies* 18:133–45.

————. 1999. "Achieving and Sustaining Social Development with Limited Resources: The Experience of Costa Rica." In *Social Development and Public Pol-*

icy: Some Lessons from Successful Experiences, ed. Dharam Ghai. London: Macmillan.

———. 1998. "Assessing Economic and Social Performance in the Cuban Transition of the 1990s." *World Development* 26, no. 5 (May): 857–76.

Mesa-Lago, Carmelo, and Jorge Pérez-López. 1985. *A Study of Cuba's National Product System, Its Conversion to the System of National Accounts, and Estimation of GDP Per Capita and Growth Rates.* Washington, D.C.: World Bank.

———. 1992. "Cuban Economic Growth in Current and Constant Prices, 1975–1988: A Puzzle on the Foreign Trade Component of the Material Product System." *Statistical Abstract of Latin America* 29, no. 1: 598–615.

Messick, Richard. 1996. *World Survey of Economic Freedom 1995–1996.* New Brunswick. N.J.: Transaction.

MIDEPLAN. 1997. *Principlaes Indicadores Sociales de Costa Rica.* San José.

Ministerio de Economía. 1998. *Cuba Informe Económico Año 1997.* Havana.

Ministry of Finance. 1997, 1998. *Chile Economic Performance.* Santiago (September and June).

Overseas Development Council (ODC). 1983. *U.S. Foreign Policy: The Third World Agenda.* New York: Praeger.

"Palabras de Carlos Lage ante el Congreso." 1997. *Granma,* October 10.

Pérez-López, Jorge. 1997. "The Cuban Economy in Mid-1997." *Cuba in Transition.* Miami: ASCE.

Population Crisis Committee 1992. *The International Human Suffering Index.* Washington, D.C.

Raczinski, Dagmar. 1997. "Social Policies in Chile: Origin and Transformations." Notre Dame: Kellogg Institute for International Studies, September 12–14.

"Resolución Económica del V Congreso del Partido Comunista de Cuba." 1998. *Granma Internacional,* February 22, Special Issue.

Rohter, Larry. 1997. "Cuba's Party Peers Ahead Chooses to March in Place." *New York Times,* October 12: 6.

Sojo, Ana. 1997. "Hacia unas nuevas reglas del juego: Los compromisos de gestión de salud en Costa Rica." Santiago: CEPAL.

"Stranded on the Farm?" 1997. *The Economist,* October 4: 84.

Trejos, Juan Diego. 1998. Poverty estimates based on household surveys. San José.

UNESCO. 1996. *Statistical Yearbook 1996.* Paris.

United Nations Development Program. 1991–97. *Human Development Report 1991 to 1997.* New York: Oxford University Press.

World Bank. 1996. *World Development Report 1996.* New York: Oxford University Press.

Index

absenteeism in Cuba, 218
absolute indicators of performance, 17
absolute ranking, 593, 595–96
acopio, in Cuba: description of, 182; inefficiency of, 268; land collectivization and, 185; under RP, 267; small farmers and, 189, 191, 205; state prices for, 186, 229, 238
Administradoras de Fondos de Pensiones (AFPs), 55–56, 71–72, 77–78, 90–91, 99, 116–17, 127, 128
Agency for International Development (USAID), 463, 466
Agrarian Reform Laws (Cuba), 176, 181, 205
agricultural lands: in Chile, 36, 49; in Costa Rica, 402–3, 413–14, 431–32, 458, 495–96
agricultural markets, *See* free peasant markets, in Cuba
Agricultural Production Cooperatives (CPA, Cuba), 229, 266, 267, 296
agriculture: in Chile, 39, 44, 52–53, 59–60, 69–70, 87, 110–11; in Costa Rica, 424–25, 452–53, 470–72; in Cuba, 186, 209–10, 216, 220, 228–30, 267, 281, 328
Aldana, Carlos, 281, 291
Alessandri (Jorge) administration, 29
Allende (Salvador) administration, 29–33
Alliance for Progress, 422, 426
Aluminum Corporation of America (ALCOA), 431
Anuario Estadístico de Cuba, 564
Arias, Oscar: agriculture policy of, 471; election of, 461; exchange rate and, 473; foreign debt and, 475–76; growth under,

486–87; housing policy of, 484; inflation under, 488–89; monetary and credit policy of, 466–67; social services under, 482–83, 496; wage-adjustment policy of, 480–81, 495
artisan and industrial markets in Cuba, 302–3
Australian system and sugarcane, 236
Aylwin, Patricio: administration of, 105–6; analysis of policy of, 131–32; economic growth with equity formula of, 109–10; election of, 80; social service policy of, 126

bananas, in Costa Rica, 416
BANHVI (Home Mortgage Bank, Costa Rica), 484
banking reform, in Cuba, 305–6
bankruptcy of financial institutions, in Chile, 59, 66–67, 68
Basic Units of Cooperative Production (UBPC), in Cuba, 295–98
biotechnology, in Cuba, 274, 311
black market, in Cuba, 191, 193, 205, 212, 267, 283, 287, 303, 558
BNC (National Bank of Cuba), 171, 177, 183, 198, 211, 304, 305, 564
Board of Port Administration and Economic Development of the Atlantic Region (JAPDEVA, Costa Rica), 414
book: approach of, 9–10; countries selected for, 9, 11–14; final part of, 17–18; issues analyzed in, 11; observation period for, 18; parts of, 10–11
Boti, Regino, 186
Büchi, Hernán, 80, 83

Budgetary Authority (Costa Rica), 464
budgetary deficits: comparison of, 571; in Chile, 32, 37–38, 51, 74, 109; in Costa Rica, 404, 410, 415, 447; in Cuba, 271, 283
budgetary finance (*sistema presupuestario*), in Cuba, 185, 200, 211, 212, 270, 304
budgets: in Chile, 68; in Costa Rica, 464; in Cuba, 185–86, 206, 211, 233, 234, 307–8, 309

CACM (Central American Common Market), 400, 418, 425, 426–27, 454–55
Calderón Fournier, Rafael Angel: agricultural development policy of, 471–72; CCSS and, 483–84, 497; Commission for State Reform and, 463; criticisms of, 496, 498–99; economic program of, 464–65; election of, 461–62; exchange rate and, 473–74; foreign debt and, 476–77; growth under, 487; housing policy of, 484–85; inflation under, 489–90; labor and employment policy of, 480, 481, 493; monetary and credit policy of, 467–68; stabilization program of, 469–70; wages under, 495
Calderón Guardia, Rafael Angel: administration of, 400, 402–5; candidacy of, 399
Canada and Cuba, 311
capital accumulation, in Cuba, 211–12
Carazo Odio, Rodrigo: candidacy of, 430; development strategy of, 439; exchange policy of, 441; growth under, 445; housing policy of, 484; industry under, 451; labor conflict under, 456–57; monetary and credit policy of, 448–49; stabilization plan of, 435–37, 544; weakness of administration of, 544
Carter (Jimmy) administration and Cuba, 240
case-study method, 5
Castro, Fidel: blame for economic problems by, 539; on capitalism, 291; on construction brigades and contingents, 277; on crime, 278; decline in economy and, 221; doctrine of humanism, 175; on education, 325; on egalitarianism, 321; on emergency adjustment program, 301; on for-

eign investment, 299; of FP, 273; on free peasant markets, 266, 301–2; goals of, 541–42; Guevarism and, 209, 227–28; implementation of market reforms by, 293–94, 303; INRA and, 198; on material incentives, 277–78; on nickel industry, 239; on private farms, 266; recentralization of decision making by, 268–69; on recentralization of work quotas and wages, 278; on self-employment, 230–31, 298; on self-financing, 270; on small business, 267; on socialism, 277; speeches on market reform by, 291; on structural approach, 293; on trade practices, 223
Castro, Raul: criticism of economic reform by, 294; on market reforms, 304; on self-employment, 319; on unemployment, 334; on unneeded workers, 318
CATs (export incentive bonds), in Costa Rica, 440–41, 471–72
cattle plan, in Cuba, 214–15, 220, 238, 274
CCS (cooperatives of credit and services), in Cuba, 296
CCSS (Costa Rican Social Insurance Fund), 403, 420, 429, 443–44, 459, 482, 483–84, 496–97
Center for the Study of National Problems (Costa Rica), 404–5
Center of Genetic Engineering and Biotechnology (Cuba), 274
Central America, economic cooperation and integration in, 478–79
Central American Common Market (CACM), 400, 417–18, 425, 426–27, 454–55
Central Bank (Chile), 84, 107
Central Bank (Costa Rica), 408–9, 415, 441–42, 466, 467, 473, 474
centrally planned economy. *See* socialist economy
Central Planning Board (JUCEPLAN, Cuba), 177, 182, 184, 198, 210, 264, 268
Chile: advantages and disadvantages of, 14, 606–8; authoritarian military regime in, 34–35; denationalization process in, 82; economic role of state in, 538, 539, 540; economic teams in power in, 67–68, 80,

vocational education, in Cuba, 325
Voisin rational pasture method, in Cuba, 274
voluntary labor, in Cuba, 217, 246

wages: in Chile, 62, 71, 98, 125; comparison
of performance in, 581–82; in Costa
Rica, 419, 442–43, 457–58, 480–81,
495; in Cuba, 245, 248, 261, 279, 286,
335–36
Wanniski, Jude, 294
water, sewerage, and sanitation, access to,
589–90; in Chile, 47, 64, 102, 129; in

Costa Rica, 429, 459, 498; in Cuba, 262,
324
Western Marxist scholars, 182
women in labor force: in Chile, 62, 76, 97,
113–14, 115, 124–25; comparison of
performance in, 584; in Costa Rica, 427–
28, 493; in Cuba, 224, 247, 260, 286
World Bank: book series, 2, 3, 5; Chile and,
85–86; Costa Rica and, 475, 476
World Development Report 1996, 3, 7

yearbooks, by international organizations, 4